Lecture Notes in Computer Science 6286

Commenced Publication in 1973
Founding and Former Series Editors:
Gerhard Goos, Juris Hartmanis, and Jan van Leeuwen

Frank S. de Boer Marcello M. Bonsangue
Stefan Hallerstede Michael Leuschel (Eds.)

Formal Methods for Components and Objects

8th International Symposium, FMCO 2009
Eindhoven, The Netherlands, November 4-6, 2009
Revised Selected Papers

Volume Editors

Frank S. de Boer
Centre for Mathematics and Computer Science, CWI
Amsterdam, The Netherlands
E-mail: F.S.de.Boer@cwi.nl

Marcello M. Bonsangue
Leiden University
Leiden Institute of Advanced Computer Science
Leiden, The Netherlands
E-mail: marcello@liacs.nl

Stefan Hallerstede
Heinrich-Heine University of Dusseldorf
Department of Computer Science
Dusseldorf, Germany
E-mail: halstefa@cs.uni-duesseldorf.de

Michael Leuschel
Heinrich-Heine University of Dusseldorf
Department of Computer Science
Dusseldorf, Germany
E-mail: leuschel@cs.uni-duesseldorf.de

Library of Congress Control Number: 2010938608

CR Subject Classification (1998): D.2.4, D.2, D.3, F.3, D.1

LNCS Sublibrary: SL 2 – Programming and Software Engineering

ISSN 0302-9743
ISBN-10 3-642-17070-6 Springer Berlin Heidelberg New York
ISBN-13 978-3-642-17070-6 Springer Berlin Heidelberg New York

springer.com

Printed in Germany

Typesetting: Camera-ready by author, data conversion by Scientific Publishing Services, Chennai, India
Printed on acid-free paper 06/3180

Preface

Large and complex software systems provide infrastructure in all industries today. In order to construct such large systems in a systematic manner, the focus in development methodologies has switched in the last two decades from functional issues to structural issues: both data and functions are encapsulated into software units that are integrated into large systems by means of various techniques supporting reusability and modifiability. This encapsulation principle is essential to both the object-oriented and the more recent component-based software engineering paradigms.

Formal methods have been applied successfully to the verification of medium-sized programs in protocol and hardware design. However, their application to the development of large systems requires more emphasis on specification, modeling and validation techniques supporting the concepts of reusability and modifiability, and their implementation in new extensions of existing programming languages like Java.

The 8th Symposium on Formal Methods for Components and Objects was held in Eindhoven, The Netherlands, November 4–6, 2009. It was realized as a concertation meeting of European projects focusing on formal methods for components and objects. This volume contains 17 revised papers submitted after the symposium by the speakers of each of the following European IST projects involved in the organization of the program:

- IST-FP6 project BIONETS on biologically inspired services evolution for the pervasive age. The contact person for work relating to FMCO is Ludovic Henrio (INRIA Sophia-Antipolis, France).
- The IST-FP7 project COMPAS on compliance-driven models, languages, and architectures for services. The contact person is Schahram Dustdar (Technical University of Vienna, Austria)
- The IST-FP6 project CREDO on modeling and analysis of evolutionary structures for distributed services. The contact person is Frank de Boer (CWI, The Netherlands).
- The IST-FP7 project DEPLOY on industrial deployment of advanced system engineering methods for high productivity and dependability. The contact person is Alexander Romanovsky (Newcastle University, UK).
- The IST-FP7 project HATS on highly adaptable and trustworthy software using formal methods. The contact person is Reiner Hähnle (Chalmers University of Technology, Sweden).
- The IST-FP7 project INESS on integrated European railway signaling system. The contact person for work relating to FMCO is Jim Woodcock (University of York, UK).
- The IST-FP7 project MOGENTES on model-based generation of tests for dependable embedded systems. The contact person for work relating to FMCO is Bernhard Aichernig (TU Graz, Austria).

- The IST-FP6 project PROTEST on property based testing. The contact person is John Derrick (University of Sheffield, UK).
- The IST-FP7 project QUASIMODO on quantitative system properties in model-driven design of embedded systems. The contact person is Kim G. Larsen (Aalborg University, Denmark).

We have also invited members of the working group on Formal Methods and Service-Oriented Architecture (FM-SOA) to participate.

The proceedings of the previous editions of FMCO have been published as volumes 2852, 3188, 3657, 4111, 4709, 5382, and 5751 of Springer's *Lecture Notes in Computer Science*. We believe that these proceedings provide a unique combination of ideas on software engineering and formal methods which reflect the expanding body of knowledge on modern software systems.

Finally, we thank all authors for the high quality of their contributions, and the reviewers for their help in improving the papers for this volume.

June 2010

Frank de Boer
Marcello Bonsangue
Stefan Hallerstede
Michael Leuschel

Organization

FMCO 2009 was part of the Formal Methods Week at Eindhoven, The Netherlands. Within the Formal Methods Week, the FMCO symposium was co-located with a host of conferences and workshops:

The Symposium on Communicating Process Architectures (CPA)
The International Workshop on Formal Aspects of Component Software (FACS)
The Workshop on Formal Aspects of Security and Trust (FAST)
The International Symposium on Formal Methods (FM)
The International Workshop on Formal Methods for Industrial Critical Systems (FMICS)
The International Workshop on Parallel and Distributed Methods in verifiCation (PDMC)
The 2009 Refine Workshop
The 21st IFIP International Conference on Testing of Communicating Systems (TESTCOM)
The 9th International Workshop on Formal Approaches to Testing of Software (FATES)
The Dutch Testing Day
The Second International FME Conference on Teaching Formal Methods (TFM)

The FMCO symposia are organized in the context of the project Mobi-J, a project founded by a bilateral research program of The Dutch Organization for Scientific Research (NWO) and the Central Public Funding Organization for Academic Research in Germany (DFG). The partners of the Mobi-J projects are: the Centrum voor Wiskunde en Informatica, the Leiden Institute of Advanced Computer Science, and the Christian-Albrechts-Universität Kiel.

This project aims at the development of a programming environment which supports component-based design and the verification of Java programs annotated with assertions. The overall approach is based on an extension of the Java language with a notion of "component" that provides for the encapsulation of its internal processing of data and composition in a network by means of mobile asynchronous channels.

Sponsoring Institutions

The Dutch Organization for Scientific Research (NWO)

Table of Contents

The INESS Project

The MOGENTES Project

The PROTEST Project

The QUASIMODO Project

A Framework for Reasoning on Component Composition

Ludovic Henrio[1], Florian Kammüller[2], and Muhammad Uzair Khan[1]

[1] INRIA – CNRS – I3S – Université de Nice Sophia-Antipolis
{mkhan,lhenrio}@sophia.inria.fr
[2] Institut für Softwaretechnik und Theoretische Informatik – TU-Berlin
flokam@cs.tu-berlin.de

Abstract. The main characteristics of component models is their strict structure enabling better code reuse. Correctness of component composition is well understood formally but existing works do not allow for mechanised reasoning on composition and component reconfigurations, whereas a mechanical support would improve the confidence in the existing results. This article presents the formalisation in Isabelle/HOL of a component model, focusing on the structure and on basic lemmas to handle component structure. Our objective in this paper is to present the basic constructs, and the corresponding lemmas allowing the proof of properties related to structure of component models and the handling of structure at runtime. We illustrate the expressiveness of our approach by presenting component semantics, and properties on reconfiguration primitives.

Keywords: Components, mechanised proofs, futures, reconfiguration.

1 Introduction

Component models focus on program structure and improve re-usability of programs. In component models, application dependencies are clearly identified by defining interfaces (or ports) and connecting them together. The structure of components can also be used at runtime to discover services or modify component structure, which allows for dynamic adaptation; these dynamic aspects are even more important in a distributed setting. Since a complete system restart is often too costly, a reconfiguration at runtime is mandatory. Dynamic replacement of a component is a sensitive operation. Reconfiguration procedures often entail state transfer, and require conditions on the communication status. A suitable component model needs a detailed representation of component organization together with precise communication flows to enable reasoning about reconfiguration. That is why we present here a formal model of components comprising both concepts.

This paper provides support for proving properties on component models in a theorem prover. Our objective is to provide an expressive platform with a wide range of tools to help the design of component models, the creation of adaptation procedures, and the proof of generic properties on the component model.

F.S. de Boer et al. (Eds.): FMCO 2009, LNCS 6286, pp. 1–20, 2010.

Indeed most existing frameworks focus on the correctness or the adaptation of applications; we focus on generic properties.

In this context, introduction of mechanised proofs will increase confidence in the properties of the component model and its adaptation procedures. We start from a formalisation close to the component model specification and implementation; then we use a framework allowing us to express properties in a simple and natural way. This way, we can convince the framework programmer and the application programmer of the safety of communication patterns, optimisations, and reconfiguration procedures.

We write our mechanised formalisation in Isabelle/HOL but we are convinced that our approach can be adapted to other theorem provers. The generic meta-logic of Isabelle/HOL constitutes a deductive frame for reasoning in an object logic. Isabelle/HOL also provides a set of generic constructors, like datatypes, records, and inductive definitions supporting natural definitions while automatically deriving proof support for these definitions. Isabelle has automated proof strategies: a simplifier and classical reasoner, implementing powerful proof techniques. Isabelle, with the proof support tool Proofgeneral, provides an easy-to-use theorem prover environment. For a precise description of Isabelle/HOL specific syntax or predefined constructors, please refer to the tutorial [20].

We present here a framework that mechanically formalizes a distributed hierarchical component model and its basic properties. We show that this framework is expressive enough to allow both the expression of component semantics and the manipulation of the component structure. Benefiting from our experiences with different possible formalisations, and from the proof of several component properties, we can now clearly justify the design choices we took and their impact[1]. The technical contributions of this paper are the following:

- formal description in Isabelle of component structure, mapping component concepts to Isabelle constructs,
- definition of a set of basic lemmas easing the proof of component-related properties,
- additional constructs and proofs to ensure well-formedness of component structures,
- proposal for a definition of component state, and runtime semantics for components communicating by asynchronous request-replies,
- application to the design and first proofs about component reconfiguration.

The remainder of the paper is organised as follows. Section 2 gives an overview of the context of this paper: it positions this paper relatively to related works and previous works on the formalisation of the GCM component model, which is also described in Section 2.2. Section 3 presents the formalisation of the component model in Isabelle/HOL highlighting design decisions and their impact on the basic proof infrastructure. We then summarize a semantics for distributed components with its properties, and present a few reconfiguration primitives in Section 4.1. Section 5 concludes and presents future directions.

[1] The GCM specification framework is available at `www.inria.fr/oasis/Ludovic.Henrio/misc`

2 Background

Component modelling is a vast domain of active research, comprising very applied semi-formal approaches to formal methods. In this section, we first give an overview of the domain, starting from well-known approaches, summarizing some community activities, and focusing on the most relevant related works. Then we present the GCM component model and existing formalisation of GCM. Finally we position this paper relatively to the other approaches presented here.

2.1 Related Work

Some well-known component models like CCA [11] are not hierarchical – their intent is the efficient building, connecting and running of components but they neglect structural aspects. We rather focus on hierarchical component models like Fractal[6], GCM[4], or SCA[5].

Recent years have shown several opportunities for the use of formal methods for the modelling and verification of component-based applications as shown in several successful conferences like FMCO, FOCLASA, or FACS.

For example, in [8, 9] the authors investigate the use of formal methods to specify interface adaptation and generation of interface adaptors, based on behavioural specification of interfaces to be connected. Also, in [10, 3] the authors focus on the verification of the behaviour of component-based application. They provide tools to specify the behaviour of a component application, and check that this application behaves correctly. Their model is applied to the GCM component model too but they prove properties of specific applications whereas we formalise the component model itself. In [18], the authors present a comprehensive formalisation of the Fractal component model using the Alloy specification language. Additionally, the consistency of resulting models can be verified through the automated Alloy Analyzer. These contributions are close to our domain but focus on the use of formal methods to facilitate the development and ensure safety of component applications, while our aim is to provide support for the design of component models and their runtime support.

SCA (Service Component Architecture) [5] is a component model adapted to Service Oriented Architectures. It enables modelling service composition and creation of service components. FraSCAti [21] is an implementation of the SCA model built upon Fractal making this implementation close to GCM. It provides dynamic reconfiguration of SCA component assemblies, a binding factory, a transaction service, and a deployment engine of autonomous SCA architecture. Due to the similarity between FraSCAti and GCM, our approach provides a good formalisation of FraSCAti implementation. There are various approaches on applying formal and semi-formal methods to Service Oriented Architectures (SOA) and in particular SCA. For example, in the EU project SENSORIA [1] dedicated to SOA, they propose Architectural Design Rewriting to formalize development and reconfiguration of software architectures using term-rewriting [7].

Creol [15, 16] is a programming and modelling language for distributed systems. Active objects in Creol have asynchronous communication by method calls and futures. Creol also offers components; the paper [12] presents a framework for component description and test. A simple specification language over communication labels is used to enable the expression of the behaviour of a component as a set of traces at the interfaces. Creol's component model does not support hierarchical structure of components. In [2], the authors present a formalisation of the interface behaviour of Creol components. Creol's operational semantics uses the rewriting logic based system Maude [19] as a logical support tool. The operational semantics of Creol is expressed in Maude by reduction rules in a structural operational semantics style enabling testing of model specifications. However, this kind of logical embedding does not support structural reasoning.

2.2 Component Model Overview

Our intent is to build a mechanised model of the GCM component model [4], but giving it a runtime semantics so that we can reason on the execution of component application and their evolution. Thus we start by describing the concepts of the GCM which are useful for understanding this paper. We will try in this paper to distinguish clearly structural concepts that are proper to any hierarchical component model and a runtime semantics that relies on asynchronous requests and replies. Structurally, the model incorporates hierarchical components that communicate through well defined interfaces connected by bindings. Communication is based on a request-reply model, where requests are queued at the target component while the invoker receives a future. The basic component model has been presented in [13] and is summarized below.

Component Structure. Our GCM-like component model allows hierarchical composition of components. This composition allows us to implement a coarse-grained component by composition of several fine-grained components. We use the term *composite component* to refer to a component containing one or more *subcomponents*. On the other hand, *primitive components* do not contain other components, and are leaf-level components implementing business functionality. A component, primitive or composite, can be viewed as a container comprising two parts. A central *content part* that provides the functional characteristics of the component and a *membrane* providing the non-functional operations. Similarly, interfaces can be functional or non-functional. In this work and in the following description, we focus only on the functional content and interfaces.

The only way to access a component is via its interfaces. *Client* interfaces allow the component to invoke operations on other components. On the other hand, *Server* interfaces receive invocations. A *binding* connects a client interface to the server interface that will receive the messages sent by the client.

For composite components, an interface exposed to a subcomponent is referred to as an *internal* interface. Similarly, an interface exposed to other components is an *external* interface. All the external interfaces of a component must have distinct names. For composites, each external functional interface has a corresponding internal one. The implicit semantics is that a call received on a server

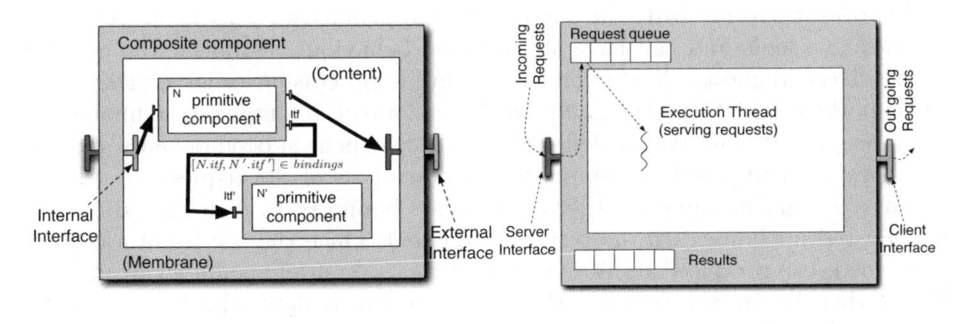

Fig. 1. component composition

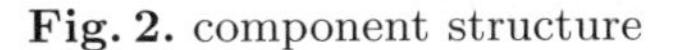
Fig. 2. component structure

external (resp. internal) interface will be transmitted – unchanged – to the corresponding internal (resp. external) client interface.

The GCM model allows for a client interface to be bound to multiple-server interfaces. For the moment, in our model, we restrict the binding cardinality such that bindings connect a client to a single server. Note that several bindings can anyway reach the same server interface.

Figure 1, shows the structure of a composite component. The composite component contains two primitive subcomponents N and N'. The binding $(N.itf, N'.itf')$ connects the client interface *itf* of subcomponent N to the server interface itf' of subcomponent N'.

Communication Model. Our GCM-like components use a simple communication model relying on asynchronous request and replies, as presented in [13]. Communication via requests is the only means of interaction between components. We avoid shared objects or component references, and use a pass-by-copy semantics for request parameters. A component receives the requests on its external server interface. The received requests are then enqueued in the *request queue*, which holds the messages until they can be treated.

Our communication model is asynchronous in the sense that the requests are not necessarily treated immediately upon arrival. Requests are only enqueued at the target component, then the component invoking the request can continue its execution without waiting for the result. Enqueuing a request is done synchronously but the receiver is always ready to receive a request. To ensure transparent handling of asynchronous requests with results, we utilise *futures*. Futures are created automatically upon request invocation and represent the request result, while the treatment of the request is not finished. Once the result of the computation is available, the future is replaced by the result value. Futures are first class objects: they can be transferred as part of requests or results.

Figure 2 gives the internal structure of a component. Incoming requests are enqueued in the *request queue*. The requests are dequeued by the execution threads, when computed; the results are placed in the *results list*.

Component Behaviour. In our model, the primitive components represent the business logic and can have any internal behaviour. Primitive components treat all the requests they receive, choosing a processing order and the way to treat them. On the other hand, the behaviour of a composite component is more restricted: it is strictly defined by its constituent subcomponents and the way they are composed. A composite component serves its requests in a FIFO manner, delegating them to other components bound to it. A delegated request is delivered unchanged to the target component. Once the service of a request is finished, the produced result is stored in the computed results for future use. It can then be transmitted to other components, as determined by the reply strategy [17, 14].

2.3 Positioning

This paper provides formalisation of hierarchical components and their structure. At our level of abstraction, this structure is shared by several component levels like Fractal, GCM, and SCA. However most implementations of SCA (except FraSCAti) do not instantiate the component structure at runtime. By contrast, to allow component introspection and reconfiguration at runtime, we consider a specification where structural information is still available at runtime. This enables adaptive and autonomic component behaviours. Indeed, component adaptation in those models can be expressed by reconfiguration of the component structure. For example, reconfiguration allows replacement of an existing component by a new one, which is impossible or very difficult to handle in a model where component structure disappears at runtime.

Most existing works on formal methods for components focus on the support for application development whereas we focus on the support for the design and implementation of component models themselves. To our knowledge, this work is the only one to support the design of component models in a theorem prover. It allows proving very generic and varying properties ranging from structural aspects to component semantics and component adaptation.

A formalisation of our communication model along with the component semantics appear in [13]. An extended version of the formal semantics is presented in [14], providing formalisation of one particular reply strategy. Other possible strategies are discussed in [17]. Compared to our previous works, this paper relies on the experience gained in specification and proof and demonstrated in [13, 14] to design a framework for supporting mechanised proofs for distributed components. In particular this paper focuses on the handling of component structure, on a basic set of lemmas providing valuable tooling for further proof, and the illustration of the presented framework to prove a few properties dealing with component semantics and reconfiguration.

3 Formalisation of Component Model in Isabelle/HOL

Our component model is a subset of the GCM component model, but with a precisely defined structure and semantics. It incorporates hierarchical components that communicate via asynchronous requests and replies. We start with formalising the structure of our components. Based on the structure defined, we present some of the various *infrastructure* operations that allow us to manipulate the components for proving properties. Then we formalise additional constructs to define component's state and request handling, and correctness of a component assembly. Finally we provide a set of very useful lemmas dealing with component structure and component correctness.

3.1 Component Structure

As we have seen in Section 2.2, a component in our model can either be a composite or primitive. A composite component comprises one or more subcomponents. On the other hand, a primitive component is a leaf-level component encapsulating the business logic.

```
datatype Component = Primitive Name Interfaces PrimState
    | Composite Name Interfaces (Component list) (Binding set) CompState
```

The above Isabelle/HOL datatype definition for `Components` has two constructors `Primitive` and `Composite`. We present below the various elements that make up the structure of our components.

NAME: Each component has a unique name. We use this name as the component identifier/reference.

INTERFACES: Each component has a number of public interfaces. All communication between components is via public interfaces. An interface can be either client or server and by construction a component cannot have two interfaces with the same name.

SUBCOMPONENTS: Composite components have a list of subcomponents, given by the `Component list` parameter. Primitive components do not have subcomponents.

BINDINGS: In composite components, a binding allows an interface of one component to be plugged to an interface of a second component. `(N1.i1, N2.i2)∈bindings` if the interface `i1` of component `N1` is plugged to the interface `i2` of `N2` where `N1` or `N2` can either be component names or *This* if the plugged interface belongs to the composite component that defines the binding.

STATE: All components, primitive or composite have an associated state. Component state is discussed in more detail in Section 3.3.

Design decisions. In the Isabelle/HOL formalisation we chose to include the name of the component into the component itself. Like for interfaces, a first intuitive approach could be rather to define subcomponents as mappings from names to components. There are, however, major advantages to our approach. When we reason about a component we always have its name, which makes the expression of several semantic rules and lemmas more natural. The main advantage of maps is the implicit elegant encoding of the uniqueness of *Name*(s). As mentioned before, *Name*(s)are used as component references. Unfortunately, this advantage of maps is quite low in a multi-layered component model because a map can only serve one level. As we want component names to be unique globally, a condition on name uniqueness is necessary.

Subcomponents are defined as lists rather than finite sets because lists come with a convenient inductive reasoning easing proofs involving component structure. Of course it is easy to define an equivalence relation to identify components modulo reordering. On the contrary the bindings of a component are defined as a set because no inductive reasoning is necessary on bindings, and sets fit better to the representation of this construct.

Having a formalisation of component structure alone, although useful, is not sufficient. An adequate infrastructure needs to be developed to help in reasoning on the component model. The next section describes some of the infrastructure operations that allow us to manipulate components inside component hierarchies.

3.2 Efficient Specification of Component Manipulation

This section provides various operations that allow us to effectively manipulate components. These include operation for accessing component fields, mechanisms for traversing component hierarchies, and means for replacing and updating components inside the hierarchical structure. All these operations are primitive recursive functions enabling an encoding in Isabelle/HOL using the `primrec` feature. Using this feature has great advantages for the automation of the interactive reasoning process. Automated proof procedures of Isabelle/HOL, like the simplifier, are automatically adapted to the new equations such that simple cases can be solved automatically. Moreover, the definitions themselves can use pattern matching leading to readable definitions.

Field access. We define a number of operations for accessing various fields. These include the function GETNAME that returns the `Name` of the component.

```
primrec getName:: Component ⇒ Name   where
        getName (Primitive N itf s) = N |
        getName (Composite N itf sub b s) = N
```

Similarly, we define `getItfs` , `getQueue`, and `getComputedResults` for getting interfaces, request queues and replies. Requests and replies are part of the component state described in Section 3.3.

Accessing component hierarchy. In order to support hierarchical components, we need a number of mechanisms to access components inside hierarchies. These range from simply finding a suitable component inside a component list to updating the relevant component with another component. The most useful of these operations are detailed below.

CPLIST: returns a list of all subcomponents of a component recursively. It uses the predefined Isabelle/HOL list operators `#` for constructing lists and `@` for appending two lists. Note that the following primitive recursive function is mutually recursive and needs an auxiliary operation dealing with component lists.

```
primrec cpList:: Component ⇒ Component list and
        cpListlist:: Component list ⇒ Component list
where
  cpList (Primitive N itfs s) = [(Primitive N itfs s)] |
  cpList (Composite N itfs subCp bindings s) =
           (Composite N itfs subCp bindings s)#(cpListlist subCp) |
  cpListlist [] = [] |
  cpListlist (C#CL) = (cpList C)@ cpListlist CL
```

CpSet: gives a set representation of the `cpList` of a component. This allows us to write properties in a much more intuitive way, for example, quantifying over sub-components is easily written as ∀ `C'` ∈ `CpSet(C)`. Note however that a few proofs require to stick to the `CpList` notation; indeed when switching to cpSet construct, one cannot reason on the coexistence of two identical components.

```
constdefs :: Component ⇒  Component set
           cpSet C == set (cpList C)
```

getCp: allows for retrieving a given component from a component list based on the component Name. The constructors `Some` and `None` represent the so-called `option` datatype enabling specifications of partial functions. Here, a component with the given name might not be defined in the list – this is nicely and efficiently modelled by a case distinction over the option type. Note the definition of `^` as an infix operator synonymous for `getCp`. This so-called pretty printing syntax of Isabelle supports natural notation of the form `CL^N = Some C'`.

```
primrec getCp:: Component list ⇒ Name ⇒ Component option where
   getCp [] N' = None |
   getCp (C#CL) N' = if (getName C=N') then Some C else (CL^N')
```

changeCp CL C: written `CL<-C` replaces the component in the list `CL` that has the same name as `C` by `C`; it does nothing if there is no component with the given name.

```
primrec changeCp::Component list ⇒ Component ⇒ Component list where
  changeCp [] C = [] |
  changeCp (C#CL) C' = if getName C=getName C' then C'#CL else C#(CL<-C')
```

removeSubCp C N: removes the subcomponent of `C` with name `N` but does nothing if there is no subcomponent with this name. Note, here the use of a `case` switch supporting again pattern matching in Isabelle/HOL definitions.

```
primrec removeSubCp:: Component ⇒ Name ⇒ Component where
  removeSubCp (Primitive N itf s) N' = (Primitive N itf s) |
  removeSubCp (Composite N itf sub b s) N' = ( case sub^N' of
          None => (Composite N itf sub b s) |
          Some C => Composite N itf (remove1 C sub) b s)
```

Similar operations are needed for dealing with requests and results. This includes operations for building lists of all referenced requests inside a component (and its subcomponents), finding a result for a given future inside a component hierarchy, etc. In all we provide almost 30 functions and predicates to help express structured component specifications efficiently.

Design decisions. It is crucial for the reasoning process whether one chooses lists or sets to represent various parts of the specified component structure. As we have seen above the basic infrastructure we have built up to handle our hierarchical components is mainly based on lists. Consequently, we can define operations over components and their constituents by primitive recursion and thereby decisively improve automated support. However, sets come with a more natural notation. Often set theoretic properties can be simply decided by boolean reasoning that poses no problems for logical decision procedures integrated in Isabelle/HOL, and Isabelle/HOL comes with numerous lemmas for reasoning on sets. On the other side, inductive reasoning on finite sets is less convenient than on lists. In places where we want to combine the merits of both worlds, the `CpSet` function provides a convenient translation.

3.3 Component State

Our component model shall not only allow structural reasoning on hierarchical components but also reasoning about dynamic component state. While the preceding sections provided a good formalisation valid for any hierarchical component model, we now define component state in order to support communication by request and replies. Those constructs are used to define our component semantics, as shown in Section 4.1. Let us first focus on the high level definition of states which provide the constructs relating the component structure with the dynamic semantics[2]. We show below the two types of component states (for composite and primitive components) used in the definition of `Component` presented in Section 3.1.

```
record CompState =                       record PrimState =
Cqueue:: Request list                    Pqueue:: Request list
CcomputedResults:: Result list           PcomputedResults:: Result list
                                         PintState:: intState
                                         behaviour:: Behaviours
```

Each state contains a queue of pending requests, and a list of results computed by this component. Additionally, primitive components have an internal state and a behaviour for encoding the business logic, see below. We use the Isabelle/HOL `record` type constructor here; it automatically defines field projection as functions, e.g. for a `Compstate s`, `(Cqueue s)` accesses its request queue. Note that uniqueness of fields identifier required us to add a 'C' or 'P' prefix to fields of component states to distinguish them.

The definition of the component state relies on the definitions of requests (characterized by a future identifier, a parameter, and a target interface), and results (characterized by the future identifier and its value).

[2] The real definition of component states contains additional fields; only the fields of interest for this paper are shown here.

```
record Request =                      record Result=
id::Fid                               fid::Fid
parameter:: Value                     fValue:: Value
invokedItf:: Name
```

An interesting construct is the representation of component behaviour. Each primitive component has an internal state. A behaviour specifies how a primitive component passes from an internal state to another. It is defined as a labeled transition system between internal states of a component:

```
typedef  Behaviours={ beh::(intState × Action × intState) set.
   (∀ s s'. ((s,Tau,s')∈ beh ⟶ (set (PRqRefs s')⊆set (PRqRefs s))
                          ∧ PcurrentReqs s' = PcurrentReqs s)) ∧
 . . . }
```

The type `Behaviours` is defined as a set of triples (internal state, action, internal state). In our case actions are: internal transition (`Tau`, shown here), request service, request emission, result reception, and end of service which associates a result to a request. More than the precise definition of our actions, it is interesting to focus on the way behaviour can be defined and further refined by constraints. Additional rules are specified to restrain the possible behaviours, preventing incorrect transitions to occur; for example, we forbid replying to a non-existing request. In the piece of code above we require conditions on the internal state before and after an internal transition: the set of referenced futures can only be smaller after an internal transition, and the set of currently served requests is unchanged. More complex conditions are imposed for other actions.

Design decisions. Isabelle/HOL extensible records are the natural choice for representing states, requests, and results. They are better suited than simple products because they support qualified names implicitly. We did, however, not use the additional extension property of records which is similar to inheritance known from object-orientation. It could have been used to factor out the shared parts of primitive and composite components but this is not worthwhile – properties specific to the shared parts are few. Hence, there is practically no overhead caused by duplicating basic lemmas. The use of lists for requests and results is important for the efficient specification and proof of structural properties (see the design decisions in the previous section). The definition of behaviours in the internal state of primitive components uses an Isabelle/HOL type definition. This way, we can encapsulate the predicate defining the set of all well-formed behaviours into a new HOL type. These constraints are thereby implicitly carried over and can be re-invoked by using the internal isomorphism with the set `Behaviours`.

3.4 Correct Component

We presented the structure of our components in Section 2.2, while the various constructs designed to manipulate hierarchical components appear in Section 3.2.

However, we only reason on a subset of all possible components that can be constructed according to the described component structure. We refer to this subset of components as *correct components*. Correct components are not only well-formed, but they adhere to some additional constraints. The various well-formedness rules along with the correctness constraints are presented in the following.

We start with specifying the structure of a well-formed component. A composite component is considered as correctly structured if it passes the criteria specified by the function `CorrectComponentStructure` given below.

```
primrec CorrectComponentStructure :: Component ⇒ bool where
 CorrectComponentStructure (Composite N itfs sub b s) =
   ((∀b∈bindings.(GetQualified(src b) (Composite N itfs sub b s =
                           Some (| kind=Client,cardinality=Single|))
    ∧ (GetQualified(dest b)(Composite N itfs sub b s) =
                           Some(| kind=Server,cardinality=Single|)))
    ∧ NoDuplicateSrc b
    ∧ distinct (map getName sub)
    ∧ (∀ Q∈ set (Cqueue s). (invokedItf Q)∈  dom itfs
                     ∧ kind (the (itfs (invokedItf Q))) = Server)
```

A composite component has a correct structure if: each binding only connects an existing client interface to another existing server interface; each client interface is connected only once; all subcomponents have distinct names; and all requests in the request queue of the composite refer to existing server interfaces. A primitive component has a correct structure if it follows the last requirement plus a couple of constraints relating its behaviour with its interfaces.

```
constdefs CorrectComponent :: Component ⇒ bool
CorrectComponent c==CorrectComponentStructure c ∧ distinct(RqIdList c)
        ∧ (ReferencedRqs c) ⊆ (set(RqIdList c))
        ∧ distinct (map getName (cpList c))
        ∧ (∀ f∈ set (RqIdList c). snd f ∈ set(map getName(cpList c)))
```

A correct component is a correctly structured component that also has uniquely defined request identifiers (`RqIdList c` gives all requests computed by `c` and its subcomponents), and all future referenced by the components should correspond to an existing request. Finally, names of all components in the composition should be unique. This differs from the well-formedness requirement which only requires the names of all direct subcomponents to be unique. The requirement of checking correct future referencing throughout the composition hierarchy is stronger than what is needed for most proofs, and can at times be relaxed resulting in a weaker correctness requirement `CorrectComponentWeak`. `CorrectComponentWeakList` gives similar constraints but for a list of components. Using `CorrectComponentWeak` eases proofs involving component hierarchy because if a component verifies `CorrectComponentWeak` then all its subcomponents also verify it.

```
constdefs CorrectComponentWeak:: Component ⇒ bool
CorrectComponentWeak c == CorrectComponentStructure c
    ∧ distinct (RqIdList c) ∧ distinct (map getName(cpList c))

constdefs CorrectComponentWeakList:: Component list ⇒ bool
CorrectComponentWeakList CL == (CorrectComponentStructureList CL)
  ∧ distinct (RqIdListList CL)∧ distinct (map getName (cpListlist CL))
```

3.5 Basic Properties on Component Structure and Manipulation

In this section, we present a few properties that we proved. They deal with the constructs presented in Section 3.2, and are unrelated to our definition of states presented in the last section. Those lemmas are the basic building blocks on which most of our proofs rely. On the set of more than 80 lemmas dealing with `cpSets` and `cpLists`, we focus on the most useful and significant ones. In particular, we choose to show rather lemmas dealing with the `cpSet` construct because it is a higher-level one and thus reasoning on sets of components is often preferable, when possible. Note however that most of the proofs dealing with distinctness of component names will rather use `cpLists`.

We start by an easy lemma quite heavily used and very easy to prove. It states that `C` is always in `cpSet(C)` (it is proved by cases on `C`).

```
  lemma cpSetFirst: C ∈ cpSet C
```

The set of components inside a composite one can be decomposed as follows. It can be separated into the composite itself plus all the components in the `cpSet` of each sub-component.

```
lemma cpSetcomposite:
cpSet (Composite N itfs sub b s)={Composite N itfs sub b s}
                                 ∪ {C.∃ C'∈set sub. C∈ cpSet C'}
```

This lemma is proved by an induction on lists of subcomponents. Conversely, we can prove that, if a component is in the `cpSet` of a subcomponent of a composite, it is in the `cpSet` of the composite. We also present a more general variant of this lemma stating that if `C''` is inside `C'` and `C'` is inside `C` then `C''` is inside `C`.

```
lemma cpSetcomposite_rev:
⟦ C∈ set sub; C'∈ cpSet C ⟧⟹ C'∈ cpSet (Composite N itfs sub b s)

lemma cpSetcpSet: ⟦C''∈ cpSet C';C'∈cpSet C⟧⟹ C''∈ cpSet C
```

Although those two lemmas are very easy to prove (by induction on the component structure), they are massively used in the other proofs.

Another theorem almost automatically proved by Isabelle, but exceedingly useful is the following one. It gives another formulation of the `getCp` construct.

```
lemma getCp_inlist: CL^N=Some C ⟹ C∈ set CL ∧ getName C=N
```

It is used to relate hypotheses in which a component name occurs and the component name, or the component structure. The reverse direction holds only if the component names inside CL are distinct as shown by the next lemma.

```
lemma getCpIdistinct:
⟦ distinct (map getName CL); getName C=N; C∈ set CL⟧ ⟹ CL^N=Some C
```

As the tools provided for the `distinct` construct in the Isabelle/HOL framework are a little weaker than for manipulating sets and lists, this proof is slightly longer and less automatic but still quite simple. Finally, the next lemma relates the `changeCp` primitive with the `getCp` one for the case that the name of the accessed component and the name of the changed one are different.

```
lemma upd_getCpunchanged: N≠getName C'⟹(CL <- C')^N = CL^N
```

Impact of design choices. As a consequence of the mapping between component structure and Isabelle's structural support, it has been relatively easy to prove properties of component structure by automatic steps plus induction on the component structure. Consequently, the basic proofs on component sets and lists were relatively easy to handle: approximately 700 lines of code for the 80 lemmas dealing with component sets, component lists, and request identifiers, including the `getCp`, `getRecSubCp`, and `changeSubCp` primitives. By contrast, the proofs dealing with the semantics or correctness are generally much longer (several hundreds of lines per proof). However, the structural lemmas presented above are heavily used in the other proofs and strongly facilitate them.

3.6 Properties on Component Correctness

Based on the infrastructure for structural reasoning on the composition structure of components, we can now prove properties on the correctness of component structure presented in Section 3.4. The properties logically relate the degree of correctness of the structure. We present some of these lemmas here.

The lemma `CorrectCompWeak` establishes the relationship between `CorrectComponent` and `CorrectComponentWeak`.

```
lemma CorrectCompWeak: CorrectComponent C ⟹ CorrectComponentWeak C
```

`CorrectComponentListComp` establishes the correctness of the list of subcomponents given that the parent composite component is correct. Similarly, a member of a weakly correct component list is also weakly correct.

```
lemma CorrectComponentListComp:
     CorrectComponentWeak (Composite N  itfs subCp bindings s)
                                   ⟹ CorrectComponentWeakList subCp
lemma CorrectComponentListComp_rev:
     ⟦CorrectComponentWeakList CL; C ∈ set CL⟧ ⟹ CorrectComponentWeak C
```

As a consequence, and as mentioned in Section 3.4, weak correctness entails weak correctness of subcomponents. Those lemmas imply that, when proving properties by induction, relying on weak correctness is very convenient as weak correctness can be used as the hypothesis of the recurrence hypothesis.

```
lemma SubComponent_CorrectComponentWeak:
    ⟦C'∈cpSet C; CorrectComponentWeak C⟧ ⟹ CorrectComponentWeak C'
```

The following property expresses a condition entailed in `CorrectComponentWeak`. `C^^N` returns the first subcomponent of `C` having the name `N`. If `C` is a weakly correct component, then there is a single component with that name, and thus the following hold:

```
lemma getRecSubCp_getName:
⟦CorrectComponentWeak C; C'∈ cpSet C⟧ ⟹ C^^(getName C') = Some C'
```

The proof of this property depends on properties on distinct names, and on the lemmas shown in this section and the preceding one.

Impact of design choices. The proofs in Isabelle/HOL are, for the most part of the correctness lemmas, almost automatic: unfolding the definitions, the proofs are mostly solved by applying the automatic tactic `auto`. Yet, these lemmas are important because they precisely relate different correctness conditions and consequently clarify subsequent proofs. They also entail properties of *compositionality*, i.e. what are the properties of a composite with respect to its constituents.

Other properties, like `getRecSubCp_getname` are harder to prove. Their proofs rely strongly on the provided infrastructure for structured components presented earlier in this section. Feasibility and readability of the proofs at the correctness level depends decisively on this clearly structured support with lemmas. Often the amount of automated proof work can be increased by adding our basic lemmas to the simplification sets of Isabelle/HOL.

4 Components at Runtime

4.1 Semantics

The formal semantics of our component model is given by a number of reduction relations defined by a set of inductive rules. These reduction relations along with the formal semantics of our component model appear in [13]; they were informally summarized in Section 2.2. This section illustrates the usefulness of the presented framework to specify and prove properties on the semantics by focusing on one reduction rule and one property. A smoothly working infrastructure of well-designed structural definitions and accompanying lemmas are prerequisite for mechanically proving properties over a structured component semantics.

We define a reduction relation $S \vdash C \rightarrow_R C', RL$ stating that in the component system S, a given component C reduces to a component C'. The list RL is used for specification of reply strategy that is not detailed here. We show below one specific communication rule CommChild, illustrated in Figure 3, and encoding the delegation of requests to a contained subcomponent.

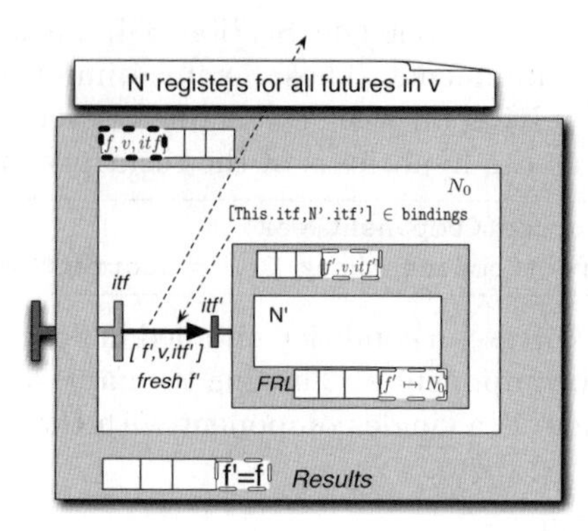

Fig. 3. COMMCHILD rule

```
COMMCHILD:
⟦ Cqueue s= R#Q; ⦇src=This(invkItf R),dest=N'.i2⦈∈bindings;
                  f'∉set (RqIdList S) ; subCp^N' = Some C'⟧  ⟹
S⊢Composite N itf sub b s→R Composite N itf
    (sub<-(C'←⦇id=f', parameter=(parameter R),invokedItf=i2⦈)) b
    (s⦇Cqueue:=Q,CcomputedResults:=CcomputedResults s @
                                          [⦇fid=id R,fValue=(0,[f'])⦈]⦈),
                            (f,N)#(map (λ id.(id,N')) (snd(parameter R)))
```

The rule expresses request delegation between a composite component N and one of its subcomponents N'. The request R (shown as its constituents $[f,\ v,\ itf]$ in Figure 3) that has been sent to the parent N is dequeued from its request queue. A new future f' is created and added to the result list (`CcomputedResults`) of the parent as the result for this request R. A new request (shown as its constituents $[f',\ v,\ itf'\ ]$) is enqueued in the subcomponent N'. In the Isabelle code snippet, we use the shortcut notation $\leftarrow$ for the enqueue operation. The target subcomponent is determined using the bindings: if *This.itf* is bound to $N'.itf'$ then the request is sent to the interface itf' of the subcomponent N', where *itf* is the external interface of N by which the request had arrived before. Note the use of the getCp primitive: `subCp^N'=Some C'` ensures that subcomponent of name `N'` exists and is `C'`. Also the `changeCp` primitive (`<-`) is quite useful here to update the subcomponent by enqueueing a new request to it.

Let us conclude this section by showing a property we proved in our framework that deals with component semantics. The following lemma shows that the set of names of components inside a component is unchanged by reduction.

```
lemma red_names_eq: ⟦S⊢c1→R c2, RL; CorrectComponentWeak c1⟧
        ⟹ getName ‘ (cpSet c2) = getName ‘(cpSet c1)
```

The proof is approximately 60 lines long, it is done by analysis on the reduction rule. It relies on a few lemmas relating names with reduction rules, and on most of the lemmas presented in Section 3. A crucial auxiliary lemma is the following one that is purely structural and unrelated with our semantics.

```
lemma upd_names_eq:
⟦CL^(getName c2)= Some c1; getName‘(cpSet c2)=getName‘(cpSet c1)⟧
        ⟹ getName‘(cpListset CL) = getName‘(cpListset (CL<-c2))
```

4.2 Reconfiguration

Reconfiguration represents all the transformations of the component structure or content that can be handled at runtime. We consider here mainly structural reconfiguration, which includes changes of the bindings, and of the content of a component. For example replacement of a primitive component by a new one is a form of reconfiguration that allows evolution of the business code.

In Fractal or GCM, configuration primitives are bind/unbind to manipulate bindings, add/remove to change the set of subcomponent of a composite component; also it is possible to start/stop a component.

Our framework enables reasoning on reconfiguration primitives and behaviour of a reconfigured component system. We illustrate below a few encodings of reconfiguration primitives and some theorems that can be proved in Isabelle/HOL thanks to our framework.

We illustrate reconfiguration capacities of our approach by defining two reconfiguration primitives and proving two related lemmas. But beforehand, we define the notion of *complete component*.

Completeness. Similarly to [6], we say that a composite component is complete if all interfaces of its sub-components and all its internal interfaces are bound. This can be easily defined in Isabelle by the following primitive recursive predicate.

```
primrec Complete::Component⇒ bool where
 Complete (Primitive N itf s) = True |
 Complete (Composite N itf sub bindings s) =
   (∀ C∈set sub. allExternalItfsBound C bindings) ∧
   (allInternalItfsBound (Composite N itf sub bindings s) bindings) ∧
   (CompleteList sub)
```

Here, `allInternalItfsBound C b` checks that all external interfaces of `C` are bound by bindings `b`, and `allExternalItfsBound C b` that all internal interfaces of `C` are bound by bindings `b`. Finally, similar to `cpListlist` in Section 3.2, `CompleteList` recursively checks that all subcomponents are complete.

As there is no notion of optional interface in our model, this definition is really straightforward. For a complete component, any request emitted by a component will arrive at a destination component.

Unbind primitive. The unbind primitive removes one of the bindings defined by a composite component.

```
primrec unbind:: Component⇒Binding⇒Component where
  unbind (Primitive N itf s) b = (Primitive N itf s) |
  unbind (Composite N itf sub bindings s) b =
         (Composite N itf sub (bindings-{b}) s)
```

Of course, un-binding does not maintain completeness, and this can be proved in our framework.

```
lemma unbinding_incomplete:
⟦b∈bindings; CorrectComponentStructure (Composite N itf sub bindings s)⟧
        ⟹ ¬ Complete (unbind (Composite N itf sub bindings s) b)
```

This lemma is proved in only 35 lines of simple Isabelle/HOL code, thanks to the properties presented in Section 3.5. The proof can be sketched as follows. `CorrectComponentStructure` imposes that in bindings `src b` is connected only once, thus, in `bindings-{b}`, `src b` is not connected anymore. Now, `src b` can be either `This N` if `b` connects an internal client interface to a sub-component, or of the form `CN.N` if it connects a sub-component to another interface. In the first case, the new component does not ensure `allInternalItfsBound` anymore, and in the second case, it is `allExternalItfsBound` that is not true for the component with name `CN`; note that `CorrectComponentStructure` ensures the existence of such a component.

Component replacement. Let us now introduce a reconfiguration primitive that would automatically maintain completeness.

```
primrec Replace:: Component⇒Name⇒Component⇒Component where
Replace (Primitive N itf s) N1 C = (Primitive N itf s) |
Replace (Composite N itf sub binds s) N1 C = addSubCp (removeSubCp
(Composite N itf sub((λb.RenameBinding b N1(getName C))`binds) s)N1) C
```

This primitive maintains completeness of a correct component as expressed in the following lemma:

```
lemma replace_complete:
 ⟦sub^(getName C')=None; sub^N'=Some oldC; getItfs oldC=getItfs C';
  Complete C'; Complete (Composite N itf sub bindings s);
  CorrectComponentStructure C';
  CorrectComponentStructure (Composite N itf sub bindings s)⟧
     ⟹ Complete (Replace (Composite N itf sub bindings s) N' C')
```

This lemma requires that all involved original components are correct and complete, that the replaced component is in the composition, but not the replacement one, and that those two components have the same interfaces. A similar lemma proving `CorrectComponentStructure` for the result of the replacement operation is also proved.

Of course, the replace primitive can be expressed by lower level reconfiguration operations, i.e. an unbind, remove, add, bind sequence. A lemma equivalent to the preceding one could also be proved. Such a lemma would be more general but a little more complex to express because it would need to relate the set of unbound bindings, the set of re-bound ones, and the component involved in the add-remove operations.

5 Conclusion

This paper presented the logical machinery of a mechanized framework for reasoning about structured component systems; especially targeting distributed components. We have first illustrated and motivated the specification of components and the provided proof infrastructure. Furthermore, we have shown this machinery in action by showing how reconfiguration of components can be formally specified, and how properties over component structure and reconfiguration can be handled. This paper also illustrated our approach by showing the specification of a semantics for components, and associated proofs. Overall, the developed framework consists of more than 4000 lines, including almost 300 lemmas and theorems, approximately 500 lines for defining the component model and its semantics, and 1800 lines focusing on properties specific to future registration which were not presented here. As usual with mechanised proofs, the main difficulty is the choice of the right structures providing the suitable level of abstraction. Some proofs are lengthy and technical but no major difficulty was encountered.

In contrast to existing works, our approach focuses on increasing confidence in global properties of component models. For this, we provide a framework and apply it to prove generally valid results. The established infrastructure of structured components with asynchronous communication provides an elegant abstraction from implementation detail while fully preserving the communication structure and defining a precise semantics. One limiting factor of our framework is that a precise semantics for components had to be chosen to allow mechanised proofs. Overall we have developed a reliable basis for the mechanical proofs of properties of hierarchical component models, and we have shown its adequacy to deal with first proofs entailing reconfiguration, or component semantics. We additionally provide subsequent support for distributed components communicating by asynchronous requests with futures.

A promising follow up project would be to analyse information flows based on this model, or properties entailing component synchronisation at reconfiguration time. More generally we expect to prove properties on reconfiguration that will entail reasoning simultaneously on component execution and on evolution of component structure. This would show the correctness of complex adaptation procedures that can be applied in autonomous component systems.

References

[1] Sensoria – software engineering for service-oriented overlay computers (2005)
[2] Ábrahám, E., Grabe, I., Grüner, A., Steffen, M.: Behavioral interface description of an object-oriented language with futures and promises. Journal of Logic and Algebraic Programming 78(1-2), 491–518 (2008)
[3] Barros, T., Ameur-Boulifa, R., Cansado, A., Henrio, L., Madelaine, E.: Behavioural models for distributed fractal components. Annales des Télécommunications 64(1-2), 25–43 (2009)
[4] Baude, F., Caromel, D., Dalmasso, C., Danelutto, M., Getov, V., Henrio, L., Pérez, C.: GCM: A Grid Extension to Fractal for Autonomous Distributed Components. Annals of Telecommunications (2008) (accepted for publication)

[5] Beisiegel, M., Blohm, H., Booz, D., Edwards, M., Hurley, O.: SCA service component architecture, assembly model specification. Technical report (March 2007), www.osoa.org/display/Main/Service+Component+Architecture+Specifications
[6] Bruneton, E., Coupaye, T., Stefani, J.B.: The Fractal Component Model. Technical report, ObjectWeb Consortium (February 2004), http://fractal.objectweb.org/specification/index.html
[7] Bruni, R., et al.: Service oriented architectural design. In: Barthe, G., Fournet, C. (eds.) TGC 2007 LNCS, vol. 4912, pp. 186–203. Springer, Heidelberg (2008)
[8] Cámara, J., Salaün, G., Canal, C., Ouederni, M.: Interactive Specification and Verification of Behavioural Adaptation Contracts. In: Ninth International Conference on Quality Software, pp. 65–75 (August 2009)
[9] Canal, C., Poizat, P., Salaün, G.: Synchronizing behavioural mismatch in software composition. In: Gorrieri, R., Wehrheim, H. (eds.) FMOODS 2006. LNCS, vol. 4037, pp. 63–77. Springer, Heidelberg (2006)
[10] Cansado, A., Madelaine, E.: Specification and verification for grid Component-Based applications: From models to tools. In: Formal Methods for Components and Objects, pp. 180–203 (2009)
[11] CCA-Forum. The Common Component Architecture (CCA) Forum home page (2005), http://www.cca-forum.org/
[12] Grabe, I., Steffen, M., Torjusen, A.B.: Executable interface specifications for testing asynchronous creol components. Technical Report Research Report No. 375, University Of Oslo (July 2008)
[13] Henrio, L., Kammüller, F., Rivera, M.: An asynchronous distributed component model and its semantics. In: de Boer, F.S., Bonsangue, M.M., Madelaine, E. (eds.) FMCO 2008. LNCS, vol. 5751, Springer, Heidelberg (2009) (to appear)
[14] Henrio, L., Khan, M.U.: Asynchronous components with futures: Semantics and proofs in isabelle/hol. In: Proceedings of the Seventh International Workshop, FESCA 2010. ENTCS (2010) (to appear)
[15] Broch Johnsen, E., Owe, O.: An asynchronous communication model for distributed concurrent objects. In: Proceedings of the Software Engineering and Formal Methods, SEFM 2004, Washington, DC, USA, pp. 188–197. IEEE Computer Society Press, Los Alamitos (2004)
[16] Broch Johnsen, E., Owe, O., Yu, I.C.: Creol: a type-safe object-oriented model for distributed concurrent systems. Theor. Comput. Sci. 365(1), 23–66 (2006)
[17] Khan, M.U., Henrio, L.: First class futures: a study of update strategies. Research Report RR-7113, INRIA (2009)
[18] Merle, P.B., Stefani, J.B.: A formal specification of the Fractal component model in Alloy. Research Report RR-6721, INRIA (2008)
[19] Meseguer, J.: Conditional reqriting logic as a unified model of concurrency. Journal of Theoretical Computer Science 96, 73–155 (1992)
[20] Nipkow, T., Paulson, L.C., Wenzel, M.: Isabelle/HOL – A Proof Assistant for Higher-Order Logic. In: Isabelle/HOL. LNCS, vol. 2283, Springer, Heidelberg (2002)
[21] OW2.Consortium. FraSCAti, Open SCA middleware platform (2009), https://wiki.objectweb.org/frascati/Wiki.jsp?page=FraSCAti

Verification of Context-Dependent Channel-Based Service Models

Natallia Kokash[1,⋆,⋆⋆], Christian Krause[1,⋆⋆⋆], and Erik P. de Vink[2]

[1] CWI, P.O. Box 94079, 1090 GB Amsterdam, The Netherlands
Natallia.Kokash@cwi.nl
[2] Technische Universiteit Eindhoven, Den Dolech 2, Eindhoven, The Netherlands

Abstract. The paradigms of service-oriented computing and model-driven development are becoming of increasing importance in the field of software engineering. According to these paradigms, new systems are composed with added value from existing stand-alone services to support business processes across organizations. Services comprising a system but originating from various sources need to be coordinated. The Reo coordination language is a state-of-the-art tool supported approach to channel-based coordination. Reo introduces various types of channels which can be composed to build complex connectors to represent various behavioral protocols. This makes Reo suitable for the modeling of service-based business processes. In previous work we presented a framework for model checking data-aware Reo connectors using the mCRL2 toolset. In this paper, we extend this result with a proof of correctness, evaluation of optimization techniques, and support for context-sensitive analysis.

1 Introduction

Service-oriented computing is a paradigm that is changing the way modern software is designed and developed. Services are autonomous, loosely coupled software components with publicly available interfaces that can be invoked by a client or composed by a third party to achieve a more complex goal. An important difference of service-oriented architectures compared to other architectural solutions is that the owner of a service-based system has very limited control over the services involved, as generally they run remotely by external companies which may not even know about each other. Conceptually this is similar to the idea of exogenous coordination which advocates the separation of computation (in this case, provided by services) and coordination [1].

One way to coordinate external services is to use a network of communication channels. Reo is an expressive channel-based coordination language with computer aided support. Reo introduces various types of channels which can be composed into complex connectors (also called circuits) to implement interaction

⋆ Corresponding author.
⋆⋆ Supported by IST COMPAS FP7-ICT-2007-1 project, contract number 215175.
⋆⋆⋆ Supported by NWO GLANCE project WoMaLaPaDiA and SYANCO.

F.S. de Boer et al. (Eds.): FMCO 2009, LNCS 6286, pp. 21–40, 2010.

protocols. Along with the graphical notation and intuitive meaning of channel behavior, several formal semantic models for Reo have been proposed [2,3]. This makes it possible to analyze the connector behavior automatically using simulation and model checking techniques as well as to generate executable code from graphical models. However, these semantic models, in particular constraint automata [2] and coloring semantics [3], require the development of special software tools to deal with them. For example, Reo animation and simulation engines [4] are developed as Eclipse plug-ins at CWI in Amsterdam to animate and simulate the execution of Reo circuits based on coloring semantics, and Vereofy [5] is a model checking tool developed by the University of Dresden to check properties of constraint automata.

Since the tailored development of reliable verification tools is a substantial effort requiring man power over an extensive time span to mature, we chose an alternative approach. In our recent work [6], we presented a framework for specifying behavior of Reo in `mCRL2`, a specification language based on the process algebra ACP, including time and data [7]. Specifications in this language can be analyzed by an extensive set of model checking and simulation tools available in the `mCRL2` toolset. The `mCRL2` model checker has proven its suitability for analyzing large scale industrial systems. Moreover, a specification can be converted into a labelled transition system (LTS) in various formats and subsequently be used as input for external model checking tools, e.g., `CADP` [8]. The `mCRL2` specification language provides means to deal with algebraic data types and user-defined functions. These features are essential for enabling data-aware analysis of Reo circuits which may accept as input structured data elements from web services and may transform them (e.g., merge, duplicate, reorder) using filter and transformer channels.

We developed a conversion tool that generates `mCRL2` specifications from Reo graphical models. These specifications are generated fully automatically and do not require any manual refinement. The mapping from Reo to `mCRL2` is performed according to the constraint automata semantics of Reo. In this paper, we establish the correctness of this mapping by proving the bisimilarity of the generated `mCRL2` specification and constraint automata semantics for a given Reo circuit. Secondly, we propose a method of step-wise `mCRL2` specification generation, that incorporates the structural information of a Reo circuit. Experimental results indicate reduced execution times for linearization of the specification, a necessary step when exploiting the `mCRL2` toolkit. Finally, we incorporate coloring information in our Reo to `mCRL2` encoding. Coloring semantics have been introduced initially to provide an animated execution of Reo circuits. In contrast to constraint automata in their basic form, coloring semantics is able to express the behavior of context-dependent Reo channels, i.e., channels whose behavior depends on the states of other channels or components. A basic example of such channels is a *synchronous lossy* channel that loses data only if it cannot simultaneously dispense it. We present an extension of our conversion tool that maps Reo channels into `mCRL2` processes that explicitly propagate the information about their states to other parts of the circuit by means of typed actions.

The rest of this paper is organized as follows. In Section 2, we summarize the basics of Reo. In Section 3, we review the mCRL2 specification language and its toolset. In Section 4, we briefly describe the translation of Reo to mCRL2. In Section 5, we formally prove the correctness of this translation. In Section 6, we discuss the coloring semantics for Reo, a more expressive semantic model that is able to deal with context dependency, and translate context-aware Reo to the process algebra mCRL2. In Section 7, we describe an updated conversion tool implemented as part of the Eclipse Coordination Tools (ECT) and evaluate its performance with and without optimization techniques based on the structural information about Reo circuits. In Section 8, we discuss related work. Finally, in Section 9, we give concluding remarks and outline future work.

2 The Reo Coordination Language

Reo is a channel-based coordination language wherein components or services are coordinated exogenously (from outside) by so-called *connectors* [9]. These connectors have a graph-like structure where the edges are user-defined communication channels and the nodes implement a standard routing policy.

Channels in Reo are entities that have exactly two ends (also referred to as *ports*), which can be either *source* or *sink* ends. Source ends accept data into, and sink ends dispense data out of their channel. Reo allows channels to have two source or two sink ends. Although channels can be defined by users in Reo, a set of basic channels suffices to implement rather complex coordination protocols. One of the most basic channels in Reo is the so-called Sync channel, which is a directed channel that accepts a data item through its source end if it can instantly dispense it through its sink end. The LossySync channel behaves similarly except that it always accepts data items through its source end. The data item is transferred if it can be dispensed through the sink end, and lost otherwise. The SyncDrain has two source ends and accepts data through them simultaneously. All accepted data items are lost. The AsyncDrain channel accepts data items through any of its two source ends, but never from both of them synchronously. The FIFO is an asynchronous channel with a buffer of size one. The basic set of Reo channels also includes channels that have data dependent behavior or perform data manipulation. For instance, the Filter channel loses the data item at its source end if the item does not match a certain pattern, which is defined in terms of a data constraint for a particular instance of this channel. Similarly one can also associate a data constraint to the SyncDrain. The channel blocks if the data constraint cannot be evaluated to *true*. Furthermore, data manipulation can be implemented using the Transform channel. It applies a user-defined function to the data item at its source end and yields the result at its sink end.

Channels can be joint together using nodes. A node can be of one out of three types: source, sink or mixed, depending on whether all coinciding channel ends are source ends, sink ends or a combination of both. Source and sink nodes together form the boundary of a connector, allowing interaction with its environment. Source nodes act as synchronous replicators, sink nodes as mergers.

Table 1. Graphical notation and semantics for channels and nodes

Channel name	Graphical notation	Constraint automaton
Sync	$A \bullet\!\!\longrightarrow\!\!\bullet B$	$\{A,B\}\ d_A = d_B$
LossySync	$A \bullet$- - -$\bullet B$	$\{A\}$; $\{A,B\}\ d_A = d_B$
SyncDrain	$A \bullet\!\!\rightarrowtail\!\!\leftarrowtail\!\!\bullet B$	$\{A,B\}$
AsyncDrain	$A \bullet\!\!\rightarrowtail\!\!\|\!\!\leftarrowtail\!\!\bullet B$	$\{B\}$; $\{A\}$
FIFO	$A \bullet\!\!-\!\!\square\!\!\rightarrow\!\!\bullet B$	$\{A\}\ d_A = 1$; $\{A\}\ d_A = 0$; $\{B\}\ d_B = 1$; $\{B\}\ d_B = 0$
Filter	$A \bullet\!\!\sim\!\!\rightarrow\!\!\bullet B$	$\{A\}\ \neg expr(d_A)$; $\{A,B\}\ expr(d_A) \wedge d_A = d_B$
Transform	$A \bullet\!\!\rhd\!\!\rightarrow\!\!\bullet B$	$\{A,B\}\ d_B = f(d_A)$
Merger	A, B $\succ\!\rightarrow C$	$\{A,C\}\ d_A = d_C$; $\{B,C\}\ d_B = d_C$
Replicator	$A \prec$ B, C	$\{A,B,C\}\ d_A = d_B = d_C$

Mixed nodes combine both behaviors by atomically consuming a data item from one sink end at the time and replicating it to all source ends.

Semantics of Reo can be given in terms of constraint automata [2]. The transitions in constraint automata are labeled with sets of synchronously firing ports, as well as with data constraints on these ports, if desired. Table 1 depicts the graphical notation and the constraint automata semantics for the basic channels and of the Merger and Replicator primitives, which can be used to construct nodes. For example, the constraint automaton for the lossy sync either has flow on ports A and B involving the same data value (right self-loop) or has flow on port A only, without further conditions (left self-loop). Note that the constraint automaton shown for the FIFO is with respect to the data domain $Data = \{0, 1\}$. Formally, constraint automata are defined as follows.

Definition 1. *A constraint automaton* $\mathcal{A} = (S, \mathcal{N}, \rightarrow, s_0)$ *consists of a set of states* S*, a set of port names* $\mathcal{N}$*, a transition relation* $\rightarrow \subseteq S \times 2^{\mathcal{N}} \times DC \times S$*, where* DC *is the set of data constraints over a finite data domain Data, and an initial state* $s_0 \in S$*.*

For a comprehensive discussion of the constraint automata semantics of Reo we refer to [2]. The intuitive idea of constraint automata is that if the data constraint is satisfied, the corresponding transition can fire and data flow is observed at the given ports. We write $s \xrightarrow{N} t$, without constraint, for a transition indicating that while going from the state s to the state t, flow is observed at the ports in the set N.

3 The mCRL2 Specification Language

We provide a brief overview of the `mCRL2` specification language and toolset. For more details we refer to [7] and to the `mCRL2` website[1].

The basic notion in `mCRL2` is the action. Actions represent atomic events and can be parametrized with data. Actions in `mCRL2` can be synchronized. In this case, we speak of multiactions which are constructed from other actions or multiactions using the so-called synchronization operator $|$, like the multiaction $a|b$ of simultaneous doing the actions a and b. The special action τ (tau) is used to refer to an internal unobservable action. Processes are defined by process expressions, which are compositions of actions and multiactions using a number of operators. The basic operators include

- *deadlock* or *inaction* δ, which does not display any behavior;
- *alternative composition*, written as $p+q$, which represents a non-deterministic choice between the processes p and q;
- *sequential composition*, written $p \cdot q$, which means that q is executed after p, assuming that p terminates;
- the *conditional operator* or *if-then-else* construct, written as $c \rightarrow p \diamond q$, where c is a data expression that evaluates to true or false;
- *summation* $\Sigma_{d:D}\ p$ where p is a process expression in which the data variable d may occur, used to quantify over a data domain D;
- the *at operator* $a@t$, which indicates that the multiaction a happens at the time t;
- *parallel composition* or *merge* $p \parallel q$, which interleaves and synchronizes the multiactions of p with those of q, where synchronization is governed by an implicit communication function;
- the *restriction operator* $\nabla_V(p)$, where V specifies which actions from p are allowed to occur, and, complementary, the *encapsulation* $\partial_H(p)$, where H is a set of action names that are not allowed to occur;
- the *renaming operator* $\rho_R(p)$, where R is a set of renamings of the form $a \rightarrow b$, meaning that every occurrence of action a in p is replaced by the action b;
- the *communication operator* $\Gamma_C(p)$, where C is a set of communications of the form $a_0|...|a_n \mapsto c$, which means that every group of actions $a_0|...|a_n$ within a multiaction is replaced by c.

The `mCRL2` language provides a number of built-in data types such as boolean, natural and positive numbers, integers and real numbers. All standard arithmetic operations for them are predefined. Custom data type definition mechanisms in `mCRL2` allow users to declare new sorts, constructors and functions. A structured type in `mCRL2` can be declared by a construct of the form

$$\textbf{sort}\, S = \textbf{struct}\ \ c_1(p_1^1{:}S_1^1, \ldots, p_1^{k1}{:}S_1^{k1})?r_1 \ \ | \ldots | \ \ c_n(p_n^1{:}S_n^1, \ldots, p_n^{kn}{:}S_n^{kn})?r_n;$$

This construct defines the type S together with constructors $c_i\colon S_i^1 \times \ldots \times S_i^{ki} \rightarrow S$, projections $p_i^j\colon S \rightarrow S_i^j$, and recognizers $r_i\colon S \rightarrow \mathit{Bool}$. Various examples of

[1] `http://mcrl2.org/mcrl2/wiki/index.php`

custom type definitions can be found in the language reference section of the mCRL2 web site.

The mCRL2 toolset provides tools that allow users to verify software models specified in the mCRL2 language. The toolset includes a tool for converting mCRL2 specifications into a compact symbolic representation of the corresponding LTS to speed up subsequent manipulations, yielding so-called linear process specifications (LPS), a tool for generating explicit LTSs from LPSs, tools for optimizing and visualizing these LTSs, and many other useful facilities. A detailed overview is provided at the mCRL2 web site.

For model checking, system properties are specified as formulae in a variant of the modal μ-calculus extended with regular expressions, data and time. In combination with an LPS such a formula is transformed into a parametrized boolean equation system (PBES) and can be solved with the appropriate tools from the toolset. Analysis at the level of LTSs is also possible by means of equivalence checking (e.g., strong and branching bisimulation or trace equivalence). In particular, the presence or absence of deadlocks/livelocks or of certain actions can be checked straightforwardly.

4 Translating Reo to mCRL2

In this section, we recall the rules for mapping Reo primitives (channels and nodes) to mCRL2 processes and briefly explain how to derive composite specifications for arbitrarily complex Reo connectors (cf. [6]).

Our mapping of the basic channels reflects the constraint automata semantics of Reo. The mCRL2 process corresponding to a channel, is based on two atomic actions modeling data flow on its respective ends. Analogously, we introduce a process for every node and actions for all channel ends meeting at the node. One important aspect of our encoding is that data constraints are translated faithfully. For this the actions corresponding to channel and node ends are extended with data parameters. In the context of a given connector, we assume a global datatype, which we model as the custom sort *Data* in mCRL2. In fact, most channels in Reo are agnostic to the actual type of data items they carry. Given such a global type, we can use the summation operator in mCRL2 to define data dependencies imposed by channels. The encodings for the primitives used in this paper are depicted in Table 2. Note that for the FIFO we need to define an additional datatype

$$\textbf{sort}\ \mathit{DataFIFO} = \textbf{struct}\ \mathit{empty?isEmpty} \mid \mathit{full}(e{:}\mathit{Data})\mathit{?isFull};$$

The encoding of the FIFO channel includes a parameter of this datatype which allows us to specify whether the buffer of the channel is empty or full, and if it is full, what value is stored in it.

As in the constraint automata approach, we construct nodes compositionally out of the Merger and the Replicator primitives. A process for a node that behaves like an exclusive router can be defined analogously. However, in practical situations a third type of node comes in handy, which we refer to as Join here.

Table 2. mCRL2 encoding for channels and nodes

$$\mathsf{Sync} = \Sigma_{d:Data}\ A(d)|B(d) \cdot \mathsf{Sync}$$
$$\mathsf{LossySync} = \Sigma_{d:Data}\ (A(d)|B(d) + A(d)) \cdot \mathsf{LossySync}$$
$$\mathsf{SyncDrain} = \Sigma_{d_1,d_2:Data}\ A(d_1)|B(d_2) \cdot \mathsf{SyncDrain}$$
$$\mathsf{AsyncDrain} = \Sigma_{d:Data}\ (A(d) + B(d)) \cdot \mathsf{AsyncDrain}$$
$$\mathsf{FIFO}(f : \mathit{DataFIFO}) = \Sigma_{d:Data}\ (\mathit{isEmpty}(f) \rightarrow A(d) \cdot \mathsf{FIFO}(\mathit{full}(d)) \diamond B(e(f)) \cdot \mathsf{FIFO}(\mathit{empty}))$$
$$\mathsf{Filter} = \Sigma_{d:Data}\ (\mathit{expr}(d) \rightarrow A(d)|B(d) \diamond A(d)) \cdot \mathsf{Filter}$$
$$\mathsf{Transform} = \Sigma_{d:Data}\ A(d)|B(f(d)) \cdot \mathsf{Transform}$$

$$\mathsf{Merger} = \Sigma_{d:Data}\ (A(d)|C(d) + B(d)|C(d)) \cdot \mathsf{Merger}$$
$$\mathsf{Replicator} = \Sigma_{d:Data}\ A(d)|B(d)|C(d) \cdot \mathsf{Replicator}$$

Such a Join synchronizes all coinciding source ends and atomically forms a tuple of the data items received at these ends and transfers it to the sink end. We define a binary join as

$$\mathsf{Join}\ =\ \Sigma_{d_1,d_2:Data}\ A(d_1)|B(d_2)|C(\mathit{tuple}(d_1,d_2)) \cdot \mathsf{Join};$$

For handling data structures formed after passing through the Join node, we need to extend our global datatype with a notion of tuples. Since mCRL2 supports standard algebraic datatypes, this is not a problem. Throughout the rest of the paper, we assume that the global datatype is generated by n user-defined datatypes, which we refer to as $\mathcal{D}_1, \ldots, \mathcal{D}_n$. In concrete cases, they are inferred from the coordinated components or services. If a circuit contains one or more Join nodes, we define the global datatype as

$$\textbf{sort}\ \mathit{Data} = \textbf{struct}\ D_1(e_1 : \mathcal{D}_1)\ |\ ...\ |\ D_n(e_n : \mathcal{D}_n)\ |\ \mathit{tuple}(p_1 : \mathit{Data}, p_2 : \mathit{Data});$$

This definition allows us to instantiate elements of any basic type as well as binary tuples, thus forming tree-like structures. Note, this datatype is suitable for circuits with Join nodes that have two incoming ends only. In the general case, for every Join node with k incoming ends a $\mathit{tuple}_k(p_1 : \mathit{Data}, ..., p_k : \mathit{Data})$ must be added to the definition.

After generating process definitions for all channels and nodes, we need to compose them into one joint process which models the whole connector. This is done using the following three steps:

1. Forming of the parallel composition of all channel and node processes.
2. Synchronizing of actions for coinciding channel and node ends.
3. Hiding of internal actions (optional).

The tentative last step is achieved by renaming into τ, an operation not introduced above. Step 2 in fact involves an application of two mCRL2 operators: communication and blocking. To elucidate the composition process, we now consider a simple example. Consider the LossyFIFO connector composed of two channels and a replication node:

$A \quad X_1\, X_2 Y_2\, Y_1 \quad B$

Following the systematic translation scheme, sorts X_1 and Y_1 are internal ports of the channels that are connected together. Although, these channel ends can be connected directly, for genericity we assume that they both connect to a node. Since the mCRL2 specification language does not allow the use of the same action name in several groups of communicating actions within a single communication operator, we introduce two ports X_2 and Y_2 to connect channel ends to the node. To keep the example small, we assume that the channel ends A and B form the boundary of the connector without connecting to nodes. Thus, the three constituents of the LossyFIFO circuit are translated to the following mCRL2 processes:

$$\begin{aligned}\mathsf{LossySync} &= \Sigma_{d:Data}\ (A(d)|X_1(d) + A(d)) \cdot \mathsf{LossySync};\\ \mathsf{Node} &= \Sigma_{d:Data}\ X_2(d)|Y_2(d) \cdot \mathsf{Node};\\ \mathsf{FIFO}(f : \mathit{DataFIFO}) &= \Sigma_{d:Data}\\ &\quad \mathit{isEmpty}(f) \rightarrow Y_1(d) \cdot \mathsf{FIFO}(\mathit{full}(d)) \diamond B(e(f)) \cdot \mathsf{FIFO}(\mathit{empty})\,;\end{aligned}$$

For obtaining the mCRL2 process for the LossyFIFO connector, we first form the parallel composition of the three processes above, force actions corresponding to the connected channel and node ends communicate, and finally hide the actions X and Y that represent the data flow at the internal node/channel ports by renaming them to τ. In the mCRL2 syntax, cf. Section 3, this reads

$$\begin{aligned}\mathsf{Connector} \;=\; &\rho_{N \rightarrow N \setminus \{X,Y\}}(\\ &\quad \partial_{\{X_1,X_2,Y_1,Y_2\}}(\\ &\quad\quad \Gamma_{\{X_1|X_2 \rightarrow X, Y_1|Y_2 \rightarrow Y\}}(\\ &\quad\quad\quad \mathsf{LossySync} \parallel \mathsf{Node} \parallel \mathsf{FIFO}\ )));\end{aligned}$$

However, this direct approach does not exploit the information about the circuit structure, and, as we show later, the further processing of the obtained specification is very inefficient. Therefore, we build up the process for a Reo connector in a stepwise fashion, i.e.,

$$\begin{aligned}\mathsf{Connector1} &= \rho_{N \rightarrow N \setminus \{Y\}}(\partial_{\{Y_1,Y_2\}}(\Gamma_{\{Y_1|Y_2 \rightarrow Y\}}(\mathsf{Node} \ \parallel\ \mathsf{FIFO})));\\ \mathsf{Connector} &= \rho_{N \rightarrow N \setminus \{X\}}(\partial_{\{X_1,X_2\}}(\Gamma_{\{X_1|X_2 \rightarrow X\}}(\mathsf{LossySync} \ \parallel\ \mathsf{Connector1})));\end{aligned}$$

In this version, we first compose the node and the FIFO, synchronize and hide their connected ends, and then continue with the rest of the circuit. This helps us to keep the intermediate state spaces relatively small. Note that we can use the topology of the connector to determine an order of the processes that significantly decreases the run-time of the linearization algorithm. A comparison of the actual run-times of the two approaches is discussed in Section 7.

5 Correctness of the Translation

In this section, we prove the correctness of the mapping of Reo to mCRL2 discussed above. For simplicity we only consider connectors with disjoint sets of port names. Note that this does not affect the generality of our approach as we can always make these sets disjoint by applying an appropriate renaming of ports.

For each state s of a given constraint automaton $\mathcal{A}$, we define the mCRL2 process $proc(\mathcal{A}, s)$ over the action set $\mathcal{P}(\mathcal{N})$ as

$$proc(\mathcal{A}, s) = \textstyle\sum_{s \xrightarrow{N} t} N \cdot proc(\mathcal{A}, t), \tag{1}$$

where $N = \prod_{x \in N} x$ represents the multiaction composed from all ports in the set. Thus, for example, $\prod_{x \in \{A,B,C\}} x = A|B|C$. In this view, it comes natural to have for the synchronization $N_1|N_2$ of actions N_1 and N_2 the union of the underlying port names $N_1 \cup N_2$. If the action N_1 claims flow at the ports of the set N_1 and the action N_2 does so for the ports of the set N_2, supposedly there is flow at the ports of the set $N_1 \cup N_2$.

As an example, consider the synchronous FIFO $\mathcal{F}$ which behaves similarly to the usual FIFO except that it also can dispense a data item from its buffer and simultaneously accept a new one. Its semantics is given by the constraint automaton and the corresponding mCRL2 processes below.

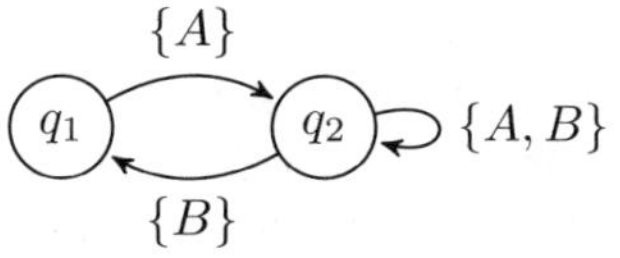

$\{A\}$ q_1 q_2 $\{A, B\}$ $\{B\}$

$$proc(\mathcal{F}, q_1) = A \cdot proc(\mathcal{F}, q_2);$$
$$proc(\mathcal{F}, q_2) = B \cdot proc(\mathcal{F}, q_1) + A|B \cdot proc(\mathcal{F}, q_2);$$

In essence, as discussed in Section 4, the translation recursively decomposes a Reo connector into two subconnectors and puts the mCRL2 processes obtained for these subconnectors in parallel, yielding the process for the main connector. To prove the correctness of this approach formally, we introduce two operations, a synchronous product $\bowtie_\gamma$ for constraint automata and a synchronized merge $\|_\gamma$ for mCRL2 processes. Thus, given a constraint automaton $\mathcal{A}$ for which we have $\mathcal{A} = \mathcal{A}_1 \bowtie_\gamma \mathcal{A}_2$, we translate the constraint automata $\mathcal{A}_1$ and $\mathcal{A}_2$, say into the mCRL2 processes P_1 and P_2, and obtain $P_1 \|_\gamma P_2$ as the translation of $\mathcal{A}$.

Definition 2. *Let $\mathcal{A}_1 = (S_1, \mathcal{N}_1, \rightarrow_1, s_0^1)$, $\mathcal{A}_2 = (S_2, \mathcal{N}_2, \rightarrow_2, s_0^2)$ be two constraint automata with disjoint sets of port names $\mathcal{N}_1$ and $\mathcal{N}_2$, respectively. A* port synchronization function *$\gamma \colon \mathcal{N} \rightarrow \mathcal{N}_1 \times \mathcal{N}_2$ is defined as $\gamma(n) = (\gamma_1(n), \gamma_2(n))$ through the pair of injective functions $\gamma_1 \colon \mathcal{N} \rightarrow \mathcal{N}_1$ and $\gamma_2 \colon \mathcal{N} \rightarrow \mathcal{N}_2$ that map port names from a new set $\mathcal{N}$ into port names from the sets $\mathcal{N}_1$ and $\mathcal{N}_2$.*

Intuitively, $\gamma(n) = (x, y)$ represents a renaming of $x \in \mathcal{N}_1$ and $y \in \mathcal{N}_2$ to the same common element $n \in \mathcal{N}$. In the context of the port synchronization function γ, we write $\mathcal{N}_1'$ for $\mathcal{N}_1 \backslash \gamma_1[\mathcal{N}]$ and $\mathcal{N}_2'$ for $\mathcal{N}_2 \backslash \gamma_2[\mathcal{N}]$. If, for subsets $N_1 \subseteq \mathcal{N}_1$, $N_2 \subseteq \mathcal{N}_2$, it holds that $\gamma_1^{-1}[N_1] = \gamma_2^{-1}[N_2]$ we write

$$N_1 \mid_\gamma N_2 = (N_1 \cap \mathcal{N}_1') \cup \gamma_1^{-1}[N_1] \cup (N_2 \cap \mathcal{N}_2'). \tag{2}$$

From Equation (2) we see that $N_1 \mid_\gamma N_2$ is the union $N_1 \cup N_2$ but with the parts of N_1 and N_2 that are identified via γ_1 and γ_2 replaced by the shared names $\gamma_1^{-1}[N_1] = \gamma_2^{-1}[N_2]$. Also, for a constraint g, we write $\gamma(g)$ for the formula obtained by replacing port names in $\gamma_1[\mathcal{N}] \subseteq \mathcal{N}_1$ and $\gamma_2[\mathcal{N}] \subseteq \mathcal{N}_2$ by the corresponding name in $\mathcal{N}$.

Definition 3. *For two constraint automata $\mathcal{A}_1$ and $\mathcal{A}_2$ with port synchronization function γ, the constraint automaton $\mathcal{A}_1 \bowtie_\gamma \mathcal{A}_2$, called the γ-synchronous product of $\mathcal{A}_1$ and $\mathcal{A}_2$, is given by $\mathcal{A}_1 \bowtie_\gamma \mathcal{A}_2 = (S_1 \times S_2, \mathcal{N}', \rightarrow, \langle s_0^1, s_0^2 \rangle)$ where $\mathcal{N}' = \mathcal{N}_1 |_\gamma \mathcal{N}_2$ and the transition relation $\rightarrow$ is determined by the following rules:*

$$\frac{s_1 \xrightarrow{N_1, g_1}_1 t_1 \quad N_1 \subseteq \mathcal{N}_1'}{\langle s_1, s_2 \rangle \xrightarrow{N_1, g_1} \langle t_1, s_2 \rangle} \qquad \frac{s_2 \xrightarrow{N_2, g_2}_1 t_2 \quad N_2 \subseteq \mathcal{N}_2'}{\langle s_1, s_2 \rangle \xrightarrow{N_2, g_2} \langle s_1, t_2 \rangle} \tag{3}$$

and

$$\frac{s_1 \xrightarrow{N_1, g_1}_1 t_1 \quad s_2 \xrightarrow{N_2, g_2}_1 t_2 \quad \gamma_1^{-1}(N_1) = \gamma_2^{-1}(N_2)}{\langle s_1, s_2 \rangle \xrightarrow{N_1 |_\gamma N_2, \gamma(g_1 \wedge g_2)} \langle t_1, t_2 \rangle} \tag{4}$$

In the above setting, for a port $n \in \mathcal{N}$, the idea is that the ports $n_1 = \gamma_1(n) \in \mathcal{N}_1$ and $n_2 = \gamma_2(n) \in \mathcal{N}_2$ synchronize. Thus, either n_1 and n_2 have both flow or n_1 and n_2 have both no flow, expressed as n having flow or no flow, respectively. The resulting automaton, the so-called synchronized product automaton $\mathcal{A}_1 \bowtie_\gamma \mathcal{A}_2$, follows the flow of $\mathcal{A}_1$ and A_2, based on the first two rules for the transition relation, but requires the flow on its ports in $\mathcal{N}$ to be agreed upon by $\mathcal{A}_1$ and $\mathcal{A}_2$.

A parallel composition $P_1 \parallel P_2$ in mCRL2, being based on the process algebra ACP [10], has its transitions derived from the steps of its left component P_1, its right component P_2, or their synchronization:

$$P_1 \parallel P_2 \;=\; P_1 \mathbin{⫗} P_2 + P_2 \mathbin{⫗} P_1 + P_1 | P_2$$

Here, $⫗$ denotes the left merge, an auxiliary operator in mCRL2. Given two processes p and q, the left merge, written $p ⫗ q$, requires p to execute an action first and thereafter continues as the parallel composition of the remainder of p and q.

In the context of the synchronization product $\mathcal{A}_1 \bowtie_\gamma \mathcal{A}_2$ of constraint automata two aspects are important. Firstly, the port synchronization function γ decides which ports synchronize, hence which sets of port names are non-trivially combined. For example, $(a \cdot Q) \mid (b \cdot Q')$ yields $c \cdot (Q \parallel Q')$ if $\gamma(a, b) = c$. If not stated otherwise, the communication operator is assumed to yield the inaction δ. Secondly, ports that are to be synchronized, i.e. $\gamma_1[\mathcal{N}] \subseteq \mathcal{N}_1$ and $\gamma_2[\mathcal{N}] \subseteq \mathcal{N}_2$, have their names erased from the alphabet. Thus, for the first issue, we define the attributes of the mCRL2 communication operator for a parallel composition as determined by a port synchronization for the synchronized product of two constraint automata. For the second issue, we will apply a specific blocking operator determined by the port synchronization.

Definition 4. *Given a port synchronization function γ with mappings $\gamma_1 \colon \mathcal{N} \rightarrow \mathcal{N}_1$, $\gamma_2 \colon \mathcal{N} \rightarrow \mathcal{N}_2$, the mCRL2 process $P_1 \parallel_\gamma P_2$, called the γ-synchronized merge of P_1 and P_2, is defined as follows:*

$$P_1 \parallel_\gamma P_2 \;=\; \partial_B(\Gamma_C(P_1 \parallel P_2))$$

where $B = \gamma_1[\mathcal{N}] \cup \gamma_2[\mathcal{N}]$ *is the set of blocked actions and* $C = \{ \gamma_1(n)|\gamma_2(n) \mapsto n \mid n \in \mathcal{N} \}$ *is the set of communications.*

We are now in a position to formulate a soundness result for our translation with respect to the parallel composition combined with appropriate synchronization, steps 1 and 2 of our translation. Lemma 1 states that the mCRL2 process associated to a synchronized product of two constraint automata is the same as the synchronized merge of the mCRL2 processes corresponding to the two individual constraint automata. For brevity we restrict to the case of a binary product. However, the result straightforwardly generalizes to an arbitrary number of constituents. Here, equality is modulo strong bisimulation [11], notation $\leftrightarroweq$. It is noted that from a logical point of view, branching bisimilar processes, hence also strongly bisimilar processes, can be used interchangeably within the mCRL2 toolset.

Lemma 1. *Let* $\mathcal{A}_1 = (S_1, \mathcal{N}_1, \rightarrow_1, s_0^1)$ *and* $\mathcal{A}_2 = (S_2, \mathcal{N}_2, \rightarrow_2, s_0^2)$ *be two constraint automata with disjoint sets of port names and let* γ *be a port synchronization for* $\mathcal{A}_1$ *and* $\mathcal{A}_2$*. Then it holds that*

$$proc(\mathcal{A}_1, s_1) \parallel_\gamma proc(\mathcal{A}_2, s_2) \leftrightarroweq proc(\mathcal{A}_1 \bowtie_\gamma \mathcal{A}_2, \langle s_1, s_2 \rangle)\,.$$

Proof. We verify, by checking the usual transfer conditions, that the relation

$$\mathcal{R} = \{ \, (proc(\mathcal{A}_1, s_1) \parallel_\gamma proc(\mathcal{A}_2, s_2), proc(\mathcal{A}_1 \bowtie_\gamma \mathcal{A}_2, \langle s_1, s_2 \rangle) \,) \mid s_1 \in \mathcal{A}_1,\ s_2 \in \mathcal{A}_2 \, \}$$

is a strong bisimulation relation. For brevity we write $proc_i(s_i)$ for $proc(\mathcal{A}_i, s_i)$, $i = 1, 2$, and $proc(s_1, s_2)$ for $proc(\mathcal{A}_1 \bowtie_\gamma \mathcal{A}_2, \langle s_1, s_2 \rangle)$.

Suppose $proc_1(s_1) \parallel_\gamma proc_2(s_2) \xrightarrow{N} P$. From the semantics of $\parallel_\gamma$ we obtain

(i) $\exists P_1$: $proc_1(s_1) \xrightarrow{N} P_1$, $N \subseteq \mathcal{N}_1'$, and $P = P_1 \parallel_\gamma proc_2(s_2)$,
(ii) $\exists P_2$: $proc_2(s_2) \xrightarrow{N} P_2$, $N \subseteq \mathcal{N}_2'$, and $P = proc_1(s_1) \parallel_\gamma P_2$, or,
(iii) $\exists P_1, P_2, N_1, N_2$: $proc_1(s_1) \xrightarrow{N_1}_1 P_1$, $proc_2(s_2) \xrightarrow{N_2}_2 P_2$, $N = N_1 \mid_\gamma N_2$ and $P = P_1 \parallel_\gamma P_2$.

By the definition of $proc_1(s_1)$ and $proc_2(s_2)$ we then have

(i) $\exists g, t_1$: $s_1 \xrightarrow{N,g}_1 t_1$, $N \subseteq \mathcal{N}_1'$, and $P = proc_1(t_1) \parallel_\gamma proc_2(s_2)$,
(ii) $\exists g, t_2$: $s_2 \xrightarrow{N,g}_2 t_2$, $N \subseteq \mathcal{N}_2'$, and $P = proc_1(s_1) \parallel_\gamma proc_2(t_2)$, or,
(iii) $\exists g_1, g_2, t_1, t_2, N_1, N_2$: $s_1 \xrightarrow{N_1,g_1}_1 t_1$, $s_2 \xrightarrow{N_2,g_2}_2 t_2$, $N = N_1 \mid_\gamma N_2$ and $P = proc_1(t_1) \parallel_\gamma proc_2(t_2)$.

Therefore, $\langle s_1, s_2 \rangle \xrightarrow{N,g} \langle t_1, s_2 \rangle$ in $\mathcal{A}_1 \bowtie_\gamma \mathcal{A}_2$, thus $proc(s_1, s_2) \xrightarrow{N} proc(t_1, s_2)$, while $proc_1(t_1) \parallel_\gamma proc_2(s_2) \; \mathcal{R} \; proc(t_1, s_2)$ regarding (i). A symmetrical remark applies regarding (ii). Finally, $\langle s_1, s_2 \rangle \xrightarrow{N,g} \langle t_1, t_2 \rangle$ with $g = \gamma(g_1 \wedge g_2)$, $proc(s_1, s_2) \xrightarrow{N} proc(t_1, t_2)$, while $proc_1(t_1) \parallel_\gamma proc_2(t_2) \; \mathcal{R} \; proc(t_1, t_2)$ regarding (iii).

Now suppose $proc(s_1, s_2) \xrightarrow{N} P$. By definition of $\mathcal{A}_1 \bowtie_\gamma \mathcal{A}_2$, either

(i) $N \subseteq \mathcal{N}_1'$ and $\exists g, t_1$: $\langle s_1, s_2 \rangle \xrightarrow{N,g} \langle t_1, s_2 \rangle$ based on $s_1 \xrightarrow{N,g}_1 t_1$, and $P = proc(t_1, s_2)$,

(ii) $N \subseteq \mathcal{N}_2'$ and $\exists g, t_2$: $\langle s_1, s_2 \rangle \xrightarrow{N,g} \langle s_1, t_2 \rangle$ based on $s_2 \xrightarrow{N,g}_2 t_2$, and $P = proc(s_1, t_2)$, or,

(iii) $N \nsubseteq \mathcal{N}_1$, $N \nsubseteq \mathcal{N}_2$ and $\exists g, g_1, g_2, t_1, t_2, N_1, N_2$: $g = \gamma(g_1 \wedge g_2)$, $\langle s_1, s_2 \rangle \xrightarrow{N,g} \langle t_1, t_2 \rangle$ based on $s_1 \xrightarrow{N_1,g_1}_1 t_1$ and $s_2 \xrightarrow{N_2,g_2}_2 t_2$ with $N = N_1 |_\gamma N_2$ and $P = proc(t_1, t_2)$.

Then, we have $proc_1(s_1) \parallel_\gamma proc_2(s_2) \xrightarrow{N} proc_1(t_1) \parallel_\gamma proc_2(s_2)$ and $proc_1(t_1) \parallel_\gamma proc_2(s_2) \mathcal{R}\, proc(t_1, s_2)$ in case of (i), a symmetrical observation in case of (ii), and $proc_1(s_1) \parallel_\gamma proc_2(s_2) \xrightarrow{N} proc_1(t_1) \parallel_\gamma proc_2(t_2)$ and $proc_1(t_1) \parallel_\gamma proc_2(t_2)$ $\mathcal{R}\, proc(t_1, t_2)$ in case of (iii).

Conclusion, $\mathcal{R}$ is a strong bisimulation relation and, for all $s_1 \in \mathcal{A}_1$, $s_2 \in \mathcal{A}_2$, it holds that $proc(\mathcal{A}_1, s_1) \parallel_\gamma proc(\mathcal{A}_2, s_2) \leftrightarroweq proc(\mathcal{A}_1 \bowtie_\gamma \mathcal{A}_2, \langle s_1, s_2 \rangle)$. □

Note that the above result, in the present setting of a parallel construct involving a port synchronization function, shows strong bisimilarity, whereas the original result of [2] claims, for general composition, language equivalence with respect to timed data streams.

Next, we turn to the final step of the translation, the optional hiding of internal flow corresponding to port names of mixed nodes. In the constraint automaton representation this amounts to restricting the observable flow, in `mCRL2` it can be captured by a proper renaming function.

Definition 5. *Let $\mathcal{A} = (S, \mathcal{N}, \rightarrow, s_0)$ be a constraint automaton and $C \subseteq \mathcal{N}$ a subset of ports. The C-restricted constraint automaton $\mathcal{A} \backslash C$ is given by $\mathcal{A} \backslash C = (S, \mathcal{N} \backslash C, \rightarrow_C, s_0)$ where $\rightarrow_C$ is given by*

$$s \xrightarrow{N,g}_C t \quad \textit{iff} \quad \exists f\, \exists M \subseteq \mathcal{N}\colon s \xrightarrow{M,f} t \wedge g = \exists C.f \wedge N = M \backslash C$$

Here, the constraint $\exists C.f$ expresses existential quantification of the port names in C for the constraint f, cf. [2]. We have that the C-restricted automaton $\mathcal{A} \backslash C$ has the same transitions as the automaton $\mathcal{A}$, but it hides the port names from C as these are considered to be internal for the underlying Reo connector. Therefore, the corresponding renaming for `mCRL2` processes needs to delete from each set of port names those in C. We have the following correctness result.

Lemma 2. *Let $\mathcal{A} = (S, \mathcal{N}, \rightarrow, s_0)$ be a constraint automaton and $C \subseteq \mathcal{N}$ a subset of ports. Then it holds that*

$$proc(\mathcal{A} \backslash C, s) \leftrightarroweq \rho_C(proc(\mathcal{A}, s))$$

where $\rho_C\colon \mathcal{N} \rightarrow \mathcal{N}$ is the renaming $N \mapsto N \backslash C$ for $N \subseteq \mathcal{N}$.

Proof. It can be checked, similar as for Lemma 1, that the relation

$$\mathcal{R} = \{\, (proc(\mathcal{A} \backslash C, s),\ \rho_C(proc(\mathcal{A}, s))) \mid s \in \mathcal{A} \,\}$$

is a strong bisimulation relation by verifying the transfer properties. □

The hiding operator as introduced in [2] differs from the hiding operator presented here. In [2], in a context of language equivalence for timed data streams, an arbitrary number of transitions with flow exclusively over hidden ports are combined within a single observable transition. In our set-up, a computation of the C-restricted automaton corresponds transition-by-transition to a computation of the unrestricted automaton. Note that the minimization of the C-restricted automaton by aggregating several transitions into a weak one can be done afterward, as branching bisimulation remains preserved.

6 Coloring Semantics

The constraint automata semantics used in the previous section has a major drawback: it cannot model context-dependency. For example, the LossySync channel is not correctly represented as its constraint automaton can pass or lose data non-deterministically, whereas according to its informal semantics the passing of data has priority over losing. To cope with this problem, different semantical models have been introduced. One of them is the so-called *coloring* semantics. The basic idea in this model is to associate flow and no-flow colors to channel ends. Clarke et al. showed in [3] that one *flow* color and two *no-flow* colors are sufficient to model context-dependency such as required by the LossySync. The names and graphical representations of these colors are shown in Figure 1(a).

Name	Symbol
flow	——
no-flow-give-reason	- ▷ -
no-flow-require-reason	- ◁ -

(a) Colors

Sync	LossySync	Merger
(1) ——→	(1) ——→	(1)
(2) - ◁ - - ◁ - ›	(2) —— - ◁ - ›	(2)
(3) - ▷ - - ▷ - ›	(3) - ▷ - - ▷ - ›	(3)
(4) - ▷ - - ◁ - ›	(4) - ▷ - - ◁ - ›	(4)

(b) Colorings for some Reo channels and nodes

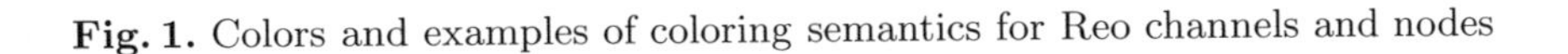

Fig. 1. Colors and examples of coloring semantics for Reo channels and nodes

Valid behaviors of channels are then expressed as colorings of their respective ends. Figure 1(b) depicts the colorings of the Sync, LossySync and Merger primitives. Note that the colors are always read from the perspective of the adjacent nodes. For instance, in coloring (2) of the Sync the sink node gives a reason for no flow, whereas the source node requires a reason. This models the behavior where data is available at the source end but the receiver at the sink end is not ready to accept data. Similarly, in coloring (3) there is no flow, because there is no data available at the source end. Finally, coloring (4) models the situation where no data is available and the receiver is also not ready to accept any data[2].

[2] This behavior is implied by the so-called *flip-rule* in [3].

The LossySync differs from the Sync channel only in one coloring, i.e. coloring (2) where the sink node is not ready to accept data, but there is data available at the source end. In this situation the LossySync permits flow at the source end and loses the data item. Otherwise, no-flow behaviors are possible only when no data is available at the source end.

Nodes are encoded in the same way as channels in the coloring semantics. As usual, we build nodes out of mergers and replicators. Figure 1 depicts the valid colorings of the Merger primitive. An interesting fact here is that intuitively the colorings allow a propagation of no-flow reasons through the connector. Note also that it is sufficient to allow no-flow reasons from both sides in channels only, which leads to a smaller number of coloring in the nodes.

To deal with context-dependency in our encoding in mCRL2 we incorporate the coloring model. We encode the different colors as simple data parameters of actions. We therefore introduce a new datatype

$$\textbf{sort}\ \mathit{Colored} \;=\; \textbf{struct}\ \mathit{flow}(\mathit{data} : \mathit{Data}) \mid \mathit{noflowG} \mid \mathit{noflowR}$$

where *Data* is the global datatype as introduced in the constraint automata encoding presented in the previous section. The idea is that we explicitly model no-flow actions and wrap actual data items into flow actions. We use here *noflowG* and *noflowR* as abbreviations for respectively *no-flow-give-reason* and *no-flow-require-reason*. With this setup, the encoding of the primitives is straightforward. For instance, the Sync channel is defined as

$$\begin{aligned}
\mathsf{Sync} = \big(&\Sigma_{d:Data}\ A(\mathit{flow}(d)) \mid B(\mathit{flow}(d)) \ + && (1)\\
&A(\mathit{noflowR}) \mid B(\mathit{noflowG}) \ + && (2)\\
&A(\mathit{noflowG}) \mid B(\mathit{noflowR}) \ + && (3)\\
&A(\mathit{noflowG}) \mid B(\mathit{noflowG})\big) \cdot \mathsf{Sync}; && (4)
\end{aligned}$$

where each line corresponds to a coloring in Figure 1(b). In the same way, the LossySync can be specified as

$$\begin{aligned}
\mathsf{LossySync} = \big(&\Sigma_{d:Data}\ A(\mathit{flow}(d)) \mid B(\mathit{flow}(d)) \ + && (1)\\
&A(\mathit{flow}) \mid B(\mathit{noflowG}) \ + && (2)\\
&A(\mathit{noflowG}) \mid B(\mathit{noflowR}) \ + && (3)\\
&A(\mathit{noflowG}) \mid B(\mathit{noflowG})\big) \cdot \mathsf{LossySync}; && (4)
\end{aligned}$$

and finally, the Merger can be encoded as

$$\begin{aligned}
\mathsf{Merger} = \big(&\Sigma_{d:Data}\ A(\mathit{flow}(d)) \mid B(\mathit{noflowG}) \mid C(\mathit{flow}(d)) \ + && (1)\\
&\Sigma_{d:Data}\ A(\mathit{noflowG}) \mid B(\mathit{flow}(d)) \mid C(\mathit{flow}(d)) \ + && (2)\\
&A(\mathit{noflowR}) \mid B(\mathit{noflowR}) \mid C(\mathit{noflowG}) \ + && (3)\\
&A(\mathit{noflowG}) \mid B(\mathit{noflowG}) \mid C(\mathit{noflowR})\big) \cdot \mathsf{Merger}; && (4)
\end{aligned}$$

The other channels are encoded analogously.

The LossyFIFO connector is a classical example where context-dependency is required (cf. [3]). Fig. 2 depicts the corresponding labeled transition systems for the basic constraint automata encoding (a), as well as the encoding based on the coloring semantics (b). For simplicity, we use the singleton set $Data = \{x\}$ as data domain. The crucial point here is that in the initial state 0, the constraint automata version can lose data (loop $A(x)$), which is an unintended behavior. However, in the coloring encoding, there is no such behavior.

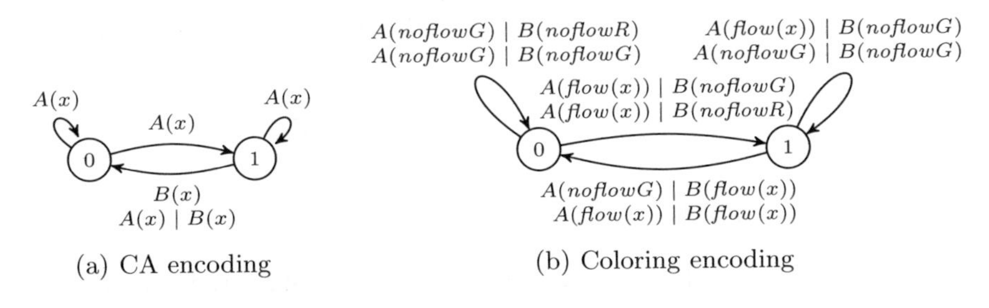

(a) CA encoding

(b) Coloring encoding

Fig. 2. Labeled transition systems for the LossyFIFO connector

Using the coloring model we can properly represent context-dependency in mCRL2. In contrast to [3], our encoding also reflects the state of the connectors and can further include data-dependency at the same time. Note also that even though the coloring encoding includes extra transitions for no-flow actions, the number of states is equal to the constraint automata version.

7 Implementation

We implemented the conversion from Reo to mCRL2 discussed above as an extension to the Eclipse Coordination Tools (ECT), see [4]. ECT is a framework for modeling, verification and execution of component-based and service-oriented systems. It consists of a set of integrated tools for the Eclipse platform[3]. The framework provides functionality for converting high-level modeling languages, such as UML, BPMN and BPEL to Reo, for editing and animation of Reo models, generation of automata-based semantical models from Reo, modeling and verification of QoS properties and tight integrations with external model checking tools such as Vereofy [5] or PRISM [12].

From our conversion tool, an mCRL2 specification can be obtained automatically from any Reo circuit simply by selecting it in the graphical Reo editor. A screenshot of the tool is shown in Figure 3. The code generation can be customized using various options. For instance, enabling the option *with components* will allow to incorporate process definitions for the components attached at the boundary of a connector. The option *with data* enables the data-aware encoding. If not enabled, data parameters and constraints are omitted. Furthermore,

[3] `http://www.eclipse.org`

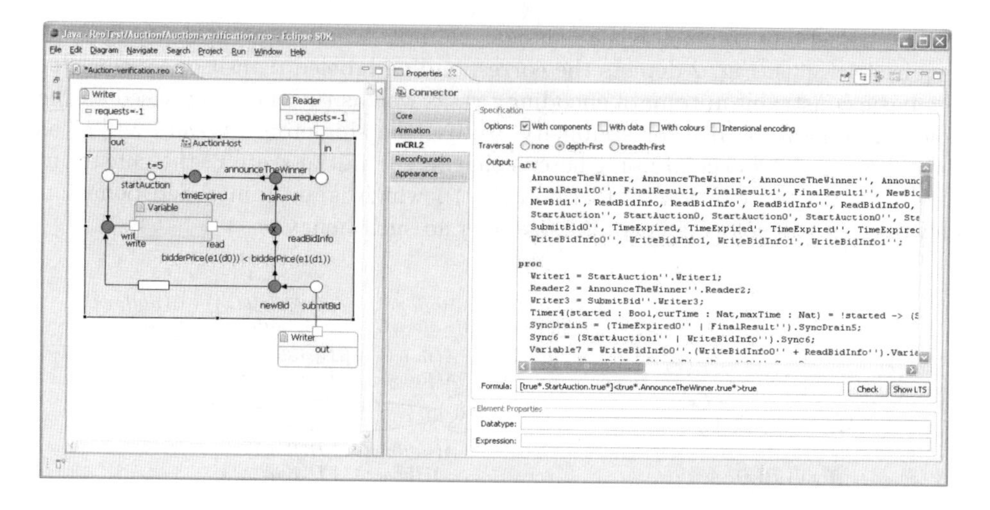

Fig. 3. Reo model of an auction process and its mCRL2 specification

the option *with colors* can be used to add support for context-dependency as described in Section 6. Moreover, data types of components or services coordinated by Reo, as well as data constraints for data dependent channels such as the Filter or Transform channel can be defined using the same interface. Note that they are saved as annotations in the Reo model and are automatically merged in when generating the final mCRL2 specification. This way we can ensure that the mCRL2 code can be regenerated at any point without manual changes if desired.

The tool further includes an integration with mCRL2's model checking and state space visualization tools. In particular, we use the mcrl22lps tool for generating linear process specifications from mCRL2 code, lps2lts and ltsconvert for generating and minimizing labeled transitions systems, lps2pbes for model checking formulas specified in modal μ-calculus, and finally ltsgraph for visualizing state spaces. Related verification tools, such as CADP[4] can be integrated in a similar fashion since they share the same format for LTSs. The integration with CADP is not implemented as yet.

In our encoding of Reo in mCRL2 we translate every primitive (channel, node or component) to a separate process, which are then run in parallel. Every primitive end corresponds to an action in this setting. Therefore, the derived specifications usually consist of a rather large number of processes and an even larger number of actions. However, the interaction between all these processes is rather local, e.g. a channel communicates only with its source and target nodes.

Our experiments show that the direct approach of naively running all processes in parallel and then performing the communication, synchronization and optionally the hiding operator leads to a state space explosion during the linearization. To overcome this problem, we add processes one by one and immediately apply the aforementioned mCRL2 operators. We use the topology information of the

[4] http://www.inrialpes.fr/vasy/cadp

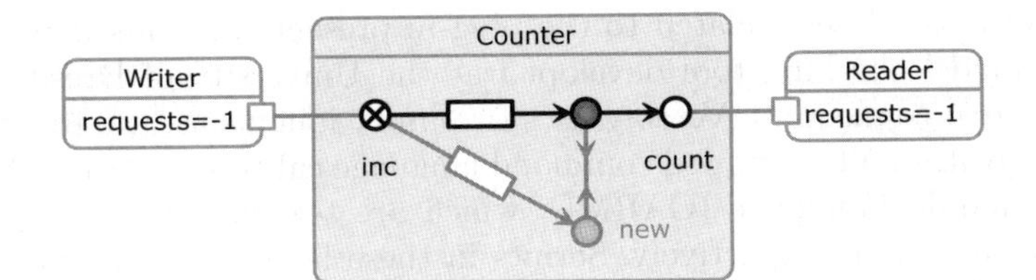

Fig. 4. Counter circuit

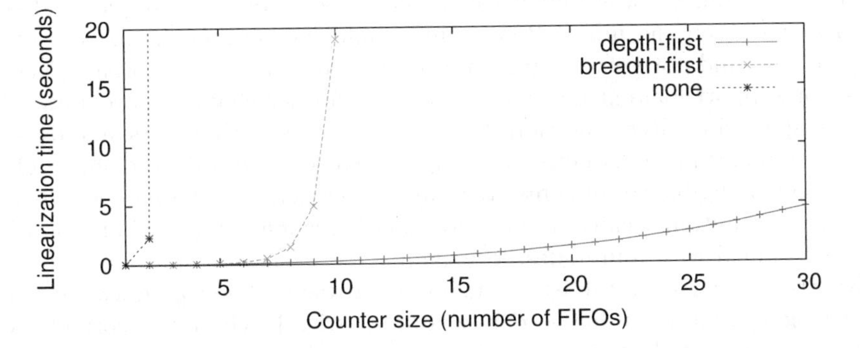

Fig. 5. Benchmarks for different encodings of the Counter circuit

connector to determine what processes communicate directly with each other. This leads to a much faster linearization process. In particular, we found out that a traversal over the connector graph is well-suited for this problem. In our experiments, the depth-first traversal showed the best results.

As an example we tested the so-called Counter circuit shown in Figure 4. This circuit consists of an exclusive router with n outputs, each connected to another FIFO, which in turn are synchronized using a SyncDrain at their sink ends. Here we are interested only in two actions: data arriving at the source end of the exclusive router and the synchronized firing of the SyncDrains. The resulting transition system consists of n states and n transitions. Benchmarks[5] of the different optimizations are depicted in Figure 5. The linearization using depth-first traversal took less than 5 seconds for the counter with 30 FIFOs. The breadth-first approach was still able to handle 10 FIFOs in 20 seconds. However, without any optimizations `mCRL2` needed more than 20 minutes to process the counter with just 3 FIFOs.

8 Related Work

In this section, we compare our framework to other tools for analyzing Reo connectors. For an overview of related work with respect to the application of our tool to business process and web service composition analysis refer to [6].

[5] Benchmarks were taken on a standard machine with 4 cores and 8GB of memory, running Linux 2.6.27 and the development version of `mCRL2` (revision 7467).

The tool most closely related to the plug-in presented in this paper is Vereofy [5], a model checking tool developed at the University of Dresden for the analysis of Reo connectors. Vereofy uses two input languages, the Reo Scripting Language (RSL), and a guarded command language called Constraint Automata Reactive Module Language (CARML) which are textual versions of Reo and constraint automata, respectively. Scripts in these languages are automatically generated from graphical Reo models and are used for the verification of circuit properties expressed in LTL and CTL-like logics. The main advantage of the tool comparing to our work is that it can generate clear counterexamples and show them as paths on the initial Reo circuit, while the counterexamples in `mCRL2` may be huge and not very useful. However, in contrast to our approach, Vereofy does not support context-dependent and transformer channels, provides a format for specifying filter conditions that is less expressive than ours, and does not allow join nodes in the circuits. Moreover, it expects the user to define a global data domain eligible to all connectors and components in the model instead of generating it automatically, and cannot handle recursive type definitions which we need to deal with join nodes, for example.

Khosravi et al. [13] establishes a mapping of Reo to Alloy, a lightweight modeling language based on first-order relational logic. To check the correctness of a circuit, the desired properties are expressed in terms of assertions which are closely related to LTL and checked by the Alloy Analyzer. The approach deals with context dependency in Reo by defining special relations that enforce maximal progress in circuit execution. However, the actual values of data passed through the channels are not considered in this work. Moreover, the authors admit to have considerable problems with performance. Bonsangue and Izadi [14] defined semantics of context-dependent Reo connectors in terms of Büchi automata and generalized standard automata based model checking algorithms to enable verification of LTL formulas for Reo connectors. However, this work is purely theoretical and is not supported by any existing software tool.

Kemper [15] presented a SAT-based approach for bounded model checking of timed constraint automata (TCA), see [16]. In this work, the behavior of TCA is represented as formula in propositional logic with linear arithmetic which can be analyzed by various SAT solvers. Since TCA provide operational semantics for timed Reo, this approach can be used for model checking timed properties of Reo connectors. However, at the moment there is no tool for generating TCA from graphical Reo circuits. The development of such a plug-in for data-aware Reo will require tools for analyzing data constraints and functions used in filter and transformer channels. In our work, we map each channel to a process in the process algebra `mCRL2` separately, and exploit the functionality provided by the `mCRL2` toolset to obtain a semantic model of the whole circuit in terms of LTS where transitions are labeled with names parametrized with data observed in these ports. Moreover, our approach can handle data manipulation using transformer channels with associated non-linear functions. Since the `mCRL2` toolset supports time analysis, the extension of our conversion tool with the ability to deal with timer channels is straightforward and belongs to our future work.

9 Conclusions

In this paper, we presented an extended approach for mapping Reo connectors to the process algebra `mCRL2`. More specifically, we proved the correctness of the mapping, extended the conversion tool with the ability to deal with context-sensitive Reo, and evaluated the tool performance in the presence of optimization techniques. Together with other tools from ECT, our plug-in provides a user-friendly environment for graphical modeling of component/service-based systems and business processes. On the one hand, this releases developers from the need to encode the behavior of their systems in the specification language `mCRL2` directly. On the other hand, the `mCRL2` toolset supports full-featured model checking for Reo.

Future work includes the application of our approach to larger examples to assess its practicality and scalability. Also, we plan to extend our approach by incorporating timer channels [16] according to their semantics in terms of TCA. This will enable the analysis of timed properties for channel-based service models. Another direction of our research is an extension of Reo semantics with various actions observable on channel ports. In particular, this will allow us to model data flow within synchronous regions of a connector and, given time delays for each channel, estimate total delays of the circuits. Finally, as mentioned before, we will integrate CADP support to our tools.

Acknowledgment. We are indebted to the reviewers for their detailed feedback and constructive comment.

References

1. Arbab, F.: The IWIM model for coordination of concurrent activities. In: Hankin, C., Ciancarini, P. (eds.) COORDINATION 1996. LNCS, vol. 1061, pp. 34–56. Springer, Heidelberg (1996)
2. Baier, C., Sirjani, M., Arbab, F., Rutten, J.: Modeling component connectors in Reo by constraint automata. Science of Computer Programming 61, 75–113 (2006)
3. Clarke, D., Costa, D., Arbab, F.: Connector coloring I: Synchronization and context dependency. Science of Computer Programming 66(3), 205–225 (2007)
4. Arbab, F., Koehler, C., Maraikar, Z., Moon, Y., Proenca, J.: Modeling, testing and executing Reo connectors with the Eclipse Coordination Tools. In: Tool demo session at FACS 2008 (2008)
5. Baier, C., Blechmann, T., Klein, J., Klüppelholz, S.: A uniform framework for modeling and verifying components and connectors. In: Field, J., Vasconcelos, V.T. (eds.) COORDINATION 2009. LNCS, vol. 5521, pp. 268–287. Springer, Heidelberg (2009)
6. Kokash, N., Krause, C., de Vink, E.: Data-aware design and verification of service composition with Reo and mCRL2. In: Shin, S.Y., et al. (eds.) Proc. SAC 2010, pp. 2406–2413. ACM, New York (2010)
7. Groote, J., Mathijssen, A., Reniers, M., Usenko, Y., van Weerdenburg, M.: The formal specification language mCRL2. In: Brinksma, E., Harel, D., Mader, A., Stevens, P., Wieringa, R. (eds.) Methods for Modelling Software Systems. IBFI, Schloss Dagstuhl (2007)

8. Garavel, H., Mateescu, R., Lang, F., Serwe, W.: CADP 2006: A toolbox for the construction and analysis of distributed processes. In: Damm, W., Hermanns, H. (eds.) CAV 2007. LNCS, vol. 4590, pp. 158–163. Springer, Heidelberg (2007)
9. Arbab, F.: Reo: A channel-based coordination model for component composition. Mathematical Structures in Computer Science 14, 329–366 (2004)
10. Baeten, J., Basten, T., Reniers, M.: Process Algebra: Equational Theories of Communicating Processes in Cambridge Tracts in Theoretical Computer Science, vol. 50. CUP, Cambridge (2010)
11. Milner, R.: Communication and Concurrency. Prentice-Hall, Englewood Cliffs (1989)
12. Kwiatkowska, M., Norman, G., Parker, D.: PRISM: Probabilistic Symbolic Model Checker. In: Field, T., Harrison, P.G., Bradley, J., Harder, U. (eds.) TOOLS 2002. LNCS, vol. 2324, pp. 200–204. Springer, Heidelberg (2002)
13. Khosravi, R., Sirjani, M., Asoudeh, N., Sahebi, S., Iravanchi, H.: Modeling and analysis of Reo connectors using Alloy. In: Lea, D., Zavattaro, G. (eds.) COORDINATION 2008. LNCS, vol. 5052, pp. 169–183. Springer, Heidelberg (2008)
14. Bonsangue, M., Izadi, M.: Automata based model checking for Reo connectors. In: Arbab, F., Sirjani, M. (eds.) Fundamentals of Software Engineering. LNCS, vol. 5961, pp. 260–275. Springer, Heidelberg (2010)
15. Kemper, S.: SAT-based verification for timed component connectors. Electronic Notes in Theoretical Computer Science (ENTCS) 255, 103–118 (2009)
16. Arbab, F., Baier, C., de Boer, F., Rutten, J.: Models and temporal logical specifications for timed component connectors. Software and Systems Modeling 6(1), 59–82 (2007)

The Credo Methodology*
(Extended Version)

Immo Grabe[1], Mohammad Mahdi Jaghoori[1], Joachim Klein[3], Sascha Klüppelholz[3], Andries Stam[6], Christel Baier[3], Tobias Blechmann[3], Bernhard K. Aichernig[5], Frank de Boer[1], Andreas Griesmayer[5], Einar Broch Johnsen[2], Marcel Kyas[9], Wolfgang Leister[8], Rudolf Schlatte[2], Martin Steffen[2], Simon Tschirner[4], Liang Xuedong[7], and Wang Yi[4]

[1] CWI, Amsterdam, The Netherlands
[2] University of Oslo, Norway
[3] Technische Universität Dresden, Germany
[4] University of Uppsala, Sweden
[5] UNU - IIST, Macau, China
[6] Almende, The Netherlands
[7] RRHF, Oslo, Norway
[8] NR, Oslo, Norway
[9] Freie Universität Berlin, Germany

Abstract. This paper is an extended version of the *Credo* Methodology [16]. *Credo* offers tools and techniques to model and analyze highly reconfigurable distributed systems. In a previous version we presented an integrated methodology to use the *Credo* tool suite. Following a compositional, component–based approach to model and analyze distributed systems, we presented a separation of the system into components and the network. A high–level, abstract representation of the dataflow level on the network was given in terms of behavioral interface automata and a detailed model of the components in terms of Creol models. Here we extend the methodology with a detailed model of the network connecting these components. The *Vereofy* tool set is used to model and analyze the dataflow of the network in detail. The behavioral automata connect the detailed model of the network and the detailed model of the components. We apply the extended methodology to our running example, a peer-to-peer file-sharing system.

1 Introduction

Current software development methodologies follow a component-based approach in modeling distributed systems. A major shortcoming of the existing methods is the lack of an integrated formalism to model highly reconfigurable distributed systems at different phases of design, i.e., systems that can be reconfigured in

* This work has been funded by the European IST-33826 STREP project CREDO on Modeling and Analysis of Evolutionary Structures for Distributed Services. (`http://credo.cwi.nl`)

F.S. de Boer et al. (Eds.): FMCO 2009, LNCS 6286, pp. 41–69, 2010.

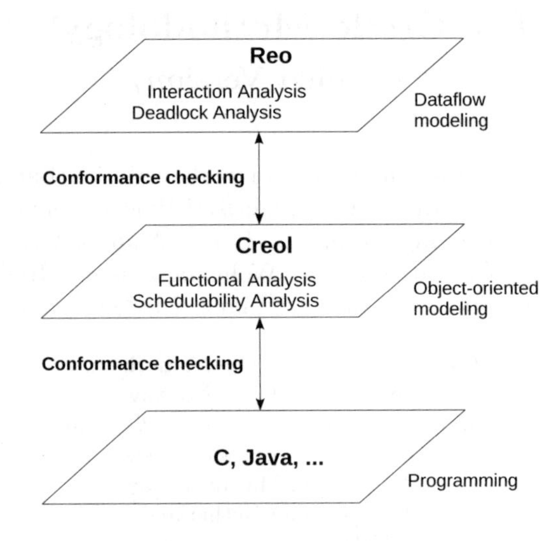

Fig. 1. Overview of modeling levels and analysis in *Credo*

terms of a change to the network structure or an update to the components. Moreover, the high complexity of such systems requires tool-supported analysis techniques.

The *Credo* methodology allows modeling on two different levels of abstraction (cf. Fig. 1). At the abstract level, i.e., the dataflow level, constraint automata [7] are used to represent the interface behavior of components and Reo [3], an executable *dataflow* language for high-level description of dynamic reconfigurable *networks*, is used to describe the glue code to connect the components. The modeling languages CARML (constraint automata reactive module language) and RSL (Reo scripting language) [6] are used for a hierarchical specification of the network and components in a compositional manner. At the concrete level, the concurrent *object-oriented* modeling language Creol [22] is used to provide an executable model of the implementation for the individual components. At this level, *Credo* offers a timed-automata framework for real-time modeling of concurrent objects. Fig. 1 illustrates the relation between the modeling languages and their relation to existing programming languages and different kinds of analysis the *Credo* tool suite provides on the chosen levels of abstraction.

In a previous version of this paper [16] we integrated the *Credo* tools and techniques into the software development life-cycle and illustrated how and when to use them during the design and analysis phases. The tools and methods presented covered a high–level model of the network and a detailed model of the components. In this paper, we extend the methodology introduced in [16] with tools and methods to model and analyze the dataflow of the network in detail. The high–level model of the network in terms of behavioral interface automata connects the detailed network model and the detailed component model; behavioral interfaces are also central to the schedulability analysis of real-time object-oriented description of a detailed component model. The connection

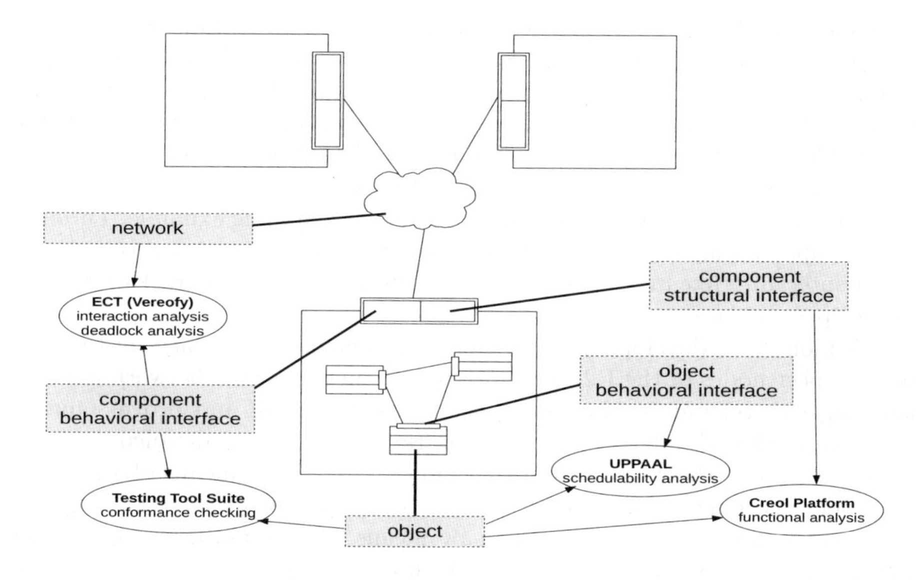

Fig. 2. End user perspective of the *Credo* Tools

between the high–level network model and the detailed component model was checked by conformance testing. In a similar approach conformance between the high–level network model and the detailed network model is established.

At the dataflow-level, which is the most abstract characterization of a system, behavioral interfaces (cf. Fig. 2) are used to describe components and the dataflow between components of a composite system. These interfaces abstract from the details of the (object-oriented) implementation of components. Instead they describe the components and the connections they use to communicate and interact with each other. *Credo* provides as an Eclipse plug-in an integrated tool-suite, ECT (Eclipse Coordination Tools) [13], including a plug-in for the model checker *Vereofy* [6,5]. *Vereofy* uses CARML and RSL as input languages and provides model checking of branching-time properties via a CTL-like logic with regular expressions to specify the observable dataflow as well as alternating-time and linear time versions thereof and bisimulation checking. The logics allow to reason about the coordination principles and the dataflow in the network as well as about the internal states of the components and behavioral interfaces.

The functional behavior of the objects within a component is modeled in Creol. Furthermore, we use the *timed automata* of UPPAAL [25,8] to create real-time models of objects and their behavioral interfaces. The *Credo* tool suite offers an automated technique for *schedulability analysis* of individual objects [21,20]. Given a specification of a scheduling policy (e.g., earliest deadline first) for an object, we use UPPAAL to analyze the object with respect to its behavioral interface in order to ensure that tasks are accomplished within their specified deadlines.

Conformance between a model of a component implementation and its behavioral interface specification is checked by the *Credo* tools [17]. Moreover, given an implementation of a component in a programming language like C, *Credo* also provides a technique to check conformance between the implementation and the Creol model [18,1]. Both techniques are based on *testing*. The abstract behavioral interface model is used to generate test cases to steer the execution.

To illustrate the *Credo* methodology we will give a running example. Throughout the paper we model and analyze a file-sharing system with hybrid peer-to-peer architecture (like in Napster), where a central server keeps track of the data in every peer node.

In Section 2, we develop the structural and behavioral interfaces of the components (peer nodes of the P2P system) and the network (the network manager managing the dynamic connections between peer nodes); and prove some example properties of different kinds. In Section 3, we give a detailed model of the network using the *Vereofy* tool suite and analyze it by means of simulation and model checking. In Section 4, we give executable object-oriented models for the components and analyze them by means of simulation and testing for conformance both with respect to the behavioral interfaces and a Creol implementation. We demonstrate schedulability analysis by analyzing the central server of the peer-to-peer example. Section 5 concludes the paper.

2 High-Level Dataflow Model

We use the exogenous coordination language Reo [3] for the high-level dataflow modeling. Reo is a channel-based formalism that supports compositional design of the network that yields the *glue-code* for a given set of components. In Reo, a system consists of a set of components connected by a network. The network exogenously controls the dataflow between the components and may be dynamically reconfigured to alter the connections between the components. At this level of abstraction, only a *facade* of each component is visible. A facade consists of port and event declarations, and its abstract behavior is specified using an automata model called constraint automata [7]. Constraint automata are variants of labeled transition systems where the transitions are labeled by sets of read and write operations on I/O-ports of components and dataflow locations of the

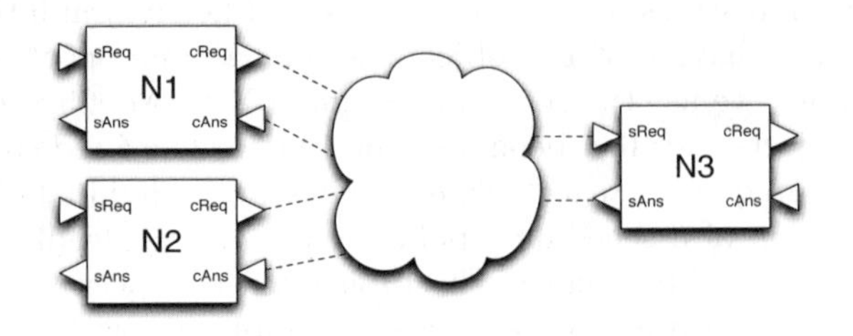

Fig. 3. Peer nodes in the P2P system

network, possibly together with data constraints for the written or read data values. Besides describing the interface behavior of the components, constraint automata also serve as a formal semantics for Reo [7]. In this section, we do not go into the details of how to compose Reo channels. Instead, we use constraint automata as a model for the network behavior directly.

Components use ports to communicate with each other via the network. Fig. 3 shows a system of components (as rectangles), their ports (as small triangles), and the network (as a cloud). Ports can be either input or output ports (implied by the direction of the triangles). By exogenous coordination, we mean that a component has no direct control on how its ports are connected. A component can only indirectly influence its connections by raising events. Events include requests/announcements of services, time-outs, or acknowledgments. These events can trigger reconfigurations of the *context-aware* network. A network manager handles the events and reconfigures the network connections according to the events. At this moment we consider the network manager to be a part of the network and we model the peer nodes independent of a concrete implementation of the network manager.

In this section, we model the peer nodes of the P2P system as components. Each peer node has two sides, a client side and a server side. Each side has a pair of request and answer ports. As a client, a peer node writes a request (a 'key' identifying the requested data) to its cReq–port and expects the result on its cAns–port. As a server, a peer node reads a request from its sReq–port and writes the result to its sAns–port. For two peer nodes to communicate, the network manager has to connect the corresponding ports of the client and the server, i.e., the cReq–port of the client with the sReq–port of the server and the cAns–port of the client with sAns–port of the server.

2.1 Structural Interface Description

To describe the facade of a component, we declare its ports and the events the component may raise. Below, we define two facades, ClientSide and ServerSide. The facade Peer inherits the ports and events declared in these two and adds another event that is needed when the two sides are combined.

```
1 facade ClientSide begin
2   port cReq : outport
3   port cAns : inport
4   sync_event openCS<req:outport,ans:inport>(in k:Data; out f:Bool)
5   sync_event closeCS<req:outport,ans:inport>()
6 end
```

```
1 facade ServerSide begin
2   port sReq : inport
3   port sAns : outport
4   sync_event openSS<req:inport,ans:outport>()
5   sync_event closeSS<req:inport,ans:outport>()
6   register<>(in keyList : List[Data]) // async_event
7 end
```

```
1 facade Peer inherits ClientSide, ServerSide begin
2   update<>(in keyList : List[Data])   // async_event
3 end
```

The network manager does not keep a centralized account of all port bindings; these are locally stored at each component. A component cannot directly change its port bindings. Before using ports, the component must request a connection by raising an open session event. An event for closing the session implies that the ports are ready to be disconnected. When requesting to open a session or reporting the end of a session the ports used in that session are send as parameters. In addition to the ports, events can have extra parameters, e.g., the 'open client session' event (written as openCS) provides the key to the data it is looking for as additional information to steer the connection process. Based on the data key the network manager can set up a connection to a server that holds the requested data.

Events are by default asynchronous. However, when expecting return values (e.g., opening or closing a session), we declare events to be synchronous (using the keyword **sync_event**). All events raised by the components are handled by the network. This is reflected in the structural interface description of the network.

Network. We give the structural interface description of a particular network manager called Broker. The keyword **networkmanager** is used to identify such interfaces (and distinguish them from those characterizing component facades). The *Credo* methodology distinguishes between the concept of a network manager and the network itself because a network in general consists of a network manager and additional coordination artifacts like *channels*, as described later in this section.

The description of the Broker declares the event handlers that it provides. For each event handler, it specifies the facade (representing a component) from which the handled event originated using the keyword **with**.

```
1 networkmanager Broker begin
2     with ServerSide
3       register<>(in keyList : List[Data])
4       sync_event openSS<in req:inport,ans:outport>()
5       sync_event closeSS<in req:inport,ans:outport>()
6     with ClientSide
7       sync_event openCS<in req:outport,ans:inport>(in k:Data; out f:Bool)
8       sync_event closeCS<in req:outport,ans:inport>()
9     with Peer
10      update<>(in keyList : List[Data])
11 end
```

2.2 Behavioral Interface Description

The behavioral description for a component facade specifies the order of raising events and the port operations. This is modeled using constraint automata [4]. In these automata, we denote port operations by port names. The corresponding

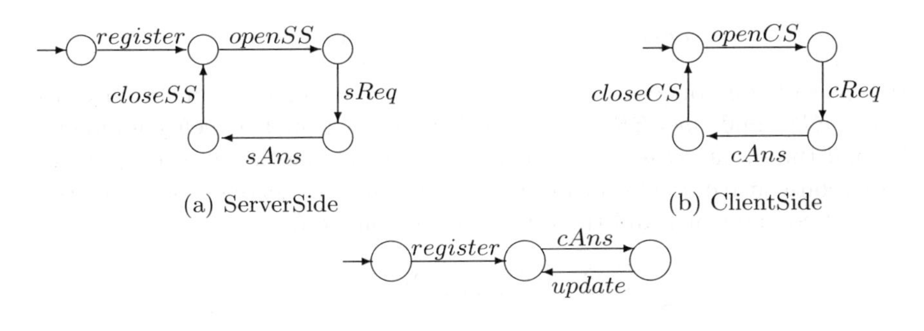

(a) ServerSide

(b) ClientSide

(c) Peer

Fig. 4. Behavioral interfaces for facades

action (read or write) is understood from the port type (given in the structural facade description).

Fig. 4 shows the behavioral specification for the facades in our example. As mentioned earlier, the port actions are enclosed by opening and closing session events in Fig. 4(a) and Fig. 4(b). A server registers its data with the network manager at initialization. We opt for a simple scenario, i.e., each server or client handles only one request at a time. We also assume at this level of abstraction, that openCS is always successful, i.e., every data item searched for is available.

The Peer facade inherits the behavior specified for ClientSide and ServerSide facades. The Peer facade introduces some additional behavior, i.e., an update to the data stored at the broker. The Peer automaton (see Fig. 4(c)) synchronizes with the ServerSide automaton (see Fig. 4(a)) to ensure that an update only takes place after the data is registered. Moreover, the data at the broker is updated after receiving new information (on the ClientSide). This is modeled by synchronization on the read operations on the *cAns*–port.

The behavior of the sub-type has to be a refinement of the behavior of its super-type [28]. This is achieved by computing the product of the automata describing the inherited behavior (ServerSide and ClientSide) and the automaton synchronizing them (Peer). In this product [4] transitions with different action names are interleaved while those with common action names are synchronized.

Network. The Broker in a peer-to-peer system connects the ports and handles the events of the components. We show how to model the synchronization of a system consisting of a fixed number of components, say n, for some $n > 0$. The observable actions of the i–th component ($i \in \{1, \dots, n\}$), i.e., the communications on its ports and its events, are denoted by $openCS_i$, $openSS_i$, $closeCS_i$, $closeSS_i$, $cReq_i$, $sReq_i$, $cAns_i$, and $sAns_i$. Synchronization of actions is modeled in the following automata by a transition labeled with the participating actions.

For clarity, we start with different automata for the synchronization of ports and events. Synchronization between the ports of a pair of components i and j is described by the following automaton.

$cReq_i, sReq_j$ $cAns_i, sAns_j$

For each pair of components i and j, the following automaton synchronizes the events $openCS_i$ and $openSS_j$ to establish a connection between components i and j and the events $closeCS_i$ and $closeSS_j$ to release the connection again. These two consecutive synchronizations together thus model one session between the client of component i and the server of component j.

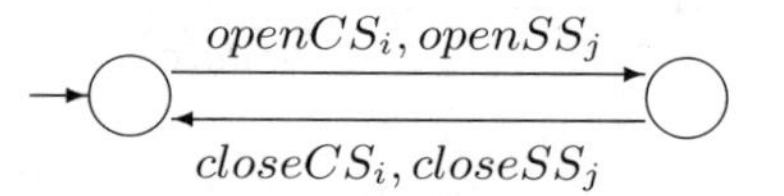

Combining the automata above models the port connections in a session (shown below). As stated before communication between components is only possible after requesting a session to be opened. After the components have finished their communication the session is closed. The *interleaving product* of these combined automata for all pairs of components results in an automaton describing the behavioral interface of the Broker.

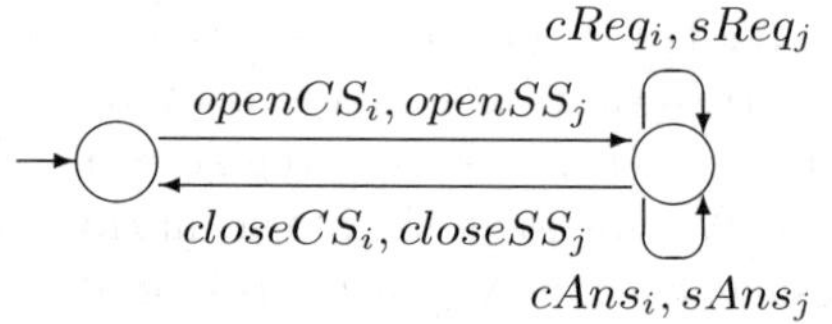

Notice that interleaving allows for components to be involved in more than one session at a time. The *synchronized product* of the network manager automaton with the component automata (from the previous subsection) describes the overall behavior of the system. The product restricts the network manager and the components to exclusive sessions, i.e. a component is involved in at most one session at a time.

Channels. We further refine the network model by introducing *channels* (which are primitive connectors) [3,19]. In general, a channel provides two (channel)-*ends*. We distinguish between input-ends (to which a component can *write*) and output-ends (from which a component can *read*). We also describe the synchronization between the two channel-ends by an automaton. For example, the automaton below models a 1-place buffer. It provides an input-end *in* and an output-end *out*. In state e the buffer is empty and in state f it is full (for simplicity, we abstract from the data transferred and stored).

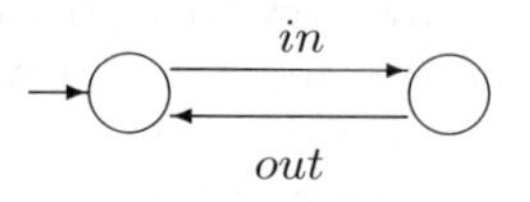

We model the data-transfer from server j to client i, i.e., the connection between the answer ports, by replacing the synchronization of $cAns_i$ and $sAns_j$ by the following synchronization with the above 1-place buffer.

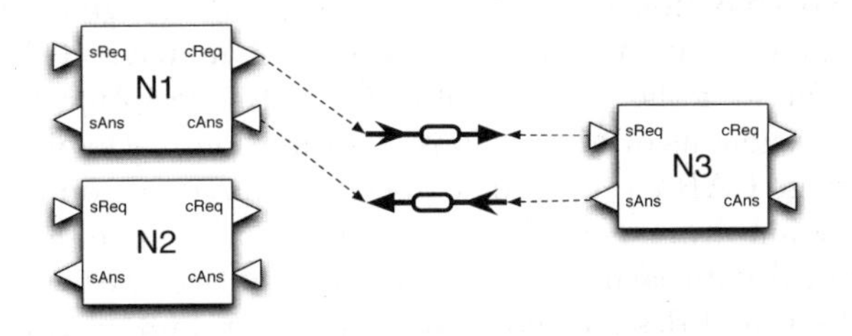

Fig. 5. Using Reo channels for modeling the network

The overall behavior of the system is described by the synchronized product of the Broker, the component automata, and the channel automata. The network itself consists of the Broker and the channels. Fig. 5 shows a configuration in which two buffer channels are used as the network connecting the components. The dashed arrows in this figure show port bindings, i.e., the channel-end to which a port is bound. The bold arrows represent the channels.

3 Dataflow Model

In this section we give a detailed model of the dataflow of our peer–to–peer example. We use the *Vereofy* [10,6,11] (see Fig. 6) tool suite for modeling and analyzing the detailed dataflow model. The *Vereofy* tool suite supports model checking and equivalence checking of components, connectors, and the composite system. Constraint automata serve as a generic operational semantics, which is used for the service interfaces of the components, the network that provides the glue code, and the composite system.

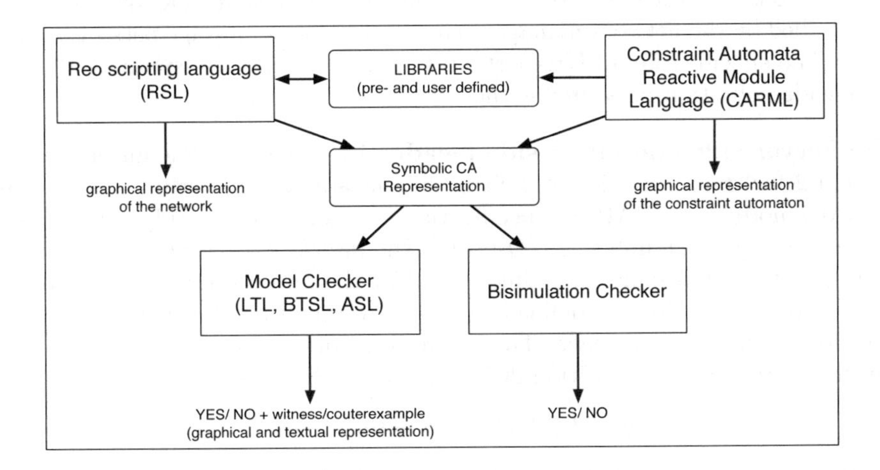

Fig. 6. The *Vereofy* tool suite

We use the specification languages Reo Scripting Language (RSL) for Reo and the Constraint Automata Reactive Module Language (CARML) to specify service interfaces of the components. While the scripting language RSL is used to specify exogenous or endogenous coordination mechanisms, the guarded command language CARML is used to specify behavioral component interfaces and component connectors. Both languages rely on the same semantic automata model. This hybrid approach allows nesting of the two specification languages, supports compositional design, modular verification and reusability of components and component connectors. *Vereofy* includes symbolic model checking tools for linear-time, branching-time and alternating-time temporal logics [24,23,5] with special operators to reason about the events and dataflow at I/O-ports of components and internal nodes of the connecting network. Furthermore *Vereofy* includes a bisimulation checker [9] for components, component connectors, and the composite system.

In the following we show how to model the network manager establishing connections in our running peer-to-peer example. We use CARML to provide textual specifications of the facades of server and client side and RSL to specify the network manager. Finally we explain how the model checking engine of *Vereofy* is used to validate the composite system. The full source code for the P2P model is available on the web:

`http://www.vereofy.de/download/examples/vereofy_p2p_example.zip`

3.1 Modeling in *Vereofy*

The facades from Section 2 serve as a starting point to model the server and client side. Facades define the interface ports together with the possible events. In this section we follow an exogenous modeling approach where the communication and coordination of the peers is handled completely outside the components by the connecting network. Thus, there are no complex events inside the component specifications, i.e., the CARML code for the server and client side. Instead, events are handled by the network manager using synchronous message passing via I/O-ports. The specification of I/O-ports in CARML differs only syntactically from the facade definition presented earlier.

The Server side and client side facades in *Vereofy*. The automata from Section 2 for the server side and client side facades are directly translated into CARML modules. A CARML specification consists of a (possibly empty) list of parameter (e.g. the number of I/O-ports), the interface declaration where source ports (for the input-ends) and sink ports (for the output-ends) of a component and its local variables are defined followed by the transition definitions specifying the behavioral interface. The evaluations of the local variables represent automata states. The transition definitions have the form

$$state\_guard \dashv [\, I/O\_guard \,] \mapsto state\_assignments;$$

where the *state_guard* represents a boolean expression on the current evaluation of the variables, *I/O_guard* is a boolean expression on the dataflow observed at the interface ports, and *state_assignments* describe the effect on the local variables. An I/O-guard specifies the list of active ports as well as restrictions to the data observed at the active ports. E.g., the I/O-guard "{A} & #A == k" states that port A is the only port active during the transition and the observable data value at A is equal to k.

To reduce the complexity of our model for demonstration purposes we (1) abstract from the update events, (2) assume that all peers have all data, and (3) the network manager establishes a connection to server_i if data_i is requested. Furthermore, we use a global data domain

$$\begin{aligned}\text{Data} = \{&0, 1, 2, 3,\\ &\text{key}_0, \text{key}_1, \text{key}_2,\\ &\text{data}_0, \text{data}_1, \text{data}_2,\\ &\text{openSignal}, \text{closeSignal}, \text{registerSignal},\\ &\text{undefined}\}\end{aligned}$$

for the requests, the data and all signals. The numbers $0, 1, 2, 3 \in$ Data are used as signals triggering a reconfiguration in the network topology. Please note, that for each message type a distinct input or output port has been introduced according to the facades definition from Section 2.1. An alternative way of modeling uses

```
1  MODULE ClientSide{
2    // interface declaration (specification of I/O-ports):
3    in: openCS;
4    in: closeCS;
5    out: myReq;
6    in: myAns;

8    // local variables:
9    var: enum{idle,open,waiting,done} status:=idle;
10   var: Data tans := undefined;

12   // transition definitions:
13   status==idle    -[ {openCS} & #openCS==openSignal ]->
14     status:=open;

16   status==open    -[ {myReq} & #myReq==key0 ]-> status:=waiting;
17   status==open    -[ {myReq} & #myReq==key1 ]-> status:=waiting;
18   status==open    -[ {myReq} & #myReq==key2 ]-> status:=waiting;

20   status==waiting -[ {myAns} ]-> status:=done & tans:=#myAns;

22   status==done    -[ {closeCS} & #closeCS==closeSignal ]->
23     status:=idle & tans:=undefined;
24 }
```

Fig. 7. CARML module for client facade of a peer

less (or even single) input and output ports and structured data types, such as disjoint unions. For the usage of structured data types we refer to the *Vereofy* user manual [11]. Fig. 7 depicts the CARML code for the client facade of a peer.

The interface of the client side facade has three input ports (openCS, closeCS, and myAns) and one output port (myReq). The variable status stores the current state of the peer (initially idle), while the variable trans stores an element from the global data domain Data when the peer receives one (initially undefined). The server side facade of the peer is modeled analogously.

The network manager. We model the network manager in the scripting language RSL which is inspired by the exogenous, channel-based coordination language Reo [3]. Both Reo and RSL yield elegant declarative frameworks for the specification of circuits, i.e., for the compositional construction of (dynamically changing) component connectors by creating channels and gluing their channels ends, the I/O-ports of components, or sub-connectors together. RSL's core language features are (1) instantiation of modules and sub-circuits (via the RSL command new); (2) gluing instances together (explicitly via the RSL command join, or implicitly by reusing port names); (3) forming a new prototype for entities for a higher modeling level (via the arrays source and sink); (4) defining networks with dynamically changing topologies (via the RSL keyword TOPO); (5) and scripting features such as variables, loops, and conditional branching.

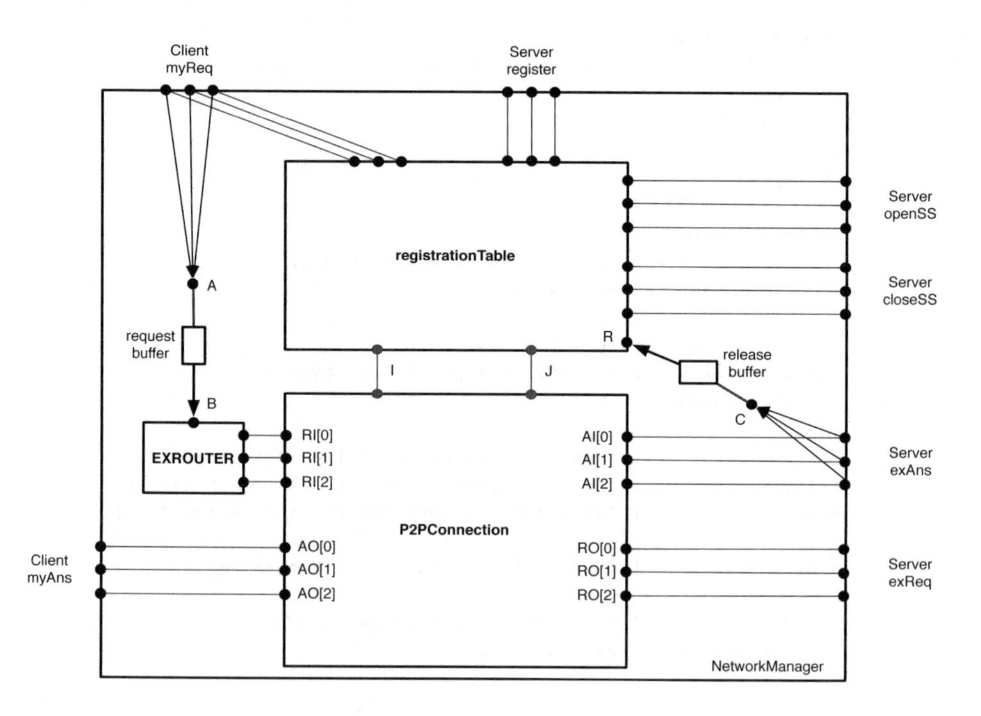

Fig. 8. The network manager

```
1  #include "builtin"
2  #include "registrationtable.carml"
3  #include "p2pconnection.rsl"

5  CIRCUIT NetworkManager{
6    // create registration table
7    Table = new registrationTable(source[0],source[1],source[2],
8                                  source[3],source[4],source[5],R;
9                                  I,J,
10                                 sink[0],sink[1],sink[2],
11                                 sink[6],sink[7],sink[8]);

13   // node A merges the requests
14   for (i=0;i<3;i=i+1){
15     Sync[i] = new SYNC(source[i+3];A);
16   }

18   // the requests are beeing buffered in the FIFO1
19   request_buffer = new FIFO1(A;B);

21   // the buffered request later goes via an exclusive router
22   // into the connections matrix (P2PConnection)
23   new EXROUTER<3>(B;RI[0],RI[1],RI[2]);

25   // create P2PConnection to direct requests and answers
26   Connections = new P2PConnection(I,J,RI[0],RI[1],RI[2],
27                                   AI[0],AI[1],AI[2];
28                                   RO[0],RO[1],RO[2],
29                                   AO[0],AO[1],AO[2]);

31   // the answers are merged into a single node C
32   for(i=0;i<3;i=i+1){
33     Sync[i+3] = new SYNC(AI[i];C);
34   }

36   // and buffered in the release_buffer for
37   // the later release (in the registration table)
38   release_buffer = new FIFO1(C;R);

40   // rest of the interface declaration
41   source[6] = AI[0]; source[7] = AI[1]; source[8] = AI[2];
42   sink[3] = RO[0]; sink[4] = RO[1]; sink[5] = RO[2];
43   sink[9] = AO[0]; sink[10] = AO[1]; sink[11] = AO[2];
44 }
```

Fig. 9. RSL script composing a network manager

An overview on the structure of the network manager is shown in Fig. 8. The network manager consists of several distinct entities, some of them are modeled in CARML while others are specified using RSL. The RSL code composing these entities to form the network manager is presented in Fig. 9. The RSL main program, which is not shown here, composes the peers and the network manager the same way.

The basic idea behind the model of the network manager is that registrationTable – specified in CARML – keeps track of the server registrations, notices requests from clients and generates indices $i, j \in \{0, 1, 2\}$ serving as reconfiguration signals for the dynamically changing P2PConnection – specified in RSL. When peer i sends the key for the ℓ-th data package (key_ℓ) indicating the request for data_ℓ, then the registrationTable is aware which of the registered servers has the requested data. If peer j is the one whose server side has already registered and has the requested data, the registrationTable opens a server session by sending the signal openSignal via the I/O-port openSS_j. Moreover it sends the indices i and j via the internal ports I and J to the P2PConnection. The P2PConnection then establishes a bidirectional connection between peer i and peer j first for the requests and then for the answers. The requests are kept in the request_buffer and delivered to exactly one of the ports $RI[0], RI[1]$ or $RI[2]$ of the P2PConnection using an exclusive router component (EXROUTER). After the connection has been established the request is routed through the P2PConnection from $RI[i]$ to $RO[j]$, i.e, to exReq of peer j. When the request is answered by the server side the data is delivered through the P2PConnection from $AI[j]$ to $AO[i]$, i.e, from port exAns of peer j to port myAns of peer i. A copy of the data package is kept in the release_buffer. In the next step the copy is forwarded to the registrationTable generating new reconfiguration signals on the internal I/O-ports I and J disconnecting the peers. Moreover, it sends the signal closeSignal via the I/O-port closeSS_j to close the server session. The network manager is now back in its initial configuration, ready for a new request-answer-cycle.

The synchronous channels (Sync), the buffers (FIFO1), and the exclusive router (EXROUTER) are part of *Vereofy*'s built-in library. The predefined channels and component connectors from the library can be instantiated like any other component. The composition of channels and components is done implicitly during the instantiation by reusing port names in the new statements. If a port name is used more than once the corresponding ports are joined. E.g. we write new FIFO1$(A; B)$; new FIFO1$(B; C)$ instead of new FIFO$(A; B1)$; new FIFO1$(B2; C)$; $B = \mathsf{join}(B1, B2)$. If the name of a port is $\mathsf{source}[i]$ (or $\mathsf{sink}[j]$) the port will be the i-th source port (j-th sink port, respectively) of the interface of the network manager. I.e., the network manager provides the interface shown in Table 1.

Dynamically changing network topologies. We now focus on the dynamically changing part of the network, i.e., the P2PConnection. As described above the registrationTable triggers a reconfiguration of the network topology. A P2PConnection manages a bidirectional communication between peer_i and peer_j on the basis of the incoming signals at the I/O-ports I and J. These signals are simultaneously

Table 1. Interface of a network manager

I/O-ports	port type	usage	data values
register_i	input	register servers sides	registerSignal
openSS_i	output	opening a server session	openSignal
myReq_i	input	handling client requests	$\text{key}_0, \text{key}_1, \text{key}_2$
exReq_i	output	forwarding requests	$\text{key}_0, \text{key}_1, \text{key}_2$
exAns_i	input	accepting answers from servers	$\text{data}_0, \text{data}_1, \text{data}_2$
myAns_i	output	forwarding answers	$\text{data}_0, \text{data}_1, \text{data}_2$
closeSS_i	output	closing a server session	closeSignal

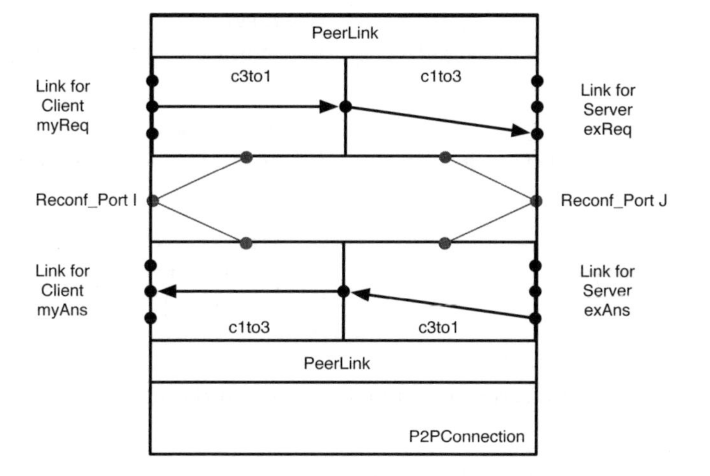

Fig. 10. P2PConnection

forwarded into two sub-circuits – one peerLink for the requests and another peerLink for the answers (see Fig. 10).

Both peerLinks consist of sub-circuits called c3to1 and c1to3. We select c3to1 as a showcase for circuits with more than one (static) topology. A dynamic circuit needs a static interface, which must not be changed within the topology descriptions. The RSL code for c3to1 consisting of the interface declaration followed by the definition of four possible topologies is shown in Fig. 11. The RSL keyword `NODE` is used to create a new I/O-port. In the RSL code of the c3to1 in Fig. 11 four nodes are created – three nodes for the input ports and one for the output port constituting the interface of the circuit.

In the first three topologies (topology 0, 1, 2) exactly one of the source ports is connected to the sink via a synchronous channel. In the last topology (topology 3) there are no connections between the sources and the sink port.

The circuit dynamically switches to topology $i \in [0..3]$ when receiving a reconfiguration signal i. As shown in Fig. 12 the initial topology can be selected on the instantiation of the sub-circuit providing the `initial_topo` option as shown

```
1 CIRCUIT c3to1{
2   outport = NODE;
3   sink[0] = outport;

5   for (i=0;i<3;i=i+1){
6     inport[i] = NODE;
7     source[i] = inport[i];
8   }

10  TOPO(0) = {
11    new SYNC(inport[0];outport);
12  }

14  TOPO(1) = {
15    new SYNC(inport[1];outport);
16  }

18  TOPO(2) = {
19    new SYNC(inport[2];outport);
20  }

22  TOPO(3) = {
23    // unconnected
24  }
25 }
```

```
1 CIRCUIT c1to3{
2   inport = NODE;
3   source[0] = inport;

5   for (i=0;i<3;i=i+1){
6     outport[i] = NODE;
7     sink[i] = outport[i];
8   }

10  TOPO(0) = {
11    new SYNC(inport;outport[0]);
12  }

14  TOPO(1) = {
15    new SYNC(inport;outport[1]);
16  }

18  TOPO(2) = {
19    new SYNC(inport;outport[2]);
20  }

22  TOPO(3) = {
23    // unconnected
24  }
25 }
```

Fig. 11. RSL script for a building block in the P2PConnection

for the peerLink. From the RSL code one can also see how the reconfiguration port becomes an additional interface port of the sub-circuits c3to1 and c1to3 and how it can be accessed. The P2PConnection is composed out of two peerLinks, one for the requests and one for the answers.

3.2 Analysis of the Model

Vereofy provides model checking for branching time properties via the CTL-like logic BTSL[24] and the alternating-time logic ASL[23], for linear time properties via $\mathsf{LTL}_{\mathsf{IO}}$[5], as well as bisimulation checking [9]. The three logics allow reasoning about the coordination principles and the dataflow in the network, i.e., between components, as well as the internal states of the components and component interfaces. BTSL (Branching Time Stream Logic) is a CTL-like logic with path quantifiers and formulas built by standard temporal operators, extended by special modalities to specify regular properties for data stream prefixes. $\mathsf{LTL}_{\mathsf{IO}}$ is likewise an extended version of LTL adapted to the constraint automata setting, where the atomic propositions are either state predicates or I/O-guards. ASL (Alternating Stream Logic) extends BTSL by means to allow reasoning about compatibility and the existence (and absence) of strategies for (alliances of) components. In this section we illustrate the type of properties expressible in BTSL,

```
1  #include "c3to1.rsl"
2  #include "c1to3.rsl"

4  CIRCUIT peerLink{
5    // instantiation with port names including the reconf. ports:
6    first = new c3to1(A[0],A[1],A[2],
7                here_is_reconf_port_first; C) with initial_topo=3;

9    second = new c1to3(C, here_is_reconf_port_second;
10                            B[0],B[1],B[2]) with initial_topo=3;

12   /*
13     defining the interface using
14     two differnt ways in accessing
15     the reconf_port of dynamic sub-circuits
16   */
17   source[0] = first.RECONF_PORT;
18   source[1] = here_is_reconf_port_second;

20   // defining the rest of the interface
21   for (i=0;i<3;i=i+1){
22     source[i+2] = A[i];
23     sink[i] = B[i];
24   }
25 }
```

Fig. 12. RSL script composing a peer link

ASL and $\mathsf{LTL_{IO}}$ by providing some examples that can be checked with the help of *Vereofy*. For this, we make use of the following notations inside the formulas:

- $\{\text{A}, \text{B}\}$ indicates that ports A and B are active and no other port is.
- #A refers to the data item observed at port A.
- `step` indicates an arbitrary step with or without observable dataflow.
- the operators ; (concatenation), * (star), and $^+$ (plus) correspond to the standard operators for regular languages.

1. Deadlock freedom, in the sense that on all paths there is always a next step, can be formalized by means of the following CTL formula.
   `AG[EX[true]]`
2. With BTSL we can formalize a condition stating the existence of a path with specific regular form. A sequence of actions is specified by a regular expression, where the atoms are constraints on a single step of the observable dataflow. This can e.g. be instrumented to check the conformance between the behavioral interfaces and the RSL model. The following formula states the existence of a path, where the first server registers, the second client opens a session and sends a request for the data with key0, the data is transferred, and the connections closed. The formula also requires that the path leads to a state where both the request and the release buffer are empty.

```
E<"{register[0]} & #register[0]==registerSignal";"step"*;
     "{openCS[1]} & #openCS[1]==openSignal";
     "{request[1],openSS[0]} & #request[1]==key0
      & #openSS[0]==openSignal";"#sendRequest[0]==key0";
     "{theAnswerIn[0],theAnswerOut[1]}
      & #theAnswerIn[0]==#theAnswerOut[1]
      & #theAnswerOut[1]==data0";
     "{closeSS[0],closeCS[1]} & #closeSS[0]==closeSignal
      & #closeCS[1]==closeSignal">
  "Manager.request_buffer.state==EMPTY
    & Manager.release_buffer.state==EMPTY"
```

3. We now provide a BTSL formula for the requirement stating that for all possible executions whenever the dataflow satisfies the dataflow specification (i.e., it is part of the language defined by the regular expression) then both buffers will be empty at the end of the execution.

```
A["{register[0]} & #register[0]==registerSignal";("step"*;
     "{openCS[1]} & #openCS[1]==openSignal";
     "{request[1],openSS[0]} & #request[1]==key0
       & #openSS[0]==openSignal";"#sendRequest[0]==key0";
     "{theAnswerIn[0],theAnswerOut[1]}
       & #theAnswerIn[0]==#theAnswerOut[1]
       & #theAnswerOut[1]==data0";
     "{closeSS[0],closeCS[1]} & #closeSS[0]==closeSignal
       & #closeCS[1]==closeSignal")+]"
  Manager.request_buffer.state==EMPTY
   & Manager.release_buffer.state==EMPTY"
```

4. The next property given in terms of an $\mathsf{LTL}_{\mathsf{IO}}$ formula asserts that whenever a server session has been closed in the next step the release buffer of the network manager will be empty.

```
G (("#closeSS[0]==closeSignal"
     | "#closeSS[1]==closeSignal"
     | "#closeSS[2]==closeSignal") ->
   X "Manager.release_buffer.state==EMPTY" )
```

5. The following $\mathsf{LTL}_{\mathsf{IO}}$ formula represents a fairness condition and ensures that enabled requests can not be ignored forever. Stated differently, if the request of a client is enabled at infinitely many positions along a path, then the request fires at infinitely many locations.

```
G F "enabled sendRequest[1]" -> G F "sendRequest[1]"
```

6. The ASL formula given below states that whether there is a strategy that controls, i.e. constraints, the possible dataflow at the three ports (theAnswerOut[0], theAnswerOut[1], and theAnswerOut[2]), such that for all remaining paths the release buffer of the network manager stays globally empty.

```
E{theAnswerOut[0], theAnswerOut[1], theAnswerOut[2]}
  G["Manager.release_buffer.state==EMPTY"]
```

All properties that have been presented in this section have successfully been validated for our model of the peer-to-peer network for which the full source code is available on the web [30]. Besides model checking for temporal logics, *Vereofy* supports checking bisimilarity of two automata, e.g., that two implementations of the network manager are bisimilar.

4 Object-Oriented Model of the Components

In this section, we model the components in Creol, an executable modeling language. To model the components, we provide interfaces for the intra-component communication and a Creol implementation of the components. Together with a Creol implementation of the network manager, we get an executable model of the whole system. Since Creol models are executable we use the terms Creol model and Creol implementation interchangeably.

We use intra-component interfaces together with the behavioral interfaces of Section 2.2 to derive test specifications to check for conformance between the behavioral models and the Creol implementation. We also use this specification to simulate the environment of a component while developing the component.

Given a C implementation of the system, we use the behavioral interfaces of Section 2.2 to derive test scenarios for checking conformance between the Creol model and an implementation in an actual programming language. Dynamic symbolic execution on the Creol implementation is used to compute test inputs for the scenarios for an improved coverage of the model [18].

Finally, we model the real-time aspects of the system using timed automata. In the real-time model, we add scheduling policies to the objects. Here, we check for schedulability, i.e., whether the tasks can be accomplished within their deadlines.

4.1 Modeling in Creol

Creol is an executable modeling language suited for distributed systems. Types are separated from classes, instead (behavioral) interfaces are used to type objects. Objects are concurrent, i.e., conceptually, each object encapsulates its own processor. Creol objects can have active behavior, i.e., during object creation a designated run method is invoked.

Creol allows for flexible object interaction based on asynchronous method calls, explicit synchronization points, and underspecified (i.e., nondeterministic) local scheduling of the processes within an object. Creol supports software evolution by means of runtime class updates [31]. This allows for runtime reconfiguration of the components. To facilitate the exogenous coordination of the components we have extended Creol with facades and an event system (cf. Section 2.1).

The modeling language is supported by an Eclipse modeling and analysis environment which includes a compiler and type-checker, a simulation platform based on Maude [12], which allows both closed world and open world simulation as well as guided simulation, and a graphic display of the simulations.

In the rest of this section, we specify the interfaces of a local data store for a peer syntactically. Then, we implement parts of a peer as an example.

Each peer consists of a client object, a server object and a data-store object. The Client interface provides the user with a search operation. The data-store provides the client object with an add operation to introduce new data and the server object with a find operation to retrieve data. We model these two perspectives on the data-store by two interfaces StoreClientPerspective and StoreServerPerspective.

The interfaces are structured in terms of inheritance and cointerface requirements. The cointerface of a method (denoted by the **with** keyword) is a static restriction on the objects that may call the method. In the model, the cointerface reflects the intended user of an interface. In Creol, object references are always typed by interfaces. The caller of a method is available via the implicit variable **caller**. Specifying a concrete cointerface allows for callbacks. Finally, method parameters are separated into input and output parameters, using **in** and **out** keywords, respectively.

```
1 interface StoreClientPerspective begin
2  with Client
3   op add(in key:Data, info:Data)
4 end

6 interface StoreServerPerspective begin
7  with Server
8   op find(in key:Data; out info:Data)
9 end

11 interface Store
12  inherits StoreClientPerspective, StoreServerPerspective
13 begin end
```

The interfaces cover the intra-component communication while the facades cover the inter-component communication (cf. Section 2.1). To implement a Creol class, we can use only the ports and events specified in the facades. Note that the use of ports is restricted to reading from an inport or writing to an outport. Since the inter-component communication is coordinated exogenously by the network, the components are not allowed to alter the port bindings; instead, they have to raise an event to request a reconfiguration of the communication network structure.

Next, we provide implementation models for the interfaces in terms of Creol classes. The client offers a search method to the user. To perform a search, the client makes a request to the broker. The event openCS<req, ans>(key; found) provides the ports req and ans to be reconfigured, plus the parameters key and found. If the data identified by key is available, the broker connects the given ports to a server holding the data and reports via found the success of the search. Otherwise, the ports are left unchanged and the failure is reported via found. If successful the client expects its ports to be connected properly and communicates the data via its ports.

For simplicity, a client only operates one search at a time. Nevertheless, the user can issue multiple concurrent search requests. The requests are buffered and served in an arbitrary order (due to the nondeterministic scheduling policy) one at a time.

```
1 class ClientImp (store:StoreClientPerspective, req:outport, ans:inport)
2    inside Peer implements Client begin

4    with User op search(in key:Data out result:Data) ==
5       var found : Boolean;
6       raise_event openCS<req, ans>(key; found);
7       if (found) then
8          req.write(key;);
9          ans.take(;result);
10         ! store.add(key, result)
11      end;
12      raise_event closeCS<req, ans>()
13 end
```

To obtain the result of the search, the client uses a synchronous call to the ans port. The update regarding the new data is sent to thc data-store asynchronously ! store.add(key, result). Using asynchronous communication the client can already continue execution while the data-store is busy processing the changes. The client is a passive object, i.e., it does not specify a run method.

The server object is active in the sense that it starts its operation upon creation. The active behavior is specified in the run method. This involves reading data requests from the req port and delivering the results on the ans port. To repeat the process, the run method issues an asynchronous self call before termination.

```
1 class ServerImp (store:StoreServerPerspective, req:inport, ans:outport)
2       inside Peer implements Server
3 begin
4    op run ==
5       var key, result:Data;
6       raise_event openSS<req, ans>();
7       req.take(;key);
8       store.find (key; result);
9       ans.write(result;);
10      raise_event closeSS<req, ans>();
11      ! run ()
12 end
```

By raising the event openSS<req,ans>(), a server announces its availability to the broker. This synchronous event returns whenever a request is made for some data on this server. Having provided the ports along the event, the server object expects to be connected to the requesting client, and reads the key to the requested data from its req port. The server looks up the data corresponding to the *key* in the data-store using the find operation. The result is sent back on the ans port. The event *closeSS* announces the accomplishment of the transaction. Finally, the server prepares for a new session by calling the run method again.

4.2 Analysis of the Model

Creol programs and models can be *executed* using the rewriting logic of Maude [12]. Maude offers different modes of rewriting and additional capabilities for validation, e.g., a search command and the means for model checking. Credo offers techniques to analyze *parts* of the system in isolation; on the lowest level, to analyze the behavior of a single (active) object in isolation.

Credo offers techniques to analyze, in a black-box manner, the behavior of a component modeled in Creol, by interaction via message passing. This allows for the description and analysis of systems in a divide-and-conquer manner. Thus the developer has the choice of developing the system bottom-up or top-down.

Although Creol allows modeling systems on a high level, the complete model might still be too large to be analyzed or validated as a whole. By building upon the analysis of the individual components, compositional reasoning still allows us to validate the system.

Conformance Testing of the Model. In the context of the Creol concurrency model, especially the *asynchrony* poses a challenge for validation and testing. Following the black-box methodology, an abstract component *specification* is given in terms of its interaction with the environment. However, in a particular execution, the actual order of outputs issued from the component may not be preserved, due to the asynchronous nature of communication. To solve this problem, the conformance of the output to the specification is checked only up-to a notion of observability [17].

The existing Creol interpreter is combined with an interpreter for the abstract behavior specification language to obtain a *specification-driven interpreter for testing and validation* [17]. It allows for *run-time assertion checking* of the Creol-models, namely for compliance with the abstract specification.

We derive a specification for an object directly from the structural interfaces and the behavioral interfaces. The specification of the implementation of the ServerSide is derived from the facade depicted in Section 2.1 and the behavioral interface depicted in Section 2.2. The facade determines the direction of a communication, i.e., whether it is incoming or outgoing communication. For the specification the direction is inverted - the specification 'interacts' with the object to analyze it. The order of the events is determined by the behavioral interface.

The specification language features, among others, choice (between communication in the same direction, i.e., incoming only or outgoing only) and recursion. As an example, we give the specification of a server:

$$\begin{aligned}\varphi_S = \ & \langle event\ register(keyList)\rangle? \ . \ \mathsf{rec}\ X \ . \ \langle event\ openSS()\rangle? \ . \\ & \langle port\ s.sReq(key)\rangle! \ . \ \langle port\ s.sAns(data)\rangle? \ . \\ & \langle event\ closeSS()\rangle? \ . \ X\end{aligned}$$

To test our executable model ServerImpl for conformance with respect to the behavioral interface description, we translate the specification to Creol and in the next step to Maude. The specification in Maude is executed together with the model. With the data-store at hand, we specify via the method parameters that the data delivered along the sAns port of the server is actually the data identified by the key. This needs to be done on the level of the Maude code.

The object is executed together with the specification in a special version of the Maude interpreter customized for the testing purpose. The programmer can track down the reason for a problem according to the Maude execution. This can be either a mistake in the executable model or a flaw in the behavioral model, i.e., the specification. The interpreter reports an error if unexpected behavior is observed, i.e., an unspecified communication from the object to the specification, or a deadlock occurs.

Simulation. The conformance testing introduced in the previous section is already a simulation of a part of the system, i.e., the object under test. We use a modified version of the above testing interpreter to eliminate the error reporting. Notice that the Maude interpreter of Creol is a set of rewrite rules which reduces the modification of the interpreter in this case to the deletion of the rules dealing with the error reporting.

Furthermore, we use the facades and behavioral interfaces of section 2 to derive a Creol skeleton of the network. By filling in the details of the network manager, we get a Creol model of the network. The model of the network and the models of the components together form a model of the entire system, which can be executed in Maude.

We use Maude to steer the execution of the model on different levels. We use the different built-in rewriting strategies to simulate different executions of the system. We use Maude's search command to search for a specific execution leading to a designated program state. And we use Maude's meta-level to control an execution by controlling the application of the rewrite rules.

To supplement the above simulation strategies, we use Maude's *model-checking* facilities. In general, the simulation is non-deterministic, which means, that only part of the specified behavior is covered. Therefore erroneous behavior might be missed. Maude's search facility allows us to explore the search space systematically. A general limitation of model checkers is the state space explosion, which makes larger systems unmanageable, when it comes to model checking. By analyzing *parts* of the system in isolation we reduce the state space explosion. Furthermore, Creol as a modeling language allows us to represent the system in a high-level, abstract manner, and concentrate on the crucial design-choices, which furthermore increases the chances of being able to model-check such a model. Since Maude is based on rewriting, dealing with the asynchronous nature of communication is natural: the asynchronicity is represented by trace–equivalence, which is directly represented as equivalence in the Maude rewriting system. This allows the execution engine to more efficiently represent the state space (by working on the normal forms instead of exploring all re-orderings one by one).

Conformance Testing of the Implementation. The testing process uses formal methods (e.g., automata and simulation of a model's formal program semantics) to provide the necessary links between behavioral interfaces, Creol models, and the actual implementation.

Behavioral interfaces provide *test scenarios*, patterns of interactions between the components. A test case created according to a test scenario represents a functional description, but does not guarantee a good coverage of the model. To optimize the coverage, *dynamic symbolic execution* is used to analyze execution paths through the Creol model to find representative test cases while avoiding redundancies in the test suite [18].

Once a test suite is created, the next step in testing is executing the tests on the implementation and reaching a test verdict to check the conformance between model and implementation. Testing a concurrent system involves validation of both functional and non–functional aspects. Functional aspects are covered by standard techniques like runtime assertions in the implementation and unit testing. To test the concurrency behavior of an implementation against its model we use the observation that typically the Creol model and the implementation share a common structure with regard to high-level structure and control flow. It is therefore reasonable to assume that, given equivalent stimuli (input data), they will behave in an equivalent way with regard to control flow.

We instrument the implementation to record *events* and use the instrumented implementation to record *traces* of observable events. Then we restrict the execution of the model to these traces. If the model can successfully play back the trace recorded from the implementation (and the implementation produces the correct result(s) without assertion failures), then the test case is successful. The Creol model is used as a test oracle for the execution of the test cases on the actual implementation [1].

4.3 Schedulability Analysis

In this section, we explain how to model the real-time aspects of the peer-to-peer system using timed automata and the UPPAAL model checker [25]. An object or component is called schedulable if it can accomplish all its tasks in time, i.e., within their designated deadlines. We demonstrate the schedulability analysis process [14,20] on the network manager object in the peer-to-peer model, which is the most heavily loaded entity in this system.

In the real-time model of an object, we add explicit schedulers to object specifications. For schedulability analysis, the model of an object consists of three parts: the behavioral interface, the methods and the scheduler.

Behavioral interface. To analyze an object in isolation, we use the behavioral interface as an abstract model of the environment. Thus, it triggers the object methods. Fig. 13 shows the behavioral interface of the network manager augmented with real-time information. The automata in this figure are derived from the behavioral interface of Peer (see Section 2.2) by removing the port operations. To send messages, we use the invoke channel, with the syntax

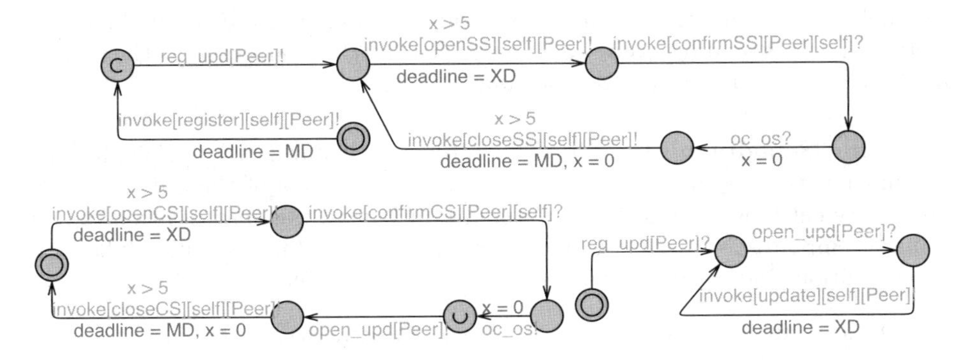

Fig. 13. The behavioral interface of broker modeled in timed automata

invoke[message][sender][receiver]!. To specify the deadlines associated to a message, we use the variable deadline.

In Fig. 13, we use the open_upd and reg_upd channels to synchronize the automata for Peer with ClientSide and ServerSide, respectively. Additionally, the automata for ClientSide and ServerSide are synchronized on the oc_os channel; this abstractly models the synchronization on port communication between the components in which the network manager is not directly involved. This model allows the client side of any peer to connect to the server side of any peer (abstracting from the details of matching the peers).

The confirmCS and confirmSS messages model the confirmation sent back from the network manager to the open session requests by the peers. In the implementation, this is an implicit reply which is therefore not modeled in the behavioral interfaces of the peers in Section 2.2. These edges synchronize with the method implementations (explained next) in order to reduce the nondeterminism in the model.

Methods. The methods also use the invoke channel for sending messages. Fig. 14 shows the automata implementation of two methods for handling the openCS and register events. In openCS, and similarly in every method, the keyword **caller** refers to the object/component that has called this method. The scheduler should be able to start each method and be notified when the method finishes, so that it can start the next method. To this end, method automata start with a synchronization on the start channel, and finish with a transition synchronizing on the finish

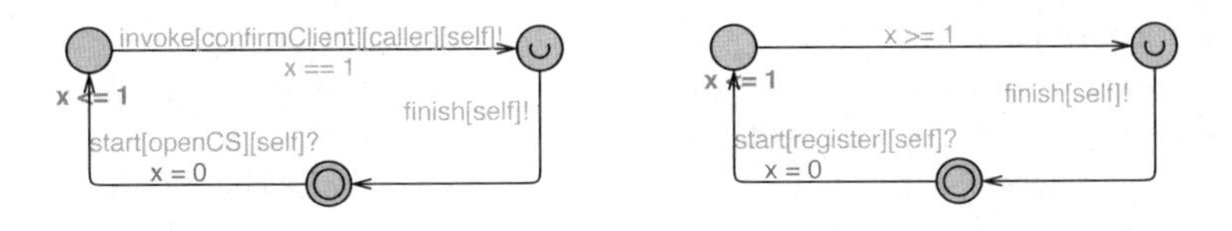

Fig. 14. Method automata for handling openCS and register events

channel leading back to the initial location. The implementation of the openCS method involves sending a message confirmCS back to the sender, while the register method is modeled merely as a time delay.

Checking Schedulability. When an object is instantiated, an off-the-shelf scheduler is selected and tailored to the particular needs of the object. For an object, we get a network of timed automata in UPPAAL by instantiating the automata templates for methods, behavioral interface and the scheduler. There are two conditions indicating that a system is not schedulable:

1. The scheduler receives a new message when the message queue is already full. In theory [20], a schedulable object needs a queue length of at most $\lceil d_{max}/b_{min} \rceil$, where d_{max} is the biggest deadline value used and b_{min} is the smallest execution time of all methods.
2. The deadline of at least one message in the queue is missed.

In either of the above cases, the scheduler automaton goes to a location called `Error`. This location has no outgoing transitions and therefore causes deadlock. Therefore, absence of deadlock implies schedulability, as well as correct output behavior for the object.

Due to the high amount of concurrency in the model, model checking is of limited use. Nevertheless, we can use the simulation feature of UPPAAL [29] to analyze bigger systems. We measure the worst-case response time for each message, which identifies a lower bound for the deadline value in a schedulable system.

5 Conclusions

We presented an extended version of the *Credo* methodology now covering also the detailed modeling and analysis of the network. The *Credo* modeling and analysis techniques addressing highly reconfigurable distributed systems presented cover a broader spectrum of the software development process. The *Vereofy* tool set is added to the picture providing modeling and analysis techniques for detailed network models.

At a high level of abstraction, the dynamic connections between the components are modeled using behavioral interface specifications. The detailed model of the network is given in terms of a Reo model specified in *Vereofy*. The detailed model of the components is given in terms of an object–oriented *Creol* model. Both models are used for analysis of functional as well as non-functional properties, e.g., schedulability, deadlock freedom. The conformance between the component and the network models is established via the behavioral interface specifications. Furthermore we can establish conformance between the *Creol* model and a given implementation by conformance testing.

The process described in this paper can be integrated in the existing software development methodologies which support component-based modeling, and thus enhance them with support for formal modeling and analysis of dynamically reconfigurable distributed systems. In the future, we intend to broaden the scope of the *Credo* modeling language and its corresponding tool suite in order to support the full development life-cycle of large-scale, open systems. This involves, on one hand, integrating models of software architecture into the process; and on the other hand, working further on deployment concerns such as scheduling.

Case Studies

The Credo methodology has been successfully applied to two industrial case studies.

ASK System. The *Credo* methodology has been applied to model and analyze the ASK system, an industrial software system developed by Almende [2]. The purpose of the ASK system is to improve communication between people by providing a mediating communication platform with knowledge about the availability, schedules, skills and past experience of users. Typical applications for ASK are workforce planning, customer service, knowledge sharing, social care and emergency response. Various communication channels can be incorporated. The ASK system is a learning system, trying to improve the quality of service according to self–monitoring and feedback mechanisms. An important part of all core components of the system are thread pools. They are used to manage the (varying) workloads of the system by distribution of individual tasks, creation of new threads to handle tasks, and destruction of threads in case of low workload to minimize the idle time. We have modeled and analyzed the different kinds of thread pools in the ASK system according to the *Credo* methodology [15].

BSN. The *Credo* methodology has been applied to model and analyze a biomedical sensor network (BSN). For the BSN case study we modeled and analyzed different routing protocols for a biomedical sensor network. The BSN case study is focused on the application of the sensor network in a hospital. Patients are monitored via medical sensors which communicate their observations via radio signals to a sink, representing the entry point to the (wired) hospital communication network. The signals are not broadcasted directly to the sink but via other sensor nodes, used as hubs. Among functional properties, like emiting an emergency signal in certain scenarios, non–functional properties, like energy consumption are of interest. Two different routing protocols have been modeled, analyzed, and compared [26,27].

References

1. Aichernig, B., Griesmayer, A., Schlatte, R., Stam, A.: Modeling and testing multi-threaded asynchronous systems with Creol. In: Proc. TTSS 2008. ENTCS, vol. 243, pp. 3–14. Elsevier, Amsterdam (2009)
2. The Almende research company, `http://www.almende.com/`
3. Arbab, F.: Reo: A channel-based coordination model for component composition. Mathematical Structures in Computer Science 14, 329–366 (2004)

4. Arbab, F., Baier, C., Rutten, J.J., Sirjani, M.: Modeling component connectors in Reo by constraint automata. In: Proc. FOCLASA 2003. ENTCS, vol. 97, pp. 25–46. Elsevier, Amsterdam (2004)
5. Baier, C., Blechmann, T., Klein, J., Klüppelholz, S.: Formal Verification for Components and Connectors. In: de Boer, F.S., Bonsangue, M.M., Madelaine, E. (eds.) FMCO 2008. LNCS, vol. 5751, pp. 82–101. Springer, Heidelberg (2009)
6. Baier, C., Blechmann, T., Klein, J., Klüppelholz, S.: A Uniform Framework for Modeling and Verifying Components and Connectors. In: Field, J., Vasconcelos, V.T. (eds.) COORDINATION 2009. LNCS, vol. 5521, pp. 247–267. Springer, Heidelberg (2009)
7. Baier, C., Sirjani, M., Arbab, F., Rutten, J.J.M.M.: Modeling Component Connectors in Reo by Constraint Automata. In: Proceedings of the 2nd International Workshop on Foundations of Coordination Languages and Software Architectures. Science of Computer Programming, vol. 61, pp. 75–113 (2006)
8. Behrmann, G., David, A., Larsen, K.G., Håkansson, J., Pettersson, P., Yi, W., Hendriks, M.: Uppaal 4.0. In: QEST, pp. 125–126. IEEE Computer Society, Los Alamitos (2006)
9. Blechmann, T., Baier, C.: Checking equivalence for Reo networks. In: Electronic Notes in Theoretical Computer Science, vol. 215, pp. 209–226 (2008)
10. Blechmann, T., Klein, J., Klüppelholz, S.: Vereofy, `http://www.vereofy.de`
11. Blechmann, T., Klein, J., Klüppelholz, S.: Vereofy User Manual. TU Dresden (2008 –2009), `http://www.vereofy.de`
12. Clavel, M., Durán, F., Eker, S., Lincoln, P., Martí-Oliet, N., Meseguer, J., Quesada, J.F.: Maude: Specification and programming in rewriting logic. Theoretical Computer Science (2001)
13. CWI Coordination Group. Eclipse coordination tools, `http://reo.project.cwi.nl/cgi-bin/trac.cgi/reo/wiki/Tools`
14. de Boer, F., Chothia, T., Jaghoori, M.M.: Modular schedulability analysis of concurrent objects in Creol. In: Arbab, F., Sirjani, M. (eds.) Fundamentals of Software Engineering. LNCS, vol. 5961, pp. 212–227. Springer, Heidelberg (2010)
15. de Boer, F.S., Grabe, I., Jaghoori, M.M., Stam, A., Yi, W.: Modeling and Analysis of Thread-Pools in an Industrial Communication Platform. In: Breitman, K., Cavalcanti, A. (eds.) ICFEM 2009. LNCS, vol. 5885, pp. 367–386. Springer, Heidelberg (2009)
16. Grabe, I., Jaghoori, M.M., Aichernig, B., Baier, C., Blechmann, T., de Boer, F., Griesmayer, A., Johnsen, E.B., Klein, J., Klüppelholz, S., Kyas, M., Leister, W., Schlatte, R., Stam, A., Steffen, M., Tschirner, S., Liang, X., Yi, W.: Credo methodology. Modeling and analyzing a peer-to-peer system in Credo. In: Johnsen, E.B., Stolz, V. (eds.) Proceedings of the 3nd International Workshop on Harnessing Theories for Tool Support in Software (TTSS 2009), ICTAC 2009 satellite Workshop. Electronic Notes in Theoretical Computer Science. Elsevier, Amsterdam (2010)
17. Grabe, I., Steffen, M., Torjusen, A.B.: Executable Interface Specifications for Testing Asynchronous Creol Components. In: Arbab, F., Sirjani, M. (eds.) Fundamentals of Software Engineering. LNCS, vol. 5961, pp. 324–339. Springer, Heidelberg (2010)
18. Griesmayer, A., Aichernig, B.K., Johnsen, E.B., Schlatte, R.: Dynamic symbolic execution for testing distributed objects. In: Dubois, C. (ed.) Tests and Proofs. LNCS, vol. 5668, pp. 105–120. Springer, Heidelberg (2009)
19. Jaghoori, M.M.: Coordinating object oriented components using data-flow networks. In: de Boer, F.S., Bonsangue, M.M., Graf, S., de Roever, W.-P. (eds.) FMCO 2007. LNCS, vol. 5382, pp. 280–311. Springer, Heidelberg (2008)

20. Jaghoori, M.M., de Boer, F.S., Chothia, T., Sirjani, M.: Schedulability of asynchronous real-time concurrent objects. J. Logic and Alg. Prog. 78(5), 402–416 (2009)
21. Jaghoori, M.M., Longuet, D., de Boer, F.S., Chothia, T.: Schedulability and compatibility of real time asynchronous objects. In: Proc. Real Time Systems Symposium, pp. 70–79. IEEE Computer Society Press, Los Alamitos (2008)
22. Johnsen, E.B., Owe, O.: An asynchronous communication model for distributed concurrent objects. Software and Systems Modeling 6(1), 35–58 (2007)
23. Klüppelholz, S., Baier, C.: Alternating-time stream logic for multi-agent systems. Science of Computer Programming. Corrected Proof (2009) (in Press)
24. Klüppelholz, S., Baier, C.: Symbolic model checking for channel-based component connectors. Science of Computer Programming 74(9), 688–701 (2009)
25. Larsen, K.G., Pettersson, P., Yi, W.: UPPAAL in a nutshell. STTT 1(1-2), 134–152 (1997)
26. Leister, W., Björk, J., Schlatte, R., Griesmayer, A.: Validation of Creol models for routing algorithms in wireless sensor networks. Report 1024, Norsk Regnesentral, Oslo, Norway (2010)
27. Leister, W., Liang, X., Klüppelholz, S., Klein, J., Owe, O., Kazemeyni, F., Bjørk, J., Østvold, B.M.: Modelling of biomedical sensor networks using the Creol tools. Report 1022, Norsk Regnesentral, Oslo, Norway (2009)
28. Rumpe, B., Klein, C.: Automata describing object behavior. In: Object-Oriented Behavioral Specifications, pp. 265–286. Springer, Heidelberg (1996)
29. Tschirner, S., Xuedong, L., Yi, W.: Model-based validation of QoS properties of biomedical sensor networks. In: Proc. Embedded software (EMSOFT 2008), pp. 69–78. ACM Press, New York (2008)
30. Vereofy source code of the peer-to-peer example (2010), `http://www.vereofy.de/download/examples/vereofy_p2p_example.zip`
31. Yu, I.C., Johnsen, E.B., Owe, O.: Type-safe runtime class upgrades in Creol. In: Gorrieri, R., Wehrheim, H. (eds.) FMOODS 2006. LNCS, vol. 4037, pp. 202–217. Springer, Heidelberg (2006)

Patterns for Refinement Automation

Alexei Iliasov[1], Elena Troubitsyna[2], Linas Laibinis[2], and Alexander Romanovsky[1]

[1] Newcastle University, UK
[2] Åbo Akademi University, Finland
{alexei.iliasov,alexander.romanovsky}@ncl.ac.uk,
{linas.laibinis,elena.troubitsyna}@abo.fi

Abstract. Formal modelling is indispensable for engineering highly dependable systems. However, a wider acceptance of formal methods is hindered by their insufficient usability and scalability. In this paper, we aim at assisting developers in rigorous modelling and design by increasing automation of development steps. We introduce a notion of refinement patterns – generic representations of typical correctness-preserving model transformations. Our definition of a refinement pattern contains a description of syntactic model transformations, as well as the pattern applicability conditions and proof obligations for verifying correctness preservation. This work establishes a basis for building a tool that would support formal system development via pattern reuse and instantiation. We present a prototype of such a tool and some examples of refinement patterns for automated development in the Event B formalism.

1 Introduction

Over the recent years model-driven development has become a leading paradigm in software engineering. System development by stepwise refinement is a *formal* model-driven development approach that advocates development of systems correct by construction. Development starts from an abstract model, which is gradually transformed into a specification closely resembling an implementation. Each model transformation step, called a *refinement* step, allows a designer to incorporate implementation details into the model. Correctness of refinement steps is validated by mathematical proofs.

The refinement approach significantly reduces the required testing efforts and, at the same time, supports a clear traceability of system properties through various abstraction levels. However, it is still poorly integrated into the existing software engineering process. Among the main reasons hindering its application are complexity of carrying proofs, lack of expertise in abstract modelling, and insufficient scalability.

In this paper we propose an approach that aims at facilitating integration of formal methods into the existing development practice by leveraging automation of refinement process and increasing reuse of models and proofs. We aim at automating certain model transformation steps via instantiation and reuse of prefabricated solutions, which we call *refinement patterns*. Such patterns generalise certain typical model transformations reoccurring in a particular development method. They can be thought of as "refinement rules in large".

In general, a refinement pattern is a generic model transformer. Essentially it consists of three parts. The first part is the pattern applicability conditions, i.e., the syntactic and

F.S. de Boer et al. (Eds.): FMCO 2009, LNCS 6286, pp. 70–88, 2010.

semantic conditions that should be fulfilled by the model to be eligible for a refinement pattern application. The second part contains definition of syntactic manipulations over the model to be transformed. Finally, the third part consists of the proof obligations that should be discharged to verify that the performed model transformation is indeed a refinement step.

Application of refinement patterns is compositional. Hence some large model transformation steps can be represented by a certain combination of refinement patterns, and therefore can also be seen as refinement patterns per se. A possibility to compose patterns significantly improves scalability of formal modelling. Moreover, reducing execution of a refinement step to a number of syntactic manipulations over a model provides a basis for automation. Finally, our approach can potentially support reuse of not only models but also proofs. Indeed, by proving that an application of a generic pattern produces a valid refinement of a generic model, we at the same time verify the correctness of such a transformation for any of its instances. This might significantly reduce or even avoid proving activity in a concrete development.

The theoretical work on defining refinement patterns presented in this paper established a basis for building a prototype tool for automating refinement process in Event B[13]. The tool has been developed as a plug-in for the RODIN platform [1] – an open toolset for supporting modelling and refinement in the Event B framework. We believe that, by creating a large library of refinement patterns and providing automated tool support for pattern matching and instantiation, we will make formal modelling and verification more accessible for software engineers and hence facilitate integration of formal methods into software engineering practice.

2 Towards Refinement Automation

In this paper we focus on automating the formal development process based on model refinement. We start this section by giving a short overview on the notion of refinement and the techniques allowing us facilitate the refinement process. Then we proceed by describing our chosen formal framework – Event B.

2.1 Formal Development by Refinement

System development by refinement is a formal model-driven development process. Refinement allows us to ensure that a refined, i.e., more elaborated, model retains all the essential properties of its abstract counterpart. Since refinement is transitive, the model-driven refinement-based development process enables development of systems that are correct-by-construction.

The precise definition of refinement depends on the chosen modelling framework and hence might have different semantics and degree of rigor. The foundations of formal reasoning about correctness and stepwise development by refinement were established by Dijkstra [9] and Hoare [12], and then further developed by Back and von Wright [5] as well as Morgan [16].

In the refinement calculus framework, a model is represented by a composition of abstract statements. Formally, we say that the statement S is refined by the statement

S', written $S \sqsubseteq S'$, if, whenever S establishes a certain postcondition, so does S' [9]. Since statement composition is monotonic with respect to the refinement relation, refinement of a model statement is also refinement of the whole model. In general, the refinement process can be seen as a way to reduce non-determinism of the abstract model, to replace abstract mathematical data structures by data structures implementable on a computer, and, hence, gradually introduce implementation decisions.

There have been several attempts to facilitate the refinement process, by generalizing the typical refinement transformations into a set of refinement rules [5,16]. These rules can be seen as generic templates (or patterns) that define the general form of the statement to be transformed, the resultant statement, and the proof obligations that should be discharged to verify refinement for that particular transformation. However, a refinement rule usually describes a small localized transformation of a certain model part. Obviously, the tools developed to automate application of such refinement rules [8,17] lack scalability.

On the other hand, such frameworks as Z, VDM, and Event B support the formal development by model transformation of the entire system. For instance, the RODIN platform – a tool supporting refinement in Event B – allows us to perform refinement by introducing many changes at once and to verify by proofs that these changes result in correct model refinement. Often a refinement step can be seen as a composition of "standard" (frequently reoccurring) localized transformations distributed all over the model. Additional research is needed, though, to answer the question whether we can employ the transformational approach to fully automate execution of these transformations by reusing the models and proofs that were constructed previously.

In this paper we propose to tackle this problem via definition and use of refinement patterns. Our definition of refinement patterns builds on the idea of refinement rules. In general, a refinement pattern is a model transformer. Unlike design patterns [10], a refinement pattern is "dynamic" in a sense that the process of pattern application takes a model as an input and produces a new model as an output. Moreover, both syntactic and semantic information about models is used to precisely define a refinement pattern.

To formalize and automate the process of pattern application, we define a pattern as a model transformer consisting of three parts. The first part is the pattern applicability conditions, i.e., the syntactic and semantic conditions that should be fulfilled by the model for a refinement pattern to be applicable. The second part contains a definition of syntactic manipulations on the model to be transformed. Finally, the third part consists of the proof obligations that should be discharged to verify that the performed model transformation is indeed a refinement step. It is easy to see that a refinement pattern manipulates a model on both syntactic and semantic level.

In principle, refinement patterns can be defined for any refinement-based modelling framework. In this paper we present our proposal for refinement patterns in the Event B formalism and also describe a prototype tool that implements them. We start by briefly introducing the Event B language and giving semantic and syntactic views on its models.

2.2 Event B

In this section we introduce our formal framework – the B Method [2]. It is an approach for the industrial development of highly dependable software. The method has been successfully used in the development of several complex real-life applications. Recently the B method has been extended by the Event B framework [3], which enables modelling of event-based (reactive) systems. In fact, this extension has incorporated the action system formalism [6,4] into the B Method.

Event B uses the Abstract Machine Notation for constructing and verifying models. An abstract machine encapsulates a state (the variables) of the model and provides operations on the state. A simple abstract machine has the following general form:

MACHINE AM
VARIABLES v
INVARIANT Inv
INITIALISATION *INIT*
EVENTS
E_1
$\ldots$
E_N

The machine is uniquely identified by its name *AM*. The state variables of the machine, *v*, are declared in the **VARIABLES** clause and initialised in *INIT* as defined in the **INITIALISATION** clause. The variables are strongly typed by constraining predicates of the machine invariant *Inv* given in the **INVARIANT** clause. The invariant is usually defined as a conjunction of the constraining predicates and the predicates defining the properties of the system that should be preserved during system execution.

The dynamic behaviour of the system is defined by a set of atomic events specified in the **EVENTS** clause. An event is defined as follows:

$$E = \textbf{WHEN } g \textbf{ THEN } S \textbf{ END}$$

where the guard *g* is conjunction of the predicates over the machine variables *v*, and the action *S* is an assignment to state variables. For simplicity, in this paper we do not consider Event B events with parameters or local variables.

The occurrence of events represents the observable behaviour of the system. The guard defines the conditions under which the action can be executed, i.e., when the event is *enabled*. The action can be either a deterministic assignment to the variables or a non-deterministic assignment from a given set or according to a given postcondition. The semantics of actions is defined as a before-after (BA) predicate as follows:

Action	Before-after predicate $BA_e(x, y, x')$
$x := E(x, y)$	$x' = E(x, y) \wedge y' = y$
$x :\in Set$	$\exists t.\ (t \in Set \wedge x' = t) \wedge y' = y$
$x :\mid P(x, y, x')$	$\exists t.\ (P(x, t, y) \wedge x' = t) \wedge y' = y$

where x and y are disjoint lists (partitions) of state variables, and x', y' represent their values in the after state.

Event B adopts interleaving semantics while treating parallelism. If several events are enabled then any of them can be chosen for execution non-deterministically. If none of the events is enabled then the system deadlocks.

To check consistency of Event B machine, we should verify two types of properties: event feasibility and invariant preservation. Intuitively, event feasibility means that execution of an event from any state where both the machine invariant and the event guard hold is possible, i.e., it can produce at least one state that satisfies the before-after predicate, i.e.,

$$Inv(v) \wedge G_e(v) \Rightarrow \exists v'.\ BA_e(v, v')$$

The invariant preservation property simply states that invariant should be maintained:

$$Inv(v) \wedge G_e(v) \wedge BA_e(v, v') \Rightarrow Inv(v')$$

The main development methodology of Event B is refinement – the process of transforming an abstract specification while preserving its correctness and gradually introducing implementation details. Let us assume that the refinement machine AM' is a result of refinement of the abstract machine *AM*:

MACHINE AM'
VARIABLES w
INVARIANT Inv'
INITIALISATION *INIT'*
EVENTS
E_1
...
E_M

In AM' we replace the abstract variables of *AM* (v) with the concrete ones (w). The invariant of AM' – Inv' – defines now not only the invariant properties of the refined model, but also the connection between the newly introduced variables (w) and the abstract variables that they replace (v). For a refinement step to be valid, every possible execution of the refined machine must correspond (via Inv') to some execution of the abstract machine. To demonstrate this, we should establish two facts – feasibility of refined events and their correctness with respect to the abstract events. To demonstrate feasibility, we should prove the following:

$$Inv(v) \wedge Inv'(v, w) \wedge G'_e(w) \Rightarrow \exists w'.\ BA'_e(w, w')$$

where $G'(w)$ is the guard of the refined event and $BA'(w, w')$ its before-after predicate.

To demonstrate that each event is a correct refinement of its abstract counterpart, we should first prove that the guard is strengthened in the refinement:

$$Inv(v) \wedge Inv'(v, w) \wedge G'_e(w) \Rightarrow G_e(v)$$

Finally, we need to demonstrate a correspondence between the abstract and concrete postconditions:

$$Inv(v) \wedge Inv'(v, w) \wedge G'_e(w) \wedge BA'_e(w, w') \Rightarrow \exists v'.\ (BA_e(v, v') \wedge Inv'(v', w'))$$

The refined model can also introduce new events. In this case, we have show that these new events are refinements of implicit empty (skip) events of the abstract model.

While presenting Event B above, we have slightly simplified matters by omitting the fact that Event B model consists of two separate parts. The static part, called context, contains the declaration of new types(sets), constants and axioms. The presented, dynamic part (machine) contains the variable declarations and events. However, this simplification is of syntactic nature and is insignificant as such. Our approach to refinement pattern definition that we are presenting next can be easily extended to compensate it.

2.3 Event-B Models as Syntactic Objects

To define refinement patterns, we now consider an Event B model as a syntactic mathematical object. For brevity, we omit representations of some model elements here, though they are supported in our tool implementation [13]. The subset of Event B models used in this paper can be described by the following data structure:

$$\begin{array}{lll} \text{model} :: \mathit{var} : \text{VAR}^* & \text{event} :: \mathit{name} : \text{EVENT} & \text{action} :: \mathit{var} : \text{VAR} \\ \qquad \mathit{inv} : \text{PRED}^* & \qquad \mathit{param} : \text{PARAM}^* & \qquad \mathit{style} : \text{STYLE} \\ \qquad \mathit{evt} : \text{event}^* & \qquad \mathit{guards} : \text{PRED}^* & \qquad \mathit{expr} : \text{EXPR} \\ & \qquad \mathit{actions} : \text{action}^* & \end{array}$$

Here VAR, PRED, EXPR, EVENT, PARAM are the carrier sets reserved correspondingly for model variables, predicates, expressions, event names and parameters. An event is represented by a tuple containing the event name, (a list of) its parameters, guards, and actions. The reserved event name `init` denotes the initialisation event. An action, in its turn, is a tuple containing a variable, an action style and an expression, where an action style denotes one of the assignment types : i.e., $\text{STYLE} = \{:=, :\in, :|\}$.

Sub-elements of a model element can be accessed by using the dot operator: $act.style$ is the style of an action act. Instances of the models, events and actions are constructed using a special notation $\langle a_1 \mid \cdots \mid a_n \rangle$. The following example shows how an Event B model is represented in our notation:

MACHINE $m0$	
VARIABLES x	$\langle\ \langle x \rangle\ \mid$
INVARIANT $x \in \mathbb{Z}$	$\langle "x \in \mathbb{Z}" \rangle\ \mid$
INITIALISATION $x := 0$	$\langle\ \langle \texttt{init} \mid - \mid - \mid \langle x \mid := \mid "0" \rangle \rangle,$
EVENTS	
$count$ = **BEGIN** $x := x + 1$ **END**	$\langle \texttt{count} \mid - \mid - \mid \langle x \mid := \mid "x + 1" \rangle \rangle \rangle \rangle$

In the example, x is an element of VAR, `init` and `count` are event names from EVENT, "$x \in \mathbb{Z}$" is a predicate, and "0", "$x + 1$" are model expressions.

Now we have set a scene for a formal definition of refinement patterns that aim at automating refinement process in general and Event B in particular.

3 Refinement Patterns

In this section we give formal definitions of transformation rules and refinement patterns. Moreover, we propose a special language allowing us to construct transformation rules, illustrating it by simple examples.

3.1 Definitions

Definition 1. *Let S be a set of all well-formed models defined according to the syntax of Event B. Then a transformation rule T is a function computing a new model for a given input model:*

$$T : S \times C \nrightarrow S$$

where C contains a set of all possible configurations (i.e., additional parameters) of a transformation rule.

Note that T is defined as a partial function, i.e., it produces a new model only for some acceptable input models s and configurations c, i.e., when $(s, c) \in \mathsf{dom}(T)$.

Definition 2. *A refinement pattern is a transformation rule* $P : S \times C \nrightarrow S$ *that constructs a model refinement for any acceptable input model and configuration:*

$$\forall s, c.(s, c) \in \mathsf{dom}(P) \Rightarrow s \sqsubseteq P(s, c)$$

where $\sqsubseteq$ *denotes a refinement relation.*

In this paper we rely on the Event-B proof theory when demonstrating that a transformation rule is indeed a refinement pattern.

3.2 The Language of Transformations

We propose a special language to construct transformation rules. The proposed language contains basic transformation rules as well as the constructs allowing to compose complex rules from simpler ones. For instance, a refinement pattern is usually composed from several basic transformation rules. These rules themselves might not be refinement patterns. However, by attaching to them additional proof obligations, we can verify that their composition becomes a refinement pattern.

The structure of the basic rules reflects the way a transformation rule or a refinement pattern is applied. First, rule applicability for a given input model and configuration parameters is checked. The applicability condition to be checked can contain both syntactic and semantic constraints on input models and configurations. Mathematically, for a transformation rule T, its applicability condition corresponds to $\mathsf{dom}(T)$. Then, the input model s for the given configuration c is syntactically transformed into the output model calculated as function application $T(s, c)$. Finally, in case of a refinement pattern, the result $T(s, c)$ should be demonstrated to be a refinement of the input model s, i.e., $s \sqsubseteq T(s, c)$. The last expression, using the proof theory of Event B, can be simplified to specific proof obligations on model elements to be verified.

A basic rule has the following general form:

rule $name(c)$
  context $Q(c, s)$
  effect $E(c, s)$
  proof obligation $PO_1(c, s)$
  ...
  proof obligation $PO_n(c, s)$

Here $name$ and c are correspondingly the rule name and the list of its parameters. The predicate $Q(c, s)$ defines the rule application context (applicability conditions), where s is the model being transformed. The effect function $E(c, s)$ computes a new model from a current model s and parameters c. The proof obligation part contains a list of theorems to be proved to establish that the rule is a (part of) refinement pattern and not just a transformation rule. From now on, we write **context**(r), **effect**(r) and **proof_obligations**(r) to refer to the context, effect computation function, and collection of proof obligations of a rule r.

As an example, let us consider two primitive rules for the Event-B method. The first transformation adds one or more new variables:

$$
\begin{array}{l}
\textbf{rule}\ newvar(vv) \\
\quad \textbf{context}\ vv \cap s.var = \varnothing \\
\quad \textbf{effect}\ \langle s.var \cup vv \mid s.inv \mid s.evt \rangle \\
\quad \textbf{proof\_obligation}\ \forall v \in vv \cdot (\exists a \cdot a \in s.\mathtt{init}.action \wedge v \in a.var)
\end{array}
$$

The rule applicability condition requires that the new variables have fresh names for the input model. The effect function simply adds the new variables to the model structure. The rule also has a single proof obligation requiring that the variable(s) is assigned in the initialisation action. Such an action would have to be added by some other basic rule for the same refinement step.

Another example is the rule for adding new model invariant(s).

$$
\begin{array}{l}
\textbf{rule}\ newinv(ii) \\
\quad \textbf{context}\ ii \subseteq \mathrm{PRED} \wedge \forall i \in ii \cdot FV(ii) \subseteq s.var \\
\quad \textbf{effect}\ \langle s.var \mid inv \cup ii \mid evt \rangle \\
\quad \textbf{proof obligation} \\
\quad\quad \forall e, v, v' \cdot e \in s.evt \wedge \\
\quad\quad\quad\quad Inv(v) \wedge Guards_e(v) \wedge BA_e(v, v') \Rightarrow Inv(v') \\
\quad \textbf{proof\_obligation}\ \exists v \cdot Inv(v)
\end{array}
$$

Here $FV(x)$ is set of free variables in x, Inv stands for $(\bigwedge_{i \in s.inv \cup ii} i)$, $Guards_e$ is defined as $(\bigwedge_{g \in e.guards} g)$ and BA_e is the before-after predicate. Both proof obligations are taken directly from the Event-B semantics (i.e., the corresponding proof obligation rules). The first obligation requires to show that the new invariant is preserved by all model events, while the second one checks feasibility of such an addition by asking to prove that the new invariant is not contradictory. This example illustrates how the underlying Event B semantics is used to derive proof obligations for refinement patterns.

The table below lists the basic rules for the chosen subset of Event B. There are two classes of rules – for adding new elements and for removing existing ones. All the rules implicitly take an additional argument – the model being transformed. A double-character parameter name means that a rule accepts a set of elements, e.g., $newgrd(e, gg)$ adds all the guards from a given set gg to an event e.

rule $newvar(vv)$	**rule** $delvar(vv)$
rule $newinv(ii)$	**rule** $delinv(ii)$
rule $newevt(ee)$	**rule** $delevt(ee)$
rule $newgrd(e, gg)$	**rule** $delgrd(e, gg)$
rule $newact(e, aa)$	**rule** $delact(e, aa)$
rule $newactexp(e, a, p)$	

To construct more complex transformations, we introduce a number of composition operators into our language. They include the sequential, $p; q$, and parallel, $p \| q$, composition constructs. In addition, there is the conditional rule construct, **if** c **then** p **end**, as well as a construct allowing us to introduce additional rule parameters – **conf** $i : Q$ **do** $p(i)$ **end**. Finally, to handle rule repetitions, generalised parallel composition is introduced in the form of a loop construct: **par** $c : Q$ **do** $p(c)$ **end**. The language summary is given in Figure 1.

$p(c) = basic(c)$	*primitive rule*
$\mid p; q$	*sequential composition*
$\mid p \| q$	*parallel composition*
$\mid$ **if** $Q(c, s)$ **then** p **end**	*conditional rule*
$\mid$ **conf** $i : Q(i, c, s)$ **do** $p(i \cup c)$ **end**	*parameterised rule*
$\mid$ **par** $i : Q(i, c, s)$ **do** $p(i \cup c)$ **end**	*generalised parallel composition*

Fig. 1. The language of transformation rules

3.3 Examples

In this section we present a couple of simple examples of refinement patterns constructed using the proposed language.

Example 1 (New Variable). A refinement step adding a new variable can be accomplished in three steps. First, the new variable is added to the list of model variables. Second, the typing invariant is added to the model. Finally, an initialisation action is provided for the variable. The following refinement pattern adds a new variable declared to be a natural number and initalised with zero:

conf $v\ : \neg\ (v \in s.var)$ **do**
  $newvar(\{v\});$
  $(newinv(\{\text{"}v \in \mathbb{N}\text{"}\}, s) \parallel newact(\texttt{init}, \{\langle v \mid:=\mid \text{"}0\text{"}\rangle\}))$
end

The only pattern parameter (apart from the implicit input s) is some fresh name for the new model variable.

A pattern application example is given below. The left-hand side model is an input model and the righ-hand side is the refined version constructed by the pattern. The example assumes that variable name q is chosen for parameter v.

MACHINE $m0$	**MACHINE** $m1$
VARIABLES x	**VARIABLES** x, q
INVARIANT $x \in \mathbb{Z}$	**INVARIANT** $x \in \mathbb{Z} \wedge q \in \mathbb{N}$
INITIALISATION $x := 0$	**INITIALISATION** $x := 0 \| q := 0$
EVENTS	**EVENTS**
$count =$ **BEGIN** $x := x + 1$ **END**	$count =$ **BEGIN** $x := x + 1$ **END**

A more general (and also useful) pattern version could accept a typing predicate and an initialisation action as additional pattern parameters.

Example 2 (Action Split). In Event B, an abstract event may be refined into a choice between two or more concrete events, each of which must be a refinement of the abstract event. A simple case of such refinement is implemented by the refinement pattern below. The pattern creates a copy of an abstract event and adds a new guard and its negation to the original and new events. The guard expression is supplied as a pattern parameter.

$$
\begin{array}{l}
\textbf{conf}\ e, en\ : e \in s.evt \wedge \neg\ (en \in s.evt)\ \textbf{do} \\
\quad newevt(en, s); \\
\quad newgrd(en, e.guard) \parallel \\
\quad newact(en, e.action); \\
\quad \textbf{conf}\ g\ : g \in \text{PRED} \wedge FV(g) \subseteq s.var \\
\quad\quad \textbf{do}\ newgrd(e, g) \parallel newgrd(en, \neg g)\ \textbf{end} \\
\textbf{end}
\end{array}
$$

The pattern configuration requires three parameters. Parameter e refers to the event to be refined from the input model s, en is some fresh event name, and g is a predicate on the model variables.

The pattern is applicable to models with at least one event. The result is a model with an additional event and a constrained guard of the original event. As an input model for this model we use the model from the previous example.

$$
\begin{array}{l}
\textbf{MACHINE}\ m1 \\
\textbf{VARIABLES}\ x \\
\textbf{INVARIANT}\ x \in \mathbb{Z} \\
\textbf{INITIALISATION}\ x := 0 \\
\textbf{EVENTS} \\
\quad count = \textbf{WHEN}\ x \bmod 2 = 0\ \textbf{THEN}\ x := x + 1\ \textbf{END} \\
\quad inc \quad\ = \textbf{WHEN}\ \neg(x \bmod 2 = 0)\ \textbf{THEN}\ x := x + 1\ \textbf{END}
\end{array}
$$

Here, the pattern parameters are instantiated as follows: e as $count$, en as inc, and x as $x \bmod 2 = 0$.

4 Pattern Composition

In the previous section we defined the notion of a basic transformation rule as a combination of the applicability conditions, transformation (effect) function, and refinement proof obligations. Moreover, In Figure 1, we also introduced various composition constructs for creating complex transformation rules. In this section we will show how we can inductively define the applicability conditions, effect, and proof obligations for composed rules.

4.1 Rule Applicability Conditions

For a basic rule, the rule applicability condition is defined in its **context** clause. For more complex rules constructed using the proposed language of transformation rules, rule applicability is derived inductively according to the following definition:

$$
\begin{array}{lcl}
\textbf{app}(basic)(c, s) & = & \textbf{context}(basic)(c, s) \\
\textbf{app}(p; q)(c, s) & = & \textbf{app}(p)(c, s) \wedge \textbf{app}(q)(c, \textbf{eff}(p)(c, s)) \\
\textbf{app}(p \| q)(c, s) & = & \textbf{app}(p)(c, s) \wedge \textbf{app}(q)(c, s) \wedge \\
 & & \quad inter(\textbf{scope}(p), \textbf{scope}(q)) = \oslash \\
\textbf{app}(\textbf{if}\ G(c, s)\ \textbf{then}\ p\ \textbf{end})(c, s) & = & G(c, s) \Rightarrow \textbf{app}(p)(c, s) \\
\textbf{app}(\textbf{conf}\ i : Q(i, c, s)\ \textbf{do}\ p(i)\ \textbf{end})(c, s) & = & \forall i \cdot Q(i, c, s) \Rightarrow \textbf{app}(p(i))(c, s) \\
\textbf{app}(\textbf{par}\ i : Q(i, c, s)\ \textbf{do}\ p(i)\ \textbf{end})(c, s) & = & \textbf{app}(\textbf{conf}\ i : Q(i, c, s)\ \textbf{do}\ p(i)\ \textbf{end})(c, s) \wedge \\
 & & \forall i, j \cdot Q(i, c, s) \wedge Q(j, c, s) \wedge i \neq j \Rightarrow \\
 & & \quad inter(\textbf{scope}(p(i)), \textbf{scope}(p(j))) = \oslash
\end{array}
$$

The consistency requirements for the sequential composition, conditional and parameterised rules are quite standard. Two rules can be applied in parallel if they are working on disjoint scopes. For instance, a rule transforming an event (e.g., adding a new guard) cannot be composed with another rule transforming the same event. A similar requirement is formulated for the loop rule, since it is realised as generalised parallel composition.

The rule scopes are calculated by using the predefined function **scope**, which returns a pair of lists, containing the model elements that the rule updates or depends on. Intersection of rule scopes is computed as an intersection of the elements updated by the transformations and the pair-wise intersection of elements updated by one rule and depended on by another:

$$inter((r_1, w_1), (r_2, w_2)) = (w_1 \cap w_2) \cup (r_1 \cap w_2) \cup (r_2 \cap w_1)$$

4.2 Effect of Pattern Application

Once the rule applicability conditions are met, an output model can be syntactically constructed in a compositional way. For a basic rule, the effect function is directly applied to transform an input model. For more complex rules, a new model is constructed according to an inductive definition of the function **eff** given below.

$$\begin{aligned}
\textbf{eff}(basic)(c,s) &= \textbf{effect}(basic)(c,s)\\
\textbf{eff}(p;q)(c,s) &= \textbf{eff}(q)(c,\textbf{eff}(p)(c,s))\\
\textbf{eff}(p\|q)(c,s) &= \textbf{eff}(q)(c,\textbf{eff}(p)(c,s)),\ \text{or}\\
&= \textbf{eff}(p)(c,\textbf{eff}(q)(c,s))\\
\textbf{eff}(\textbf{if}\ G(c,s)\ \textbf{then}\ p\ \textbf{end})(c,s) &= \textbf{eff}(p)(c,s),\ \text{if}\ G(c,s)\\
&= s,\ \text{otherwise}\\
\textbf{eff}(\textbf{conf}\ i : Q(i,c,s)\ \textbf{do}\ p(i)\ \textbf{end})(c,s) &= \textbf{eff}(p(i))(c,s),\ \text{if}\ Q(i,c,s)\\
&= s,\ \text{otherwise}\\
\textbf{eff}(\textbf{par}\ i : Q(i,c,s)\ \textbf{do}\ p(i)\ \textbf{end})(c,s) &= \textbf{eff}(\| i \in Q(i,c,s) \cdot p(i))\,(c,s),\\
&\quad\ \text{if}\ \exists\, i,c,s \cdot Q(i,c,s)\\
&= s,\ \text{otherwise}
\end{aligned}$$

As expected, the result of sequential composition of two rules is computed by applying the second rule to the result of the first rule. For parallel composition, the result is computed in the same manner but the order of the rules should not affect the overall result. The resulting model of the loop construct is computed as generalised parallel composition of an indexed family of transformation rules. The last three cases depend on some additional application conditions (i.e., $G(c, s)$ or $Q(i, c, s)$). If these conditions are not true, rule application leaves the input model unchanged.

The rule application procedure based on the presented definition can be easily automated. The only interesting detail is in providing input values for the rule parameters. In our tool implementation for the Event-B method, briefly covered later, the user is requested to provide the parameter values during rule instantiation, while appropriate contextual hints and descriptions are provided by the tool.

4.3 Pattern Proof Obligations

To demonstrate that a rule is a refinement pattern, we have to discharge all the proof obligations of individual basic rules occurring in the rule body. These proof obligations cannot be discharged without considering the context produced by the neighbour rules. The following inductive definition shows how the list of proof obligations is built for a particular refinement pattern. The context information for each proof obligation is accumulated, while traversing the structure of a pattern, as a set of additional hypotheses that can be then used in automated proofs.

$$
\begin{array}{ll}
\mathbf{po}(\Gamma, basic)(c,s) & = \{\Gamma \models \mathbf{proof\_obligations}(basic)\} \\
\mathbf{po}(\Gamma, p; q)(c,s) & = \mathbf{po}(\Gamma \cup \{s' = \mathbf{eff}(p;q)(c,s)\}, p(c,s')) \cup \\
 & \quad\ \mathbf{po}(\Gamma \cup \{s' = \mathbf{eff}(p;q)(c,s)\}, q(c,s')) \\
\mathbf{po}(\Gamma, p \| q)(c,s) & = \mathbf{po}(\Gamma, p) \cup \mathbf{po}(\Gamma, q) \\
\mathbf{po}(\Gamma, \mathbf{if}\ G(c,s)\ \mathbf{then}\ p\ \mathbf{end})(c,s) & = \mathbf{po}(\Gamma \cup \{G(c,s)\}, p) \\
\mathbf{po}(\Gamma, \mathbf{conf}\ i : Q(i,c,s)\ \mathbf{do}\ p(i)\ \mathbf{end})(c,s) & = \bigcup i \in Q(i,c,s) \cdot \mathbf{po}(\Gamma \cup \{Q(i,c,s)\}, p(i)) \\
\mathbf{po}(\Gamma, \mathbf{par}\ i : Q(i,c,s)\ \mathbf{do}\ p(i)\ \mathbf{end})(c,s) & = \mathbf{po}(\Gamma, \mathbf{conf}\ i : Q(i,c,s)\ \mathbf{do}\ p(i)\ \mathbf{end})(c,s)
\end{array}
$$

Here Γ is a set of accumulated hypothesis containing pattern parameters c and the initial model s as free variables. For each basic rule, we formulate a theorem whose right-hand side is a list of the rule proof obligations and the left-hand side is a set of hypotheses containing the knowledge about the context in which the rule is applied.

4.4 Assertions

The described procedure for building a list of proof obligations tries to include every possible fact as a proof obligation hypothesis. This can be a problem for larger patterns as the size of a list of accumulated hypotheses makes a proof obligation intractable. To rectify the problem, we allow a modeller to manually add fitting hypotheses, called assertions, that can be inferred from the context they appear in. An assertion would be typically simple enough to be discharged automatically by a theorem prover. At the same time, it can be used to assist in demonstrating the proof obligations of the rule immediately following the assertion.

An assertion is written as $\mathbf{assert}(A(c,s))$ and is delimited from the neighboring rules by semicolons. An assertion has no effect on rule instantiation and application. The following additional cases of the *po* definition are used to generate additional proof obligations for assertions as well as insert an asserted knowledge into the set of collected hypotheses of a refinement pattern.

$$
\begin{array}{ll}
\mathbf{po}(\Gamma, p; \mathbf{assert}(A(c,s)))(c,s) & = \Gamma \cup \{s' = \mathbf{eff}(p)(c,s)\} \models A(c,s') \\
\mathbf{po}(\Gamma, \mathbf{assert}(A(c,s)); p)(c,s) & = \mathbf{po}(\Gamma \cup \{A(c,s)\}, p)(c,s)
\end{array}
$$

5 Triple Modular Redundancy Pattern

Triple Modular Redundancy (TMR) [15] is a fault-tolerance mechanism in which the results of executing three identical components are processed by a voting element to produce a single output that takes the majority view. This mechanism is schematically shown in Figure 2.

The purpose of the mechanism is to mask a single component failure. In this section we will demonstrate how to generalize a refinement step introducing the TMR arrangement into a model as a refinement pattern.

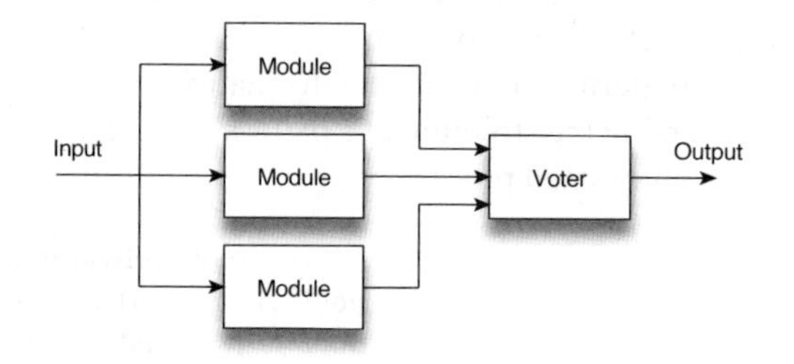

Fig. 2. TMR Arrangement

Before creating our new pattern, we have to decide on its applicability conditions. First, our input model should have a variable representing the output of the component for which TMR will be introduced. Moreover, it should have an event that models the behaviour of a component by non-deterministically updating this variable. Non-determinism is used here to model unpredictable (possibly faulty) results produced by the component. We do not make any assumptions about the variable type. Furthermore, the event can contain some additional actions on other variables. Finally, our input model should also contain an event that handles the component failure.

In the refined model, we replace the single abstract component with three similar components. The outputs of the new components are modelled by fresh variables. The variable types and initialisation of these variables are simply copied from their abstract counterpart in the input specification.

The TMR pattern that we define uses a number of configuration parameters, as shown below. The parameter s identifies a variable modelling the output of a component; u is an event updating the variable s (in addition to possible update of other variables); zz is an event handling a failure of the component modelled by u; finally, a is an action from u updating the variable s.

conf s, u, zz, a :
  $s \in var \wedge u \in evt \wedge zz \in evt \wedge u \neq zz \wedge$
  $a \in u.actions \wedge a.style \neq (:=) \wedge \{s\} = a.var$
do
  conf $ph, s_1, s_2, s_3, r_1, r_2, r_3$:
    $\{s_1, s_2, s_3, r_1, r_2, r_3, ph\} \subseteq (\mathrm{VAR} - var) \wedge$
    $part(\{\{s_1\}, \{s_2\}, \{s_3\}, \{r_1\}, \{r_2\}, \{r_3\}, \{ph\}\})$
  do
    $variables;\ events;\ voter;\ abort;\ invariant$
  end
end

As a result of pattern application, the new variables ph, s_i and r_i are introduced into the refined model. The variable ph keeps track of the current phase in the TMR implementation, i.e., reading from the new components, voting on them, or delivering the final result; the variables s_i, $i = 1..3$, are used to record the outputs produced by the components; finally, the flags r_i reflect availability of new outputs in the respective output variables s_i.

The pattern consists of four major parts: the rules declaring the types and initialisation of new variables of the refined model; the definition of new events; the refinement rules for transforming a single abstract event representing the functionality of a sole component into the voter event; and, finally, the addition of an invariant characterising the behaviour of a TMR block. The condition using the operator $part$ simply states that its arguments are disjoint sets.

$$
\begin{aligned}
&variables \stackrel{\text{df}}{=} \\
&\quad (newinv(\text{"}ph \in BOOL\text{"}); newini(\langle ph \mid :=\mid \text{"}FALSE\text{"}\rangle)) \parallel \\
&\quad (newinv(\text{"}s_1 \in s.type\text{"}); newini(\langle s_1 \mid init(s).style \mid init(s).expr\rangle)) \parallel \\
&\quad (newinv(\text{"}r_1 \in BOOL\text{"}); newini(\langle r_1 \mid :=\mid \text{"}FALSE\text{"}\rangle)) \\
&\quad \ldots
\end{aligned}
$$

Each new variable definition should come with a typing invariant and an initialisation action. These are normally grouped together so that the related proof obligation rules would work with a smaller context. For the sake of brevity, we omit showing here the rules defining the types and initialisation for the variables s_2, s_3 and r_2, r_3 (the omitted part is indicated by $\ldots$). The shortcut notation $newini(a)$ used in the pattern description stands for declaration of the initialisation action: $newini(a) \stackrel{\text{df}}{=} newact(\texttt{init}, a)$. The shortcut $init(v)$ refers to an action of the initialisation event assigning to the variable v.

The refined model specifies the behavior of three components of TMR (we call them replicated components) as copies of the behaviour of the component specified in the input model. Since we assumed that a component is represented by a single event, the replicated components are created by adding three new events into the refined model in the following way.

The guard of the event modelling behaviour of a replicated component essentially coincides with the guard of an abstract component. However, it also contains an extra conjunct ensuring that the event is executed before passing control to the voter. The event actions essentially copy the corresponding actions of the abstract component (given as the pattern parameter a). The only difference is that each replicated event records the result into a separate variable s_i (for the copy i) instead of the abstract variable s. In addition, a component copy also assigns to r_i to indicate the availability of result in s_i.

$$
\begin{aligned}
&events \stackrel{\text{df}}{=} \\
&\textbf{conf}\ u_1, u_2, u_3\ : \\
&\quad \{u_1, u_2, u_3\} \subset \text{EVENT} \setminus s.evt \wedge part(\{\{u_1\}, \{u_2\}, \{u_3\}\}) \\
&\textbf{do} \\
&\quad copy_1 \parallel copy_2 \parallel copy_3 \\
&\textbf{end}
\end{aligned}
$$

The above creates three component copies, each constructed according to the following rule.

$$
\begin{aligned}
©_1 \stackrel{\text{df}}{=} \\
&\quad newevt(\langle u_1 \mid - \mid \{\text{"}r_1 = FALSE\text{"}\} \cup u.guards \mid \\
&\qquad \langle s_1 \mid a.style \mid a.expression\rangle, \langle r_1 \mid :=\mid \text{"}TRUE\text{"}\rangle, \langle ph \mid :=\mid \text{"}FALSE\text{"}\rangle\rangle \\
&\quad \ldots
\end{aligned}
$$

The above rule $\langle s_1 \mid a.style \mid a.expression\rangle$ constructs an action from the abstract action a in such a way that it would have the same effect but update the new variable s_1. Here $a.style$ is one of non-deterministic assignment styles.

The voter event is simply a refined version of the event modelling the abstract component. Whereas the abstracted version was computing results itself, its refined counterpart votes on the results of component copies. The voter is enabled once all the components have produced a result (which is ensured by the first guard in the rule below). The final result is computed according to a simple majority voting protocol. The event parameter rr is set to the voting outcome in the second guard.

$$
\begin{aligned}
&voter \stackrel{\mathrm{df}}{=}\\
&\quad newpar(u, "rr");\\
&\quad newgrd(u, "r_1 = TRUE \wedge r_2 = TRUE \wedge r_3 = TRUE");\\
&\quad newgrd(u, "(s_1 = s_2 \vee s_1 = s_3 \wedge rr = s_1) \vee (s_2 = s_1 \vee s_2 = s_3 \wedge rr = s_2");\\
&\quad (delact(u, a); newact(u, \langle s \mid:=\mid "rr"\rangle));\\
&\quad (newact(u, \langle r_1 \mid:=\mid "FALSE"\rangle) \parallel\\
&\qquad newact(u, \langle r_2 \mid:=\mid "FALSE"\rangle) \parallel\\
&\qquad newact(u, \langle r_3 \mid:=\mid "FALSE"\rangle));\\
&\quad newact(u, \langle ph \mid:=\mid "TRUE"\rangle)
\end{aligned}
$$

As a result, the abstract action a of the component is replaced by a deterministic assignment (to the same variable s) of the result of the winning component. The flags r_i and ph are reset in preparation for the next iteration.

In case all the component copies disagree, no final result may be computed. This corresponds to an *abort* event of the abstract specification. The refined model simply constraints the guard of the event so it only gets enabled in the situations when the voting has failed.

$$
\begin{aligned}
&abort \stackrel{\mathrm{df}}{=}\\
&\quad newgrd(zz, "r_1 = TRUE \wedge r_2 = TRUE \wedge r_3 = TRUE");\\
&\quad newgrd(zz, "s_1 \neq s_2 \wedge s_2 \neq s_3 \wedge s_1 \neq s_3");
\end{aligned}
$$

Finally, a new invariant is added to the refined model to characterise the state of the refined system after voting is completed. It summarises the cases when the majority voting on component results succeeds.

$$
\begin{aligned}
&invariants \stackrel{\mathrm{df}}{=}\\
&\quad newinv("ph = TRUE \wedge (s_1 = s_2 \vee s_2 = s_3)) \Rightarrow s = s_1");\\
&\quad newinv("ph = TRUE \wedge s_2 = s_3) \Rightarrow s = s_2")
\end{aligned}
$$

Application of the pattern to a fairly simple abstract model (containing only two events and two variables) saves a user from analysing and discharging 14 proof obligations, three of which would have to be done manually in an interactive theorem prover. For larger models or more elaborated patterns, the benefits are even greater.

6 Tool for Refinement Automation

A proof of concept implementation of the pattern tool for the Event B method has been realised as a plug-in to the RODIN Platform [1]. The plug-in seamlessly integrates with the RODIN Platform interface so that a user does not have to switch between different tools and environments while applying patterns in an Event B development. The plug-in

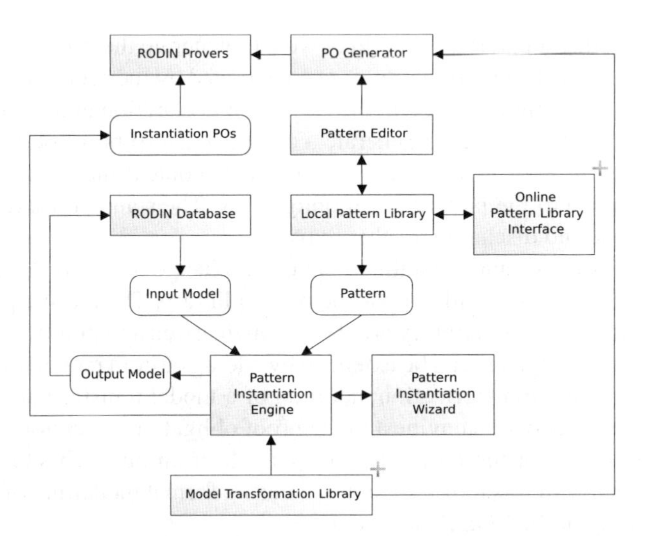

Fig. 3. The Event-B refinement patterns tool architecture

relies on two major RODIN Platform components: the Platform database, which stores models, proof obligations and proofs constituting a development; and the prover which is a collection of automated theorem provers supplemented by the interactive prover.

The overall tool architecture is presented in Figure 3. The core of the tool is the *pattern instantiation engine*. The engine uses an input model, imported from the Platform database, and a pattern, from the pattern library, to produce a model refinement. The engine implements only the core pattern language: the sequential and parallel composition, and *forall* construct. The method-specific model transformations (in this case, Event-B model transformations) are imported from the *model transformation library*.

The process of a pattern instantiation is controlled by the *pattern instantiation wizard*. The wizard is an interactive tool which inputs pattern configuration from a user. It validates user input and provides hints on selecting configuration values. Pattern configuration is constructed in a succession of steps: the values entered at a previous step influence the restrictions imposed on the values of a current step configuration.

The result of a successful pattern instantiation is a new model and, possibly, a set of instantiation proof obligations - additional conditions that must be verified every time when a pattern is applied. The output model is added to a current development as a refinement of the input model and is saved in the Platform database. The instantiation proof obligations are saved in an Event B *context* file. The RODIN platform builder automatically validates and passes them to the Platform prover.

The tool is equipped with a *pattern editor*. The current version (0.1.7)[13] uses the XML notation and an XML editor to construct patterns. The next release is expected to employ a more user-friendly visual editor. The available refinement patterns are stored in the *local pattern library*. Patterns in the library are organised in a catalogue tree, according to the categories stated in pattern specifications. A user can browse through the library catalogue using a graphical dialogue. This dialogue is used to select a pattern for instantiation or editing.

When constructing a pattern, a user may wish to generate the set of pattern correctness proof obligations. Proof obligations are constructed by the proof obligation generator component. The component combines a pattern declaration and the definitions of the used model transformations to generate a complete list of proof obligations, based on the rules given in Section 4.3. The result is a new context file populated with theorems corresponding to the pattern proof obligations. The standard Platform facilities are used to analyse and discharge the theorems.

We believe it is important to facilitate pattern exchange and thus the tool includes a component for interfacing with an on-line pattern library. The on-line pattern library and the model transformation library are the two main extension points of the tool. The pattern specification language can be extended by adding custom model transformations to the library of model transformation; addition of a model transformation should not affect the pattern instantiation engine and the proof obligation generator.

The current version of the tool is freely available from our web site [13]. Several patterns developed with this tool were applied during formal modelling of the Ambient Campus case study of the RODIN Project [14].

7 Conclusions

In this paper we proposed a theoretical basis for automation of refinement process. We introduced the notion of refinement patterns – model transformers that generically represent typical refinement steps. Refinement patterns allow us to replace a process of devising a refined model and discharging proof obligations by a process of pattern instantiation. While instantiating refinement patterns, we reuse not only models but also proofs. All together, this establishes a basis for automation. In this paper we also demonstrated how to define refinement patterns for the Event B formalism and described a prototype tool allowing us to automate refinement steps in Event B.

Our work was inspired by several works on automation of refinement process. The Refinement Calculator tool [8] has been developed to support program development using the Refinement Calculus theory by R.Back and J. von Wright. [5] The theory was formalised in the HOL theorem prover, while specific refinement rules were proved as HOL theorems. The HOL Window Inference library[11] has been used to to facilitate transformational reasoning. The library allows us to focus on and transform a particular part of a model, while guaranteeing that the transformation, if applicable, will produce a valid refinement of the entire model.

A similar framework consisting of refinement rules (called tactics) and the tool support for their application has been developed by Oliveira, Cavalcanti, and Woodcock [17]. The framework (called ArcAngel) provides support for the C.Morgan's version of the Refinement Calculus. The obvious disadvantage of both these frameworks is that the refinement rules that can be applied usually describe small, localised transformations. An attempt to perform several transformations on independent parts of the model at once, would require deriving and discharging additional proof obligations about the context surrounding transformed parts, that are rather hard to generalise. However, while implementing our tool, we found the idea of using the transformational approach for model refinement very useful.

Probably the closest to our tool is the automatic refiner tool created by Siemens/Matra [7]. The tool automatically produces an implementable model in B0 language (a variant of implementable B) by applying the predefined rewrite rules. A large library of such rules has been created specifically to handle the specifications of train systems. The use of this proprietary tool resulted in significant growth of developer productivity. Our work aims at creating a similar tool yet publicly available and domain-independent. The idea of reuse via instantiation of generic Event B models has also been explored by Silva and Butler [18]. However, they focus on the instantiation of the static part of the model – the context – while our approach mainly manipulates its dynamic part. Nevertheless, these two approaches are complementary and can be integrated.

Obviously the idea to use refinement patterns to facilitate the refinement process was inspired by the famous collection of software design patterns [10]. However in our approach the patterns are not just descriptions of the best engineering practice but rather "active" model transformers that allow a designer to refine the model by reusing and instantiating the generic prefabricated solutions.

As a future work we are planning to further explore the theoretical aspects of the proposed language of refinement patterns as well as extend the existing collection of patterns. Obviously, this work will go hand-in-hand with the tool development. We believe that by building a sufficiently large library of patterns and providing designers with automatic tool supporting refinement process, we will facilitate better acceptance of formal methods in practice.

Acknowledgements

This work is supported by IST FP7 DEPLOY project. We also would like to thank the anonymous reviewers for their valuable comments.

References

1. RODIN Event-B Platform (2007), `http://rodin-b-sharp.sourceforge.net/`
2. Abrial, J.R.: The B-Book: Assigning Programs to Meanings. Cambridge University Press, Cambridge (2005)
3. Abrial, J.-R.: Extending B without Changing it. In: Proceedings of 1st Conference on the B Method, Nantes, France, pp. 169–191. Springer, Heidelberg (1996)
4. Back, R., Sere, K.: Superposition refinement of reactive systems. Formal Aspects of Computing 8(3), 1–23 (1996)
5. Back, R., von Wright, J.: Refinement Calculus: A Systematic Introduction. Springer, Heidelberg (1998)
6. Back, R.-J., Sere, K.: Stepwise Refinement of Action Systems. In: Proceedings of the International Conference on Mathematics of Program Construction, 375th Anniversary of the Groningen University, London, UK, pp. 115–138. Springer, Heidelberg (1989)
7. Burdy, L., Meynadier, J.-M.: Automatic Refinement. In: Workshop on Applying B in an industrial context: Tools, Lessons and Techniques - Toulouse, FM 1999 (1999)
8. Butler, M., Grundy, J., Långbacka, T., Rukšenas, R., von Wright, J.: The Refinement Calculator: Proof Support for Program Refinement. In: Proc. of Formal Methods Pacific (1997)
9. Dijkstra, E.W.: A Discipline of Programming. Prentice-Hall, Englewood Cliffs (1976)

10. Gamma, E., Helm, R., Johnson, R., Vlissides, J.: Design Patterns. Addison-Wesley, Reading (1995) ISBN 0-201-63361-2
11. Grundy, J.: Transformational Hierarchical Reasoning. The Computer Journal 39(4), 291–302 (1996)
12. Hoare, C.A.: An Axiomatic Basis for Computer Programming. Communications of the ACM 12(10), 576–583 (1969)
13. Iliasov, A.: Finer Plugin (2008), http://finer.iliasov.org
14. Iliasov, A., Romanovsky, A., Arief, B., Laibinis, L., Troubitsyna, E.: On Rigorous Design and Implementation of Fault Tolerant Ambient Systems. In: Proceedings of the 10th IEEE International Symposium on Object and Component-Oriented Real-Time Distributed Computing, ISORC 2007, Washington, DC, USA, pp. 141–145. IEEE Computer Society Press, Los Alamitos (2007)
15. Lyons, R.E., Vanderkulk, W.: The Use of Triple-Modular Redundancy to Improve Computer Reliability. IBM Journal, 200–209 (April 1962)
16. Morgan, C.: Programming From Specifications. Prentice Hall International (UK) Ltd., Englewood Cliffs (1994)
17. Oliveira, M., Cavalcanti, A., Woodcock, J.: Arcangel: a tactic language for refinement. Formal Asp. Comput. 15(1), 28–47 (2003)
18. Silva, R., Butler, M.: Supporting Reuse of Event-B Developments through Generic Instantiation. In: Breitman, K., Cavalcanti, A. (eds.) ICFEM 2009. LNCS, vol. 5885, pp. 466–484. Springer, Heidelberg (2009)

Applying Event-B Atomicity Decomposition to a Multi Media Protocol

Asieh Salehi Fathabadi and Michael Butler

University of Southampton
asf08r,mjb@ecs.soton.ac.uk

Abstract. Atomicity Decomposition is a technique in the Event-B formal method, which augments Event-B refinement with additional structuring in a diagrammatic notation to support complex refinement in Event-B. This paper presents an evaluation of Event-B atomicity decomposition technique in modeling a multi media case study with the diagrammatic notation. Firstly the existing technique and the diagrammatic notation are shown. Secondly an evaluation is performed by developing a model of a Media Channel System. A Media Channel is established between two endpoints for transferring multi-media data. Finally some extensions to the existing diagrammatic notation are proposed and applied to the multi-media case study.

Keywords: Event-B, Refinement, Atomicity Decomposition, Structured Event Refinement.

1 Introduction

Event-B [1, 2] is a formal method that uses the concept of refinement [3, 4] in modeling. Event-B modeling starts with an abstraction of a system and adds details during refinement levels in order to gain a final model close to the implementation. Moreover mathematical proofs are incorporated into Event-B to verify the correctness of refinement steps.

The most important benefit of using Event-B is its capability to use abstraction and refinement. In this approach the modeling process starts with an abstraction of the system which speifies the goals of the system. In our case study, a media channel system, establishing and modifying the established channel are the main system goals. The abstract level of our Event-B model shows these goals in a very general way, and then during refinement levels, features of the protocol are modeled and the goals are achieved in a detailed way. Moreover tool support is another benefit of using Event-B. The Rodin tool [5] supports proof obligation generation and automated proof. Through a refinement approach, we prove that the abstract goals concerning establishment and modification of media channels are satisfied by the detailed protocol. In the developed Event-B models of the media channel system reported here, all proofs are generated and discharged by the Rodin tool.

F.S. de Boer et al. (Eds.): FMCO 2009, LNCS 6286, pp. 89–104, 2010.

Modeling of large and complex systems can result in large and complex models and difficult proofs [6]. Refinement techniques can address this complexity. In Event-B refinement, rather than having a single large model, it is common to represent a desired outcome as an abstract atomic event and then decompose that into smaller sub-events in subsequent refinement levels. If the abstraction gaps between refinement levels are small, it means relatively small details are added in each refinement level and proof obligations would be relatively easy to discharge. Most of proof obligations are related to consistency between refinement levels, so with the small gaps these proofs become easier to discharge. This will be explained more in the next section when we introduce invariants.

Although refinement offers the advantages outlined above, the Event-B refinement method does not explicitly represent all refinement connections between abstract and concrete events. *Atomicity decomposition* diagrams provide a structuring technique which addresses this through a diagrammatic notation. The atomicity decomposition technique helps to structure refinement in Event-B. This technique is introduced in [7]. It is intended to make the standard refinement rules clearer and their application more systematic. In Event-B refinement there is no clear connection between certain actions of different refinement levels. The diagrammatic notation of atomicity decomposition shows relationships between refinement levels. In this approach usually a single event shows the goal in the abstract level, and then it is decomposed to sub-events in refinement.

The contribution of this paper is applying existing Event-B atomicity decomposition technique to a multi media case study. An evaluation of this technique in modeling the multi media system is presented. There are several contributions in this evaluation. First we will see how system goals are modeled in the abstract level with single events. Then details of the protocol are added gradually during refinement levels. For applying these details we will see how the atomicity decomposition diagrammatic notation will help us to structure refinement in an explicit way. Finally this development leads to discharge of all proof obligations using the Rodin tool-set.

In this paper after a short background about Event-B, we will explore how the diagrammatic notation for atomicity decomposition of [7] can help to structure refinement in Sect. 3. Then an incremental development of an existing multi-media protocol using this technique will be presented. In this protocol, a media channel is a point-to-point and dynamic channel, established for transferring multi-media data between two endpoints, called initiator and acceptor. In the previous paper [7] the connection between the requirements of a system and the decomposition technique was not explicitly discussed. In this paper we will see how requirements of the system are linked with levels in the atomicity decomposition diagram. The current atomicity decomposition technique provides sufficient patterns in development of media channel system in most of refinement levels. However some extensions to the diagrammatic technique are proposed and applied to the case study.

2 Event-B Background

Event-B [1, 2] is a formal method for specifying, modeling and reasoning about systems. Event-B has evolved from Classical B [8] and Action Systems [9]. Key features of Event-B are modeling and reasoning. The modeling notation is based on set theory and predicate logic. Building a model in Event-B typically starts with a very abstract level, and continues in different levels by use of refinement technique. Event-B use mathematical proof to verify consistency between refinement levels.

An Event-B model [1, 10] consists of *contexts* and *machines*. In other words, a model is made of several components of these two types. Contexts contain the static part of a model while a machines contain the dynamic part. There are various relationships between contexts and machines. A context can be "extended" by other contexts and "referenced" or "seen" by machines. A Machine can be "refined" by other machines and refers to contexts as its static part. The structure is shown in Fig. 1.

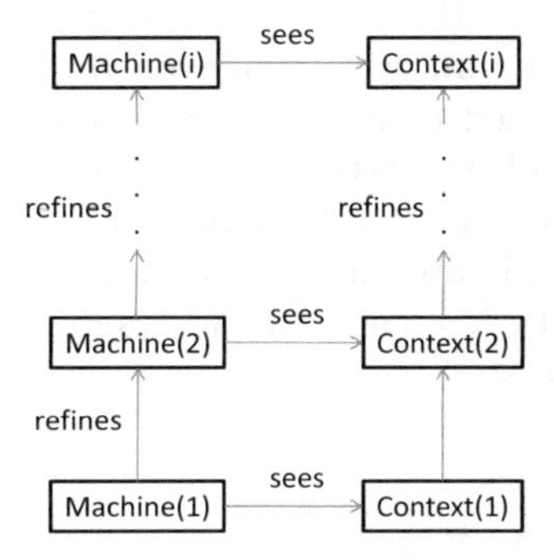

Fig. 1. Event-B Structure

Building a model usually starts with a very abstract model of the system, and then gradually details are added through several modeling steps in such a way that leads us towards a suitable implementation; this approach is called refinement [3, 4]. Thus, instead of building a single model in a flat manner, we have a sequence of models, where each of them is supposed to be a refinement of the previous.

From a given model M1, a new model M2 can be built as a refinement of M1. In this case, model M1 is called an abstraction of M2, and model M2 is said to be a concrete version of M1. A concrete model is said to refine its abstraction. Each event of a concrete machine refines an abstract event or refines *skip*. An event that refines *skip* is referred to as a new event since it has no counterpart in the abstract model.

In the introduction we stated that small gaps between refinement levels results in simplicity in proof obligations. Most of proof obligations are related to consistency between refinement levels. Ensuring consistency is done by some gluing invariants. Invariants constrain variables, and are supposed to be maintained whenever variables are changed by an event. A gluing invariant connects the abstract variables to the concrete ones. In other words, it glues the state of the concrete model to that of its abstraction. When just small changes are applied to a new level of refinement, the abstract model and the concrete model are similar, so invariants which glue the state of these two models would be simple. Therefore it can be said that small gaps between refinement levels result in simple gluing invariants, and simple gluing invariants result in simplicity in proofs related to them.

3 Atomicity Decomposition in Event-B

This section highlights the motivation for the atomicity decomposition technique and presents the technique introduced in [7] as a background to development of our case study.

Although the refinement technique in Event-B provides a flexible approach to modeling, it does not show all the relations between abstract events and concrete events. In the atomicity decomposition approach of [7], a graphical technique is proposed which is intended to make the relationships between abstract and concrete events clearer and easier to manage than simply using the standard Event-B refinement method. In this technique course-grained atomicity can be refined to more fine-grained atomicity. Sub-atomic events are treated in two ways, some refine abstract events and the others are viewed as hidden events in abstract level which refine *skip*.

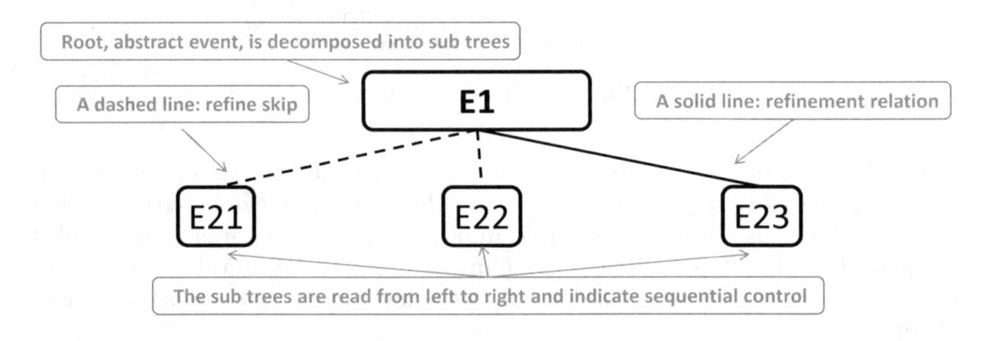

Fig. 2. Atomicity Decomposition Diagram

The tree structure notation of atomicity decomposition is illustrated in Fig. 2. In [7] this is called an event refinement diagram. The abstract atomic event, *E1* in this case, appears in the root node, which is decomposed to sub-events in the next refinement level. There is a sequential control from left to right between sub-events; in other words, the events, E21, E22, E23 in this figure, are read from left to right and are executed in this order. One important feature in the structure is the distinction between solid lines and dashed lines. The sub-event corresponding to dashed line, E21, E22, are new events which refine *skip* in the abstract level. The child node with a solid line, E23, is a main event which should be proved to refine the abstract one, E1. The hierarchical and sequential structure is influenced by the structure diagrams of Jackson System Development (JSD) [13].

In this case, E21, E22 should execute before E23 in order to reach a state that enables event E23. This is done by some control variables in Event-B model. An Event-B model of this diagram is illustrated in Figs. 3, 4 and 5. VarE21, VarE22 and VarE23 are control variables. Event E22 is guarded by VarE21 which indicates the sequential execution of E21 and E22. Also event E23 is guarded by VarE22. Event E23 can be executed only when E22 has been executed, and event E22 can be executed only when E21 has been executed.

The possible execution traces of the model are presented here. The only event trace in abstract machine, which contains abstract event E1, is

$< E1 >$

and the execution of E21, E22, and E23 is given by the only trace of the refined model:

$< E21, E22, E23 >$

The event refinement diagram is used because it explicitly illustrates our intention that the effect achieved by E1 at the abstract level is realized at the refined level by execution of E21 followed by E22 followed by E23. In the standard Event-B method E21 and E22 are refinements of *skip* and there is no explicit connection to E1. Technically, E23 is the only event that refines E1 but the diagram indicates that we break the atomicity of E1 into events E21, E2 and E23.

```
E21  ≙
STATUS
  ordinary
WHEN
  grd1  :  VarE21 = FALSE
THEN
  act1  :  VarE21 := TRUE
END
```

Fig. 3. Event-B Model Part a

Atomicity decomposition has been applied to a distributed file system in [7]. It can be used for many types of system, including sequential, concurrent and distributed systems. It is important to note that the technique of using refinement of *skip* is standard in action systems [9] and Event-B [1] and its use can also be found in Z refinement [11].

```
E21   ≙
STATUS
  ordinary
WHEN
  grd1   :   VarE21 = FALSE
THEN
  act1   :   VarE21 ≔ TRUE
END
```

Fig. 4. Event-B Model Part b

```
E21   ≙
STATUS
  ordinary
WHEN
  grd1   :   VarE21 = FALSE
THEN
  act1   :   VarE21 ≔ TRUE
END
```

Fig. 5. Event-B Model Part c

4 An Overview of Media Channel System Requirements and Multi Media Protocol

Media Channel Properties

All properties described in this section are based on a Spin model in [12]. This case study has a protocol for establishing, modifying and closing a media channel. We believe that using the atomicity decomposition technique eases understanding and development of the models.

Each Media Channel has one source, one sink, a codec type and a specific direction. A Media Channel is point-to-point and dynamic, established for transferring multi-media data.

A codec is a specific data format by which data is encoded. The codec choice in the media channel is dynamic; it means that each endpoint of the channel is allowed to change the codec in the middle of data transfer. Although each endpoint can interpret more than one codec, the source and sink of a media channel have to know which codec they are supposed to send or receive with. So any two endpoints of a media channel should have at least one common codec.

Note that in our Event-B model, we are not modeling just a single media channel, rather we are modeling a system that manages an arbitrary number of channels simultaneously by interleaving events associated with separate channels.

4.1 Requirements for Establishing a Media Channel

Either end of a channel, sender or receiver, can attempt to open a media channel by sending an *open* signal. The other end can respond affirmatively with *openAck* (Open Acknowledge) or negatively with *close.* A media flow can be established between two media endpoints if and only if both media endpoints agree.

Each *open* signal carries the medium being requested, and a descriptor. A descriptor is a record in which an endpoint describes itself as a receiver of media. A descriptor contains an IP address, port number, and priority-ordered list of codecs that it can handle. If the endpoint does not wish to receive media, then the only offered codec is *noMedia.* Each *openAck* signal also carries a descriptor, describing the channel acceptor as a receiver of media.

A selector is a response to a descriptor. A selector is a record in which an endpoint describes itself as a sender of media. It contains the identification of the descriptor it is responding to, the IP address of the sender, and the port number of the sender. If the selecting endpoint does not wish to send media, then the selector contains *noMedia*; otherwise, it contains a single codec selected from the list in the descriptor. The only legal response to a descriptor *noMedia* is a selector *noMedia.*

After sending an *open* signal by the *initiator* side of the channel, and sending an *openAck* signal by the other side, called the *acceptor*, both endpoints have to respond to descriptors carried by the *open* and *openAck* signal, by sending a *select* signal carrying a selector. As said before, it is a rule of the protocol that a selector should be sent in order to respond to receiving a descriptor. A media channel is established by the endpoint, initiator or acceptor, which receives a real codec in a select signal. Fig. 6 illustrate a life cycle of a media channel starting with establishing the channel.

4.2 Requirements for Modifying an Established Media Channel

Modifying an established media channel may involve changing the codec and changing the port of each endpoint. At any time after sending the first selector in response to a descriptor, an endpoint can choose a new codec from the list in the descriptor, send it as a selector in a select signal, and begin to send media in the new codec. In Fig. 6, *select(sel'2)* shows this possibility.

At any time after sending or receiving *oAck*, an endpoint can send a new descriptor for itself in a describe signal. The endpoint that receives the new descriptor must begin to act according to the new descriptor. This might mean sending to a new address or choosing a new codec. In any case, the receiver of the descriptor must respond with a new selector in a select signal, if only to show that it has received the descriptor. In Fig. 6, describe(desc3) and select(sel3) illustrate this interaction. Finally at any time after sending or receiving *oAck*, an endpoint can send a new port and describe itself by a new port.

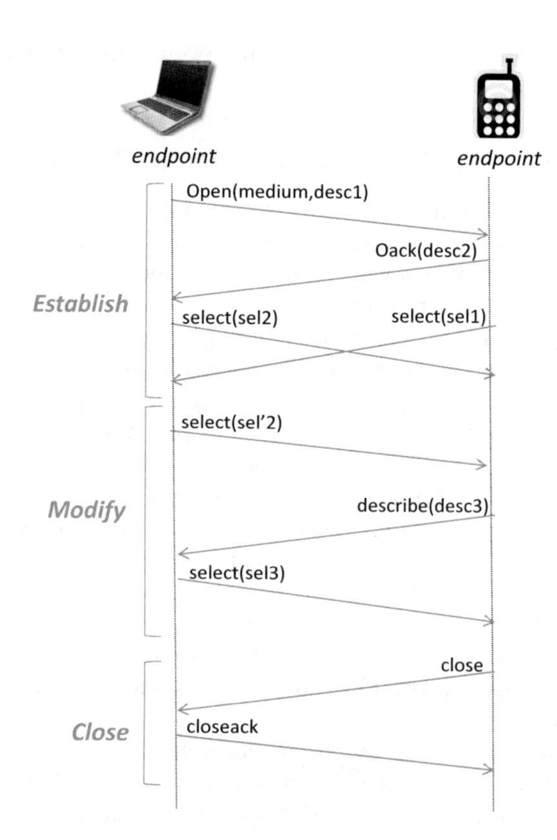

Fig. 6. Protocol of Media Channel System

4.3 Requirements for Closing an Established Media Channel

Either endpoint can close the media channel at any time by sending close, which must be acknowledged by the other end with a *closeAck* (close Acknowledge). Figure 6 illustrates the case that the acceptor side closes a channel.

5 Linking Requirements and Atomicity Decomposition

5.1 Abstract Specification

The abstract events are illustrated in an informal diagram that aids understanding, Fig. 7. It is not a formal decomposition diagram. These events happened sequentially from left to right. The circle containing "*", shows that multiple execution, zero or more, of the related event, *modify* in this case, is possible. So first a media channel is established by execution of *establishMediaChannel* event, then it can be modified zero or more times by execution of the *modify* event and then closed.

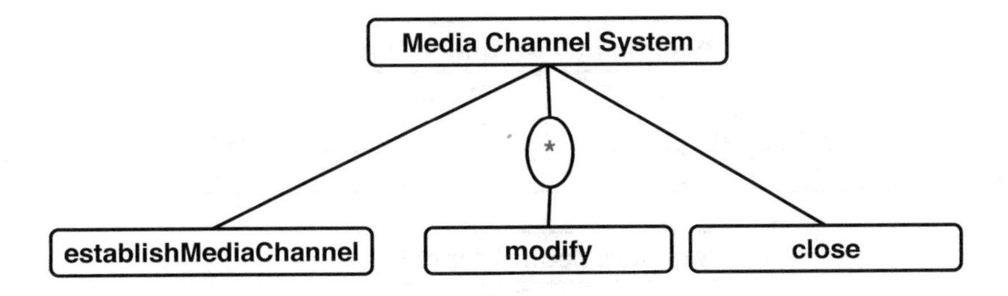

Fig. 7. Initial Model of Media Channel System

As described before, this ordering is ensured by event guards in the Event-B model. The abstract model contains a variable called *mediaChannel* containing established media channels, and a function *codec* which maps each established channel to its chosen the codec. The first event, *establishMediaChannel*, is guarded by

$ch \notin mediaChannel$

So if a channel has not been added to *mediaChannel* set, it means it has not been established then by execution of this event it would be added to *mediaChannel*:

$mediaChannel = mediaChannel \cup \{ch\}$

Events, *modify* and *close* can be executed for a channel if it was established, it is done by this guard:

$ch \in mediaChannel$

In *modify* event the codec of a channel can be changed and in *close* event, the channel is removed from *mediaChannel*.

5.2 Refinement 1: Breaking the Atomicity of Establish Media Channel

In the abstract model, we saw that a media channel is established in a single atomic step. However first phase of Fig. 6 has shown that establishing a media channel is not atomic. Instead, an open request should be sent by the initiator endpoint and should be responded to by an *openAck* signal from the acceptor side.

Following the protocol steps of Fig. 6, breaking the atomicity of establishing a media channel is outlined diagrammatically in Fig. 8. Two cases are possible. The initiator can send an open signal containing a list of codecs in a descriptor and define itself as a receiver, in this case the acceptor sends an open acknowledge signal without any codec and then selects a codec from received list in select signal. In this case the direction is from acceptor to initiator.

In the other case open signal does not contain a list of codecs and instead the acceptor sends a list of codecs in open acknowledge signal and defines itself as the receiver and the initiator selects a specific codec in select signal. The direction in this case is from initiator to acceptor. In both cases after receiving

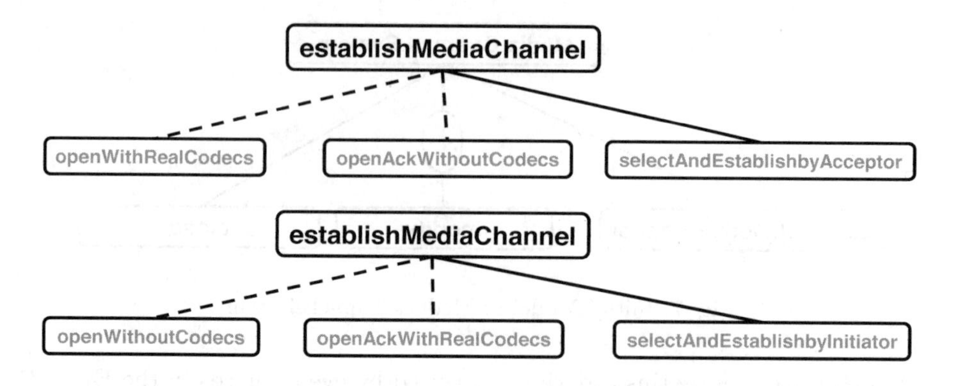

Fig. 8. Breaking the Atomicity of Establish a Media Channel

a select signal carrying a real codec, selected from the priority list of codecs of the received descriptor, the media channel can be established.

Similar to the abstract model, this sequencing the Event-B model is done by some control variables. In the first case, by execution of *openWithRealCodecs*, a channel is added to a specific set variable, *openWithCodecsSet* and the next event *openAckWithoutCodecs* can be executed only for a channel which is in *openWithCodecsSet*. The other events are encoded in a similar way.

5.3 Refinement 2: Breaking the Atomicity of Modify Media Channel

Up to this level, *modify* was considered as an atomic event that simply changes the codec of an established media channel. In this refinement we break the atomicity of the *modify* event. There are different ways of modifying the properties of an established channel. The *modify* event is decomposed to sub-events in three diagrams, presented in Fig. 9. This decomposition fulfills the modification requirements which was shown in second phase of Fig. 6.

First, in Case A, after establishing a media channel the endpoint which plays the role of the media sender can select a new codec from the list of acceptable codecs of the receiver, which has been received at the time of establishing the media channel.

In Case B, the receiver side of an established media channel, can send a new list of codecs in a *describe* signal. As described in Sect. 4, the other endpoint, has to respond to a descriptor by choosing a codec from the new list and send it via a selector.

It is shown that each endpoint, either initiator or acceptor, can describe itself with a new port by sending a describe signal carrying the new port property. It is represented as Case C.

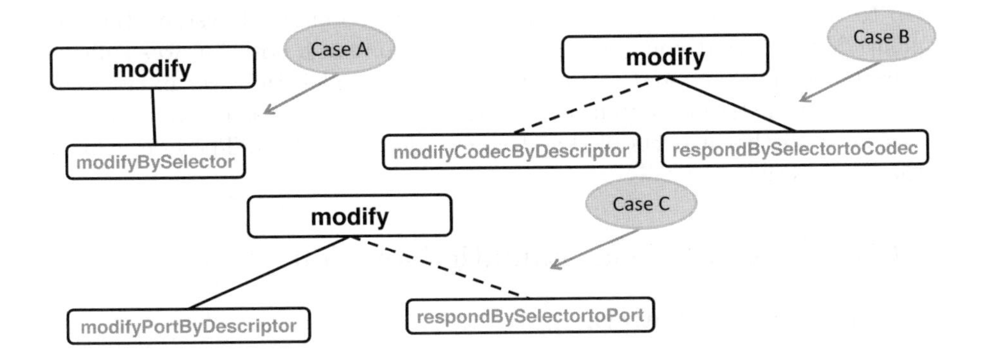

Fig. 9. Breaking the Atomicity of Modify a Media Channel

5.4 Refinement 3: Breaking the Atomicity of Close Media Channel

This is a simple refinement in which the atomicity of close is broken into two events (see Fig. 10). *CloseRequest* can be sent by each side of the channel, the sender of receiver. This figure satisfies the closing requirements shown in the last phase of Fig. 6.

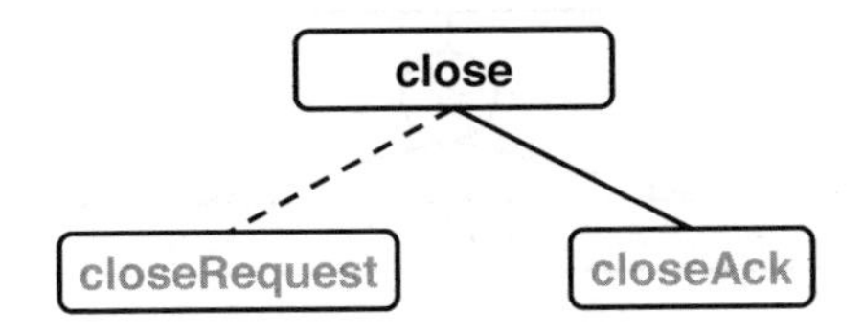

Fig. 10. Breaking the Atomicity of Close Media Channel

In Event-B model, by execution of *closeRequest* event, the channel is added to a set called *closeReqSet*, and then *closeAck* event is guarded by checking the set membership of $(ch \in closeReqSet)$.

5.5 Assessment

The refinement and atomicity decomposition technique for Event-B of [7] provides a manageable incremental development of media channel system. The overall behaviour of a media channel is modeled abstractly as three atomic events, *establish*, *modify* and *close*. Then each event has been decomposed to sub-events during refinement levels and details have been added to the model gradually. The event decomposition is presented by atomicity decomposition diagrams. The atomicity decomposition technique helps to present the relationships between an abstract atomic event and concrete sub-events in a hierarchical and sequential structure and it is specified by some guarded events in Event-B model.

Up to the fourth level of refinement of the media channel system, the basic sequential atomicity decomposition of the diagrammatic notation was sufficient for decomposing events and adding details to the model. However in the fourth level we identified some extensions to the notation that were convenient for representing further aspects of the atomicity decomposition. These are covered in the next section.

6 Extending the Diagrammatic Notation

6.1 Case Splitting Pattern

We found it convenient to introduce a diagrammatic notation to represent case splitting in a refinement. With the case splitting notation, an event is split to several sub-events is a way that execution of the abstract event is realized by execution of any of the refined events. It is presented by a circle containing an "or", as can be seen in Fig. 11. Jackson's JSD diagrams also includes case splitting [13].

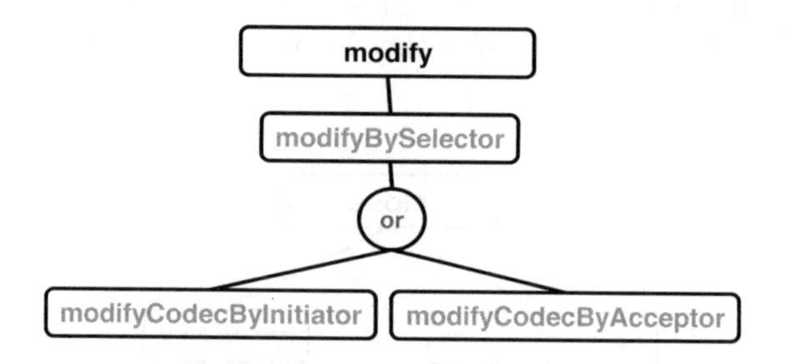

Fig. 11. Case Splitting, Level 4 of Refinement

In our model the case splitting is achieved by adding only one guard to each refined event which constrains the direction of the media channel. If the direction is from initiator to acceptor, *ItoA*, only the Initiator can modify the codec, because it has received the list of codecs belonging to acceptor, so can choose a new codec whenever it wants; and if the direction is from acceptor to initiator, *AtoI*, the one which has received the list of codecs is acceptor, so in this case it may modify the codec.

6.2 Weak Sequencing and Guard Lines

Consider the diagram in Fig. 12(a) where abstract event X is sequentially split into events *M1* and *M2* and where *M1* and *M2* are respectively further refined into sequential sub-events. Clearly, in abstract level *M2* occurs after *M1*, and in the next level *ReceiveM1* occurs after *SendM1* and *ReceiveM2* occurs after *SendM2*. Since *ReceiveM1* refines *M1* and *ReceiveM2* refines *M2*, and *M2* occurs after *M1*, clearly *ReceiveM2* occurs after *ReceiveM1*, i.e., the ordering constraint

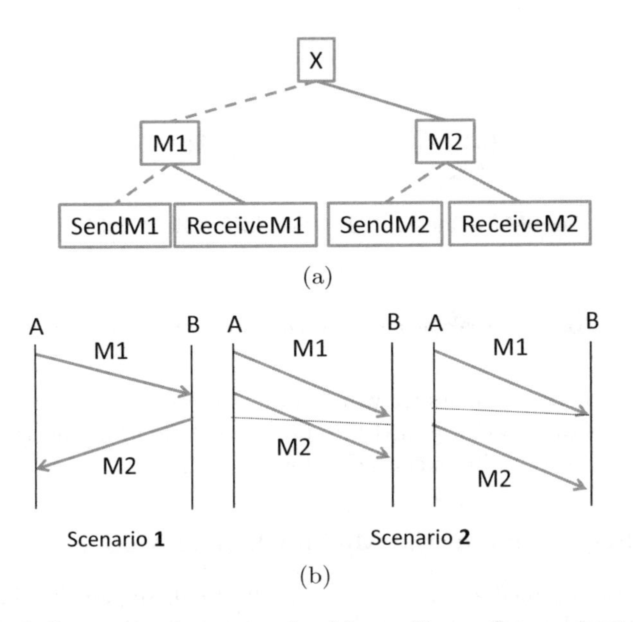

Fig. 12. Weak Sequencing interpretation Versus Strong Sequencing interpretation

between *M1* and *M2* is inherited by *ReceiveM1* and *ReceiveM2* via the solid refinement lines in Fig. 12(a).

An important question is whether there is an ordering constraint between *ReceiveM1* and *SendM2*. Two interpretations are possible. First it is possible for *SendM2* to occur before or after *ReceiveM1*. This is represented by an example of the message sequencing in Scenario 2 in Fig. 12(b) where the sequencing between these two events does not matter. We refer to this lack of sequencing as *weak* sequencing. In this sample it assumed that the channel is a fifo channel, message *M1* is sent before sending message *M2* and also message *M1* is received before receiving message *M2*, but there is not any sequencing order between receiving *M1* and sending *M2*. *Strong* sequencing, on the other hand, would be represented by the message sequencing sample in Scenario 1 in Fig. 12(b), where it is important that *SendM2* would executed only after *ReceiveM1*.

While not being explicit about this, [7] implicitly assumes that there is no ordering constraint between *ReceiveM1* and *SendM2*. This means that Butler in [7] implicitly accepts weak sequencing. Jackson's JSD diagrams allow multiple levels of decomposition but since they are intended to represent sequential processes, they implicitly assume strong sequencing [13].

If we accept weak sequencing as the default interpretation (which is useful for many distributed systems), then we need additional notation to indicate further sequencing. For our purposes we found the use of explicit *guard* lines to be convenient. A guard line is an explicit line from one event to another, indicating that the target event must occur after the source event. An example is shown in Fig. 13. In this figure, according to our default there is weak sequencing between events, as a result *SendM2* can be occur after or before *ReceiveM1*. In the case

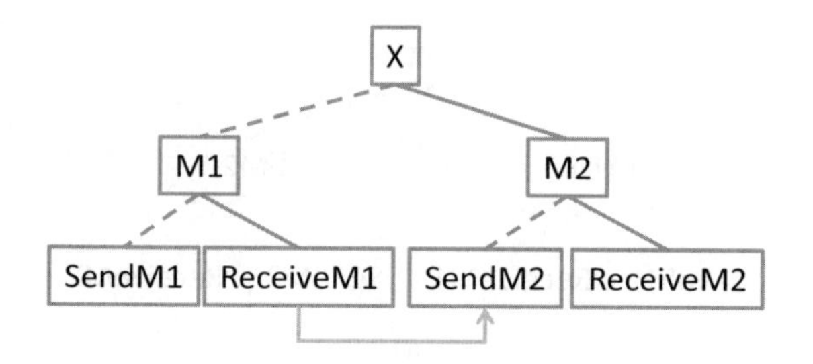

Fig. 13. Weak Sequencing Diagram with guard line

that according to requirements we would want to force them to be executed in a specific ordering, we insert a guard line between them. The inserted guard line means *ReceiveM1* should be executed before *SendM2*.

6.3 Weak Sequencing in the Media Channel Model

In our model of the media channel system the weak sequencing interpretation is used in further decomposition of the *close* event. As shown in Fig. 6, *receiveCloseRequest* should execute before *sendCloseAck*. This constraint is illustrated by a guard line in Fig. 14. It means that for sending the close acknowledge signal, a close request should be received before.

This guard line influences the Event-B model by adding a new guard to the *sendCloseAck* event requiring prior execution of the *receiveCloseRequest* event.

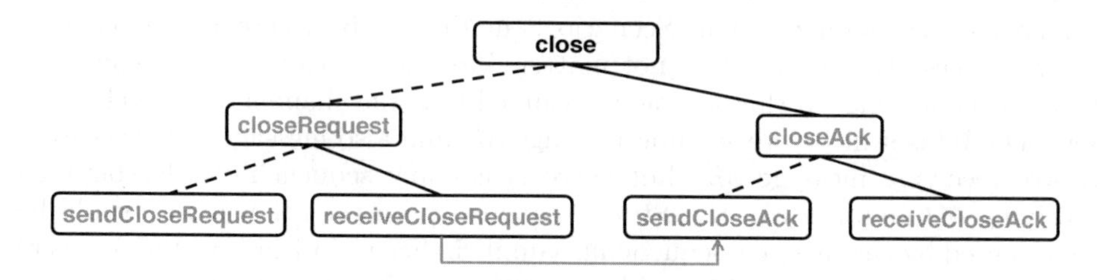

Fig. 14. Weak Sequencing Diagram in Decomposing Close Event

7 Conclusion and Directions for Future Work

An explicit representation of the sequencing of sub-events and refinement relationships, called atomicity decomposition has been used and assessed. The hierarchical diagrams introduce control structure in an incremental modeling of a case study. In abstraction media channel requirements are considered as three phases, establish, modify and close. In this paper we have shown that how each phase refine to detailed refinement using the benefits of atomicity decomposition technique in structuring requirements.

Building models of large and complex systems is not an easy task; the main reason is that it can result in very complex models and difficult proofs. Applying this technique to the multi media system partly shows that the technique can help overcome some of the complexity problems. Based on our experience in this case study, we believe that atomicity decomposition can be scaled to complex systems. The atomicity decomposition technique makes the standard refinement more systematic and visual. Sequential relations between levels of refinement during incremental modeling of a system are structured in atomicity decomposition diagrams.

It is interesting to compare our approach to the media channel system with the approach taken by Zave and Cheung [12]. Zave and Chueng present Promela models of the behaviour of each end of the protocol (sender and initiator respectively) and use the Spin model checker to verify that these models satisfy certain safety and liveness properties. In our approach with Event-B, we start with a more global view of the intension of the protocol and then use atomicity decomposition to arrive at models that have similar levels of detail to the Promela models since they include sending and receiving of messages by agents.

Sequential decomposition [7] appears to be a common pattern, but we illustrated two other patterns: the case splitting pattern and the guard line. Also we believe that the graphical technique provides representing ways of other reusable patterns. By modeling a wider range of systems on the future we anticipate the discovery of more patterns. Providing a structured refinement guideline can be considered as a future direction.

Atomicity decomposition provides a clear view of refinement steps, and can help in constructing models. At this stage building Event-B models corresponding to atomicity decomposition diagrams is done by hand, with some control variables and guarded events. An automatic model builder from atomicity decomposition diagrams will be developed in the future.

Acknowledgement

Partly supported by the EU research project ICT 214158 DEPLOY (Industrial deployment of system engineering methods providing high dependability and productivity) www.deploy-project.eu.

References

[1] Abrial, J.R.: Modeling in Event-B: System and Software Engineering. Cambridge University Press, Cambridge (2010)
[2] Butler, M.: Incremental Design of Distributed Systems with Event-B. In: Marktoberdorf Summer School 2008 Lecture Notes. IoS (November 2008)
[3] de Willem Roever, P., Engelhardt, K.: Data Refinement: Model-oriented Proof Theories and their Comparison Cambridge Tracts in Theoretical Computer Science, vol. 46. Cambridge University Press, Cambridge (1998)
[4] Rezazadeh, A., Butler, M., Evans, N.: Redevelopment of an Industrial Case Study Using Event-B and Rodin. In: BCS-FACS Christmas 2007 Meeting - Formal Method. In: Industry (2007)

[5] Abrial, J.-R., Butler, M., Hallerstede, S.: Rodin: An Open Toolset for Modelling and Reasoning in Event-B. International Journal on Software Tools for Technology Transfer, STTT (2010)
[6] Abrial, J.-R.: Refinement, Decomposition and Instantiation of Discrete Models. In: Abstract State Machines, pp. 17–40 (2005)
[7] Butler, M.: Decomposition Structures for Event-B. In: Leuschel, M., Wehrheim, H. (eds.) IFM 2009. LNCS, vol. 5423, Springer, Heidelberg (2009)
[8] Abrial, J.R.: The B-book: assigning programs to meanings. Cambridge University Press, New York (1996)
[9] Back, R.-J., Kurki-Suonio, R.: Distributed cooperation with action systems. ACM Trans. Program. Lang. Syst. 10(4), 513–554 (1988)
[10] Hallerstede, S.: Justifications for the Event-B Modelling Notation. In: Julliand, J., Kouchnarenko, O. (eds.) B 2007. LNCS, vol. 4355, pp. 49–63. Springer, Heidelberg (2006)
[11] Woodcock, J., Davies, J.: Using Z: Specification, Refinement, and Proof. Prentice-Hall, Englewood Cliffs (1996)
[12] Zave, P., Cheung, E.: Compositional Control of IP Media. IEEE Trans. Software Eng. 35(1), 46–66 (2009)
[13] Jackson, M.A.: System Development. Prentice-Hall, Englewood Cliffs (1983)

Abstract Certification of Global Non-interference in Rewriting Logic*

Mauricio Alba-Castro[1,2], María Alpuente[1], and Santiago Escobar[1]

[1] ELP-DSIC, U. Politécnica de Valencia, Spain
{alpuente,sescobar}@dsic.upv.es
[2] U. Autónoma de Manizales, Colombia
malba@autonoma.edu.co

Abstract. *Non–interference* is a semantic program property that assigns confidentiality levels to data objects and prevents illicit information flows from occurring from high to low security levels. In this paper, we present a novel security model for global non–interference which approximates non–interference as a safety property. We also propose a certification technique for global non-interference of complete Java classes based on rewriting logic, a very general *logical* and *semantic framework* that is efficiently implemented in the high-level programming language Maude. Starting from an existing Java semantics specification written in Maude, we develop an extended, information–flow Java semantics that allows us to correctly observe global non-interference policies. In order to achieve a finite state transition system, we develop an abstract Java semantics that we use for secure and effective non-interference Java analysis. The analysis produces certificates that are independently checkable and are small enough to be used in practice.

1 Introduction

Confidentiality is a property by which information that is related to an entity or party is not made available or disclosed to unauthorized individuals, entities, or processes. A *non-interference policy* [11] is a confidentiality policy that allows programs to manipulate and modify confidential data as long as the observable data generated by those programs do not improperly reveal information about the confidential data, i.e., confidential data does not interfere with publicly observable data. Thus, ensuring that a program adheres to a non-interference policy means analyzing how information flows within the program. The mechanism for transfering information through a computing system is called a *channel.* Variable updating, parameter passing, value return, file reading and writing, and network communication are channels. Channels that use a mechanism that is not designed for information communication are called *covert channels* [20]. There are covert channels such as the control structure of a program, termination, timing, exceptions, and resource exhaustion channels. The information flow that occurs

* This work has been partially supported by the EU (FEDER) and the Spanish MEC/MICINN under grant TIN 2007-68093-C02-02.

F.S. de Boer et al. (Eds.): FMCO 2009, LNCS 6286, pp. 105–124, 2010.

through channels is called *explicit flow* [11] because it does not depend on the specific information that flows. The information flow that occurs through the control structure of a program (conditionals, loops, breaks, and exceptions) is called an *implicit flow* [11] because it depends on the value of the condition that guards the control structure. In this paper, we are interested in both explicit and implicit flows for non-interference analysis of deterministic Java programs. However, we do not consider covert channels such as termination, timing, exceptions, and resource exhaustion channels.

In [1,2], we proposed an abstract methodology for certifying safety properties of Java source code. It is based on *Rewriting logic* (RWL) and is implemented in Maude [8], which is a high-performance language that implements RWL. In [1], we considered integer arithmetic properties that we analyzed as a safety property, whereas in [2] we dealt with (local) non–interference of Java methods. Non-interference is usually defined as a hyperproperty [7], i.e., a property defined on a set of sets of traces, and cannot be established by simply checking a (safety) property on a set of runs (essentially, no single run of a system can violate non-interference). However, we are able to analyze non-interference by observing a stronger property which can be checked as a safety[1] property using an instrumented flow-sensitive semantics.

The methodology of [1,2] is as follows. Consider a Java program together with a specification of the Java semantics. The Java program is a concrete expression (i.e., term) that represents the initial state of the Java interpreter running the considered Java program. The Java semantics is a specification in Maude. Given a safety property (i.e., a system property that is defined in terms of certain events that do not happen), the unreachability of the system states that denote the events that should never occur allows us to infer the desired safety property. Unreachability analysis is performed by using the standard Maude (breadth–first) search command, which explores the entire state space of the program from an initial system state. In the case where the unreachability test succeeds, the corresponding rewriting proofs that demonstrate that those states cannot be reached are delivered as the expected outcome certificate. We achieve a finite search space by using abstraction [9]. This methodology is an instance of Proof–carrying code (PCC), a mechanism originated by Necula [19] for ensuring the secure behavior of programs.

This article provides a comprehensive and full-fledged formulation of the abstract non–interference certification methodology of [2]. In that work, we focused on the methodology as well as the PCC and rewriting-based particulars of our approach with a specific emphasis on practicality and good performance. This paper, however, formalizes more foundational semantic security aspects, namely: (i) the characterization of non-interference as a safety property on extended Java computations; (ii) the conditions required by Java programs in order to ensure the correctness of our methodology; (iii) the observational capabilities of an attacker; and (iv) the soundness of our abstract non-interference analysis

[1] There are other approaches for proving non–interference as a safety property, which use self-composition [10,5] or flow-sensitive security types [16].

technique. In our previous work [2], we analyzed (local) non–interference of Java functional methods (i.e. methods that return values). However, in this paper, we are able to analyze entire Java programs, and thus, we consider *global non-interference.*

This paper is organized as follows. In Section 2, we recall the notion of non–intereference and describe a mechanism to specify non-interference policies in JML. In Section 3, we recall the specification of the Java semantics in rewriting logic. In Section 4, we extend this semantics to handle confidential information and formulate a non–interference certification methodology that is based on the unreachability of undesired states in the extended semantics. In Section 5, we develop an approximation of the extended Java semantics that produces a finite search space for any input Java program. By using this abstract semantics (which we implement as a source-to-source transformation of the extended semantics in Maude) we formulate our non-interference analysis and prove its soundness. We include some experiments in Section 6. A thorough discussion of related work is presented in Section 7. Finally, Section 8 presents our conclusions.

2 Non–interference

A non-interference policy establishes a confidentiality level for each source program variable of primitive datatypes. It guarantees that actual values of variables with a higher confidentiality level do not influence the output of a variable with a lower confidentiality level during program execution [11,15,20,23]. It is implicitly assumed that constants that appear in a program always have the lowest confidentiality level (i.e., the considered program is authorized to access secret data, but it does not contain secret data in its code).

A non-interference policy can be represented by a *partially ordered set* $\langle Labels, \leq \rangle$ and a labeling function $Labeling : Var \rightarrow Labels$, where $Labels$ is the finite set of confidentiality levels, $\leq$ is a partial order between confidentiality levels, and Var is the set of source program variables [22,4,16]. There are usually two confidentiality levels: $Labels = \{\texttt{Low}, \texttt{High}\}$. These represent public non-secret data (low confidentiality) and secret data (high confidentiality), respectively. $\langle Labels, \leq \rangle$ forms a lattice where `Low` is the greatest lower bound or *bottom* element ($\bot$), `High` is the least upper bound or *top* element ($\top$), and $\texttt{Low} < \texttt{High}$. The *join* operator ($\sqcup$) is defined as $\texttt{Low} \sqcup \texttt{Low} = \texttt{Low}$; otherwise, $X \sqcup Y = \texttt{High}$. Enforcing non-interference means that the values of `High`-labeled source variables cannot flow to `Low`-labeled source variables, whereas the values of `Low`-labeled source variables can flow to `High`-labeled source variables. The attacker model for global non–interference that we formalize below assumes that the attacker is passive and can only see the `Low`-labeled source variables of the Java program at the initial and final states and not at the intermediate states. Our methodology can certify programs that have temporal breaches and are still non-interferent.

In order to express confidentiality policies, we use the *Java modeling language* JML [17], which is a property specification language for Java modules. The text of a JML annotation can either be in one line after the `//@` marker, or in many lines enclosed between the markers `/*@` and `@*/`. They are ignored by traditional compilers. The initial confidentiality level of a variable in a Java program is written with the word `setLabel` as a JML annotation (e.g. `setLabel(var, High)`). The confidentiality label of program variables is `Low` if nothing is specified (i.e., program variables are public by default). These JML annotations, together with the default assumption, define the labeling function of the non–interference policy.

Example 1. Consider the following Java program borrowed from [10] that models a bank account and the initial state given by the execution of the function `main`:

```
public class Account { int balance; //@ setLabel(balance, High);
  public boolean extraService;
  public Account() { balance = 0; extraService = false; }
  public void writeBalance(int amount) { balance = amount;
     if (balance>=10000) extraService=true; else extraService=false; }
  private int readBalance() {return balance;}
  public boolean readExtra() {return extraService;}
}
class System { static Account a = new Account();
  public static void main(String[] args) {
     int initbalance; //@ setLabel(initbalance, High);
     initbalance = Integer.parseInt(args[0]);
     a.writeBalance(initbalance); System.out.println(readExtra());  }}
```

This non-interference policy specifies that the object field `balance` of the global object `a` and the initialization parameter `initbalance` (i.e., `args[0]`) hold secret data. This program is insecure w.r.t. this policy since an observer with low access rights can obtain partial information about the variable `balance` via an observation of the non–secret variable `extraService`.

We assume a fixed Java program P_{Java}. $Vars(P_{\text{Java}})$ denotes the set of `static` source variables that may be initialized by the `main` function call. We denote the set of *Low* program variables as $Low(P_{\text{Java}}) = \{var \in Vars(P_{\text{Java}}) \mid Labeling(var) = \texttt{Low}\}$. A program state St is a set of value assignments to program variables. Given $var \in Vars(P_{\text{Java}})$ and a state St, $St[var]$ denotes the value of variable var in St. We model a *Java program* P_{Java} as a state transition system between pairs $\langle P, St\rangle$, where P is the current, still-to-be-executed part of the Java program P_{Java} and St represents the current program state. $\langle P_{\text{Java}}, St_0\rangle$ denotes the initial *configuration* of standard program execution and $\langle \checkmark, St\rangle$ denotes a final *configuration*, where $\checkmark$ stands for the empty program. Note that we assume that every Java program properly terminates for each set of input data (i.e., we do not consider non-terminating programs, deadlocks, or runtime errors). We also assume deterministic Java programs, without threads or exceptions. $\mapsto_{\text{Java}}$ is the transition relation that describes any possible one-step transition between any two Java program states. An *execution* (or trace) of P_{Java} is a sequence $\langle P_{\text{Java}}, St_0\rangle \mapsto_{\text{Java}} \cdots \langle P_i, St_i\rangle \mapsto_{\text{Java}} \cdots \mapsto_{\text{Java}} \langle \checkmark, St_n\rangle$, which is simply denoted by $\langle P_{\text{Java}}, St_0\rangle \mapsto^*_{\text{Java}} \langle \checkmark, S_n\rangle$ if the intermediate states are irrelevant. We can also abbreviate $\langle \checkmark, S_n\rangle$ by $\langle S_n\rangle$.

We define program non–interference by using an equivalence $=_{Low}$ relationship between states [20,22,4]. Roughly speaking, non-interference establishes that any two terminating runs of a program that start from indistinguishable initial states produce indistinguishable final states.

Definition 1 (State equality [20]). *Given a Java program P_{Java}, two states St_1 and St_2 for P_{Java} are* indistinguishable *at the confidentiality level* `Low`*, written $St_1 =_{Low} St_2$, if for all $var \in Low(P_{\text{Java}})$, $St_1[var] = St_2[var]$.*

What the attacker can see from a final state is determined by a relation $\approx_{\texttt{Low}}$. Two executions of a program P_{Java} are related by $\approx_{\texttt{Low}}$ if they are indistinguishable to the attacker [20]. The notion of non–interference is therefore parametric on $\approx_{\texttt{Low}}$. A program is non–interferent if, whenever different initial program states are indistinguishable at level `Low`, this implies that the corresponding final states are also indistinguishable at level `Low`.

Definition 2 (Non–interference [20]). *A Java program P_{Java} is* non–interferent *if for every pair of different program initial states St_1 and St_2, and for their corresponding final program states St'_1, St'_2 such that $\langle P_{\text{Java}}, St_1\rangle \mapsto^*_{\text{Java}} \langle St'_1\rangle$ and $\langle P_{\text{Java}}, St_2\rangle \mapsto^*_{\text{Java}} \langle St'_2\rangle$, we have that $St_1 =_{Low} St_2$ implies $St'_1 \approx_{Low} St'_2$.*

In this paper, we follow the standard approach in the literature that considers $St \approx_{Low} St'$ iff $St =_{Low} St'$. Then, the non–interference condition of Definition 2 is understood as the lack of any *strong dependence* [20] of `Low`-labeled variables on any of the `High`-labeled variables.

3 The Rewriting Logic Semantics of Java

In the following, we briefly recall the rewriting logic semantics of Java that was originally given in [12]. We refer the reader to [18] for further technical details on rewriting logic semantics.

In [12], a sufficiently large subset of full Java 1.4 language is specified in Maude, including inheritance, polymorphism, object references, multithreading, and dynamic object allocation. However, Java native methods and many of the available Java built–in libraries are not supported. The specification of Java operational semantics is a rewrite theory: a triple $\mathcal{R}_{\text{Java}} = (\Sigma_{\text{Java}}, E_{\text{Java}}, R_{\text{Java}})$ where Σ_{Java} is an order–sorted *signature*; $E_{\text{Java}} = \Delta_{\text{Java}} \uplus B_{\text{Java}}$ is a set of Σ_{Java}–equational *axioms* where B_{Java} are algebraic axioms such as associativity, commutativity and unity, and Δ_{Java} is a set of terminating and confluent (modulo B_{Java}) equations. Finally, R_{Java} is a set of Σ_{Java}–rewrite rules that are not required to be confluent nor terminating.

Intuitively, the sorts and function symbols in Σ_{Java} describe the static structure of the Java program state space as an algebraic data type; the equations in Δ_{Java} describe the operational semantics of its deterministic features; and the rules in R_{Java} describe its concurrent features. Following the rewriting logic framework we denote by $u \rightarrow^r_{\text{Java}} v$ the fact that the concrete terms

```
eq k((E > E') -> K) = k((E, E') -> > -> K) . ---Evaluate arguments
eq k((int(I), int(I')) -> > -> K) = k(bool(I > I') -> K) . ---Resolve
```

Fig. 1. Continuation-based equations for the Java greater-than operator on integers

```
--- Evaluates boolean expression keeping the then and else statements
eq k((if E S else S') -> K) = k(E -> (if(S, S') -> K)) .
eq k(bool(true) -> (if(S, S') -> K)) = k(S -> K) .
eq k(bool(false) -> (if(S, S') -> K)) = k(S' -> K) .
```

Fig. 2. Continuation-based equations for if-then-else statement

u, v (which denote Java program states) are rewritten (at the top position, see [12]) by using r, which is either a rule in R_{Java} or an equation in Δ_{Java} (both of which are applied modulo B_{Java}). We simply write $u \rightarrow_{\text{Java}} v$ when the applied rule or equation is irrelevant. We denote by $\rightarrow^*_{\text{Java}}$ the extension of $\rightarrow_{\text{Java}}$ to multiple rewrite steps (i.e., $u \rightarrow^*_{\text{Java}} v$ if there exist $u_1, \ldots, u_k$ such that $u \rightarrow_{\text{Java}} u_1 \rightarrow_{\text{Java}} u_2 \cdots u_k \rightarrow_{\text{Java}} v$).

The rewrite theory $\mathcal{R}_{\text{Java}}$ is defined on terms of a concrete sort State, with the main state attributes (represented by means of constructor symbols of the algebraic type State) such as `fstack` for handling function calls, `lstack` for handling loops, `env` for assignments of variables to memory locations, and `store` for assignments of memory locations to their actual values. They define an algebraic structure that is parametric w.r.t. a generic sort Value that defines all the possible values returned by Java functions or stored in the memory. For instance, the `int` and `bool` constructor symbols describe Java integer and boolean values and are defined in Maude as "`op int : Int → Value .`" and "`op bool : Bool → Value .`", where `Int` and `Bool` are the internal built–in Maude sorts that define integer and boolean data types. Intuitively, equations in Δ_{Java} and rules in R_{Java} are used to specify the changes to the program state (i.e., the changes to the memory, input/output, etc). Since we consider only deterministic Java programs, our specification of the Java semantics in rewriting logic contains only equations and no rules. The reader can find a RWL specification of the semantics of a programming language with threads in [18,1,2].

The semantics of Java is defined in a *continuation-based style* [18] and specified in Maude itself. Continuations maintain the control context, which explicitly specifies the next steps to be performed. The sequence of actions that still need to be executed are stacked. We use letters `K`, `K'` to denote continuation variables, letters `E`, `E'` to denote expressions to be evaluated, and `Val`, `Val'` to denote values (i.e., the result of evaluating an expression). Once the expression e on the top of a continuation (e `->` k) is evaluated, its result will be passed on to the remaining continuation k. For instance, in Figure 1, the Java greater-than operation on Java integers is specified by using continuations, where `k` is the constructor symbol used to denote a continuation, `->` is the constructor symbol used to concatenate continuations, `bool` is the constructor symbol used to denote a Java boolean data, and `int` is the constructor symbol used to denote a Java integer number.

```
--- Stack loop and transform while expression into while continuation
eq k((while E S) -> K) lstack(Lstack)
 = k(while(E,S) -> popLStack -> K) lstack(while(E,S) -> K, Lstack) .
--- A while continuation is transformed into an if-then-else
eq k(while(E,S) -> K) = k(E -> if(S while ( E , S ),{}) -> K) .
--- Add semantics for popLStack
eq k(popLStack -> K) lstack(LItem,Lstack) = k(K) lstack(Lstack) .
```

Fig. 3. Continuation-based equations for while statement

```
--- The state is restored from the loop stack
eq k(break -> K) lstack(while(E,S) -> K', Lstack) = k(K') lstack(Lstack).
```

Fig. 4. Continuation-based equations for while break statement

The if-then-else statement is shown in Figure 2. The semantics of while statements (loops) is specified in Figure 3, where the term `while E S` denotes the Java iteration statement, the term `while`(E, S) denotes both the while continuation and the while statement that is expressed in terms of the `if`(S, S′) continuation, and `lstack` denotes a stack of loops currently being executed, which is needed for a proper control of the Java `break` statement. Figure 4 shows the semantic specification of the `break` statement, that simply pops the stack of loops. This is important, since it can also abruptly change the information flow. Method calls are not shown in this paper; their semantics is simply defined by eager evaluation of all arguments of the method (whose values are stored in new memory locations) and by creating a new local environment that contains location assignments for formal method parameters and local variables. Due to space limitations we do not discuss heap manipulation here. We refer the reader to [18] for further details.

The following example illustrates the mechanization of the Java semantics.

Example 2. Consider again the Java program of Example 1 and two program executions, respectively fed with 5000 and 10000 for the initialization parameter `initbalance`. Note that the corresponding initial states are indistinguishable at the `Low` confidentiality level (e.g. the only `Low`-labeled variable, `extraService`, is set to `false` in both of them). The Maude command `search` provides built–in breadth-first search. We ask for the final Java program state of each execution trace (actually, in order to visualize the results, we show the output of `println` Java instructions). The Maude terms `EX1-MAUDE` and `EX2-MAUDE` stand for the Java program with the corresponding initial call (for input value 5000 and 10000, respectively), which are compiled into a Maude expression by using a suitable Java wrapper[2]:

```
search in PGM-SEMANTICS :
java((preprocess(EX1-MAUDE) noType . 'main < new string [i(0)] > noVal))
=>! JO:Output .
Solution 1 JO:Output --> pl(bool(false))
No more solutions.
```

[2] See `http://fsl.cs.uiuc.edu/index.php/Rewriting_Logic_Semantics_of_Java`

```
search in PGM-SEMANTICS :
java((preprocess(EX2-MAUDE) noType . 'main < new string [i(0)] > noVal))
=>! JO:Output .
Solution 1 JO:Output --> pl(bool(true))
No more solutions.
```

If the attacker observes these two final states, she will appreciate the two different values for the variable `extraService`.

4 Proving Non–interference by Using an Extended Instrumented Semantics

Non–interference is usually understood to be a security property and is therefore defined as a *hyperproperty* [7] (i.e., a property defined on a set of sets of traces). For instance, in Example 2, the verification process for non–interference should check the (possibly infinite) set of (possibly infinite) sets of final states issued from the (possibly infinite) sets of indistinguishable initial configurations. Note that checking the final states issued from `EX1-MAUDE` and `EX2-MAUDE` is just one of the combinations to be analyzed. In contrast, the verification process for a safety property should simply check the traces issuing from the (possibly infinite) set of initial configurations, which is simpler.

In this paper, we prove non-interference as a safety property by instrumenting the Java semantics in order to dynamically keep track of the change of the confidentiality labels of program variables. Intuitively, the semantic instrumentation is defined as follows:

1. Attach a confidentiality label to each memory location; this allows us to observe their confidentiality level at the final execution state.
2. Attach a confidentiality label to the evaluation of program expressions; this allows us to know whether the evaluation of an expression involves high confidentiality data.
3. Associate a confidentiality label to the evaluation of program statements, particularly those involving conditional expressions or guards; this allows us to determine whether the control flow at a given execution point depends on the actual value of high confidential variables. However, this label is not attached to each program statement. Rather it is kept as an extra attribute of a state in the extended Java semantics. This corresponds to the notion of a *context label* being updated after each evaluation step in [11,23,16], which is introduced in the following example.

Example 3. Consider the following Java[3] program `TestClass` that is borrowed from [23]. We endow it with the attached non-interference policy:

```
public class Testclass {static int low=0, high; //@ setLabel(high, High);
  public static void main(String[] args) {
    high = Integer.parseInt(args[0]); while (high > 0) {high--;low++;} }}
```

[3] We omit the semantics of some Java operators such as _++, ++_, and _+=_, since they can be defined in terms of addition (_+_) and assignment (_=_), as usual [18].

Here there is an an illicit and implicit information flow from the `High`-labeled source variable `high` to the `Low`-labeled source variable `low`. For instance, when the variable `high` contains the value `0` or `1`, the variable `low` is assigned the value `0` and `1`, respectively. This implicit flow would be detected using the context label, which is set to `High` after evaluating the expression `high>0`, and which forces variable `low` to be set to `High` independently of the confidentiality level of the expression `low++`.

In contrast to [2] where local non-interference was studied, here we consider global non-interference (i.e., we are able to ensure a non-interference policy at the final state of the whole Java program execution, which contains several methods, classes, and function calls). This important improvement in the verification power (which has been hardly explored in the related literature) requires the following two modifications to the non-interference analysis of [2]. These changes avoid the difficult (or costly) process of tracing the current confidentiality label of a memory location back to the point where this location was created.

1. We introduce an additional confidentiality label ($\texttt{Low} \gg \texttt{High}$), which allow us to represent not only the current confidentiality label of a memory location but also to keep track, at a global level, of hazardous transitions from an initial confidentiality label `Low` to `High`. Similarly, we introduce the confidentiality label ($\texttt{High} \gg \texttt{Low}$), in order to avoid false positives where a `High`–labeled variable is updated with the value of a `Low`–labeled expression and then updated again with the value of a `High`–labeled expression.
2. In [2], we used the context label only when updating the value of a variable in memory, as in [23,16,14], and when returning values as in [14]. In this paper, we use the context label during expression evaluation, as in [4].

We describe the information-flow extended version of the rewriting logic semantics of Java by the rewrite theory $\mathcal{R}_{\text{Java}^{\text{E}}} = (\Sigma_{\text{Java}^{\text{E}}}, E_{\text{Java}^{\text{E}}}, R_{\text{Java}^{\text{E}}})$, $E_{\text{Java}^{\text{E}}} = \Delta_{\text{Java}^{\text{E}}} \uplus B_{\text{Java}^{\text{E}}}$ and its corresponding $\rightarrow_{\text{Java}^{\text{E}}}$ rewriting relation. In the new semantics, program data not only consist of standard concrete values but each value is decorated with its corresponding confidentiality label. Formally, we consider the label change $LabelChange = \{\texttt{Low} \gg \texttt{High}, \texttt{High} \gg \texttt{Low}\}$ so that the domain of program variables in the extended semantics is $Value \times (Labels \cup LabelChange)$. We write `<Value,LValue>` for a pair consisting of a concrete value and its corresponding confidentiality label in $Labels \cup LabelChange$.

Thanks to the modularity of the rewriting logic approach to formalizing program semantics [12], our changes to the semantics of Section 3 are incremental and minimal. The assignment computes the new confidentiality label in terms of the previous label at the memory location, namely `NewVal = LVal' >>> LVal`. The new operator $\ggg$ is defined in Figure 5.

The context label can only change due to a conditional control flow statements. According to [11,4,23,16], the evaluation of its boolean guards returns a confidentiality level that is associated to the resulting `true` or `false` value and, possibly, a modified context label. The extended semantic equations for the if-then-else of Figure 2 need some slight revision, which is motivated by the following example.

Previously Stored Label	$\ggg$	New Label	=	New Stored Label
L	$\ggg$	L	=	L
Low	$\ggg$	High	=	Low $\gg$ High
High	$\ggg$	Low	=	High $\gg$ Low
$L_1 \gg L_2$	$\ggg$	L_1	=	L_1
$L_1 \gg L_2$	$\ggg$	L_2	=	$L_1 \gg L_2$

Fig. 5. Updating memory locations

Example 4. Consider the following Java method, where the value computed for the variable `low` does not actually depend on the value of the high confidentiality variable `high` (which only affects the temporal variable `aux`). This program does fulfill the non-interference policy at the final state, which can be proved by using our non-interference verification methodology.

```
class Testclass { static int low=0, high; //@ setLabel(high, High);
  public static void main(String[] args) {
      high = Integer.parseInt(args[0]);
      int aux=0; if (high > 2) aux = 1; else aux = 0; low = 0; } }
```

In order to avoid false positives during the evaluation of conditional statements, we dynamically restore the previous context label after its execution. The extended semantics equations for the if-then-else are shown in Figure 6, where a new continuation symbol `restoreLEnv` is used to restore the previous confidentiality label. However, restoring the previous context label has to be carefully considered in the presence of `break` or `continue` statements within a loop, since they can abruptly change the information flow as shown in the following example.

Example 5. Consider a variation of Example 3 where the while loop has a bogus guard together with a `break` statement to exit the loop:

```
public class Testclass {static int low=0, high; //@ setLabel(high, High);
 public static void main(String[] args) {high = Integer.parseInt(args[0]);
    int aux=0; while (true) {high--; low++; if (high == 0) break;} } }
```

As in Example 3, when the while loop ends, the variable `low` has the initial value of the variable `high`. Whenever `high` $\neq 0$, the `break` statement is not executed. In this case, the conditional guard uses `High`-labeled data, and the conditional statement should not restore the previous context label. In other words, the critical component here is not the `break` statement but rather the else branch that does not contain the `break`.

In order to solve this problem, we check in Figure 6 whether either of the two branches of a conditional statement contains a `break` or `continue` statement and no other conditional statement or `while` loop in between. If there is such a statement, `restoreLEnv` is not used. This case was not considered in [23] or in [2], which only considered `break` statements within `High` guarded while loops.

Method invocation propagates the context label without changes as proposed in [23] and, thus, is not shown here. Since while statements were expressed in terms of if-then-else statements, they need a slight extension to introduce the

```
--- Evaluates boolean expression keeping the then and else statements
ceq k((if E S else S') -> K) lenv(CL)
  = k(E -> (if(S, S') -> restoreLEnv(CL) -> K)) lenv(CL)
 if not break-or-continue(S) and not break-or-continue(S') .
ceq k((if E S else S') -> K) lenv(CL) = k(E -> (if(S, S') -> K)) lenv(CL)
 if break-or-continue(S) or break-or-continue(S') .
eq k(<bool(true),LVal> -> (if(S, S') -> K)) lenv(CL)
 = k(S -> K) lenv(CL join LVal) .
eq k(<bool(false),LVal> -> (if(S, S') -> K)) lenv(CL)
 = k(S' -> K) lenv(CL join LVal) .
--- New equation to restore previous context label
eq k(restoreLEnv(CL) -> K) lenv(CL') = k(K) lenv(CL) .
```

Fig. 6. Extended equations for the if-then-else

```
--- Stack loop and transform while expression into while continuation
eq k((while E S) -> K) lstack(Lstack) lenv(CL)
 = k(while(E,S) -> restoreLEnv(CL) -> popLStack -> K)
   lstack(while(E,S) -> K, Lstack) lenv(CL) .
```

Fig. 7. Extended equations for while statement

`restorelEnv` continuation (shown in Figure 7). The semantic specification of the `break` statement stays the same as shown in Figure 4: the context label `lenv(CL)` is not modified and the `restoreLEnv` expression introduced by the while statement is removed.

4.1 Proving Non-interference as a Safety Property

Now, we are ready to formulate a novel characterization of non-interference that allows us to check it as a property that is verified for each possible execution trace instead of being verified for each set of indistinguishable execution traces.

Definition 3 (Strong Non-Interference). *A Java program P_{Java} is* strongly non–interferent *for a given labeling function if for every extended initial state St_1^E and for its corresponding final program state St_2^E given by $\langle P_{\text{Java}}, St_1^E\rangle \mapsto^*_{\text{Java}^{\text{E}}} \langle St_2^E\rangle$, we have that for all $var \in Low(P_{\text{Java}})$, $St_2^E[var] = \langle Val, \texttt{Low}\rangle$ for a value Val.*

Since in our model, a public variable can only have the label `Low` or the label `Low` $\gg$ `High`, this means that in the extended execution of a program that is not strongly non-interferent, the label of at least one program variable is `Low` $\gg$ `High`. Given an initial state St and a given labeling function, we denote the corresponding extended state by St^E.

Lemma 1. *Consider a Java program P_{Java} and two initial states St_1 and St_2 such that $St_1 =_{Low} St_2$. Consider the two corresponding final program states St_1' and St_2' given by $\langle P_{\text{Java}}, St_1\rangle \mapsto^*_{\text{Java}} \langle St_1'\rangle$ and $\langle P_{\text{Java}}, St_2\rangle \mapsto^*_{\text{Java}} \langle St_2'\rangle$. If there exists $var \in Low(P_{\text{Java}})$ such that $St_1'[var] \neq St_2'[var]$, then*

$\langle P_{\text{Java}}, St_1^E\rangle \mapsto^*_{\text{Java}^{\text{E}}} \langle St^E\rangle$ *and* $St^E[var] = \langle Val, \texttt{Low} \gg \texttt{High}\rangle$ *for a value* Val.

From Lemma 1 we derive that strong non-interference implies non-interference, as given by the following result.

Theorem 1 (Strong Non-Interference Soundness). *Given a Java program* P_{Java}*, if* P_{Java} *is strongly non–interferent (Definition 3), then* P_{Java} *is non–interferent (Definition 2).*

The following example illustrates the mechanization of our verification methodology.

Example 6. Consider again the Java program of Example 1. Now, we compute the final state in the extended Java program execution for `EX1-MAUDE` (for simplicity we show only the value of variable `extraBalance`).

```
search in PGM-SEMANTICS-EXTENDED :
java((preprocess(EX1-MAUDE) noType .  'main < new string [i(0)] > noVal))
=>! M:Store .
Solution 1 M:Store --> store([l(6),<bool(false),Low >> High>] ...)
No more solutions.
```

The execution for `EX2-MAUDE` will also contain the label `Low` $\gg$ `High` for variable `extraBalance`.

In other words, we transform non-interference into a stronger property which can be effectively checked in the extended semantics. Obviously, we are not able to certify the security of all the programs that are secure, as shown in Example 7.

Example 7. Consider the following Java program borrowed from [23].

```
class Testclass { static int low=0, high; //@ setLabel(high, High);
 public static void main(String[] args) {high = Integer.parseInt(args[0]);
      low = high; low = low - high;}  }
```

Apparently, there is an explicit flow from variable `high` to variable `low` through the two assignment statements. However for any execution, when program ends, the value of variable `low` is always `0` so that the variable `low` does not depend on the variable `high`. According to Definition 2, the program is non–interferent. However, we give a false positive by using our notion of strong non-interference since the assignment "`low` = `high`" assigns to the variable `low` a high confidentiality label `Low` $\gg$ `High` and the last statement "`low` = `low` − `high`" does not revert the label back to `low`.

The program of Example 7 cannot be verified by traditional type inference approaches [22,26,4] either, since they fail to verify (type check) any program with temporary breaches, e.g. Examples 4 and 7 above, whereas Example 4 is effectively verified by using our methodology.

5 Approximating Non–interference by Using an Abstract Semantics

The extended, instrumented Java semantics defined so far allows us to develop a technique for proving non–interference. However, this technique is still not feasible in general because there are too many possible initial states to consider for the safety property to be checked. In the following, we develop an abstract, rewriting logic Java semantics that allows us to statically analyze global non–interference. Similar to [2], the purpose of the abstract semantics is to correctly approximate the extended computations in a finite way. Given the extended Java semantics, where there are concrete labeled values, we simply get rid of the values in the abstract semantics, and use their confidentiality labels as the abstract values instead.

In the following, we develop an abstract version of the extended rewriting logic semantics of Java developed in Section 4, which we describe by the rewrite theory $\mathcal{R}_{\text{Java}\#} = (\Sigma_{\text{Java}\#}, E_{\text{Java}\#}, R_{\text{Java}\#})$, $E_{\text{Java}\#} = \Delta_{\text{Java}\#} \uplus B_{\text{Java}\#}$ and its corresponding $\rightarrow_{\text{Java}\#}$ rewriting relation. As in Section 4, our approach for the abstract Java semantics consists of modifying the original theory $\mathcal{R}_{\text{Java}^{\text{E}}}$ (taking advantage of its modularity) by abstracting the domain to $Labels \cup LabelChange$ and introducing approximate versions of the Java constructions and operators tailored to this domain.

An *abstract interpretation* (or abstraction) [9] of the program semantics is given by an *upper closure operator* $\alpha : \wp(\mathsf{State}) \rightarrow \wp(\mathsf{State})$, which is *monotonic* (for all $SSt_1, SSt_2 \in \wp(\mathsf{State})$, $SSt_1 \subseteq SSt_2$ implies $\alpha(SSt_1) \subseteq \alpha(SSt_2)$), *idempotent* (for all $SSt \in \wp(\mathsf{State})$, $\alpha(SSt) \subseteq \alpha(\alpha(SSt))$), and *extensive* (for all $SSt \in \wp(\mathsf{State})$, $SSt \subseteq \alpha(SSt)$). In our framework, each Java program state $St \in \mathsf{State}$ is abstracted by its closure $\alpha(\{St\})$. Our abstraction function $\alpha : \wp(\mathsf{State}^E) \rightarrow \wp(\mathsf{State}^E)$ is a simple homomorphic extension to sets of states of the function $2nd : \mathsf{Value} \times (Labels \cup LabelChange) \rightarrow (Labels \cup LabelChange)$, meaning that we disregard the actual values of data.

In the abstract Java semantics, several alternative computation steps of $\rightarrow_{\text{Java}^{\text{E}}}$ are mimicked by a single abstract computation step of $\rightarrow_{\text{Java}\#}$, reflecting the fact that several distinct behaviors are compressed into a single abstract state (i.e. set of states). The instrumentalization of the Java semantics for dealing with a set of states instead of one single state implicitly means too many modifications. Therefore, we adopt a different approach. When several $\rightarrow_{\text{Java}^{\text{E}}}$ rewrite steps are mimicked by a single abstract rewriting state leading to an abstract Java state, and those rewrite steps apply different rules or equations, we use concurrency at the Maude level. Despite the fact that our extended Java semantics contains only equations and no rules, the abstract Java semantics does contain rules in $R_{\text{Java}\#}$ to reflect the different possible evolutions of the system.

The abstract semantics is mainly a straightforward extension of the extended semantics. The only difference is that any set of equations that was confluent and terminating in the extended semantics but might become non confluent or non terminating in the abstract semantics is transformed into rules. As a representative example, the abstract rules associated to two of the equations of the extended semantics of the if-then-else statement are shown in Figure 8.

Now, we are ready to formalize the abstract rewriting relation $\rightarrow_{\text{Java}\#}$, which intuitively develops the idea of applying only one rule or equation from the concrete Java semantics to an abstract Java state while exploring the different

```
rl k(LVal -> (if(S,S') -> K)) lenv(CL) => k(S -> K) lenv(CL join LVal).
rl k(LVal -> (if(S,S') -> K)) lenv(CL) => k(S' -> K) lenv(CL join LVal).
```

Fig. 8. Abstract rules for the if-then-else

alternatives in a non-deterministic way. By abuse, we denote the abstraction of a rule $\alpha(\{l\}) \rightarrow \alpha(\{r\})$ by $\alpha(\{l\} \rightarrow \{r\})$. $\mathcal{P}_{\text{Java}}$ denotes the sort of Java programs P_{Java} (i.e. $P_{\text{Java}} \in \mathcal{P}_{\text{Java}}$).

Definition 4 (Abstract rewriting). *We define abstract rewriting* $\rightarrow_{\text{Java}\#} \subseteq (\mathcal{P}_{\text{Java}} \times \wp(\mathsf{State}^E)) \times (\mathcal{P}_{\text{Java}} \times \wp(\mathsf{State}^E))$ *by* $\langle P_{\text{Java}_1}, SSt_1\rangle \rightarrow_{\text{Java}\#} \langle P_{\text{Java}_2}, SSt_2\rangle$ *if* $\exists u \in SSt_1, \exists v \in SSt_2$ *s.t.* $\langle P_{\text{Java}_1}, u\rangle \rightarrow_{\text{Java}^{\text{E}}} \langle P_{\text{Java}_2}, v\rangle$.

We denote by $\rightarrow^*_{\text{Java}\#}$ the extension of $\rightarrow_{\text{Java}\#}$ to multiple rewrite steps.

Lemma 2. *If* $\langle P_{\text{Java}}, St_1^E\rangle \rightarrow^*_{\text{Java}^{\text{E}}} \langle St_2^E\rangle$, *then there exists* $SSt_3 \in \wp(\mathsf{State}^E)$ *s.t.* $\langle P_{\text{Java}}, \alpha(\{St_1^E\})\rangle \rightarrow^*_{\text{Java}\#} \langle SSt_3\rangle$ *and* $St_2^E \in SSt_3$.

A program is non–interferent for a given labeling function if the abstract values (the confidentiality labels) of the *Low* variables in the final state of an abstract program execution do not have the label `Low` $\gg$ `High`.

Theorem 2 (Abstract Non-Interference Soundness). *Given a Java program* P_{Java}, P_{Java} *is non–interferent (Definition 2) if for all* $SSt_1 \in \wp(\mathsf{State}^E)$ *s.t.* $\langle P_{\text{Java}}, SSt_1\rangle \mapsto^*_{\text{Java}\#} \langle SSt_2\rangle$, *for all* $St \in SSt_2$, *and for all variables* $var \in Low(P_{\text{Java}})$, $St[var] = \langle Val, \texttt{Low}\rangle$ *for a value* Val.

The following example illustrates the mechanization of the Java non-interference analysis.

Example 8. Consider again the Java program of Example 1. By virtue of the abstraction, we consider just one abstract initial state that safely approximates any extended initial state and compute the corresponding abstract final states.

```
search in PGM-SEMANTICS-ABSTRACT :
java((preprocess(EX1-MAUDE) noType . 'main < new string [i(0)] > noVal))
=>! M:Store .
Solution 1 M:Store --> store([l(6),Low >> High] ...)
No more solutions.
```

Due to the transformation of some equations into rules in the abstract semantics, there may be several execution paths but all lead to the same abstract final state.

6 Experiments

Our methodology generates a safety certificate which essentially consists of the set of (abstract) rewriting proofs that implicitly describe the program states which can (and cannot) be reached from a given (abstract) initial state, as illustrated in Example 8. Since these proofs correspond to the execution of the

Table 1. Code measures, certificate sizes, and generation times

Code Examples → Experiment Measures ↓	1	2	3	4	5
Code size in LOC	27	31	48	80	117
Code size in bytes	869	924	1981	3305	3504
Code cyclomatic complexity	1	1	4	16	192
Full Cert. size (Kb)	1134	1251	4223	10619	24176
Red. Rules Cert. size (Kb)	6.1	6.3	21.1	47.1	21.3
Red. Labels Cert. size (Kb)	1.8	1.8	2.6	3.7	5.2
Full Cert. Gen. Time (ms)	10408	23574	29482	45709	84331
Red. Rules Cert. Gen. Time (ms)	7057	7030	7527	8215	9547
Red. Labels Cert. Gen. Time (ms)	7030	6700	7190	8198	9537

abstract Java semantics specification, which is made available to the code consumer, the certificate can be unexpensively checked on the consumer side by any standard rewrite engine by means of a rewriting process that can be very simplified. Actually, it suffices to check that each abstract rewriting step in the certificate is valid and that no rewriting chain has been disregarded, which essentially amounts to using the matching infrastructure available within the rewriting engine. Note that, according to the different treatment of rules and equations in Maude, where only transitions caused by rules create new states in the space state, an extremely reduced certificate can be delivered by just recording the rewrite steps given with the rules, while the rewritings using the equations are omitted.

The abstract certification methodology described here has been implemented in Maude[4]. The prototype system offers a rewriting-based program certification service, which is able to analyze global confidentiality program properties related to non–interference. Our certification tool can generate three types of certificates: (i) the full certificates consist of complete rewriting sequences including all rewrite steps; (ii) the reduced rules certificates only contain the rewrite steps that use rules; and (iii) the reduced labels certificates only record the labels of the used rules.

In Table 1, we analyze three key points for the practicality of our approach: the size and complexity of the program code, the size of the three types of certificates, and the certificate generation times. The running times are given in milliseconds and were averaged over a sufficient number of iterations. We considered three code measures, the code size in LOC (lines of source code), the code size in bytes, and the cyclomatic complexity, which counts the execution paths of a program. The experiments were performed on a laptop with a Pentium M 1.40 GHz processor and 0.5 Gb RAM.

Program `1` consists mainly of a simple non–interferent code example borrowed from [23]. The program has been structured into two classes. The first class has one secret variable and one public variable, a constructor method, two get methods, and a method that contains the non–interferent piece of code of [23]. The second class is the main class with four method invocations. Similarly, program 2

[4] The tool is provided with a Web interface written in Java and is publicly available at `http://www.dsic.upv.es/users/elp/toolsMaude/GlobalNI.hml`

is a simple non–interferent example borrowed from [16]. It is structured into two classes. Program 3 includes three simple methods in two classes: one of which is an interferent method borrowed from [23]. The main method has a sequence of method invocations such that the last invocation calls a non–interferent method, and thus the entire program is non–interferent. Program 4 includes six simple methods, the three methods included in program 3 and three other interferent methods also borrowed from [23], including a method with a `while` loop and a method that calls another method. In this case, the last invoked method as well as the whole example program are non-interferent. Similarly, program 5 includes nine simple methods, the six examples included in program 4 plus three other interferent methods: two interferent variations of the loop example of program 5 and an interferent method with a return statement within a conditional statement. The source code of our benchmarks is provided within the distribution package.

The experiments are very encouraging since they show that the reduction in size of the certificate is very significant in all cases, with the quotient "Red. Rules Cert. Size/Full Cert. Size" ranging from 0.54% in program 2 to 0.09% in program 5. Note that the biggest reduction occurs for the largest program. When the time employed to generate the full and reduced rules certificates are compared, the reduced certificate generation time vs the full certificate generation time range from 11, 32% to 67.80%. The reduction for the biggest example (program 5) was the largest one (11, 32%). Note that the generation time for the reduced labels certificate were not significantly lower than the reduced rules certificate. These results show that the technique scales up better when reduced certificates are considered.

7 Related Work

Goguen and Meseguer [15] formalized non–interference of deterministic and terminating systems as a system hyperproperty [7], i.e., a security property that is defined for pairs of system output traces that are indistinguisable for an observer. In [13], Foccardi and Gorrieri defined a stronger, security–based notion of non–interference that considers pairs of system input/output traces. In contrast to [13], our safety-based notion of strong non–interference only considers secret outputs, similarly to [15].

Barthe et. al [5] develop a methodology to prove non–interference of deterministic terminating programs in an imperative language with loops, conditionals, and mutable data structures (i.e. objects). Their methodology relyies on using Hoare logic and separation logic, and handles non–interference as a safety property by using program self–composition with variable renaming (i.e., they compose a program with a copy of itself without sharing memory positions). Their method can verify non–interference of secure programs with temporary breaches such as "`low` = `high`; `low` = 2", whereas imprecise conservative type systems [22,26,4] cannot. Also, their method can deal with Examples 4 and 7, whereas we cannot ensure security for the last example. This proposal is complete and sound, but the criterion is undecidable, and for the best of our knowledge no approximation has yet been implemented. Existing Java verification tools that use standard JML [17] as a property specification language do not support non–interference certification (see [2] for a further discussion). A flow-sensitive and termination-insensitive analysis for object-oriented programs based on Hoare logic is proposed in Amtoft et. al [3]. This analysis considers pointer aliasing that can leak confidential information. The non–interference property is specified by using independence assertions that are written in JML. In order to compute postconditions, the analysis uses an algorithm that is sound and complete given some assumptions, but it does not generate a program security proof.

Although non–interference has not been considered in current PCC implementations, there are some proposals that are based on type systems (see [2] for some key references). However, none of these use JML to express non–interference policies and none of them have yet been implemented. In [16], Hunt and Sands propose a flow sensitive, dynamic type system that has not yet been implemented. It tracks syntactical dependences between program variables in a simple imperative language without objects or function calls [16]. Moreover, we have shown that our analysis can achieve more precision than traditional, type-based approaches, thanks to the combination of static analysis and dynamic labeling. Wasserrab et. al present in [24] the first machine-checked correctness proof for information-flow control that is based on program dependence graphs using static intraprocedural slicing. The proof is formalized in Isabelle/HOL. The analysis applies to deterministic terminating programs and is flow-sensitive, object-sensitive and context-sensitive. The machine-checked proof was instantiated for a simple imperative language with loops and for a subset of Jinja (a definition of Java bytecode), which must be manually annotated with security labels. This work does not consider method calls, classes, or objects. Bavera and Bonelli [6] present a flow-sensitive type system for verifying non–interference of bytecode, where class fields may have different confidentality labels for different instance objects. This methodology does not consider method calls and it does not generate checkable proofs. Moreover, as is usually the case in type-based analysis, once the object fields and the variable labels are determined, they remain fixed throughout the analysis. A proposal that deals with dynamic information-flow policies is [21]. This technique is based on runtime tracking of indirect dependencies between program points. While our confidentiality label tracking is also dynamic, our approach is based on static analysis rather than runtime monitoring, similarly to [16,23].

Some proposals also exist for non–interference verification that are based on abstract interpretation (see [26,25] and [2] for further references). However, these proposals do not generate a certificate as an outcome of the verification process, and they do not use JML to express non–interference policies. The idea of first enriching the original semantics of the language by pairing each data value to its security level, and then approximating it by only considering the security level was also proposed in [4,26]. By using classes and class hierachies as abstract domains, Zanardini adopts a different perspective of abstract non–interference for classes in [25], where the abstract value of a concrete object is its class. Two objects (values) are indistinguishable at an abstraction level (class) if the objects belong to the given class or if the given class is a superclass of object classes. An algorithm for checking abstract non–interference of Java classes is proposed that relies on class–based dependencies.

In previous work [2], we dealt with (local) non–interference of function methods regarding explicit inputs by parameter passing and explicit outputs by value returning. The local non–interference policies considered there were required to explicitly establish the confidentiality labels for all method parameters and variables. In this work, however, we consider global non–interference of complete Java classes and we do not need to explicitly state the confidentiality level for all program variables. In [2], we worked directly with an implementation level definition of non–interference; in this work, we provide a general and language-independent characterization as well as a formal and rigorous relation between the approximate properties and the security model. As in [11,4,20,23,16], we take into account implicit information flows by considering the context confidentiality label in expression evaluation (the context label is joined with the confidentiality label of the expression) and also by modifying the context label during the evaluation of guards of conditionals and while loops. Our global policies are very flexible since the security levels of object variables, local variables, and method parameters may change temporarily as in [16,23,4,14,5].

8 Conclusion

In this paper, we formalize a framework for automatically certifying global non–interference of Java programs. Our methodology relies on an (abstract) extended semantics for Java written in rewriting logic that can be model–checked in Maude by using Maude's breadth-first search space exploration. In the extended semantics, non-interference becomes a safety property, and we formally demonstrate that the safety property in the extended semantics entails the semantic, non-interference security property in the standard Java semantics. In this work, we provide a general and abstract definition as well as a rigorous link between the approximate properties and the security model that we consider, whereas in our previous work [2], we worked directly with a program-level definition of non–interference. The proposed framework fully accounts for explicit as well as implicit flows, and allows not only the inference of rewriting logic safety proofs but also the checking of existing ones, thus providing support for proof-carrying code. Actually, the steps that the abstract semantics takes are recorded in order to construct a certificate ensuring that the program satisfies the desired property. By turning a potentially infinite labelled state space of a Java program into a finite abstract space, the abstract semantics not only makes the approach feasible, but also greatly reduces the size of the certificates that must be checked on the consumer's end.

The Java operational semantics in rewriting logic that we have used is modular and has 2635 lines of code in 4 files [12]. We have modified less than 20 of the

1527 lines of code in the main file of the original Java semantics. The abstract operational Java semantics was developed as a source–to–source transformation in rewriting logic and consists of 650 lines of extra code. This is equivalent to saying that, in our current system, the *trusted computing base* (TCB)[5] is less than a fourth of the size of the original Java semantics (at least one order of magnitude smaller than the standard rewriting infrastructure, and even much smaller than other PCC systems).

Since our approach is based on a rewriting logic semantics specification of the full Java 1.4 language [18], the methodology developed in this work can be easily extended to cope with exceptions, heaps, and multithreading since they are considered in the Java rewriting logic semantics.

References

1. Alba-Castro, M., Alpuente, M., Escobar, S.: Automatic certification of Java source code in rewriting logic. In: Leue, S., Merino, P. (eds.) FMICS 2007. LNCS, vol. 4916, pp. 200–217. Springer, Heidelberg (2008)
2. Alba-Castro, M., Alpuente, M., Escobar, S.: Automated certification of non-interference in rewriting logic. In: Cofer, D., Fantechi, A. (eds.) FMICS 2008. LNCS, vol. 5596, pp. 182–198. Springer, Heidelberg (2009)
3. Amtoft, T., Bandhakavi, S., Banerjee, A.: A logic for information flow in object-oriented programs. In: Conference record of the 33rd ACM SIGPLAN-SIGACT Symposium on Principles of Programming Languages, POPL 2006, pp. 91–102 (2006)
4. Barbuti, R., Bernardeschi, C., Francesco, N.D.: Abstract interpretation of operational semantics for secure information flow. Information Processing Letters 83(22), 101–108 (2002)
5. Barthe, G., D'Argenio, P., Rezk, T.: Secure information flow by self-composition. In: Proceedings of the 17th IEEE workshop on Computer Security Foundations, CSFW 2004, pp. 100–114 (2004)
6. Bavera, F., Bonelli, E.: Type-based information flow analysis for bytecode languages with variable object field policies. In: SAC 2008, pp. 347–351 (2008)
7. Clarkson, M.R., Schneider, F.B.: Hyperproperties. In: Proc. IEEE Computer Security Foundations Symposium, CSF 2008 (2008)
8. Clavel, M., Durán, F., Eker, S., Lincoln, P., Martí-Oliet, N., Meseguer, J., Talcott, C. (eds.): All About Maude - A High-Performance Logical Framework. LNCS, vol. 4350. Springer, Heidelberg (2007)
9. Cousot, P., Cousot, R.: Systematic Design of Program Analysis Frameworks. In: Proc. of Sixth ACM Symp. on Principles of Programming Languages, pp. 269–282 (1979)
10. Darvas, A., Hahnle, R., Sands, D.: A theorem proving approach to analysis of secure information flow. In: Hutter, D., Ullmann, M. (eds.) SPC 2005. LNCS, vol. 3450, pp. 193–209. Springer, Heidelberg (2005)
11. Denning, D.E., Denning, P.J.: Certification of programs for secure information flow. Commun. ACM 20(7), 504–513 (1977)

[5] The TCB is the part of the code that is used to check if other code can be safely run, and it is assumed to be trusted.

12. Farzan, A., Chen, F., Meseguer, J., Rosu, G.: JavaRL: The rewriting logic semantics of Java (2007), http://fsl.cs.uiuc.edu/index.php/Rewriting_Logic_Semantics_of_Java
13. Focardi, R., Gorrieri, R., Focardi, R., Gorrieri, R.: A classification of security properties for process algebras. Journal of Computer Security 3, 5–33 (1994)
14. Francesco, N.D., Martin, L.: Instruction-level security typing by abstract interpretation. International Journal of Information Security 6(2-3), 85–106 (2007)
15. Goguen, J.A., Meseguer, J.: Security policies and security models. In: IEEE Symposium on Research in Security and Privacy, pp. 11–20 (1982)
16. Hunt, S., Sands, D.: On flow-sensitive security types. In: Conference record of the 33rd ACM SIGPLAN-SIGACT Symposium on Principles Of Programming Languages, POPL 2006, pp. 79–90 (2006)
17. Leavens, G., Baker, A., Ruby, C.: Preliminary design of JML: A behavioral interface specification language for Java. ACM SIGSOFT Software Engineering Notes 31(3), 1–38 (2006)
18. Meseguer, J., Rosu, G.: The rewriting logic semantics project. Theoretical Computer Science 373(3), 213–237 (2007)
19. Necula, G.C.: Proof carrying code. In: Proceedings of the 24th ACM SIGPLAN-SIGACT Annual Symposium on Principles of Programming Languages POPL 1997, Paris, France, pp. 106–119 (1997)
20. Sabelfeld, A., Myers, A.: Language-based information-flow security. IEEE Journal on Selected Areas in Communications 21(1), 5–19 (2003)
21. Shroff, P., Smith, S., Thober, M.: Dynamic dependency monitoring to secure information flow. In: CSF 2007: Proceedings of the 20th IEEE Computer Security Foundations Symposium, pp. 203–217. IEEE Computer Society, Los Alamitos (2007)
22. Volpano, D., Smith, G., Irvine, C.: A sound type system for secure flow analysis. Computer Security 4(4), 167–187 (1996)
23. Warnier, M.: Language Based Security for Java and JML. PhD thesis, Radboud University Nijmegen (2005)
24. Wasserrab, D., Lohner, D., Snelting, G.: On pdg-based noninterference and its modular proof. In: Proceedings of the ACM SIGPLAN Fourth Workshop on Programming Languages and Analysis for Security (PLAS 2009), pp. 31–44 (2009)
25. Zanardini, D.: Analysing non–interference with respect to classes. In: Proc. 10th italian Conference on Theoretical Computer Science (ICTCS 2007), pp. 57–69 (2007)
26. Zanotti, M.: Security typings by abstract interpretation. In: Hermenegildo, M.V., Puebla, G. (eds.) SAS 2002. LNCS, vol. 2477, pp. 375–2002. Springer, Heidelberg (2002)

Interleaving Symbolic Execution and Partial Evaluation*

Richard Bubel, Reiner Hähnle, and Ran Ji

Department of Computer Science and Engineering
Chalmers University, 41296 Gothenburg, Sweden
{bubel,reiner,ran.ji}@chalmers.se

Abstract. Partial evaluation is a program specialization technique that allows to optimize programs for which partial input is known. We show that partial evaluation can be used with advantage to speed up as well symbolic execution of programs. Interestingly, the input required for partial evaluation comes from symbolic execution itself which makes it natural to interleave partial evaluation and symbolic execution steps in a software verification setup.

1 Introduction

Symbolic execution [1] and partial evaluation [2] both are generalizations of standard interpretation of programs, however, they generalize in different ways: while symbolic execution permits interpretation of a program with symbolic (i.e., unspecified) initial values, the aim of partial evaluation is to transform a program with partially specified input values into a (hopefully, more efficient) program that has only the unspecified arguments as input. For fully specified input arguments the result of both mechanisms is standard program interpretation.

In this paper we show that both technologies not only are compatible with each other, but that there is considerable potential for synergies. Specifically, we integrate a simple partial evaluator for a JAVA-like language into the logic-based symbolic execution engine of the software verification tool KeY [3]. This allows to interleave symbolic execution and partial evaluation steps within a uniform (logic-based) framework in a sound way. Intermittent partial evaluation during symbolic execution has the effect that the remaining program that is yet to be executed is continuously simplified relative to the current path conditions and the current symbolic state in each symbolic execution trace.

This paper is organized as follows: in the next section we introduce a small object-oriented programming language which is used for the formal definitions (the actual system is implemented for nearly full-fledged sequential JAVA); we also provide background on symbolic execution and partial evaluation. Sect. 3 defines the program logic and deduction system that we use as a framework for

* This work has been partially supported by the EU project FP7-ICT-2007-3 HATS *Highly Adaptable and Trustworthy Software using Formal Methods* and the EU COST Action IC0701 *Formal Verification of Object-Oriented Software.*

F.S. de Boer et al. (Eds.): FMCO 2009, LNCS 6286, pp. 125–146, 2010.

the integration. In Sect. 4 we introduce a version of a program specialization operator that is suitable for logic-based verification and we extend the symbolic execution calculus with sound rules that permit intermittent partial evaluation. In Sect. 5 we show the context in which the resulting calculus is applied, and in Sect. 6 we evaluate the integrated system using formal verification tasks for a number of JAVA programs. This is followed by a discussion of related work (Sect. 7). We stress that the particular combination of symbolic execution and partial evaluation explored in the present paper is by far not the only possible one. We sketch further possibilities in the final section on future work.

2 Background

2.1 A Simple Programming Language

The object-oriented programming language PL described in this section is basically a simplified JAVA variant and closely related to the language defined in [4]. We briefly sketch the differences to JAVA:

Unsupported Features. Multi-threading, graphics, dynamic class loading, generic types or floating point datatypes are *not* supported by PL nor by the actual implementation in the KeY tool. Formal specification and verification of these features is a topic of ongoing research, therefore, left out completely.

Restricted Features. For ease of presentation PL imposes some additional restrictions compared to JAVA. The KeY tool and the prototype implementation of our ideas evaluated in Sect. 6 do not impose these restrictions, but model and respect the JAVA semantics faithfully. The following restrictions apply to PL:

Inheritance and Polymorphism. For the sake of a simple semantics for dynamic dispatch of method invocations PL abstains from JAVA-like interfaces and method overloading. Likewise, with exception of the `Null` type, the type hierarchy induced by user-defined class types has a tree structure with class `Object` as root.
Prohibiting method overloading allows to identify a method within a class unambiguously by its name and number of parameters. We allow polymorphism (i.e. methods can be overwritten in subclasses) but require that their signature must be exactly the same, otherwise it is a compile-time error.

Visibility. All classes, methods and fields are publicly visible. This restriction contributes also to a simpler dynamic dispatch semantics.

No Exceptions. PL has no support for exceptions. Instead of runtime exceptions like `NullPointerExceptions` the program will simply not terminate in these cases.

No class/object Initialization. In JAVA the first active usage of a type or creation of a new instance triggers complex initialization. PL supports only instance creation, but does not initialize fields upon creation. In particular, PL does not support static or instance initializers. Constructors are also missing in PL, a new instance is simply created by the expression `new` $T()$.

Primitive Types. Only `boolean` and `int` are available. To keep the semantics of standard arithmetic operators simple, `int` is an unlimited datatype representing the whole numbers $\mathbb{Z}$ rather than a finite datatype with overflow.

A PL program `p` is a non-empty set of class declarations with at least one class of name `Object`. The class hierarchy is a tree with class `Object` as root. A class $Cl := (cname, scname_{opt}, fld, mtd)$ consists of (i) a classname *cname* unique in `p`, (ii) the name of its superclass *scname* (only omitted for $cname =$ `Object`), and (iii) a list of field *fld* and method *mtd* declarations.

The syntax for class declaration is the same as in JAVA. The only lacking features are constructors and static/instance initialization blocks. PL knows also the special reference type `Null` which is a singleton with `null` as the only element. It may be used in place of any reference type and is the only type that is a subtype of all class types.

To keep examples short we agree on the following convention: if not explicitly stated otherwise, any given sequence of statements is seen as if it would be the body of a static, void method declared in a class `Default` with no fields declared.

The syntax of the executable fragment needed for the purpose of this paper as follows:

```
Statements
stmnt ::= stmnt stmnt | lvarDecl | locExp '=' exp ';' | cond | loop
loop ::= while '(' exp ')' '{' stmnt '}'
lvarDecl ::= Type IDENT ( '=' exp)_opt ';'
cond ::= if '(' exp ')' '{' stmnt '}' else '{' stmnt '}'
Expressions
exp ::= (exp .)_opt mthdCall | opExp | locExp
mthdCall ::= mthdName '(' exp_opt (',' exp)* ')'
opExp ::= f (exp_opt (, exp)*) | ℤ | TRUE | FALSE | null
f ::= ! | - | < | <= | >= | > | == | & | | | * | / | % | + | -
Locations
locExp ::= IDENT | exp . IDENT
```

Dynamic dispatch works in PL as follows: we need to determine the implementation of a method on encountering a method invocation such as `o.m(a)`. To do so, first look up the dynamic type T of the object referenced by `o`. Then scan all classes between T and the static type of o for an implementation of a method named m and the correct number of parameters. The first match is taken.

2.2 Symbolic Execution

Symbolic execution is an idea from the 1960s [1], but it has only recently been realized efficiently for industrially relevant programming languages. Symbolic execution is a central, very versatile program analysis technique that is used for formal program verification [3,5,6], extended static checking and verification [7], debugging [8], and automatic test case generation [9,10].

In the last decade a number of efficient symbolic execution engines for real heap-based programming and intermediate languages were created including KeY (for JAVA, C, Creol, see [3]), KIV (for JAVA, see [11]), Bogor/Kiasan (for BIR, see [12]), Pex (for MSIL, see [9]), and VeriFast (for C, JAVA, see [13]).

In symbolic execution one permits either uninitialized program locations or, more generally, program locations that are initialized with symbolic expressions. The following PL program orders the values of x and y: after its execution x contains the maximum of x_0, y_0 and y their minimum.

```
int x = x0; int y = y0; int z = max(x,y);
if (x < z) {y = x; x = z;}
```

We use location-value pairs to represent states in symbolic execution. The expression $\{\mathtt{l}_1 := t_1 \,||\, \cdots \,||\, \mathtt{l}_n := t_n\}$ denotes a symbolic state in which each program location of the form $\mathtt{l}_i$ has the expression t_i as its symbolic value.

After symbolic execution of the first three statements of the program above we obtain the symbolic state $\mathcal{U} = \{\mathtt{x} := x_0 \,||\, \mathtt{y} := y_0 \,||\, \mathtt{z} := \max(x_0, y_0)\}$. Symbolic execution of the conditional splits the execution into two branches, because the value $x_0 < \max(x_0, y_0)$ of the guard expression is symbolic and cannot be reduced. The (negated) value of the guard becomes a *path condition* relative to which symbolic execution continues. Under the path condition $P_1 \equiv x_0 < \max(x_0, y_0)$ the body of the conditional is executed which results in the final symbolic state $\mathcal{U}' = \{\mathtt{x} := \max(x_0, y_0) \,||\, \mathtt{y} := x_0 \,||\, \mathtt{z} := \max(x_0, y_0)\}$. From P_1 and properties of max one can infer $\max(x_0, y_0) \doteq y_0$ which simplifies $\mathcal{U}'$ to $\{\mathtt{x} := y_0 \,||\, \mathtt{y} := x_0 \,||\, \mathtt{z} := y_0\}$. The other branch terminates immediately in state $\mathcal{U}$ under path condition $P_2 \equiv x_0 \geq \max(x_0, y_0)$ $(\equiv x_0 \doteq \max(x_0, y_0))$.

It is obvious already from this small example that simplification of intermediate states wrt first-order theories is essential for efficiency and to obtain intuitive results. Modern symbolic execution engines use SMT solvers [9,13] and also powerful built-in theorem provers [3,11] for this purpose.

The example suggests that a single state during symbolic execution of a program p consists of the following three components:

1. A program pointer to the next executable statement of the remaining statements in p that have to be executed.
2. A path condition P relative to which the remaining statements are executed.
3. A symbolic state $\mathcal{U}$ relative to which the remaining statements are executed.

Symbolic execution of a program is then arranged as a *symbolic execution tree* whose nodes are triples consisting of program pointer, path condition, and symbolic state.

In general it is not possible to symbolically execute a program fully, because unbounded loops give rise to infinitely many branches with differing symbolic path conditions. Loop invariants or induction are required to turn symbolic execution into a complete method for computing strongest post-states of programs.

2.3 Partial Evaluation

The ideas behind partial evaluation go back in time even further than those behind symbolic execution: Kleene's well-known s_{mn} theorem from 1943 states that for each computable function $f(\boldsymbol{x}, \boldsymbol{y})$ where $\boldsymbol{x} = x_1, \ldots, x_m$, $\boldsymbol{y} = y_1, \ldots, y_n$ there is an $m+1$-ary primitive recursive function s_n^m such that $\phi_{s_n^m(f,\boldsymbol{x})} = \lambda \boldsymbol{y}.f(\boldsymbol{x},\boldsymbol{y})$. Partial evaluation can be characterized as the research programme to prove Kleene's theorem under the following conditions:

1. $\phi_{s_n^m(f,\boldsymbol{x})}$ is supposed to run more efficiently than f.
2. f is a program from a non-trivial programming language, not merely a recursive function.
3. The construction of $\phi_{s_n^m(f,\boldsymbol{x})}$ is efficient, i.e., its runtime should be comparable to compilation of f-programs.

In contrast to symbolic execution the result of a partial evaluator is not the value of output variables, but another program. The known input (named $\boldsymbol{x}$ above) is also called *static input* while the general part $\boldsymbol{y}$ is called *dynamic input*. The partial evaluator or *program specializer* is often named `mix`. Fig. 1 gives a schematic overview of partial evaluation.

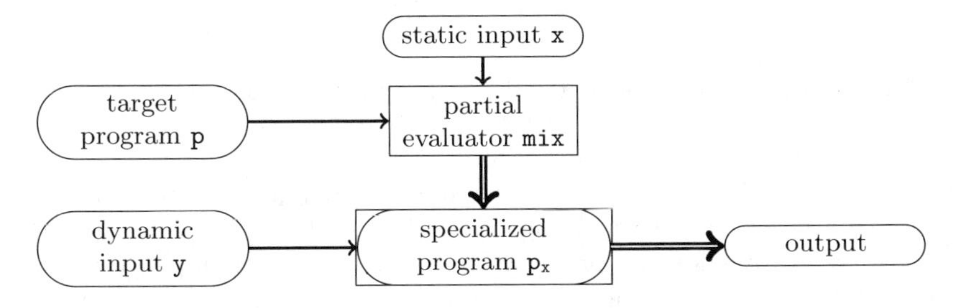

Fig. 1. Partial evaluation schema [2]

The first efforts in partial evaluation date from the mid 1960s and were targeted towards Lisp. Due to the rise in popularity of functional and logic programming languages the 1980s saw a large amount of research in partial evaluation of such languages. A seminal text on partial evaluation is the book by Jones et al. [2].

There has been relatively little research on partial evaluation of JAVA. The paper [14] summarizes the state-of-art until 2002 and discusses the JAVA specializer JSPEC which worked by cross-translation to C as an intermediate language. JSPEC seems to be no longer maintained. We found only one other (commercial) JAVA partial evaluator called JPE[1], but its capabilities and underlying theory is not documented.

The application context of partial evaluation is rather different from that of symbolic execution: in practice, partial evaluation is not only employed to boost the efficiency of individual programs, but often used in meta-applications such as parser/compiler generation.

We illustrate the main principles of partial evaluation by a small control circuit PL program depicted in Fig. 2 on the left. The program approximates the value of variable `y` to a given `threshold` with accuracy `eps` by repeatedly increasing or decreasing it as appropriate.

[1] `http://www.gradsoft.ua/products/jpe_eng.html`

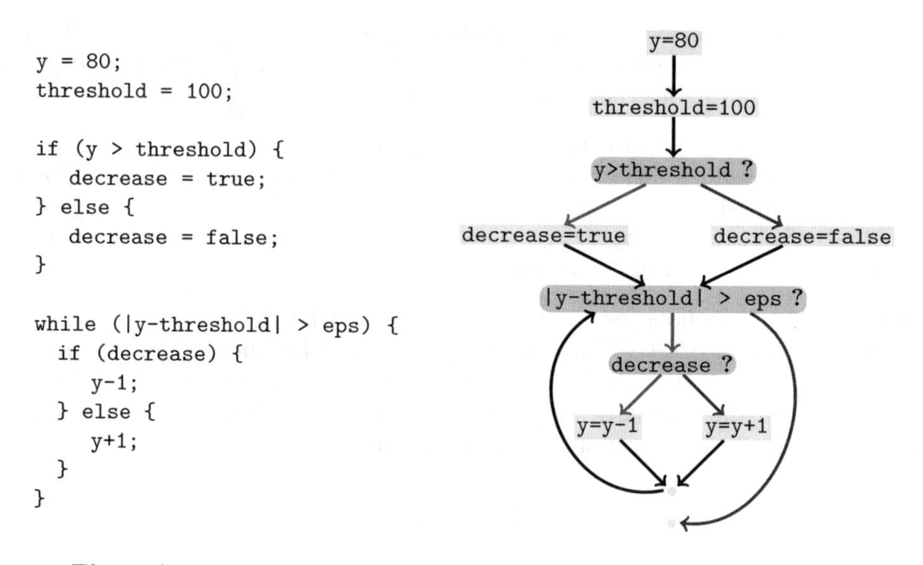
y = 80;
threshold = 100;
if (y > threshold) {
decrease = true;
} else {
decrease = false;
}
while (|y-threshold| > eps) {
if (decrease) {
y-1;
} else {
y+1;
}
}
y=80
threshold=100
y>threshold ?
decrease=true
decrease=false
|y-threshold| > eps ?
decrease ?
y=y-1
y=y+1

Fig. 2. A simple control circuit PL program and its control flow graph

We can imagine to walk a partial evaluator through the control flow graph (for the example on the right of Fig. 2) while maintaining a table of concrete (i.e., constant) values for the program locations. In the example, that table is empty at first. After processing the two initial assignments it contains $\mathcal{U} = \{\mathtt{y} := 80 \,||\, \mathtt{threshold} := 100\}$ (using the update notation of Section 2.2).

Whenever a new constant value becomes known, the partial evaluator attempts to propagate it throughout the current control flow graph (CFG). For the example, this *constant propagation* results in the CFG depicted in Fig. 3 on the left. Note that the occurrences of y that are part of the loop have *not* been replaced. The reason is that y might be updated in the loop so that these latter occurrences of y cannot be considered to be static. Likewise, the value of decrease after the first conditional is not static either. The check whether the value of a given program location can be considered to be static with respect to a given node in the CFG is called *binding time analysis* (BTA) in partial evaluation.

Partial evaluation of our example proceeds now until the guard of the first conditional. This guard became a *constant expression* which can be evaluated to false. As a consequence, one can perform *dead code elimination* on the left branch of the conditional. The result is depicted in Fig. 3 in the middle. Now the value of decrease is static and can be propagated into the loop (note that decrease is not changed inside the loop). After further dead code elimination, the final result of partial evaluation is the CFG on the right of Fig. 3.

Partial evaluators necessarily approximate the target programming language semantics, because they are supposed to run fast and automatic. In the presence of such programming language features as exceptions, inheritance with complex localization rules (as in JAVA), and aliasing (e.g., references, array entries) BTA becomes very complex [14].

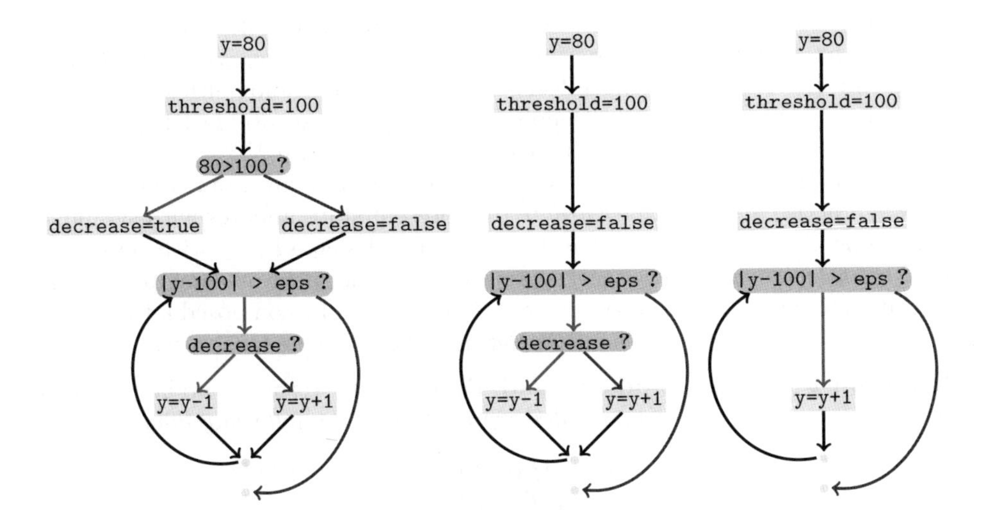

Fig. 3. Partial evaluation example

3 Dynamic Logic with Updates

3.1 Program Logic

As program logic for PL we use a sorted first-order dynamic logic instantiated by a given PL program p. We define formally the family of first-order dynamic logics DPL used to reason about PL programs. Each concrete instance of this family is associated to exactly one PL program which is then referred to as the *context program* or sometimes the *program context* of that logic.

Definition 1 (Signature). *For any* PL *program* p *a* DPL signature $\Sigma_{\mathtt{p}}$ *is defined as a tuple* (Types, FSym, PSym, VSym)*, where* Types *is a set of sort names that contains at least* $\{\top, \mathtt{boolean}, \mathtt{int}, \mathtt{Object}, \mathtt{Null}\} \cup classes(\mathtt{p})$*. Further,* FSym *is a set of function symbols,* PSym *a set of predicate symbols, and* VSym *a set of logic variable symbols (we omit the subscript* p *in* $\Sigma_{\mathtt{p}}$ *whenever it can be unambiguously derived from the context). Function, predicate, and logic variable symbols have a fixed sorted signature. Sorts are ordered wrt a sort hierarchy* $\preceq$*. The order* $\preceq$ *models* p*'s type hierarchy with maximum element* $\top$*.*

We distinguish between *rigid* and *non-rigid* function and predicate symbols. Intuitively, the semantics of rigid symbols does not depend on the current state of program execution while non-rigid symbols are state-dependent. (Local) program variables, arrays, static, and instance fields are modeled as non-rigid function symbols and together form a separate class of non-rigid symbols called *location* symbols. Specifically, local program variables and static fields are modeled as non-rigid constants, instance fields as unary non-rigid functions, and array access as a binary non-rigid function. For example, an instance field `size` of type `int` declared in a class `List` is modeled as a unary non-rigid function $size@List$: `List` $\rightarrow$ `int`. For terms representing field accesses, such as $size@List(head)$, we use the more readable short form $head.size$, if no ambiguities arise (and similar for array accesses). Π_Σ denotes the set of all executable PL programs (i.e., sequence of statements) with locations over signature Σ.

The inductive definition of terms and formulas is standard, but we introduce a new syntactic category called *update* to represent state updates with symbolic expressions. An *elementary update* has the general shape $l := t$ with terms l, t and l being a *location term* (i.e., a program variable, field or array access). It has the same semantics as an assignment. Updates can be composed into *parallel updates* $l_1 := t_1 \,||\, l_2 := t_2$ or *quantified updates* $\mathtt{for}\ T\ x;\ \phi;\ l(x) := t(x)$.

Definition 2 (Terms, Updates and Formulas). Terms t, updates u *and* formulas ϕ *are* well-sorted *first-order expressions of the following kind:*

$$
\begin{aligned}
t &:= x \mid f(t_1, \ldots, t_n) \mid if\,(\phi)\,then\,(t)\,else\,(t) \mid \{u\}t \\
u &:= l := t \mid u \,||\, u \mid \mathtt{for}\ T\ x;\ \phi;\ u \\
\phi &:= q(t_1, \ldots, t_n) \mid \neg\phi \mid \phi \circ \phi \ (\circ \in \{\wedge, \vee, \rightarrow, \leftrightarrow\} \mid \\
&\quad\ \{u\}t \mid \mathcal{Q}x; \phi \ (\mathcal{Q} \in \{\exists, \forall\}) \mid if\,(\phi)\,then\,(\phi)\,else\,(\phi) \\
&\quad\ [s]\phi \mid \langle s \rangle \phi \\
s &:= any\ element\ of\ \Pi_\Sigma
\end{aligned}
$$

The formula $[\mathtt{p}]\phi$ has the intuitive meaning that *if* the program `p` terminates *then* in its final state the formula ϕ must hold (*partial correctness*). The formula $\langle \mathtt{p} \rangle \phi$ means that `p` terminates *and* in its final state ϕ holds (*total correctness*).

All formulas, terms and updates are evaluated with respect to a DPL-Kripke structure whose states correspond to program states.

Definition 3 (DPL-Kripke structure). *A* DPL-*Kripke structure is a tuple* $\mathcal{K} = (D, I, \mathcal{S}, \rho)$ *where:*

- D *is a non-empty* domain *together with a domain function* $\delta : D \rightarrow \mathsf{Types}$ *mapping each domain element to its (*run-time*) type.*
  $D_T = \{d \in D \mid \delta(d) \preceq T\}$ *denotes the projection of* D *to elements of sort* T *or any subsort of* T*. We ensure* $D_T \neq \emptyset$*, for all* $T \in \mathsf{Types}$ *by setting* $D_{\mathtt{Null}} = \{\mathit{null}\}$, $D_{\mathtt{int}} = \mathbb{Z}$, $D_{\mathtt{boolean}} = \{true, false\}$.
- I *is an interpretation mapping each* rigid *function symbol* $f : T_1 \times \ldots \times T_n \rightarrow S$ *to a total function* $I(f) : D_{T_1} \times \ldots \times D_{T_n} \rightarrow D_S$ *and each* rigid *predicate symbol* $p : T_1 \times \ldots \times T_n$ *to a relation* $I(p) \subseteq D_{T_1} \times \ldots \times D_{T_n}$.
- $\mathcal{S}$ *is a set of* states*. Each state* $s \in \mathcal{S}$ *is an interpretation of the non-rigid function and predicate symbols.*
- $\rho : \Pi \times \mathcal{S} \times \mathcal{S}$ *is a* state transition relation *relating two states* s, t *by a program* `p` *iff* `p` *started in state* s *terminates in the final state* t*. Any set of final states* $\rho(\mathtt{p})(s)$ *is either a singleton set or empty as* PL *is deterministic.*

As usual in first-order logic, to define evaluation of terms and formulas in addition to a structure we need the notion of a *variable assignment.* This is a function $\beta : \mathsf{VSym} \rightarrow D$ assigning to logical variables a value in D. The evaluation function $val_{\mathcal{K},s,\beta}$ is then defined as usual and summarized in Fig. 4. Due to space

$$val_{\mathcal{K},s,\beta}(f(t_1,\ldots,t_n)) = I(f)(val_{\mathcal{K},s,\beta}(t_1),\ldots,val_{\mathcal{K},s,\beta}(t_1))$$
$$val_{\mathcal{K},s,\beta}(q(t_1,\ldots,t_n)) = tt \text{ iff } (val_{\mathcal{K},s,\beta}(t_1),\ldots,val_{\mathcal{K},s,\beta}(t_1)) \in I(q)$$
$$val_{\mathcal{K},s,\beta}(\phi \wedge \psi) = \begin{cases} tt, & \text{if } val_{\mathcal{K},s,\beta}(\phi) = tt \text{ and } val_{\mathcal{K},s,\beta}(\phi) = tt \\ ff, & otherwise. \end{cases}$$
$$\ldots$$
$$val_{\mathcal{K},s,\beta}([\mathtt{s}](\phi)) = \begin{cases} val_{\mathcal{K},s',\beta}(\phi), & \text{if } \exists\ s \in \mathcal{S} \text{ such that } \rho(p)(s,s') \\ tt, & otherwise \end{cases}$$

Fig. 4. Definition (excerpt) of evaluation function *val*

reasons we do not give a formal semantics of updates and refer to [3] for details on updates. Instead we explain the meaning intuitively along some examples:

- Elementary updates $\mathtt{i} := \mathtt{j}$ have exactly the same meaning as assignments: in a DPL-Kripke structure $\mathcal{K}$ and state s, an update application $\{\mathtt{i} := \mathtt{j}\}\ \xi$ on a term/formula ξ yields the same value as if evaluating ξ in $\mathcal{K}, s'$ where s' is identical to s except at $\mathtt{i}$ which is evaluated to $val_{\mathcal{K},s,\beta}(\mathtt{j})$ in s'.
- Parallel updates $u_1 \,||\, u_2$ are evaluated simultaneously and do not interfere with each other. Content swapping of two program variables can thus be expressed by $\mathtt{i} := \mathtt{j} \,||\, \mathtt{j} := \mathtt{i}$.
- Quantified updates $\mathtt{for}\ T\ x;\ \phi;\ u$ allow to update arbitrarily many locations simultaneously. The update "$\mathtt{for\ int}\ i;\ i \geq 0 \wedge i < a.length;\ a[i] := 0$", for example, assigns all array components the value 0.
- In case of parallel and quantified updates conflicts may arise when the same location is assigned different values as in $\mathtt{i} := \mathtt{0} \,||\, \mathtt{i} := \mathtt{1}$. Conflict resolution for parallel updates utilizes a last-wins semantics where the previous update is equivalent to $\mathtt{i} := \mathtt{1}$. Conflict resolution for quantified updates requires a well-founded order on T and the update with the smallest value for the quantified variable wins [3].

To summarize, updates are similar to explicit substitutions and allow to express state changes concisely at the syntactic level.

Definition 4 (Satisfiability and Validity). *A DPL-formula ϕ is*

- satisfiable *iff there exists a* DPL-*Kripke structure* $\mathcal{K} = (D, I, \mathcal{S}, \rho)$, *a state* $s \in \mathcal{S}$ *and a variable assignment* β *such that* $val_{D,I,s,\beta}(\phi) = tt$ *(or in short:* $\mathcal{K}, s, \beta \models \phi$*);*
- valid in a DPL-Kripke structure $\mathcal{K}$ *(we also say that* $\mathcal{K}$ *is a* model *for* ϕ *and write* $\mathcal{K} \models \phi$*) iff for all states* $s \in \mathcal{S}$ *and variable assignments* β *we have* $\mathcal{K}, s, \beta \models \phi$*;*
- logically valid *iff all* DPL-*Kripke structures* $\mathcal{K}$ *are models for* ϕ*.*

We introduce two notions which we will need later on. For technical reasons we must have the possibility to extend a logic's signature.

Definition 5 (Signature Extension). *Let* Σ, Σ' *denote two signatures.* Σ' *is called a* signature extension *of* Σ *if there is an embedding* $\sigma(\Sigma) \subset \Sigma'$ *that is unique up to isomorphism and enjoys the following properties:*

- $\sigma(\mathsf{Types}_\Sigma) = \mathsf{Types}_{\Sigma'}$
- $\sigma(\mathsf{FSym}_\Sigma) \subseteq \mathsf{FSym}_{\Sigma'}$ *where for any arity countably infinite additional function symbols exist (analogously for predicates and logic variables)*
- $\sigma(\Pi_\Sigma) \subseteq \Pi_{\Sigma'}$

An important property of signature extensions is the following:

Lemma 1. *Let $\Sigma' \supseteq \Sigma$ denote a signature extension in the sense of Def. 5. If a* DPL*-formula ϕ over Σ has a counter example, i.e., a* DPL*-Kripke structure $\mathcal{K}_\Sigma$, $s \in \mathcal{S}_\Sigma$ with $\mathcal{K}, s \not\models \phi$ then $\sigma(\mathcal{K}, s) \not\models \phi$. In words, signature extensions are counter example preserving.*

Finally, we define the notion of an *anonymizing update.* The motivation behind anonymizing updates is to erase knowledge about the values of the fields included in the set *mod* of locations that can be modified by a program. This is achieved by assigning fresh constant or function symbols to those locations. For example, the anonymizing update for the modifier set $mod_\Sigma = \{i, j\}$ is $i := c_i \,||\, j := c_j$ where c_i, c_j are constants freshly introduced in the extended signature Σ'.

Definition 6 (Anonymizing Update). *Let mod denote a set of terms built from location symbols in Σ. An* anonymizing update *for mod is an update $\mathcal{V}_{mod}$ over an extended signature Σ' assigning each location $l(t_1, \ldots, t_n) \in mod$ a term $f_l'(t_1, \ldots, t_n)$ where $f_l' \in \Sigma' \backslash \Sigma$.*

3.2 Sequent Calculus

The calculus for reasoning in DPL is a *sequent calculus.* A sequent is an expression of the form $\Gamma \Rightarrow \Delta$ with Γ, Δ being sets of DPL-formulas. We call Γ the *antecedent* and Δ the *succedent* of the sequent. A sequent has the same meaning as the formula

$$\bigwedge_{\phi \in \Gamma} \phi \rightarrow \bigvee_{\psi \in \Delta} \psi \ .$$

Sequent rules have the general form

$$\mathsf{name}\ \frac{s_1 \quad \cdots \quad s_n}{s}$$

where $s, s_1, \ldots, s_n$ are sequents. The sequents above the line are the rule's *premises* while sequent s is called the rule's *conclusion.* A sequent without any premises is an *axiom.*

A *sequent proof* is a tree whose nodes are labelled with sequents and with a sequent whose validity is to be proven at its root. This *proof tree* is constructed by applying sequent rules r to leaf nodes n whose sequent matches the conclusion r. The premises of r are then added as children of n. A branch of a proof tree is *closed* iff it contains an application of an axiom. A proof tree is closed iff all its branches are closed.

As usual, sequent rules are written in schematic form using schema variables (pattern variables with matching restrictions):

$$\mathsf{andLeft}\ \frac{\Gamma, \phi, \psi \Longrightarrow \Delta}{\Gamma, \phi \wedge \psi \Longrightarrow \Delta} \qquad \mathsf{close}\ \frac{*}{\Gamma, \phi \Longrightarrow \phi, \Delta}$$

Here, ϕ, ψ (Γ, Δ) are schema variables that can be instantiated with any formula (set of formulas). The sequent rule andLeft is applicable at any leaf sequent that contains a disjunctively connected formula in its antecedent.

To handle formulas containing programs within our sequent calculus we aim to model symbolic execution (see Sect. 2.2). Recall that a node in a symbolic execution tree contains a program pointer to the next active statement, path condition, and a symbolic state relative to which symbolic execution is executed. Accordingly, nearly all sequent rules for programs work on a *first active statement* `s` and a current *update* $\mathcal{U}$ in the following general form of a conclusion:

$$\Gamma \Longrightarrow \{\mathcal{U}\}[\pi\ \texttt{s;}\ \omega]\phi, \Delta$$

In addition, π stands for an inactive prefix containing labels, opening braces or method-frames (see below) and ω for the remaining program. Path conditions are represented by suitable formulas and accumulate in the antecedent Γ.

Symbolic execution in our DPL-calculus can be roughly organized into two phases. The first is the *rewriting phase* where the first active statement is replaced with an equivalent series of simpler statements. A typical rule is

$$\mathsf{evalIfGuard}\ \frac{\Gamma \Longrightarrow \{\mathcal{U}\}[\pi\ \texttt{boolean b = nse; if (b) \{s1\} else \{s2\}}\ \omega]\phi, \Delta}{\Gamma \Longrightarrow \{\mathcal{U}\}[\pi\ \texttt{if (nse) \{s1\} else \{s2\}}\ \omega]\phi, \Delta}$$

where `nse` is a schema variable matching any non-simple PL-expression (basically, an expression that is neither a literal nor a program variable). As these kind of rules are pure rewrite rules that can be applied in any possible syntactic context (antecedent, succedent, box, diamond) we use the short form $\xi \rightsquigarrow \xi'$ to express that a term/program ξ is replaced with an equivalent term/program ξ':

$$\texttt{if (nse) \{s1\} else \{s2\}} \rightsquigarrow \texttt{boolean b = nse; if (b) \{s1\} else \{s2\}}$$

After the first active statement has been reduced to an elementary statement it is translated into a first-order representation of its semantics with the help of rules belonging to the second phase. For instance, if the first active statement is a conditional whose guard is a simple expression (a program variable or a boolean literal) then the rule

$$\mathsf{ifElseSplit}\ \frac{\begin{array}{c}\Gamma, \{\mathcal{U}\}(b \doteq TRUE) \Longrightarrow \{\mathcal{U}\}[\pi\ \texttt{\{s1\}}\ \omega]\phi, \Delta \\ \Gamma, \{\mathcal{U}\}(b \doteq FALSE) \Longrightarrow \{\mathcal{U}\}[\pi\ \texttt{\{s2\}}\ \omega]\phi, \Delta\end{array}}{\Gamma \Longrightarrow \{\mathcal{U}\}[\pi\ \texttt{if (b) \{s1\} else \{s2\}}\ \omega]\phi, \Delta}$$

splits the current proof branch into two branches, one for the case when the guard evaluates to true, and the other covering the `else` case. Further important representatives of the rules in this phase are assignment rules like

$$\text{writeAttribute}\ \frac{\Gamma, \{\mathcal{U}\}\ \neg(\mathtt{o} \doteq \mathtt{null}) \Longrightarrow \{\mathcal{U}\}\{o.a := se\}[\pi\,\omega]\phi, \Delta}{\Gamma \Longrightarrow \{\mathcal{U}\}[\pi\ o.a = se;\ \omega]\phi, \Delta}$$

where o is a schema variable matching program variables, a matches fields and se matches simple expressions without side-effects that can be directly translated into a logic term. Fig. 5 shows a small excerpt of a sequent proof illustrating symbolic execution. Finally, we discuss how dynamic dispatch of a method is

$$\dfrac{\dfrac{\dfrac{\begin{matrix}\vdots & & \vdots\\ \Gamma, \{\mathcal{U}\}\ (\mathtt{b} \doteq \mathit{TRUE}) \Longrightarrow \{\mathcal{U}\}\ [\mathtt{s1}]\phi, \Delta & & \Gamma, \{\mathcal{U}\}\ (\mathtt{b} \doteq \mathit{FALSE}) \Longrightarrow \{\mathcal{U}\}\ [\mathtt{s2}]\phi, \Delta\end{matrix}}{\Gamma \Longrightarrow \{\mathcal{U}\}\ [\mathtt{if\ (b)\ then\ s1\ else\ s2;}]\phi, \Delta}}{\Gamma \Longrightarrow [\mathtt{boolean\ b\ =\ (i>=0);\ if\ (b)\ then\ s1\ else\ s2;}]\phi, \Delta}}{\Gamma \Longrightarrow [\mathtt{if\ (i>=0)\ then\ s1\ else\ s2;}]\phi, \Delta}$$

where $\mathcal{U}$ is the update $\mathtt{b} := \mathit{if}\ (\mathtt{i} \geq 0)\ \mathit{then}\ (\mathit{TRUE})\ \mathit{else}\ (\mathit{FALSE})$

Fig. 5. Excerpt of a proof demonstrating symbolic execution

realized in the calculus. The rule for method invocation translates a dynamic dispatch into a cascade of concrete method calls:

methodInvocation

$$\frac{\begin{array}{l}\Gamma, \{\mathcal{U}\}\ \neg(\mathtt{o} \doteq \mathtt{null}) \Longrightarrow \{\mathcal{U}\}[\pi\\ \qquad\qquad \mathtt{if\ (o\ instanceof}\ T_n\mathtt{)\ res=o.m(se)@}T_n;\\ \qquad\qquad \mathtt{else\ if\ (o\ instanceof}\ T_{n-1}\mathtt{)\ res=o.m(se)@}T_{n-1};\\ \qquad\qquad \ldots\\ \qquad\qquad \mathtt{else\ res=o.m(se)@}T_1;\\ \qquad\qquad \omega]\phi, \Delta\end{array}}{\Gamma \Longrightarrow \{\mathcal{U}\}\ [\pi\ \mathtt{res\ =\ o.m(se);}\ \omega]\phi, \Delta}$$

- `o`, `res` are schema variables for program variables.
- `res=o.m(se)@`T are so called *method-body* statements. A method-body statement is a place holder for an actual method body namely exactly the method body of method `m` with the specified number of parameters as implemented in class T.
- $T_1, \ldots, T_n$ are all the subtypes of the static type of the program variable against which o is matched and that contain an actual implementation of the method `m`. As the most specific implementation has to be taken, the list $T_1, \ldots, T_n$ fulfills the condition that for all $0 < i < j \leq n : T_i \not\preceq T_j$.

4 Interleaving Symbolic Execution and Partial Evaluation

4.1 General Idea

Recall from Section 2.2 that a symbolic execution tree unwinds a program's control flow graph (CFG). As a consequence, identical code is (symbolically) executed in many branches, however, under differing path conditions and symbolic states. Merging back different nodes is usually not possible without approximation or abstraction [15,16].

The hope with employing partial evaluation is that it is possible to factor out common parts of computations in different branches by evaluating them partially *before* symbolic execution takes place. The naïve approach, however, to *first* evaluate partially and *then* perform symbolic execution fails miserably. The reason is that for partial evaluation to work well the input space dimension of a program must be significantly reducible by identifying certain input variables to have static values.

Typical usage scenarios for symbolic execution like program verification are not of this kind. For example, in the program of Fig. 2 in Sect. 2.3 it is unrealistic to classify the value of y as static. If we redo the example without the initial assignment y=80 then partial evaluation can only perform one trivial constant propagation. The fact that input values for variables are not required to be static can even be considered to be one of the main advantages of symbolic execution and is the source of its generality: it is possible to cover all finite execution paths simultaneously and one can start execution at any given source code position without the need for initialization code.

The central observation that makes partial evaluation work in this context is that *during* symbolic execution static values are accumulated continuously as path conditions added to the current symbolic execution path. This suggests to perform partial evaluation *interleaved* with symbolic execution.

To be specific, we reconsider the example shown in Fig. 2, but we remove the first statement assigning the static value 80 to y. As observed above, no noteworthy simplification of the program's CFG can be achieved by partial evaluation any longer. The structure of the CFG after partial evaluation remains exactly

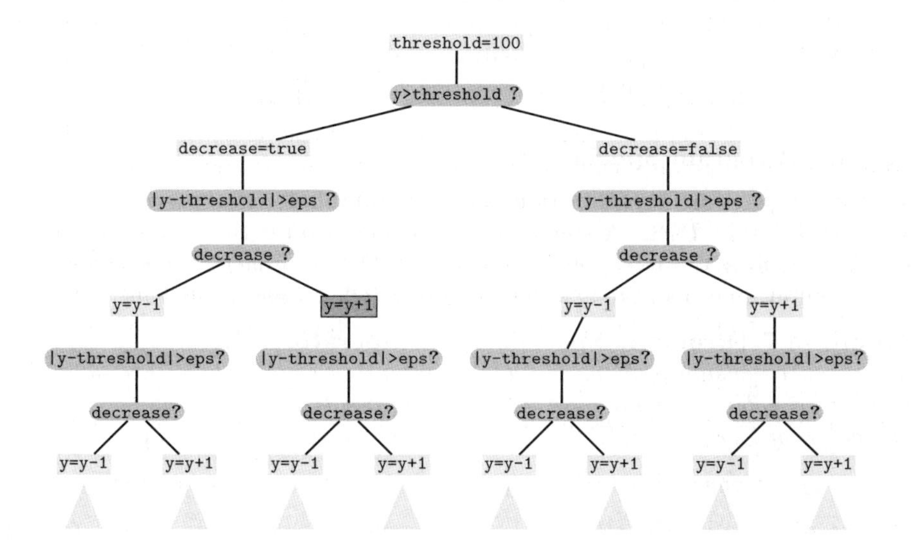

Fig. 6. Symbolic execution tree of the control circuit program

the same and only the occurrences of variable `threshold` are replaced by the constant value `100`. If we perform symbolic execution on this program, then the resulting execution tree spanned by two executions of the loop is shown in Fig. 6. The first conditional divides the execution tree in two subtrees. The left subtree deals with the case that the value of `y` is too high and needs to be decreased. The right subtree with the complementary case.

All subsequent branches result from either the loop condition (omitted in Fig. 6) or the conditional expression inside the loop body testing the value of `decrease`. As `decrease` is not modified within the loop, some of these branches are infeasible. For example the branch below the boxed occurrence of `y=y+1` (filled in red) is infeasible, because the value of `decrease` is true in that branch. Symbolic execution will not continue on these branches (at least for simple cases like that), but abandon them as infeasible by *proving* that the path condition is contradictory. Since the value of `decrease` is only tested *inside* the loop, however, the loop must still be first unwound and the proof that the current path condition is contradictory must be repeated. Partial evaluation can replace this potentially expensive proof search by *computation* which is drastically cheaper.

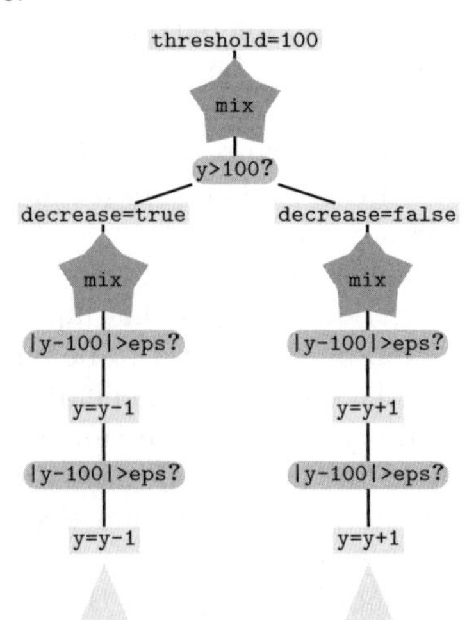

Fig. 7. Symbolic execution with interleaved partial evaluation

In the example, specializing the remaining program in each of the two subtrees after the first assignment to `decrease` eliminates the inner-loop conditional, see Fig. 7 (the partial evaluation steps are labelled with `mix`). Hence, interleaving symbolic execution and partial evaluation promises to achieve a significant speed-up by removing redundancy from subsequent symbolic execution.

4.2 The Program Specialization Operator

We define a program specialization operator suitable for interleaving with symbolic execution in DPL. A soundness condition ensures that the operator can be safely integrated into the sequent calculus. This approach avoids to formalize the partial evaluator in DPL which would be tedious and inefficient.

Definition 7 (Program Specialization Operator). *Let Σ be a signature and Σ' an extension of Σ as in Def. 5 containing countably infinite additional program variables and function symbols for any type and arity. Let σ be the embedding of Σ in Σ' ($\sigma(\Sigma) \subseteq \Sigma'$). The* program specialization operator

$$\downarrow_{\Sigma' \supseteq \Sigma}: ProgramElement \times Updates_{\Sigma'} \times For_{\Sigma'} \to ProgramElement$$

takes as arguments a PL*-statement (-expression), an update and a* DPL*-formula and maps these to a* PL*-statement (-expression), where all arguments and the result are over Σ'.*

The intention behind the above definition is that $\texttt{p} \downarrow_{\Sigma' \supseteq \Sigma} (\mathcal{U}, \varphi)$ denotes a "simpler" but semantically equivalent version of p under the assumption that both are executed in a state coinciding with $\mathcal{U}$ and satisfying φ. The signature extension allows the specialization operator to introduce new temporary variables or function symbols.

A program specialization operator is *sound* iff for all DPL-formulas $\psi \in For_\Sigma$, DPL-Kripke structures $\mathcal{K}_{\Sigma'}$, and states $s \in \mathcal{S}_{\Sigma'}$

$$\mathcal{K}_{\Sigma'}, s \models \langle (\texttt{p}) \downarrow_{\Sigma' \supseteq \Sigma} (\mathcal{U}, \varphi) \rangle \psi \Rightarrow \mathcal{K}_{\Sigma'}, s \models \mathcal{U}(\varphi \rightarrow \langle \texttt{p} \rangle \psi) \ .$$

In words, the specialized program $\texttt{p} \downarrow_{\Sigma' \supseteq \Sigma} (\mathcal{U}, \varphi)$ must be able to reach at least the same post-states as the original program p when started in a state coinciding with $\mathcal{U}$ in which (path condition) φ holds.

Interleaving partial evaluation and symbolic execution is achieved by introduction rules for the specialization operator. The simplest possibility is:

$$\textsf{introPE} \ \frac{\Gamma \Longrightarrow \{\mathcal{U}\} \, [(\texttt{p}) \downarrow (\mathcal{U}, true)]\phi, \Delta}{\Gamma \Longrightarrow \{\mathcal{U}\} \, [\texttt{p}]\phi, \Delta}$$

4.3 Specific Specialization Actions

We instantiate the generic program specialization operator of Def. 7 with some possible actions. In each case we derive soundness conditions.

Specialization Operator Propagation. The specialization operator needs to be propagated along the program as most of the different specialization operations work locally on single statements or expressions. During propagation of the operator, its knowledge base, the pair $(\mathcal{U}, \phi)$, needs to be updated by additional knowledge learned from executed statements or by erasing invalid knowledge about variables altered by the previous statement. Propagation of the specialization operator as well as updating the knowledge base is realized by the following rewrite rule

$$(\texttt{p;q}) \downarrow (\mathcal{U}, \phi) \quad \rightsquigarrow \quad \texttt{p} \downarrow (\mathcal{U}, \phi)\texttt{;}\ \texttt{q} \downarrow (\mathcal{U}', \phi')$$

This rule is unsound for arbitrarily chosen $\mathcal{U}'$, ϕ'. Soundness is ensured under a number of restrictions:

1. Let *mod* denote the set of all program locations possibly changed by p. Then we require that the DPL-formula "$\{\mathcal{U}\}$ respectStrongModifies(p, *mod*)" is valid where the predicate respectStrongModifies abbreviates a formula that is valid iff p changes at most locations included in *mod*. "Strong" means that *mod* must contain even locations whose values are only changed temporarily. Such a formula is expressible in DPL, see [17] for details.
2. Let $\mathcal{V}_{mod}$ be the anonymizing update for *mod* (Def. 6). By fixing $\mathcal{U}' := \mathcal{U}\mathcal{V}_{mod}$ we ensure that the program state reached by executing p is covered by at least one interpretation and variable assignment over the extended signature[2].

[2] It is sufficient to let $\mathcal{U}'$ be any update more general than $\mathcal{U}\mathcal{V}_{mod}$.

3. ϕ' must be chosen in such a way that if $\mathcal{K}_\Sigma \models \{\mathcal{U}\}\langle \mathtt{p} \rangle \phi$ then there exists also an extended DPL-Kripke structure $\mathcal{K}_{\Sigma'}$ over an extended signature Σ' such that $\mathcal{K}_{\Sigma'} \models \{\mathcal{U}'\}\phi'$. This ensures that the post condition of p is correctly represented by ϕ'. One possible heuristic to obtain ϕ' consists of symbolic execution of p and applying the resulting update to ϕ. This yields a formula ϕ'' from which we obtain a candidate for ϕ' by "anonymizing" all occurrences of locations in it that occur in *mod*.

The first two soundness conditions can be expressed in DPL, the third one only in absence of quantified updates. In the latter case, the necessary proofs could be added as additional nodes that spawn side proofs. A more efficient (and generally necessary) approach is to show once and for all that the oracle used to determine *mod* and ϕ' is correct wrt the conditions.

Constant propagation and constant expression evaluation. Constant propagation is one of the most basic operations in partial evaluation and often a prerequisite for more complex rewrite operations. Constant propagation entails that if the value of a variable v is known to have a constant value c within a certain program region (typically, until the variable is potentially reassigned) then usages of v can be replaced by c. The rewrite rule

$$(v)\!\downarrow(\mathcal{U}, \varphi) \rightsquigarrow c$$

models the replacement operation. To ensure soundness the rather obvious condition $\mathcal{U}(\varphi \rightarrow v \doteq c)$ has to be proved where c is a rigid constant. The above rule can be easily modified to include constant expression evaluation.

Dead-Code Elimination. Constant propagation and constant expression evaluation result often in specializations where the guard of a conditional (or loop) becomes constant. In this case, unreachable code in the current state and path condition can be easily located and pruned. A typical example for a specialization operation eliminating an infeasible symbolic execution branch is the rule

$$(\mathtt{if\ (b)\ \{p\}\ else\ \{q\}}) \downarrow (\mathcal{U}, \phi) \qquad \rightsquigarrow \qquad \mathtt{p} \downarrow (\mathcal{U}, \phi)$$

which eliminates the else branch of a conditional if the guard can be proved true. The soundness condition of the rule is straightforward and self-explaining: $\mathcal{U}(\phi \rightarrow \mathtt{b} \doteq \mathtt{TRUE})$.

Safe Field Access. Partial evaluation can be used to mark expressions as safe that contain field accesses or casts that may otherwise cause non-termination. We use the notation @(e) to mark an expression e as safe, for example, if we can ensure that $\mathtt{o} \neq \mathtt{null}$, then we can derive the annotation @(o.a) for any field a in the type of o. The advantage of safe annotations is that symbolic execution can assume that safe expressions terminate normally and needs not to spawn side proofs that ensure it. The rewrite rule for safe field accesses is

$$\mathtt{o.a} \downarrow (\mathcal{U}, \phi) \quad \rightsquigarrow \quad \mathtt{@(o.a)} \downarrow (\mathcal{U}, \phi) \ .$$

Its soundness condition is $\mathcal{U}(\phi \rightarrow \neg(\mathtt{o} \doteq \mathtt{null}))$.

Type Inference. For deep type hierarchies dynamic dispatch of method invocations may cause serious performance issues in symbolic execution, because a long cascade of method calls is created by the method invocation rule (Sect. 3.2, p. 136). To reduce the number of implementation candidates we use information from preceding symbolic execution to narrow the static type of the callee as far as possible and to (safely) cast the reference to that type. The method invocation rule can then determine the implementation candidates more precisely:

$$res = o.m(a_1, \ldots, a_n); \downarrow (\mathcal{U}, \phi) \quad \rightsquigarrow$$
$$res = @((C)o \downarrow (\mathcal{U}, \phi)).m(a_1 \downarrow (\mathcal{U}, \phi), \ldots, a_n \downarrow (\mathcal{U}, \phi));$$

The accompanying soundness condition $\mathcal{U}(\phi \rightarrow \exists\ \mathtt{C}\ x; (\mathtt{o} \doteq x))$ ensures that the type of o is compatible with C in any state specified by $\mathcal{U}$, ϕ.

5 Application

As an application of interleaving symbolic execution and partial evaluation, consider the verification of a GUI library. It includes standard visual elements such as `Window`, `Icon`, `Menu` and `Pointer`. An element has different implementations for different platforms or operating systems. Consider the following program snippet involving dynamic method dispatch:

```
framework.ui.Button button = radiobuttonX11;
button.paint();
```

The element `Button` is implemented in one way for Max OS X, while it is implemented in a different way for the X Window System. The method `paint()` is defined in `Button` which is extended by `CheckBox`, `Component`, and `Dialog`. Altogether, `paint()` is implemented in 16 different classes including `ButtonX11`, `ButtonMPC`, `RadioButtonX11`, `MenuItemX11`, etc. The complete type hierarchy is shown in Fig. 8. In the code above `button` is assigned an object with type `RadioButtonX11` which implements `paint()`. As a consequence, it should always terminate and the DPL-formula $\langle \mathtt{gui} \rangle \mathit{true}$ should be provable where `gui` abbreviates the code above.

First, we employ symbolic execution alone to do the proof. During this process, `button.paint()` is unfolded into 16 different cases by the method invocation rule (Sect. 3.2, p. 136), each corresponding to a possible implementation of `button`

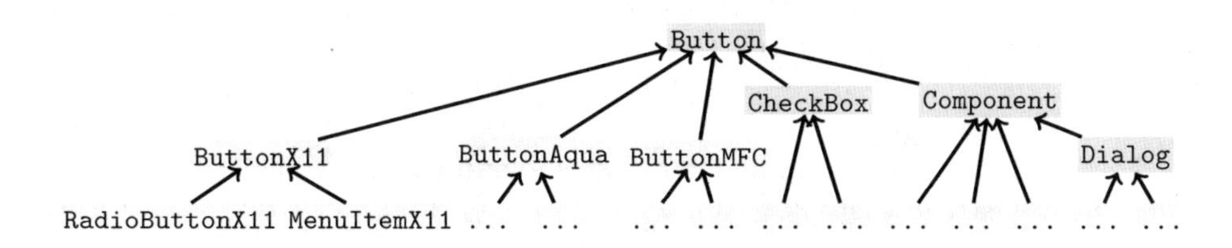

Fig. 8. Type hierarchy for the GUI example

in one of the subclasses of `Button`. The proof is constructed automatically in KeY with 161 nodes and 10 branches in the proof tree.

In a second experiment, we interleave symbolic execution and partial evaluation to prove the same claim. The partial evaluator propagates with the help of the *Type Inference* rule in the previous section the information that the runtime type of `button` is `RadioButtonX11` and the only possible implementation of `button.paint()` is `RadioButtonX11.paint()`. All other possible implementations are pruned. Only 24 nodes and 2 branches occur in the proof tree when running KeY integrated with a partial evaluator.

6 Evaluation

We implemented a simple partial evaluator for JAVA and interleaved it with symbolic execution in the KeY system as described above. We formally verified a number of JAVA programs with KeY with and without partial evaluation.

Table 1 shows the experimental results for a number of small JAVA programs which can be found in the KeY distribution. The column "Program" shows the name of the program we prove, the column "Strategy" shows the strategy we choose to perform the proof where "SE" means symbolic execution and "SE+PE" means interleaving symbolic execution and partial evaluation; the column "#Nodes" shows the total number of nodes in the proof; the column "#Branches" shows the total number of branches in the proof. The results show that interleaving symbolic execution with partial evaluation significantly speeds up the proof for `complexEval`, `constantPropagation`, `dynamicDispatch`, `safeAccess`, and `safeTypeCast` which can all be considered to be amenable for partial evaluation. Table 2 shows the experimental results of verifying a larger and more realistic JAVA e-banking application used in [3, Ch. 10]. The column "Proof Obligation" shows which property we prove; the remaining columns are as in Table 1. The results show that symbolic execution interleaved with partial evaluation can speed up verification proofs even for larger applications. As is

Table 1. Symbolic execution and partial evaluation for small JAVA programs

Program	Strategy	#Nodes	#Branches
`complexEval`	SE	261	15
	SE+PE	158	3
`constantPropagation`	SE	65	1
	SE+PE	56	1
`dynamicDispatch`	SE	161	10
	SE+PE	24	2
`methodCall`	SE	113	4
	SE+PE	108	3
`safeAccess`	SE	28	4
	SE+PE	24	3
`safeTypeCast`	SE	73	5
	SE+PE	45	3

Table 2. Symbolic execution and partial evaluation for an e-banking application

Proof Obligation	Strategy	#Nodes	#Branches
`ATM.insertCard (EnsuresPost)`	SE	949	20
	SE+PE	805	13
`ATM.insertCard (PreservesInv)`	SE	2648	89
	SE+PE	2501	79
`ATM.enterPIN (EnsuresPost)`	SE	661	7
	SE+PE	654	8
`ATM.enterPIN (PreservesInv)`	SE	1524	45
	SE+PE	1501	44
`ATM.confiscateCard (EnsuresPost)`	SE	260	2
	SE+PE	255	2
`ATM.confiscateCard (PreservesInv)`	SE	739	19
	SE+PE	695	19
`ATM.accountBalance (EnsuresPost)`	SE	1337	35
	SE+PE	1271	29
`ATM.accountBalance (PreservesInv)`	SE	2233	57
	SE+PE	2223	59
`Account.checkAndWithdraw (EnsuresPost)`	SE	16174	136
	SE+PE	17023	135
`Account.checkAndWithdraw (PreservesInv)`	SE	14076	89
	SE+PE	10478	78

to be expected, depending on the structure of the program the benefit varies. It is noteworthy that none of the programs and proof obligations used in the present section have been changed in order to make them more amenable to partial evaluation. In no case we have to pay a significant performance penalty which seems to indicate that partial evaluation is a generally useful technology for symbolic execution and should generally be applied.

The case study in Sect. 5 suggests that it could pay off to take partial evaluation into account when designing programs, specifications, and proof obligations.

7 Related Work

Partial evaluation as a technique has been applied in a variety of areas including program optimization, compiler generation and meta-compilation. Partial evaluation has been applied successfully in logic programming [18] as well as for imperative and object-oriented languages like C [19] and JAVA [14]. A good overview including many references is given in [2]. As far as we know, the present paper is the first application of partial evaluation in formal verification.

Our approach is also related to supercompilation [20]. Supercompilation goes beyond partial evaluation by being able not only to specialize but also to generalize a program to achieve a functionally equivalent but better performing program even in the absence of static input.

Partial evaluation is used in [21] to generate test cases and test case generators for given target programs. Instead of using a dedicated symbolic execution engine, they use partial evaluation to obtain an executable version of the implementation under test in the language CLP. CLP programs can then be executed on symbolic values returning a set of constraints on those input values. Partial evaluation is used as an approximation and replacement for a fully precise symbolic execution engine while we are interested in using partial evaluation to speed up symbolic execution in a dedicated symbolic execution engine.

There is a close relationship between the rule for specialization operator propagation (SOP) in Sect. 4.3 and what is known as *binding time analysis* (BTA) in partial evaluation. Partial evaluation techniques roughly categorize program variables into those which are known to have a constant value independent from any input and those whose value may vary. BTA in partial evaluation determines to which of these categories a variable belongs to. The precision of the analysis has a significant impact on the power of partial evaluation as too early binding prevents certain optimizations. The modifier set *mod* in the SOP rule influences directly the precision of the BTA performed by our specialization operator. If the oracle determining *mod* is too conservative (imprecise) too much knowledge of the current state $\mathcal{U}$ will be lost and cannot be utilized in later specializations.

8 Conclusions and Future Work

In this paper we concentrated on deductive program verification as the main application scenario, however, as pointed out in Sect. 2.2, symbolic execution has other important usages, such as automatic test case generation [10,9]. It would be interesting to investigate whether partial evaluation can lead to a reduction of redundant test cases.

We showed that a fairly naïve partial evaluator can be used to boost performance of a symbolic execution engine. In Sect. 7 we pointed out that symbolic execution in connection with assignable-clauses amounts to a relatively precise binding time analysis (BTA). As BTA becomes rather tricky for complex languages such as JAVA, it would be interesting to use symbolic execution and our simple partial evaluator to bootstrap a sophisticated partial evaluator for JAVA. It could also be interesting to use symbolic execution in addition to partial evaluation to improve precision, for example, in the test case generation approach of [21] discussed in the previous section.

The example in Sect. 5 shows that interleaving partial evaluation and symbolic execution has potential for speed-up especially for programs that are written generically. This is the case for two software development paradigms that gained much popularity in recent times: *model-driven development* (MDD) and *software product line* (SWPL) engineering. In both cases, development takes place as much as possible on a generic level: in MDD programs are modelled in abstract notations (the Platform Independent Model) and code generation is used to derive Platform-Specific Models and actual code; in SWPL one separates Domain Engineering which includes feature modeling and library development from Application Engineering where code is derived via instantiation and composition.

In either case the executable code has been derived from generic artefacts and, therefore, verification is likely to benefit from the ability to partially evaluate specific information. We are currently experimenting with an SWPL scenario where we plan to use interleaved partial evaluation and symbolic execution.

References

1. King, J.C.: A program verifier. PhD thesis, Carnegie-Mellon University (1969)
2. Jones, N.D., Gomard, C.K., Sestoft, P.: Partial evaluation and automatic program generation. Prentice-Hall, Englewood Cliffs (1993)
3. Beckert, B., Hähnle, R., Schmitt, P. (eds.): Verification of Object-Oriented Software: The KeY Approach. LNCS, vol. 4334. Springer, Heidelberg (2006)
4. Beckert, B., Platzer, A.: Dynamic logic with non-rigid functions: A basis for object-oriented program verification. In: Furbach, U., Shankar, N. (eds.) IJCAR 2006. LNCS (LNAI), vol. 4130, pp. 266–280. Springer, Heidelberg (2006)
5. Heisel, M., Reif, W., Stephan, W.: Program verification by symbolic execution and induction. In: Knuth, E., Neuhold, E.J. (eds.) Operating Systems 1982. LNCS, vol. 152, Springer, Heidelberg (1985)
6. Pasareanu, C.S., Visser, W.: Verification of Java programs using symbolic execution and invariant generation. In: Graf, S., Mounier, L. (eds.) SPIN 2004. LNCS, vol. 2989, pp. 164–181. Springer, Heidelberg (2004)
7. Barnett, M., Leino, K.R.M., Schulte, W.: The Spec# programming system: an overview. In: Barthe, G., Burdy, L., Huisman, M., Lanet, J.-L., Muntean, T. (eds.) CASSIS 2004. LNCS, vol. 3362, pp. 49–69. Springer, Heidelberg (2005)
8. Baum, M.: Debugging by visualizing of symbolic execution. Master's thesis, Dept.of Computer Science, Institute for Theoretical Computer Science (June 2007)
9. de Halleux, J., Tillmann, N.: Parameterized unit testing with Pex. In: Beckert, B., Hähnle, R. (eds.) TAP 2008. LNCS, vol. 4966, pp. 171–181. Springer, Heidelberg (2008)
10. Engel, C., Hähnle, R.: Generating unit tests from formal proofs. In: Gurevich, Y., Meyer, B. (eds.) TAP 2007. LNCS, vol. 4454, pp. 169–188. Springer, Heidelberg (2007)
11. Stenzel, K.: A formally verified calculus for full Java Card. In: Rattray, C., Maharaj, S., Shankland, C. (eds.) AMAST 2004. LNCS, vol. 3116, pp. 491–505. Springer, Heidelberg (2004)
12. Deng, X., Lee, J.: Robby: Bogor/Kiasan: a k-bounded symbolic execution for checking strong heap properties of open systems. In: Proc. 21st IEEE/ASM Intl. Conference on Automated Software Engineering, Tokyo, Japan, pp. 157–166. IEEE Computer Society, Los Alamitos (2006)
13. Jacobs, B., Piessens, F.: The VeriFast program verifier. Technical Report CW-520, Department of Computer Science, Katholieke Universiteit Leuven (August 2008)
14. Schultz, U.P., Lawall, J.L., Consel, C.: Automatic program specialization for java. ACM Transactions on Programming Languages and Systems 25 (2003)
15. Bubel, R., Hähnle, R., Weiss, B.: Abstract interpretation of symbolic execution with explicit state updates. In: de Boer, F.S., Bonsangue, M.M., Madelaine, E. (eds.) FMCO 2008. LNCS, vol. 5751, pp. 247–277. Springer, Heidelberg (2009)

16. Weiß, B.: Predicate abstraction in a program logic calculus. In: Leuschel, M., Wehrheim, H. (eds.) IFM 2009. LNCS, vol. 5423, pp. 136–150. Springer, Heidelberg (2009)
17. Engel, C., Roth, A., Schmitt, P.H., Weiß, B.: Verification of modifies clauses in dynamic logic with non-rigid functions. Technical Report 2009-9, Department of Computer Science, University of Karlsruhe (2009)
18. Sahlin, D.: Mixtus: an automatic partial evaluator for full prolog. New Gen. Comput. 12(1), 7–51 (1993)
19. Glenstrup, A.J., Makholm, H., Secher, J.P.: C-mix: Specialization of c programs. Partial Evaluation, 108–154 (1998)
20. Turchin, V.F.: The concept of a supercompiler. ACM Trans. Program. Lang. Syst. 8(3), 292–325 (1986)
21. Albert, E., Gomez-Zamalloa, M., Puebla, G.: PET: a partial evaluation-based test case generation tool for Java bytecode. In: ACM SIGPLAN WS on Partial Evaluation and Semantics-based Program Manipulation. ACM Press, New York (2010)

The Use of Model Transformation in the INESS Project

Osmar M. dos Santos, Jim Woodcock, Richard F. Paige, and Steve King

University of York
Department of Computer Science
York, UK
{osantos,jim,paige,king}@cs.york.ac.uk

Abstract. The INESS (INtegrated European Signalling System) Project is an effort, funded by the FP7 programme of the European Union, to provide a common, integrated, railway signalling system within Europe. It comprises 30 partners, including 6 railway companies. INESS experts have been using the Executable UML (xUML) language to model the proposed integrated signalling system. Because of the safety-critical aspects of these systems, one key idea is to use formal verification techniques to analyse the xUML models for inconsistencies in the requirements and against core properties provided by professional railway engineers. Our objective in the project is to equip our INESS partners with an automated tool to carry out this analysis. Therefore, we have devised a formal verification strategy that uses model transformation technology to automatically translate xUML models to the input language of existing, state-of-the-art, model checking tools. In this paper we describe this formal verification strategy in more detail: we present initial results on implementing the automatic generation of PROMELA models that can be analysed using the SPIN model checker.

1 Introduction

INESS (INtegrated European Signalling System) [8] is an industry-focused project funded by the FP7 programme of the European Union, comprising 30 partners, including 6 railway companies. The objective is to provide a common railway signalling system that integrates existing European ones. The motivation is cost effectiveness: there is increasing competition from other kinds of transport and from manufacturers outside Europe. The European Commission, which is committed to revitalise rail transport, sees as the main obstacle to further development the lack of infrastructure and interoperability between networks and systems. Signalling systems are perhaps the most significant part of the railway infrastructure: they are essential for the performance and the safety of train operations. Two of the objectives of INESS are to produce a common core of validated, standardised functional requirements for future interlockings, and to provide safety-verified test tools and techniques to enable the testing and commissioning of future signalling applications.

F.S. de Boer et al. (Eds.): FMCO 2009, LNCS 6286, pp. 147–165, 2010.

UML is the *de facto* language for modelling software systems in industry. In particular, one of its profiles, Executable UML (xUML) [19], augments a subset of UML with an action language that adds enough information to enable, amongst other features, creating objects, establishing references and performing operations. From the developer's viewpoint, this has the benefit of providing means to quickly prototype the system at the modelling level, which can then have its behaviour analysed, for instance by simulation.

INESS experts have been using xUML to model a specification of the proposed integrated signalling system. The idea is to use the specified xUML models to check for inconsistencies in the requirements and against core properties of the system provided by professional railway engineers. Currently, xUML models can be analysed only via simulation. Due to safety-critical requirements involved in railway signalling systems, using formal verification to analyse the model is of vital importance. Therefore, our task in the project, together with partners from the Universities of Eindhoven, Twente and Southampton is to equip railway experts with an automatic tool able to analyse the models formally.

Similar to most work found in the literature targeting the automatic verification of xUML models (*e.g.*, [28,9,27]), we have focused our research on generating code that can be used as input to a state-of-the-art model-checking tool. For this technique to succeed in the context of the INESS project, three challenges have to be faced:

1. The translation[1] of the xUML model to the input language of the model-checking tool has to be automatic.
2. The specification of verification properties has to be given in terms of the xUML model, and the translation of properties to the model-checking tool has to be automatic and transparent.
3. It must be possible to accurately trace back the results of the analysis from the model-checking tool (*i.e.*, success or a counter-example) to the abstraction level of the xUML model.

In order to tackle these challenges, we define a verification strategy that uses model transformation technology to automatically and transparently generate code from xUML models, which can then be used as input to model-checking tools. Model transformation technology provides a major opportunity to automate all the steps necessary to achieve this task. In particular, for the transformation of models, we use the Epsilon tool-set [11], based on the Eclipse platform [25]. We take a diverse approach in our verification strategy. We focus on translating xUML models to different model-checking tools, which may yield different and potentially better verification results under certain verification scenarios.

In this paper, we describe the results obtained so far in the INESS project:

– The verification strategy for the different transformations of xUML to input languages of different model-checkers.

[1] The terms translation and transformation are used interchangeably in this paper.

- A translation of xUML models of railway signalling systems to the PROMELA language, used as input by the SPIN model-checker [6].
- The implementation of an automated translation of this definition, using the Epsilon tool-set.

This work forms the basis for automating future translations, defined by us and our University partners, from xUML to different model-checking input languages. Our idea is to reuse as much as possible of this work, *e.g.*, transformation rules and meta-models, in future translations.

This paper is structured as follows. The next section provides background material on the behaviour of the xUML models we are working with (along with a very simple example of a railway signalling system), basic features of the PROMELA language, an overview of the Epsilon tool-set, and related work. In Section 3, we explain the verification strategy for xUML models. The definition of a translation of xUML models to PROMELA is described in Section 4. Section 5 details the implementation of this translation using the Epsilon tool-set. Finally, Section 6 presents closing remarks and future work.

2 Background

2.1 xUML Models of Railway Signalling Systems

The Executable UML (xUML) language augments a subset of UML with an action language. INESS experts have been using the tool Cassandra [10], a plug-in for the UML modelling tool Artisan Studio [2], to model railway signalling systems and simulate their execution. The Cassandra tool defines its own action language. In our work, we follow Cassandra's action language, since our intention in the project is to provide experts with the possibility of formally analysing their current railway signalling system models.

The xUML models used to describe railway signalling systems in INESS are composed of class diagrams and states machines. Every class diagram has an associated state machine that describes the behaviour of the class once instantiated (the object). Some characteristics of the classes include the use of integer attributes and derived attributes, which can have a very complex behaviour. Amongst other features, the action language is used to send messages between objects, create objects and set references. To illustrate the xUML models we are dealing with, we present some parts of a very small interlocking example, which we call the Micro model, provided by INESS partners.

Fig. 1 shows the class diagram of the Micro model, which is composed of six different classes. In addition to inheritance and the use of references in the models, we also have integer attributes, like the *id* described in Fig. 1. In particular, a class called *application*, which does not reference any other classes, is specified to represent an initial scenario for executing the model.

Fig. 2 depicts the state machine for the *route* class. State machines can only have initial and normal states. Moreover, they can have concurrent regions (not shown in this particular example) and can execute actions when entering and

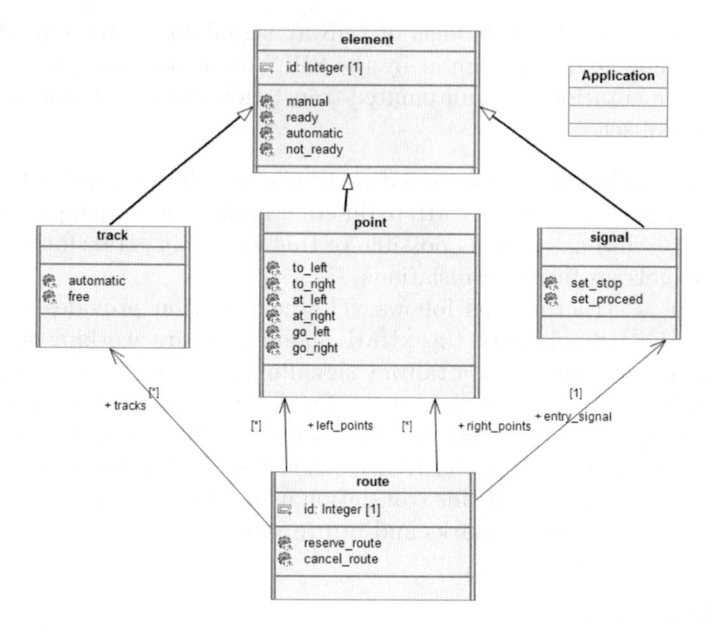

Fig. 1. Micro model - class diagrams

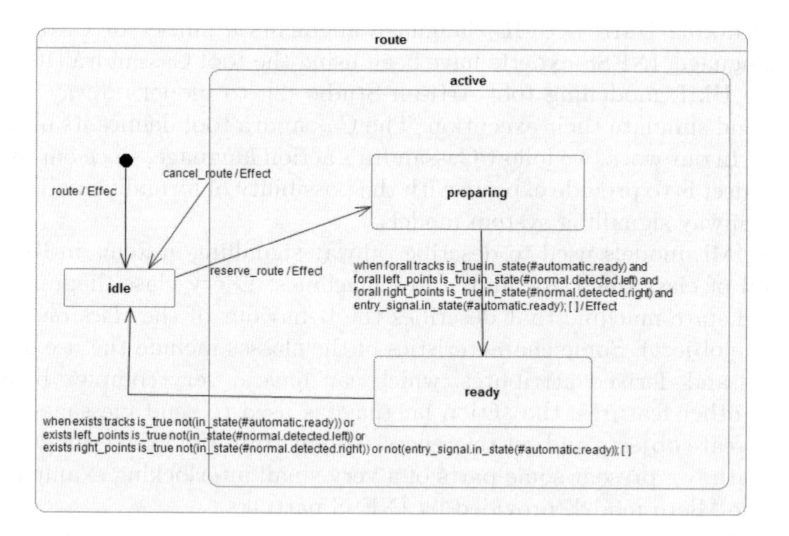

Fig. 2. Micro model - route state machine

exiting states. With respect to transitions, the following are possible: (i) *signal*-transitions, triggered once a signal is received; (ii) *after*-transitions, executed after a given time specified in the guard has passed; and (iii) *change*-transitions, taken once the condition of the *when* guard becomes true.

INESS experts have been using the Cassandra tool to analyse the xUML models via simulation. We have taken the behaviour implemented by this tool as the operational semantics for the execution of the model. Cassandra imposes some important constraints. Firstly, (a) even though *after*-transitions are possible in the model, there is no notion of progressive increase of time during simulation. During simulation, if two transitions are enabled (and one of them is an *after*-transition), the system can choose (nondeterministically) which one to execute. Secondly, (b) an enabled *change*-transition will always be executed, even if other transitions are enabled. This means that, if the system still has an active *change*-transition, it will be processed before any attempt to handle other events, like an arriving signal. Thirdly, (c) the same signal arriving in a state machine can generate different transitions (if they are enabled) in different concurrent regions.

Continuing, Fig. 3 shows an example scenario for the Micro model specified in the xUML action language. The same scenario is represented by an example of a Track Layout diagram in Fig. 4. The Track Layout is a closer abstraction for railway engineers. It effectively has an one-to-one correspondence to the xUML model. Later, in Section 4 we describe the verification strategy used in the project, which relates different levels of abstraction (from Track Layout down to verification code).

```
1  create T1 from track by track;
2  create T2 from track by track;
3  create T3 from track by track;
4  create S1 from signal by signal;
5  create P1 from point by point;
6  create R1 from route by route;
7  create R2 from route by route;
8  link R1 via route with T1 via tracks;
9  link R1 via route with T3 via tracks;
10 link R1 via route with P1 via left_points;
11 link R1 via route with S1 via entry_signal;
12 link R2 via route with T1 via tracks;
13 link R2 via route with T2 via tracks;
14 link R2 via route with P1 via right_points;
15 link R2 via route with S1 via entry_signal;
```

Fig. 3. Micro model - scenario in the xUML action grammar

For specifying the xUML models of railway signalling systems, we have been using a modified version of the Papyrus UML modelling tool [21], an open-source tool based on Eclipse. The use of a homogeneous platform, in this case Eclipse, for modelling and developing the transformation (with Epsilon), makes it easier to provide one integrated tool. A key element of this modified version is that we have integrated it with another Eclipse plugin, called EMFText [23], which enables us to define an action grammar and automatically parse this grammar from code to a model. This approach facilitates the translation between models, since the xUML action grammar can be viewed as a model with well-defined constraints, which is also part of the UML model. Section 5 provides more details about our current xUML action grammar.

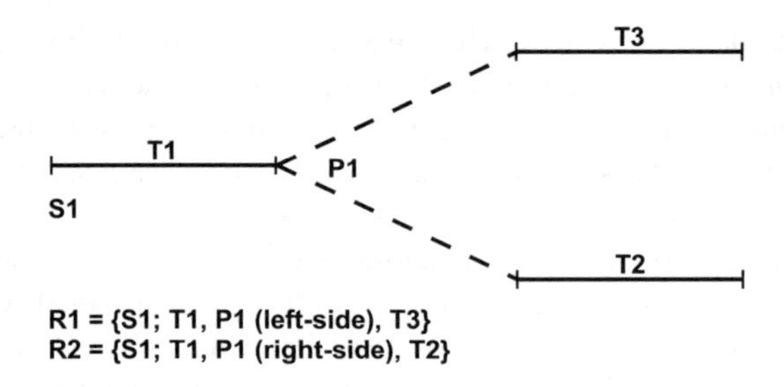

Fig. 4. Micro model - example of a possible Track Layout for the scenario

2.2 PROMELA

PROMELA [7] is a process-based language, used by the SPIN model-checker [6] for the specification of models. It is possible to define properties using LTL (Linear Temporal Logic) formulas, and verify if the formulas are true for a given specification.

The language has a *C-like* syntax and constructs for receiving and sending messages similar to the ones found in CSP (Communication Sequential Processes) [5]. Processes in PROMELA can be created statically or dynamically (*proctype* keyword). There is a special process, called *init*, used to initialize a specification. Processes can exchange information through message channels (*chan* keyword) or global variables (variables declared outside the scope of the processes). Message channels can be asynchronous (the buffer of the message channel can have N messages, being $N > 0$). Message channels are typed, in the sense that one has to explicitly declare the types of variables a channel might receive. As well, PROMELA offers several functions used to check, for example, if a channel is not full (*nfull(channel)*), not empty (*nempty(channel)*), empty (*empty(channel)*), and others [7].

In PROMELA, nondeterminism is modeled in condition (*if ... fi*) or repetition (*do ... od*) structures. The entries of condition and repetition structures are composed of guarded commands. Once the condition of a guarded command is not satisfied, the entry is blocked, possibly blocking the process that contains it. This blocking occurs until the condition is satisfied. In condition and repetition structures, nondeterminism occurs when several entries have their conditions satisfied. In this case, one of the possible paths is chosen in a nondeterministic way. It is possible to define atomic structures (*atomic* { ... }) for a specification, *i.e.*, a sequence of statements that must be executed without interleaving with the execution of statements of other processes. However, if there are guarded commands inside an atomic structure and they are not satisfied, the structure will lose its atomicity characteristic and will interleave its statements with other processes. We can define enumeration types in PROMELA (*mtype* keyword). One can insert assertions in a PROMELA specification. An assertion statement evaluates an expression (*assert(expression)*) to true or false, each time the statement is executed. If the expression evaluates to false, an error is generated and the verification procedure stops. Finally, the language provides a special boolean *timeout* keyword. This keyword is initially false, only becoming true when the system gets to a stage where it can no longer progress (a deadlock occurs). The *timeout* keyword can then be used in a guard in order to ensure that the system can progress.

2.3 Epsilon

Epsilon [11] is both a platform for task-specific model management languages and a framework for implementing *new* model management languages by exploiting the existing ones. Epsilon is currently a component of the Eclipse Generative Modeling Technologies (GMT) research incubator project. More specifically, Epsilon provides a language for direct manipulation of models (EOL) [13], and further languages for model merging (EML) [12], model comparison (ECL) [16], model-to-model transformation (ETL) [17], model validation (EVL) [15] model-to-text transformation (EGL) [22], model migration, and unit testing of model management operations (EUnit).

EOL is the core language in Epsilon, providing OCL-like [20] model navigation and modification facilities; all the other languages of the platform build on EOL and its runtime environment in different ways. As a result, all the languages in Epsilon are highly interoperable. For example, an *operation* defined using EOL can be imported as-is by the model-to-model and the model-to-text transformation languages. Because all languages in Epsilon share a common runtime, modules of different languages can exchange variables with each other [14]. With regard to supported modelling technologies, the architecture of Epsilon allows users to manage models of different technologies such as MDR and EMF models and XML documents and even implement support for additional formats. In this work we are using both model-to-model (ETL) and model-to-text (EGL) transformation languages.

2.4 Related Work

Related work [28,9,27] has targeted the automatic verification of xUML models using model-checking technology. The idea followed is basically the same, translate xUML models to the input language of an existing model-checker that is then used to analyse the model. In [28], the COSPAN model-checker [4] is used as the target for the verification of xUML models. Similarly, the SPIN model-checker [6] is used in [9]. Neither work uses transformation technology, nor does either address certain features, like the use of derived attributes, of the xUML action grammar that are used in the INESS models. More recent work translates xUML models to CSP || B [27,26], where the FDR model-checker [3] is then used to analyse the system. This work uses model transformation, but the xUML models being translated make substantially less use of the action language than the railway signalling systems we are analysing.

3 The Verification Strategy

The verification strategy of INESS consists of defining a methodology for the verification of railway signalling system models specified in xUML. Fig. 5 illustrates this methodology, where three different levels of abstraction are presented:

1. Track Layout level: We use a Domain-Specific Language (DSL) for describing the scenario (diagram) of railway signaling systems for verification. In the INESS Project, the xUML language is used to specify different European railway signalling systems and how they integrate together. This culminates in the definition of a set of components that can be combined in different ways. In this sense, the Track Layout level provides an abstraction, understood by railway engineers, that facilitates the definition of analysis scenarios. A component at this level provides a direct mapping to an xUML component (at the xUML level). Moreover, we are currently looking into method to specify verification properties at this level.
2. xUML level: This represents the xUML level used to model the integrated railway signalling system. An important element is the xUML Library of railway signalling components that can be put together in order to define an analysis scenario. We focus our work on providing a verification method at this abstraction level. Given a transformed xUML model of the desired Track Layout, we provide transformation rules to generate a model in the target language (used as input to a model-checking tool) integrating the model and the encoded verification property. Although we have initial results in translating the xUML to PROMELA (see Section 4), we are still working on a way to express verification properties in terms of the xUML model.
3. Verification level: This level represents the target verification model, already encoded with the desired verification properties. Once the model has been translated, the task is to generate the verification code, which is actually used by the model checker for the automated formal verification. After verification, it is necessary to translate the results back from the verification level to the xUML level, so that users can view the same abstraction level (transparency, with respect to the verification, is obtained).

Starting from the top level, the verification strategy should work with the definition of a Track Layout scenario. This is mapped to an xUML model. The xUML model is then translated to the input language of a model checking tool (Target Model), being analysed (Verification Code and Results) and have its results transformed back to the abstractions found in the Track Layout (Counter Examples chain from Verification to Track Layout levels).

Note that, in our current work, we have not focused on the Track Layout level, since it provides a direct and straightforward mapping of one-to-one to the xUML level. In other words, the Track Layout level only facilitates transparency of verification, since railway engineers do not have to even understand the xUML model in order to use the verification facilities. However, one of our industrial partners has already successfully defined a Track Layout level and mapped it

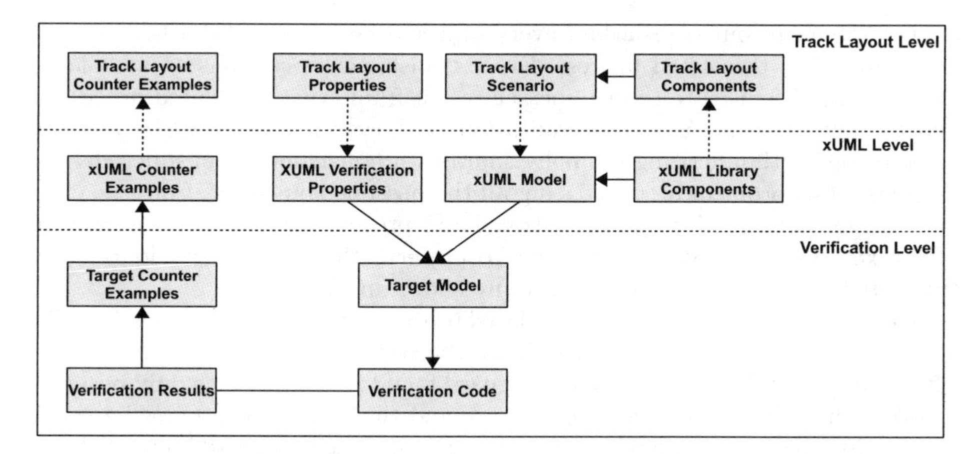

Fig. 5. Illustration of the verification strategy

to the xUML level, where the model can be simulated – as opposed to formally verified, as we aim to achieve in our work.

We use model transformation technology to implement every transition between levels of the strategy. At its most basic form, model transformation consists of defining transformation rules that are executed in order to translate a model A (conforming to a given meta-model) to a new model B (which conforms to another meta-model). In the verification strategy, two different types of model transformation techniques found in Epsilon are used: model-to-model (ETL) and model-to-text (EGL).

For translating an xUML model to a target input language, we firstly define a meta-model for the target language. Secondly, we specify transformation rules for populating the target model (using the elements of the xUML model), which must conform to the meta-model of the target language. We show how this is done in terms of the PROMELA language in Section 5. The same should happen when translating the counter-examples from the verification level back to the xUML level. Although, in this case we can potentially reuse the already defined meta-models for verification and xUML.

4 Translation of xUML into PROMELA

In this section we describe how the xUML constructs are translated to PROMELA. The translation is divided in two different parts. The first describes the translation of the class diagrams and state machines that compose the objects. Then, in Subsection 4.2 we show the translation of the initial scenario of the system, where objects are created and references between these objects are set.

4.1 Class Diagrams, State Machines and Objects

In the xUML model every class diagram has an associated state machine, although only objects (the basic computation units) are used in the execution of the system. In our translation, every object becomes a PROMELA process, which we call a translated process. Every translated process has an associated channel, which is used to receive messages sent from other translated processes, and the environment. Since generalisation is allowed in the xUML model, we need to cope with inheriting the behaviour of state machines from super classes. We tackle this problem by translating all the possible transitions from the class and its super classes into a single translated process, flattening the structure of the xUML object. With the intent to preserve the xUML behaviour, every translated process has the basic structure shown in Fig. 6.

According to this structure, a translated process enters in a loop (lines 1 to 17). There are two types of guards in this loop: guards used for translated *change* and *after* transitions (lines 2 to 7), and the guard found in line 8, which only becomes enabled when the *timeout* keyword is true and the translated process has messages in its associated channel (*nempty* function). Once this guard is enabled, the translated process gets a message from its associated channel (line 9) and tries to find a *signal*-transition that is triggered by that particular message (lines 11 to 13). Note that all the actions from lines 8 to 16 occur atomically.

```
1  do
2  :: /* Change-Transition 1 */
3     ...
4  :: /* Change-Transition N */
5  :: timeout && ... /* Time-Transition 1 */
6     ...
7  :: timeout && ... /* Time-Transition N */
8  :: atomic { timeout && nempty(obj_chan);
9       obj_chan?msg_name;
10      if
11      :: /* Signal-Transition 1 */
12         ...
13      :: /* Signal-Transition N */
14      ::else -> skip;
15      fi;
16    }
17 od;
```

Fig. 6. Basic structure for translated xUML objects

As presented in Subsection 2.2, the *timeout* keyword only becomes true when the system gets to a deadlock stage where no more transitions can occur. The basic idea for encoding the xUML behaviour in PROMELA is as follows. The system starts and tries to apply all possible *change*-transitions in the different translated processes. Once all *change*-transitions have occurred, the system gets to a deadlocked situation and the *timeout* keyword becomes true. At this stage, it may happen that translated processes have messages in their associated channels (guard in line 8 becomes true). This leads to the translated process trying to apply *signal*-transitions, and the *timeout* keyword becoming false. The applied *signal*-transition may generate new *change*-transitions in the system. The system enters the cycle once again, waiting for inputs to occur. There may be a case where no translated processes have messages in their buffer and the system stops. In this case, the initial process emulates the environment by generating a nondeterministic input to the system. Below we describe in more details how specific xUML components are translated to PROMELA.

Attributes and References. Attributes and references are part of the class diagram definition. However, they have there values instantiated at the creation of the process. We translate both attributes and references to parameters passed during the creation of the translated process. Fig. 7 illustrates this in terms of a translated route object $R1$, where the input parameters of the process are presented. Channel *obj_chan* is the process associated channel. The *id* attribute is translated to the *route_id* variable. The other channels are references for the different objects in the system.

```
1 proctype R1(chan obj_chan; int route_id; chan point_P1;
2             chan track_T1; chan track_T3; chan signal_S1) {
3    ...
4 }
```

Fig. 7. Process parameters for the route object $R1$

States and Transitions. In order to keep the state-based structure found in xUML, we decided to translate regions of a state machine to global variables. This way, the states became constants in PROMELA that are set to the correct global variable once the state is changed. Moreover, transitions are translated to *transition blocks*. A transition block is an entry in a PROMELA condition or repetition structure. It has a guard, which uses the global variables to match the current state of the translated process. If a guard is true, other statements corresponding to the actions of the xUML transition are executed. At the end of the execution of the transition block, the new state is set for the translated process. Examples of translated *change* and *signal* transitions are shown in Fig. 8.

```
1  /* Change-Transition */
2  :: atomic { (route_active_active[id] == preparing) &&
3              (route_route[id] == active) &&
4              ((((track_element[0] == automatic) &&
5                (track_automatic_automatic[0] == ready)) &&
6               ((track_element[2] == automatic) &&
7                (track_automatic_automatic[2] == ready))) &&
8               (((point_point[0] == normal) &&
9                (point_normal_detected[0] == left))) &&
10              (((signal_element[0] == automatic) &&
11               (signal_automatic_automatic[0] == ready))));
12      assert(nfull(signal_S1));
13      signal_S1!set_proceed;
14      route_active_active[id] = ready;
15      route_route[id] = active;
16     }
17     ...
18 /* Signal-Transition */
19 :: (msg_name == reserve_route) && (route_route[id] == idle);
20      assert(nfull(point_P1));
21      point_P1!to_left;
22      route_active_active[id] = preparing;
23      route_route[id] = active;
```

Fig. 8. Example of *change* and *signal* transitions for route object $R1$

The guard of a translated *change*-transition (lines 2 to 16) is composed of global variables checking the correctness of: (a) the source state of the translated process (lines 2 and 3); and (b), the other states of translated processes (lines 4 to 11). Amongst the actions, the translated process can generate a message (line 13), although before sending a message it checks if the target channel is not full (line 12), maintaining the atomicity of the whole transition. Finally, it sets the target state by changing the values of the global variables (lines 14 and 15). A translated *signal*-transition (lines 19 to 23) is similar to the *change*-transition. The only difference is that it incorporates a message name (*msg_name*), which is the signal triggering the transition (line 19).

4.2 The Initial Scenario

In Fig. 3 the definition of a scenario uses the action grammar of the xUML language in order to create the objects and define their references. We translate an initial scenario of xUML (the *application* class and its associated state machine) to a special PROMELA initial process.

A part of a translated PROMELA initial process, describing only the translation of the track object $T1$, is presented in Fig. 9. In the translation, the initial process has three different purposes. Firstly, it creates the channel that is associated to the translated object (line 3). Then, it creates the process by passing as parameters the associated channel and, if necessary, other channel references needed by the process (line 5). Both the creation of the channels and the processes occur atomically (lines 2 to 7).

The final purpose of the initial process is to generate inputs from the environment for the execution of the verification scenario. Therefore, it enters in an atomic loop (lines 8 to 19) that has only one guard (line 9) stating that the system can no longer execute (*timeout* keyword) and all the other channels associated to translated processes are empty (*empty* function). Once this guard

```
1  init {
2    atomic {
3      chan T1_ = [5] of { mtype };
4      ...
5      run T1(T1_);
6      ...
7    }
8    do
9    :: atomic { timeout && empty(T1_) && ...;
10        if
11        ::(track_track[0] == free) -> T1_!occupied;
12        ::(track_track[0] == occupied) -> T1_!free;
13        ::(track_track[0] == free) -> T1_!automatic;
14        ::(track_element[0] == automatic) -> T1_!manual;
15        ::(track_element[0] == manual) -> T1_!automatic;
16        ...
17        fi;
18      }
19    od;
20 }
```

Fig. 9. Partial PROMELA initial process for the Micro model

becomes true, the initial process checks different states of each process and, if more than one process is in the correct state for receiving the signal, it nondeterministically selects an input to be generated (a signal to be sent via the channel). The list of possible states and generated inputs for the translated process $T1$ are presented from lines 11 to 15.

5 Implementation of the Transformation

The previous section completed the description of the translation from xUML to PROMELA, now we show how this translation is implemented. A key aspect of our work is the use of model transformation technology to implement the translation between the different languages. As an underlying basis, model transformation requires the use of meta-models to provide the basic structure that models must conform to. In Subsection 5.1 we provide an overview of the meta-models we are using for both the xUML action language and the PROMELA translation. We describe the translation to PROMELA in Subsection 5.2. The generation of code from translated PROMELA models is presented in Subsection 5.3.

5.1 Meta-Modelling

The meta-model is used to define a structure that models must conform to. By using Eclipse and associated tools (Papyrus, EMFText and Epsilon), we have defined our meta-models using the Eclipse Modelling Framework (EMF). Our meta-models are composed of classes, references and basic attributes, such as string and integer variables. In particular, we have defined two different meta-models: one is for representing the xUML action language; another represents the translated PROMELA model. We do not have to define a meta-model for the UML files, since we use the UML2 project meta-model [24] found in Eclipse – also produced as output by the Papyrus tool. UML2 provides an implementation of the UML OMG meta-model standard in Eclipse.

Fig. 10 shows the meta-model used to represent the xUML action grammar in the Papyrus tool-set. This is supposed to be a simple model, since we intend to keep extending it in order to accommodate new actions in the language. As shown in Fig. 10, all the actions are contained in a body class. Currently, we have actions for the creation of links (set references), assignments, send messages, create objects and rules for checking the state of different objects (used in the change transitions).

In the PROMELA meta-model (Fig. 11) we have defined a model composed of constants (state and message names from the xUML model), processes (from class diagrams and associated state machines) and an initial process (*Init*). Amongst the most important features, note that the processes include transitions, states and references to their super classes (generalization) – much like the structure of a UML class diagram. Translated processes (objects) are represented by *ProctypeDef*'s, contained in the initial process. When translating verification

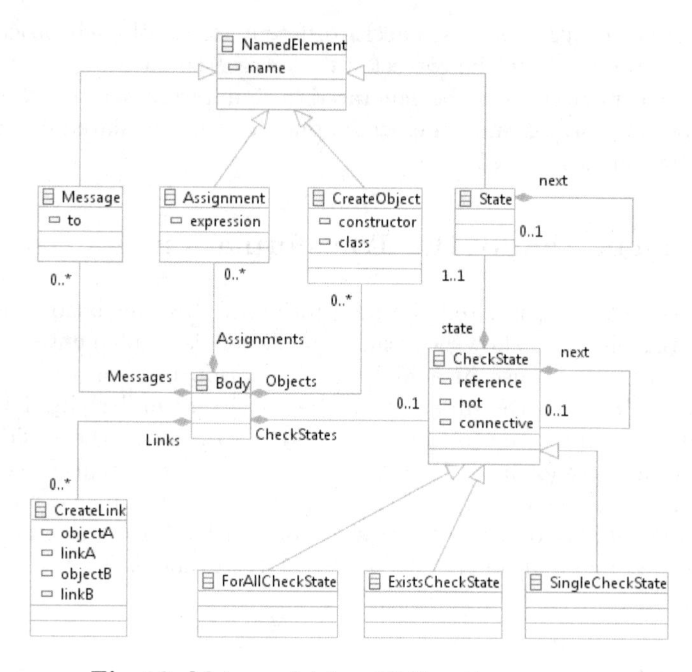

Fig. 10. Meta-model for xUML action grammar

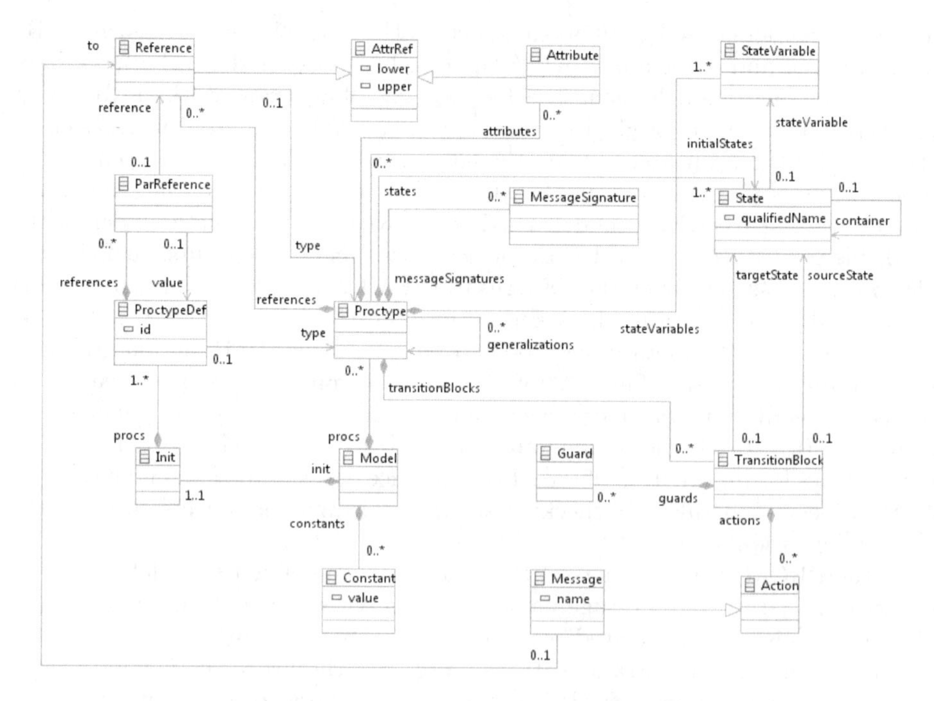

Fig. 11. Meta-model for PROMELA

code, the transformation task is to generate code for every *ProctypeDef* defined in the model. Due to its complexity, we present in Fig. 11 a subset of the PROMELA meta-model necessary for understanding the translation process.

5.2 xUML Models to PROMELA Models

Rules in ETL (Epsilon Transformation Language) are defined in order to construct a PROMELA model from the original xUML model. As shown previously, the PROMELA model (according to its meta-model) has constants, processes and an initial process. We define rules to translate each one of these elements and a further rule to put them together inside a complete PROMELA model.

In order to illustrate the use of Epsilon, we present in Fig. 12 the ETL rule used to transform a class and its associated state machine to a PROMELA

```
1 rule UMLClassToPROMELAProctype
2   transform class : UML!Class
3   to proctype : PROMELA!Proctype {
4
5   -- Application class defines the scenario: it is a PROMELA init proctype
6   guard : class.name <> 'Application' and class.name <> 'application'
7
8   -- Sets the proctype name
9   proctype.name := class.name;
10
11  -- Transform generalizations
12  -- Find if it is a generalisation and link the superclasses if they have
13  -- been transformed, otherwise, trigger the transformation superclasses
14  var generalizations := class.generalization;
15  if (generalizations.isDefined()) {
16    for (g in generalizations) {
17      for (c in g.target) {
18        var proc := PROMELA!Proctype.all.select(t|t.name = c.name).first();
19        if (proc.isDefined()) {
20          proctype.generalizations.add(proc);
21        } else {
22          proctype.generalizations.add(c.equivalent());
23        }
24      }
25    }
26  }
27
28  -- Associate to the proctype, the messages that it can receive
29  -- Used in the code transformation to generate inputs from the environment
30  for (s in class.ownedReception) {
31    var msg := PROMELA!MessageSignature.createInstance();
32    msg.name := s.signal.name;
33    proctype.messageSignatures.add(msg);
34  }
35
36  -- Generate the attributes and references for this class
37  GenerateAttributesAndReferences(class, proctype);
38
39  -- Generate states and state variables according to the state machine
40  GenerateStateAndStateVariables(class, proctype);
41
42  -- Generate the transition blocks according to the state machine
43  GenerateTransitionBlocks(class, proctype);
44 }
```

Fig. 12. ETL rule transforming a class and its state machine to a PROMELA process

process (*Proctype*). The first lines are used to define the name of the rule (line 1), specify the original element being transformed (UML class, line 2) and to what element it is being mapped to (PROMELA *Proctype*, line 3). This informs the transformation engine that for every class element in the UML model, this rule must be called. However, we specify a guard (line 6) stating that any class with the name *application* shall not be transformed. The *application* class defines the initial scenario and is transformed in a different rule.

The name of the class is maintained in the target process element (line 9). If the class diagram has generalisations (line 15), it makes sure that they are translated as well (lines 20 and 22). The function *equivalent()* is used to trigger an implicit rule. This way, if the super class has not been transformed yet, its transformation rule is triggered in order to set the correct references in the target model. We also translate the messages that a class can receive (lines 30 to 34) in order to correctly build the environment. Finally, we define three different operations that are used for translating attributes and references (line 37), states and state variables (line 40) and the transition blocks obtained from the associated state machine (line 43).

5.3 PROMELA Models to PROMELA Code

The Epsilon Generation Language (EGL) is used to generate the verification code starting from the obtained PROMELA model. In EGL definitions, we define templates of the final text (which are not to be changed) and specify dynamic structures used to add information gathered from the model. This way, we have specified in total, four different templates. They are used for declaring the

```
1  [%
2  for (p in ProctypeDef.allInstances) {
3          var s;
4  %]
5  proctype [%=p.name%](chan obj_chan[%=p.generateParameters()%]) {
6    atomic {
7      mtype msg_name;
8      int id = [%=p.id%];
9  [%=p.initialStates()%]
10   }
11   do
12 [%=p.transitionBlocks()%]
13 [%=p.changeTransitionBlocks()%]
14 [%=p.timeTransitionBlocks()%]
15   ::atomic { timeout && nempty(obj_chan);
16     obj_chan?msg_name;
17 [%=p.signalTransitionBlocks()%]
18   }
19   od;
20 }
21 [%
22 }
23 %]
```

Fig. 13. EGL rule for generating translated processes in PROMELA

PROMELA constants, the global variables of the processes (used to represent the states), define the translated processes and generate the initial process.

We illustrate the use of Epsilon to generate verification code in Fig. 13. This code generates translated processes (transformed xUML objects). We translate all the possible instances of *ProctypeDef*'s (lines 2 to 22). For each instance, we define the header of the process, with its name and its input parameters (line 5). The global variables associated to the translated process are initialised with the correct states in line 9. Then, we generate all the transitions for the process (lines 12, 13, 14 and 17). The transitions are used to populate the basic structure (shown previously, in Fig. 6) used to maintain the behaviour of the xUML models in the PROMELA language (lines 11 to 19).

6 Final Remarks

In this paper we presented the verification strategy for INESS, devised for analysing xUML models of railway signalling systems, which is being currently modelled by our Industry partners. At the core of our strategy is the use of model transformation to facilitate the implementation and extension of the translation, as new features (from the action language) used in the xUML models need to be encoded in the verification tool. The strategy has three different levels of abstraction: (a) Track Layout level; (b) xUML level; (c) Verification level. We have focused our efforts on implementing the automatic transformation from xUML models down to verification code. This has been explained by exemplifying the translation of xUML model to PROMELA verification code.

In this paper we have not shown the formal analysis of the xUML models. We have focused on describing how model transformation can be used to automate the translation of models. In fact, as we are currently developing a technique to specify verification properties in terms of xUML and translate them to the verification model, our only possibility of analysing the models is to encode verification properties directly in SPIN. When doing that, we have analysed basic properties of the Micro model, such as no two different routes can be active at the same time. In terms of SPIN, this can be easily expressed as a temporal formula stating that (in terms of the Micro model of Section 2.1) objects $R1$ and $R2$ are never in the *active* state at the same time. During verification, false results were obtained. Given the simplicity of the Micro Model, which is being used as a starting example for our translations, this was an expected result. Currently, we are starting to analyse more complex models obtained from our partners.

As an immediate future work, we aim to complete our current ongoing work on defining the specification of properties in terms of xUML and how to translate them to the verification model. We also plan to start tackling the automatic translation of counter-examples from the Verification level to the xUML abstractions. SPIN's counter-example result is made of a text file with the execution of the model until the property under verification had a false result. In this case, we can use text-to-model transformation from the counter-example file to a specified meta-model representing the model's execution. Moreover, we are starting to implement the automatic translation of xUML models to other target languages such as CSP [5] and mCRL2 [1] with our partners from the Universities of Twente and Eindhoven. With respect to the validation of the translation, we are currently using testing to guarantee that the translated model indeed maintains the behaviour of the xUML model [16,18].

Another important future work is to revise our current translation to PROMELA. For instance, one of the restrictions in our current work is the use of global variables. This has direct consequences on the use of the Partial Order Reduction algorithm found in SPIN. Therefore, if there are errors in the model that can be easily detected, as in the Micro model shown in this paper, this may not be a problem, since SPIN dynamically generates the state space during verification stopping once an error is found. However, as the models have fewer errors, checking the whole state space without the use of the Partial Order Reduction algorithm may prove to be difficult, due to the increased state space.

Acknowledgment. The work in this paper was funded by the European Commission via the INESS project, Seventh Framework Programme (2008-2011).

References

1. Alexander, M., Gardner, W. (eds.): Process Algebra for Parallel and Distributed Processing. CRC Press, USA (2008)
2. Artisan Software Tools Inc. Artisan studio UML modelling tool (2010), `http://www.artisansoftwaretools.com/`
3. Formal Systems (Europe) Ltd. FDR 2.83 manual (2007)
4. Hardin, R.H., Har'El, Z., Kurshan, R.P.: COSPAN. In: Alur, R., Henzinger, T.A. (eds.) CAV 1996. LNCS, vol. 1102, pp. 423–427. Springer, Heidelberg (1996)
5. Hoare, C.A.R.: Communicating Sequential Processes. Prentice Hall, USA (1985)
6. Holzmann, G.J.: The model checker SPIN. IEEE Transactions on Software Engineering 23(5), 279–295 (1997)
7. Holzmann, G.J.: The SPIN Model Checker: Primer and Reference Manual. Addison-Wesley, USA (2003)
8. INESS Project. INtegrated European Signalling System (INESS) Project Web Page (2010), `http://www.iness.eu/`
9. Jussila, T., Dubrovin, J., Junttila, T., Latvala, T., Porres, I.: Model checking dynamic and hierarchical UML state machines. In: 3rd Workshop on Model design and Validation, Italy, pp. 94–110 (2006), `http://modeva.itee.uq.edu.au/accepted_papers/main.pdf`
10. KnowGravity Inc. Cassandra/xUML User's Guide (2008), `http://www.knowgravity.com/eng/value/cassandra.htm`
11. Kolovos, D.S.: Extensible Platform for Specification of Integrated Languages for mOdel maNagement Project Website (2010), `http://www.eclipse.org/gmt/epsilon`
12. Kolovos, D.S., Paige, R.F., Polack, F.: Merging Models with the Epsilon Merging Language (EML). In: Nierstrasz, O., Whittle, J., Harel, D., Reggio, G. (eds.) MoDELS 2006. LNCS, vol. 4199, pp. 215–229. Springer, Heidelberg (2006)

13. Kolovos, D.S., Paige, R.F., Polack, F.: The Epsilon Object Language (EOL). In: Rensink, A., Warmer, J. (eds.) ECMDA-FA 2006. LNCS, vol. 4066, pp. 128–142. Springer, Heidelberg (2006)
14. Kolovos, D.S., Paige, R.F., Polack, F.: A framework for composing modular and interoperable model management tasks. In: Workshop on Model Driven Tool and Process Integration, Germany, pp. 79–90. Fraunhofer-Verlag (2008)
15. Kolovos, D.S., Paige, R.F., Polack, F.: On the Evolution of OCL for Capturing Structural Constraints in Modelling Languages. In: Abrial, J.-R., Glässer, U. (eds.) Rigorous Methods for Software Construction and Analysis. LNCS, vol. 5115, pp. 204–218. Springer, Heidelberg (2009)
16. Kolovos, D.S., Paige, R.F., Polack, F.A.: Model comparison: a foundation for model composition and model transformation testing. In: 1st International Workshop on Global Integrated Model Management, Shanghai, China, pp. 13–20. ACM Press, New York (2006)
17. Kolovos, D.S., Paige, R.F., Polack, F.A.: The Epsilon Transformation Language. In: Vallecillo, A., Gray, J., Pierantonio, A. (eds.) ICMT 2008. LNCS, vol. 5063, pp. 46–60. Springer, Heidelberg (2008)
18. Kolovos, D.S., Paige, R.F., Rose, L.M., Polack, F.A.: Unit testing model management operations. In: 5th IEEE Workshop on Model Driven Engineering Verification and Validation, Norway, pp. 97–104. IEEE Computer Society Press, Los Alamitos (2008)
19. Mellor, S.J., Balcer, M.J.: Executable UML. Addison Wesley, USA (2002)
20. OMG: Object Constraint Language, Version 2.2, OMG document number formal/2010-02-01 (2010)
21. Papyrus UML - CEA LIST. Open source tool for graphical UML2 modelling (2008), http://www.papyrusuml.org/
22. Rose, L.M., Paige, R.F., Kolovos, D.S., Polack, F.A.: The Epsilon Generation Language. In: Schieferdecker, I., Hartman, A. (eds.) ECMDA-FA 2008. LNCS, vol. 5095, pp. 1–16. Springer, Heidelberg (2008)
23. Software Technology Group - Dresden University of Technology. Emftext concrete syntax mapper (2010), http://www.emftext.org/
24. The Eclipse Foundation. Eclipse UML2 Web Page (2010), http://www.eclipse.org/uml2
25. The Eclipse Foundation. Eclipse Web Page (2010), http://www.eclipse.org/
26. Treharne, H., Turner, E., Paige, R.F., Kolovos, D.S.: Automatic generation of integrated formal models corresponding to UML system models. In: GI-Fachtagung 1975. LNBIP, vol. 33, pp. 357–367. Springer, Heidelberg (2009)
27. Turner, E., Treharne, H., Schneider, S., Evans, N.: Automatic generation of CSP || B skeletons from xUML models. In: Fitzgerald, J.S., Haxthausen, A.E., Yenigun, H. (eds.) ICTAC 2008. LNCS, vol. 5160, pp. 364–379. Springer, Heidelberg (2008)
28. Xie, F., Levin, V., Kurshan, R.P., Browne, J.C.: Translating software designs for model checking. In: Wermelinger, M., Margaria-Steffen, T. (eds.) FASE 2004. LNCS, vol. 2984, pp. 324–338. Springer, Heidelberg (2004)

Suitability of mCRL2 for Concurrent-System Design: A 2 × 2 Switch Case Study

Frank P.M. Stappers, Michel A. Reniers, and Jan Friso Groote

Department of Computer Science, Eindhoven University of Technology, P.O. Box 513, NL-5600MB Eindhoven, The Netherlands

Abstract. Specifying concurrent systems can be done using a variety of languages. These languages have different features and therefore are not necessarily equally suitable for capturing concepts from reality with respect to both expressivity and ease-of-use.

This paper addresses these aspects for the specification language mCRL2 by considering the 2 × 2 Switch case study. This case study has been used before to compare other specification languages, more specifically TLA+, Bluespec, Statecharts and ACP. The case study primarily focuses on two important features, namely multi-party communication and priority of certain actions over other actions. We show that mCRL2 is appropriate for the specification of these features, especially multi-party communication. Moreover, we express some of the requirements of the original case study in terms of modal μ-calculus formulae and establish that these are indeed satisfied by the model.

1 Introduction

In today's world, there are many different ways to specify system's behavior. At first, many specification languages seem suitable for describing system behaviour, as they are applied to case studies and toy examples that are specially tailored to assess certain features of a language. Unfortunately, when actual systems need to be specified, it often turns out that a language cannot express a certain amount of behavior, as the language is too generic or too limited, and therefore not vigorous enough to express complex behavioral patterns. This way, designers are required to deviate from the system's behaviour or they have to apply abstractions such that inexpressible behavior becomes irrelevant.

When designs are finished, it is difficult to ensure that a system meets the requirements that were agreed upon in advance. In many cases human reasoning is applied to validate that a system meets these requirements. However, a proof or guarantee cannot be given. Especially for mission critical systems, but also for concurrent systems, this might yield to undesired behaviour, which can result into catastrophic disasters.

Selecting a suitable language for system design is a difficult task. To guide designers, the authors of [6] have recently compared the specification languages TLA+, Bluespec, Statecharts, and ACP for a particular case study. The authors of [6] compare these languages with respect to the following three criteria:

F.S. de Boer et al. (Eds.): FMCO 2009, LNCS 6286, pp. 166–185, 2010.

1. the *local* (as opposed to global and temporal) reasoning that is required by the designer in order to specify behaviour,
2. *adaptability* to variations in design intent, and
3. checking whether a specification *captures* the corresponding design intent.

The case study they selected, deals with a switch that internally routes packets from input buffers to output buffers. These packets are routed according to a set of rules that specify priority amongst selected packets as well as simultaneous packet transfers. As these rules are complementary to each other, they illustrate contradictive concerns and emphasize on the possible weaknesses of the specification languages. In [6] it is concluded that each of the used specification languages performs poorly for at least two of these criteria.

In extension to the framework, presented in [6], this paper puts mCRL2 [9] to the same test. The goal of this paper is to show that the specification language mCRL2 is better suited than the other specification languages, at least for the presented case study.

mCRL2 is a specification language, especially targeted for describing communication behaviour among systems. The behavioural part of the language is based on process algebra [1]. For the purpose of specifying behaviour, mCRL2 facilitates a data part which is based on higher-order abstract equational data types. It allows quantifiers, (unbounded) integers, (infinite) sets and bags, structured types, lists and real numbers, that are set up as close as possible to their mathematical counterparts.

The models that we present for the cases are obtained in a relatively straightforward way from the informal description. It turns out that multi-party communication is easily captured by the advanced communication mechanisms of mCRL2. mCRL2 has no direct support for specifying priority. Nevertheless we are able to describe the types of priority used in the cases at hand.

For the manipulation, analysis and visualisation of specifications, the language is equipped by a range of tools [7,10]. These tools allow amongst others the verification of requirements that are described in the modal μ-calculus [13].

This paper is structured as follows. Section 2 gives a brief introduction to the relevant fragments of the language mCRL2 and the modal μ-calculus. The switches are modelled in Sections 3,4 and 5. Section 6 elaborates on the requirements that have been verified on the constructed models. Section 7 compares the work presented here to that of others. Section 8 describes our conclusions and future work.

2 Preliminaries

2.1 Syntax and Semantics of mCRL2

An mCRL2 process is built from data-parameterized multi-actions and a collection of process operators. In this paper, a fragment of the syntax of the un-timed mCRL2 language is used. It is given by the following *BNF*:

$$\begin{aligned} P &::= \alpha \mid P + P \mid P \cdot P \mid c \to P \mid \textstyle\sum_{x:D} P \mid P \parallel P \\ &\mid \partial_B(P) \mid \tau_B(P) \mid \Gamma_V(P) \mid X(\boldsymbol{d}) \\ \alpha &::= \tau \mid a(\boldsymbol{d}) \mid \alpha \,|\, \alpha \end{aligned}$$

The small $\mid$ indicates a choice between symbols in the expression of the BNF. In this syntax α denotes a multi-action. A multi-action consists of actions combined by the big $|$. The empty multi-action is denoted by τ. An action $a(\boldsymbol{d})$ consists of an action name a and possibility a data parameter vector $\boldsymbol{d}$ (the syntax of which is left unspecified). A multi-action represents the simultaneous execution of the constituent actions.

Processes are denoted by P. For processes, $+$ denotes non-deterministic choice, i.e., a choice between behaviors, $\cdot$ denotes sequential composition, i.e., a process followed by another process. The conditional operator, written as $c \to p$, denotes that if c data expression of sort $\mathbb{B}$ holds, then process P is executed. The non-deterministic choice among processes is denoted by $\sum_{x:D} P$, where x is a variable of sort D and P is a process expression in which the variable x may occur. The parallel composition of processes is represented by $\parallel$ operator, that denotes the concurrent execution of both processes. The operator ∂_B blocks all actions from set B of action names, i.e., prevents the occurrence of the specified actions. The operator τ_B replaces all occurrences of actions from B by τ. Γ_V applies the communications described by the set V to a process. A communication in the set V is of the form $a_1 \mid \cdots \mid a_n \to a$. Application of Γ_V to a process means that any occurrence of the multi-action $a_1(\boldsymbol{d}) \mid \cdots \mid a_n(\boldsymbol{d})$ is replaced by $a(\boldsymbol{d})$, for any $\boldsymbol{d}$. $X(\boldsymbol{d})$ is a reference to a process definition of the form $X(\boldsymbol{x}) = P$, i.e., the process $X(\boldsymbol{d})$ behaves as prescribed by P with $\boldsymbol{x}$ replaced by $\boldsymbol{d}$.

The semantics associated with an mCRL2 process, as used in the mCRL2 tool set, is a transition system where the transitions are labelled by multi-actions. A more elaborate description of the syntax and (timed) semantics are given in [9,10].

2.2 Modal μ-Calculus

Modal μ-calculus formulae are used to describe behavioral properties. These properties are verified against a behavioral model described in mCRL2. In this paper, requirements are specified in a variant of the modal μ-calculus extended with regular expressions [8] and data. The restricted fragment of the modal μ-calculus used, is as follows:

$$\begin{aligned} \phi &::= \mathit{false} \mid \phi \Rightarrow \phi \mid \phi \land \phi \mid [\rho]\phi \mid \langle\rho\rangle\phi \mid \forall_{x:D}\phi \mid c \\ \rho &::= \alpha \mid \rho \cdot \rho \mid \rho^* \\ \alpha &::= a(\boldsymbol{d}) \mid \neg\alpha \mid \alpha \,|\, \alpha \mid \mathit{true} \end{aligned}$$

In this syntax, ϕ represents a property, ρ represents a set of sequences of actions and α represents the absence or presence of a multi-action. An arbitrary multi-action is denoted by *true*. The property *false* holds for no model. The property $[\rho]\phi$ states the property that ϕ holds in all states that can be reached by a sequence described by ρ. The property $\langle\rho\rangle\phi$ describes that ϕ holds in some state that can be reached by a sequence from ρ. To describe action sequences concatenation and iteration can be used. A more elaborate description of the modal μ-calculus and its semantics can be found in [5,8].

3 Specification of the Simple 2 × 2 Switch

The 2 × 2 Switch case study consists of three separate cases that gradually increase in difficulty. These cases are referred to as the "Simplified Switch", the "Original Switch" [4] and the "Modified Switch". In the specification of the three cases, we follow the informal description from [6] as closely as possible. This means that we introduce a single process for each of the four buffers. By means of the advanced communication mechanisms offered in mCRL2, we describe their non-trivial interaction. In this section, and in the sections to follow, we discuss the way in which we have dealt with the modeling challenges posed by the case studies.

The Simplified Switch contains two input FIFO buffers and two output FIFO buffers. All buffers have a unique identity, w.r.t. the type of buffer, e.g. each input or output buffer corresponds to a numerical value, and a finite capacity for storing packets. All buffers have the same capacity.

Each packet consists of 32 bits. Packets enter the system via the input buffers and depart the system via the output buffers. Packets are transferred from an input buffer to one of the output buffers based on the first bit of the packet: If the first bit of a packet is 0, it is routed to the output buffer with identity 0, and otherwise it is routed to the output buffer with identity 1.

The packets may only be transferred if the relevant output buffer is not full. A buffer operates per clock cycle and can do at most one operation, namely receive a packet, send a packet, or nothing. Furthermore, we require maximum throughput, e.g. a packet should be transferred if it has the ability to. Next to that, if packets from different input buffers are available for transferral to the same output buffer, transferral of the packet from input buffer 0 gets priority over transferral of the packet from input buffer 1.

3.1 Bits and Packets

The data type of bits consists of two different values. In mCRL2, this is defined as:

sort Bit = **struct** zero | one;

In the case study, packets consist of 32 bits. This implies that a single packet can be represented by 2^{32} different configurations. mCRL2 allows the description of such a data type without any problems; e.g., by a structured sort that composes 32 bits by:

sort $Packet$ = **struct** $packet(b_1, b_2, \ldots, b_{32} : Bit)$;

From a modelling point of view, we do not object to such a representation or see any difficulty to write it down in an mCRL2 specification. Unfortunately, for a formal analysis with tools that require an explicit state space generation such as model-checking tools, this has an apparent drawback. It gives rise to 2^{32} different potential contents for each position in each of the considered buffers. This number is usually too big to be handled by current state-of-the-art model-checking tools. For that reason we require an appropriate abstraction.

Investigation shows that only two types of data packets are relevant for the Simplified Switch. First, those data packets for which the first bit of the packet is 0, and second, those data packets for which the first bit is 1. According to the first bit, packets are respectively routed to output buffer 0 or to output buffer 1. For this reason, we choose to abstract from the irrelevant bits of a packet, by only modeling the first bit. Consequently, the structure of a packet is redefined as:

sort $Packet = $ **struct** $packet(b_1 : Bit)$;

To route packets, we require a function that assigns a destination to a given packet. So, we define a mapping *dest* that expresses the relation between the data within the packet and the output buffer to which the packet is to be routed.

map $dest : Packet \rightarrow \mathbb{N}$;
eqn $dest(packet(\mathsf{zero})) = 0$;
$dest(packet(\mathsf{one})) = 1$;

3.2 Capacity of the Buffers

The system consists of four queues. Each buffer has the same capacity *cap*, which is assumed to be at least 1. In order to specify the case study without referring to an explicitly defined value we introduce the following constant.

map $cap : Pos$;

By means of an equation we may assign a specific value to this mapping. This is necessary for state space generation and simulation of the specification. This way changing the capacity, if desired, needs to be done in one place only.

eqn $cap = 3$;

3.3 Information Exchange between the Processes

To observe packets that enter and leave the 2×2-switch, two parameterized actions are introduced, namely one for adding an element to an input buffer (*enter*) and another one for removing an element from an output buffer (*leave*). The first data parameter refers to the identity of an input buffer (for *enter*-actions) or an output buffer (in case of *leave*-actions). The second data parameter is used to represent the actual data for the packet itself.

$$\textbf{act}\quad \begin{array}{ll} \mathit{enter} & : \mathbb{N} \times \mathit{Packet}; \\ \mathit{leave} & : \mathbb{N} \times \mathit{Packet}; \end{array}$$

The sending of a packet from an input buffer to an output buffer is described by means of the *send* action. Similarly, for the receipt of a packet by an output buffer, the action *recv* is used. To synchronize actions, mCRL2 provides synchronous communication between processes, if all the action data parameters in the synchronizing actions have the same value. To show (and observe) that a send and receive synchronize, we use the action *comm*, which reflects the successful synchronization of a *send* and a *recv*.

The actions *send*, *recv* and *comm* are each modeled with three data parameters. The first parameter is used to denote the identity of the input buffer that sends the package, the second parameter denotes the identity of the output buffer that receives the package, and the last parameter denotes the packet that is actually being transferred. The first and second parameter provide handles to observe the routing of packets; i.e., they are used to express and verify requirements later on. The last data parameter is required to transfer and observe the data flow between buffers. Note that the second parameter is a cosmetic addition, as its can also be obtained from the data of the packet itself.

$$\textbf{act}\quad \begin{array}{ll} \mathit{send} & : \mathbb{N} \times \mathbb{N} \times \mathit{Packet}; \\ \mathit{recv} & : \mathbb{N} \times \mathbb{N} \times \mathit{Packet}; \\ \mathit{comm} & : \mathbb{N} \times \mathbb{N} \times \mathit{Packet}; \end{array}$$

In the Simplified Switch case study, the packet exchange between an input buffer, say i, and an output buffer, say o, not only depends on the behavior expressed in the processes, but also on the contents of the other input buffer. In mCRL2, it is possible to use multi-party communication to establish the involvement of another process. This means that we require actions that reveal information about a third party in the communication. We introduce actions *grant* and *free* for this purpose. Both $\mathit{grant}(i,j,p)$ and $\mathit{free}(i,j,p)$ denote that input buffer i is granted permission to send a packet p to output buffer j. One of these actions is used for establishing priority and the other one for simultaneous packet transfer. A more detailed explanation is provided later in this section.

$$\textbf{act}\quad \begin{array}{ll} \mathit{grant} & : \mathbb{N} \times \mathbb{N} \times \mathit{Packet}; \\ \mathit{free} & : \mathbb{N} \times \mathbb{N} \times \mathit{Packet}; \end{array}$$

3.4 The Output Buffers with Capacity *cap*

In mCRL2, a FIFO buffer *Output* with capacity *cap* is given by the following process specification:

$$\begin{array}{l} \textbf{proc}\ \mathit{Output}(i:\mathbb{N}, c:\mathit{List}(\mathit{Packet})) = \\ \qquad \#c < \mathit{cap} \rightarrow \sum_{s:\mathbb{N}} \sum_{p:\mathit{Packet}} \mathit{recv}(s,i,p) \cdot \mathit{Output}(i, p \triangleright c) \\ \quad + \ c \not\approx [\,] \qquad \rightarrow \mathit{leave}(i, \mathit{rhead}(c)) \cdot \mathit{Output}(i, \mathit{rtail}(c)); \end{array}$$

The first line in the above model specifies the name of the process and declares the associated process parameters. In this case the buffer has two parameters. The first process parameter represents the identity of an output buffer. The second process parameter captures the contents of the queue as a list of packets. As already described, an arbitrary packet can be received as long as the buffer is not yet full ($\#c$ denotes the number of elements in the list c). So the first summand, specifies that when a packet is received, it is appended to the buffer. Appending a packet p to a buffer contents c is denoted by $p \triangleright c$. The second summand describes that the packet (if any) that has been inserted into the queue (so the buffer is not empty, $c \not\approx []$) first ($rhead(c)$ denotes this element), it exits the switch by means of the *leave* action and is removed from the queue ($rtail(c)$). Note that modeling the buffer in this way, the specification of the output buffer does not rely in any way on the fact that only packets with a specific first bit will be send to it, e.g. it accepts packets regardless of their content.

For both the output buffer as described in this subsection and the input buffer described in the following subsection we have chosen to allow it to perform at most one action at the same time.

3.5 The Input Buffers with Capacity *cap*

The main challenges of this modeling exercise are to deal appropriately with the priority of input buffer 0 over input buffer 1 in case both buffers want to transfer a packet to the same destination; and to deal with the required simultaneous packet transfer in case both buffers want to transfer packets to different destinations. In this section we gradually shape the model, by defining the interaction between the different processes, as well as specifying the input buffer such that it eventually complies to the settled design intent.

We start by modeling the behavior of the input buffer analogously to the output buffer:

$$
\begin{aligned}
&\textbf{proc}\ Input(i:\mathbb{N}, c: List(Packet)) = \\
&\qquad \#c < cap \rightarrow \sum_{p:Packet} enter(i,p) \cdot Input(i, p \triangleright c) \\
&\qquad + c \not\approx [] \rightarrow send(i, dest(rhead(c)), rhead(c)) \cdot Input(i, rtail(c));
\end{aligned}
$$

Next, we setup the basic communication between input buffers and output buffers. We first specify that the four buffers require to run in parallel. Furthermore, we specify that a successful synchronization of *send* and *recv* actions, results in a *comm* action. This is expressed by means of the subscript parameter $send|recv \rightarrow comm$ in the communication operator Γ. We only allow successful communications, therefore we encapsulate all *send* and *recv* actions that do not result in a successful synchronization. This way, insertion or removal of a packet can be done simultaneously, while other buffers transfer packets. Combining the instantiated process definitions with the communication and encapsulated operators, leads to the following initialization:

$$\textbf{init} \;\; \partial_{\{send,recv\}}(\Gamma_{\{send|recv \rightarrow comm\}}(\\ \quad Input(0,[\,]) \parallel Input(1,[\,]) \parallel Output(0,[\,]) \parallel Output(1,[\,])));$$

To acquire the simultaneous packet transfer and prioritized packet transfer, the model needs to be adapted in two ways. The first step takes care of the prioritized packet transfer if packets route to the same destination. The second step takes care of the required simultaneous packet transfer to different output buffers.

Prioritized packet transfer. The way in which we deal with the prioritized packet transfer is as follows. The input buffer signals which transfers are allowed for execution by the other input buffer by means of the *grant*-action. If a buffer is empty it grants permission for any transfer in the other process of the input queue. If the buffer is not empty it only grants permission for a transferral of packets from each input buffer with a lower identity to the same output buffer.

$$\begin{aligned}
&\textbf{proc } Input(i:\mathbb{N}, c: List(Packet)) = \\
&\qquad \#c < cap \rightarrow \sum_{p:Packet} enter(i,p) \cdot Input(i, p \triangleright c) \\
&\qquad + c \not\approx [\,] \rightarrow send(i, dest(rhead(c)), rhead(c)) \cdot Input(i, rtail(c)); \\
&\qquad + c \approx [\,] \rightarrow \sum_{n,m:\mathbb{N}} \sum_{p:Packet} grant(n,m,p) \cdot Input(i,c) \\
&\qquad + c \not\approx [\,] \rightarrow \sum_{n:\mathbb{N}} n < i \rightarrow grant(n, dest(rhead(c)), rhead(c)) \cdot Input(i,c)
\end{aligned}$$

To ensure that the *grant*-action synchronizes with the other corresponding *send*- and *recv*-actions another communication function is added:

$$\textbf{init} \;\; \partial_{\{send,recv,grant\}}(\Gamma_{\{send|recv \rightarrow comm\}}(\Gamma_{\{send|recv|grant \rightarrow comm\}}(\\ \quad Input(0,[\,]) \parallel Input(1,[\,]) \parallel Output(0,[\,]) \parallel Output(1,[\,]))));$$

The nesting of the communication functions this way is necessary to ensure that priority is given.

Maximal communication. In order to meet the second requirement, the input buffer announces that it allows a simultaneous transferral of packets (from the other input buffer) with a different destination via the *free*-action.

$$\begin{aligned}
&\textbf{proc } Input(i:\mathbb{N}, c: List(Packet)) = \\
&\qquad \#c < cap \rightarrow \sum_{p:Packet} enter(i,p) \cdot Input(i, p \triangleright c) \\
&\qquad + c \not\approx [\,] \rightarrow \sum_{n:\mathbb{N}} \sum_{p:Packet} n \not\approx i \wedge dest(p) \not\approx dest(rhead(c)) \rightarrow \\
&\qquad\qquad send(i, dest(rhead(c)), rhead(c)) | free(n, dest(p), p) \cdot Input(i, rtail(c)) \\
&\qquad + c \not\approx [\,] \rightarrow send(i, dest(rhead(c)), rhead(c)) \cdot Input(i, rtail(c)) \\
&\qquad + c \approx [\,] \rightarrow \sum_{n,m:\mathbb{N}} \sum_{p:Packet} grant(n,m,p) \cdot Input(i,c) \\
&\qquad + c \not\approx [\,] \rightarrow \sum_{n:\mathbb{N}} n < i \rightarrow grant(n, dest(rhead(c)), rhead(c)) \cdot Input(i,c);
\end{aligned}$$

By adapting the communications in the outermost communication operator to $\{send|recv|free \rightarrow comm\}$ we achieve that packet transfers are only allowed in case the other input buffer grants permission. This way simultaneous packet transfers are achieved whenever possible. All possible communications are now permitted by either a *grant*- or a *free*-action.

$$\textbf{init}\ \partial_{\{send,recv,grant,free\}}(\Gamma_{\{send|recv|grant \rightarrow comm\}}(\Gamma_{\{send|recv|free \rightarrow comm\}}(\\ \quad Input(0,[]) \parallel Input(1,[]) \parallel Output(0,[]) \parallel Output(1,[]))));$$

The order in which the communication operators are applied to the parallel composition of the buffers is of no importance. It is not allowed to declare both communication operators by means of one communication operator since the left-hand sides of the communication patterns share an action, which might lead to a non-unique solution. For that reason the communication operators are placed in a hierarchial composition. We conjecture that the order of these communication operators is of no importance. To provide (partial) evidence, we have validated this claim, by using the mCRL2 tool set to establish that the respective labelled transition systems are strongly bisimilar (even isomorphic) for the case that the capacity of the buffers is 1, 2 and 3.

4 Specification of the Original 2 × 2 Switch

The Original Switch is an extension of the Simplified Switch. The Original switch contains an additional counter, that counts interesting packets that are transferred from input to output buffers. A packet is considered interesting if its second, third, and fourth bit are all 0. The counter is restricted. Therefore the value can only be incremented by one per clock cycle. So when both input buffers are capable of transferring interesting packets, priority is given to the transferral of packets from input buffer 0 and the transferral of packets from input buffer 1 is delayed. Thus, we may only transfer packets simultaneously if they are not both interesting. In all other cases a process needs to either take or grant priority as in the Simplified Switch case study.

In this section, we adapt the model of the Simplified Switch to obtain a model that corresponds to the design intent of the Original Switch. Thereto, we need to extend a part of the data specification and adapt the behaviors of the buffer processes slightly.

4.1 Packets

The fact that the second, third and fourth bit of a packet have become relevant for the behaviour of the switch means that we have to reconsider our definition of the data type representing packets. We can introduce packets with four bits (all relevant ones) in a way similar to the current definition. Instead, and more abstractly, we decide to model packets as before but now with an additional

Boolean parameter indicating whether the packet is interesting (*true*) or not (*false*).

$\textbf{sort}\ \ Packet = \textbf{struct}\ packet(b_1 : Bit,\ int : \mathbb{B});$

By extending the structured sort, we are required to update the definition of the mapping for routing packets. As the second, third, and fourth bit have no effect on the destination of a packet, the adaptation is straightforward.

$$\begin{array}{ll} \textbf{map} & dest : Packet \to \mathbb{N}; \\ \textbf{var} & b : \mathbb{B}; \\ \textbf{eqn} & dest(packet(\mathsf{zero}, b)) = 0; \\ & dest(packet(\mathsf{one}, b)) = 1; \end{array}$$

4.2 The Act of Counting

There are several ways of modelling the counting of interesting packets. One way is to introduce a parameter that reflects the number of interesting packets that have been transferred. Another way is to introduce an action to indicate a transferral of an interesting packet. We have chosen the latter solution. Thus, the act of counting interesting packets will be performed by executing an action *inc*, that has no data parameters.

$\textbf{act}\ \ inc;$

Another decision that must be made is which entity actually performs the counting. One solution is to introduce a separate process for this purpose. Another option is to enhance the functionality of either the input or the output buffers. We have chosen to enhance the functionality of the output buffers. It should be said that implementing the other solutions poses no real problems for mCRL2.

To accommodate this behavior, the first summand of the output buffer from the Simplified Switch is split into two cases, one for receiving and counting an interesting packet and one for receiving a non-interesting packet. To decide if a packet is interesting, the projection function *int* is used. The projection function for a specific field of a structured sort is specified in the sort declaration. For the sort *Packet* there are projection functions b_1 and *int* for obtaining the values of the first and second field, respectively.

$$\begin{array}{l} \textbf{proc}\ Output(i : \mathbb{N}, c : List(Packet)) = \\ \qquad \#c < cap \to \sum_{s:\mathbb{N}} \sum_{p:Packet} (int(p) \to recv(s,i,p) | inc \cdot Output(i, p \rhd c) \\ \qquad\qquad\qquad\qquad\qquad\quad + \neg int(p) \to recv(s,i,p) \cdot Output(i, p \rhd c)) \\ \qquad + c \not\approx [\,] \qquad \to leave(i, rhead(c)) \cdot Output(i, rtail(c)); \end{array}$$

4.3 Adapting the Input Buffer

The Original Switch poses an additional restriction on the cases in which communication between input and output buffer can be performed.

We may only transfer packets simultaneously if they have different destinations and at most one packet is interesting. This is expressed in the second summand below.

In case both input buffers contain an interesting packet and these packets have different destinations, priority is granted to any input buffer with lower identity. See the fifth summand below.

We are required to grant priority to both interesting and non-interesting packets if the local packet is non-interesting. For that reason, the last summand is adapted as well.

$$
\begin{array}{l}
\textbf{proc } \mathit{Input}(i:\mathbb{N}, c:\mathit{List}(\mathit{Packet})) = \\
\qquad \#c < \mathit{cap} \rightarrow \sum_{p:\mathit{Packet}} \mathit{enter}(i,p) \cdot \mathit{Input}(i, p \rhd c) \\
\quad + c \not\approx [] \rightarrow \\
\qquad \sum_{p:\mathit{Packet}} \mathit{dest}(p) \not\approx \mathit{dest}(\mathit{rhead}(c)) \wedge (\neg \mathit{int}(p) \vee \neg \mathit{int}(\mathit{rhead}(c))) \rightarrow \\
\qquad \sum_{n:\mathbb{N}} n \not\approx i \rightarrow \mathit{send}(i, \mathit{dest}(\mathit{rhead}(c)), \mathit{rhead}(c)) | \mathit{free}(n, \mathit{dest}(p), p) \cdot \\
\qquad\qquad \mathit{Input}(i, \mathit{rtail}(c)) \\
\quad + c \not\approx [] \rightarrow \mathit{send}(i, \mathit{dest}(\mathit{rhead}(c)), \mathit{rhead}(c)) \cdot \mathit{Input}(i, \mathit{rtail}(c)) \\
\quad + c \approx [] \rightarrow \sum_{n,m:\mathbb{N}} \sum_{p:\mathit{Packet}} \mathit{grant}(n,m,p) \cdot \mathit{Input}(i,c) \\
\quad + c \not\approx [] \wedge \mathit{int}(\mathit{rhead}(c)) \rightarrow \sum_{p:\mathit{Packet}} \mathit{dest}(p) \approx \mathit{dest}(\mathit{rhead}(c)) \vee \mathit{int}(p) \rightarrow \\
\qquad \sum_{n:\mathbb{N}} n < i \rightarrow \mathit{grant}(n, \mathit{dest}(p), p) \cdot \mathit{Input}(i,c) \\
\quad + c \not\approx [] \wedge \neg \mathit{int}(\mathit{rhead}(c)) \rightarrow \sum_{p:\mathit{Packet}} b_1(p) \approx b_1(\mathit{rhead}(c)) \rightarrow \\
\qquad \sum_{n:\mathbb{N}} n < i \rightarrow \mathit{grant}(n, \mathit{dest}(\mathit{rhead}(c)), p) \cdot \mathit{Input}(i,c);
\end{array}
$$

5 Specification of the Modified 2 × 2 Switch

The modified 2 × 2 switch alters the way the priority is handled amongst colliding transfers in the case that the packets are both interesting and have a different destination. We have defined two conditions, namely both head packets have the same destination (C1) and both head packets are interesting (C2). If either one of these conditions holds, priority is given to the transferral of the packet from input buffer 0.

Now, in the Modified Switch, we keep that if C1 holds, the first input buffer will be given priority over the second buffer. However if C1 does not hold, while C2 holds, priority is given to transferral of the packet from input buffer 1.

This only requires the adaptation of the model of the input buffers. In the relevant case this time priority is granted to the input buffer with the higher identity. The last but one summand of the specification of the input buffer of the Original Switch is split in these two cases.

$$
\begin{array}{l}
\textbf{proc } \mathit{Input}(i:\mathbb{N}, c:\mathit{List}(\mathit{Packet})) = \\
\quad \#c < \mathit{cap} \rightarrow \sum_{p:\mathit{Packet}} \mathit{enter}(i,p)\cdot \mathit{Input}(i, p \triangleright c) \\
\quad + c \not\approx [] \rightarrow \\
\qquad \sum_{p:\mathit{Packet}} \mathit{dest}(p) \not\approx \mathit{dest}(\mathit{rhead}(c)) \wedge (\neg \mathit{int}(p) \vee \neg \mathit{int}(\mathit{rhead}(c))) \rightarrow \\
\qquad \sum_{n:\mathbb{N}} n \not\approx i \rightarrow \mathit{send}(i, \mathit{dest}(\mathit{rhead}(c)), \mathit{rhead}(c)) | \mathit{free}(n, \mathit{dest}(p), p)\cdot \\
\qquad\qquad \mathit{Input}(i, \mathit{rtail}(c)) \\
\quad + c \not\approx [] \rightarrow \mathit{send}(i, \mathit{dest}(\mathit{rhead}(c)), \mathit{rhead}(c)) \cdot \mathit{Input}(i, \mathit{rtail}(c)) \\
\quad + c \approx [] \rightarrow \sum_{n,m:\mathbb{N}} \sum_{p:\mathit{Packet}} \mathit{grant}(n,m,p)\cdot \mathit{Input}(i,c) \\
\quad + c \not\approx [] \wedge \mathit{int}(\mathit{rhead}(c)) \rightarrow \sum_{p:\mathit{Packet}} \mathit{dest}(p) \approx \mathit{dest}(\mathit{rhead}(c)) \rightarrow \\
\qquad \sum_{n:\mathbb{N}} n < i \rightarrow \mathit{grant}(n, \mathit{dest}(p), p)\cdot \mathit{Input}(i,c) \\
\quad + c \not\approx [] \wedge \mathit{int}(\mathit{rhead}(c)) \rightarrow \sum_{p:\mathit{Packet}} \mathit{dest}(p) \not\approx \mathit{dest}(\mathit{rhead}(c)) \wedge \mathit{int}(p) \rightarrow \\
\qquad \sum_{n:\mathbb{N}} n > i \rightarrow \mathit{grant}(n, \mathit{dest}(p), p)\cdot \mathit{Input}(i,c) \\
\quad + c \not\approx [] \wedge \neg \mathit{int}(\mathit{rhead}(c)) \rightarrow \sum_{p:\mathit{Packet}} b_1(p) \approx b_1(\mathit{rhead}(c)) \rightarrow \\
\qquad \sum_{n:\mathbb{N}} n < i \rightarrow \mathit{grant}(n, \mathit{dest}(\mathit{rhead}(c)), p)\cdot \mathit{Input}(i,c);
\end{array}
$$

6 Properties of the Models

In [6], the authors presented their models without any form of formal verification. For Statecharts this already led to a model that did not meet the design intent, according to [6]. Their model contained a flaw when both buffers contain interesting head packets and one of the buffers was full while the other was not. In that case, one packet should be delayed while the other head packet was routed. This however was not covered.

To convince readers that our models capture the design intent, we formulate some requirements and verify that the models satisfy them. These requirements relate to deadlock analysis, overflowing buffers, packet collection and maximum progress. The requirements are expressed in terms of modal μ-calculus formulae. The mCRL2 tool set allows for checking the validity of such formulae on labelled transition systems obtained from mCRL2 models.

6.1 Deadlock Detection

Deadlock is a specific condition that brings the system into a halt, from which it cannot execute any behavior for any future. Deadlock can be caused by various reasons, amongst others due to circular resource dependencies or when processes cannot fulfill their precondition in order to execute an extension.

We claim that all of the presented models are free from deadlock. Deadlock freedom is expressed by the following modal μ-calculus formula:

$$[\mathit{true}^\star]\langle \mathit{true}\rangle \mathit{true} \tag{1}$$

6.2 Absence of Overflowing Buffers

We have used the standard mCRL2 type construction of lists for modeling the contents of the buffer. Thought the lengths of such lists are not fixed or bound from above, the use in combination with the constant *cap* guarantees that there can be no overflows of the buffers. By means of adding the alternative summand:

$$\#c > \mathit{cap} \rightarrow \mathit{overflow} \cdot \mathit{Input}(i, c)$$

to the input buffers, and the summand

$$\#c > \mathit{cap} \rightarrow \mathit{overflow} \cdot \mathit{Output}(i, c)$$

to the output buffers, we can easily check that this situation can never occur by verifying the validity of the modal formula

$$[\mathit{true}^{\star} \cdot \mathit{overflow}]\mathit{false} \tag{2}$$

on the model that is obtained after abstracting from all actions besides *overflow*. This formula then expresses that there can be no execution that performs the action *overflow*.

6.3 Absence of Colliding Packets

The property that no simultaneous packet transfers are possible to the same output buffer is specified by means of the following modal μ-calculus formula:

$$\forall_{p,q:Packet} \forall_{i,j,k:\mathbb{N}}\ [\mathit{true}^{*}.(\mathit{comm}(i, j, p)|\mathit{comm}(k, j, q))]\mathit{false} \tag{3}$$

This formula must be checked on the model after abstraction from all other actions. This means that for the Simplified Switch the following model has been used

$$\textbf{init}\ \tau_{\{enter,leave\}}(\partial_{\{send,recv,grant,free\}}(\Gamma_{\{send|recv|grant \rightarrow comm\}}(\Gamma_{\{send|recv|free \rightarrow comm\}}(\mathit{Input}(0, []) \parallel \mathit{Input}(1, []) \parallel \mathit{Output}(0, []) \parallel \mathit{Output}(1, []))))));$$

In a similar way, abstract models for Original and Modified Switch can be defined.

It is not allowed to send two interesting packets simultaneously. This is verified by checking the modal μ-calculus formula

$$\forall_{p,q:Packet} \forall_{i,j,k,l:\mathbb{N}}\ (\mathit{int}(p) \wedge \mathit{int}(q)) \Rightarrow [\mathit{true}^{\star}.(\mathit{comm}(i, j, p)|\mathit{comm}(k, l, q))]\mathit{false} \tag{4}$$

on the system where all environmental actions are abstracted from.

Requirement 3 is relevant for all three models discussed in this paper and Requirement 4 is only relevant for the latter two models.

6.4 Maximal Progress

A property we would like to verify is *maximal progress*. In the context of this case study, the property can be phrased as: "It is impossible to transfer a single packet from an input buffer to an output buffer in case a simultaneous packet transfer is possible." A modal μ-calculus formula that captures this (provided that it is checked on the model after abstraction of environmental actions) is the following:

$$\begin{aligned}\forall_{p,q:Packet}\, ([true^{\star}](\langle comm(0, dest(p), p) | comm(1, dest(q), q)\rangle true \\ \Rightarrow ([comm(1, dest(p), p)]false \wedge [comm(1, dest(q), q)]false))) \end{aligned} \tag{5}$$

Note that this way of expressing maximal progress does *not* enforce that packet transfer takes priority over environmental actions.

6.5 Verification Results

The requirements have been checked for the all the (relevant) models, for which the buffers have capacity 3. This buffer capacity has been chosen because it still allows for a reasonably fast analysis. The analysis has been conducted with the mCRL2 tool set (Release 2010, January), on an x86-64 GNU/Linux, running kernel 2.6.31.12, with an Intel® Core™ 2 Duo Mobile Processor T9600 and 4GB of RAM.

The results of the formal analysis are captured in Table 1. Requirements that hold w.r.t. a particular model are marked with "✓". The time that the verification took is also indicated. Requirements that are irrelevant for a specific model are marked with a "-". It shows that for each of the models all relevant formulae hold. It should be noted that we have not attempted to reduce these numbers as much as possible by using state space reduction techniques.

Table 1. Results of verifying properties on the models

Requirement	Simplified	Original	Modified
1	✓, 3.550s	✓, 5m3.863s	✓, 5m16.921s
2	✓, 3.729s	✓, 7m35.686s	✓, 7m35.202s
3	✓, 3.778s	✓, 4m44.647s	✓, 4m49.101s
4	–	✓, 5m29.906s	✓, 5m39.844s
5	✓, 3.301s	✓, 4m22.232s	✓, 4m33.786s

7 Comparison

This case study originates form work, gathered in [6]. There, the authors discuss the same case studies, described in the specification languages: TLA+, Bluespec, State-charts and ACP. As we have elaborated on the construction of the different models with their underlying design decisions in mCRL2, this section describes the deviation of the formalisms with respect to the case study. The comparison focusses on three aspects, namely locality of reasoning, adaptability of the language and maximal throughput. Furthermore we extend the focus by taking verification into account.

Before explaining the comparison, we give a brief description of the four languages. First, TLA+ (the Temporal Logic of Actions) is a complete specification language, that uses logic for the specification and reasoning about concurrent and reactive systems. It is designed for writing specifications consisting of non-temporal mathematics with temporal logic and tries to capture a complete system in a single formula [14]. Second, Bluespec [12] is a guarded command language, based on an operation centric description, where the behavior of a system is described as a collection of atomic operations in the form of rules. These rules are defined by a predicate condition and the effect on the state of the system. During execution several rules are concurrently executed in a clock cycle. Third we consider Statecharts, which are an extension of conventional state-transition diagrams with three elements, dealing, with hierarchy, concurrency and communication [11]. The graphical hierarchy presentation enables designers to adapt to the required level of detail of the system. Finally, the comparison covers the Algebra of Communicating Processes (ACP) [3]. ACP is a finite axiomatisation based framework for specifying and manipulating the behaviour of models. It facilitates the behavioural description for non-deterministic choices, sequential operations, parallel composition, deadlock and communication.

7.1 Maximal Throughput

Within the specification maximal throughput is achieved by executing multiple actions in a single clock cycle. Therefore, this comparison narrows down the scope to the behaviour for simultaneous actions.

It is not possible to describe the simultaneous transfer of packets in TLA+ and ACP. Therefore a designer is required to apply a spatial reasoning to verify that indeed packets are transferred simultaneously. As we compare the formalism to mCRL2, we see that within mCRL2, it is possible to define multi-actions. We believe that these multi-actions are more suitable for specifying the throughput behavior as they relate better to the simultaneous packet transfers in the system. Therefore it is not necessary for a designer to reason about multiple transitions.

For Bluespec specifications, a greedy run-time scheduler tries to acquire maximal throughput. It should be noted that in some cases a maximal throughput cannot be obtained, even though all conflict-free rules are selected. To minimize latency, the scheduler may chose a maximal set of actions of the design for execution during each hardware clock cycle. Therefore it is possible that this set does violate the maximal throughput requirement [15]. As exploration in mCRL2 is exhaustive, and latency is no issue, maximal throughput can be guaranteed, by means of synchronizing actions and guards. Furthermore, although not specified here, we believe that it possible to use the mCRL2 time operator to enforce throughput in different ways, e.g. by enforcing the execution of actions at predefined timestamps.

Regarding Statecharts, the authors of [6] did not give a suitable description in their paper, as they specified a wrong model. Therefore a comparison for maximal throughput, renders useless as a throughput analysis on Statecharts is omitted. Note that this does not mean that it is impossible to give a correct model using Statecharts.

7.2 Priority

The locality of reasoning is derived from the way priority is assigned to the routing of packets.

To reduce the amount of global reason, w.r.t. the communication we have generalized from the specific implementations of the input buffers. This allows us to reason on a local level about priorities. This shows if we compare our models to those as given in ACP. Note that within mCRL2, we have modelled priority by means of permissions, and therefore the contents of the buffers are invisible to other processes. In the given ACP models, the queues are directly inspected by the other processes. This requires a more spatial reasoning in ACP, in order to derive the priority.

Within TLA+, the priority of a packet transfer is handled at a local level. So with respect to assigning priority to executing actions, mCRL2 and TLA+ are comparable. We do have to note that the input queues, as well as the output queues are grouped in TLA+. This makes it possible for TLA+ actions to directly observe the queue of another process, at a local level. When comparing this method to the one given in our models, we believe that it is possible in mCRL2 to apply reasoning on a more local level.

The Bluespec specification defines rules that implicitly deal with mutually exclusive access to shared resources. When multiple rules access the same resource, access is given to the resource defined first in the priority hierarchy. In this way, priority amongst packet transfers is ensured. Note that priority rules are defined on a spatial level. Therefore, the reasoning that needs to be applied is more spatial than the one used in mCRL2.

Within Statecharts all the behavior of the buffers are locally specified, however global temporal reasoning is required to establish the priority among packet transfers. A simultaneous transfer requires a global spatial reasoning over at least four individual Statecharts.

7.3 Adaptability

In [6], the authors only explain TLA+ for the simple switch. Though they claim that TLA+ relates to Bluespec, they do not show models for the original and modified switch. For that reason, the adaptability of TLA+ is unclear, since we are no experts in it. This does not permit us to judge whether mCRL2 performs better or worse in terms of adaptability.

A similar reasoning holds for Statecharts. The authors describe in a fairly easy way how to obtain a simple switch from the original switch. However, the subsequent discussion they show that the presented model of the original switch is incorrect and requires a more complicated model to capture the design intent. Since this correct complicated model is not given, it is not fair to make a comparison.

For modeling the modified switch in Bluespec, the authors require an entire redesign of the original switch, such that each priority separately defines rules. This leads to almost a duplication of the model. As we compare the same extension for our modified switch in mCRL2, we only have to split a summand and alter a guard, which is a rather small modification.

ACP serves well in terms of adaptability for this case study. As mCRL2 falls in the same category as ACP, this also holds for mCRL2. Therefore in terms of adaptability, mCRL2 and ACP are comparable.

Furthermore, we have set up the processes of the buffers in such a way that they can be easily reused for a more general specification, e.g. a $N \times M$ specification. To do so, we are required to add extra process references in the initialisation, and add extra rules to the data equations for routing packets. Within the current models we allow, that only one packet can be send simultaneously within a clock cycle. By adding more processes, this bound will not change. To increase the throughput, e.g. allowing more message transfers per clock cycle, we need to add summands that grant this communication. We argue that these modifications can be done at a local level.

7.4 Verification

The authors of [6] are unable to convince themselves that the specification they give are correct with respect to the design intent. As their remark essentially holds for all specifications, it already shows the first pitfalls in concurrent system design.

In line with the authors of [6], we agree that global reasoning is required on a specification across all the processes to verify system requirements. This however is a difficult task. As the description of the models is fairly simple, their explicit behaviour is not. In Figure 1 we have taken the opportunity to show, that even for a small system like the simplified switch, it already leads to systems that cannot be overlooked by human reasoning[1]. For a buffer capacity of three elements, we generate a state-space of 3600 states with 41137 transitions[2]. Nevertheless, with the automated methods of the mCRL2 tool set it turns out to be possible to verify interesting properties of the modelled systems. This does not require reasoning by humans, which is the case for establishing properties using the formalisms used in [6].

[1] These numbers are obtained, without applying any reduction techniques. We are aware that these numbers can be reduced. Note that the number of states and the number of transitions are given on a logarithmic scale.

[2] Please note that multi-actions that contain precisely the same actions are only taken into account once. Otherwise, the numbers of transitions would have been much larger.

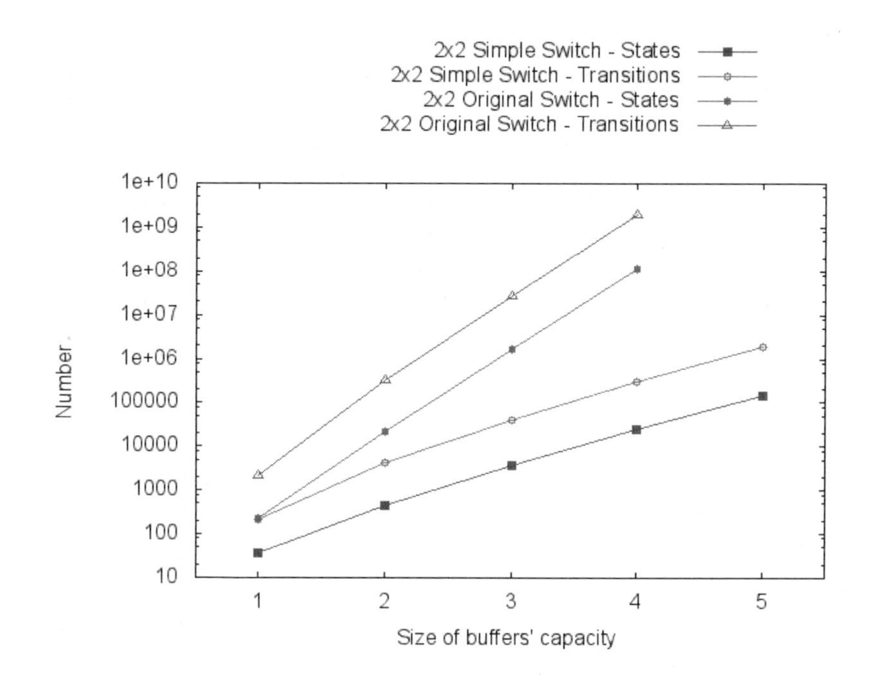

Fig. 1. Complexity of the model expressed in number of states and transitions for the simplified and original switch models

8 Conclusion and Future Work

In this paper, we have shown, in a case-study, that mCRL2 is suitable for the modelling and subsequent analysis of a system in which multi-party communications combined with priority-based communication occur. We have tried to apply local reasoning as much as possible, by generalizing the behavior of the buffers by type, thereby preserving both the possibility to send prioritized packets as well as sending packets simultaneously. As a consequence, it is possible to re-use the models in a more general setting. Furthermore, we showed that with mCRL2, we were also able to verify some properties, that has led to an increase in confidence that the model represents the design intent. Thereby, we have shown that mCRL2 is at least comparable to the formalisms used in [6], and in some cases more suitable for specifying complex system designs.

We should note that the comparison is based on subjective grounds. For a fair comparison, one should study the possible language constructs for each of the formalisms and point out the differences. This requires an expert over multiple formalisms or a cooperation among experts of different formalisms. Since the case study is centered around a specific specification, for which the models are created according to the level of expertise of the designers, the outcome of the comparison is subjective. As the authors of this paper can be considered experts when it comes to mCRL2 specifications, and are familiar with ACP and Statecharts, we are confident about the claims made between these formalisms.

We have shown that it is possible to capture relative performance requirements, without explicitly stating time. Since mCRL2 falls into the category of timed process algebra's [2], it allows designers to specify real-time behaviour. Nevertheless, we have chosen not to do so for several reasons. First, we would like to have a fair comparison between the untimed formalisms. Second, timed requirements tend to be complex in general and require challenging manipulations on the mCRL2 models before one can verify requirements. Nevertheless, we believe that the case study considered in this paper can be formulated in a timed specification, and can serve as subject of study for reduction and analysis techniques for timed systems.

References

1. Baeten, J.C.M., Basten, T., Reniers, M.A.: Process Algebra: Equational Theories of Communicating Processes. Cambridge tracts in theoretical computer science, vol. 50. Cambridge University Press, Cambridge (2010)
2. Baeten, J.C.M., Kees Middelburg, C.A.: Process Algebra with Timing. In: EATCS Monographs, Springer, Berlin (2002)
3. Bergstra, J.A., Klop, J.W.: Process algebra for synchronous communication. Information and Control 60(1-3), 109–137 (1984)
4. Bluespec: Automatic Generation of Control Logic with Bluespec SystemVerilog (Februari 2005), `http://www.bluespec.com/forum/download.php?id=63`
5. Bradfield, J.C.: Verifying Temporal Properties of Systems. In: Progress in Theoretical Computer Science, Birkhäuser, Basel (1992)
6. Daylight, E.G., Shukla, S.K.: On the difficulties of concurrent-system design, illustrated with a 2×2 switch case study. In: Cavalcanti, A., Dams, D.R. (eds.) FM 2009. LNCS, vol. 5850, pp. 273–288. Springer, Heidelberg (2009)
7. Groote, J.F., Keiren, J., Mathijssen, A., Ploeger, B., Stappers, F., Tankink, C., Usenko, Y., van Weerdenburg, M., Wesselink, W., Willemse, T., van der Wulp, J.: The mCRL2 toolset. In: Proceedings International Workshop on Advanced Software Development Tools and Techniques, WASDeTT 2008 (2008)
8. Groote, J.F., Mateescu, R.: Verification of temporal properties of processes in a setting with data. In: Haeberer, A.M. (ed.) AMAST 1998. LNCS, vol. 1548, pp. 74–90. Springer, Heidelberg (1998)
9. Groote, J.F., Mathijssen, A., Reniers, M., Usenko, Y., van Weerdenburg, M.: The formal specification language mCRL2. In: Brinksma, E., Harel, D., Mader, A., Stevens, P., Wieringa, R. (eds.) Methods for Modelling Software Systems (MMOSS). Dagstuhl Seminar Proceedings, vol. 06351, Internationales Begegnungs- und Forschungszentrum fuer Informatik (IBFI), Schloss Dagstuhl, Germany (2007)
10. Groote, J.F., Mathijssen, A.H.J., Reniers, M.A., Usenko, Y.S., van Weerdenburg, M.J.: Analysis of distributed systems with mCRL2. In: Alexander, M., Gardner, W. (eds.) Process Algebra for Parallel and Distributed Processing, ch. 4, pp. 99–128. Taylor & Francis, Abington (2009)
11. Harel, D.: Statecharts: A visual formalism for complex systems. Sci. Comput. Program. 8(3), 231–274 (1987)

12. Hoe, J.C., Arvind: Synthesis of operation-centric hardware descriptions. In: Proceedings of the 2000 IEEE/ACM international conference on Computer-aided design, ICCAD 2000, Piscataway, NJ, USA, pp. 511–519. IEEE Press, Los Alamitos (2000)
13. Kozen, D.: Results on the propositional mu-calculus. Theor. Comput. Sci. 27, 333–354 (1983)
14. Lamport, L.: Specifying Systems, The TLA+ Language and Tools for Hardware and Software Engineers. Addison-Wesley, Reading (2002)
15. Singh, G., Shukla, S.K.: Verifying compiler based refinement of Bluespec^{TM} specifications using the spin model checker. In: Havelund, K., Majumdar, R., Palsberg, J. (eds.) SPIN 2008. LNCS, vol. 5156, pp. 250–269. Springer, Heidelberg (2008)

Mapping UML to Labeled Transition Systems for Test-Case Generation

A Translation via Object-Oriented Action Systems*

Willibald Krenn[1], Rupert Schlick[2], and Bernhard K. Aichernig[1]

[1] Institute for Software Technology, Graz University of Technology, Austria
{wkrenn,aichernig}@ist.tugraz.at
[2] Austrian Institute of Technology, Vienna, Austria
Rupert.Schlick@ait.ac.at

Abstract. The Unified Modeling Language (UML) is a well known and widely used standard for building software models. While it is familiar to many software engineers, it lacks standardized formal semantics. In this paper, we extend on the formalism of object-oriented action systems (OOAS) and describe a mapping of a selected UML-subset to OOAS by choosing one of the several possible semantics of UML. This mapping, together with the introduction of a trace semantics for OOAS, paves the way for applying tools for and theory of labeled transition systems to UML-models. As a running example, we use a car alarm system in the context of model-based test-case generation and show how the UML mapping is done.

1 Introduction

Today, embedded computer systems constitute an integral part of almost all technology surrounding us. They are increasingly integrated in safety-relevant systems, either in any kind of vehicles, medical equipment, or industrial or public control systems. Evidently, any possible measure has to be taken to ensure the dependability of such systems, from early planning and design to final installation and maintenance.

The standards EN 50128 and IEC 61508 recommend the use of formal methods, especially at higher Safety Integrity Levels (SILs). However, despite the decades of research dedicated to formal methods, most engineers still lack experience and confidence in this field. Techniques like theorem proving or model checking are rarely applied to large and complex systems.

Therefore, testing remains the preferred method of verification, despite the fact that it is very expensive. In general, about half of the overall effort of a project is dedicated to testing, and for safety-relevant projects the amount of time spent on testing is even higher. Consequently, there is a huge demand for

* Research herein was funded by the EU FP7 project ICT-216679, Model-based Generation of Tests for Dependable Embedded Systems (MOGENTES).

F.S. de Boer et al. (Eds.): FMCO 2009, LNCS 6286, pp. 186–207, 2010.

reliable automatic test case generation tools grounded on solid foundations. The European FP7 project MOGENTES serves these demands.

MOGENTES stands for Model-based Generation of Tests for Dependable Embedded Systems and its goal is to significantly enhance testing and verification of dependable embedded systems by means of automated generation of efficient test cases relying on development of new approaches as well as innovative integration of state-of-the-art techniques. In particular, MOGENTES aims at the application of these technologies in large industrial systems, simultaneously enabling application domain experts (with rather little knowledge and experience in usage of formal methods) to use them with minimal learning effort.

The industrial partners in the project identified UML as their future modeling paradigm and hence, require test case generation tools to process UML models. This need conflicts with the requirement that our test case generation technique has to be build on solid foundations, because UML lacks a standard formal semantics. However, a formal semantics is essential for our testing techniques based on precise fault-models and formal notions of conformance. Therefore, we decided to treat UML as a front-end modeling language and translate it to a formal back-end formalism on which our test case generators will work on.

In this paper, we give insights into this translation process. A car alarm system serves as a running example. Section 2 presents the UML model of the car alarm system including the technique to express the testing interface in UML class diagrams. Then, Section 3 presents and motivates our back-end formalism, namely Object-Oriented Action Systems (OOAS), a formalism well-suited for expressing object-oriented models of embedded systems. This section also presents a further level of semantic mapping: the behavior of state-rich OOAS is interpreted as a series of controllable and observable events. It is this event-level on which our test case generators work. This gives us the advantage that we can base our formal testing approach on the existing testing theory on labeled-transition systems. Next, in Section 4 we discuss our semantic mapping, including the translation of non-trivial UML state charts with nested states, parallel regions and time triggers. In Section 5 we discuss the case study. Finally, in Section 6 we draw our conclusion and give an outlook on future and related work.

2 A UML-Model

We use a very simplified car alarm system as an example for discussing the concepts and issues of the transformation of UML models to action systems. The example is taken from Ford's automotive demonstrator within MOGENTES and the main purpose of this rather simple example within the project is to test and validate the test-case generation work flow on a basic level. Notice that we are dealing with black-box testing here, as, e.g., Ford wants to test components provided by an external partner based on the requirements that were given to this company.

Before we can generate any test-cases, we need to build a model from the requirements. For our simplified car alarm system (CAS), we were given the following three textual requirements.

Requirement 1: Arming. The system is armed 20 seconds after the vehicle is locked and the bonnet, luggage compartment and all doors are closed.

Requirement 2: Alarm. The alarm sounds for 30 seconds if an unauthorized person opens the door, the luggage compartment or the bonnet. The hazard flasher lights will flash for five minutes.

Requirement 3: Deactivation. The anti-theft alarm system can be deactivated at any time, even when the alarm is sounding, by unlocking the vehicle from outside.

When trying to construct an animated model based on textual requirements it is often the case that conflicts or underspecified situations become apparent. One might think that the simplistic car alarm system is sufficiently described by these three textual requirements – the contrary is the case. What is left unspecified is the case of what happens when an alarm is ended by the five minute timeout: does the system go back to armed directly, or does it need to wait for all doors to be closed again before returning to armed?

2.1 Testing Interface and Instantiation

The UML model of the car alarm system comprises four classes and four signals, as shown in Fig. 1. The class *AlarmSystem* is marked as system under test (SUT) and may receive any of the *Lock*, *Unlock*, *Close*, or *Open* signals. At the same time, the SUT calls methods of the classes *AlarmArmed*, *AcousticAlarm*, and *OpticalAlarm* – all of them marked as being part of the environment.

Notice that the context diagram specifies the observations (all calls to methods being part of the environment) we can make and the stimuli the system under test can take (all signals). In effect, this diagram specifies our testing interface.

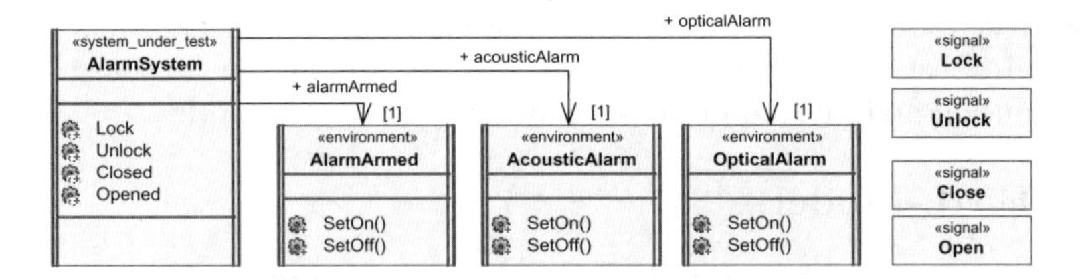

Fig. 1. Car Alarm System - Testing Interface

We use an initialization diagram (not shown) to specify the system configuration: we create a singleton object for each of the classes.

2.2 State Machine

Fig. 2 shows the CAS state-machine diagram. From the state *OpenAndUnlocked* one can traverse to *ClosedAndLocked* by closing all doors and locking the car.

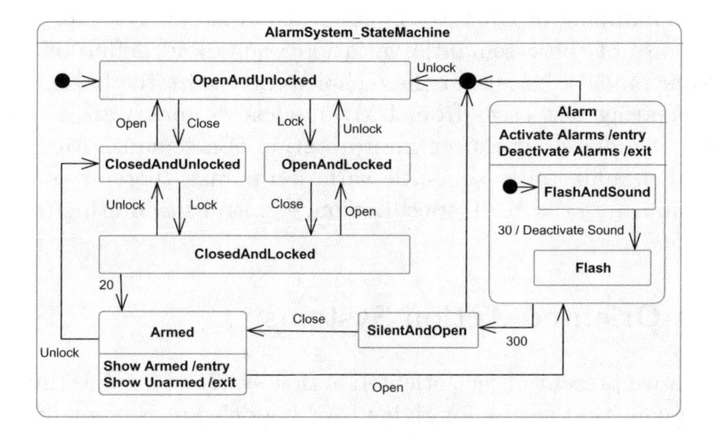

Fig. 2. Car Alarm System - State Machine

Actions of closing, opening, locking, and unlocking are modeled by corresponding signals *Close*, *Open*, *Lock*, and *Unlock*. As specified in the first requirement, the alarm system is armed after 20 seconds in *ClosedAndLocked*. Upon entry of the *Armed* state, the model calls the method *AlarmArmed.SetOn*. Upon leaving the state, which can be done by either unlocking the car or opening a door, *AlarmArmed.SetOff* is called. Similar, when entering the *Alarm* state, the optical and acoustic alarms are enabled. When leaving the alarm state, either via a timeout or via unlocking the car, both acoustic and optical alarm are turned off. When leaving the alarm state after a timeout (cf. second requirement) we decided to interpret the requirements in a way that the system returns to an armed state only in case it receives a close signal. Turning off the acoustic alarm after 30 seconds, as specified in the second requirement, is reflected in the time-triggered transition leading to the *Flash* sub-state of the *Alarm* state.

2.3 Semantic Variation Points

Despite being machine readable, the presented UML model lacks precise semantics. As an example, the event processing-machinery within a state machine is not fully specified within the UML standard:

> No assumptions are made about the time intervals between event occurrence, event dispatching, and consumption. This leaves open the possibility of different semantic variations such as zero-time semantics. It is a semantic variation whether an event is discarded if there is no appropriate trigger defined for them. *[1], Trigger, p. 456*

These intentionally underspecified areas in the UML standard are called "semantic variation points" and are used within the UML specification to *provide leeway for domain-specific refinements of the general UML semantics ([1], p. 17)*. Other semantic variation points affect, e.g., time events and signal events. When we discuss the mapping of UML to object-oriented action systems in Section 4, we will make use of these semantic variation points and define one particular behavior of our models. Note that these choices may form the basis for semantic tests: when creating test cases from UML models we may want to find implementations that violate our chosen interpretation of a semantic variation point! Note also that in addition to semantic variation points, there are other sources of non-determinism in the UML specification, e.g., transition firing (cf. *[1], State Machine, p. 566*).

3 Object-Oriented Action Systems

In this section we present object-oriented action systems, our intermediate-level modeling language that we use for giving UML models precise semantics. Object-oriented action systems are an extension to the action system formalism initially proposed by Back et al. in [2,3]. The object-oriented extension presented here is based on the work of Bonsangue et al., published in [4]. We also use a prioritized composition operator that has already been introduced by Sekerinski et al. in [5]. Notice, however, that our work is the first to combine object-oriented action systems (with custom extensions), prioritized composition, complex data types, and a trace semantics of action systems. We start our description of object-oriented action systems with the introduction of normal (non-object-oriented) action systems.

3.1 Action Systems

Syntactically, we may represent an action system AS comprising m functions, a named actions, d non-deterministically composed anonymous actions, and a set F_I of imported functions syntactically as follows.

$$\begin{array}{lll} AS =_{df} |[& \textbf{var} & V : T = I \\ & \textbf{functions} & F_n^1 = F_b^1; \ldots; F_n^m = F_b^m \\ & \textbf{actions} & N_n^1 = N_b^1; \ldots; N_n^a = N_b^a \\ & & \textbf{do } A_1 \,\Box \ldots \Box\, A_d \textbf{ od} \\ \quad]| : F_I & & \end{array}$$

Notice that functions have a name, a body and may return a value. Named actions are similar to functions but may not have a return value. In the remainder of this paper, we assume that named actions may only be called from within the **do od**-block (that is, not from within named actions or functions), and that function-calls may not be recursively nested. We also demand that each named action has the form of a guarded command. Relying on these assumptions, we are allowed to re-write the action system in a more classical form, where only the actions within the **do od**-block are left:

$$\begin{array}{ll} AS =_{df} |[& \textbf{var } V : T = I \\ & \quad \textbf{do } A_1 \,\Box \ldots \Box\, A_d \textbf{ od} \\ \quad]| : Z & \end{array}$$

Within this representation, V is a vector of variables of types T, initialized with values I, all A_i $(1 \leq i \leq d)$ are actions, and $\Box$ stands for non-deterministic, demonic choice. Demonic choice of actions means that when an aborting action is enabled, this action is chosen. Notice that after "inline'ning" all imported functions $\in F_I$, Z denotes the set of imported variables of the environment that was accessed by the imported functions.

After eliminating all function calls, the action system consists of basic actions only (cf. Table 1) and all actions are part of the **do od**-block, also known as Dijkstra's guarded iteration statement [6]. The guarded iteration statement can be thought of as being a loop that selects one enabled action A_i for execution in each iteration. In case there is no action enabled, execution of the action system ceases as execution of the loop terminates.

We can determine the enabledness of an action A_i by computing the enabledness guard: Because we do not want an action A_i to be enabled for states in which it is guaranteed to establish any postcondition, i.e. behave miraculously, the enabledness guard is defined as $g.A =_{df} \neg wp(A, false)$, where $wp : Action \times (State \mapsto Bool) \mapsto (State \mapsto Bool)$ is the weakest precondition predicate transformer. For example, the precondition of a guarded command is given by

$$wp(\text{requires } guard : A \text{ end}, q) \equiv guard \Rightarrow wp(A, q)$$

with "$\Rightarrow$" denoting logical implication. Table 1 lists the weakest preconditions of all actions for any given predicate q.

Table 1. Semantics of Basic Actions

Action	Notation	$wp(Action, q)$
Sequential Composition	$S_1; \ldots; S_n$	$wp(S_1, wp(\ldots, wp(S_n, q)))$
Nondeterministic Composition	$S_1 \Box S_2$	$wp(S_1, q) \wedge wp(S_2, q)$
Prioritizing Composition	$S_1 // S_2$	$wp(S_1, q) \wedge$ $(\neg g.S_1 \Rightarrow wp(S_2, q))$
Guarded Command	requires p: S_1 end	$p \Rightarrow wp(S_1, q)$
Multiple Assignment	$y := e$	$q[y := e]$
Nondeterministic Assignment	$z := z'$ with Q	$(\forall z' \in Q.z \cdot q[z := z'])$
Local Variables	var $x_1 : T_1; \ldots; x_n : T_n : S$	$\forall x_1 \ldots x_n : wp(S, q)$
Skip	**skip**	q
Abort	**abort**	*false*

In Table 1, S_1, S_2 each denote an action, y lists of variables, z, z' variables, e is a list of expressions, p is a predicate over the state of the action system, $g.S_1$ is the enabledness guard of action S_1, and Q is a predicate over z, z' (and the state). The nondeterministic assignment assigns to variable z the value of z' for which Q holds. The statement aborts if this is not possible [3]. Notice that an action will terminate if the *termination guard* $t.A = wp(A, true)$ holds.

For any of the defined actions, the monotonicity (1) and conjunctivity (2) properties hold:

$$(p \Rightarrow q) \implies (wp(A,p) \Rightarrow wp(A,q)) \tag{1}$$

$$wp(A,P) \wedge wp(A,Q) \equiv wp(A,P \wedge Q) \tag{2}$$

In addition, we require an action to be bounded non-deterministic. The parallel composition of two action systems is done by joining all actions and variables. (Some variables may be shared between the systems.) As an example, the parallel composition $AS^1 \parallel AS^2$ of two action systems

$$\begin{aligned} AS^1 &= |[\ \textbf{var} \ X : T^1 = I^1; \\ &\quad \textbf{do} \ A_1^1 \ \Box \ \ldots \ \Box \ A_m^1 \ \textbf{od}]| : u^1 \\ AS^2 &= |[\ \textbf{var} \ Z : T^2 = I^2; \\ &\quad \textbf{do} \ A_1^2 \ \Box \ \ldots \ \Box \ A_n^2 \ \textbf{od}]| : u^2 \end{aligned}$$

yields $AS^{1\|2}$:

$$\begin{aligned} AS^{1\|2} = |[\ & \textbf{var} \ X : T^1 = I^1; Z : T^2 = I^2; \\ & \textbf{do} \ A_1^1 \ \Box \ \ldots \ \Box \ A_m^1 \\ & \Box \ A_1^2 \ \Box \ \ldots \ \Box \ A_n^2 \ \textbf{od} \\ ]| & : (u^1 \cup u^2) \setminus (v^1 \cup v^2) \end{aligned}$$

where v^i denotes all variables used (exported) from action system AS^i.

3.2 Object Orientation

We use the work of Bonsangue et al. [4] as the basis for object-oriented action systems: in particular we share the transformation step from object-oriented action systems to action systems. We differ in the notion of named actions and procedures and we add the ability to prioritize objects of a particular class with respect to objects of another class. Within our methodology, we use a very simple form of inheritance: A class C^2 is a valid subclass of C^1 if and only if the (syntactic) superposition (cf. [7]) refinement holds between the classes. Roughly speaking this means that C^2 may introduce additional variables and actions. However, none of the additional actions may have any effect on the variables of C^1, it must be guaranteed that when only considering the new actions and the initial state the system terminates, and the exit condition of C^2 must imply the exit condition of C^1. The subclass C^2 may override (refine) actions of C^1 in a way that the guard is strengthened and values to the additional variables are assigned.

Like most object-oriented programming languages, objects are constructed at runtime from classes with the help of a constructor statement $o := new(C)$, where o represents the instance (object) and C stands for some class. Similar to [4], a class C is a named type and can be represented as tuple $C =_{df} (C_n, C_b)$

where $C_n \in \mathcal{CN}$ is a class name from the set of class-names $\mathcal{CN}$ and C_b is the body of the type definition:

$$
\begin{array}{lll}
C_b =_{df} |[& \textbf{var} & V : T = I \\
 & \textbf{methods} & M_n^1 = M_b^1; \ldots; M_n^m = M_b^m \\
 & \textbf{actions} & N_n^1 = N_b^1; \ldots; N_n^a = N_b^a \\
 & \textbf{do}\ A\ \textbf{od} & \\
\quad]| : M_I & &
\end{array}
$$

Similar to our definition of action systems, V denotes a vector of state-variables of types T, initialized with a value of I. A class may have m methods, each one having a name and a body: $M^i =_{df} (M_n^i, M_b^i)$ $(1 \leq i \leq m)$. As in action systems, the class may import a set of methods M_I from other classes. Like before, we do not allow for recursive calls of methods (so we can easily in-line the calls), and named actions may only be called from within the **do od**-block. Notice that this implies that methods are "public", as they can be called by any other method or action. Again, methods are free to return a value while named actions may only take input parameters.

We restrict an object-oriented action system to a finite set of classes $\mathcal{C} =_{df} \{C^1, \ldots, C^k\}$ and a finite set of objects. Practically, this means that we allow object-instantiation only during state-variable initialization, which permits us a rather easy check of finiteness. When a class in an object-oriented action system is marked as *autocons*, one instance of the class will be created automatically at system start and is called a "root object".

We assume that all objects of one class have the same priority. Between objects of different classes, however, we allow ordering with the help of the prioritized composition operator: we introduce a so-called system assembling block (SAB). The SAB, which is an extension to the work of [4], specifies the ordering of priorities between objects of different classes. We rely extensively on this feature in order to model, e.g., event broadcasting, as is discussed in Section 4.4. The syntax of the system assembling block is defined by the following grammar.

$$SAB ::= C_n \ ((\ \Box \mid //\ )\ SAB)?$$

Notice that the non-deterministic choice operator denotes parallel composition and the prioritizing composition operator expresses a prioritizing composition of objects. As an example, $C^1 // C^2$ means that only if there is no action enabled in any of the C^1 objects, actions of any of the C^2 objects will be looked at.

Hence, we define an object-oriented action system as a 3-tuple $(\mathcal{C}, \mathcal{R}, SAB)$, where $\mathcal{C}$ is a finite set of classes $\{C^1, \ldots C^k\}$, $\mathcal{R} \subseteq \mathcal{C}$ is a set of classes that need to be instantiated once at system start, and SAB is the system assembling block. Within the system assembling block, each class-name $C_n^i \in \mathcal{C}$ must be listed once, and all listed names must be from $\mathcal{CN}$.

The semantics of object-oriented action systems are given by a mapping to action systems which is based on the work presented in [4]. The main idea of the mapping is to create one action system per object and join all action systems as specified in the system assembling block.

After generating the set of all object names $\mathcal{ON} =_{df} \cup_{C^i \in \mathcal{C}} \mathcal{ON}_{C^i}$, in a first step every action of a class C^i is translated into an action of an action system. During this step, method calls are transformed into function calls of action systems. Because a function call in an action system needs to statically specify the target action system name and the function name, i.e. looks like *ActionSystemName.FunctionName*(...), and the name of the target object (action system) is not known until runtime, the translation needs to split the method call into a non-deterministic choice over calls to all possible action systems (objects) created for the target type. Notice that an implementation may do this more efficiently: here we only show how an object-oriented action system could be directly specified using the action system syntax. Also notice that during the transformation of an object-oriented action system all named actions and methods get renamed so that the names are unique.

In a second step, each single class C^i of an object-oriented action system is translated into an action system: for the class C^i itself and for each object of C^i an action system is constructed. Remember that the methods have already been translated in the previous step. All action systems that were built in this step are then parallel composed and form the action system $A(C^i)$ describing class C^i.

Finally composing all action systems $A(C^i)$ as specified in the system assembly block completes the mapping of the object-oriented action system OO to an action system $A(OO)$.

3.3 Prioritizing Composition

Given two actions S_1 and S_2, then the prioritizing composition $S_1 \;//\; S_2$ can be re-written using non-deterministic choice and the enabledness guard as follows (cf. Table 1).

$$S_1 \;//\; S_2 \equiv S_1 \;\Box\; (\text{requires } \neg g.S_1 : S_2 \text{ end})$$

Hence, in case the enabledness guard of action S_1 does not hold, the system will deterministically choose action S_2 provided S_2 is enabled. However, if S_1 is enabled, the system will only choose S_1 because action S_2 is guarded by $\neg g.S_1$.

When prioritizing composition is applied to action systems AS^1 and AS^2 (as in the SAB), it is defined such that priority is given to the actions of AS^1 over the actions of AS^2. As an example, the prioritized composition $AS^1 \;//\; AS^2$ of two action systems

$$\begin{aligned} AS^1 = |[\; &\mathbf{var}\; X : T^1 = I_0^1; \\ &\mathbf{do}\; A_1^1 \;\Box\; \ldots \;\Box\; A_m^1 \;\mathbf{od}]| : u^1 \\ AS^2 = |[\; &\mathbf{var}\; Z : T^2 = I_0^2; \\ &\mathbf{do}\; A_1^2 \;\Box\; \ldots \;\Box\; A_n^2 \;\mathbf{od}]| : u^2 \end{aligned}$$

yields $AS^{1\;//\;2}$:

$$\begin{aligned} A^{1\;//\;2} = |[\; &\mathbf{var}\; X : T^1 = I_0^1; Z : T^2 = I_0^2; \\ &\mathbf{do}\; (A_1^1 \;\Box\; \ldots \;\Box\; A_m^1) \end{aligned}$$

$$// (A_1^2 \,\Box\, \ldots \,\Box\, A_n^2) \textbf{ od}$$
$$]| : (u^1 \cup u^2) \setminus (v^1 \cup v^2)$$

where v^i denotes all variables exported from action system AS^i.

Like on actions, prioritizing composition is associative on action systems. However, it does not in general distribute over parallel composition to the right when used on action systems. This is due to local variables that would be duplicated.

3.4 Complex Data Types

Finally we add complex data types, such as maps, lists, and tuples (besides objects) to our language of OOAS. Most operators on these complex types were taken from the set of operators defined in the Vienna Development Method (VDM) [8,9] and include domain/range restrictions, and distributed union/intersection among other standard operators. We also allow array-like access of list elements and set operators to be working on lists.

3.5 Trace Semantics

For black-box test-case generation purposes, we are interested in the abstract computation sequences, i.e. traces, of an action system. In [2] the computation of an action system starting from an initial state γ_0 is defined as a possibly infinite sequence t of the form

$$t =_{df} \gamma_0 \xrightarrow{S_i} \gamma_1 \cdots$$

with each $g.S_i$ enabled in the transition's initial state.

We will use the concept of named actions to define more abstract computation traces: we extend the name of named actions to include markers for *observable* and *controllable* actions. All methods and all unmarked actions are considered *internal*. Hence, any name N_n^i of a named action is built according to the following grammar.

$$N_n^i ::= (\text{ 'obs' } | \text{ 'ctr' } | \text{' '})\text{' '}\ \textit{Identifier}$$

Informally, an abstract computation sequence starting from an initial state γ_0 is a possibly empty or infinite sequence t_{abs} of the form

$$t_{abs} =_{df} \gamma_0 \xrightarrow{N_n^i} \gamma_1 \cdots$$

where $\xrightarrow{N_n^i}$ means the application (call) of the action body N_b^i of action N^i when $g.N_b^i$ holds at the transition's initial state or there is some sequence of basic actions (including method calls) $\gamma_j \xrightarrow{S_i} \cdots$ starting at the current state γ_j and leading to a state where $g.N_b^i$ holds.

Notice that the concept of labeled actions can already be found in [2] and that in [10] a similar event-based view of action systems is taken.

4 Chosen UML Semantics

Since many UML constructs represent rather complex behavior, mapping to OOAS means also implementing these constructs in OOAS. Because of the size of UML, not only would full feature support be a major effort, but many elements simply are not useful in the context of behavioral test models. Therefore, we limit the transformation tool to a subset of UML.

In the following subsections, we describe the selected subset along with some motivation and then four of the more interesting aspects of the transformation are discussed, along with the taken decisions regarding semantic interpretation.

4.1 Used UML Subset

In the context of embedded and safety critical systems, modeling with state machines is quite common and fits the needs of the domain. The UML subset supported by the transformation therefore comprises class diagrams, state machines and a subset of OCL. The selection is mainly based on the needs of the demonstrator applications within MOGENTES; some state-machine concepts that were intentionally left out, like deferred triggers and history states, could be added when needed. Table 2 summarizes all supported UML elements. In the table, *"Simple" Inheritance* means that we do not support any polymorphism or late-binding. It is set in brackets as our tool-support for inheritance is not yet complete. Also, while the transformation in principle supports the float data type, we do not use it currently. Method and effect opaque behavior bodies are filled using a minimal custom language that can be used to express signal sending/broadcasting, method calling and assignment. If needed, this small language can easily be replaced by another one, e.g., the Object Action Language (OAL).

In the transformation, we strive for following UML v2.2 Standard. Nonetheless we have made some design choices, aside from the selected elements: object

Table 2. Supported UML Elements

“Types”	Class Enums Signal Bool Int (Float)	Classes	Active/Passive Associations (“Simple” Inheritance) Member Fields Methods Def. + Body Signal Reception	OCL	and, or, not, implies =, <, >, <=, >= union, intersect select, collect exists, forall, oclIsInState Literals (Numbers, Bool)
State Machines	Substate Machine Orthogonal Regions (Final-, Initial-, Pseudo-) State Entry, Exit Action Transitions with Effects Trigger with Change/Signal/Call/Time Events Constraints (OCL) Junctions, Choice				

instantiation is limited to the initialization phase while destruction of objects is not used at all. This fits well into the current practice in embedded systems design, where a constant, limited and predictable memory footprint is wanted. This also avoids some of the semantic variation points on deletion/creation in context of composition and aggregation relations between classes.

Classes, member-fields and method definitions map easily to the respective counterparts in the OOAS as described in the previous section. Mapping of inheritance is also straight forward, provided the subclass is a valid superposition-refinement of the superclass. Behavioral aspects are mainly expressed with state machines in the selected UML subset; while there is a similarity between state machine transitions and guarded actions, some of the features of UML state machines need some more thought on how to implement them in OOAS.

4.2 Events

Transitions in UML state machines are triggered by events. There are four trigger types: *signal triggers, call triggers, change triggers* and *time triggers*. All events concerning an object are stored in the object's event pool until they are consumed, e.g., by transitions. Although we assume that there is always only one external input event at a time, multiple objects might be interested in an event, e.g., a signal reception event, and processing the event might produce further events before the initial events are consumed in the other objects. Hence the need to implement an event-management logic.

Most models are developed with an assumption of in order processing of events, therefore we decided to use event queues, implemented as lists in OOAS. The event distribution logic of the respective event type adds the event at the end of the list. State machine transitions consume events from the front of the list. Providing real pool behavior with OOAS can be easily done by non-deterministically choosing the event to process next, at the cost of increased non-determinism.

A transition path (one direct transition between states or a series of transitions connected by choice pseudo-states) is implemented as a named action of the following form:

```
1 transition_OpenAndLocked_to_ClosedAndLocked =
2   requires (state = OpenAndLocked) and
3            (events <> [nil]) and
4            (hd events)[0] = received_AlarmSystem_Close):
5     state := ClosedAndLocked
6   end;
7 /* .. other transitions .. */
8 dequeue =
9   requires events <> [nil] :
10    events := tl self.events
11  end
```

The *requires* expression (guard) of the transition tests if the object is in the source state, and whether the first event in the event queue is one of the trigger events of the transition. In case the transition has a guard, it is also checked. All actions modeling transitions are combined by non-deterministic choice as follows.

```
1 do
2    ( (transition_Armed_to_Alarm;
3        call_AlarmArmed_SetOff;
4        call_OpticalAlarm_SetOn;
5        call_AcousticAlarm_SetOn )
6      [] transition_OpenAndLocked_to_ClosedAndLocked
7      [] /* .. other transitions .. */
8    ) //  dequeue()
9 od
```

As can be seen, entry and exit actions, e.g., *call_AlarmArmed_SetOff*, are sequentially composed with the transition action. Transition effects, if present, are treated in the same manner. Dequeuing of the event is done in the *dequeue* action by removing the head-element of the event-list. The dequeue action is enabled only if there is no enabled transition left. This allows modeling of events triggering multiple transitions as well as events that enable no transition, as required by the standard (cf. *[1], State Machine, p.566*). We discuss the handling of multiple transitions for one event in detail in Subsection 4.3.

Calls and Signals. After an object has received a signal or a method of the object was called, the corresponding events are added to the object's event queue. (Currently, there is no support for handling synchronous method calls.) We represent these events in the OOAS as data-tuples, hence the event queue is a list of tuples, and is initially empty.

```
1   types
2     t_eventname_AlarmSystem = {__received_AlarmSystem_Close,
          __received_AlarmSystem_Lock, ... }; /*enumeration*/
3     t_event_AlarmSystem = (t_eventname_AlarmSystem) /*tuple*/
4   var
5     /* object event queue */
6     events : list[7] of t_event_AlarmSystem = [nil]
7
8   methods
9        /* add a lock event to queue */
10    __rcv_Lock =
11        events := events ^ [t_event_AlarmSystem(
              __received_AlarmSystem_Lock)]
12    end;
```

If there are call parameters and signal properties, the event-type has to be extended to provide place for the event name itself and all parameters. In the example above, there are no properties or parameters, hence *t_event_Alarmsystem* is a 1-tuple.

According to the UML standard, signal transmission might be lossy, out of order, or even allow duplication of signals. As a practical example we may consider a distributed embedded system using the CAN bus: there, message transmission is based on priorities. If we want to model this kind of behavior, we need to explicitly represent it in the UML-model as our transformation guarantees in-order message processing.

4.3 Object Concurrency and Regions

There are two different sources of concurrency in UML models. One source are active classes, the other one are orthogonal regions in state machines. Since the

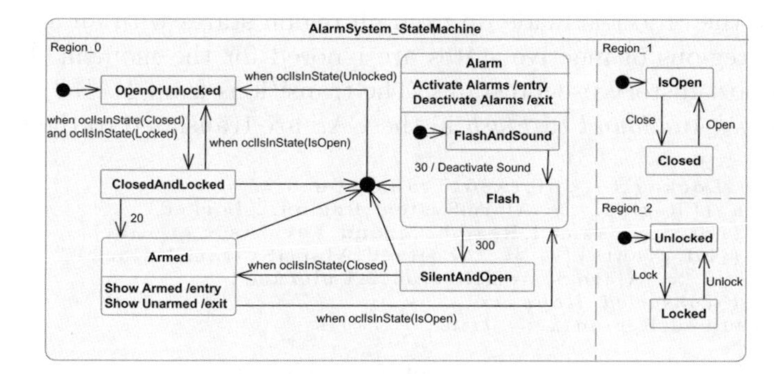

Fig. 3. Car Alarm System - State machine implemented using orthogonal regions

UML standard does not request true parallel execution we decided to use the interleaving semantics provided by the non-deterministic choice operator. Therefore, concurrent execution of active classes can be trivially mapped to a parallel composition of classes of an OOAS (cf. Section 3). The resulting interleavings of the active objects represent all possible "sequentializations".

The second source of concurrency are orthogonal regions of state machines. State machines and states may be split into two or more parallel active regions, so called orthogonal regions. To discuss our support of orthogonal regions, we extend the testing-model presented in Section 2. Instead of permitting an input signal, e.g., *Open*, only at certain places, we take a more realistic view and add two orthogonal regions. Each of the new regions has two states and the state machine may flip between these states when encountering a matching input signal. This may happen at any time and "runs" in parallel with the main-logic of the car-alarm-system. Fig. 3 shows the resulting state machine that includes all behavior that was possible in our first CAS-version. Notice that the UML standard does not specify the order in which parallel enabled and selected transitions have to fire (cf. *[1], State Machine, p. 566*). Hence we are allowed to map this type of concurrency to non-deterministic choice over enabled transitions again.

Since we need to memorize the state of each region of the state machine (notice that sub-states of a state automatically lie in a separate region) we need to introduce a state variable for every region in the OOAS. Below we sketch the state variable definitions for the CAS with regions.

```
1  types
2      /* enumeration types for class state variables */
3      AlarmSystem_Region_2 = {AlarmSystem_Region_2_Unlocked, ...};
4      AlarmSystem_Region_0__Alarm__Region_0 = {
           AlarmSystem_Region_0__Alarm__Region_0_Initial_0, ...};
5      AlarmSystem_Region_0 = {AlarmSystem_Region_0_Initial_0, ...};
6      AlarmSystem_Region_1 = {AlarmSystem_Region_1_Initial_0,
           AlarmSystem_Region_1_IsOpen, AlarmSystem_Region_1_Closed}
7  var
8      /* class state variables */
9      Region_2 : AlarmSystem_Region_2 = AlarmSystem_Region_2_Initial_0;
10     Region_0__Alarm__Region_0 : AlarmSystem_Region_0__Alarm__Region_0
           = ...;
11     Region_0 : AlarmSystem_Region_0 = ...;
12     Region_1 : AlarmSystem_Region_1 = ...;
```

The state of the object is made up from all region states with an active parent region. Sub regions of inactive states are ignored for the moment, but can be used to support history pseudo states. The transitions from *Locked* to *Unlocked* and from *FlashAndSound* to *Flash* in the CAS are translated to the following:

```
1 transition_Locked_to_Unlocked_Transition_0 =
2   requires ((Region_2 = AlarmSystem_Region_2_Locked)
3      and (not __consumed_Region_2) and (events <> [nil])
4      and ((hd events)[0] = __received_AlarmSystem_Unlock)) :
5     Region_2 := AlarmSystem_Region_2_Unlocked;
6     /* set consumed flags */
7     __consumed_Region_2 := true
8   end;
9 transition_FlashAndSound_to_Flash_Transition_0 =
10  requires ((Region_0__Alarm__Region_0 =
11       AlarmSystem_Region_0__Alarm__Region_0_FlashAndSound)
12       and (Region_0 = AlarmSystem_Region_0_Alarm)
13       and (not __consumed_Region_0__Alarm__Region_0)
14       and (events <> [nil])
15       and ((hd events)[0] = __time_trigger_FlashAndSound_30_Flash)) :
16    Region_0__Alarm__Region_0 :=
          AlarmSystem_Region_0__Alarm__Region_0_Flash;
17    /* set consumed flags */
18    __consumed_Region_0__Alarm__Region_0 := true
19  end
```

The consumed flags in the OOAS-code are necessary to guarantee standard-conforming behavior of transitions in orthogonal regions that are triggered by the same event. When the *consumed* flag for a region is set, it means that the event has already been processed by the region. Hence the transitions of the region depending on events must not fire as long as the flag is set: each transition tests for its region's consumed flag being false and sets it when it is done. The *dequeue* action then resets all flags. Transitions in sub-states may also consume events for the region and in fact have priority over transitions with the same trigger in higher level regions. To ensure this behavior, before processing the next transition, the consumed flags for regions whose child regions have the flag set, are set. Furthermore, transitions within sub-state machines are put first in a prioritized composition to mirror the priority of transitions given by the standard, as can be seen below.

```
1 actions
2   mark_Region_0_conditional_consumed =
3     requires __consumed_Region_0 = false
4        and (__consumed_Region_0__Alarm__Region_0):
5       __consumed_Region_0 := true
6     end;
7   /* other actions */
8 do
9     ( transition__FlashAndSound_to_Flash_Transition_0;
10      call_AcousticAlarm_SetOff)
11  //
12     mark_Region_0_conditional_consumed()
13  //
14    (
15          transition_Unlocked_to_Locked_Transition_0 =
16      [] /* other transition paths */
17    )
18  // dequeue()
19 od
```

4.4 Input / Output

There is no canonical form to express borders of a system and I/O across these borders in UML. For our purposes, we use a self-defined, minimal UML profile, providing the class stereotypes `<<system under test>>` and `<<environment>>` as we have already shown in Fig. 1. Classes without one of these stereotypes are considered to be part of the SUT.

There are several ways of communication between the SUT and its environment classes:

Incoming signals. In UML, incoming signals are modeled by signal receptions either in the SUT class or in an interface implemented by the SUT class. The latter is used for signals not directly handled by the SUT class but delegated to another class. In the OOAS code, this is modeled by a controllable action that puts the signal event into the event queues of all objects registered as listeners on this signal.

Outgoing signals. Outgoing signals are modeled as signal receptions in the environment classes in the UML model. In the OOAS code, this is mapped to an observable action that is called when the signal sending occurs.

Outgoing calls. In UML, outgoing calls are modeled as methods of environment classes (like the *setOn/setOff* methods in the Car Alarm System). In the OOAS this is mapped to a call of an observable action. If the callee has a return value, the observable action is directly followed by a controllable action.

Incoming calls. Incoming calls are modeled as method invocations of the SUT class in UML. In the OOAS this is reflected by a call of a controllable action. If the callee has a return value, the controllable action is directly followed by an observable action.

The classes in the OOAS directly derived from classes in the UML model are accompanied by two additional classes: *__model* and *__environment*. The *__model* class is put before the SUT class in a prioritized composition and provides housekeeping functionality like distributing broadcast signals and time triggers (see next subsection). The *__environment* class is put after the SUT class in a prioritized composition in the SAB and contains all the controllable actions like signal receptions. The system assembling block for the CAS is shown below.

```
1 /* all definitions before */
2 system
3   __model // AlarmSystem // __environment
```

External inputs are put last in the OOAS execution because internal operations are assumed to happen in zero time steps and therefore would always be completed before the next input can happen - resulting in a run-to-completion behavior.

One important semantical difference between the behavior of the OOAS- and the UML model concerns the handling of input events that do not enable any transition in the current state of the state-machine. In the UML standard for state-machines (this is a semantic variation point for protocol state-machines) it is requested that these inputs are ignored (cf. *[1], State Machine, p. 566*). We deviate from the behavior specified in the UML standard and only allow inputs that enable transitions. The reasons for this design choice are among the following.

- Firstly, we use the input-output conformance relation (IOCO [11]) for testing. This conformance relation enables us to work with partial models, which is an advantage we want to preserve. Allowing all input events at all times would make the testing model *input complete* and disallow the use of several partial models working on the same inputs for test-case generation. Notice that IOCO assumes the implementation to be input-enabled.
- Secondly, disallowing inputs that are ignored also has the benefit of shrinking the state-space, which is an advantage during test-case generation: models of other demonstrators within the MOGENTES project are significantly more complex than the car alarm system.

Hence, we limit the OOAS to a non-input-enabled system. Within the OOAS-code, enabling and disabling of controllables is controlled via flags that are managed by the *__model* class.

4.5 Time Triggers

A time triggered transition fires a given amount of time after entering the source state if the state has not been left before. Object-oriented action systems, as described, have no notion of time, hence we need to emulate it. We also need to say that our support of time is restricted to cases of observable, variable delay: we do not control the SUT via timeouts.

We use an additional action *after(t)*, which is non-deterministically composed with the actions representing input from the environment, to mark the observation of passing time. Notice that we do not allow the waiting time to be split: two consecutive *after(t)* may not occur without either the first causing a time trigger to fire or a controllable action is used between them. This avoids series of *after(t)* actions which can be represented by one having a larger t parameter.

The time trigger functionality is realized by managing an ordered list of active timers. When a state with a leaving time triggered transition is entered, the timer is registered with the value of the time trigger.

The occurrence of *after(t)* reduces all timers in the list by the value of t. When a timer value is reduced to zero this way, the corresponding time trigger event is added to the event queue of the registered object. To simplify the implementation, we limit the allowed value of t to the minimum value of all registered timers. The following pseudo-code sketches the after action.

```
1 obs after (c_waittime : t_time) =
2   requires c_waittime > 0 and wait_allowed and
3       (len m.get_timers() > 0) and (t = min_timeout(m.get_timers())):
4     /*update timers and event queue*/
5 end
6
7 do
```

```
8       var t : t_time : after(t)
9     []
10      receive_external_signal_Close()
11      /* further receptions */
12 od
```

Always taking the minimum time of the next timer due as a waiting time disallows certain behaviors, as is demonstrated in Fig. 4.

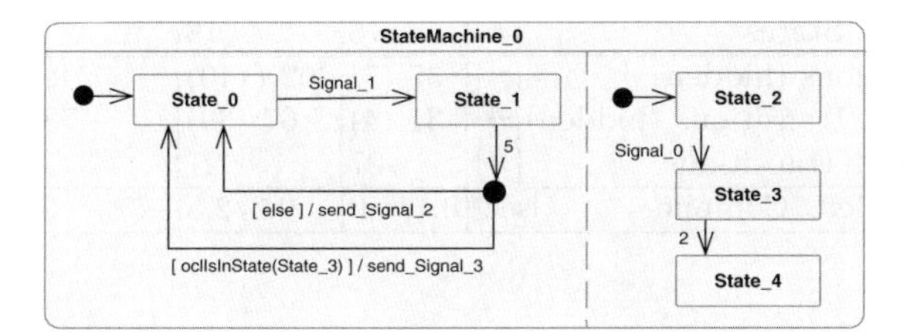

Fig. 4. Simple State Machine Example with Interdependent Time Triggers

In the example, due to the restriction to move to the next timer firing, a trace like

```
ctr Signal_1, obs after(4), ctr Signal_0 ,after(1), obs Signal_3
```

cannot be taken any longer. Therefore we lose the observation *Signal_3* in the example. In order to mitigate this shortcoming without the need to enumerate every time value that is smaller than the time value of the next timer firing, we propose to add non-deterministic transitions in the UML model that explicate these additional interleavings. Notice that this might be done on the fly by a tool that over-approximates such situations and adds the relevant transitions.

5 Results

We have implemented the presented transformations in a tool chain comprising two applications. The first utility takes a UML model and generates the object-oriented action system code. The second tool ("Argos") then converts the OOAS to an action system that is the input for our test-case generator called "Ulysses" [12,13]. As a second option, Argos is able to generate an implicit labeled-transition system in CADP-style (cf. [14]). All figures in this section were produced using this second back-end of Argos and the CADP tools.

Table 3 shows some basic figures for three different models of the car alarm system. The two one-region-only models are branching bisimilar [15] and included (modulo branching equivalence) in the multi-region model. Within the table, *B-Min.* stands for a minimization using strong bisimulation [16], while *W-Min.* stands for a sequence of weak-trace minimization that eliminates all

Table 3. Comparison of CAS Models

		One Region		Mult. Regions
LoC UML	[#]	–	263	273
LoC OOAS	[#]	105	720	790
LoC impl. LTS	[#]	2880	13 420	14 430
States	[#]	28	167	503
B-Min. States	[#]	22	58	159
W-Min. States	[#]	18	18	26
Transitions (hidden)	[#]	37 (7)	202 (140)	742 (662)
B-Min. Transitions (hidden)	[#]	31 (4)	67 (39)	178 (134)
W-Min. Transitions	[#]	27	27	42
Time Gen./Compile	[sec]	0.1/1.0	0.3/2.5	0.4/2.5

internal transitions followed by a minimization using strong bisimulation. The lines-of-code (LoC) figures as well as the time figures are reproduced only in order to give a hint on the complexity and performance. The experiments were carried out within a virtual machine running Ubuntu 9.04 on a Lenovo T400 laptop running Windows Vista. During the development of the models (and tools), we extensively used the animation, model-checking, minimization, and bisimulation capabilities offered by the CADP toolbox.

The first (left-to-right) model in the table is a hand-crafted OOAS model of our one-region car alarm system. It serves the purpose of showing the minimal number of lines necessary to model the CAS behavior. The second model is the UML-model presented in Fig. 2, and the third one is the multiple-regions CAS-model that was presented in Fig. 3.

Because the first model omits any event-handling overhead it has significantly less lines of code than the second model. It can also be seen that the percentage of hidden, i.e. internal, transitions is much lower for the first model: the event processing machinery contributes a lot of hidden transitions. These additional transitions also blow up the non-minimized state space, as can be seen in the table (167 vs. 28 states). Notice that the third model defines more testable behavior, which is reflected in additional states and transitions. In particular the third model allows for tests that send *Open* and *Close* events while being in the alarm state. However, it can be proved that under branching bisimulation (we are not interested in internal transitions) all the behavior specified in the second model (Fig. 2) is still present in the third one (Fig. 3).

While for the first model only one object is instantiated, models two and three comprise three objects each: the first object is used for event processing and house keeping, the second one models the alarm system itself, and the last one models the environment and it's capabilities of sending events.

Finally, Fig. 5 shows the explored state-space (weak-trace minimized) of our running one-region example. Notice the appearance of the observable "after", that models the observation of passing time.

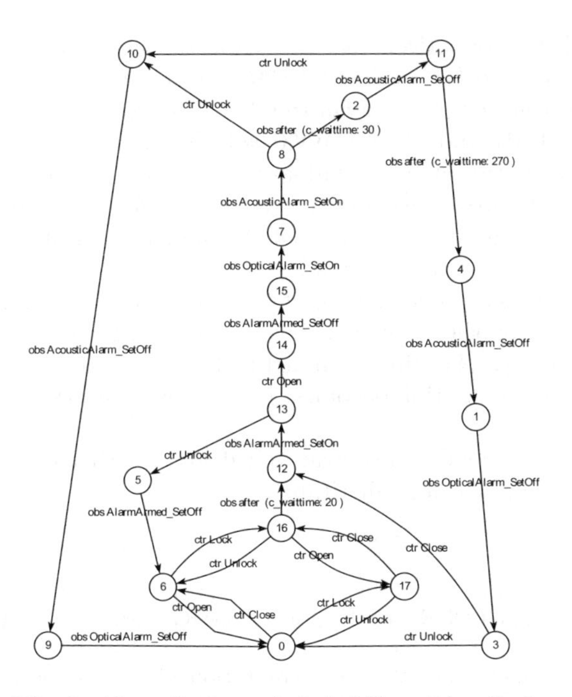

Fig. 5. Alarm System - Labeled Transition System

6 Conclusion

We have presented our mapping of a UML-subset to object-oriented action systems. It turns out that the mapping is relatively straight forward. In particular, we map concurrency to standard conformant non-deterministic choice, treat event processing as in-order and loss-less, and support time triggered transitions via timer queues. Having said that, some of our design decisions give our models a behavior that deviates from the UML standard: In case of time triggered transitions, we have proposed a way around this limitation, while in the case of the non-input-enabledness of the model we argue with the support of partial test-models. It is important to say that none of these choices constitute a principal limitation of our approach.

Other contributions of this paper are the extension of object-oriented action systems with prioritized composition and a system assembling block, the presentation of a tool chain that maps UML diagrams to labeled transition systems, and the discussion of a case study taken from industry. We have also demonstrated our ability to check that a refined model preserves the behavior of the more abstract one and we have given hints on how we validate our tools.

It is out of the scope of this paper to review all UML semantics, however, closest to our work on mapping UML to action systems is work on defining a UML profile for action systems (cf. [17]). This work is exactly the opposite of ours, as it aims to add a special UML profile that maps one-to-one to action systems. There has also been work on defining a mapping of UML to B which, according to [18], did not entirely meet the expectations as *schematic translations that attempt to cover a broad class of UML models usually result in B models that are hard to read and quite unnatural.* Because we do not aim at supporting a broad class of UML models in MOGENTES – in fact we are interested in supporting (partial) test models that are made from the requirements – and since the mapping to object-oriented action systems feels very natural, we do not suffer from the problem of 'unnatural' OOAS models. (Automatically generated code, however, always is a pity to read.)

By giving the action systems abstract trace semantics and generating labeled transition systems for them, we can leverage existing tools, such as the well-known CADP toolbox: checking of model-inclusion, absence of particular properties, and test-case generation becomes the problem of invoking the right CADP tool.

Finally, future work will concentrate on dealing with more complex models and finishing tool support for inheritance.

References

1. OMG: OMG Unified Modeling Language (OMG UML), superstructure, Version 2.2. (2009)
2. Back, R.J., Kurki-Suonio, R.: Decentralization of process nets with centralized control. Distributed Computing 3(2), 73–87 (1989); Appeared previously in 2nd ACM SIGACT-SIGOPS Symp. on Principles of Distributed Computing (1983)
3. Back, R.J., Sere, K.: Stepwise refinement of action systems. Structured Programming 12, 17–30 (1991)
4. Bonsangue, M.M., Kok, J.N., Sere, K.: An approach to object-orientation in action systems. In: Jeuring, J. (ed.) MPC 1998. LNCS, vol. 1422, pp. 68–95. Springer, Heidelberg (1998)
5. Sekerinski, E., Sere, K.: A theory of prioritizing composition. Technical Report 5, Turku Centre for Computer Science (1996)
6. Dijkstra, E.W.: A Discipline of Programming. Prentice Hall, Inc., Englewood Cliffs (1976)
7. Back, R.J., Sere, K.: Superposition refinement of parallel algorithms. In: Proceedings of the IFIP TC6/WG6.1 Fourth International Conference on Formal Description Techniques for Distributed Systems and Communication Protocols, FORTE 1991, pp. 475–493. North-Holland Publishing Co, Amsterdam (1992)
8. Fitzgerald, J., Larsen, P.G.: Modelling systems: practical tools and techniques in software development. Cambridge University Press, New York (1998)
9. Lucas, P.: Formal semantics of programming languages: VDL. IBM J. Res. Dev. 25(5), 549–561 (1981)
10. Butler, M., Morgan, C.: Action systems, unbounded nondeterminism, and infinite traces. Formal Aspects of Computing 7, 37–53 (1995)
11. Tretmans, J.: Test generation with inputs, outputs and repetitive quiescence. Software - Concepts and Tools 17(3), 103–120 (1996)
12. Brandl, H., Weiglhofer, M., Aichernig, B.K.: Automated conformance verification of hybrid systems. In: QSIC (2010) (under review)
13. Aichernig, B.K., Brandl, H., Jöbstl, E., Krenn, W.: Model-based mutation testing of hybrid systems. In: Proceedings of Formal Methods for Components and Objects FMCO 2009 (2010) (under review)

14. Garavel, H., Mateescu, R., Lang, F., Serwe, W.: CADP 2006: A toolbox for the construction and analysis of distributed processes. In: Damm, W., Hermanns, H. (eds.) CAV 2007. LNCS, vol. 4590, pp. 158–163. Springer, Heidelberg (2007)
15. Glabbeek, R.v., Weijland, W.: Branching time and abstraction in bisimulation semantics (extended abstract). In Ritter, G., ed.: Information Processing 89, Proceedings of the IFIP 11th World Computer Congress, San Fransisco 1989, North-Holland (1989) 613–618 Full version in *Jounal of the ACM* 43(3), 1996, pp. 555–600.
16. Park, D.: Concurrency and automata on infinite sequences. In: Proceedings of the 5th GI-Conference on Theoretical Computer Science, London, UK, pp. 167–183. Springer, Heidelberg (1981)
17. Westerlund, T., Seceleanu, T.: An UML profile for action systems. Technical Report 581, Turku Centre for Computing Science (December 2003)
18. Fekih, H., Ayed, L.J.B., Merz, S.: Transformation of B specifications into UML class diagrams and state machines. In: Proceedings of the 2006 ACM Symposium on Applied Computing, SAC 2006, pp. 1840–1844. ACM, New York (2006)

Mutation-Based Test Case Generation for Simulink Models*

Angelo Brillout[1], Nannan He[2], Michele Mazzucchi[1], Daniel Kroening[2], Mitra Purandare[1], Philipp Rümmer[2], and Georg Weissenbacher[1,2]

[1] Computer Systems Institute, ETH Zurich
[2] Computing Laboratory, Oxford University

Abstract. The Matlab/Simulink language has become the standard formalism for modeling and implementing control software in areas like avionics, automotive, railway, and process automation. Such software is often safety critical, and bugs have potentially disastrous consequences for people and material involved. We define a verification methodology to assess the correctness of Simulink programs by means of automated test-case generation. In the style of fault- and mutation-based testing, the coverage of a Simulink program by a test suite is defined in terms of the detection of injected faults. Using bounded model checking techniques, we are able to effectively and automatically compute test suites for given fault models. Several optimisations are discussed to make the approach practical for realistic Simulink programs and fault models, and to obtain accurate coverage measures.

1 Introduction

Model-based design is a development methodology for modern software artifacts. It promotes the use of powerful and specialized modeling languages, allowing the engineer to focus on the domain-specific aspects of the system under development. The implementation of the system is either generated or derived manually from high-level models. The goal is to identify design flaws as early as possible in the development cycle, thereby avoiding costly late-stage design fixes.

The Matlab/Simulink language, developed by The MathWorks,[1] has emerged as the predominant modeling formalism in the automotive industry and is also widely deployed for avionic applications. A software glitch in these application domains may result in high cost and considerable damage of reputation. Due to the safety-critical nature of these domains, defects in the software may put human lives at stake. Accordingly, international safety standards such as DO-178B or IEC 61508 demand the application of rigorous verification techniques. In particular, they require the test engineers to provide a set of test cases that exercise the implementation of the system according to certain coverage metrics. The

* Supported by the EU FP7 STREP MOGENTES (project ID ICT-216679) and the ARTEMIS CESAR project.

[1] http://www.mathworks.com/products/simulink/

F.S. de Boer et al. (Eds.): FMCO 2009, LNCS 6286, pp. 208–227, 2010.

effort to create appropriate test suites is substantial, and the execution of the test suites is time consuming. There is therefore a strong incentive to automate the generation of test cases and to keep the resulting test suite small.

Model-based testing is an application of model-based design for deriving test cases from a model of the design, which promises better scalability and is applicable before the implementation phase. In the context of model-based testing, the question of suitable coverage metrics has to be reconsidered: traditional metrics such as location or branch coverage are no longer meaningful, since the test cases are not derived from implementation source code. In this paper, we focus on *mutation testing*: the quality of the test suite is assessed by injecting mutations into the model and by measuring which percentage of these modifications can be detected when exercising the test cases. We say that a modification is detected if we can observe that the modified and the original model generate different output signals. The resulting test vectors can be used to check that the model satisfies requirements or can be applied to an implementation of the design.

The generation of test suites that achieve high mutation coverage is difficult. We use *model checking* [1] for this task, as it is also able to address the issue of *equivalent mutants*. The application of model checking to generate high-coverage test suites has become commonplace (see, for instance, [2] for an application in the automotive domain). Test case generation for Simulink models is complicated by the fact that the Simulink language lacks a formal semantics and makes heavy use of floating-point arithmetic.

Contribution. We describe an application of the bounded model checking engine CBMC [3] to generate test suites for Simulink models with high mutation coverage. The implementation features precise reasoning with respect to the floating-point semantics of the models. The computational complexity of the underlying model checking algorithm requires us to deploy a number of heuristics to achieve the desired coverage if the number of mutations is large. Moreover, these heuristics also serve the orthogonal purpose of keeping the number of redundant test cases small in order to reduce the time required to execute the test suite.

Related Work. We briefly relate our work to other tools that generate test-vectors by means of software model checkers. A number of papers report applications of CBMC or similar techniques for generating high-coverage test suites [4,5,6]. These implementations are very similar to ours. There are also reports of the use of predicate abstraction in test-vector generation, e.g., using SLAM [7] and BLAST [8].

We refer the reader to [9] for a broad survey on mutation testing. We only consider mutant models with single mutations, whereas other authors also consider combinations of faults [10]. Do and Rothermel [11] proposes to use mutations to prioritise test cases to increase a test suite's rate of fault detection.

Schuler et al. [12] discusses the impact of *equivalent mutations* (mutations that keep the semantics of the model unchanged) and presents an approach to detect such mutations by means of checking dynamic invariants. We propose a similar approach in Section 5, but we rely on invariants statically generated by means of verification techniques such as k-induction.

We also relate our work to other methods for analyzing Simulink models. Most tools that aim at formal analyses of Simulink models focus on a particular and usually relatively small fragment. In particular, models that contain ANSI-C are often not considered [13,14,15]. Strichman and Ryabtsev [16] uses an automated decision procedure to validate code generated by Simulink against a set of verification conditions extracted from the model.

Another issue is the floating-point semantics of Simulink. Tools such as the Simulink Design Verifier rely on approximations of floating point arithmetic by means of infinite-precision rational numbers [17]. In contrast to that, we use a bit-accurate representation of floating-point arithmetic, as presented in [18]. We are therefore able to analyse the exact behaviour of the model rather than an approximation. Furthermore, our bit-level technique enables the use of mutations such as bit-flips in data values.

Outline. Section 2 describes the transformation of Simulink diagrams into an intermediate representation amenable to static analysis. This translation process conclusively determines the semantics of the model. Section 3 discusses how fault injection and mutations of the model and (bounded) model checking can be used to generate test cases. For this purpose, we rely on a model checking technique able to deal with floating-point arithmetic. We present a novel algorithm which aims at identifying efficient test cases that cover more than one mutation, thus reducing the size of the test suite and improving the performance of the test-case generation process in Section 4. In Section 5, we discuss strategies to detect mutations that do not have an observable impact on the model.

2 Simulink Models

The Simulink language is a graphical modeling language comprising block diagrams and an extensive set of block libraries. An example of a Simulink model is presented in Figure 1. Due to the complexity of the language and the lack of formal semantics, Simulink models are not directly amenable to automated analysis. We present a front-end to transform these models into intermediate ANSI-C programs with well-defined semantics. This transformation is performed fully automatically and allows us to separate the ambiguity issues in the Simulink semantics from our test case generation process.

Each Simulink block is associated with a type. We define the meaning of blocks of a particular type by means of C code, which is organized in a library. This library can be independently refined or modified (e.g., to add a new block-type definition) without the need to change the transformation process.

A *block-type* `X` is defined with the following artifacts:

- `X_in_t`: a C struct that defines the input ports of `X`.
- `X_out_t`: a C struct that defines the output ports of `X`.
- `X_props_t`: a C struct that specifies the verification-relevant properties of `X`.
- `X_semfun`: a C function that defines the semantics of `X` as a mapping from input ports to output ports. Its declaration format is
  `X_out_t* X_semfun(X_props_t *prop, X_in_t *in)`.

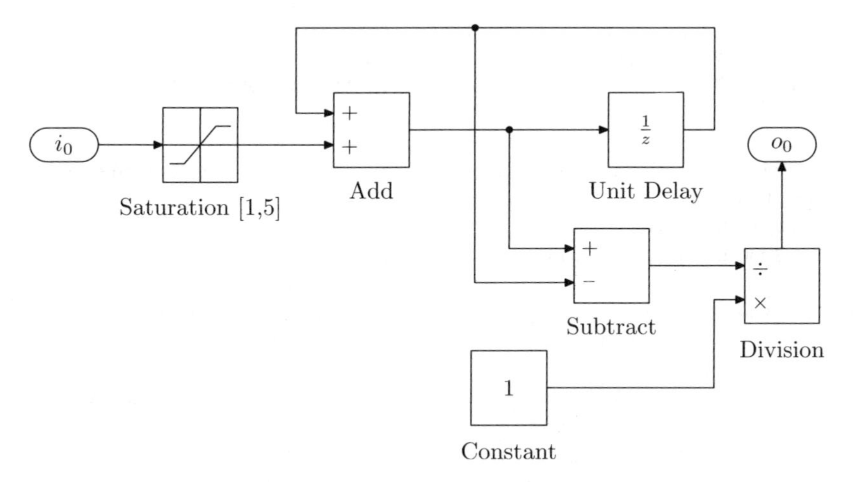

Fig. 1. A Simulink model example

Currently, our Simulink front-end supports a set of commonly used block types that belong to a variety of Simulink libraries, such as *Math, Discrete, Logic and Bit, Sinks, Sources, Ports&Subsystems, Discontinuities, Signal Routing, Signal Attributes* and *Model Verification.* Some important block types include *Subsystems*, *Unit Delay* that forms feedback loops, *Switches*, and *From/Goto* pairs. With our uniform definition artifacts, further block types can easily be added to the library as needed. Support for Stateflow diagrams is under development.

The transformation source is a Simulink model composed of a set of interconnected blocks, organized into a hierarchy of subsystems. The front-end parses the model, flattens the hierarchy and derives an appropriate block execution order which determines the simulation order of blocks in the resulting ANSI-C model. The front-end identifies the type and property specifications of each individual block instance and maps it to the corresponding block-type definition in the library. Then, it determines which C block-type definitions need to be included and assigns values to block properties. Some analyses like type inference are also performed during the transformation to resolve ambiguities in the Simulink model.

Figure 2 shows the basic structure of the C code transformed from the model in Figure 1 with the front-end. Our analysis and test-case generation approach based on the resulting C code is introduced in the sections below.

3 Generating Test Cases Using Mutations

3.1 Overview

Many existing test case generation techniques permit the generation of test suites that satisfy structural coverage criteria such as condition or statement coverage. One approach to achieve such coverage is to use a *model checker*, which can generate counterexamples that demonstrate the reachability of certain statements or conditions.

```
/*1.Links to blocktypes definitions */
#include <Sum.h>     // Corresponds to the Add block
...

/*2.Declaration and initialization of block instances */
Sum_in_t b3_in;
Sum_out_t b3_out;
const Sum_prop_t b3_props={.Inputs="++"}; ...

/*3.Simulation loop: define data dependencies w.r.t.
   block connections extracted from the model */
int main() {
  for(sim_time=START; sim_time<END; sim_time+=sim_step) {
    b3_in.port1 = b7_out.port1;
    b3_in.port2 = b2_out.port2;
    b3_out = *Sum_semfun(&b3_props, &b3_in); ...
  }
}
```

Fig. 2. Structural overview of the C code transformed from a Simulink model

The following sections present mutation-based test case generation (TCG) using *bounded model checking* (see Section 3.2). We describe how test cases can be extracted automatically from a model or implementation M by injecting mutations or faults into M (producing in a *mutant model* M') and checking the equivalence of M and M' by means of model checking. If M and M' are not equivalent, a model checking tool is able to generate a witness for the inequality (a counterexample for equality). This counterexample determines a set of input values for which the executions of M and M' produce different outputs.

The coverage criteria for fault-based testing in our work are based on syntactic and semantic modifications of the model. Given a modification to the model, the aim is to generate a test case that demonstrates the resulting change of the behavior. Simple structural coverage metrics are not sufficient, since even exhaustive coverage criteria such as modified condition/decision coverage (MC/DC) provide no guarantee that the error resulting from the modification of the model has a visible impact on the behavior generated by exercising the test suite.

The fault-driven test case generation approach is inspired by mutation testing and fault injection:

- **Mutation testing** denotes the method of making (syntactic) modifications to the source code of the implementation. The intention is to evaluate a given test suite based on whether it is able to detect the introduced faults and to aid the generation of additional meaningful test cases.
- **Fault injection.** Fault injection triggers the occurrences of faults in the system under test. The main purpose of this technique is to evaluate the error handling mechanisms of the system.

Examples for injected faults and mutations are provided in Section 3.5. The common idea underlying both approaches is to make modifications to the system and to run test cases that demonstrate the impact of these changes.

The following subsection provides a brief overview over the formal verification techniques we apply to generate test suites from models containing mutations or failure modes.

3.2 Bounded Model Checking

Model checking, in the most general sense, is a technique that explores the reachable states of a model in order to determine whether a given specification is satisfied [1]. It differs from testing in so far as it aims at an exhaustive exploration of the state space of the model or program under test, thereby providing a correctness guarantee that is rarely achieved by means of testing. If the specification is violated, model checking tools are often able to provide a *counterexample*, i.e., a witness that demonstrates how the specification can be violated in the model.

Bounded model checking (BMC) is a variation of model checking which restricts the exploration to execution traces up to a certain (user-defined) length k. BMC either provides a guarantee that the first k execution steps of the program are correct with respect to the property P or a counterexample of length at most k. The ability to report counterexamples is the essential feature we use to generate test cases. The disadvantage of model checking is that it does not scale as well as testing.

Figure 3a illustrates the schema of a Simulink model with a feedback loop. Simulink diagrams comprise blocks instances and signals and wires representing the connections between these blocks. These components determine the input and output signals (i and o, respectively) and the transition function R represented by the model. A bounded model checking algorithm unwinds such models as indicated in Figure 3b; the signals i_i and o_i refer to the input and output signals in the ith step (or point in time), respectively, and $\star$ denotes an undefined/non-deterministic signal value.

For the purpose of test case generation it suffices to determine whether certain states in a model are reachable. A model is specified by a formula representing a (possibly partial) transition relation R (e.g., specified by means of a Simulink diagram or ANSI-C program) and a predicate I that determines the valid initial states of the model. The transition relation R relates the current state of the model to its successor states (i.e., the potential states after one step). The structure of R may be further detailed by means of a *control flow graph*, which partitions R into a separate transition function for each program location. This simple formalism is sufficiently general to allow imperative models (such as C programs or state charts) as well as data flow models (such as Simulink models). Furthermore, the predicate I characterizes the set of valid initial states of the model (this may be the safe or reset state of the system), i.e., $I(s)$ holds if s is a valid initial state.

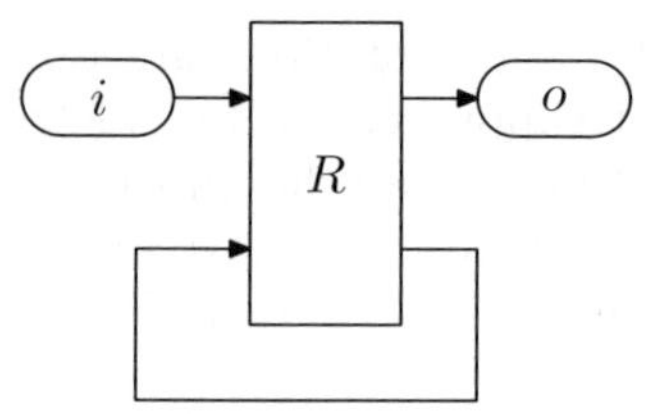

(a) Schema of a Simulink model with a loop

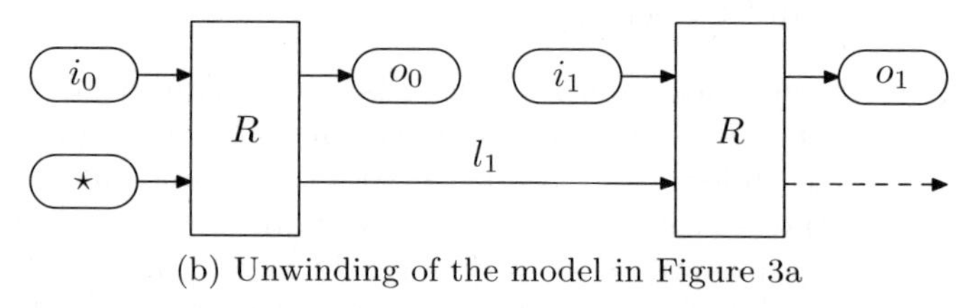

(b) Unwinding of the model in Figure 3a

Fig. 3. Unwinding Simulink models

A *path* (or execution trace) π of the model is a sequence of states $s_0, s_1, \ldots, s_n$ such that the adjacent pairs s_i, s_{i+1} of states in that sequence are related by R (i.e., $\bigwedge_{i=0}^{n-1} R(s_i, s_{i+1})$), and $I(s_0)$ holds (i.e., s_0 is a valid initial state). A state is induced by the values of the variables (or wires and signals) of the model. In reactive models, the variables are typically partitioned into input variables, hidden (or internal) variables, and output variables. The observable part of an execution trace is therefore the sequence of inputs and the resulting sequence of outputs. Given a state s_i, we use $s_i.i$ to refer to the input, and $s_i.o$ to denote the output.

3.3 Equivalence Checking

Formal Equivalence Checking is a technique used to formally prove that two models M and M' exhibit the same observable behavior [19]. This is achieved by comparing the input and the output behavior of the two models. To construct a test-scenario (i.e., a sequence of input/output pairs), we are interested in checking whether for a given input sequence the outputs in the first k steps of the executions of the models match. This notion of "k-equivalence" is decidable, assuming that the input and output values have a finite range.

Whether two given models are k-equivalent can be decided using model checking. Given two models M and M' (comprising the transition functions R and R' and the initial state predicates I and I', respectively), we can check (assuming that the size of the states is finite) whether the following is satisfiable:

$$\underbrace{\bigwedge_{i=0}^{k} s_i.i = s'_i.i}_{\text{equality of all inputs}} \quad \wedge \underbrace{I(s_0) \wedge \bigwedge_{i=0}^{k-1} R(s_i, s_{i+1}) \wedge}_{\text{first model}} \\ \underbrace{I'(s'_0) \wedge \bigwedge_{i=0}^{k-1} R'(s'_i, s'_{i+1}) \wedge}_{\text{second model}} \quad \underbrace{\bigvee_{i=0}^{k} s_i.o \neq s'_i.o}_{\text{inequality of an output}} \tag{1}$$

Any satisfying assignment to this formula represents two executions of M and M' that yield a different output sequence. The models are equivalent (up to k steps) if Formula (1) is unsatisfiable.

Checking software equivalence is more complicated, since the two programs rarely perform input/output in lockstep. Algorithmic details of equivalence checking using BMC are covered in [3]. An approach based on predicate abstraction [20] is presented in [21].

3.4 Floating-Point Arithmetic

Simulink models make heavy use of floating-point arithmetic (FPA). Although reasoning about FPA is an active field of research, existing methods are primarily tailored to interactive proof assistants (e.g., [22,23]) or abstract floating-point number to intervals of the reals (e.g., [24,25]). The methods of the first kind are unsuitable for automated tools, while the latter ones are not able to construct models for satisfiable formulae and therefore cannot be used for test-case generation. Currently, there are only few model checkers that handle FPA accurately.

In our model checker CBMC, we use the mixed abstraction framework described in [18]. By using both over- and under-approximations simultaneously, combined with a novel abstraction refinement approach, we are able to achieve both accurate reasoning and a significantly better performance than ordinary bit-blasting approaches [26].

Previous work on test case generation for Simulink programs, for instance in the Simulink Design Verifier [17], employs approximations of floating-point arithmetic by means of infinite-precision rational numbers. While this allows efficient reasoning in the case of models only containing linear arithmetic, rationals do not faithfully reflect the actual behavior of Simulink programs: in equivalence checking, it can happen that Simulink models are erroneously reported as equivalent (although they are not with FPA semantics), or that equivalent Simulink models are erroneously reported as non-equivalent. This is particularly relevant because unexpected over- or underflows due to FPA semantics can be hard to detect, but can have profound consequences.

We illustrate the inconsistencies between rational arithmetic and FPA using the Simulink model in Figure 1. The model contains a feedback loop that computes the consecutive sums

$$t_n = \sum_{j=1}^{n} i_j$$

given the stream $i_1, i_2, i_3, \ldots$ of inputs. Furthermore, in each time frame, the quotient

$$\frac{1}{t_n - t_{n-1}}$$

is computed. Because the inputs are constrained to the interval $[1, 5]$ with the help of a `Saturation` block, and since $t_n = t_{n-1} + i_n$, the computation of the fraction will always succeed when computing with infinite-precision rational numbers. If the model is implemented and executed using floating-point numbers, however, the stream of sums $t_1, t_2, t_3, \ldots$ will eventually get stationary due to lack of precision: in FPA, it is the case that $a + b = a$ if a is a very large and b a very small number. As soon as $t_n = t_{n-1}$ occurs in the sequence of sums, the computation of the quotient will raise a division-by-zero exception.

The use of a bit-accurate decision procedure has further advantages in the context of mutation testing: Many fault models are based on bit-level modifications (such as *single-bit-stuck-at* faults). The effect of these mutations is trivial to model using a propositional formula, and SAT-solvers can deal with the resulting encoding very efficiently. For instance, modeling a single-bit-stuck-at-1 fault corresponds to setting a single propositional variable to true. Modern SAT-solving algorithms deal with this case by using unit propagation, which is extremely efficient. If, on the other hand, a decision procedure for reasoning about real arithmetic was used, encoding the same fault would be complicated and would result in constraints that are very hard to solve.

3.5 Mutation Testing and Fault Injection

From an abstract point of view, mutations as well as injected faults are simply modifications to the behavior of the model.

Example 1. Consider the simple Simulink diagram in Figure 4a. The input signals i_1 and i_2 are related to the output signal o by means of the formula $o = i_1 \times i_2$, i.e., the transition function is

$$R(s_i, s_{i+1}) \stackrel{def}{=} s_i.o = s_i.i_1 \times s_i.i_2 \wedge s_{i+1}.o = s_{i+1}.i_1 \times s_{i+1}.i_2 \,.$$

A possible syntactic mutation is to replace the multiplication ($\times$) with an addition:

$$R'(s_i, s_{i+1}) \stackrel{def}{=} s_i.o = s_i.i_1 + s_i.i_2 \wedge s_{i+1}.o = s_{i+1}.i_1 + s_{i+1}.i_2 \,.$$

This mutation can be implemented in the diagram using an *enable* signal, allowing us to switch the mutation on and off (see Figure 4b).

In our formalism, such a modification can be modeled by replacing the transition relation R of our model M' with a slightly modified transition relation R' (and possibly a modified condition I' for the initial state). The faults introduced into the system may be either permanent, transient, or intermittent (i.e., occur repeatedly). The former case can be simply modeled by permanently altering the transition relation R, and applying the resulting relation R' in each step:

$$\underbrace{I'(s_0) \wedge R'(s_0, s_1) \wedge R'(s_1, s_2) \wedge R'(s_2, s_3) \wedge R'(s_3, s_4)}_{\text{permanent fault}} \wedge \ldots$$

To model transient or intermittent faults, we have to take the temporal aspect into account, i.e., the alteration becomes only effective at certain points in time.

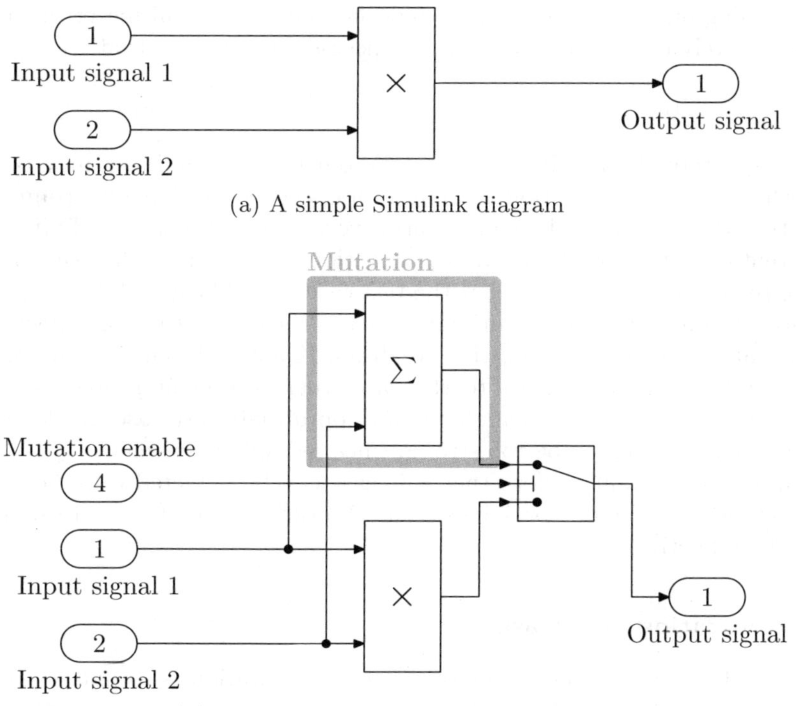

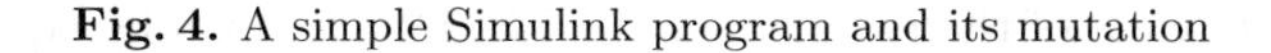

Fig. 4. A simple Simulink program and its mutation

Accordingly, a typical execution satisfies the following constraint:

$$I(s_0) \wedge R(s_0, s_1) \wedge R(s_1, s_2) \wedge \underbrace{R'(s_2, s_3)}_{\text{intermittent fault}} \wedge R(s_3, s_4) \wedge \ldots$$

Transient or intermittent faults can be modeled by referring to a global timer. Let R' be a transition function with a permanently enabled mutation. Furthermore, given a state s_i, let $s_i.t$ denote a signal tracking progression of time during the execution. A transition function R'' with an intermittent fault occurring every c execution steps can be modeled as

$$R''(s_i, s_{i+1}) \stackrel{def}{=} \begin{cases} R'(s_i, s_{i+1}) & \text{if } (s_i.t = 0 \bmod c) \\ R(s_i, s_{i+1}) & \text{if } (s_i.t \neq 0 \bmod c) \end{cases} .$$

Mutations are small syntactic changes of the model, whereas simulated hardware faults require semantic changes to the model that reflect physical faults of the system as accurately as possible. Conceptually, however, there is no difference when it comes to their integration into the transition relation: The implementation of faults in the model M requires syntactic changes to M.

Depending on the extent of these modifications, the resulting error may not be immediately observable, i.e., it is not necessarily the case that

$$s_0.i = s'_0.i \wedge R(s_0, s_1) \wedge R'(s'_0, s'_1) \Longrightarrow s_1.o \neq s'_1.o$$

holds. Even though s_1 differs from s'_1, the outputs $s_1.o$ and $s'_1.o$ may be indistinguishable: the modification of R may not necessarily have an (immediate) impact on the observable behavior. Intuitively, a test case is "good" if it yields a different outcome for M and M'. In mutation testing, the term *weak mutation testing* refers to the condition that the test cases should cause different program states for the mutant and the original model. In the case that the affected part of the state is not observable, this condition is not sufficient for our purpose. *Strong mutation testing* refers to the case where the error propagates to the output of the model and is caught by an appropriate test case. In dependable systems, this notion may be too strong, since redundant systems may tolerate a certain number of faults. Note that this case can be detected using a *complete* model checking technique or k-induction. A brief outline of these techniques is provided in Section 5.1.

3.6 Generating Test Cases

One way of generating test cases that detect a mutation is to find a satisfying assignment to Formula (1). Such a satisfying assignment provides the inputs that yield a different output sequence during the first k steps and, provided the observable behaviors of the two models M and M' are not fully equivalent, such a solution must exist for some k.

Encoding Combinations of Faults. Assume that the objective is to generate a test suite that detects single faults (or mutations). The naïve approach to create such a test suite is to generate a new model M' for each conceivable fault or mutation and to generate an instance of Formula (1) for each pair of models M and M'. In practice, this approach is very wasteful, since modern satisfiability checkers such as MiniSAT [27] are able to solve problem instances *incrementally*. Encoding M' in a way such that faults or mutations can be activated or deactivated by adding constraints to the formula allows the SAT solver to (partially) reuse the information it has already derived.

Therefore, we propose to generate a modified model M' that contains all faults and mutations for which we want to generate test cases. We use the same idea as in Figure 4b and introduce a Boolean flag f for each modification that allows us to activate (deactivate) the respective fault/mutation by setting f to true (false). Assume that R is the transition relation of the original model M and that R'_i is the transition relation of the model M'_i that contains the ith of the n modifications in question. We define the model R_μ as follows:

$$R_\mu(s_0, s_1, f^1, \ldots, f^n) := \begin{cases} R(s_0, s_1) & \text{if } \bigvee_{i=1}^n f^i = \mathsf{F} \\ R'_1(s_0, s_1) & \text{if } f^1 = \mathsf{T} \wedge \left(\bigvee_{=2}^n f^i\right) = \mathsf{F} \\ R'_2(s_0, s_1) & \text{if } f^2 = \mathsf{T} \wedge f^1 = \mathsf{F} \wedge \left(\bigvee_{=3}^n f^i\right) = \mathsf{F} \\ \vdots & \\ R'_n(s_0, s_1) & \text{if } f^n = \mathsf{T} \wedge \left(\bigvee_{=1}^{n-1} f^i\right) = \mathsf{F} \end{cases} \quad (2)$$

We use M_μ to denote the model with the transition relation R_μ.

Given the resulting transition relation R_μ (as defined in (2)) we can construct an instance of Formula (1). A fault in the modified model M_μ can be triggered by adding a constraint of the form

$$F^j := f^j \wedge \bigwedge_{0<i\leq n, i\neq j} \neg f^i \, . \quad (3)$$

Example 2. Figure 5 shows a mutation and a fault injected into the Simulink diagram in Figure 4a. The first diagram shows the implementation of a signal-stuck-at-0 fault. The diagram below combines this fault and the mutation in Figure 4b into one model. The model provides two flags allowing us to trigger the mutations.

The decision procedure of CBMC, the model checker which our test case generation tool COVER is based on, performs bit-level accurate reasoning by transforming the instance of Formula (1) into an equi-satisfiable propositional formula EQ_k in Conjunctive Normal Form[2] (CNF). This formula is then handed over to the satisfiability checker MINISAT [27]. The decision process of MINISAT is incremental, i.e., it allows

- to add additional clauses, and
- to add or remove a constraint F^j of the form described in (3)

without reinitializing the solver, meaning that the solver can reuse intermediate results if it has to solve similar problem instances.

Let EQ_k denote the CNF of the instance of Equation (1) derived from the models M and M_μ. We can generate a test suite covering all n mutations in question by iteratively computing satisfiable assignments to

$$EQ_k \wedge F^i, \quad i \in \{1, \ldots, n\} \, . \quad (4)$$

We say that a test case t *independently* covers a mutation if it corresponds to a satisfying assignment of (4) for that mutation i. If each of the instances of Formula (4) has a solution, we obtain n (not necessarily different) test cases that cover all mutations injected into the model M_μ.

[2] A propositional formula in conjunctive normal form is a conjunction of disjunctions of literals, where a literal l is a propositional variable or its negation (e.g., a or $\neg a$). A *clause* is a disjunction of literals.

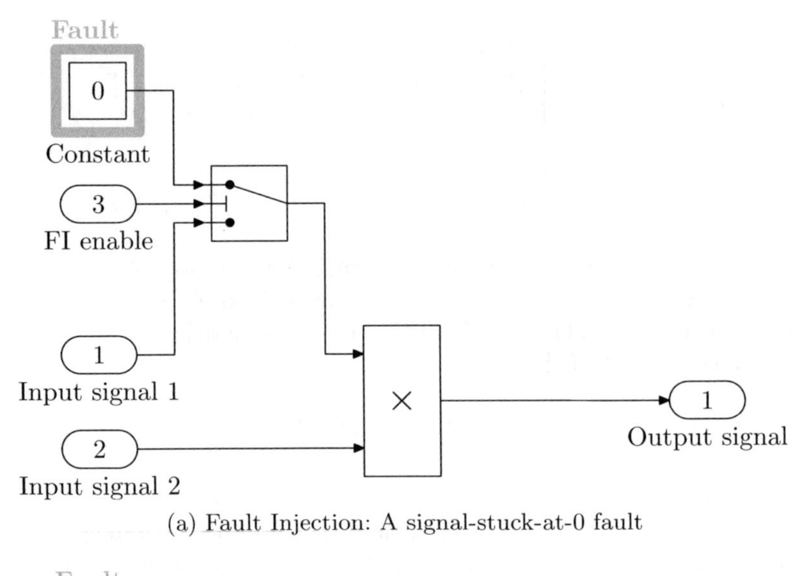

(a) Fault Injection: A signal-stuck-at-0 fault

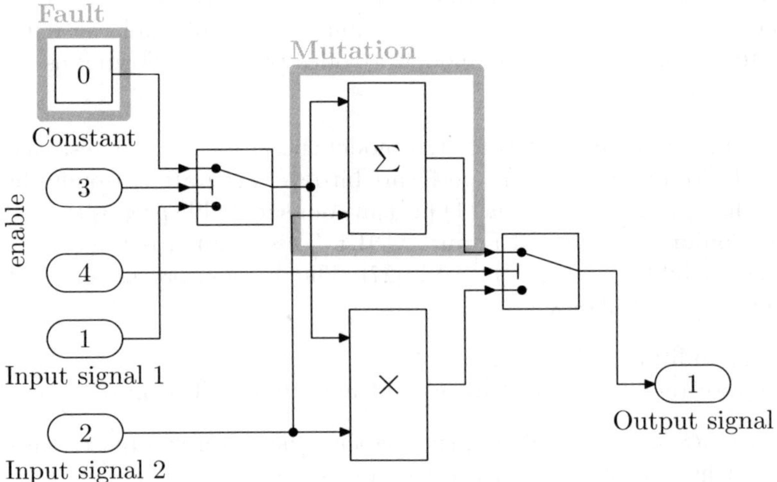

(b) The fault and the mutation from Figure 4b combined in one model

Fig. 5. Mutations and Faults injected into a simple Simulink model

4 Generating Test-Cases for Many Mutations

In this section, we propose an optimisation of the mutation-based test-case generation approach discussed in Section 3.

4.1 Finding an Efficient and Sufficient Test-Suite

The technique described in Section 3.6 uses a SAT-solver to extract n test cases from Formula (4), each of which corresponds to one mutation. If the number of mutations (n) is large, this may lead to an equally large number of test cases. These test-cases are computationally expensive to generate and time-consuming to execute. Therefore, it is desirable to minimize the size of the test-suite.

Example 3. Consider the Simulink diagrams in Figures 4a, 4b, and 5. Assume that we use the model in Figure 5b to generate a test case. Consider the test case $s.i_1 = 1.2$ and $s.i_2 = 23.4$. The following table lists the observable outputs of the model for all possible combinations of enable flags:

Input signal 1	Input signal 2	Fault	Mutation	Output
1.2	23.4	off	off	28.08
1.2	23.4	on	off	0.0
1.2	23.4	off	on	24.6
1.2	23.4	on	on	23.4

This test case is sufficient to detect the syntactic mutation, the signal-stuck-at-0 fault, as well as the combination of these modifications.

The observation in Example 3 suggests that it is not strictly necessary to generate a separate test case for each single modification. In the setting presented in Example 3, the test vector $t = \{i_1 \mapsto 1.2, i_2 \mapsto 23.4\}$ can be obtained from the model in which *both* modifications are enabled. This can be achieved by generalizing the constraint F^j (see (3)) accordingly, i.e., for a set T of indices corresponding to mutations or faults

$$F^T := \bigwedge_{0<i\leq n} ((i \in T) \Rightarrow f^i) \wedge ((i \notin T) \Rightarrow \neg f^i) \ . \tag{5}$$

Notably, t is sufficient to cover the fault and the mutation independently.

It follows that it is possible that a test-case t derived from a model M_μ with a combination of several mutations $\{\nu_1, \nu_2, \ldots\}$ detects the independent mutations, too. This can be efficiently checked by evaluating the behavior of the mutated models $M_{\nu_1}, M_{\nu_2}, \ldots$ for the input defined by the test-vector t. The execution of a given test-case on a model is very efficient compared to the model checking-based computation of a new test-vector for M_{ν_i}.

Example 4. We continue working in the setting of Example 4. Consider the test case $s.i_1 = 0.0$ and $s.i_2 = 23.4$. We can compute the outcome for all different models for this input by simply executing the test cases:

Input signal 1	Input signal 2	Fault	Mutation	Output
0.0	23.4	off	off	0.0
0.0	23.4	on	off	0.0
0.0	23.4	off	on	23.4
0.0	23.4	on	on	23.4

This test case is sufficient to detect the combination of the syntactic mutation and the injected signal-stuck-at-0 fault, as well as the single syntactic mutation. However, it fails to detect the signal-stuck-at-0 fault.

Example 4 shows that it is not always the case that a test-case that detects a combination of mutations and faults also covers each mutation independently. While we have found a test vector $t = \{i_1 \mapsto 0.0, i_2 \mapsto 23.4\}$ which "kills" the mutation, the same test vector fails to cover the fault. We are forced to generate an additional test case for the injected fault, which can be achieved by deactivating the enable flag for the fault and starting another incremental run of the SAT solver.

We propose to analyze the model systematically, starting with a set of mutations T. The corresponding algorithm is outlined in Figure 6. We generate a test case which covers this set of mutations T and check whether it independently covers the single elements of T. The advantage of the algorithm is that it is possible to prune entire subsets of mutations if C in step ③ is non-empty. If this is not the case, we have to split T recursively. In the worst case, we still require n test-cases to cover all n mutations.

Input: A model and a set of mutations T
Output: A test-suite S covering the mutations in T.

① If $T = \emptyset$, terminate.
② Compute a test case t satisfying $EQ_k \wedge F^T$ (as defined in (5)). ($C = \emptyset$ if there is no such t).
③ Let $C \subseteq T$ be the set of mutations independently covered by t:
  ❶ If $C \neq \emptyset$, let $T := T \setminus C$. Add t to the test suite and proceed to ①.
  ❷ If $C = \emptyset$, partition T into T_1 and T_2 s.t. $T = T_1 \cup T_2$, and $T_1 \cap T_2 = \emptyset$. Call the algorithm recursively with $T := T_1$ and $T := T_2$, respectively.

Fig. 6. An algorithm for systematic test-case generation

The success or failure of this approach depends inherently on the structure of the mutations and the model M. In the following, let ν_1 and ν_2 be two mutations for M. Furthermore, let $s_0, \ldots, s_n$ be an execution trace of M, and $s'_0, \ldots, s'_n$ be an execution trace of M with both mutations enabled.

Assume that ν_1 and ν_2 affect different output signals, i.e., given a fixed input sequence $s_0.i, \ldots s_n.i$, the set of signals changed by activating the mutation ν_1 is disjoint from the set of signals changed by enabling the mutation ν_2. Then, we can increase the chance of finding a test case that covers both mutations independently by trying to maximize the difference between $s_0.o, \ldots s_n.o$ and $s'_0.o, \ldots s'_n.o$.

Unfortunately, such an independence cannot be assumed in general, since there may be a mutual influence between mutations. In particular, two mutations may cancel each other out. Checking whether two mutations are independent in the sense explained above is computationally as expensive as model checking and therefore not a feasible strategy.

5 Detecting Non-observability of Mutations

In traditional mutation-based testing, the difficulty to identify mutations without observable effect on the system outputs is known to be one of the main obstacles. Assume that one instance $EQ_k \wedge F^c$ of (4) (with $i = c$) is unsatisfiable. This indicates that the injected fault corresponding to f^c (see Formula (2)) does not result in an error that propagates to an observable output within k steps. There are two possible reasons for this phenomenon:

1. The bound k is not sufficiently large to reveal the error.
2. The model contains redundancy and the injected fault does not result in an observable change of its behavior. We say that the model *tolerates* the fault. The mutant is an *equivalent mutant.*

A *complete* model checking algorithm can distinguish both cases. The first case can be addressed by simply increasing the bound k. In the second case, the mutation is not *strong* enough to have any impact on the observable behavior of the model and the model checking tool provides a *proof* for the equivalence of the mutated and original model. This concept is explained in the following subsection.

5.1 Model Checking, Induction, and Invariants

BMC is only capable of providing a guarantee that a property P is not violated within at most k execution steps. In this section, we briefly discuss two techniques to lift this restriction: k-induction [28] and finding invariants by means of fixed-point detection [1].

k-Induction. This technique generalizes the standard induction principle, and has been used before for test-vector generation for Simulink models [2]. The base case is established by means of BMC. The following equation holds if and only if the property P is not violated in the first k execution steps:

$$I(s_0) \wedge \bigwedge_{i=0}^{k-1} R(s_i, s_{i+1}) \wedge \bigwedge_{i=0}^{k} P(s_i) \tag{6}$$

If the base case (6) holds, the technique proceeds to show by induction that P holds for any arbitrary $k \in \mathbb{N}$:

$$\left(\bigwedge_{i=0}^{k} R(s_i, s_{i+1}) \wedge \bigwedge_{j=0}^{k} P(s_j) \right) \Rightarrow P(s_{k+1}) \tag{7}$$

Formula (6) in combination with (7) implies that the sequence of states can be extended to a path of arbitrary length without ever violating P. Thus, if we can find a k for which the conjunction of (6) and (7) holds, then the model is safe.

To check whether this conjunction holds for a given k, we rely on efficient decision procedures (SAT solvers such as [27], in particular). Let $G = (6) \wedge (7)$. If

G holds, modern decision procedures are able to generate a *proof*. In our setting, a proof is a directed acyclic graph (V, E, ℓ), where V is a set of vertices, E is a set of edges, and ℓ is a labeling function. Each initial vertex v has in-degree 0 and $\ell(v)$ is an axiom or a sub-conjunct of G. Each internal vertex has in-degree m, $m \geq 1$. The label of each inner node w is derived from the labels of its predecessors $\{v_1, \ldots, v_m\}$ by means of a deduction rule $\ell(v_1), \ldots, \ell(v_m) \vdash \ell(w)$. The final vertex u has out-degree 0 and $\ell(u)$ is the conclusion of the proof. SAT solvers typically generate proofs that $\neg G$ is unsatisfiable, that is, the conclusion is F.

Fixed-Points and Invariants. For finite-state systems, iterating the transition function until no new states are found is a viable verification technique, known as fixed-point detection. This technique relies on an efficient symbolic representation of sets of states such as binary decision diagrams [29]. The following recursive equations are iterated until $\mathcal{S}_i = \mathcal{S}_{i+1}$:

$$\mathcal{S}_0 = \{s_0 | I(s_0)\}, \quad \mathcal{S}_{i+1} = \mathcal{S}_i \cup \{s_{i+1} | s_i \in \mathcal{S}_i \wedge R(s_i, s_{i+1})\} \tag{8}$$

Let J be a symbolic representation of the final $\mathcal{S}_i$ in this sequence. Then J is an inductive invariant, i.e., it holds that

$$I(s_0) \Rightarrow J(s_0), \quad \text{and} \quad J(s_i) \wedge R(s_i, s_{i+1}) \Rightarrow J(s_{i+1}). \tag{9}$$

A popular technique to find invariants is the over-approximation of the set of safe states by means of Craig interpolation [30].

5.2 Reusing Proofs and Invariants for Proving Unobservability

Proof Analysis. The techniques presented in this section are based on work recently presented by Purandare et al. [31]. Consider a system M and a mutated system M_o in which all the mutations are introduced, but disabled using $F^{\emptyset}$, i.e. $\forall i. \neg f^i$. Thus, M and M_o are equivalent, i.e. $s_i.o = s_i'.o$ at all times. The equivalence checking Formula (1) is unsatisfiable for all k. As stated in Section 5.1, k-induction is one possibility to prove equivalence of M and M_o. Let T be a set of indices corresponding to all possible mutations (cf. Section 4.1). The formulae that k-induction checks to establish equivalence of M and M_o are as follows:

$$\underbrace{I(s_0) \wedge \bigwedge_{i=0}^{k-1} R(s_i, s_{i+1})}_{\text{original model}} \wedge \underbrace{I'(s_0') \wedge \bigwedge_{i=0}^{k-1} R'(s_i', s_{i+1}')}_{\text{mutated model}} \wedge \underbrace{\bigwedge_{j \in T} \neg f^j}_{\text{disable T}} \wedge \underbrace{\bigwedge_{i=0}^{k} s_i.o = s_i'.o}_{\text{equality of output}} \tag{10}$$

$$\left(\bigwedge_{i=0}^{k} (R(s_i, s_{i+1}) \wedge R'(s_i', s_{i+1}')) \wedge \bigwedge_{j \in T} \neg f^j \wedge \bigwedge_{j=0}^{k} s_j.o = s_j'.o \right) \Rightarrow s_{k+1}.o = s_{k+1}'.o \tag{11}$$

The following theorem states that those mutations that do not appear in the final proof of $G = (10) \wedge (11)$ checked during k-induction are non-observable [31].

Theorem 1. *A mutation corresponding to an enabling variable f^j that does not appear in the final proof of G is unobservable.*

Proof. A variable absent in the proof does not influence the conclusion of the proof. Thus, enabling a flag f^j absent in the proof does not invalidate the proof of k-inductivity and hence, does not break equivalence.

Thus, mutations absent in the proof do not need to be checked as these are unobservable.

Inductive Invariant. An inductive invariant represents a set of safe states with respect to a certain property of the model. Consider the composition of the two models M and M_o (where $\forall i\,.\,(s_i.i = s'_i.i)$) and let $\forall i\,.\,(s_i.o = s'_i.o)$ be the property in question.

Theorem 2. *Let $J(s, s')$ represent an invariant over the state space of the two models that warrants the equivalence of M and M_o, i.e., that $\forall i\,.J(s_i, s'_i) \Rightarrow (s_i.o = s'_i.o)$ holds. Furthermore, let R' be the transition function of M_o, only that the jth mutation is enabled ($f^j = \mathsf{T}$). If*

$$I(s_0) \wedge I'(s'_0) \Rightarrow J(s_0, s'_0) \text{ and}$$
$$J(s_i, s'_i) \wedge R(s_i, s_{i+1}) \wedge R'(s'_i, s'_{i+1}) \Rightarrow J(s_{i+1}, s'_{i+1})$$

holds, then the jth mutation is unobservable.

Proof. The inductive invariant J is also an inductive invariant of the resulting mutated system and therefore establishes equivalence.

6 Conclusion

We have defined a methodology for automated test case generation for Simulink models. By formulating test coverage and goals in terms of fault models, we achieve a flexible and general framework that subsumes standard coverage criteria and is directly related to functional and non-functional requirements specifications. The use of equivalence checking and bounded model checking makes it possible to explore the behavior of models with high precision, taking intricate details such as the actual floating-point semantics of execution platforms into account. We implemented this approach in our test-case generation tool COVER, which is based on the model checker CBMC. The evaluation of COVER on industrial case studies developed in the European projects MOGENTES and CESAR is currently in progress.

In order to handle the size of real-world Simulink models, we have introduced two main concepts to keep the complexity of test case generation manageable: a strategy to compute small test suites by maximizing the number of mutations that are covered by each test case, and techniques to efficiently detect unobservability of mutations. An experimental evaluation of both techniques is planned as future work.

References

1. Clarke, E., Grumberg, O., Peled, D.: Model Checking. MIT Press, Cambridge (1999)
2. Gadkari, A., Yeolekar, A., Suresh, J., Ramesh, S., Mohalik, S., Shashidar, K.C.: AutoMOTGen: Automatic model oriented test generator for embedded control systems. In: Gupta, A., Malik, S. (eds.) CAV 2008. LNCS, vol. 5123, pp. 204–208. Springer, Heidelberg (2008)
3. Kroening, D., Clarke, E.M., Yorav, K.: Behavioral consistency of C and Verilog programs using bounded model checking. In: Design Automation Conference (DAC), pp. 368–371. ACM, New York (2003)
4. Holzer, A., Schallhart, C., Tautschnig, M., Veith, H.: FShell: Systematic test case generation for dynamic analysis and measurement. In: Gupta, A., Malik, S. (eds.) CAV 2008. LNCS, vol. 5123, pp. 209–213. Springer, Heidelberg (2008)
5. Angeletti, D., Giunchiglia, E., Narizzano, M., Puddu, A., Sabina, S.: Automatic test generation for coverage analysis using CBMC. In: Moreno-Díaz, R., Pichler, F., Quesada-Arencibia, A. (eds.) Computer Aided Systems Theory - EUROCAST 2009. LNCS, vol. 5717, pp. 287–294. Springer, Heidelberg (2009)
6. Holzer, A., Schallhart, C., Tautschnig, M., Veith, H.: Query-driven program testing. In: Jones, N.D., Müller-Olm, M. (eds.) VMCAI 2009. LNCS, vol. 5403, pp. 151–166. Springer, Heidelberg (2009)
7. Ball, T.: A theory of predicate-complete test coverage and generation. In: de Boer, F.S., Bonsangue, M.M., Graf, S., de Roever, W.-P. (eds.) FMCO 2004. LNCS, vol. 3657, pp. 1–22. Springer, Heidelberg (2005)
8. Beyer, D., Chlipala, A.J., Henzinger, T.A., Jhala, R., Majumdar, R.: Generating tests from counterexamples. In: International Conference on Software Engineering (ICSE), pp. 326–335 (2004)
9. Jia, Y., Harman, M.: An analysis and survey of the development of mutation testing. IEEE Transactions on Software Engineering, TSE (2010)
10. Kupferman, O., Li, W., Seshia, S.A.: A theory of mutations with applications to vacuity, coverage, and fault tolerance. In: Formal Methods in Computer-Aided Design (FMCAD), pp. 1–9. IEEE, Los Alamitos (2008)
11. Ruthruff, J.R., Burnett, M.M., Rothermel, G.: Interactive fault localization techniques in a spreadsheet environment. IEEE Transactions on Software Engineering (TSE) 32, 213–239 (2006)
12. Schuler, D., Dallmeier, V., Zeller, A.: Efficient mutation testing by checking invariant violations. In: International Symposium on Software Testing and Analysis (ISSTA), pp. 69–80. ACM, New York (2009)
13. Meenakshi, B., Bhatnagar, A., Roy, S.: Tool for translating simulink models into input language of a model checker. In: Liu, Z., He, J. (eds.) ICFEM 2006. LNCS, vol. 4260, pp. 606–620. Springer, Heidelberg (2006)
14. Fehnker, A., Krogh, B.H.: Hybrid system verification is not a sinecure: The electronic throttle control case study. In: Wang, F. (ed.) ATVA 2004. LNCS, vol. 3299, pp. 263–277. Springer, Heidelberg (2004)
15. Joshi, A., Heimdahl, M.P.E.: Model-based safety analysis of Simulink models using SCADE design verifier. In: Winther, R., Gran, B.A., Dahll, G. (eds.) SAFECOMP 2005. LNCS, vol. 3688, pp. 122–135. Springer, Heidelberg (2005)
16. Ryabtsev, M., Strichman, O.: Translation validation: From simulink to c. In: Bouajjani, A., Maler, O. (eds.) Computer Aided Verification. LNCS, vol. 5643, pp. 696–701. Springer, Heidelberg (2009)

17. The Mathworks: Simulink design verifier user's guide. version 1.5 (2009), http://www.mathworks.com/access/helpdesk/help/toolbox/sldv/
18. Brillout, A., Kroening, D., Wahl, T.: Mixed abstractions for floating-point arithmetic. In: Formal Methods in Computer-Aided Design (FMCAD), pp. 69–76. IEEE, Los Alamitos (2009)
19. Kuehlmann, A., van Eijk, C.A.J.: Combinational and sequential equivalence checking. In: Logic Synthesis and Verification. Kluwer International Series in Engineering and Computer Science Series, pp. 343–372. Kluwer, Norwell (2002)
20. Graf, S., Saïdi, H.: Construction of abstract state graphs with PVS. In: Grumberg, O. (ed.) CAV 1997. LNCS, vol. 1254, pp. 72–83. Springer, Heidelberg (1997)
21. Kroening, D., Clarke, E.: Checking consistency of C and Verilog using predicate abstraction and induction. In: IEEE/ACM International Conference on Computer-Aided Design, pp. 66–72. IEEE, Los Alamitos (2004)
22. Victor, A.C.: Interpretation of IEEE-854 floating-point standard and definition in the HOL system. Technical report, NASA Langley (1995)
23. Harrison, J.: Formal verification of square root algorithms. Formal Methods in System Design (FMSD) 22, 143–153 (2003)
24. Blanchet, B., Cousot, P., Cousot, R., Feret, J., Mauborgne, L., Miné, A., Monniaux, D., Rival, X.: A static analyzer for large safety-critical software. In: Programming Language Design and Implementation (PLDI), pp. 196–207. ACM, New York (2003)
25. Miné, A.: Relational abstract domains for the detection of floating-point run-time errors. In: Schmidt, D. (ed.) ESOP 2004. LNCS, vol. 2986, pp. 3–17. Springer, Heidelberg (2004)
26. Kroening, D., Strichman, O.: Decision Procedures. Springer, Heidelberg (2008)
27. Eén, N., Sörensson, N.: An extensible SAT-solver. In: Giunchiglia, E., Tacchella, A. (eds.) SAT 2003. LNCS, vol. 2919, pp. 502–518. Springer, Heidelberg (2004)
28. Sheeran, M., Singh, S., Stålmarck, G.: Checking safety properties using induction and a SAT-solver. In: Johnson, S.D., Hunt Jr., W.A. (eds.) FMCAD 2000. LNCS, vol. 1954, pp. 108–125. Springer, Heidelberg (2000)
29. Bryant, R.E.: Graph-based algorithms for Boolean function manipulation. IEEE Transactions on Computers 35, 677–691 (1986)
30. McMillan, K.L.: Interpolation and SAT-based model checking. In: Hunt Jr., W.A., Somenzi, F. (eds.) CAV 2003. LNCS, vol. 2725, pp. 1–13. Springer, Heidelberg (2003)
31. Chockler, H., Kroening, D., Purandare, M.: Coverage in interpolation-based model checking. In: Design Automation Conference (DAC), ACM, New York (2010)

Model-Based Mutation Testing of Hybrid Systems*

Bernhard K. Aichernig, Harald Brandl, Elisabeth Jöbstl, and Willibald Krenn

Institute for Software Technology, Graz University of Technology
{aichernig,hbrandl,ejoebstl,wkrenn}@ist.tugraz.at

Abstract. This paper presents a novel model-based testing approach developed in the MOGENTES project. The aim is to test embedded systems controlling a continuous environment, i.e., hybrid systems. We present our two key abstractions against which we systematically test for conformance. (1) Classical action systems are used to model the discrete controller behavior. (2) Qualitative differential equations are used to model the evolutions of the environment. The latter is based on a technique from the domain of Artificial Intelligence called qualitative reasoning. Mutation testing on these models is used to generate effective test cases. A test case generator has been developed that searches for all test cases that would kill a mutant. The mutant models represent our fault models. The generated test cases are then executed on the implementation in order to systematically exclude the possibility that a mutant has been implemented.

1 Introduction

The EU FP7 project MOGENTES aims at significantly enhancing testing of dependable embedded systems by means of automated generation of test cases. As its full name Model-based Generation of Tests for Dependable Embedded Systems indicates the approach to address this aim is model-based testing.

In model-based testing a (formal) model of the system under test (SUT) serves two purposes, to generate the input stimuli and as a test oracle for the expected behavior. Figure 1 gives the general picture. A tester produces a model and generates test cases from it. The tests are automatically executed. If all possible tests pass, we have conformance between the model and the SUT. However, since exhaustive testing is impractical, we have to select a proper subset of possible test cases. Hence, the aim is to show non-conformance, i.e., to find bugs in the SUT.

Since the project deals with highly critical systems, e.g., in the transportation domain, the techniques have to be well-grounded. Therefore, a formal testing approach is required implying, (1) models with precise semantics, (2) well-defined notions of conformance, and (3) an explicit notion of fault models and coverage. The latter is addressed by applying mutation testing techniques to the modeling level.

* Research herein was funded by the EU FP7 project ICT-216679, Model-based Generation of Tests for Dependable Embedded Systems (MOGENTES).

F.S. de Boer et al. (Eds.): FMCO 2009, LNCS 6286, pp. 228–249, 2010.

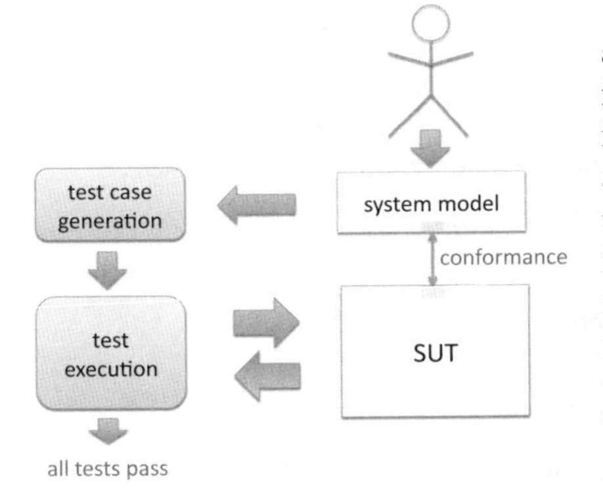

Fig. 1. Model-based testing: (1) a tester develops a model of the system under test, (2) test cases are generated from the model, (3) the test cases are executed on the system under test (SUT) to check for conformance

Mutation testing is a way of assessing and improving a test suite by checking if its test cases can detect a number of injected faults in a program. The faults are introduced by syntactically changing the source code following patterns of typical programming errors [10,9]. However, in MOGENTES we apply model-based mutation testing. The idea is to mutate the models and generate those test cases that would kill a set of mutated models. The generated tests are then executed on the SUT and will detect if a mutated model has been implemented. Hence, model-based mutation testing tests rather against non-conformance than for conformance. In terms of epistemology, we are rather aiming for falsification than for verification. It is a complementary fault-centered testing approach, well-suited for dependability analysis.

In the past, we have successfully applied model-based mutation testing to test communication protocols: e.g., HTTP [3] and SIP [18]. Furthermore, we have investigated its semantic foundations [4]. In this paper we extend our model-based mutation testing approach to models of hybrid systems. Hybrid systems involve discrete and continuous state updates as typically found in controllers interacting with a physical environment. Many embedded systems interact with a continuous environment and hence there is a strong interest in applying model-based testing to such systems.

The key technique is abstraction. Note that our models are abstract test models capturing the requirements. They are not implementation models for code generation as, e.g., found in model-driven development. The requirements of hybrid systems are largely qualitative and hence, as testers we are mainly interested in the qualitative changes of the system over time. As a consequence, in our test models we are able to abstract away from continuous environmental changes to qualitative changes. We use techniques from the field of Qualitative Reasoning (QR) [13] to model and reason over the qualitative behavior of the continuous environment. In QR modeling, numerical values are abstracted to relevant qualitative symbolic values. The behavior of these models is described in so called Qualitative Differential Equations. In order to model both, the controller and the environment, we have integrated these Qualitative Differential Equations into classical Action System before [2]. We call this extension Qualitative Action Systems (QAS).

The main contribution of this paper is the new combination of model-based mutation testing and qualitative reasoning. This involves a new test case

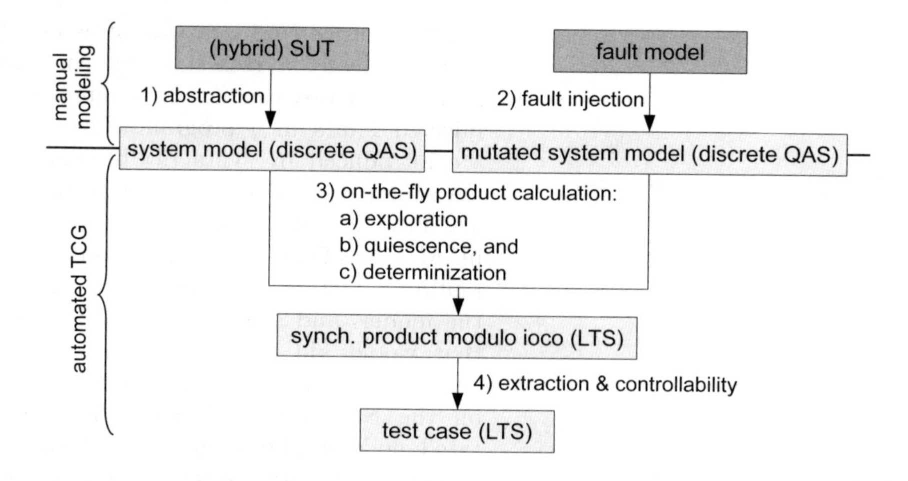

Fig. 2. Overview of our approach: Based on two QAS (a model of the SUT and a mutated system model), we calculate the synchronous product modulo ioco on-the-fly, i.e., we explore both QAS to gain the LTS semantics, add quiescence where needed, and determinize the resulting LTS in parallel. Finally, we extract a controllable test case from the synchronous product.

generator that combines a qualitative reasoning engine with an equivalence (conformance) checker. Note that we rely on classical notions of conformance defined over labeled transition systems (LTS). This is achieved by interpreting an action system as an LTS via a labeling of actions. We distinguish between input, output and internal labels representing the communication events between tester and SUT.

Figure 2 gives an overview of our test case generation approach. It relies on two inputs: (a) a model of the SUT in the form of a QAS and (b) a mutated system model, which is derived from the original QAS by applying a certain fault model. Note that modeling (cf. Step 1) as well as fault injection (cf. Step 2) have to be carried out manually. By the exploration of qualitative action systems, we are able to give them an LTS semantics. Our testing approach relies on the well-known input-output conformance relation *ioco* [17]. For test case generation, we check if the mutated model conforms to the original one. If not, a counter-example is turned into a test case. The conformance check is implemented as an on-the-fly calculation of the synchronous product modulo ioco of the two given QAS, i.e., we explore both QAS to gain the LTS semantics, add ioco's additional quiescence observation where needed (see Section 5.2), and determinize the resulting LTS in parallel (cf. Step 3). In this way, only parts of the QAS which are relevant for the test case generation are explored. Finally, we extract a controllable test case, which is an LTS again.

In the rest of this paper we present the details of this approach. Section 2 introduces our running hybrid systems example. Section 3 presents the qualitative abstraction of continuous functions and Section 4 describes the modeling of a hybrid system by means of QAS. Then, we discuss how test cases are identified via mutation testing in Section 5 and show how to select test cases in Section 6. Finally, we draw our conclusions, discuss related work and give an outlook to future work in Section 7.

2 Hybrid Systems

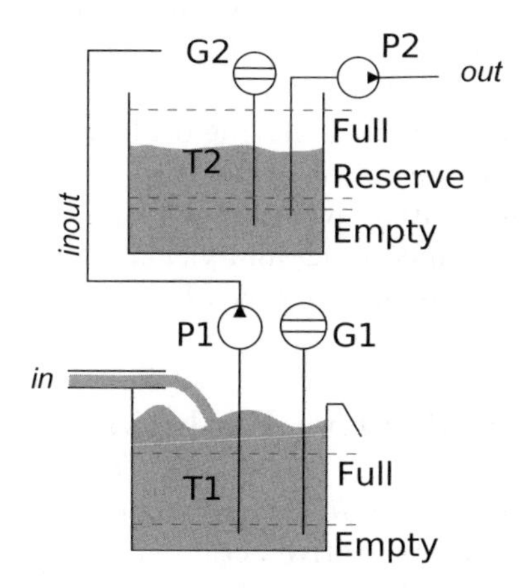

Fig. 3. A Two-Tank System with two pumps

Hybrid systems provide a closed-loop view on control programs operating in their environment. This closed-loop view, which incorporates continuous (environment) and discrete (controller) behavior, allows to draw more conclusions than by looking at the controller in isolation. For example, properties about the system's stability or its long term behavior.

Consider the example hybrid system of Figure 3 and the task to automatically derive tests. The first step towards a hybrid system model is to know the (informal) *system requirements*: in the two-tank system in Figure 3 tank $T1$ is on a lower level than the tank $T2$. $T1$ is being filled with water having some inflow rate *in*. Both tanks ($T1$, $T2$) are connected by the pump $P1$ that is controlled such that: if the water level in $T2$ decreases below a certain *Reserve* mark and $T1$ is full, pump $P1$ starts pumping water until $T2$ is full or $T1$ gets empty. In addition, the controller needs to control the pump $P2$ that is pumping water out of $T2$: $P2$ shall be turned on as long as a button *WaterRequest* is pressed and there is enough water in $T2$ ($T2$ not *Empty*). Note that the signal *WaterRequest* and the inflow rate *in* are not controllable, hence *T1* may overflow.

Given these requirements, one is able to derive a formal model. In this example, the continuous dynamics of the system is expressed by two coupled differential equations:

$$\dot{x}_1 = (in - inout)/A_1 \quad and \quad \dot{x}_2 = (inout - out)/A_2. \tag{1}$$

Here, A_1 and A_2 are the base areas of the two tanks and x_1 and x_2 denote the current level in the tanks. The variables *in*, *inout*, and *out* denote the flow rates into $T1$, between $T1$ and $T2$, and out of $T2$ respectively.

Observe that for testing whether some given implementation of this two-tank system conforms to the stated requirements we do not need to know the exact numerical value of the water level at all times, nor do we care about the exact time information. We would also need to incorporate additional knowledge, such as the exact base areas of the tanks in order to solve these equations numerically: in reality we might not have all information that is required for such a detailed model. Informal requirements, as in our example, mostly describe evolutions of hybrid systems in a qualitative manner like "when something increases to a certain value another thing will start decreasing". Finally, in order to transform the informal requirements to the differential equation model, one needs experience in physics and applied mathematics. To put a long story short: for our purposes of model-based mutation testing, the full differential model – most of the time – requires (and carries) too much detail. Hence, we abstract away these unnecessary details by using a technique called *qualitative abstraction.* After applying qualitative abstraction to the continuous behavior of our hybrid system we obtain a discrete model which we discuss in the next section. Having dealt with the continuous parts of the hybrid system, we then use action systems to formalize the discrete part. How action systems and qualitative evolutions can be joined to a hybrid system model has already been described in [2] and yields a formalism called *Qualitative Action Systems (QAS).* This provides us a framework for modeling and analyzing hybrid systems.

3 Environment Modeling with Qualitative Evolutions

In difference to most hybrid system models that use *Ordinary Differential Equations (ODEs)* to model continuous evolutions, a qualitative action system only knows about discrete, qualitative evolutions. Each of these qualitative evolutions forms a transition system that is constructed from *Qualitative Differential Equations (QDEs)* by applying a technique called *Qualitative Reasoning (QR)* [13]. Qualitative Reasoning originates from the area of Artificial Intelligence and is applied in common sense reasoning about physical systems with incomplete knowledge. The technique is based on the well founded theory of QDEs which are an abstraction of ODEs. Solutions to QDEs are usually found by inference systems like *QSIM* [13]. Qualitative reasoning relies on two abstractions: (1) value abstraction and (2) time abstraction.

Value abstraction is a data abstraction mapping the continuous real-valued variables of a physical environment to discrete variables with symbolic values. These symbolic variables are called *quantities* and have a finite domain of symbolic values. This finite domain of a quantity variable, i.e., its type, is called quantity space. There are two kinds of symbolic values in a quantity space: *landmark values* and *open intervals.*

Landmark values are the "natural joints" that break a continuous set of values into qualitatively distinct regions. A landmark value is a symbolic name for a particular real number, whose numerical value may or may not be known. It serves as a precise boundary for a qualitative region. For example, the landmark values of our water level in tank $T2$ are $Zero$, $Empty$, $Reserve$ and $Full$. These names indicate the interesting points where a behavior changes from a qualitative point of view. Hence, in our qualitative abstraction, the water level x_2 may evaluate to the landmark values, e.g., $x_2 = Empty$. Furthermore, the landmark values are defined to form a strict total order. In our example $Zero < Empty < Reserve < Full$ holds.

The qualitative values of a quantity variable are not only the landmark values, but also the open intervals between them. Hence, a quantity evaluates either to a landmark value or to an interval between landmarks. For example, the water level of tank T_2 can evaluate to seven different symbolic values:

$$x_2 \in \{Zero, Zero..Empty, Empty, Empty..Reserve,\\ Reserve, Reserve..Full, Full\}$$

Please note, in this abstraction the syntax *Empty..Reserve* represents a symbolic value expressing the imprecise knowledge that the concrete real value is somewhere in between those landmarks. For modeling, it is sufficient to define a list of landmarks, the interval values are implicit.

In order to describe the dynamics of a continuous system on a qualitative level, the symbolic values alone would be insufficient. Therefore, the direction of change $\delta =_{df} \{-, 0, +\}$ is also part of the abstract value space. This is an abstraction of the first derivation of the continuous behavior. Hence, the type of a qualitative variable is a pair consisting of a qualitative value and δ. For example, $x_2 = (Reserve, -)$ expresses the state of tank T_2 when its water-level reaches the reserve level and the water-level is still decreasing.

A typical evolution of the water level x_2 when filling up the tank would be

$$(Zero, 0), (Zero..Empty, +), (Empty, +), (Empty..Reserve, +),\\ (Reserve, +), (Reserve..Full, +), (Full, 0).$$

Note that jumps in the qualitative evolution are forbidden. The water level cannot go from increasing to decreasing without first being steady. Furthermore, the qualitative value cannot jump from one landmark value to the next without the interval value in between.

Time abstraction. Time intervals in which the qualitative behavior does not change are abstracted away. As a consequence, we abstract from continuous time to a temporal ordering of qualitative states. Figure 4 shows the relation between a continuous function v (top-right) and the according qualitative behavior q (bottom-left). Here, four landmarks split the value space into three regions of interest. The symbolic values show if a value is on a landmark or in between as well as its direction of change. The symbols in the qualitative trace denote steady behavior (circle), increasing behavior (arrow pointing upward), and decreasing behavior (arrow pointing downward). In addition, the abstraction s of the time intervals to steps in the evolution is also made explicit (bottom-right diagram).

The intended qualitative behavior is specified via Qualitative Differential Equations (QDEs). Like Ordinary Differential Equations, a QDE defines the dynamics of a system via relating the symbolic variables and their first derivations. Auxiliary variables may be used to link a set of QDEs. Our running example serves to illustrate the modeling approach.

In order to model the controller environment of our example we have to define the domains of the model quantities. The quantities x_1 and x_2 denoting the fill

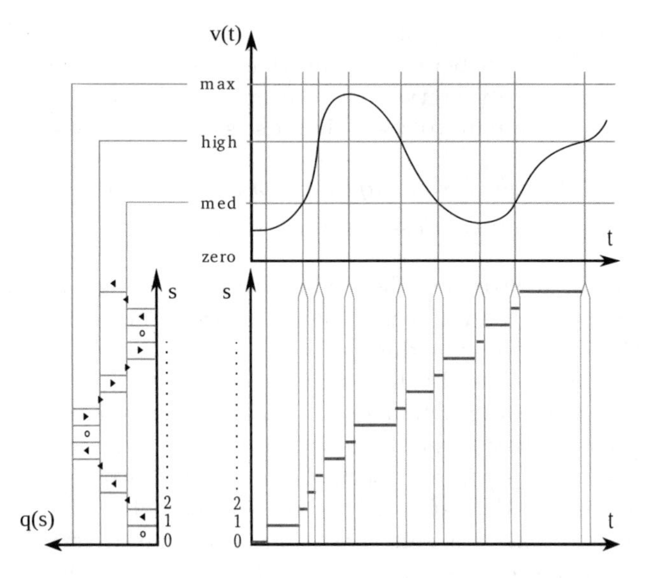

Fig. 4. Abstracting a continuous state evolution to a qualitative trace

levels in the two tanks have the quantity spaces $T1 =_{df} \{Zero, Empty, Full\}$ and $T2 =_{df} \{Zero, Empty, Reserve, Full\}$ respectively (see Figure 3). Remember that the implicit intervals between the landmarks are part of the quantity spaces. The flow rates have the quantity space $FR =_{df} \{Zero, Max\}$. We also need to introduce auxiliary quantities in order to be able to set up the QDEs. The auxiliary quantities $diff_1$ and $diff_2$ have to link the different QDEs. Hence, they only need a coarse quantity space $NZP =_{df} \{minf, Zero, inf\}$.

We use two types of qualitative constraints to formulate the QDEs of the water tank example: *add* and d/dt. The constraint $add(x, y, z)$ denotes the qualitative addition of two qualitative values $x + y = z$. It is defined over sign algebra and simply expresses facts like that two positive qualitative values will also be positive, etc. Table 1 shows the full definition of this qualitative addition. Note that in contrast to the real-valued algebra, here the addition is a relation rather than a function. This is because the result of adding opposing signs cannot be uniquely determined. The second constraint $d/dt(x, y)$ denotes that y is the qualitative derivation of x. This means that the sign of y determines the direction of change of x. The qualitative model of the two-tank system is given by the conjunction of the following QDEs:

Table 1. Qualitative Addition

add	+	0	−
+	+	+	+/0/−
0	+	0	−
−	+/0/−	−	−

$$add(diff_2, out, inout) \wedge add(diff_1, inout, in) \wedge d/dt(x_1, diff_1) \wedge d/dt(x_2, diff_2) \quad (2)$$

Since QR only deals with symbolic values and monotonic function relations (e.g., if x increases then y decreases) constant factors have no influence on the qualitative behavior. For example, the continuous functions $f_1(t) = t^2$ and $f_2(t) =$

$3 \cdot t^2$ with $t > 0$ both map to the same qualitative value $(0..inf, +)$ denoting some unknown function increasing in the interval $(0, \infty)$. Hence, the base areas of the two tanks in Equation 1 are not considered by the qualitative model.

Starting from a given initial state, a qualitative inference engine like QSIM [13] derives all possible behaviors which may evolve over time. This qualitative inference process results in a transition system. It represents the set of all possible behaviors, which is the set of all state sequences starting from the initial state, referred to as traces.

Behavior inference relies on solving constraints between the quantities expressed as QDEs and on transition rules between the current state and successor states imposed by the qualitative theory. For example, the earlier mentioned *continuity law* preventing jumps in the qualitative evolution is such a transition rule. A behavior is extended with a new state if at least one of the model quantities changes its value and the new state satisfies the QDEs and transition constraints.

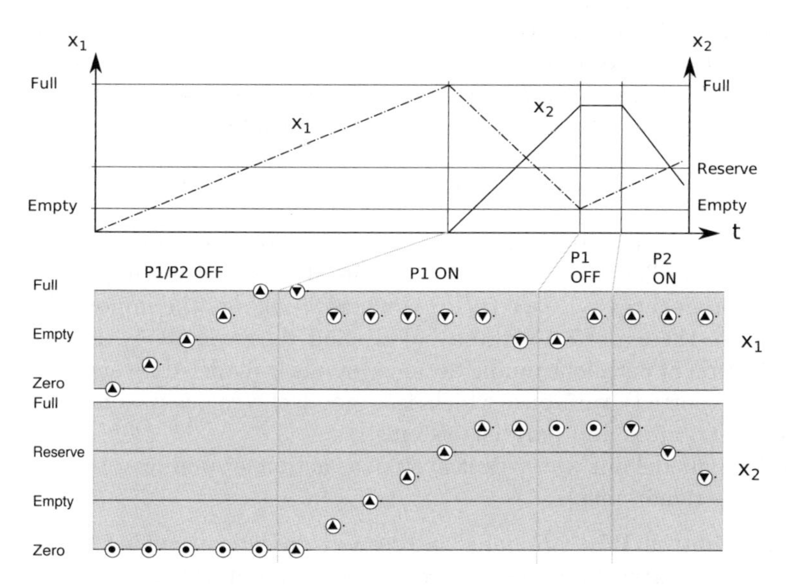

Fig. 5. Qualitative evolution of the two-tank system

Figure 5 shows an example evolution of our system. The upper diagram shows a concrete evolution while the lower diagram shows the corresponding qualitative evolution. In hybrid systems theory, a continuous region is denoted as mode. The scenario comprises four different modes. Discrete controller actions may cause non-continuous changes in the system as can be observed for the quantity x_1 at the change from mode *P1 ON* to *P1 OFF* in the qualitative trace. Here, the water level x_1 changes directly from decreasing to increasing. Of course, in a real system the changes would be continuous as mass inertia requires changes to take some time.

For a more detailed description of the process of qualitative behavior inference and the possible qualitative constraints see [13]. The following section presents the hybrid model of our running example.

4 System Modeling with Qualitative Action Systems

In the previous section, we have developed a set of QDEs expressing the continuous evolutions of our running example. For our hybrid system model to be complete, we now have to merge the qualitative evolutions of the environment with the behavior of the controller into a single qualitative action system model. Qualitative action systems are based on the formalism of action systems by Back et al. [5] that provide a framework for describing discrete and distributed systems. The actions are statements in the form of Dijkstra's guarded commands where the semantics is defined via weakest precondition predicate transformers. An action system (see Equation 3) consists of a block of variable declarations followed by an initialization action S_0 assigning to each variable an initial value and a **do od** block looping over the non-deterministic choice of all actions. Variables declared with a star are exported by an action system and can be imported by others in the import list I at the end of the action system block. Exported variables have to be unique among all other exported variables.

$$AS =_{df} |[\textbf{var}\ Y : T \bullet S_0; \textbf{do}\ A_1 \Box \ldots \Box A_n \textbf{od}\ ]| : I \qquad (3)$$

In order to specify distributed concurrent systems, several action systems can be composed in parallel. For two action systems A_1 and A_2 the import list of the resulting system gets $(u_1 \cup u_2) \backslash (v_1 \cup v_2)$ where u_1, u_2 are the imported variables and v_1, v_2 are the exported variables of A_1 and A_2 respectively. It follows that communication of parallel running action systems is modeled by access to shared (imported/exported) variables which is a good choice (easy semantics) when modeling distributed and parallel systems.

In order to model our water-tank system as action system, we have to be more precise on its requirements:

1. If a button *WaterRequest* is pressed (on) and provided $T2$ is not empty (water level above *Reserve*), start pump P2 and pump water out of tank $T2$.
2. If P2 is running and *WaterRequest* is not pressed, stop P2.
3. If P2 is running and the water level of $T2$ drops to *Empty*, stop P2.
4. If tank $T2$ gets empty (water level below *Reserve* mark) and $T1$ is full, pump water out of tank $T1$ into tank $T2$ by starting pump P1.
5. If pump P1 is running and the water level in tank $T1$ drops to *Empty*, then stop P1.
6. If pump P1 is running and the water level in tank $T2$ reaches *Full*, then stop P1.

The formal model of the system is given in Figure 6 and comprises three sections. In the *var* section all variables are declared and initialized: the system starts with both tanks empty, both pumps turned off, and some non-zero inflow rate into tank $T1$. The two keywords *alt* and *with* are used to denote the principle of hybrid alternation: the discrete actions in the *alt* block are alternated with the continuous action in the *with* block. In order to model reactive behavior, we give the controller priority over the environment. In other words, whenever an action of the *alt* block (which models the controller) is enabled for execution, a possibly running continuous action terminates and the action of the *alt* block is executed. This type of alternation is called *interrupting prioritized alternation*. Notice that the controller eventually has to reach a stable state in its computation where it waits for environmental updates. Otherwise, the environment and hence the progress of time would be blocked. The work in [15] discusses various kinds of hybrid alternation.

In order to apply standard LTS-based testing techniques we label each action with a name, denoting an event. For environmental changes (the execution of qualitative actions) we introduce the so-called *qual* event which may have parameters. The parameters determine the valuation of certain model quantities at the end of an evolution. This event view provides a further level of abstraction since, for blackbox testing, we are only interested in the external event behavior of a system. If the tester is only interested in the discrete controller events, the environmental *qual* events can also be hidden and considered as internal. Even in this case, a wrong environmental behavior can be detected if it has influence on the discrete controller events. Internal events are denoted with τ.

By executing a (qualitative) action system we obtain the set of all possible event sequences starting from the initial state. This gives us the trace (LTS) semantics of the action system. The trace semantics of qualitative action systems is described in [6]. Hence, our test model is an LTS obtained by exploration rather than the action system itself.

We need to create five discrete actions in order to model the controller. Each discrete action has a name (label) followed by a guard and an action body. When the action guard holds in a certain computation state, the body is executed and the model variables are updated accordingly. For instance, the first discrete action

$$PUMP1\_ON : g_1 \rightarrow p1\_running := true; inout := (0..Max, 0)$$

has some guard g_1 and switches on pump $P1$ by setting the Boolean variable *p1_running* to true and the pump to some non-zero, steady flow rate. The action system in Figure 6 still has general guards g_1 to g_5 instead of concrete ones. Hence, we need to find the correct guards so that our controller behavior matches the requirements. Starting with the first requirement that specifies when P2 should be enabled we can replace g_3 by:

$$g_3 =_{df} wr \wedge \neg p2\_running \wedge x_2 > Empty$$

Requirements 2 and 3, dealing with cases when to stop P2, can be translated into guard g_4:

$$g_4 =_{df} p2\_running \wedge (\neg wr \vee x_2 \leq Empty)$$

$$
\begin{array}{lll}
\multicolumn{3}{l}{System =_{df}} \\
\|[\ \mathbf{var} & & x_1 : T1, x_2 : T2, out, inout : FR, \\
 & & diff_1, diff_2 : NZP, \\
 & & p1\_running, p2\_running, wr : Bool \\
 & \bullet & x_1 := (0,0); x_2 := (0,0); \\
 & & out := (0,0); inout := (0,0); wr := false \\
 & & p1\_running := false; p2\_running := false \\
\quad \mathbf{alt} & & PUMP1\_ON : g_1 \rightarrow p1\_running := true; \\
 & & inout := (0..Max, 0) \\
 & \Box & PUMP1\_OFF : g_2 \rightarrow p1\_running := false; \\
 & & inout := (0,0) \\
 & \Box & PUMP2\_ON : g_3 \rightarrow p2\_running := true; \\
 & & out := (0..Max, 0) \\
 & \Box & PUMP2\_OFF : g_4 \rightarrow p2\_running := false; \\
 & & out := (0,0) \\
 & \Box & WATER\_REQ(X) : g_5 \rightarrow wr := X \\
\quad \mathbf{with} & & \neg(g_1 \vee g_2 \vee g_3 \vee g_4 \vee g_5) :\rightharpoondown \\
 & & add(diff_2, out, inout) \wedge add(diff_1, inout, in) \wedge \\
 & & d/dt(x_1, diff_1) \wedge d/dt(x_2, diff_2) \\
]| : in & &
\end{array}
$$

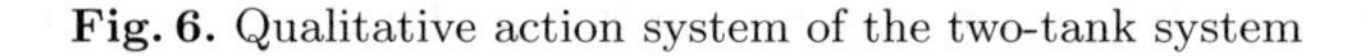

Fig. 6. Qualitative action system of the two-tank system

Similarly, g_1 and g_2 can be given as follows:

$$
\begin{aligned}
g_1 &=_{df} x_2 < Reserve \wedge x_1 = Full \wedge \neg p1\_running \\
g_2 &=_{df} p1\_running \wedge (x_1 < Empty \vee x_2 = Full)
\end{aligned}
$$

The first four controller actions are observable by a user of the system. The fifth discrete action *WATER_REQ(X)* is controllable and models a user scenario where water is requested when tank $T2$ is full and the water is being turned off as soon as the water level drops below the *Reserve* level. Guard g_5 expresses this behavior:

$$
g_5 =_{df} (\neg wr \wedge x_2 = Full \wedge X = true) \vee (wr \wedge x_2 < Reserve \wedge X = false)
$$

Since *WATER_REQ(X)* is a controllable action, the tester sets the Boolean parameter X for requesting water or not depending on the described user scenario. All discrete actions are combined via demonic choice.

The qualitative action in the *with* section consists of an *evolution guard (EG)*, the $:\rightharpoondown$ arrow denoting a qualitative action, and a body comprising a set of QDEs. If the EG holds in a certain state, the corresponding evolution consists of the set of qualitative traces which terminate in post-states where EG does not hold anymore. If there exist no post-states, the evolution does not terminate. The weakest precondition (wp) semantics of qualitative actions is described in [2] and can be interpreted as a non-deterministic update statement. The action relates the initial state of a qualitative evolution to a set of post-states. From these post-states further actions or evolutions can proceed. The wp semantics of qualitative action systems ensures that only terminating actions are executed.

The qualitative differential equation in (2) is totally defined, which means that we could use predicate *true* as evolution guard. However, since the evolution is considered atomic, it would never terminate and as a result the controller would not be able to interrupt it once it is run. So in order to realize the interrupted prioritized alternation between discrete and qualitative actions, we conjoin the negated guards of all discrete actions to strengthen the evolution guard. This guarantees that whenever the controller has something to do, it can interrupt the evolution of the environment.

The imported variable in denotes that the inflow rate into the lower tank is external to the system. In our example we assume a steady, non-zero inflow rate, i.e., $in = (0..Max, 0)$. This concludes the description of the model and we proceed with the testing techniques applied to our running example.

5 Model-Based Mutation Testing

Given the hybrid system model of the previous section, we derive test cases by mutation: we compare the behavior of the original model with mutated ones and extract behavior traces (tests) that allow us to distinguish implementations conforming to the original specification from implementations that do not.

5.1 Mutation Testing

Classical mutation testing is a way of assessing and improving a test suite by checking if its test cases can detect a number of injected faults in a program. The faults are introduced by syntactically changing the source code following patterns of typical programming errors. These deviations in the code are called mutations. The resulting faulty versions of the program are called mutants. Usually, each mutant includes only one mutation. Examples of typical mutations include renaming of variables, replacement of operators, e.g., an assignment for an equivalence operator, and slightly changing Boolean and arithmetic expressions. The number and kind of mutations depend on the programming language and are defined as so called mutation operators. A mutation operator defines a rewrite rule how certain terms in the programming language are replaced by mutations. For every occurrence of the term the mutation operator rewrites the original program into a new mutant. After a set of mutants has been generated, the test cases are run both on the original and on each mutant. If a test case can distinguish a mutant from the original program, i.e., a different output behavior can be observed, we say that this test case kills a mutant. The goal is to develop a test suite that kills all mutants. This technique of program testing has been invented by Hamlet [10] and DeMillo et al. [9] in the 70-ies.

Mutation testing has three basic assumptions: (1) the *competent programmer* assumption assumes that programmers make only small errors. This argument supports the use of small variations in the code to represent the fault models, i.e., the typical faults of programmers; (2) the chosen *mutation operators* are a representative set of those errors; (3) via a *coupling effect*, more subtle errors can be detected by testing against the simple errors only.

However, even with this assumptions there is a fundamental difficulty in this approach. Not all mutations represent actual faults producing observable failures. For example, a mutation in dead code, i.e., code that is never executed, will not lead to failures. Mutants with such an equivalent behavior are called *equivalent mutants* and can never be killed by any test case. This posed a serious limitation to the mutation testing technique: for a mutant surviving the tests, i.e., it is not killed, we do not know if this is due to our inability to come up with a proper test case or due to the fact that there is no such test case. Unfortunately, the problem is undecidable in general.

In recent years, however, with the advent of model checking techniques, the situation improved considerably: Today, the equivalence of two mutants can be decided for a growing class of programs assuming finite datatypes. This may explain the returning interest in mutation testing. For abstract models of a SUT the situation is even better. We have implemented such an equivalence checker, more precisely a conformance checker, for deciding if two action systems are equivalent. In case of non-equivalence (non-conformance) we generate a discriminating test case.

Hence, in *model-based mutation testing* we mutate the models of a SUT and generate test cases that would kill an implementation of a mutated model. The test cases are generated with the help of a conformance checker. In the following, we describe this test case generation technique in more detail.

5.2 Test Case Generation via Conformance Checking

As explained above, conformance or equivalence checking is at the heart of our test case generation technique. The reason why we prefer the term conformance checking to equivalence checking is the fact that our models are non-deterministic. Therefore, conformance is formally a pre-order relation, but not an equivalence relation.

In testing, we are only interested in external events. By interpreting our action systems in terms of their labeled actions, we map qualitative action systems to a labeled transition system (LTS) semantics. Furthermore, we distinguish between controllable (input), observable (output), and internal (τ) actions. Based on this LTS semantics we apply the input-output conformance relation *ioco* [17] for generating mutation-based test cases. Therefore we implemented an *ioco* checker in SICStus Prolog[1] which verifies the conformance between two given qualitative action systems by computing the synchronous product modulo *ioco* [6]. The result of the check is again an LTS which, in the case of non-conformance, contains *fail* states. These *fail* states are then used in the step of test case extraction to obtain test cases which reveal the mutated behavior.

The *ioco* relation states that for all *suspension* traces in the specification the outputs of the implementation after such a trace must be allowed in the specification after the same trace. Here, *suspension* traces are traces of the specification over inputs, outputs, and quiescence. These traces are obtained from a

[1] `http://www.sics.se/sicstus/`

specification by adding quiescence (δ) self loops in states where no output event is observable. Such states are called quiescent states. The purpose of quiescence is to exploit the absence of any observable events as an observation itself. Quiescence is realized as timeout event, i.e., if the implementation does not send any output within a specified timeout then δ can be observed. Thus, the timeout associated with δ has to be greater than the maximum response time of all other output events in the system. In Example 2, we discuss how the observation of quiescence can be employed to resolve decision conflicts during synchronous testing. Such conflicts arise in states where the tester has the choice between either applying an input or observing outputs. After adding δ self loops in quiescent states, determinization is applied resulting in the suspension automaton.

Environmental changes in qualitative action systems are designated by *qual* events. These events mark the firing of the qualitative action. If a tester's choice depends on a previous environmental update, such *qual* events have to be observable by the tester. Referring to our running example, a tester's input to the system is the controllable *WATER_REQ(X)* event, where X is a Boolean parameter for requesting water or not. Note that the guard of this input action depends on the water level of tank $T2$. Hence, we have to declare qualitative evolutions as observable events. Otherwise, the nondeterminism of the model would prevent the enabledness of the controllable action according to the controllability condition (4), discussed in section 5.3.

Example 1. Figure 7 shows a part of the conformance verification result between the system specification and a mutant. In the mutant, the action

$$PUMP1\_OFF : g_2 \rightarrow p1\_running := \textbf{true}; inout := (0, 0)$$

has been modified such that the Boolean flag denoting the state of pump $P1$ remains *true* although it should be set to *false*. The *ctr* prefix of actions means that the action is controlled by a tester while *obs* denote observations a tester can make from the implementation. As can be seen in Figure 7, the mutation is revealed when the tester tries to turn off pump $P1$ twice which is in difference to the specified behavior. After unexpected output behavior, not permitted by the specification, *fail* states are appended in the product LTS. The behavior of a mutant following after *pass* states is allowed by the *ioco* relation. Furthermore, the parametric values of *qual* events denote the environmental condition at the end of an evolution. For example, the first evolution after the initial state fills the lower tank to the *Full* level and the upper tank remains empty. Then pump $P1$ is turned on which subsequently causes another evolution filling the upper tank $T2$. Here, depending on the flow rates and tank volumes several outcomes are possible.

Applying the conformance verification step to several different mutants yields the results shown in Table 2. In the first column *ASO* stands for the *Association Shift Operator* which changes the association between variables in Boolean expressions. *ENO* is the shorthand for the *Expression Negation Operator*, *ERO*

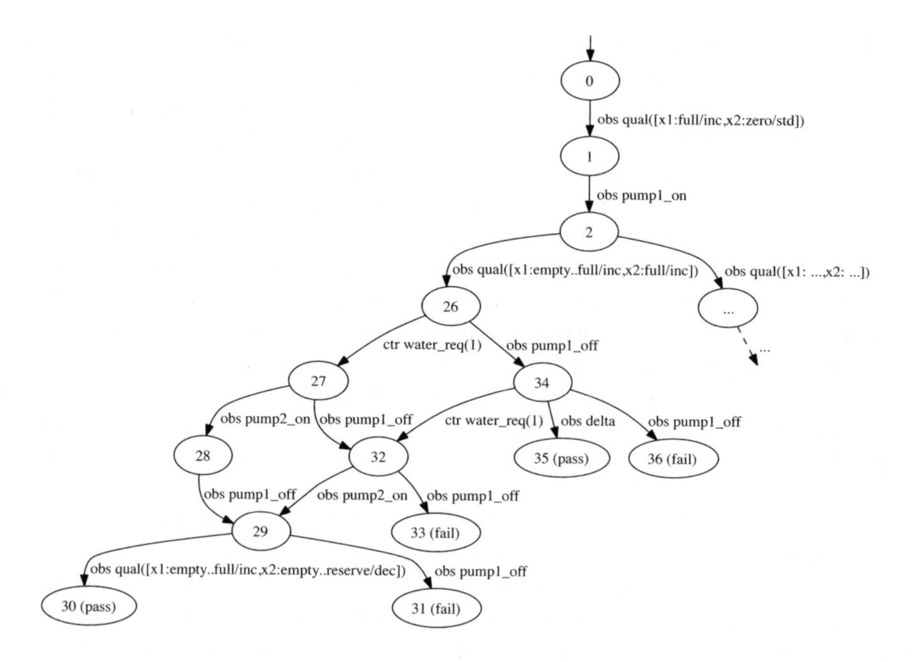

Fig. 7. Part of the result of the conformance check between the original and the mutated specification

Table 2. Results when applying conformance verification to mutated specifications

Mut. Op.	No. Mutants	Avg.Time [s]	Average No. States	Average No. Trans.	≠	= No.	= Perc.
ASO	10	13.9	64	117	7	3	30%
ENO	6	7.6	68	120	5	1	17%
ERO	20	12.9	62	110	20	0	0%
LRO	13	12.8	93	168	9	4	31%
MCO	16	12.8	70	126	10	6	38%
RRO	12	12.0	40	73	10	2	17%
Total	77	12.0	66	119	61	16	21%

means the *Event Replacement Operator*, *LRO* stands for *Logical Operator Replacement*, *MCO* denotes the *Missing Condition Operator*, and *RRO* is the abbreviation for the *Relational Replacement Operator*. The second column shows the number of generated mutants for each of the different operators. The average time needed for the conformance verification is given in the third column. The average number of states and transitions of the resulting product graphs are given in the fourth and fifth column, while the next to last column shows how many equivalent mutants were found: from a total of 77 mutants, 16 (about 21%) were found to be equivalent and cannot contribute any test cases. All conformance results were derived using unbounded search, i.e., the results are exact. The state space of the original specification comprises 59 states and 107 transitions.

5.3 Ensuring Controllability in Presence of Non-determinism

The *ioco* relation is a global property referring to label traces of the specification rather than to states like simulation relations. This implies that the local information in a certain state, in general, is not enough to decide conformance. That is the case for non-deterministic specifications where the same trace leads to different states. Here the outputs of both states have to be considered by *ioco* which requires preceded determinization. Our *ioco* checker applies the computation of the suspension automaton on-the-fly while computing the product LTS of two given QAS. However, care has to be taken during determinization regarding the enabledness of events. In action systems, events can only occur if the action's enabledness guard is satisfied in the current state. This guard is defined as $g(A) =_{df} \neg wp(A, false)$, ensuring that the action will not terminate in an undefined post-state. Here, *wp* denotes the weakest precondition.

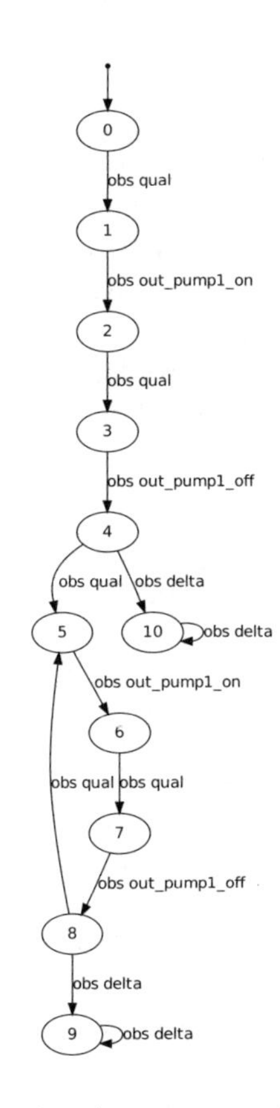

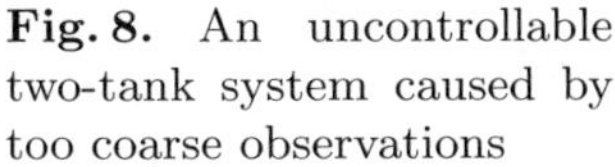

Fig. 8. An uncontrollable two-tank system caused by too coarse observations

In the case of black-box testing, the state of a system is internal and cannot be observed from outside. If an action system model contains non-determinism, i.e., internal actions and nondeterministic updates, determinization of its labeled transition system via subset construction leads to sets of states. In the action system model, however, for each of these states different subsequent events (actions) could be enabled. Due to the abstraction to an LTS we lose this information and in the LTS the union of all enabled events would be indicated as valid subsequent actions. This information loss leads to a problem during test case execution, as the implementation might make another internal decision than the test driver. In the end, the tester might not know in which state the SUT is in and worse, which events are allowed. Because we require the SUT to be input-enabled, the tester might not even notice the loss of synchronization immediately: the SUT has to ignore all inputs that are not allowed. Of course, if the tester subsequently encounters an unexpected observation, it would issue a fail verdict - which would be wrong in this case, as the SUT made a valid internal choice.

To overcome this problem, we need to synchronize the test case execution with the internal state decisions of the implementation. Since this is not possible in blackbox testing, the alternative is to disallow input events with guards that do not hold for all internal states. We denote the occurrence of an event a in a state s as $s \xrightarrow{a}$. The following property states that an action from the set of input actions L_I is enabled in a state $s \in S$ of the suspension automaton iff the action is enabled in all sub-states of s:

$$\forall a \in L_I, s \in S \bullet (\forall s_i \in s \bullet g(a)(s_i)) \Longleftrightarrow s \xrightarrow{a} \tag{4}$$

According to *ioco* this is a valid abstraction since input behavior can get stronger, which reduces the number of testing scenarios. If this causes the loss of many input events then this is an indication that the tester needs more observations to control the implementation. The work in [19] exploits the observation of quiescence to resolve the internal decision of the implementation to either accept inputs or to produce outputs. The enabledness of (additional) output events causes no problem since the *ioco* relation allows weaker output behavior in the specification. For events in the output alphabet L_U we get the property:

$$\forall a \in L_U, s \in S \bullet (\exists s_i \in s \bullet g(a)(s_i)) \Longleftrightarrow s \xrightarrow{a} \tag{5}$$

To sum up, the suspension automaton is a valid abstraction of the event traces generated during the exploration of the action system regarding *ioco*.

Example 2. Consider an internal choice between two events, i.e., $(\tau; a) \Box (\tau; b)$, where τ denotes an internal event, $?a$ is an input event, $!b$ is an output event, the semicolon denotes sequential composition, and $\Box$ is the external choice. The first (left-to-right) LTS in Figure 9 shows the LTS of the internal-choice example. Notice that states with output quiescence are augmented with δ self loops. The suspension automaton in LTS 2 is obtained after determinization of LTS 1 by computing the τ closure. A problem arises here since both events $?a$ and $!b$ can occur at the initial state which is not the behavior specified by the internal choice. We can only apply input $?a$ if the implementation is in the according internal state. Hence, we forbid event $?a$ in the initial state, see LTS 3. Then two things can happen: either the output event $!b$ or no output is observed. In the case of quiescence, the tester changes to a state where the input event is enabled.

Due to the inherent non-determinism of qualitative actions, controllability is a major issue. Figure 8 shows the complete LTS of the two-tank system in the case where the parameters of *qual* events are omitted. This weaker environmental behavior causes the loss of controllability which means that the tester has

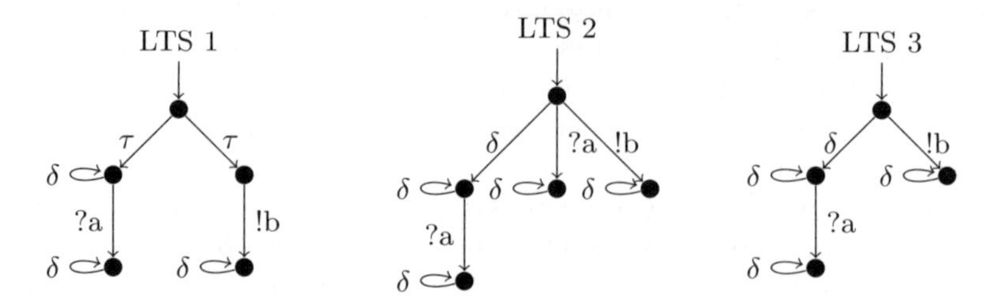

Fig. 9. Internal choice between an input and an output action

not enough information to control the system under test. In this example all controllable actions have been removed since no state satisfies condition (4), i.e., in every state a controllable action may be disabled. Such a system model is restricted to monitoring the behavior of an implementation.

In the following section we discuss the test case extraction from the product LTS.

6 Test Case Extraction

From the resulting product LTS, which will be referred to as *test graph* in the following, test cases that aim at detecting the mutation can be generated. Note that in order to generate proper test cases, the labels in the test graph are divided into two categories: (1) Observables (keyword *obs*) denote actions that are observable by the tester, i.e., they denote outputs of the implementation under test. (2) Controllables (keyword *ctr*) denote actions that are controllable by the tester, i.e., they denote inputs of the implementation under test.

The resulting test cases must fulfill certain properties in order to form valid ioco test cases. One characteristic is *controllability*, which means that a test case must not contain choices between several controllables or between controllables and observables. Furthermore, each final state of the test case has to be labeled with a verdict, which can be *pass*, *fail*, or *inconclusive*. Pass means that the implementation has successfully passed the test case. Fail denotes that the implementation does not conform to the specification. Fail verdicts may be expressed implicitly by defining that each unspecified behavior causes a fail verdict. Inconclusive says that the implementation behaved correctly but that the goal of the test case, the so-called *test purpose*, could not be reached. A test purpose describes what shall be tested by the test case. In our case, the test purpose is to pass so-called *unsafe states*. An unsafe state denotes the direct predecessor of a fail state of the test graph, which indicates a mutation. If a fail state cannot be reached any more, i.e., if its unsafe state has been passed and the fail state has not been reached, then the fault injected into the mutant used for test case generation could not be identified in the implementation by the test case. In this case, the verdict has to be pass. Note that the verdicts of the test cases are assigned during test case extraction. They are not specified by the pass and fail states generated throughout the product calculation described in the previous section.

There exists more than just one approach to extract test cases that detect the injected fault from a given test graph. Describing all of them in detail would go beyond the scope of this paper. Hence, in the following we will only outline several of our ideas for selecting test cases from our test graph. Our first approach, called *A1* in the following, is to unfold the test graph and subsequently select one controllable test case for each unsafe state in the resulting tree. The extracted test cases have a special structure. They consist of one main branch representing the path to the unsafe state. All other branches not leading to the unsafe state are cut right after one observation and terminated via an inconclusive verdict. This is also illustrated by our example test case depicted in Figure 10 . This test

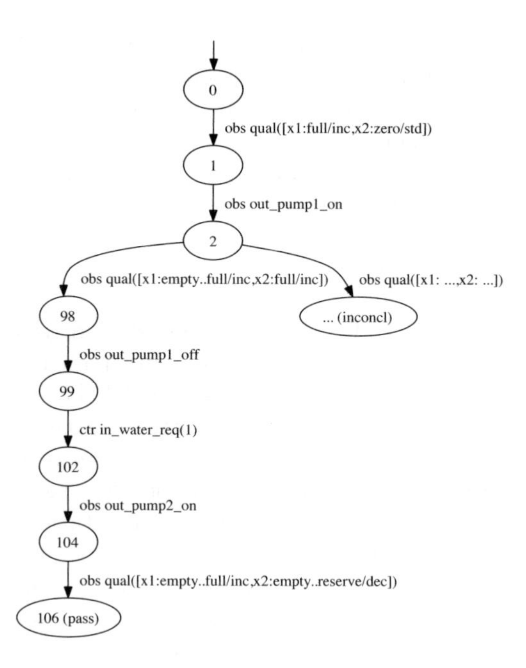

Fig. 10. Example test case for our two-tank system extracted from the test graph (product LTS) depicted in Figure 7 by applying approach *A1*. Several inconclusive states have been merged for the sake of clarity. Fail verdicts are implicit.

case for our two-tank example has been extracted from the test graph (product LTS) depicted in Figure 7. Note that several inconclusive states have been merged for the sake of clarity and that fail verdicts are implicit. This first approach yields one test case for each path to an unsafe state and hence a possibly huge number of test cases is produced.

Our second approach *A2* significantly reduces the number of generated test cases. It works directly on the test graph and in contrast to *A1* produces *adaptive* test cases, i.e., the controllables depend on previously made observations. Figure 11 shows a test case for the two-tank system that has been generated in this way. The test case contains more than just one path leading to the unsafe state, which is numbered by 6. For the sake of simplicity, *qual* events are internal, i.e., not visible. Our third approach *A3* results in even less test cases, since it works globally over all injected faults. Again, we successively generate test cases in order to generate a test suite which kills all mutants. But this strategy checks whether an already generated test case is able to kill other mutants for which in turn no further test cases need to be generated and added to the test suite. Again, the extracted test cases are adaptive and have the same structure as those resulting from *A2*. The evaluation of these three approaches is ongoing work. It has to be assessed, which of the strategies provides sufficient coverage on the implementation under test in order to gain a satisfactory test suite.

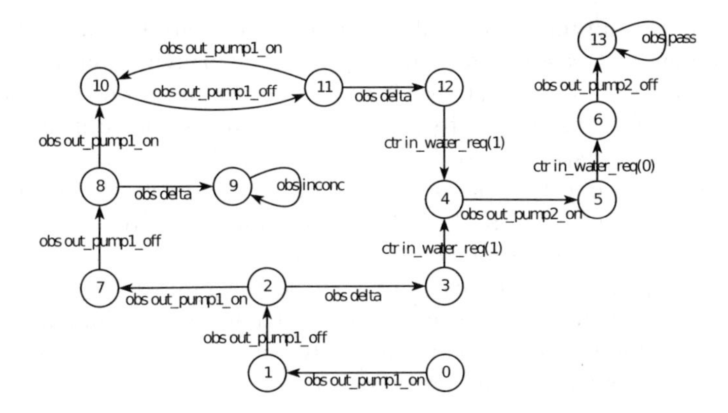

Fig. 11. Adaptive example test case for our two-tank system. For the sake of simplicity, *qual* events are internal, i.e., not visible.

7 Concluding Remarks

We have presented two key abstractions for testing a hybrid system: action systems and qualitative differential equations. The core of the paper covers our tool-supported mutation testing approach including empirical results of the running example. In addition, we have discussed the different possibilities for selecting test cases.

To our knowledge this is the first work on model-based mutation testing for hybrid systems. The modeling formalism [2] and the conformance checker [6] have been published previously, but the testing approach is a new contribution of this paper. Furthermore, we added parameters to the qualitative events to guarantee controllability. The idea of model-based mutation testing can be traced back to Budd and Gopal, who mutated specifications in the form of predicate calculus [7]. For a thorough overview of related work on model-based mutation testing we refer to our theory paper on mutation testing [4]. With respect to the LTS interpretation of action systems our work is close to other integrated approaches combining state-based modeling languages and process algebras, e.g., [8]. The *B* model specifies the abstract state and the operations of the system while the *CSP* model describes the order in which the operations occur. The combined semantics is a parallel composition of the models which synchronize on common operations (events). This combination of B [1] and CSP [12] has been implemented in the *ProB* tool [14], a model checker and animator for B that can also check for CSP's notions of (event) refinement. *ProB* also relates to our conformance checker from an implementation point of view: both are implemented in SICStus Prolog. Finally, with respect to hybrid system analysis, we refer to Henzinger's work on hybrid automata [11]. However, our extension of action systems was mainly inspired by Rönkkö et al. [16].

The test case generation process via conformance checking between a specification and a mutant is costly. Therefore, in practise we delay this process as long as possible. We start with a set of randomly generated test cases and run these against the mutants. This will kill many simple mutants without the need to generate new test cases for them. Only for the surviving mutants, we check their conformance. If a new test case is generated, we use it on the other surviving mutants. Unfortunately, there will always remain some equivalent mutants for which the whole state space has to be explored. However, we could start with a lower search-depth in the beginning and only increase it later on. We are currently experimenting with these heuristics. Furthermore, we are currently working on the test execution of the hybrid systems.

The next step in our research is to analyse the fault-detection rate of our testing technique. In addition, we are working on methods to eliminate redundant mutations. Our final objective is to integrate the presented technique into the testing process of our industrial partners.

References

1. Abrial, J.-R.: The B-book: assigning programs to meanings. Cambridge University Press, New York (1996)
2. Aichernig, B.K., Brandl, H., Krenn, W.: Qualitative action systems. In: Breitman, K., Cavalcanti, A. (eds.) ICFEM 2009. LNCS, vol. 5885, pp. 206–225. Springer, Heidelberg (2009)
3. Aichernig, B.K., Delgado, C.C.: From faults via test purposes to test cases: on the fault-based testing of concurrent systems. In: Baresi, L., Heckel, R. (eds.) FASE 2006. LNCS, vol. 3922, pp. 324–338. Springer, Heidelberg (2006)
4. Aichernig, B.K., He, J.: Mutation testing in UTP. Formal Aspects of Computing Journal 21(1-2), 33–64 (2009)
5. Back, R.-J., Kurki-Suonio, R.: Decentralization of process nets with centralized control. In: Proceedings of the 2nd ACM SIGACT-SIGOPS Symp. on Principles of Distributed Computing, Montreal, Quebec, Canada, pp. 131–142. ACM, New York (1983)
6. Brandl, H., Weiglhofer, M., Aichernig, B.K.: Automated conformance verification of hybrid systems. In: QSIC (2010) (in press)
7. Budd, T.A., Gopal, A.S.: Program testing by specification mutation. Comput. Lang. 10(1), 63–73 (1985)
8. Butler, M., Leuschel, M.: Combining CSP and B for specification and property verification. In: Fitzgerald, J.S., Hayes, I.J., Tarlecki, A. (eds.) FM 2005. LNCS, vol. 3582, pp. 221–236. Springer, Heidelberg (2005)
9. DeMillo, R., Lipton, R., Sayward, F.: Hints on test data selection: Help for the practicing programmer. IEEE Computer 11(4), 34–41 (1978)
10. Hamlet, R.G.: Testing programs with the aid of a compiler. IEEE Transactions on Software Engineering 3(4), 279–290 (1977)
11. Henzinger, T.A.: The theory of hybrid automata, pp. 278–292. IEEE Computer Society Press, Los Alamitos (1996)
12. Hoare, C.A.R.: Communicating sequential processes. Commun. ACM 26(1), 100–106 (1983)
13. Kuipers, B.: Qualitative Reasoning: Modeling and Simulation with Incomplete Knowledge. MIT Press, Cambridge (1994)
14. Leuschel, M., Butler, M.: ProB: A model checker for B. In: Araki, K., Gnesi, S., Mandrioli, D. (eds.) FME 2003. LNCS, vol. 2805, pp. 855–874. Springer, Heidelberg (2003)

15. Rönkkö, M., Ravn, A.P.: Switches and jumps in hybrid action systems. Technical Report 152, Turku Centre for Computer Science (1997)
16. Rönkkö, M., Ravn, A.P., Sere, K.: Hybrid action systems. Theoretical Computer Science 290, 937–973 (2003)
17. Tretmans, J.: Test generation with inputs, outputs and repetitive quiescence. Software - Concepts and Tools 17(3), 103–120 (1996)
18. Weiglhofer, M., Aichernig, B., Wotawa, F.: Fault-based conformance testing in practice. International Journal of Software and Informatics 3(2-3), 375–411 (2009)
19. Weiglhofer, M., Wotawa, F.: Asynchronous input-output conformance testing. In: Ahamed, S.I., Bertino, E., Chang, C.K., Getov, V., Liu, L., Ming, H., Subramanyan, R. (eds.) COMPSAC (1), pp. 154–159. IEEE Computer Society, Los Alamitos (2009)

Property-Based Testing - The ProTest Project

John Derrick[1], Neil Walkinshaw[1], Thomas Arts[2], Clara Benac Earle[4], Francesco Cesarini[3], Lars-Ake Fredlund[4], Victor Gulias[5], John Hughes[6], and Simon Thompson[7]

[1] Department of Computing, University of Sheffield, Sheffield, S1 4DP, UK
[2] Goteborgs Universitet, Goeteboug, Sweden
[3] Erlang Solutions Ltd, London
[4] Universidad Politecnica de Madrid, Madrid, Spain
[5] Lambdastream Servicios Interactivos SL, A Coruna, Spain
[6] Quviq AB, Savedalen, Sweden
[7] University of Canterbury, Canterbury, Kent, UK
J.Derrick@dcs.shef.ac.uk

Abstract. The ProTest project is an FP7 STREP on property based testing. The purpose of the project is to develop software engineering approaches to improve reliability of service-oriented networks; support fault-finding and diagnosis based on specified properties of the system. And to do so we will build automated tools that will generate and run tests, monitor execution at run-time, and log events for analysis.

The Erlang / Open Telecom Platform has been chosen as our initial implementation vehicle due to its robustness and reliability within the telecoms sector. It is noted for its success in the ATM telecoms switches by Ericsson, one of the project partners, as well as for multiple other uses such as in facebook, yahoo etc. In this paper we provide an overview of the project goals, as well as detailing initial progress in developing property based testing techniques and tools for the concurrent functional programming language Erlang.

1 Introduction

Communication networks, based on telephony, wireless and Internet, have over the last few years been converging. At the present time and for the foreseeable future, more and more services will be added to these merging networks. Moreover, these services are becoming more complex, both in themselves and in their interactions with each other and their end users. The telecoms industry has an admirable record in providing reliability and robust services to its clients, and indeed it is the telecoms industry that can point to 5-nines reliability: that is 99.999% reliability, of their core systems.

This context provides the motivation of the ProTest project - namely that of maintaining 5-nines reliability in future service-oriented networks and systems.

The software for new services and network devices is rapidly growing in complexity, among other things because of the variety of formats and multiplicity of delivery modes evident in modern communication protocols (with thousands

F.S. de Boer et al. (Eds.): FMCO 2009, LNCS 6286, pp. 250–271, 2010.

of optional fields, for instance). In addition, such software needs to be context-aware, since the requirements vary when the same software is used in different ways. There are several ingredients for ensuring that such complex systems provide the expected reliability, among them choosing a good architecture, using the right technologies, improving the software process, and also being extremely thorough and efficient in *testing.*

Testing of complex systems is difficult and time-consuming in the extreme, and in the ProTest project we build upon the innovative idea of using properties as objects for testing software. In order to deliver dynamic services and interoperable network applications with guaranteed properties, we focus testing around these properties.

The economic motivator is that testing with properties as objects improves the competitiveness of software developers, since they can deliver higher quality software for a lower price. It also allows collaborating companies to improve the definition of their software interfaces and therewith improve the compatibility between their services.

Our objective is to deliver methods and tools to support property-based development of systems, and in order to do so we need tools to integrate property-based testing into the development life cycle. To this extent we are conducting work along four technical themes as follows:

Property discovery. Current testing is based on sets of test cases embedded in test suites; over the lifetime of the project we will aim to provide tools to aid the software developers to extract properties from this test data. Current specifications and models are often informal: so we will develop specialised property languages to ease the formalisation of existing specifications.

Test and property evolution. All software systems are subject to change and evolution; we will thus provide tools to support the evolution of tests and properties in line with the evolution of the system itself.

Property monitoring. Not all properties can be tested in advance of systems being executed, and so we will provide tools to support the post hoc examination of trace details for conformance to (or indeed violation of) particular constraints.

Analysing concurrent systems. At the heart of service oriented systems is concurrency: servers will provide services to multiple clients in a seamlessly concurrent way; services will federate to provide complex functionality through concurrently performing parts of a task. We will provide tools by which such concurrent systems can be analysed for fundamental properties by way of model-checking and testing.

In subsequent sections of this paper we explain work in progress under each of these themes.

2 Background

The ProTest project aims to introduce property-driven development into the software engineering process. Property-driven development can be used in a variety of programming languages and systems. The particular platform chosen for initial implementation of the project is Erlang/OTP (Open Telecom Platform), but a crucial aspect of our proposal is the dissemination and adoption of the approach much more widely, particularly into the model driven development arena (UML) and other implementation languages (C/C++, Java, etc).

Erlang/OTP has been chosen as the implementation vehicle because of its robustness and reliability within the telecoms sector; witness, for example, its success in the implementation of the AXD301 ATM telecoms switch by Ericsson, one of the project partners. Erlang [AVWW96] is a concurrent functional language with specific support for the development of distributed, fault-tolerant systems with soft real-time requirements. Language and implementation design have aimed from the start to support a concurrency-oriented programming paradigm and the massively concurrent systems that it leads to.

The project consortium contains a balance of academics from Universities of Sheffield, Kent, Politecnica de Madrid, Goteborg, Chalmers University of Technology, SMEs, and a larger company. One of the SMEs is Quviq which is a spin-off from academia, founded to commercialise the property-based testing tool QuickCheck. The remaining industrial partners are system builders (Ericsson, LambdaStream) together with Erland Solutions who are consultants, system developers and trainers. These partners provide invaluable insights into what is required of practical tools, what properties will need to be checked, and ways of fitting the results from the project into practical software development methods.

Our own work on QuickCheck [AHJW06] combines random test case generation, with a flexible language for specifying generators, with the use of properties to adjudge success [CH00]. The inevitable *noise* in random test cases is removed by automatic simplification, using an approach resembling Zellers delta-debugging [ZH02]. This technique enabled us to isolate subtle faults in industrial telecommunications software [AHJW06], and has also been used successfully to test software for space missions [GHJ07].

Refactoring has become a well-known technique, particular in the realm of object oriented software development. It is standard for Integrated Development Environments, such as Eclipse, NetBeans and IntelliJ IDEA, to support a selection of refactorings, particularly those to do with the structure of the code base. Refactorings are also commonly discussed in the context of transforming code so that it conforms to a particular design pattern or coding standard. Here we build on existing work undertaken at Kent who have developed refactoring tool support for functional programming [Tho04] in the languages Erlang [LT08] and Haskell [LTR05] and their relationship [LT06].

Trace analysis is a natural extension to testing. Instead of only studying the outcome of a test case, all events (at some appropriate level of detail) during the test execution are recorded in a trace. By analyzing the trace in an intelligent way more information can be extracted from a single test. The Erlang run-time system has a built-in trace recording functionality, which has lead to wide-spread use of trace analysis as a verification technique for Erlang systems. Trace analysis for Erlang systems has been studied by [AF02] and further by [ACS04]. Our previous work on trace analysis for Erlang includes trace abstraction, in which an approximation of a system's state space is built from an actual concrete trace. This is done using an abstraction function; the resulting state space is called an abstract trace.

Model checking offers the promise of a push-button solution for verification, and during the last twenty years many researchers have been pursuing that goal. In practise the technique still suffers from the well known state explosion problem, i.e. models become too large for analysis. Thus a priority is developing tractable models by abstracting from the full complexity of the artefact being verified. Our work in the project on model checking will investigate the integration of property-based testing and model checking techniques for Erlang. As model checking inevitably fails to fully verify a piece of software (e.g., due to state explosion or the problem of constructing an accurate model from a complex program), we have to resort to testing. But, in fact, testing and model checking are often complementary techniques. In ProTest we will explore their combination in model based testing (to provide accurate estimations of space coverage, to provide a test oracle, etc) and to explore non-exhaustive model checking as an alternative to testing for highly concurrent and complex distributed systems.

3 Property Discovery

Our work on property discovery covers two main aspects, one dealing with obtaining properties from a specification, the other dealing with obtaining properties from a library of existing test cases.

3.1 Properties from Specifications

To enhance how QuickCheck can be applied to other languages, we have produced a library for testing finite state machines, which has been used in an industrial project in which the UML design tool Rose/RT was connected to QuickCheck, allowing systems designed in Rose/RT to be using QuickCheck's finite state machine library. We have also developed a general approach to test C software with QuickCheck. In this way, all QuickCheck libraries developed in the ProTest project also become available to Rose/RT and C programmers.

We have also developed two ways of obtaining properties from specification, viz. obtaining properties from data type definitions and from databases. The methods have been evaluated in a number of industrial projects, and some subtle errors were identified in the financial systems of these companies and the methods proved useful [ACH08]. The novelty here is that one is assured that the properties together span the complete set of all possible tests.

Going further we have developed a fully automatic method to generate properties from purely functional descriptions for both Haskell and Erlang. This tool, called QuickSpec [Hug08], can automatically generate properties for a given library of functions. QuickSpec reads in an API of an Erlang module or a Haskell module, and automatically produces a list of equations that hold for the functions in that module. The method uses random testing to do this (no heavy theorem proving is performed); the only extra input the tool might require is some information on how to generate test data.

For example, given the function names of the standard list functions append (++), reverse, tail, cons, empty list ([]), insert and sort, the tool produces the following algebraic properties of the functions, fully automatically, in about 1 second:

```
1: insert(X,[]) = [X]
2: insert(X,[X|Xs]) = [X|[X|Xs]]
3: insert(Y,[X]) = insert(X,[Y])
4: insert(Y,insert(X,Xs)) = insert(X,insert(Y,Xs))
5: reverse([]) = []
6: reverse([X]) = [X]
7: reverse(reverse(Xs)) = Xs
8: sort([]) = []
9: sort([X|Xs]) = insert(X,sort(Xs))
10: sort(insert(X,Xs)) = insert(X,sort(Xs))
11: sort(reverse(Xs)) = sort(Xs)
12: sort(sort(Xs)) = sort(Xs)
13: sort(Ys++Xs) = sort(Xs++Ys)
14: stail([]) = []
15: stail([X|Xs]) = Xs
16: Xs++[] = Xs
17: []++Xs = Xs
18: [X|Xs]++Ys = [X|Xs++Ys]
19: reverse(Xs)++[X] = reverse([X|Xs])
20: reverse(Xs)++reverse(Ys) = reverse(Ys++Xs)
21: stail(Xs)++Xs = stail(Xs++Xs)
22: (Xs++Ys)++Zs = Xs++(Ys++Zs)
```

The basic method we use is the following. We start by generating a finite set of well-typed terms that contain variables (in the above example there are 2298 such terms of depth 3). Next, we compute equivalence classes of these terms, by means of random testing and refining: we start by assuming that all terms are in the same equivalence class, and partition equivalence classes into smaller ones by running random tests and inspecting the values of the terms (in the above example, this results in 1931 equivalence classes). For each equivalence class, we pick one representative, and produce equations between that representative and all other terms in an equivalence class. For the example, this results in 367 equations, these are all equations that are true, but there are clearly too many to be useful, thus we spent some effort into producing a list of non-overlapping algebraic equations.

When one naively generates equations that hold between terms, many of which are not independent. To reduce the number, we have developed several filtering algorithms that remove superfluous equations. Choosing the right filtering algorithm constitutes finding a balance between (1) not keeping too many equations,

(2) how expensive is it to check that equations follow from other equations, (3) not removing too many equations (even though an equation follows from other ones, it might still be useful to have in the list). The algorithm we finally settled for uses a congruence closure algorithm to approximate if an equation follows from a set of equations.

We have applied QuickSpec to a number of concrete Erlang and Haskell modules. Most notably, we applied it on the Erlang standard functional array library, and on a library for fixed-point arithmetic that was written by a company in South Africa. Exploring the properties that QuickSpec produced (and the properties it did not produce!) was a great way of understanding code that someone else had written, and has lead us to come up with a number of concrete techniques that may be used for applying QuickSpec in this way. Other applications of QuickSpec include providing a cheap and easy way for programmers and testers to start writing properties.

3.2 Reverse Engineering

We have developed two methods to extract properties from test cases - one dynamic, the other static. That is, in the first approach, the test cases are run, generating traces for the program. From these traces a finite state machine can be abstracted. This is described fully in the companion paper [WD09] as well as in [WDG09].

The second approach works on the level of the source code of the test cases. It is a guided automatic approach; testers know best what part of the test case they like to generate and what part they want to keep specific. Recent work with test suites from Ericsson, and with tests from an Open Source project (Engineyard's Natter application) confirm that this approach is a fruitful one.

3.3 Building Domain Specific Languages

QuickCheck has long provided a DSL (Domain Specific Language) for specifications based on abstract state machines; however, this DSL represents states as arbitrary Erlang data values - for example, a list of key-value pairs if modeling a key-value store. With this approach, each operation of the API under test is applicable in every state, unless an explicit precondition is given to restrict this. Software is commonly specified instead via a state transition diagram, in which states are distinguished by name, and operations are typically applicable only in a certain named state.

Of course, such a specification can be based on the previous state machine library, but doing so in effect encodes the structure of the diagram in an ugly way in many different places in the code.

To help overcome this, we have developed a new FSM library, implemented on top of the original one, which separates state names and state data. Specifications using the new library are much more concise and perspicuous than the equivalent specification using the old one. Our FSM library allows weights to be assigned to transitions, but assigning weights well is difficult, since changing a weight on one transition can affect the execution frequency of many others in quite non-obvious ways. We have therefore developed an optimization criterion for weighting (which essentially tries to distribute test effort as evenly as possible across the transitions in the state diagram), and an approximation algorithm for assigning weights automatically. Although the algorithm is not optimal (and finding an optimal solution appears to be NP-hard), it usually produces good results.

The weight assignment algorithm can take priorities into account - for example, if the user specified that testing the lock transaction is 10x as important as testing others (for example, because it contains new code), then the weight assignment algorithm results in the distribution to the left. Note that unlock is also assigned a higher weight necessary, since without an unlock, we can never perform more than one lock in a test case. The new library has now been released as a part of Quviqs product.

4 Refactoring

Our second strand of work addresses software evolution and the way that this impacts on testing, and in particular property-based testing. The Wrangler refactoring tool [LT08, ST08], developed at Kent, is used to support refactorings of tests, test-aware refactorings and property discovery.

Initial work has investigated the impact of various refactorings on testing as practised in three systems:

- EUnit (for unit testing of Erlang systems),
- Quviq QuickCheck (for property-based testing of Erlang systems), and
- Common Test / OTP Test Server (for system testing)

and we describe a selection of work below.

4.1 Duplicate/Similar Code Detection in Wrangler

Duplicated/similar code is common in software, especially in test cases. For example, in industrial test suites, some test case functions only differ in an atom and a record definition. It would be desirable to have a generalised abstraction of these similar test case functions, and make each test case an instance of the generalised abstraction.

Wrangler's support for "duplicated code detection" and "expression search" is able to report code fragments that are syntactically identical after semantic-preserving renaming of variable names, ignoring variations in literals, layout and comments.

The requirement of "syntactic identity" is somehow restrictive because it could not detect code fragments that look similar but are not syntactically identical. For instance, Wrangler's original "expression search" would not report the following two pieces of code as clones because of the slight syntactical difference in the record field "codec" though they look very similar.

```
Code fragment 1:
%%%%%%%%%%%%%%%%%%%%%%%%%%%%%%%%%%%%%%%%%
?COMMENT("Test case create_2 started.",[]),
%%%%%%%%%%%%%%%%%%%%%%%%%%%%%%%%%%%%%%%%%
SidMux = {mux_id_1, h223_id_1},
{TdmSid, LocalData, _, _} = precond_one_blade_tdm_mux_create(SidMux),
?CHECK(ok, hcfTraceServerSupport, start, [[{brchDspRhI, exported}]]),
SidLc = {mux_id_1, audio_id_1},
CreateData = #brchMuxLcAccess{sid = SidLc,
stream_type = ?BRCH_AUDIO,
local_data = LocalData,
codec = {?AMR,
{?R_122, ?BRCH_DISABLED,
?BRCH_DISABLED, ?BRCH_BIT},
33, 44, 40},
event_module = iptermCb},
?CH(1, brchShI, create, [[CreateData]]),
?CHECK([], hcfTraceServerSupport, get_trace_list, []),
clean_up([SidLc, SidMux, TdmSid]),
?RESULT("DONE", []).

Code fragment 2:
%%%%%%%%%%%%%%%%%%%%%%%%%%%%%%%%%%%%%%%%%
?COMMENT("Test case create_3 started.",[]),
%%%%%%%%%%%%%%%%%%%%%%%%%%%%%%%%%%%%%%%%%
SidMux = {mux_id_1, h223_id_1},
{TdmSid, LocalData, _, _} = precond_one_blade_tdm_mux_create(SidMux),
?CHECK(ok, hcfTraceServerSupport, start, [[{brchDspRhI, exported}]]),
SidLc = {mux_id_1, audio_id_1},
CreateData = #brchMuxLcAccess{sid = SidLc,
stream_type = ?BRCH_AUDIO,
local_data = LocalData,
codec = {?G723_1, {?R_53, ?BRCH_DISABLED},
33, 44, 40},
event_module = iptermCb},
[{ok, [{SidLc, _IntCep}], ?BRCH_REPLICATION_NEEDED}] =
?CH(1, brchShI, create, [[CreateData]]),
?CHECK([], hcfTraceServerSupport, get_trace_list, []),
clean_up([SidLc, SidMux, TdmSid]),
?RESULT("DONE", []).
```

To be able to detect this kind of similarity, we have extended Wrangler with a "Similar expression search" . The functionality allows the user to search for expressions that are similar to the expression selected according to a similarity score specified by the user.

Furthermore, "Similar expression search" also automatically generates the least general common abstraction of those similar expressions found, which is also known as anti-unifier. With the example above, Wrangler would suggest the generalised abstraction as:

```
new_fun(NewVar_1, NewVar_2, NewVar_3) ->
?COMMENT(NewVar_1, []),
SidMux = {mux_id_1, h223_id_1},
{TdmSid, LocalData, _, _} = precond_one_blade_tdm_mux_create(SidMux),
?CHECK(ok, hcfTraceServerSupport, start, [[{brchDspRhI, exported}]]),
SidLc = {mux_id_1, audio_id_1},
CreateData = #brchMuxLcAccess{sid=SidLc,
stream_type = ?BRCH_AUDIO,
local_data=LocalData,
codec={NewVar_2, NewVar_3, 33, 44, 40},
event_module=iptermCb},
[{ok, [{SidLc, _IntCep}], ?BRCH_REPLICATION_NEEDED}] =
?CH(1, brchShI, create, [[CreateData]]),
?CHECK([], hcfTraceServerSupport, get_trace_list, []),
clean_up([SidLc, SidMux, TdmSid]),
?RESULT("DONE", []).
```

Being able to generate the least general abstraction automatically speeds up the similar code elimination process, because the user does not need to inspect the differences manually, and generalise the function step by step.

The notion of least general abstraction (anti-unifier) and the definition of "similarity" need to be refined further, but for the moment we have a working definition. We are now also in the process of designing a more efficient algorithm so that we could apply "similar code detection" to large projects, as well as investigating a more general notion of "similarity" than having a non-trivial common generalisation.

Apart from the work on duplicate code detection and the introduction of "similar expression search", a number of new refactorings have also been added including the introduction macros (optionally with parameters), folding expressions against a macro definition, and the normalisation of record expressions.

4.2 Extension to Wrangler to Refactor EUnit Test Data

We have been working on the extension of the Wrangler tool to accompany the basic refactorings in Wrangler with refactorings of EUnit test data. This extension has two aspects:

1. When application code is refactored, Wrangler should make sure that the test code of the application code is also refactored consistently.
2. Since test code is also Erlang code, it can be refactored in its own right, but Wrangler needs to make sure the refactoring of test code preserves the test framework's particular idioms, such as naming conventions.

The extension affects all the refactorings that change module/function/macro interfaces, such as renaming, generalisation, move function between modules, function extraction, etc.

The major challenge with extending Wrangler to the EUnit test framework lies in the interpretation of symbolic representation of test data, and the multiple roles of atoms in the Erlang language. For example, with EUnit's test data representation, a single module name, which is an atom, can be used to represent the whole test set from the exported test functions of the named module; so when the named module is renamed, Wrangler needs to make sure all the related uses of this module name in the test data are renamed, and also make sure that atoms with the same name, but not used as a module name are not renamed.

To ensure that Wrangler refactors test data correctly, we designed some invariants which should hold for a refactoring. For example, for each test generation function, F say, affected by a renaming refactoring, suppose F becomes F' after the refactoring, then the following invariant should hold:

```
rename(parse(F())) == parse(F'())
```

where function *parse* transforms the test set representation into a normal form, *rename* does renaming in the normal form in which each atom's role can be decided precisely. If the above invariant does not hold for a particular test generation function, Wrangler will ask the user for manual inspection.

4.3 Wrangler and Eclipse: Integration with Erlide

Another strand of work has been to support the integration of Wrangler into the Eclipse binding for Erlang, Erlide. Erlide is under active development at Ericsson, as well as being made available freely to the Erlang community. Wrangler is currently a part of the standard Erlide distribution, freely available for download.

Integration with Eclipse through Erlide provides a number of advantages over emacs. For example, it has a well-defined notion of project, and so this gives a scope to refactorings which affect more than one module; it has a well-defined distribution and update mechanism, which means that users will automatically pick up the latest version of the tool (should they choose to); it provides multiple views of a code base, so that users can access refactorings in different ways. In addition, through its refactoring API, it provides some facilities "for free" such as preview of the effect of refactorings (across multiple modules), and through its interface it is possible to present results of searches or the effect of a multisite refactoring in a more explicit way than emacs. For instance, search results can be browsed, and choices for multi-site refactorings be specified through a series of check boxes.

Future work will see the creation of a new integration structure which relies more on Erlide. With this development it will be possible to access the refactorings through the Outline, Navigator and Duplicated Code views as well as through the Refactor menu at present. This will in turn simplify the User Interface, and eliminate a number of current error possibilities which arise as a consequence of the form of the interface.

5 Property Monitoring

The final goal of the audit-trace analysis is to be able to monitor properties determining the correct behaviour of the system, be in real time through analysis of trace events, or offline , through the analysis of audit-log batches. Online and offline analysis requires a way to aggregate data and rigidly specify what should be checked. These requirements resulted in tools allowing the user to describe inter-log-file relations and merge live traces originating across a cluster of nodes.

Work on developing a monitoring tool for offline analysis was concentrated on a prototype that automatically analyses a set of log files, given a description of what constitutes the key and what is the interesting value. This simple analysis will track a session ID through several separate log files, or track a single request by focusing on a request ID. Events are either sorted by appearance in the log files or by their timestamps. The sequences are presented graphically using the graphviz visualization package. The prototype is also able to check sessions against a specification (represented as a state machine).

In audit trails used for offline analysis, the content and format of the audit logs are usually defined by developers. In online analysis, however, there is a de facto standard defined by a set of live tracing tools. These tools are based on the Erlang trace BIFs, and support different tracing scenarios. However, we found that for tracing of multi-node environments, no tool offered the combination of user-friendliness and power that we needed. We developed to close that gap in the OTP trace tool suite. The next step is to examine the aggregated traces with the analysis tools built for the offline tracing tool, merging offline and online tracing analysis.

The current versions of the tools show there is a need to design audit trails which facilitate the definition of properties to be verified. Our research has used a simple example of an SMS Log System to design the criteria and standards needed to provide a testing basis, not only for our tools, but for any valid audit trail.

5.1 Exago, the Offline Monitoring Tool

Exago is an offline monitoring tool that allows property monitoring via audit log file analysis. The applicability of the tool is independent of the implementation language of the target system, placing requirements on the syntax and semantics of the log files.

Exagos approach is to parse the log files, creating abstract representations of the live events over a predefined time interval, and re-evaluate them against a model of the system. If these abstract commands are accepted by the model, the system behaves as expected. If they are not accepted, Exago reveals the system anomalies in the information provided in the audit trails.

To use Exago, the relevant information of the events should be identified in each log file:

- The timestamp of the events
- The identifier of the session the event belongs to
- An abstract value which describes the type and the details of the event.

Events belonging to the same session will be tracked through the session id across different log files. Optionally, a transaction id can be specified, aggregating together events that belong to the same transaction.

When some of the required information is only present implicitly, inter-log-file relations can be described to resolve them. The timestamp can also be adjusted with an offset for each different log file, allowing event sequences to be sorted and reconstructed in their proper order.

The data extracted from the log files will then be abstracted into events. Testers have to specify the method of how the abstraction is achieved by defining first order functions. Exago will then check each session of abstract events against a Finite State Machine model of the system. It will generate an abstracted events report with the point of failure and the visualization of the state machine.

The first prototype of the tool was developed by testing a simple SMS log example. Two case studies on commercial systems, an SMS gateway that had been in production for years and an SMSC system under development were used.

In the SMS gateway case study, over 20000 sessions were analyzed. During this small timeframe (The system handles millions of SMS messages a day), Exago found discrepancies in the logs, which when analysed, were narrowed down to bugs.

We find this result particularly satisfying, as the SMS gateway had been in commercial operation for several years, and by all reasonable accounts was a well tested system; yet there was evidence of malfunction in the logs that went unnoticed. The obvious reason is that the amount of data in the logs makes it extremely hard to find spurious faults through manual inspection.

Exago was also used in the early stages of development of an SMSC system. This experience indicated that integrating Exago into the test-driven design flow helps designers to develop an optimal level of detail in the audit log output.

5.2 Onviso, Simple and Intuitive Tracing Environment

In order to obtain data for property testing or debugging, it is often necessary to use live tracing. Whereas there are established tracing tools for Erlang (Erlang Trace BIFs, the dbg library), for the more complex cases where multiple nodes are involved, the current trace tool interfaces are confusing. As far as we can determine, very few people use the existing multi-node tracing facilities.

In order to establish a good and user-friendly platform for integration with our property-based testing tools, we created Onviso. Onviso builds on the existing OTP tool, Inviso. Whereas Inviso provides the online tracing for small and large systems, Onviso provides default settings that suit most setups, making it user-friendly and re-usable.

It is now possible to set up tracing across multiple nodes and merge the result in a variety of combinations. Tracing can be re-enabled if the traced node restarts. Additionally, for convenience when using Onviso as an ad-hoc tracing tool, it is also possible to retrieve the status of the recent traces run and the configuration that was used.

For merging the traces, there are a number of options provided. The simplest of them is to write every trace to a file in the order that it was generated. The merge functionality can also be used to conduct property checking or profiling the system. Moreover, it is possible to merge the same data multiple times with different specifications, making it possible to check for various properties with every merge.

Onviso Example. The following example demonstrates one of the simplest use-cases of Onviso. The user specifies the patterns which can be either local or exported functions of any module on any of the following nodes. A pattern is specified as `{Module, Format, Arguments, Match_specification}`. Obviously any number of patterns can be specified.

```
1> onviso:trace([{heart, send_heart_beat, '_', []},
                 {io, format, '_', return}],
                ['server@linux', 'client@linux'],
                {all, [call]}).
{ok, 1}

2> onviso:merge(1, void, void, shell).

...
{server@linux, Pid, call, {io,format,["~p,~p~",[jacques, derida]]},
{1250,585321,791722}}
...
{ok, 15}
```

As seen in the second trace pattern, defined above, it is possible to use short-cuts for the most common match specification actions (like return).

If desired one can, of course, write custom functions for merging. The following example illustrates writing trace data into a file (as this is a common use case, there is another shortcut provided so that it is not necessary to write the funs by hand).

```
3> BeginFun = fun(_InitData) ->
                  case file:open("output.txt", [write]) of
                      {ok, FD} ->
                          {ok, FD};
                      {error, Reason} ->
                          {error, Reason}
                  end
              end,
#Fun<erl_eval.6.13229925>

4> WorkFun = fun(Node, Trace, _, FD) ->
                 io:format(FD, "~p >> ~p~n", [Node, Trace]),
                 {ok, FD}
             end,
#Fun<erl_eval.4.105156089>
```

```
5> EndFun = fun(FD) ->
                  file:close(FD)
            end,
#Fun<erl_eval.6.13229925>

6> onviso:merge(1, BeginFun, WorkFun, EndFun).
{ok, 15}
```

It is important to note that these only demonstrate basic usage. It is, of course, possible to build significantly more complex functions for evaluating the traces collected.

Future Work. Currently two components comprise Onviso: Trace Setup API, used to run, stop and analyse traces and Trace Management API used to manage units called trace cases, which keep together trace options, merge options and trace data. In order to encourage their usage, we plan to include our APIs into existing OTP applications, namely runtime-tools for Trace Setup API and observer for Trace Management API. We will also develop necessary documentation and tutorials.

For Exago, we plan to run further pilot projects, e.g. on systems developed using other technologies and targeting different domains. We will improve documentation and also experiment with other ways to define the specification.

6 Analysing Concurrent Systems

Our work on support for concurrent system analysis has included a number of themes. Part of this is working out how to shrink counter-examples resulting from an error found in a system, and to support repeatable testing. Another major theme is development of McErlang, a model-checker for Erlang.

6.1 Shrinking Trace Counter-Examples

The goal here is to investigate, and implement, methods to shrink trace counter-examples (resulting from testing or model checking concurrent systems) to ease the task of understanding the reason for a fault detected during testing. As such trace counter-examples frequently grow very large, having such a reduction facility is highly desirable. Our work has resulted in the development of a new tool, PULSE, which is now implemented as part of the commercial QuickCheck distribution. PULSE has been used for finding race conditions in industrial software. See [CPS+09] for more information.

To achieve property-based testing of concurrent software, several challenges have to be overcome. We must be able to decide whether tests have passed, and to run tests repeatably.

Our approach to automatically simplifying failing tests is based on running many simpler variations on the first failing test found, culminating in a minimal example that provokes a fault in the software under test. Finding such minimal failing tests is invaluable in speeding fault diagnosis. Yet our approach depends fundamentally on being able to repeat a test, with the same result as the first time it was run; finding minimal failing tests then requires that we can repeat smaller tests, in the same way as the original failing test was run. In concurrent programs, where the scheduling can vary from run to run, achieving repeatable behaviour is already a challenge.

Our first goal is thus to enable repeatable testing of concurrent Erlang code. This could be achieved by modifying the underlying Erlang virtual machine to use a custom, controllable process scheduler. But in practice, users will not be interested in using a custom version of the Erlang VM to test their systems - in fact, many projects continue to use outdated virtual machines long after upgrades are released, to avoid problems in their own software that might be caused by changes in the behaviour of the VM. Thus we consider it essential to achieve repeatable testing without changing the underlying Erlang VM. As multicore systems become more and more prevalent, it will be less and less reasonable to assume that the underlying scheduler can be replaced.

Our approach is instead to instrument the code under test, to make it communicate with a scheduler of our own design, written in Erlang, such that our scheduler can impose purely deterministic execution on the code under test, regardless of the underlying concurrent execution. We have developed an instrumenting compiler (in only 400LOC) which handles almost full Erlang, and an associated scheduler which takes control of the order of delivery of interprocess messages. By varying this order, we can even test the behaviour of distributed systems (which have a different semantics for message passing) on a single Erlang node. In addition we created a way to visualize the scheduling of events, such that the analysis of error cases becomes much easier. The scheduler currently makes random scheduling choices, and has proven quite effective in revealing race conditions in the examples studied so far.

6.2 Developing Model-Checking Techniques for Erlang

The other strand of work in our support for concurrency involves development of model checking as a complementary verification technique to the use of testing. Our initial goal was to deliver a model checker that supports a very large fragment of the Erlang language (e.g., with full support for all Erlang data types, the distributed Erlang API, and many OTP behaviours) to ease the task of constructing a verifiable model from an Erlang program.

A prototype model checker existed at the start of the project, and we have concentrated on delivering a number of enhancements to it, including:

– support for model checking a much larger language fragment. To achieve this a new source-to-source translation was realised as a number of transformations on HiPE Core Erlang code – an intermediate code level in the Erlang compiler. In addition more OTP behaviours are handled (gen_fsm, gen_event, partial support for ets tables, ...). In fact we are able to use the source code for some Erlang/OTP modules, without changes, in model checking.

- the implementation of an alternative small-step Erlang semantics which is able to detect more program errors, but which may yield substantially larger state spaces,
- initial support for using multiple processors (SMP) for model checking,
- improved handling of Linear Temporal Logic claims through the integration of a new translator from Linear Temporal Logic to Buchi automata (see discussion below),
- support for combining simulation and model checking algorithms to reduce the state space needed to verify a program. This is used to reduce the cost of using OTP behaviours such as e.g. the supervisor behaviour,
- providing user documentation, including a tutorial, a user manual, and a web page.

This has resulted in the production of the McErlang model checker which has been released as open source under the agreed project license (a BSD variant); more documentation and the option to download it is available at the tool web site: `https://babel.ls.fi.upm.es/trac/McErlang/`.

A sign of the increasing maturity of the tool is that we were able to analyse a RoboCup simulation league team programmed in Erlang (comprising some 8500 lines of Erlang code) using the McErlang tool, see [EFIL08]. A number of recent improvements to the McErlang tool realised in the ProTest project are described in [EF09].

LTL-to-Buchi Translation. One of the additions made to McErlang during the ProTest project was to add the possibility of expressing and checking correctness properties expressed in Linear Temporal Logic (LTL). This is fairly straightforward, since LTL expressions can be automatically translated into Buchi automata. However, for model checking to be efficient it is important to produce as small an automaton as possible, thus a good translator was needed. The obvious solution was to use an existing implementation. However, this was not done for two reasons: by developing an in-house translator we avoided licensing problems (our in-house translator is licensed under the same BSD license as McErlang unlike, e.g., the LTL2Buchi translator used in the JavaPathfinder project), and secondly its proper integration into the McErlang verification framework enabled a better end-user experience (e.g., with regards to formula parsing/deparsing, conversion to an executable Erlang module, and so on).

The LTL-to-Buchi translator we have developed [Sve09] consists of the following three parts: - A rewrite engine, which aims to simplify the LTL formula. It uses a fixed set of (heuristically chosen) rewrite rules. - A core translation algorithm Construction of the Buchi automaton from the re-written LTL formula. We use a tableau-based algorithm. - A reduction step, where optimizations such as simulation reductions and removal of non-reachable and non-accepting states, are applied to the Buchi automaton.

The efficiency of the LTL-to-Buchi translator was evaluated against two reference implementations; the LTL2Buchi translator in the JavaPathfinder and the Wring tool. Our translator clearly outperforms Wring; moreover the evaluation also uncovered a few remaining errors in the Wring tool. The resulting automata generated by our tool and LTL2Buchi are very similar in size, perhaps not very surprising since similar translation algorithms are used. However, on average our implementation generates about 1% smaller automata, when tested on randomly generated LTL formulas.

The development process (the implementation was carried out using property driven development supported by the QuickCheck tool) for the LTL-to-Buchi translator, as well as the implementation and the result of the evaluation are described in [EF09].

7 Tool Integration

In addition to work on the individual tools and methods described above, we aim to integrate the tools we are building in a number of ways. As a first step, we focused on the verification of the global process registry with an approach that combined QuickCheck and McErlang. Here, the QuickCheck tool was used to generate a number of test sequences for the global process registry; these were then fed to McErlang which explored all possible interleavings of the test sequences using its model checking algorithms. Finally the results (a set of sequences of return values of a set of API calls) were checked using the QuickCheck tool. Early results are promising, as the combined tool set was also able to discover race conditions in the global process registry.

We are also working on a integration of the other relevant tools. Essentially we want to be able to run a set of QuickCheck tests where the program under test is capable of being controlled by different schedulers: (i) either using the standard Erlang program scheduler, or (ii) using the PULSE scheduler which offers more control over scheduling and a more random behaviour, or (iii) the program is controlled by the McErlang model checker which in theory can fully explore the state space corresponding to any given test case.

As an example of how the tools and methodologies can be integrated consider the following example, where we describe how we can refactor a test suite into properties.

7.1 Example

The test suite in this example is 2228 lines of code, containing 4 groups of test cases:

- 5 test cases in the create group,
- 4 test cases in the set_topology group,
- 11 test cases in the modify group,
- 10 test cases in the delete group.

It is clear that certain test cases have some similarity. For example, we have a number of occurrences where a test case for audio is repeated for video. There are two ways in which we can work with this in the refactoring tool: We can search for expressions identical to this, or we can perform a general search for code clones in the existing file (or indeed in a complete project). Currently under development is a facility to search for "similar" code.

Using this approach we automatically find that test cases create_2, create_3 and create_4 only differ in an atom and a record definition. The test cases create_2 and create_3 are for audio, the test case create_4 is for video.

```
create_2(id) -> "create_2";
create_2(doc) -> "Create basic VIG MUX + audio LC AMR segment";
create_2(setupimg) -> "";
create_2(fts) ->
"/vobs/mgwblade/HCF/HCF_CRA1190072/test/doc/15241/XYZ_FTS.fm";
create_2(class) -> auto;
create_2(time) -> {{00,00,00},{00,00,00}};
create_2(config) -> [];
create_2(main) ->
%%%%%%%%%%%%%%%%%%%%%%%%%%%%%%%%%%%%%%%%%%%%%%%%%%%%%%%
?COMMENT("Test case create_2 started.",[]),
%%%%%%%%%%%%%%%%%%%%%%%%%%%%%%%%%%%%%%%%%%%%%%%%%%%%%%%
SidMux = {mux_id_1, h223_id_1},
{TdmSid, LocalData, _, _} = precond_one_blade_tdm_mux_create(SidMux),
?CHECK(ok, hcfTraceServerSupport, start, [[{brchDspRhI, exported}]]),
SidLc = {mux_id_1, audio_id_1},
CreateData = #brchMuxLcAccess{sid = SidLc,
stream_type = ?BRCH_AUDIO,
local_data = LocalData,
codec = {?AMR,
{?R_122, ?BRCH_DISABLED,
?BRCH_DISABLED, ?BRCH_BIT},
33, 44, 40},
event_module = iptermCb},
[{ok, [{SidLc, _IntCep}], ?BRCH_REPLICATION_NEEDED}] =
?CH(1, brchShI, create, [[CreateData]]),
?CHECK([], hcfTraceServerSupport, get_trace_list, []),
%%%%%%%%%%%%%%%%%%%%%%%%%%%%%%%%%%%%%%%%%%%%%%%%%%%%%%%
%% Clean up this test case
%%%%%%%%%%%%%%%%%%%%%%%%%%%%%%%%%%%%%%%%%%%%%%%%%%%%%%%
clean_up([SidLc, SidMux, TdmSid]),
?RESULT("DONE", []).
```

If we select the body of the create_2(main) clause and search for expressions (i.e., similar code), we will find create_4, but also a create_3, which is also for audio, but which differs much less. We found out that generalizing code further apart from each other will result in being able to automatically include code closer to the original copy.

Using the facilities in Wrangler to generate this, we automatically get the most general antiunifier of the code, that is, variables replace subterms that are different. The most general part is copied into a new function create_234, since it combines the 3 test cases create_2, create_3 and create_4.

Another refactoring ("folding") lets us now replace the bodies of create_2, create_3 and create_4 to function calls to create_234 with different arguments.

So far, this is pure refactoring, the code that we produce has the same semantics as the original test cases. Now we introduce a step that helps us to lift test cases to properties. We collect all calls to create_234 in one generator that randomly selects one of the alternatives and we create a property that does test each of these 3 alternatives:

```
create_234_gen() ->
oneof([{audio_id_1,?BRCH_AUDIO,{?G723_1, {?R_53, ?BRCH_DISABLED}, 33,
44, 40}},
{audio_id_1,?BRCH_AUDIO,{?AMR, {?R_122, ?BRCH_DISABLED,
?BRCH_DISABLED, ?BRCH_BIT}, 33, 44, 40}},
{video_id_1,?BRCH_VIDEO,{?H264, ?BRCH_NO_OPTION, 33, 44, 40}}
]).

prop_create_234() ->
?FORALL({Media,Channel,Codec},create_234_gen(),
create_234(Media,Channel,Codec)).
```

The property should be a bit more complex, since it should return true or false, not the result of create_234, but for reasons of clarity we keep it simple here.

Now normal refactoring steps should be used to refactor the generator in this property to more detailed generators. We know how to do this manually, and automation will possible, and is in our future plans.

The result will be:

```
media() ->
oneof([audio_id_1,video_id_1]).

streamtype(audio_id_1) ->
?BRCH_AUDIO;

streamtype(video_id_1) ->
?BRCH_VIDEO.

codec(audio_id_1) ->
oneof([{?G723_1, {?R_53, ?BRCH_DISABLED}, 33, 44, 40},
{?AMR, {?R_122, ?BRCH_DISABLED, ?BRCH_DISABLED, ?BRCH_BIT}, 33,
44, 40}
]);

codec(viedo_id_1) ->
{?H264, ?BRCH_NO_OPTION, 33, 44, 40}
```

This requires that we know that there is a dependency between the different fields and it also requires automatic refactoring of the property as soon as the generators are refined:

```
prop_create_234() ->
?FORALL(Media,media(),
?FORALL(Channel,streamtype(Media),
?FORALL(Codec,codec(Media),
create_234(Media,Channel,Codec)).
```

Now the tester can add additional alternatives to the generator which will automatically increase the number of tests, without having to copy and paste test cases. In addition, the test code becomes more structured and readable.

This example shows how refactoring and related transformations in Wrangler can be used to support the extraction of Quick Check properties from 'free' tests. A similar approach allows Quick Check properties to be extracted from EUnit tests, and we anticipate implementing a suite of transformations supporting in the near future.

8 Conclusions

Our work on property discovery has already shown very promising results. Working with our industrial partners we are now close to having automatic support for extracting properties from test cases. In addition, we have worked on two other ways of obtaining properties from specification, viz. obtaining properties from data type definitions and from databases. The methods have been evaluated by the Swedish company Klarna, and Ericsson's OTP team, and have shown their immediate benefit. We have developed a tool, called QuickSpec that can automatically generate properties for a given library of functions.

We have developed two methods to extract properties from test cases. One is dynamic, the other static. In the first approach, the test cases are run, generating traces for the program, from these traces a finite state machine can be abstracted. The second approach works on the level of the source code of the test cases. It is a guided automatic approach; testers know best what part of the test case they like to generate and what part they want to keep specific.

Our work on test and property evolution has concentrated on the development of the Wrangler refactoring tool that can be used to support refactorings of tests, test-aware refactorings and property discovery. We have investigated the impact of various refactorings on the industrial practise of testing using: EUnit, QuickCheck, and Common Test / OTP Test Server, and have worked on extending Wrangler with refactorings of EUnit test data. We have begun the integration of Wrangler into the Eclipse binding for Erlang, Erlide.

In property monitoring we have developed a prototype tool that automatically analyses a set of log files given a description of what constitutes the 'key' and what is the interesting 'value', and is capable of handling some non-trivial inter-log-file relations.

We have made significant progress in our work on analysing concurrent systems. Our work on developing methods to shrink trace counter-examples (resulting from testing or model checking concurrent systems) has resulted in the development of a new tool, PULSE, which is now implemented as part of the commercial QuickCheck distribution. PULSE has been successfully used to find race conditions in software provided by an industrial partner.

In addition we have developed a model checker, McErlang, which was released as open source under the agreed project license that supports a very large fragment of the Erlang language to ease the task of constructing a verifiable model from an Erlang program.

References

[ACH08] Arts, T., Castro, L.M., Hughes, J.: Testing Erlang data types with Quviq QuickCheck. In: Teoh and Horváth DBLP:conf/erlang/2008, pp. 1–8 (2008)

[ACS04] Arts, T., Claessen, K., Svensson, H.: Semi-formal Development of a Fault-Tolerant Leader Election Protocol in Erlang. In: Grabowski, J., Nielsen, B. (eds.) FATES 2004. LNCS, vol. 3395, pp. 140–154. Springer, Heidelberg (2005)

[AF02] Arts, T., Fredlund, L.-Å.: Trace analysis of Erlang programs. In: Page, R.L., Hughes, J. (eds.) Erlang Workshop, pp. 16–23. ACM, New York (2002)

[AHJW06] Arts, T., Hughes, J., Johansson, J., Wiger, U.: Testing Telecoms Software with Quviq Quickcheck. In: Feeley, M., Trinder, P.W. (eds.) Proceedings of the 2006 ACM SIGPLAN Workshop on Erlang (Erlang 2006), pp. 2–10. ACM Press, New York (2006)

[AVWW96] Armstrong, J., Virding, R., Wikström, C., Williams, M.: Concurrent Programming in Erlang, 2nd edn. Prentice-Hall, Englewood Cliffs (1996)

[CH00] Claessen, K., Hughes, J.: QuickCheck: a lightweight tool for random testing of Haskell programs. In: ICFP, pp. 268–279 (2000)

[CPS+09] Claessen, K., Palka, M., Smallbone, N., Hughes, J., Svensson, H., Arts, T., Wiger, U.: Finding race conditions in Erlang with QuickCheck and PULSE. In: ICFP, pp. 149–160. ACM, New York (2009)

[EF09] Earle, C.B., Fredlund, L.-Å.: Recent improvements to the McErlang model checker. In: Erlang Workshop, pp. 93–100 (2009)

[EFIL08] Earle, C.B., Fredlund, L.-Å., Iglesias, J.A., Ledezma, A.: Verifying robocup teams. In: Peled, D.A., Wooldridge, M.J. (eds.) MoChArt 2008. LNCS, vol. 5348, pp. 34–48. Springer, Heidelberg (2009)

[ET09] Earle, C.B., Thompson, S.J. (eds.): Proceedings of the 8th ACM SIGPLAN Workshop on Erlang, Edinburgh, Scotland, UK, September 5. ACM, New York (2009)

[GdM08] Glück, R., de Moor, O. (eds.): Proceedings of the 2008 ACM SIGPLAN Symposium on Partial Evaluation and Semantics-based Program Manipulation, PEPM 2008, San Francisco, California, USA, January 7-8. ACM, New York (2008)

[GHJ07] Groce, A., Holzmann, G.J.: Randomized differential testing as a prelude to formal verification. In: ICSE, pp. 621–631. IEEE Computer Society, Los Alamitos (2007)

[Hug08] Hughes, J.: Formal Specification for Free!. In: Erlang Workshop (2008)

[LT06] Li, H., Thompson, S.: Comparative Study of Refactoring Haskell and Erlang Programs. In: SCAM, pp. 197–206. IEEE Computer Society, Los Alamitos (2006)

[LT08] Li, H., Thompson, S.J.: Tool support for refactoring functional programs. In: Glück and de Moor/pepm/2008, pp. 199–203 (2008)

[LTR05] Li, H., Thompson, S., Reinke, C.: The Haskell Refactorer, HaRe, and its API. Electr. Notes Theor. Comput. Sci. 141(4), 29–34 (2005)

[ST08] Sultana, N., Thompson, S.J.: Mechanical verification of refactorings. In: pepm, pp. 51–60 (2008)

[Sve09] Svensson, H.: Implementing an ltl-to-büchi translator in erlang: a protest experience report. In: Erlang Workshop, pp. 63–70 (2009)

[TH08] Teoh, S.T., Horváth, Z. (eds.): Proceedings of the 7th ACM SIGPLAN workshop on ERLANG, Victoria, BC, Canada, Se ptember 27. ACM, New York (2008)

[Tho04] Thompson, S.: Refactoring functional programs. In: Vene, V., Uustalu, T. (eds.) AFP 2004. LNCS, vol. 3622, pp. 331–357. Springer, Heidelberg (2005)

[WD09] Walkinshaw, N., Derrrick, J.: Incrementally discovering testable specifications from program executions. In: FMCO (2009)

[WDG09] Walkinshaw, N., Derrick, J., Guo, Q.: Iterative refinement of reverse-engineered models by model-based testing. In: Cavalcanti, A., Dams, D.R. (eds.) FM 2009. LNCS, vol. 5850, pp. 305–320. Springer, Heidelberg (2009)

[ZH02] Zeller, A., Hildebrandt, R.: Simplifying and isolating failure-inducing input. IEEE Trans. Software Eng. 28(2), 183–200 (2002)

Incrementally Discovering Testable Specifications from Program Executions

Neil Walkinshaw and John Derrick

Department of Computer Science, The University of Sheffield, Sheffield, UK

Abstract. The ProTest project[1] is an EU FP7 project to develop techniques that improve the testing and verification of concurrent and distributed software systems. One of the four main work packages is concerned with the automated identification of specifications that could serve as a suitable basis for testing; this is currently a tedious and error-prone manual task that tends to be neglected in practice. This paper describes how this problem has been addressed in the ProTest project. It describes a technique that uses test executions to refine the specification from which they are generated. It shows how the technique has been implemented and applied to real Erlang systems. It also describes in detail the major challenges that remain to be addressed in future work.

1 Introduction

The ProTest project [1] is motivated by the need to develop improved testing and verification techniques for concurrent and distributed software systems. This paper describes a particular programme of work within the project that aims to reverse-engineer testable models. The work is targeted at systems that are implemented in Erlang [2], and makes use of QuickCheck, the most popular model-based testing framework for Erlang systems.

Erlang is the leading platform for the development of distributed and concurrent software systems. With its Open Telecom Platform (OTP) libraries, Erlang applications can be rapidly developed and deployed across a large variety of hardware platforms. This has caused it to become increasingly popular, not only within large telecoms companies such as Ericsson, but also with a variety of SMEs in different areas. It is increasingly used to develop applications that are business-critical, from financial transaction systems (e.g. it forms the basis for Klarna's services [2]), telephone switches, and web-based communication services.

However, in contrast to the extensive support for rapid program development, the verification and validation of Erlang systems is to-date largely unsupported. Consequently there is an inherent danger that important functionality remains untested and undocumented. The ProTest project is intended to develop a suite of tools and techniques that help to address this problem.

[1] `http://www.protest-project.eu`
[2] `http://www.klarna.com`

F.S. de Boer et al. (Eds.): FMCO 2009, LNCS 6286, pp. 272–289, 2010.

As a part of this effort, we have developed an automated technique to infer testable specifications from Erlang systems [3]. This does not completely eliminate the need for manual intervention – it has to be inspected and perhaps slightly amended to represent the correct system – but the required effort is nonetheless substantially reduced. Specifications of the actual system behaviour can be obtained relatively cheaply; they can serve as a useful guide to understanding system behaviour as-is, and can form a suitable basis for regression testing if the current system behaviour is deemed to be correct.

The technique operates by reverse-engineering a specification from traces of program executions. As with most techniques that are based on program traces (referred to as dynamic analysis techniques), the selection of traces is critical [4]. One of the key novelties of our technique is that, instead of relying on the developer to record and supply traces, they are obtained automatically by using a model-based test-set generator. The resulting traces are used to refine the model at each iteration, until no further tests that contradict the hypothesised model can be found.

This paper provides details on how the technique works. It shows how the technique has been combined with an Erlang TCP-testing framework to automatically reverse-engineer a model for a Linux TCP implementation. This is followed by a substantial discussion of the main areas that need to be addressed by future work.

2 Background

To provide a motivation for our work, we show in section 2.1 how Erlang applications are currently tested with the QuickCheck tool, a commonplace Erlang model-based testing framework. Its weakness is that it currently relies on the developer to supply the models to be tested. An overview of the challenges of reverse-engineering models is given in section 2.2.

2.1 Model-Based Testing of Erlang Applications

QuickCheck [5] is an automated model-based testing tool for Erlang. It has become one of the standard testing tools used by Erlang developers. The 'model' is conventionally provided by the developer, as a set of simple properties that must hold for the program to behave correctly, and these have conventionally been expressed as logical properties in Erlang itself. For example, the following property would check that the reverse function for lists behaves as expected:

```
prop_reverse() ->
      ?FORALL(Xs,list(int()),
      lists:reverse(lists:reverse(Xs)) == Xs).
```

The property prop_reverse generates lots of lists of random length, filled with random integers. For each list (assigned to the variable Xs) it ensures that the list is the same as the reverse of the reverse. Were this not the case, it would have found a bug in the lists:reverse function.

As part of the ProTest project, QuickCheck has been extended to so that it is possible to test an implementation against a finite state machine (rather than just a simple property). The use of a finite state machine enables the developer to specify the permitted sequences of program functions, along with their effect on the data-state of the system. QuickCheck tests an implementation by selecting random paths through the state machine, with the aim of verifying their behaviour in the implementation (i.e. checking that pre-/post-conditions hold on the data state once a transition is executed). Given state-machine model, QuickCheck can produce the requisite sequences of inputs (with the necessary data parameters) to automatically test any path in the model against the actual software system (this is important to with respect to our reverse-engineering technique described later).

The key problem with model-based techniques such as QuickCheck is the reliance upon a model that is both accurate and complete. In practice, large and complex systems are often developed under restrictive time-constraints, across multiple sites by different developers, and are constantly evolving. Under such circumstances a developer can at best provide a partial model. This is undermined further as the system evolves due to changes in requirements and bug-fixes.

2.2 Reverse-Engineering State Machines

Reverse-engineering techniques aim to address this problem. Broadly speaking, these approaches can be separated into two categories: Those based on source-code analysis (c.f. [6]), and those based on the analysis of execution traces. Here we focus on the latter (dynamic) approaches. They are based on the analysis of program traces, which are sequences of events (e.g. function calls, message-passing events etc.), that may optionally be annotated with variable values. The traces can be recorded by instrumenting the source code, or by using tracing tools. For Erlang several such tools are included in the OTP framework.

From a given set of traces, the challenge for reverse-engineering techniques is to produce a candidate state machine that conforms to the provided set of traces. This is not a new problem. Its roots can be traced back to to the 50s, in Moore's work on "gedanken experiments" on state machines [7] and Nerode's work on the synthesis of machines from equivalence relations [8]. However it was Gold's work on Grammar Inference in 1967 that was arguably most influential, establishing the theoretical limits of regular grammar (i.e. deterministic state machine) learnability [9]. Most reverse-engineering techniques in the field of software engineering are inspired by techniques that were initially devised as grammar-inference techniques [10,11,12,4].

It is unrealistic to expect an inference technique to be able to infer a machine that is 100% accurate from any arbitrary set of traces. An inference technique will only produce an accurate result if the provided set of traces is *characteristic* of the behaviour of the underlying software system [11,4]. In terms of state machines, this must include enough information about what the program can and cannot do to enable the inference technique to identify every state transition, and to distinguish between every pair of non-equivalent states. Thus the key challenges lie in (a) *identifying* the relevant subset of executions and (b) *collecting* them - a potentially expensive and time-consuming process.

Current reverse-engineering techniques force the user to make a difficult compromise between accuracy and practical applicability. On the one hand, there are several *passive* inference techniques [10,13,14] that are reasonably easy to apply and cheap to use, but these can result in inaccurate models unless the user has a prior comprehensive knowledge of the system that can be used to obtain required set of traces [4]. On the other hand, they can choose *active* inference techniques (e.g. based on Angluin's L^* algorithm [15,16]), that guarantee an accurate model, but are usually prohibitively expensive and fail to scale to larger, more complex systems.

3 An Iterative, Test-Driven Model Inference Approach

This section describes a specification inference technique that was developed by the authors as part of the ProTest project [3]. It circumvents the problems that are intrinsic to conventional passive approaches. It does not rely on a human user to supply it with traces, but instead resorts to a model-based test set generator to identify and collect the traces automatically. The model from which these tests are generated is updated and refined with each iteration, until no more tests can be found that conflict with the model.

The approach is underpinned by the Erlang QuickCheck tool described in section 2.1. The presented technique will infer state machine transition structures, which are represented as Labelled Transition Systems. An LTS[3] is a quadruple $A = (Q, \Sigma, \delta, q_0)$, where Q is a finite set of states, Σ is a finite alphabet, $\delta : Q \times \Sigma \rightarrow Q$ is a partial function and $q_0 \in Q$. In this work we assume that an LTS is deterministic.

The rest of this section describes the basic (passive) algorithm that can be used to infer state machines from traces. We use the EDSM Blue-Fringe algorithm [17]. This is followed by a description of how the EDSM algorithm can be combined with the QuickCheck testing framework, so that traces are automatically extracted from the subject system.

3.1 Inferring State Machines from Traces

We begin by describing the underlying algorithm for inferring state machines from traces. State machine inference techniques in the software engineering domain tend to use the k-tails algorithm [10,18]. This is however prone to several weaknesses (see previous work by the authors [4]). Instead we use the more recent EDSM algorithm that has emerged from the closely related field of regular grammar inference [17].

The EDSM algorithm is presented in Algorithm 1. The algorithm works on the basis of two types of trace: a set *Pos* of traces that represent valid program

[3] References to "state machines" are henceforth assumed to refer to their LTS.

Input: (Pos, Neg)
1 $LTS \leftarrow generateAPTA(Pos, Neg)$;
2 **while** $(q, q') \leftarrow selectStatePair(LTS)$ **do**
3 | $LTS' \leftarrow merge(PLTS, (q, q'))$;
4 | **if** $Compatible(PLTS', Pos, Neg)$ **then**
5 | | $LTS \leftarrow LTS'$;
6 | **end**
7 **end**
8 **return** LTS

Algorithm 1. EDSM algorithm

executions, and a set Neg of traces that represent either infeasible executions, or executions that terminate with an exception or failure[4]. These traces are first arranged into a tree-structured state machine that exactly accepts the given set of traces (this is referred to as an *Augmented Prefix Tree Acceptor*). In the algorithm this is carried out by the *generateAPTA* function in line 1. The process of inferring the state machine subsequently consists of repeating the following process: A pair of states that are deemed to be equivalent is selected, (2) the pair is merged, and (3) the resulting machine is checked against Pos and Neg to ensure that it is still compatible – if not the merge is ignored. The process terminates when no further mergable state-pairs are found.

The key to the effectiveness of the EDSM algorithm is the *selectStatePair* function. It does not simply select the first pair of states that are deemed to be compatible. It computes a "similarity score" for each pair, and then merges pairs in the order of their scores (highest to lowest). The similarity score is computed by counting the extent to which their outgoing paths overlap with each other. The greater the overlap, the greater the score. Thanks to the availability of negative traces, it is also possible to rule-out state merges if they have a conflicting set of outgoing paths (i.e. a sequence is deemed to be possible from one state but not from another). If this is the case, the pair is assigned a score of -1 to prevent a merge from occurring.

The *merge* function (Line 3) takes two states q and q', along with the current state machine A. In effect, the state q' is removed, all of its incoming transitions are routed to q instead and all of its outgoing transitions are routed from q. Every time a pair of states is merged, the resulting state machine may be non-deterministic. Nondeterminism is eliminated by recursively merging the targets of non-deterministic transitions.

A comprehensive description of the EDSM algorithm itself is beyond the scope of this paper, and the reader is referred to the original paper by Lang *et al.* [17] for a more complete description. In practice, our implementation does not compare *every* pair of states at any given point. It uses a windowing-strategy to compare only

[4] Traditional dynamic analysis approaches presume that all traces represent positive / valid executions. However, in our work, traces that lead to a program failure (i.e. an exception) are interpreted as "invalid" and so added to the Neg set in the EDSM algorithm.

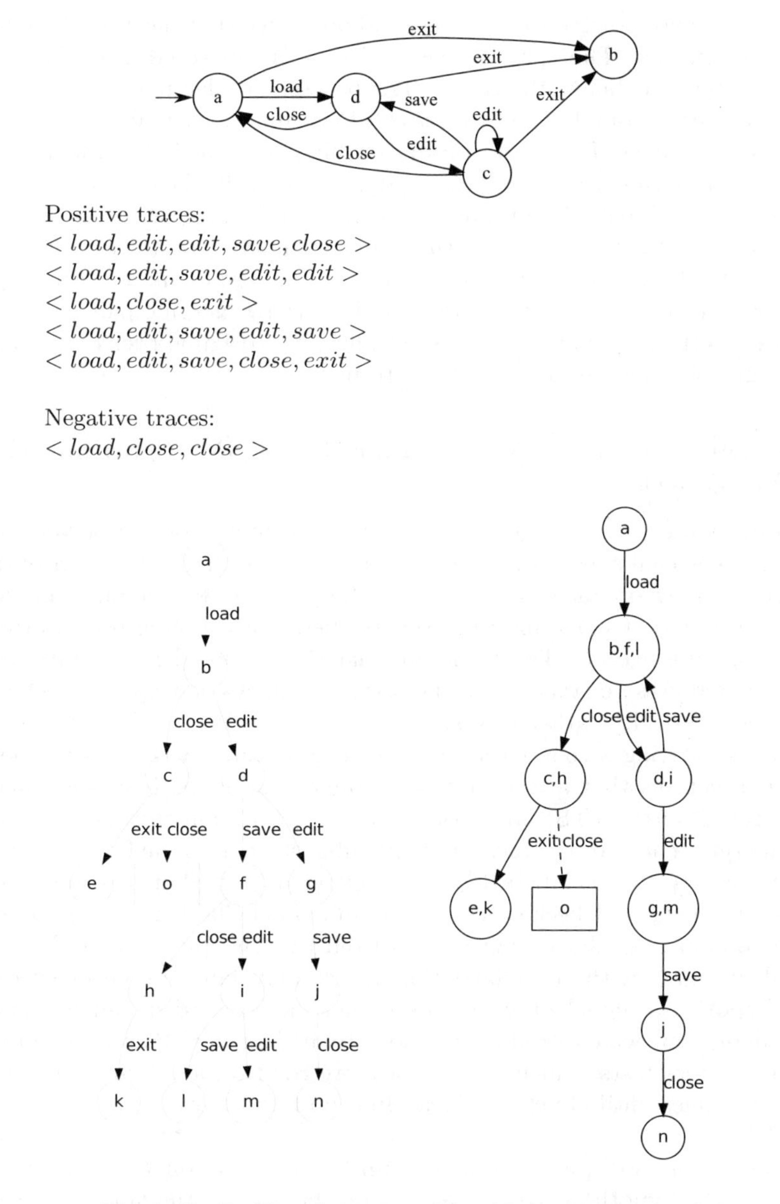

Fig. 1. Prefix Tree Acceptor with added negative trace

those states that are most likely to produce high scores called the "Blue-Fringe" strategy. A detailed description is provided by Lang *et al.*, or in a subsequent survey of grammar inference techniques by Cicchello and Kremer [19].

To provide the reader with an intuition of how the algorithm operates, we refer to the example in Figure 1. The state machine at the top represents a simple, fictional text editor. The task is to infer it from the set of traces given below, where there are five valid traces, and one trace that has been found to be impossible / invalid. The "prefix acceptor" that is generated from these traces is shown to the left, below the traces. The process of selecting state pairs to be merged (as carried out by the *selectStatePair* function) is illustrated with a selection of examples. Pair (b, f) produce a high score of 5; by tracing out the sub-trees from both states there are 5 matching labels in the outgoing sub-trees. On the other hand, pair (b, c) produce a score of -1, because a "close" is possible from b, but not from c. Any pair that involves node a produces a score of 0, because a "load" only appears once in the machine and cannot be matched to any other edges in the tree. Thus, we would begin by merging pair (b, f), which would lead to the machine shown to the right of the original prefix tree, and the search begins for the next pair of states to merge.

3.2 Automating Trace Collection for the EDSM Algorithm with QuickCheck

When using traces to reverse-engineer state machines (or any other type of model), the key challenge is to supply the technique with a suitable set of traces. The sheer number of traces required, and the prior knowledge and time on the part of the user that is required to execute these traces, often renders the task infeasible in practice [4]. The technique that is presented here addresses this problem; it requires no traces from the user, and shows how QuickCheck can be used to automatically gather traces.

Instead of starting with a set of traces, we begin simply with the set of possible inputs or functions that are to label the transitions in the final state machine (i.e. the set Σ in the LTS), and also supply the program that is to be tested. Our technique generates the most basic possible state machine from Σ – a single state with a loop that is labelled by every element in Σ. This is translated into a corresponding QuickCheck specification, and QuickCheck attempts to execute a set of random tests that are generated from this general machine. Invariably, tests will disagree with the model (i.e. a test may fail, but be deemed valid by the hypothesis model or vice versa); these are recorded and fed into the EDSM algorithm, which produces a more refined model. This is in turn used to generate more tests, which produce a more refined model, and the iterative process continues until QuickCheck can find no further tests that disagree with the model.

The algorithm is displayed in algorithm 2. The notation L^{LTS} refers to the *language* of the hypothesis LTS. If a sequence belongs to the language, it represents a sequence of events that should be permitted according to the LTS. The *runTest* function refers to QuickCheck executing a test, and *generateTests* refers to the automated random test set generation process implemented by QuickCheck. The process broadly consists of executing the tests, observing if they pass or fail, and then checking (in lines 8 and 14) whether these are in agreement with the hypothesis LTS.

A QuickCheck state machine specification consists of more than just an LTS. It corresponds to an extended state machine [20]; for each element in Σ it can

```
   Input: Prog, Σ
 1 Pos ← ∅; Neg ← ∅;
 2 LTS ← generateInitLTS(Σ);
 3 Test ← generateTests(LTS);
 4 foreach test ∈ Test do
 5 |   (trace, pass) ← runTest(test, Prog);
 6 |   if pass then
 7 |   |   Pos ← Pos ∪ {trace};
 8 |   |   if trace ∉ L^LTS then
 9 |   |   |   LTS ← EDSM(Pos, Neg);
10 |   |   |   Test ← generateTests(LTS);
11 |   |
12 |   else
13 |   |   Neg ← Neg ∪ {trace};
14 |   |   if trace ∈ L^LTS then
15 |   |   |   LTS ← EDSM(Pos, Neg);
16 |   |   |   Test ← generateTests(LTS);
17 |   |
18 |   end
19 end
20 return LTS
```

Algorithm 2. InferWithTests

contain data transformations that manipulate some underlying memory. As it stands, the inference algorithm is restricted to inferring the LTS, and extending it to deal with data-constraints will be discussed in section 5. In its current form, these elements are supplied by the user in the form of a template. The data-state, along with the way elements in Σ change it, is specified by the user and made available as a template file.

The EDSM algorithm has been implemented by the authors in their StateChum tool [12,21]. Traces are recorded by using the comprehensive tracing framework that is built into the Erlang OTP [2]. Given the template file generated by the user, a simple Bash script is used to orchestrate the interaction between the QuickCheck testing/tracing process and the StateChum model inference framework.

4 Case Study - Reverse-Engineering a TCP Stack

The ProTest project has involved a selection of case studies, to explore the efficacy of the various tools and techniques that are being developed. One of those case studies is a comprehensive QuickCheck testing specification for TCP stacks, which was developed by Paris and Arts [22]. To provide a preliminary assessment of our technique, we have applied it to this case-study, with the aim of reverse-engineering an accurate model of a Linux TCP/IP implementation (via a TCP testing extension of the QuickCheck framework).

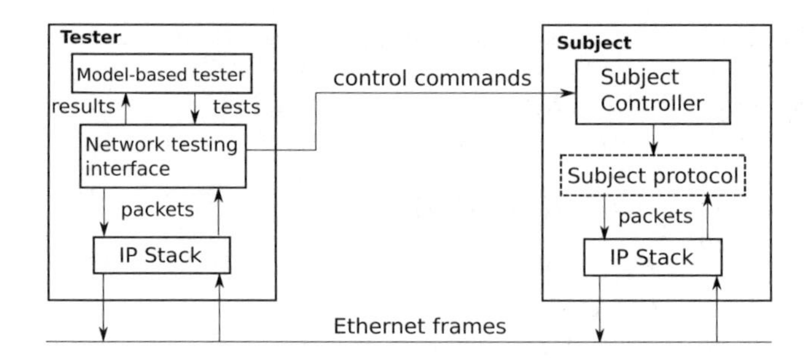

Fig. 2. Communication between tester and subject

Paris and Arts developed a network interface for QuickCheck that enables it to check network protocols on remote machines. The basic process is shown in Figure 2. They use two channels to interact with the system under test; one channel is used to induce certain behaviour from the subject (invoking behaviour by invoking functions with Erlang messages), and the other is the network-level channel, which is used to inspect the actual packets that are sent over the network as a result, and to send packets over the network to the subject. The model on the tester machine contains certain constraints that the messages are expected to adhere to, and every time a message is received, it is checked against those constraints. The model then uses the information on these packets to generate valid replies and transition the subject stack through the state machine. Using these two channels enables black box testing of the subject by observing and steering the behaviour using the two interfaces the stack has: to the user through the API (managed through the subject controller), and to the network (using the network channel).

Paris and Arts have used this framework, along with a QuickCheck specification that they have manually generated from the TCP RFC [23]. They have used this as the basis for testing a number of TCP stacks, including the Linux kernel release, as well as a specialised Erlang TCP implementation. As mentioned previously, the state machine is not complete; there are some legal transitions which are not explicitly stated in the graph. There are also many self transitions which are not represented in the graph, but are referred to in the natural language of the RFC. Therein lies the rationale for applying the approach presented here; we want to find the real specification, and not merely an idealized one, so that we have a more authoritative basis for understanding how the system works.

4.1 Results

Any testing technique for TCP implementations is necessarily limited by the time taken waiting for responses for the server. Some of the operations could take several minutes to execute (mainly due to waiting for time-outs, or packets that may have been lost on the network). Consequently, the process of collecting tests was a very time-consuming process. For this reason, the process was limited to

474 iterations (which took 9 hours to collect). In total 1085 tests were executed, 611 of which passed, and 474 of which failed. It is important to bear in mind that this would have been virtually impossible if it was up to a human to collect the traces, and that the diversity of the traces would have been substantially less if the collection process had not been guided by the inference algorithm.

To provide some intuition of the process, the test executions generated for the first 10 test iterations are shown in Figure 3, with the hypothesis model generated for the 10th iteration shown at the bottom and the reference model shown on the right. Failed tests are prefixed with a '-', and passed tests are prefixed with a '+'. At the beginning, the process starts with the most general LTS, where everything loops to the same state. The first tests are very short, because most of them fail instantly. Nonetheless, these already form a model that has some important commonalities with the reference model; any communication must either start with a `listen` or an `open`. An `open` must be followed by a `syn_ack` before anything else can happen, and a `send_last_ack` returns to the initial state.

As more tests are executed, and more possible and impossible sequences are identified, the model is gradually refined. Every test that conflicts with the current model leads to a new, improved model. Depending on the current hypothesis model, QuickCheck will generate tests that exercise scenarios that were not envisaged. In Figure 3, the test `listen, send_last_ack, listen, passive_close` passes (does not cause a program or pre/post-condition failure), even though it should not be possible according to the reference model (also in Figure 3). To provide an intuition of the extent of the final set of traces that the technique ended up with, the final APTA is shown in Figure 4. Although far too small to read the labels[5], it does show that the iterative test-generation-and-mode-refinement process was successful at collecting a broad range of program executions.

The final model consists of 38 states, with 277 permitted and 157 forbidden transitions. Structurally, the inferred machine is completely different from the reference model. It is however important to bear in mind that the reference model is only partial – it only describes the small portion of behaviour that is *expected*, and does not account for what may happen if unexpected sequences of events are produced. For this to be the case it would have to account for every operation at every state. It is this more complete spectrum of behaviour that is represented by the inferred model.

Although more representative of the actual TCP implementation, the inferred model inevitably still contains inaccuracies. The trace-collection process is hampered by the fact that it had to wait for timeouts. More traces would inevitably have led to a more accurate machine. Nonetheless, given that no inference algorithm has been empirically shown to outperform the EDSM algorithm yet [17], the inferred model is the most accurate one possible with current state machine inference techniques.

---

[5] The PDF version of this paper does permit the user to zoom in to read the labels.

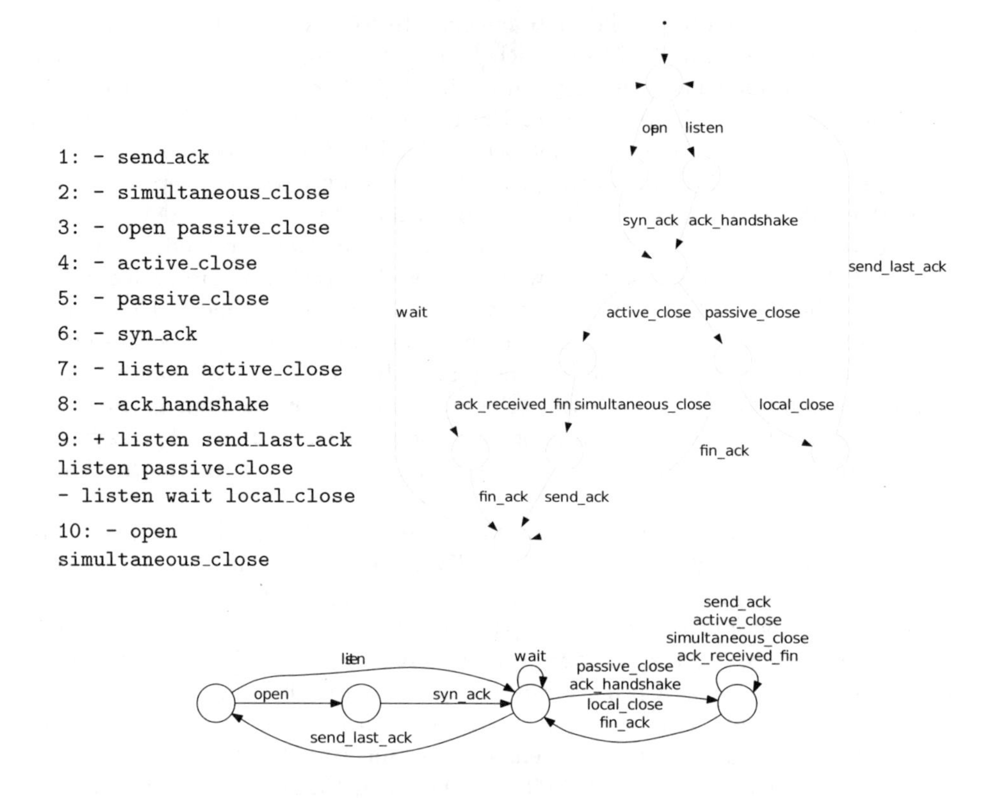

Fig. 3. Test cases for 10 iterations on the left, with the reference TCP model on the right and the hypothesis model after 10th iteration below (Forbidden transitions are omitted for readability)

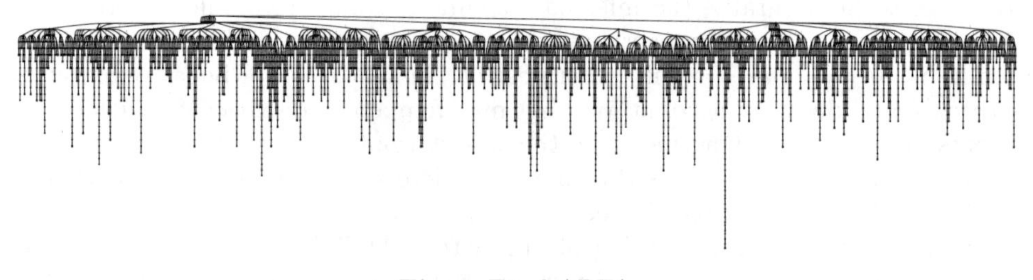

Fig. 4. Final APTA

5 Improving the Inference Process

The presented technique is promising. The combination of QuickCheck with the StateChum model inference framework can seek out the necessary traces, automatically record them, and use them as a basis for inferring a model. All this without the need for interventions from the developer.

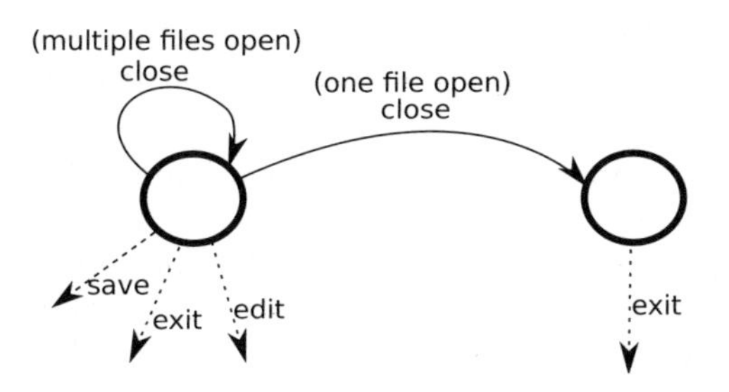

Fig. 5. Behaviour of "close" function in extended text editor

There are however still aspects of the technique that do require expertise and effort on the part of the developer. Currently, the QuickCheck template file (minus LTS) has to be generated by hand. This must include any relevant data state information, along with appropriate data transformations. Furthermore, the developer has to manually identify a mapping from the low-level trace events to abstract transition labels in the machine. Both can involve a substantial amount of effort, which we aim to reduce in future work. This section will elaborate on these problems, and will provide some preliminary suggestions for solutions.

5.1 Inferring Extended State Machines

The current approach, with the help of the EDSM algorithm, infers labelled transition systems. In practice however, software behaviour cannot be completely described by a simple LTS. In reality, the sequence of events or functions in a program is also dependent upon the memory of the system; a particular function may behave differently (and affect the state of the system in a different way) depending on the state of the system when it is invoked.

To illustrate this problem, we envisage a slightly more sophisticated text editor than the example in Figure 1. Imagine that, instead of only being able to open one file at a time, the editor can open and edit multiple files concurrently. This system can no longer be represented in a straightforward LTS with the same labels we use in Figure 1. As a simple example, we focus in on the "close" function. As illustrated in Figure 5, if multiple files are open, its behaviour ultimately depends on how many files are open; if multiple files are open, it is possible to close one of them and subsequently edit / save / close others. However, if only one file is open, it is subsequently impossible to do any further editing or saving. There are two different ways in which "close" can affect the subsequent behaviour of the software system, and this depends on the underlying state of the system. This more complex, data state-dependent behaviour cannot be represented on a simple deterministic LTS.

There are two approaches that attempt to address this problem. The first approach, which is currently adopted by the authors, is to ensure that functions are chosen in such a way that the different data constraints are encompassed in the labels. The second approach is to adopt a state-labelling procedure that augments states in the PTA or the LTS with data constraints.

Decomposition into Atomic Functions. The decomposition approach works as follows. Instead of using data-sensitive functions such as the "close" example above, it can be decomposed into separate sub-functions, based on the different ways it can affect the system state. The approach is analogous to the Category Partition method used in functional testing [24]. So the "close" function could be divided into "close" and "close_last", making the distinction between the two different types of close behaviour. The data constraints remain implicit, but the data state-based behaviour is represented more accurately by the labels.

This approach places a significant burden on the developer. They have to be aware not only of the individual functions in the system, but also of their potential to change the state of the system. Furthermore, the process of trace collection becomes more intricate. It is no longer sufficient to simply list the functions in the order in which they occur. Every time a data state-dependent function is executed, the data state has to be interpreted, and mapped to the appropriate re-labelled function name that represents the new sub-function. For example, the execution of "close" could no longer be simply listed in the trace as "close", but would have to be mapped to either "close" or "close_last" depending on the current data state.

Labelling States with Data Constraints. Both Dupont *et al.* [25,11] and Lorenzoli *et al.* [26] describe techniques for integrating data-constraints into the inference process. They deal with different settings; Dupont *et al.* assume a forward-engineering scenario, where the developer can manually provide the relevant rules for particular sets of states, whereas Lorenzoli *et al.* describe a reverse-engineering scenario, where they have to mine data constraints from the variable values in a given set of traces.

In the approach proposed by Dupont *et al.*, additional domain knowledge about the system is added in the form of *fluents*. A fluent is in effect a proposition that is given an initial state, and this state can be altered by a selection of events in Σ. Given that the relevant fluents are specified for the initial state, the rest of the states in the state machine can be annotated in terms of the fluents by symbolic execution. Consequently, these state annotations can be fed into the inference process, preventing states that correspond to distinct *data* states from being merged.

Lorenzoli *et al.* approach the problem from a reverse-engineering angle. In their setting, there is no well-informed developer who can supply suitable fluent-like constraints. Instead, they extract data constraints from variable values in execution traces. Data constraints are obtained with the Daikon tool [27], and state comparisons take account of these constraints. Although they describe the approach with respect to the problematic k-tails algorithm, there is no reason why it cannot be adapted to other algorithms such as EDSM.

The approach proposed by Lorenzoli *et al.*, of extracting data constraints directly from the traces, is appealing. It provides additional information without increasing the expense in terms of the human effort involved in using the technique. The idea of using data constraint inference to augment the EDSM process forms part of our future work.

Such an approach can however not be applied as-is to large-scale models, derived from realistic traces. Its effectiveness is dependent on the effectiveness of the constraint-inference technique. Daikon (used by Lorenzoli *et al.*) has some important limitations. It was only designed to identify simple, linear constraints, and any constraint types have to be pre-supplied to the tool.

With respect to our technique, we intend to extend it in the manner of Lorenzoli *et al.*. To apply to realistic traces, it will necessitate the investigation of more powerful data constraint / function identification techniques – techniques that can identify more relevant complex data transformations, that perhaps incorporate nonlinear variable relationships (c.f. work by Bongard and Lipson on identifying non-linear functions from data [28]).

5.2 Identifying the Primary Functions in a Trace

All current reverse-engineering approaches, including those discussed in the previous subsection, make the assumption that the functions used to label the edges are trivially known (i.e. "edit" and "save"). It is presumed that these functions clearly map to a given trace (i.e. "edit" corresponds to a method in the trace called "edit" etc.). This is fine if the trace contains only a small number of different types of event (such as the traces for the TCP example used above). However, when traces scale up to larger and more complex systems, this becomes impossible. A trace of a trivial Java system for example will often encompass hundreds of thousands calls to thousands of different methods. A simple operation to load a text file might encompass hundreds of different input/output library methods to read the file, and hundreds of font-rendering library methods to render the characters onto the screen for example. Given such a trace, how do we reduce it to a sequence of symbols that can be used to infer a state machine?

To illustrate the problem, we use a simple example of an openly-available Java drawing application called JHotDraw. We may want an abstracted state machine that describes its core functionality. To do so, it is executed and record the trace is recorded: we create three new drawings, and insert five figures into each drawing. The figure in 6 shows the result in JHotdraw.

The problem facing us is this: the ensuing trace contains 161,087 method calls to 1489 different methods[6]. To reverse-engineer a machine from such a system, we need to map this extremely large trace to a sequence of symbols that will result in a machine that is readable and can be readily understood by the developer. So far, model inference work implies that this is a relatively straightforward process [14]; but it can be a very challenging task - especially if the developer is not familiar with the functionality, let alone the architecture of the underlying system.

[6] The trace was recorded by Cornelissen *et al.* [29] and can be downloaded from their website.

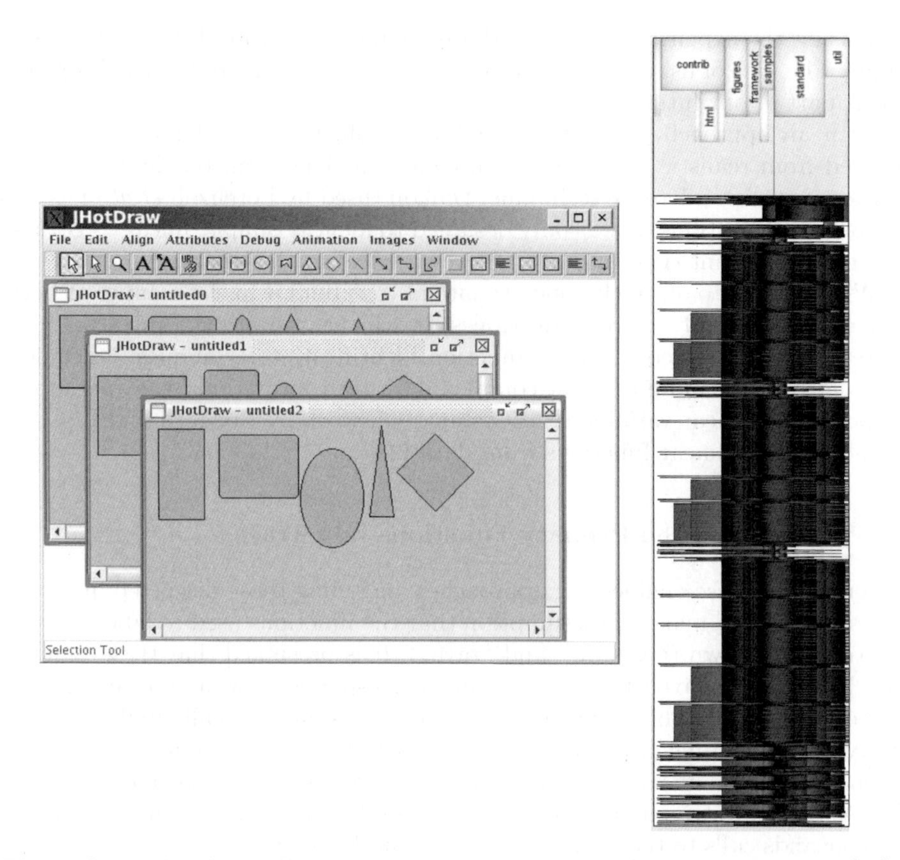

Fig. 6. Screenshot from JHotDraw along with phase-visualisation of the trace [29]

In practice, a trace is not just an homogeneous series of calls to different methods. It consists of patterns; processing of text file might contain a loop to read in characters that causes the repetition of a few specific methods for a long period of time, followed by a different loop of method calls to display these characters etc. These *phases* of activity tend to correspond to high-level units of behaviour, and are what we are looking to identify from these traces for our purpose of trace abstraction.

The solution lies in the identification of those 'segments' of the trace that correspond to a particular item of functionality (i.e. rendering a figure). In the trace-analysis community this is refered to as *phase analysis*. Phase analysis is an established problem [29]. Current solutions rely on visualisation techniques. The trace is visualised as a vast message sequence chart, which is compressed into a bitmap that fits to the screen. As an example see the trace-visualisation produced by Cornelissen *et al.* to the right in Figure 6. Despite the size of the trace, it is clear that the trace consists of distinct phases of activity. The three repeated actions of drawing figures on the three canvasses is clearly visible in the visualisation.

For the purposes of inferring models however, visualisations are not enough. They only produce bitmaps, as opposed to sequences of symbols that can be used for state machine executions. Visualisations are left to the developer to interpret, and although two phases may look visually identical, they can hide significant differences.

Solving this problem is the focus of ongoing work within the ProTest project. The authors are investigating the application of string compression algorithms such as the LZW algorithm [30] and the SEQUITUR algorithm [31,32]. These can automatically identify and label repeated patterns of method invocations, to pull out sequences of high-level functions from a trace, without requiring the expensive and tedious intervention of identifying these functions by hand.

6 Conclusions

This paper has presented the challenge of inferring testable models, with a specific focus on testing Erlang systems. The basic reverse-engineering challenge is to find a set of program executions that sufficiently exercise a program to ensure that the reverse-engineered model is accurate. This problem has traditionally been overlooked; developers have supplied sets of traces that are effectively arbitrary; without extensive prior knowledge about the program, it is virtually impossible to collect an adequate set of traces [4].

As part of the ProTest project, the authors have devised a technique [3] that, instead of relying on the manualy supply of traces, automates the trace collection process. It requires a template specification that contains the necessary input values for the functions, but does not need to know the order in which they can be executed. Once this is supplied, it combines a model-based test generation tool [5] with a state machine inference framework [12,17] to automatically collect the traces and home-in on a more accurate specification. Its feasibility has been demonstrated with respect to a TCP implementation [22].

One of the main aims of this paper was to present the main remaining challenges in this area, of which there are several. Current reverse-engineering techniques only have crude approaches to dealing with data-constraints in the model. They also make the big assumption that it is trivial to abstract a program execution trace to a corresponding abstract sequence of symbols. This paper has presented potential avenues of research in these areas, some of which are already being pursued in the context of the ProTest project.

References

1. Derrick, J., Walkinshaw, N.: Property-based testing: The protest project. In: FMCO (2009)
2. Armstrong, J.: Programming Erlang: Software for a Concurrent World. Pragmatic Bookshelf (July 2007)
3. Walkinshaw, N., Derrick, J., Guo, Q.: Iterative refinement of reverse-engineered models by model-based testing. In: Cavalcanti, A., Dams, D.R. (eds.) FM 2009. LNCS, vol. 5850, pp. 305–320. Springer, Heidelberg (2009)

4. Walkinshaw, N., Bogdanov, K., Holcombe, M., Salahuddin, S.: Improving Dynamic Software Analysis by Applying Grammar Inference Principles. Journal of Software Maintenance and Evolution: Research and Practice (2008)
5. Claessen, K., Hughes, J.: Quickcheck: A Lightweight Tool for Random Testing of Haskell Programs. In: Proceedings of the International Conference on Functional Programming (ICFP), pp. 268–279 (2000)
6. Walkinshaw, N., Bogdanov, K., Ali, S., Holcombe, M.: Automated discovery of state transitions and their functions in source code. Software Testing, Verification and Reliability 18(2) (2008)
7. Moore, E.F.: Gedanken–experiments on sequential machines. In: Shannon, C.E., McCarthy, J. (eds.) Annals of Mathematics Studies (34), Automata Studies, pp. 129–153. Princeton University Press, Princeton (1956)
8. Nerode, A.: Linear automata transformations. Proceedings of the American Mathematical Society 9, 541–544 (1958)
9. Gold, E.: Language Identification in the Limit. Information and Control 10, 447–474 (1967)
10. Biermann, A., Feldman, J.: On the Synthesis of Finite-State Machines from Samples of their Behavior. IEEE Transactions on Computers 21, 592–597 (1972)
11. Dupont, P., Lambeau, B., Damas, C., van Lamsweerde, A.: The QSM Algorithm and its Application to Software Behavior Model Induction. Applied Artificial Intelligence 22, 77–115 (2008)
12. Walkinshaw, N., Bogdanov, K., Holcombe, M., Salahuddin, S.: Reverse Engineering State Machines by Interactive Grammar Inference. In: 14th IEEE International Working Conference on Reverse Engineering, WCRE (2007)
13. Cook, J., Wolf, A.: Discovering Models of Software Processes from Event-Based Data. ACM Transactions on Software Engineering and Methodology 7(3), 215–249 (1998)
14. Ammons, G., Bodík, R., Larus, J.: Mining Specifications. In: 29th SIGPLAN-SIGACT Symposium on Principles of Programming Languages (POPL), Portland, Oregon, pp. 4–16 (2002)
15. Angluin, D.: Learning Regular Sets from Queries and Counterexamples. Information and Computation 75, 87–106 (1987)
16. Shahbaz, M., Groz, R.: Inferring mealy machines. In: Cavalcanti, A., Dams, D.R. (eds.) FM 2009. LNCS, vol. 5850, pp. 207–222. Springer, Heidelberg (2009)
17. Lang, K., Pearlmutter, B., Price, R.: Results of the Abbadingo One DFA Learning Competition and a New Evidence-Driven State Merging Algorithm. In: Honavar, V.G., Slutzki, G. (eds.) ICGI 1998. LNCS (LNAI), vol. 1433, pp. 1–12. Springer, Heidelberg (1998)
18. Biermann, A.W., Krishnaswamy, R.: Constructing programs from example computations. IEEE Trans. on Software Engineering SE 2, 141–153 (1976)
19. Cicchello, O., Kremer, S.: Inducing grammars from sparse data sets: A survey of algorithms and results. Journal of Machine Learning Research 4, 603–632 (2003)
20. Cheng, K., Krishnakumar, A.: Automatic functional test generation using the extended finite state machine model. In: 30th ACM/IEEE Design Automation Conference, pp. 86–91 (1993)
21. Walkinshaw, N., Bogdanov, K.: Inferring Finite-State Models with Temporal Constraints. In: Proceedings of the 23rd International Conference on Automated Software Engineering, ASE (2008)
22. Paris, J., Arts, T.: Automatic testing of tcp/ip implementations using quickcheck. In: Proceedings of the 8th ACM SIGPLAN workshop on Erlang, Erlang 2009, pp. 83–92. ACM, New York (2009)

23. Postel, J.: Transmission control protocol. Technical Report 793, DDN Network Information Center, SRI International, RFC (September 1981)
24. Ostrand, T., Balcer, M.: The category-partition method for specifying and generating functional tests. Communications of the ACM 31(6), 676–686 (1988)
25. Damas, C., Lambeau, B., Dupont, P., van Lamsweerde, A.: Generating Annotated Behavior Models from End-User Scenarios. IEEE Transactions on Software Engineering 31(12), 1056–1073 (2005)
26. Lorenzoli, D., Mariani, L., Pezzè, M.: Automatic generation of software behavioral models. In: Proceedings of the 30th international conference on Software engineering, ICSE 2008, pp. 501–510. ACM, New York (2008)
27. Ernst, M., Cockrell, J., Griswold, W., Notkin, D.: Dynamically Discovering Likely Program Invariants to Support Program Evolution. Transactions on Software Engineering 27(2), 1–25 (2001)
28. Bongard, J.C., Lipson, H.: Nonlinear system identification using coevolution of models and tests. IEEE Trans. Evolutionary Computation 9(4), 361–384 (2005)
29. Cornelissen, B., Zaidman, A., Holten, D., Moonen, L., van Deursen, A., van Wijk, J.: Execution trace analysis through massive sequence and circular bundle views. Journal of Systems and Software 81(12), 2252–2268 (2008)
30. Afshan, S., McMinn, P., Walkinshaw, N.: Using dictionary compression algorithms to identify phases in program traces. Technical Report CS-10-01, Department of Computer Science, The University of Sheffield (2010)
31. Walkinshaw, N., Afshan, S., McMinn, P.: Using compression algorithms to support the comprehension of program traces. In: Proceedings of the Eighth International Workshop on Dynamic Analysis (WODA 2010). ACM, New York (2010)
32. Nevill-Manning, C., Witten, I.: Compression and explanation using hierarchical grammars. Computer Journal 40(2/3), 103–116 (1997)

Methodologies for Specification of Real-Time Systems Using Timed I/O Automata

Alexandre David[1], Kim G. Larsen[1], Axel Legay[2], Ulrik Nyman[1], and Andrzej Wąsowski[3]

[1] Computer Science, Aalborg University, Denmark
[2] INRIA/IRISA, Rennes Cedex, France
[3] IT University of Copenhagen, Denmark

Abstract. We present a real-time specification framework based on Timed I/O Automata and a comprehensive tool support for it. The framework supports various design methodologies including: top-down refinement—for decomposition of abstract specifications towards increasingly detailed models; bottom-up abstraction—for synthesis of complex systems from more concrete models; and step-wise modularisation of requirements—to factor out behaviours given by existing available components from a complex global requirements specification to be implemented. These methodologies are realized by consecutive applications of operators from the following set: refinement, consistency checking, logical and structural composition and quotienting. Additionally, our tool allows combining the component-oriented design process with verification of temporal logic properties increasing the flexibility of the process.

1 Context and Motivation

Industries developing complex embedded systems, such as aerospace and automotive, have undergone deep organisational changes with tremendous impact on development processes. In the past, they were vertically integrated companies, internally supporting all design activities from specification to implementation. Today they rely increasingly on external suppliers and on independent teams to provide essential components of systems. It is no longer possible for a single team to control the entire design process from specification to implementation.

Complex systems emerge from assembling multiple components. These components are designed by independently working teams, who adhere to a common agreement, a *contract*, on what the interface of each component should be. Such an interface defines the behaviours expected from the component as well as the environment in which it can be used. The main advantage is that it abstracts from the way the component can be implemented.

In practice interfaces are described using textual documents or modelling languages such as UML or WSDL. Unfortunately, such specifications are ambiguous and thus are subject to interpretation. We instead recommend relying on mathematically sound formalisms to reduce ambiguities. In this context, the vibrant research area of *compositional reasoning* [20] gives the foundations that allow to

F.S. de Boer et al. (Eds.): FMCO 2009, LNCS 6286, pp. 290–310, 2010.

reason about properties of the global system based on properties of individual components. The essential advantage of compositional reasoning is its support for safe reuse of components, well known from other engineering disciplines.

Building specification theories is a subject of intensive studies [11, 14]. One particularly successful direction are interface automata [14, 15, 23, 31]. In this framework, an interface is represented by an input/output automaton [29], where transitions are typed as *input* and *output*. The semantics is given by a two-player game: the *input* player represents the environment, and the *output* player represents the component itself. Contrary to the input/output model of [29], this semantic offers an optimistic treatment of composition: two interfaces can be composed if there exists an environment in which they can safely interact.

The existing interface theories focus primarily on composition (and sometimes on refinement). There hardly exist supporting tools that could be used by engineers. Over the years of interaction with industrial partners, we have collected the following requirements for interfaces theories. Notice that they significantly exceed the usual scope of studying composition and refinement.

1. It should be decidable whether an interface admits an implementation.[1]
2. There must be a mechanism to safely replace a component by another one. Technically this corresponds to the requirements of precongruence and completeness for *Refinement*. Refinement (written $\leq$), which is a preorder on the set of interfaces, should satisfy the following property:
   Every implementation satisfying a refinement of an interface should also satisfy this interface.
3. To control design complexity, one should be able to decide whether there exists an interface that refines two different interfaces (a *shared refinement*).
4. Different aspects of systems are often specified by different teams. The issue of dealing with multiple aspects or multiple viewpoints is thus essential. It should be possible to represent several interfaces (viewpoints) for the same component, and to combine then in a conjunctive fashion. Conjunction (written $\wedge$) should satisfy the following property:
   Given two viewpoints represented by two interfaces, any implementation that satisfies the conjunction must satisfy the two viewpoints.
5. The framework should provide a combination operation reflecting the standard interaction between systems. It should respect the refinement to support independent development:
   Given two implementations of two interfaces, the composition of the implementations satisfies the composition of their interfaces.
6. It should be possible to factor in existing components into general requirements, in order to facilitate reuse of accumulated assets. In interface theories this is realized using a quotient operator.
7. Conjunction and composition must be associative and commutative, so that the emergent behaviour of the system depends only on the specifications, not on the order in which they have been combined.

[1] In our theory, an implementation shall not be viewed as a program in a concrete programming language but rather as an abstract mathematical object that represents a set of programs sharing common properties.

8. There must exist a specification language to specify properties of interfaces as well as a procedure to decide whether the interface satisfies the properties.
9. All the above operations and properties should be performed and checked with efficient algorithms.
10. User-friendly tools providing comprehensible feedback to the user must be available. For example, if an implementation violates a specification, a useful feedback inspires the designer on how to correct it.

In [16], a timed extension of the theory of interface automata has been introduced, motivated by the fact that time can be a crucial parameter in practice, for example in embedded systems. The results of [16] focus mostly on structural composition. Recently [12] we have proposed what seems to be the first complete interface theory for timed systems (with respect to the above requirements). Our specifications are *timed* input/output automata [21]—timed automata whose sets of discrete transitions are split into *input* and *output* transitions. Contrary to [16] and [21] our theory distinguishes between implementations and specifications. This is done by assuming that the former have fixed timing behaviour and they can always advance either by producing an output or delaying. The theory also provides a game-based algorithm to decide whether a specification is consistent, i.e. whether it has at least one implementation. The latter reduces to deciding existence of a strategy that despite the behaviour of the environment will avoid states that cannot possibly satisfy the implementation requirements.

A *pruning* facility removes all the states not covered by the strategy. It can drastically reduce the state-space of the system. Following a similar principle, it is possible to constrain an interface with a timed temporal logic formula [1]. For example, like in [16], one can use a Büchi objective to remove states allowing Zeno behaviours. Our theory is rich in the sense that it captures all the good operations for a compositional design theory presented above. Also all the algorithms have been implemented. This implementation (available at [36]) comes as an extension of the UPPAAL-TIGA tool-set [3]. UPPAAL-TIGA is a tool that implements a series of algorithms for solving timed games [9] as well as checking timed temporal logic properties. Working within UPPAAL-TIGA allows us to propose a state-of-the-art user interface for verification tools.

In this paper our objectives are (1) to give more insight into design choices made in [12], (2) to report on challenges of the implementation, (3) to discuss design methodologies compatible with our theory, (4) to evaluate the implementation, and (5) to compare our results with other results in the same field.

2 Specifications and Implementations

We shall now introduce our component model.

Definition 1. *A Timed I/O Transition System (TIOTS) is a quadruple* $S = (St^S, s_0, \Sigma^S, \rightarrow^S)$*, where* St^S *is an infinite set of states,* $s_0 \in St$ *is the initial state,* $\Sigma^S = \Sigma_{\mathrm{i}}^S \oplus \Sigma_{\mathrm{o}}^S$ *is a finite set of actions partitioned into inputs* (Σ_{i}^S) *and outputs* (Σ_{o}^S) *and* $\rightarrow^S : St^S \times (\Sigma^S \cup \mathbb{R}_{\geq 0}) \times St^S$ *is a transition relation. We* *write* $s \xrightarrow{a}^{S} s'$ *instead of* $(s, a, s') \in \rightarrow^{S}$ *and use* $i?$, $o!$ *and* d *to range over inputs, outputs and* $\mathbb{R}_{\geq 0}$ *respectively. In addition any TIOTS satisfies the following:*

[time determinism] whenever $s \xrightarrow{d}^{S} s'$ *and* $s \xrightarrow{d}^{S} s''$ *then* $s' = s''$

[time reflexivity] $s \xrightarrow{0}^{S} s$ *for all* $s \in St^{S}$

[time additivity] for all $s, s'' \in St^{S}$ *and all* $d_1, d_2 \in \mathbb{R}_{\geq 0}$ *we have* $s \xrightarrow{d_1 + d_2}^{S} s''$ *iff* $s \xrightarrow{d_1}^{S} s'$ *and* $s' \xrightarrow{d_2}^{S} s''$ *for an* $s' \in St^{S}$

TIOTSs are semantic objects that represent timed interactive processes. In our framework we use *Timed I/O Automata* as a syntactic domain in which *specifications* and *implementations* are represented.

Definition 2. *A* Timed I/O Automaton *(TIOA) is a tuple* $A = (Loc, q_0, Clk, E, Act, Inv)$ *where* Loc *is a finite set of locations,* $q_0 \in Loc$ *is the initial location,* Clk *is a finite set of clocks,* $E \subseteq Loc \times Act \times \mathcal{B}(Clk) \times \mathscr{P}(Clk) \times Loc$ *is a set of edges with* $\mathcal{B}(Clk)$ *being a set of clock constraints,* $Act = Act_{\mathrm{i}} \oplus Act_{\mathrm{o}}$ *is a finite set of actions, partitioned into inputs and outputs respectively, and* $Inv : Loc \mapsto \mathcal{B}(Clk)$ *is a set of location invariants.*

As for timed automata, a *state* of A is a pair (q, V) where q is a location and $V : Clk \mapsto \mathbb{R}_{\geq 0}$ is a *valuation function* that assigns a non-negative value to each clock in Clk. We write $u + d$ to denote a valuation such that for any clock r we have $(u + d)(r) = x + d$ iff $u(r) = x$. Given $d \in \mathbb{R}_{\geq 0}$, we write $u[r \mapsto 0]_{r \in c}$ for a valuation which agrees with u on all values for clocks not in c, and returns 0 for all clocks in c. We use $\mathbf{0}$ to denote the constant function mapping all clocks to zero. The *initial state* of A is the pair $(q_0, \mathbf{0})$.

We visualise TIOAs using classical Timed Automata notation, extending it with two types of transitions (inputs and outputs). See example in Figure 1.

The semantics of a TIOA $A = (Loc, q_0, Clk, E, Act, Inv)$ is a TIOTS $[\![A]\!]_{\mathrm{sem}} = (Loc \times (Clk \mapsto \mathbb{R}_{\geq 0}), (q_0, \mathbf{0}), Act, \rightarrow)$, where $\rightarrow$ is the largest transition relation generated by the following rules:

- Each $(q, a, \varphi, c, q') \in E$ gives rise to $(q, u) \xrightarrow{a} (q', u')$ for each clock valuation $u \in [Clk \mapsto \mathbb{R}_{\geq 0}]$ such that $u \models \varphi$ and $u' = u[r \mapsto 0]_{r \in c}$ and $u' \models Inv(q')$.
- Each location $q \in Loc$ with a valuation $u \in [Clk \mapsto \mathbb{R}_{\geq 0}]$ gives rise to a transition $(q, u) \xrightarrow{d} (q, u + d)$ for each delay $d \in \mathbb{R}_{\geq 0}$ such that $u + d \models Inv(q)$.

Observe that the TIOTSs induced by a TIOAs naturally satisfy the three axioms of Definition 1. In the rest of the paper, we will only consider deterministic TIOAs, whose corresponding TIOTSs are deterministic.

A TIOTS represents a two-player *timed game* [9]. The *Input* player (the environment) controls the input transitions of the TIOTS. The *Output* player (the system) controls the output transitions. The formal definitions of strategy and move outcomes for such a game are given in [12]. The set of *winning states* from which one of the players has a strategy to satisfy a safety or a reachability objective can be computed with algorithms presented in [9]—efficient symbolic versions of well-known controller synthesis algorithms of [30].

We now define implementations and specifications in terms of TIOAs.

Definition 3. *A specification automaton is a TIOA that is input-enabled, i.e., in each state all the inputs should be available.*

The assumption of input-enabledness, also seen in many interface theories [28, 18, 34, 37, 32], reflects our belief that an input cannot be prevented from being sent to a system, but it might be unpredictable how the system behaves after receiving it. Input-enabledness encourages explicit modelling of this unpredictability, and compositional reasoning about it; for example, deciding if an unpredictable behaviour of one component induces unpredictability of the entire system. Observe that it is easy to check whether a TIOA is input-enabled. In practice tools can interpret absent input transitions in at least two reasonable ways. First, they can be interpreted as ignored inputs, corresponding to location loops in the automaton. Second, they may be seen as unavailable ('blocking') inputs, which can be achieved by assuming implicit transitions to a designated error state. Later, in Section 4.2 we will call such a state *strictly undesirable* and give a rationale for this name.

The role of specifications in a specification theory is to abstract, or underspecify, sets of possible implementations. *Implementations* are concrete executable realizations of systems. We will assume that implementations of timed systems have fixed timing behaviour (outputs occur at predictable times) and systems can always advance either by producing an output or delaying. Formally:

Definition 4. *An implementation is a specification that satisfies the two following conditions:*

1. **Independent progress:** *implementations cannot get stuck in a state where it is up to the environment to induce progress. In each implementation state either an output is possible or one can delay until an output is enabled.*
2. **Output urgency:** *if an output is available, then it cannot be delayed.*

Since specifications and implementations are TIOAs, their semantics are still given in terms of TIOTs. We refer the interested reader to [12] for more details.

Example. Figure 1a specifies a vending machine that can serve tea or coffee. A possible implementation of this machine can be found in Figure 1b. Both automata are deterministic. Note that the output transitions of the implementation Impl arrive at a fixed moment in time and cannot be delayed, which guarantees output urgency (the invariant guarantees progress and the guard constrains the transition). Each time the output tea! from Idle to Idle is taken, the clock y is reset. Without this reset, independent progress would not be guaranteed for valuations of the clock y that are greater than 6.

We now introduce *refinement*—a notion of comparison between two specifications and a way to relate implementations to specifications. Refinement should satisfy the following *substitutability* condition. If A_S refines A_T, it should be possible to replace A_T with A_S in every context and obtain an equivalent system. Contrary to the other operations, refinement is defined at the level of TIOTSs.

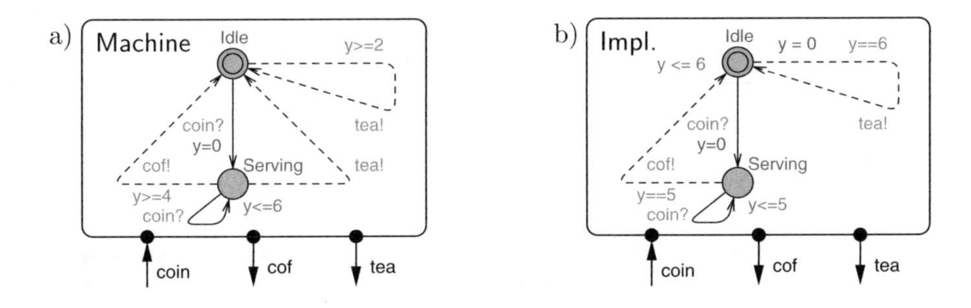

Fig. 1. a) Specification of a coffee and tea Machine and b) an implementation

Definition 5. *Let A_S and A_T be two specification automata and $S = (St^S, s_0, \Sigma, \rightarrow^S)$ and $T = (St^T, t_0, \Sigma, \rightarrow^T)$ be their corresponding timed transition systems. We say that A_S refines A_T, written $A_S \leq A_T$, iff there exists a binary relation $R \subseteq St^S \times St^T$ containing (s_0, t_0) and for all states sRt implies:*

1. *whenever $t \xrightarrow{i?}{}^T t'$ for some $t' \in St^T$ then $s \xrightarrow{i?}{}^S s'$ and $s'Rt'$ for some $s' \in St^S$*
2. *whenever $s \xrightarrow{o!}{}^S s'$ for some $s' \in St^S$ then $t \xrightarrow{o!}{}^T t'$ and $s'Rt'$ for some $t' \in St^T$*
3. *whenever $s \xrightarrow{d}{}^S s'$ for $d \in \mathbb{R}_{\geq 0}$ then $t \xrightarrow{d}{}^T t'$ and $s'Rt'$ for some $t' \in St^T$*

It is easy to see that the refinement is reflexive and transitive, so it is a preorder on the set of all specifications. Refinement can be checked for specification automata by reducing the problem to a specific refinement game, and using a symbolic representation to reason about it. See Section 5 for more details.

Satisfaction is a simple application of refinement. More precisely, we say that an implementation satisfies a specification automaton iff it refines this specification. As an example, observe that the automaton in Figure 1b is a refinement of the one in Figure 1a, and thus it is also an implementation of it.

The set of all implementations of A is denoted $[\![A]\!]_{\text{mod}}$. In [12], we have shown that the refinement relation is complete for our specification model, i.e, A_S refines A_T iff the set of implementations that satisfy A_S is included in the set of implementations that satisfy A_T.

A specification may be *locally inconsistent* in the sense that it may contain *bad states*, i.e., states that do not satisfy the *independent progress* property[2]. We say that a specification is *consistent*, and thus useful, if it admits at least one implementation. It is important to have a procedure to decide whether a specification admits at least one implementation. In [12], we have shown that this question reduces to the one of deciding if there exists a strategy for the system (Output player) to avoid reaching *bad states* in the specification. A *pruning* facility removes from the TIOA all the behaviours that are not covered by the strategy. It can drastically reduce the state-space of the automaton. In the rest of the paper, we assume that bad states are always pruned away.

[2] In section 4, we shall observe that the combination of two specifications without bad states may lead to a specification with bad states.

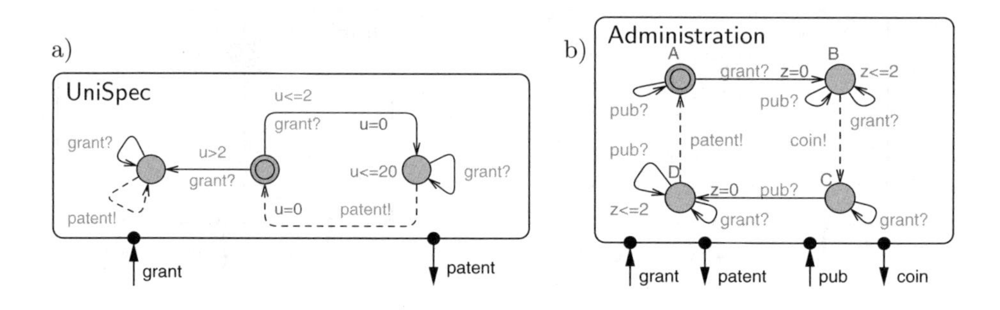

Fig. 2. a) University specification UniSpec. b) Specification of an Administration.

3 Design Methodologies

In the following we introduce three different development methodologies supported by our framework. These development methodologies are in no way in conflict with each other, but should more be seen as prototype work-flows that in a concrete development process would be combined. First we present the running example that will be used in presenting the methodologies.

The example is based on a very simplified view of a modern university. The purpose of the university is to file as many patents as possible. More precisely the requirements imposed on the university is given by the TIOA UniSpec as presented in Figure 2a. The border around the specification shows the input and output sort by incoming and outgoing arrows respectively. The initial state of the specification is marked by a double circled state. Given that the university receives a grant (solid transition marked with grant?) after a delay of less than two time units it will output (dashed transition marked with patent!) a patent within the next 20 time units. If the first grant comes after more than two time units or any subsequent grant comes more than two time units after a patent has been filed then the behaviour of the university becomes unpredictable, which is modelled by the leftmost state in the specification.

Stepwise Refinement. The first methodology presented is the classic top-down development through *stepwise decomposition and refinement.* Starting from the overall specification of Figure 2a one can refine this into a specification that contains several parallel components. The refinement is based on a knowledge of how the system under design is supposed to meet the overall requirements. This refined specification can again be refined further, until the desired level of detail has been reached. It is important to note that the *independent implementability* property allows for these refinement steps to be taken for individual components, greatly increasing the scalability of the framework through compositional design.

We will decompose the University specification into three components: an Administration, a Coffee/Tea machine and a Researcher. The responsibility of the Administration (Figure 2b) is to convert the grants provided to the University into coins that can be used in the coffee and tea machine. The coffee and tea

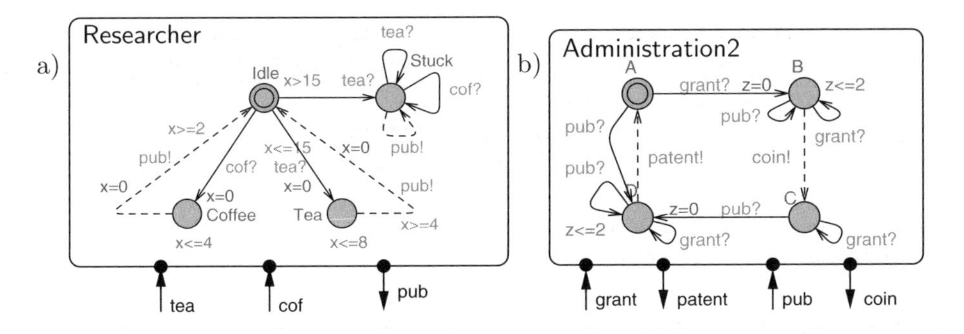

Fig. 3. Specifications for the a) Researcher and b) Administration2

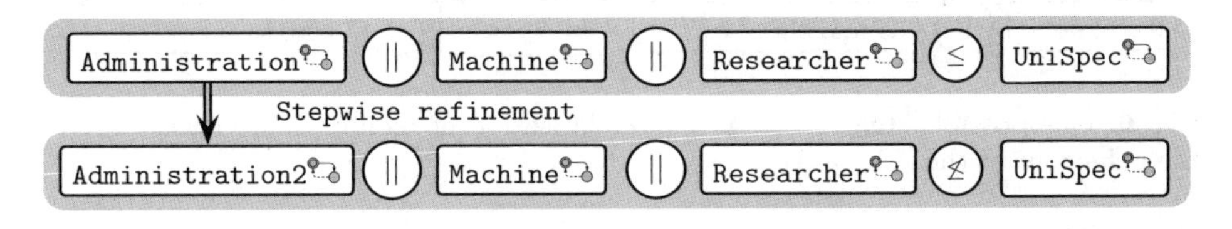

Fig. 4. One possible step in Top-down development: Modifying a component and rechecking refinement

Machine (Figure 1a) will then in turn provide the Researcher (Figure 3a) with coffee and tea so that the researcher can produce publications. The Administration component also has the responsibility of converting publications into patents.

The top line in Figure 4 shows a successful refinement check which shows that the three components together refine the overall specification.

The bottom part of Figure 4 shows an additional step in the refinement process. Here a single component is updated (Administration to Administration2). This new version (Figure 3b) differs in a single transition. If it receives a publication (pub?) in the initial, left most state, then it will not loop but instead shift to the lower left state indicating that it is ready to output a patent based on this publication. This new version of the administration is thus able to receive and process free publications that it has not payed for.

Figure 4 shows that the refinement check fails after this update of the model. By the independent implementability property this could also have been discovered by checking whether Administration2 refines Administration, which indeed it does not. This might come as a surprise to the developer as it seems like a reasonable improvement to be able to accept free publications. We defer the discussion of how to solve this issue to Section 5.

In stepwise refinement this step of decomposing and refining individual components is applied iteratively, until a suitable level of detail is reached.

Bottom-up Synthesis. The second development methodology that our framework supports is a bottom-up development process through *stepwise composition.* Here we assume that actual implementations of some components already exist and

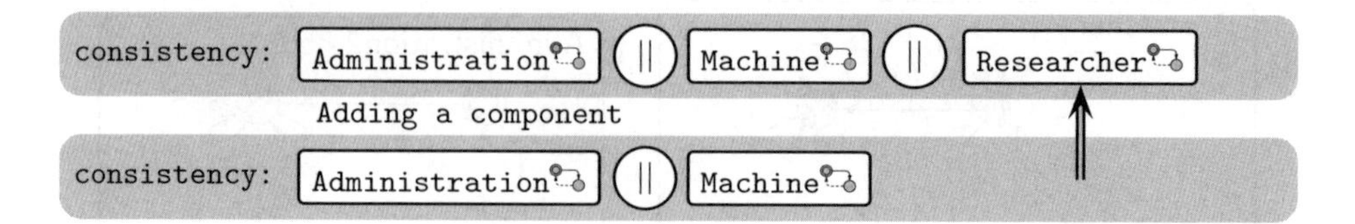

Fig. 5. One possible step in Bottom-up development: Checking consistency before and after adding an extra component

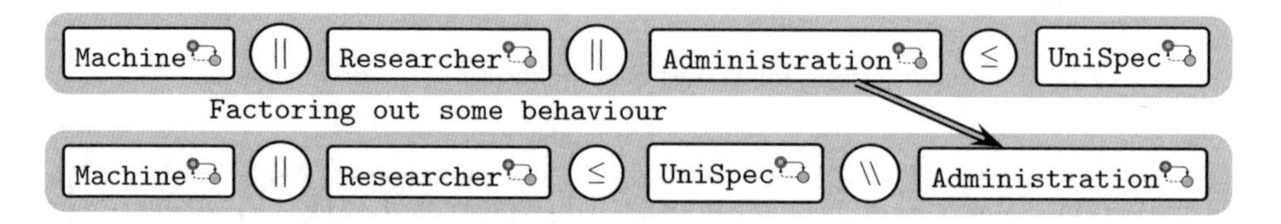

Fig. 6. One possible step in Stepwise modularisation of requirements: Factoring out the behaviour of the Administration

that models are made that describe the behaviour of these components. The aim of the bottom-up development in our setting is to verify that a complete system can be built from the preexisting components. Figure 5 shows one possible step in a bottom-up development process. Here a consistency check is performed on the parallel composition of two components after which another component is added and the consistency check is redone. The bottom up development methodology could easily be combined with refinement checking where the overall requirements are stepwise refined to see what the actual combination of components can guarantee in terms of behaviour and timing.

Stepwise Modularisation of Requirements. The third and more novel type of development methodology that our framework supports is the *Stepwise modularisation of requirements.* Here the idea is, like for the *top-down development* to start with a general specification of the requirements to the system and then using the *quotient* operator to factor out behaviour that is already implemented by existing components, so that one is left with a specification for the missing behaviour. This specification, which is synthesised by the tool, can now be further refined to provide the implementation of missing functionality in terms of new components. In that this process generalises stepwise refinement and bottom-up synthesis. Figure 6 shows how one component can be moved from one side of the refinement check to the other by factoring out the behaviour.

Another aspect of our framework that can be used orthogonally to the three described development ideas is conjunction. Conjunction allows to specify different aspects or requirements to a component and then compose these using logical conjunction, such that an implementation would have to individually satisfy each conjunct in order to satisfy the conjunction. Figure 7 shows an example of two specifications that each handle one aspect of the responsibilities

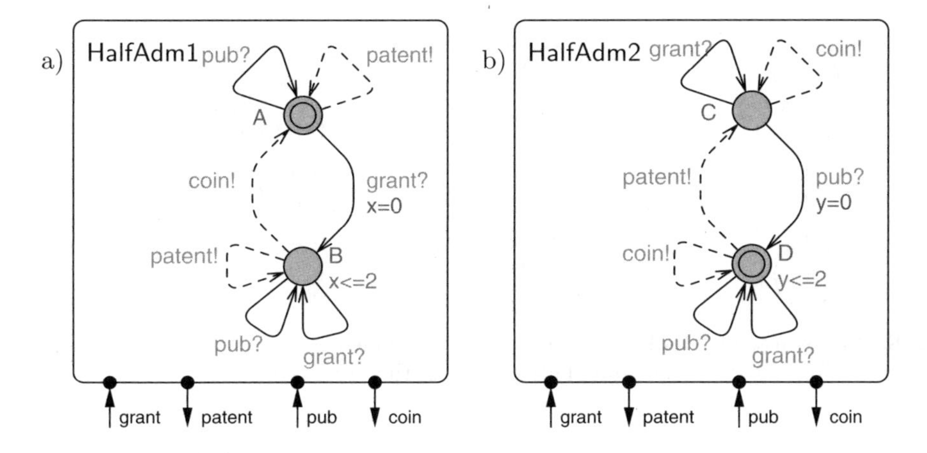

Fig. 7. Example of two conjuncts, each handling one aspect, that make up a different model of the Administration component

of the Administration component. Figure 7a describes an alternation between the coin! and grant? while Figure 7b describes the alternation between patent! and pub?. Together these form an alternative and slightly more loose specification of the administration. It is the case that both Administration and Administration2 refine the conjunction HalfAdm1∧HalfAdm2, while the opposite is not the case.

Finally the tool is able to verify TCTL* [1] properties on the specifications. This feature is made possible thanks to the modified underlying verification engine. This will be exemplified in section 5.

4 Combining Specification Automata

In this section, we discuss the three main operations defined on specification automata, namely: conjunction, composition, and quotient. All of these were used to support different design processes described in the previous section.

In the rest of the section, we will consider two specification automata $A_S = (Loc_1, q_0^1, Clk_1, E_1, Act^1, Inv_1)$ and $A_T = (Loc_2, q_0^2, Clk_2, E_2, Act^2, Inv_2)$. For technical reasons, we also assume that $Clk_1 \cap Clk_2 = \emptyset$.

4.1 Conjunction

Conjunction allows to test whether several specifications can be simultaneously met by the same component. In our framework, conjunction can only be defined if $Act_i^S = Act_i^T$ and $Act_o^S = Act_o^T$. The operation reduces to check whether the two specifications can progress in the same way. Formally the conjunction of A_S and A_T, denoted $A_S \wedge A_T$, is the TIOA $A = (Loc, q_0, Clk, E, Act^S, Inv)$ given by: $Loc = Loc_S \times Loc_T$, $q_0 = (q_0^S, q_0^T)$, $Clk = Clk_S \uplus Clk_T$, $Inv((q_S, q_T)) = Inv(q_S) \wedge Inv(q_T)$. The set of edges E is defined by the following rule:

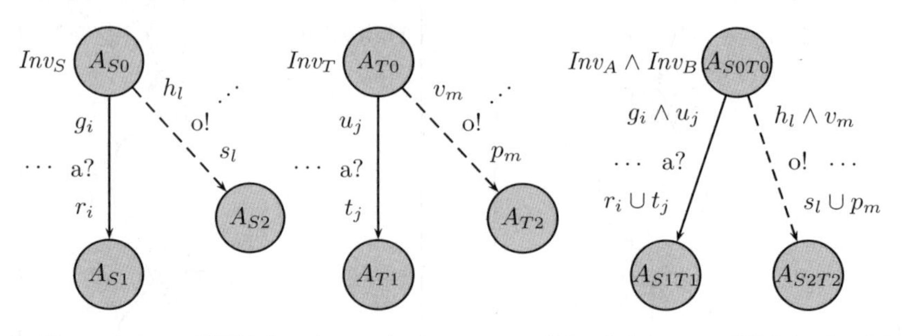

Fig. 8. Two states of TIOAs A_S and A_T are combined into one TIOA A with the conjunction operator for one step. This process is then iterated.

- If $(q_S, a, \varphi_S, c_S, q'_S) \in E_S$ and $(q_T, a, \varphi_T, c_T, q'_T) \in E_T$ this gives rise to $((q_S, q_T), a, \varphi_S \wedge \varphi_T, c_S \cup c_T, (q'_S, q'_T)) \in E$.

An example of how the conjunction of two specific states from two different TIOA with example input and output transitions will look is given in Figure 4.1.

Conjunction may introduce locally inconsistent states. For example, assume that A_S reaches a state from s where the only available action is the output a and A_T reaches a state t from where the only available action is the output b. Assume also that A_S and A_T cannot delay in s and t. In (s, t), the conjunction will not issue any output and will not be able to delay, which violates the *independent progress* property. As stated in Section 2, locally inconsistent states can be removed with the help of a pruning operation. In the rest of the paper, we assume that each conjunction is immediately followed by a pruning.

In [12], we have shown the following results:

- The set of implementations satisfying a conjunction is the intersection of the implementation sets of the operands: $[\![(A_S \wedge A_T)]\!]_{\text{mod}} = [\![A_S]\!]_{\text{mod}} \cap [\![A_T]\!]_{\text{mod}}$.
- The conjunction of A_S and A_T corresponds to the greatest lower bound of their implementations sets: if $A \leq A_S$ and $A \leq A_T$ we have that $A \leq A_S \wedge A_T$.
- The conjunction operation (also if combined with pruning) is associative and commutative, so among others: $[\![(A_S \wedge A_T) \wedge A_U]\!]_{\text{mod}} = [\![A_S \wedge (A_T \wedge A_U)]\!]_{\text{mod}}$.

4.2 Composition

We shall now define *structural composition*, also called *parallel composition*, between specifications. Roughly speaking, this operation computes the classical product between timed specifications [21], where components synchronise on common inputs/outputs. Two components are *composable* iff the intersection between their output alphabets is empty. Formally the *parallel composition* of A_S with A_T, denoted $A_S || A_T$, is the TIOA $A = (Loc, q_0, Clk, E, Act, Inv)$ given by: $Loc = Loc_S \times Loc_T$, $q_0 = (q_0^S, q_0^T)$, $Clk = Clk_S \uplus Clk_T$, $Inv((q_S, q_T)) = Inv(q_S) \wedge Inv(q_T)$ and the set of actions $Act = Act_i \uplus Act_o$ is given by $Act_i =$

$Act_i^S \setminus Act_o^T \cup Act_i^T \setminus Act_o^S$ and $Act_o = Act_o^S \cup Act_o^T$. The set of edges E is defined by the following rules:

1. If $(q_S, a, \varphi_S, c_S, q'_S) \in E_S$ with $a \in Act_S \setminus Act_T$ then for each $q_T \in Loc_T$ this gives $((q_S, q_T), a, \varphi_S, c_S, (q'_S, q_T)) \in E$
2. If $(q_T, a, \varphi_T, c_T, q'_T) \in E_T$ with $a \in Act_T \setminus Act_S$ then for each $q_S \in Loc_S$ this gives $((q_S, q_T), a, \varphi_S, c_S, (q_S, q'_T)) \in E$
3. If $(q_S, a, \varphi_S, c_S, q'_S) \in E_S$ and $(q_T, a, \varphi_T, c_T, q'_T) \in E_T$ with $a \in Act_S \cap Act_T$ this gives rise to $((q_S, q_T), a, \varphi_S \wedge \varphi_T, c_S \cup c_T, (q'_S, q'_T)) \in E$.

The first rule represent all the cases where A_S makes an individual move, be it input or output, because a is not in the signature of A_T. Similarly the second rule handles all individual moves by the second component A_T. The third rule handles all synchronisations between the two components, no matter the combination of input and/or output. The rule is so simple because the type of the resulting transition is given by the sets Act_i and Act_o. The new output set, Act_o, is just a simple union of the outputs, while the input set, Act_i, is all the inputs that are not outputs of the other component.

Observe that if we compose two locally-consistent specifications using the above product rules, then the resulting product is also locally consistent. Moreover, unlike [16], our specifications are input-enabled, and there is no way to define an error state in which a component can issue an output that cannot be captured by the other component. The absence of "model-related" error states allows us to define more elaborated errors specified by the designer [12]. As an example, a temporal property written in some logic such as TCTL* can be interpreted over our specification, which when analysed by a model checker, will result in partitioning of the states into good ones (say satisfying the property) and bad ones (violating the property).

In contrast to conjunction, parallel composition is used to reason about external use of two (or more) components. We assume an independent implementation scenario, where the two composed components are implemented by independent designers. The designer of any of the environment components can only assume that the composed implementations will adhere to original specifications being composed. Consequently if an error occurs in parallel composition of the two specifications, the *environment* is the only entity that is possibly in a position to avoid it. Thus, each composition is followed by a pruning operation where all the states from which the environment has no strategy to avoid the set of bad states are removed.

In [12], we have shown the following important results regarding composition.

- Any implementation of composition can be realized by implementations of composed specifications: $[\![(A_S||A_T)]\!]_{\mathrm{mod}} = [\![A_S]\!]_{\mathrm{mod}}||[\![A_T]\!]_{\mathrm{mod}}$.
- The composition operation (also if combined with a pruning) is associative and commutative, so among others: $[\![(A_S||A_T)||A_U]\!]_{\mathrm{mod}} = [\![A_S||(A_T||A_U)]\!]_{\mathrm{mod}}$.
- Refinement is a precongruence with respect to parallel composition; for any specifications A_S, A_T, and A_U such that $A_S \leq A_T$ and A_S composable with

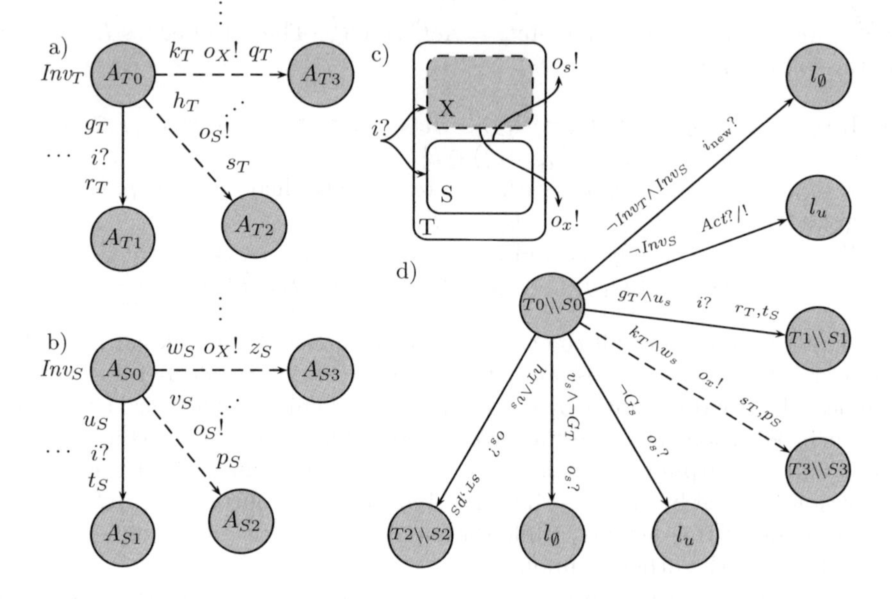

Fig. 9. Initial states of two example TIOA a) A_T, b) A_S, c) an overview of the communication flow and d) the initial state of the resulting quotient

A_U, we have that A_T composable with A_U and $A_S||A_U \leq A_T||A_U$. Moreover if A_T compatible with A_U then A_S compatible with A_U.

4.3 Quotient

An essential operator in a complete specification theory is the one of *quotienting*. It allows for factoring out behaviour from a larger component. If one has a large component specification A_T and a small one A_S then $A_T \backslash\backslash A_S$ is the specification of exactly those components that when composed with A_S refine A_T. In other words, $A_T \backslash\backslash A_S$ specifies the work that still needs to be done, given availability of an implementation of A_S, in order to provide an implementation of A_T. This is a non trivial operation which reduces to synthesis of a timed game. To the best of our knowledge, we are the first to compute the quotient in a timed setting.

We require that for the dividend A_T and the divisor A_S the following relations on action sets hold: $\Sigma_{\mathrm{i}}^S \subseteq \Sigma_{\mathrm{i}}^T$ and $\Sigma_{\mathrm{o}}^S \subseteq \Sigma_{\mathrm{o}}^T$. If these requirements on the input and output sets are met, then the quotient of A_T by A_S, which is denoted $A_T \backslash\backslash A_S$ is the TIOA given by: $Loc = Loc_T \times Loc_S \cup \{l_u, l_\emptyset\}$, $q_0 = (q_0^T, q_0^S)$, $Clk = Clk_T \uplus Clk_S \uplus \{x_{\mathrm{new}}\}$, $Inv((q_T, q_S)) = Inv(l_u) = \mathit{true}$ and $Inv(l_\emptyset) = \{x_{\mathrm{new}} \leq 0\}$. The two new states l_u and $l_\emptyset$ are respectively universal and inconsistent. The set of actions $Act = Act_i \uplus Act_o$ is given by $Act_i = Act_i^T \cup Act_o^S \cup \{i_{\mathrm{new}}\}$ and $Act_o = Act_o^T \setminus Act_o^S$. The set of edges E is defined by the following rules:

1. if $q_T \in Loc_T, q_S \in Loc_S, a \in Act$ then $((q_T, q_S), a, \neg Inv_S(q_S), \{x_{\mathrm{new}}\}, l_u) \in E$
2. if $q_T \in Loc_T, q_S \in Loc_S$ then $((q_T, q_S), i_{\mathrm{new}}, \neg Inv_T(q_T) \wedge Inv_S(q_S), \{x_{\mathrm{new}}\}, l_\emptyset) \in E$

3. if $(q_T, a, \varphi_T, c_T, q'_T) \in E_T$ and $(q_S, a, \varphi_S, c_S, q'_S) \in E_S$ this gives $((q_T, q_S), a, \varphi_T \wedge \varphi_S, c_T \cup c_S, (q'_T, q'_S)) \in E$
4. for each $(q_S, a, \varphi_S, c_S, q'_S) \in E_S$ with $a \in Act_o^S$ this gives rise to $((q_T, q_S), a, \varphi_S \wedge \neg G_T, \{x_{\text{new}}\}, l_\emptyset)$ where $G_T = \bigvee\{\varphi_T \mid (q_T, a, \varphi_T, c_T, q'_T)\}$
5. if $(q_T, a, \varphi_T, c_T, q'_T) \in E_T$, $a \notin Act_S$ then $((q_T, q_S), a, \varphi_T, c_T, (q'_T, q_S)) \in E$
6. for each $(q_T, a, \varphi_T, c_T, q'_T) \in E_T$ with $a \in Act_o^S$ this gives rise to $((q_T, q_S), a, \neg G_S, \{\}, l_u)$ where $G_S = \bigvee\{\varphi_S \mid (q_S, a, \varphi_S, c_S, q'_S)\}$
7. for each $a \in Act_i$ this gives rise to $(l_\emptyset, a, x_{\text{new}} = 0, \{\}, l_\emptyset)$
8. for each $a \in Act$ this gives rise to $(l_u, a, \mathit{true}, \{\}, l_u)$

The quotients input set, Act_i, consists of the inputs to the outer component A_T and the outputs of the existing inner component A_S (See Figure 9c) and a new fresh input action i_{new}. The output set of the quotient, Act_o, is simply the output set of the outer component, A_T, minus the outputs handled by the existing inner component A_S. The resulting quotient has two new special states l_u and $l_\emptyset$. The first *universal* state, l_u, represents all the cases where the existing inner component A_s has violated the guarantees of the outer component A_T and thus there are no restrictions on the future behaviour of the quotient. The second *inconsistent* state, $l_\emptyset$, represents all the cases where the quotient by taking this action would itself violate the assumptions of the other components.

In the above definition we have eight rules. The first rule creates a new transition leading to the *universal* state with a guard that equals the original invariant of the existing inner specification. The second rule reflects the case where the invariant of A_T is not satisfied while the invariant of A_S is. The third rule handles all regular synchronisation where the guards of both components are satisfied. The fourth rule handles the case where the inner component generates an output at a time where it is not allowed by any of the matching guards in the outer component A_T. The fifth rule handles the cases where A_T takes an action which is not in the action set of A_S. The sixth rule represents all the cases where A_T takes an action which is not allowed by any of the matching guards in A_S thus leading to the universal state. Finally the seventh rule makes the $l_\emptyset$ state inconsistent and the eighth rule ensures that the universal state has all possible behaviour. Figure 9 illustrates one step in the computation of a quotient.

Like Conjunction, the quotient operation may produce (locally) inconsistent specifications. Hence, each quotient operation has to be followed by a pruning.

In [12], we have shown that the quotient operation produces the most liberal specification with respect to refinement. Formally we have the following theorem.

Theorem 1. *For any two specification automata A_S and A_T such that the quotient is defined, and for any implementation X over the same alphabet as $T\backslash\backslash S$ we have that $S||X$ is defined and $S||X \leq T$ iff $X \leq T\backslash\backslash S$.*

5 Tool Implementation

We begin with summarising the functionality of the tool, and proceed later to present a running example.

Our specification theory has been implemented as an extension of UPPAAL-TIGA [3], which is an engine for solving timed games. We have made two major modifications to the original engine. The first modification was to enrich the input language in order to allow for the description of specifications/implementations and operations between them; the second one was to modify the timed-game algorithms in order to take the compositional reasoning methodology into account.

Modelling Language. The input syntax of UPPAAL-TIGA is identical to the one of UPPAAL [4, 26] – a tool for specifying, combining and verifying properties of timed automata. The user-friendly interface of UPPAAL is divided in two parts: 1) the *specification interface* where automata are specified in a graphical manner, and 2) the *query interface* where one can ask verification questions. The main difference between the input language of UPPAAL-TIGA and UPPAAL is that, due to the game interpretation, transitions are typed with control modalities. The specification interface of our tool is similar to the one of UPPAAL-TIGA, except that we decorate transitions with *input* and *output* modalities, which allows the user to specify timed I/O automata. Like timed automata, interfaces can communicate via broadcast channels, but global variables are not permitted. The query interface allows the user to (a) check whether a TIOA is a proper implementation or a specification, (b) to apply composition operations and (c) to check refinement relations. More details can be found at [36].

Each time we specify a TIOA, the tool automatically checks whether it is deterministic and input-enabled. In case of an implementation, the tool also checks whether it satisfies the output urgency and independent progress properties. Also, the tool automatically computes the set of states for which the specification is consistent. When the specification is combined with another one, this information is used in order to avoid involving bad states.

Timed Interface Operators. We have implemented the composition, conjunction, and refinement operators. Quotient is being implemented. These operators are available from the query interface. We now give details regarding the modifications we have made on the original version of UPPAAL-TIGA.

As we have seen, the operations of *conjunction*, *composition*, and *quotienting* may produce specifications with *bad* states. Such states need to be identified and pruned away. For doing so, we have adapted the game algorithm implemented in UPPAAL-TIGA. The main challenge, in terms of implementation, is that the original algorithms work on fixed input automata. In our case the automata are not known in advance since they result from the successive pruning operations.

The problem of checking whether A_S refines A_T reduces to the one of solving a timed game between two players on the graph-product of A_S and A_T [12]. The first player, or *attacker*, plays outputs on A_S and inputs on A_T, whereas the second player, or *defender*, plays inputs on A_S and outputs on A_T. One can show that Refinement does not hold if and only if the attacker can put the defender in a bad state. There are two kinds of bad states in this game: 1) the attacker may delay and violates invariants on A_T, which is, the defender cannot match a delay, and 2) the defender has to play a given action and cannot do so, i.e., a deadlock with respect to the game. In [8], we have proposed and implemented an efficient algorithm for solving such a game.

We illustrate the input language and the functionalities of the tool with the university example presented in Section 3. We fist consider the part of the example in which the administration is split in two parts (see Figure 7). We thus have four implementations (Machine, HalfAdm1, HalfAdm2, and Researcher) and one specification (UniSpec). All of these machines can easily be drawn in the specification interface. In the query interface, specifications and implementations are declared as follows: specification: UniSpec, and implementation: HalfAdm1. The tool automatically plays a safety-game followed by a pruning in order to remove locally inconsistent states. The tool also makes sure that the implementation and the specification satisfy Definitions 3 and 4. If this is not the case, or if the specification admit no implementation, then the tool stops.

We combine implementations with composition and conjunction operators as follows. The interface of the administration is the conjunction of two interfaces, one specifying when to output coins (after grants) and the other when to deliver a patent (after a publication). This is a better (and less restrictive approach) than to specify manually the combination of both. Then we compose the interfaces of the researcher, the university, and the machine. To check if this composition refines our original specification we check the following query

```
refinement: (Researcher || (HalfAdm1 && HalfAdm2) || Machine) <= UniSpec.
```

Figure 10 illustrates the different steps of the verification. The checker explores each component locally and prunes them from inconsistent states. The results of the exploration of the two "half-administrations" are conjuncted and pruned. Then the three automata are composed and pruned. The same is done for the specification and then the safety-game algorithm is used to check whether refinement holds. If at any step an automaton turns to be inconsistent then the check stops and the tool reports the error to the user. In this latter case, the user can invoke the simulator of UPPAAL-TIGA which will play the game until it breaks down. This information can be used to improve/change the design of the specification or of the implementation.

For the above example, it turns out that the refinement does not hold. The tool reveals that the UniSpec interface does not allow patents to be produced without a preceding grant. However, the composition allows researchers to publish with free tea, which is accepted by the conjunction of the two half administrations, which results in a patent. If we check instead

```
refinement: (Researcher || Administration || Machine) <= UniSpec.
```

with the administration of Figure 2b then the refinement holds as mentioned in Section 3 because this administration does not accept patents without grants first. However, specifying the administration manually exhibits a restricting behaviour that is not present in the cleaner conjunction of the two smaller specifications. Here the right correction would be to allow for free patents in UniSpec. The conclusion is that the user should not try to make the conjunction by hand and use conjunctions to specify more accurate specifications.

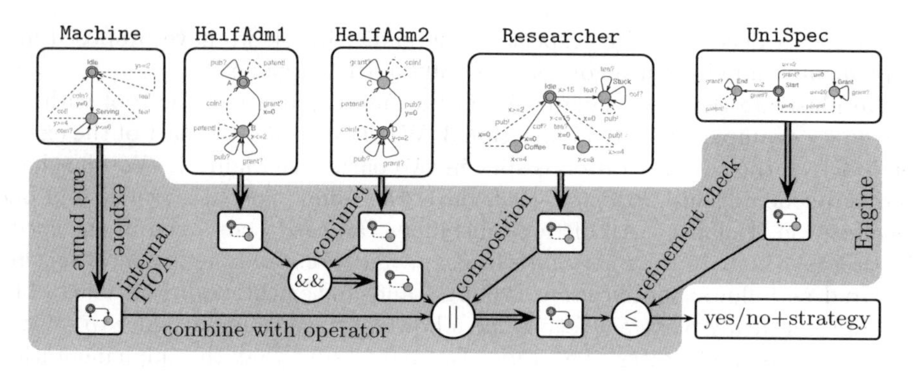

Fig. 10. Illustration of the steps performed in a concrete refinement check. The grey box represents the part carried out internally by the verification engine.

Finally, we illustrate the advantage of being capable to model check TCTL properties on TIOAs. We would like to avoid considering zeno behaviours. The idea is to combine our specification with an observer and then make sure that the observer visits infinitely often a state in which time advances. The latter can be specified with a TCTL property. The observer Obs has two states reset and advance and a witness clock w. The observer issues a non shared output from reset to advance if $w > 1$. Then it directly moves back to reset and resets the clock. The observer is then composed with the specification. There will be no synchronisation between the observer and the specification. Non zeno behaviours in the composition are those where Obs visits the state advance infinitely often. We use the following property that checks for refinement with an additional Büchi condition constraining the composition.

```
refinement: (Researcher || Administration2 || Machine || Obs
            : A[] A<> Obs.advance) <= UniSpec.
```

6 Related Work

In this section, we compare our results with other timed interface theories.

Input/Output automata model There have been several other attempts to propose an interface theory for timed systems (see [14, 16, 13, 7, 6, 10, 35, 17, 27] for some examples). Our model shall definitely be viewed as an extension of the timed input/output automaton model proposed by Lynch et al. [21]. The major differences are in the game-based treatment of interactions and the addition of quotient and conjunction operators.

Timed Interfaces by de Alfaro et al. In [16], de Alfaro et al. proposed *timed interfaces*, a timed extension of the interface model they introduced in [14]. Like for specification automata, the syntax of a timed interface is similar to the one of a *timed input/output automaton* [22] and the semantic is given by a timed game. However, unlike specification automata, timed interfaces are not forced to be deterministic or input-enabled. The absence of input-enabledness allows for defined error states in the composition where one component can issue an output that cannot be captured by the other component. Two timed interfaces are said to be compatible if there exists an environment in which they can work together while avoiding such error states. This definition of compatibility allows to capture the timing between interfaces: "what are the temporal ordering constraints on communication events between components?". Unfortunately, the work in [16] is incomplete. Indeed there is no notion of implementation and refinement. Moreover, conjunction and quotient are not studied. Also, de Alfaro et al. did not consider more elaborated error states specified by the user with some timed temporal logic. Finally, the theory has only been implemented in a prototype tool called TICC [13], which does not handle continuous time. A main drawback of TICC is its textual input language that is far from modern graphical specification languages used by engineers.

Timed Modal Specifications In [23] Larsen proposes *modal automata*, which are deterministic automata equipped with transitions of the following two types: *may* and *must*. The components that implement such interfaces are simple labelled transition systems. Roughly, a must transition is available in every component that implements the modal specification, while a may transition need not be. Recently [7, 6] a timed extension of *modal* automata was proposed, which embeds all the operations presented in the present paper. However, modalities are orthogonal to inputs and outputs, and it is well-known [24] that, contrary to the game-semantic approach, they cannot be used to distinguish between the behaviours of the component and those of the environment. Aside from the orthogonality between input/output and may/must modalities. Our model does not allow to combine/compare automata that share common clock names, while in [7, 6] they restrict themselves to even-clock automata [2] for doing so. We are convinced that our theory directly extends to an event-clock automata version of TIOA with shared clocks. Finally, our work is implemented, while the work in [7, 6] is not implemented.

7 Conclusion

We have proposed a complete game-based specification theory for real time systems, in which we distinguish between a component and the environment in which it is used. To the best of our knowledge, our contribution is the first game-based approach to support both refinement, consistency checking, logical and structural composition, and quotient. Our results have been implemented in the UPPAAL tool family [3].

In the future one could extend our model with global variables. This was already suggested by Berendsen and Vaandrager in [5], but only for structural composition and refinement and without the game-based semantic.

One could also investigate whether our approach can be used to perform scheduling of timed systems (see [13, 19, 17] for examples). For example, the quotient operation could perhaps be used to synthesise a scheduler for such problems. It would also be of interest to add stochastic features to the model.

In [33, 25], we have proposed a model which takes advantages of both interface automata and modal specifications. One should follow a similar direction in the timed setting and combine our model with the one proposed in [7, 6].

Finally, our notion of error states is still primitive and in the future we plan to allow the users to define their own error states. This will be done with the help of some temporal logic, just like it was done for a refinement in [8].

References

1. Alur, R., Dill, D.L.: A theory of timed automata. Theor. Comput. Sci. 126(2), 183–235 (1994)
2. Alur, R., Fix, L., Henzinger, T.A.: Event-clock automata: A determinizable class of timed automata. Theoretical Computer Science 211, 1–13 (1999)
3. Behrmann, G., Cougnard, A., David, A., Fleury, E., Larsen, K.G., Lime, D.: Uppaal-tiga: Time for playing games? In: Damm, W., Hermanns, H. (eds.) CAV 2007. LNCS, vol. 4590, pp. 121–125. Springer, Heidelberg (2007)
4. Behrmann, G., David, A., Larsen, K.G., Håkansson, J., Pettersson, P., Yi, W., Hendriks, M.: Uppaal 4.0. In: QEST, pp. 125–126. IEEE Computer Society, Los Alamitos (2006)
5. Berendsen, J., Vaandrager, F.W.: Compositional abstraction in real-time model checking. In: Cassez, F., Jard, C. (eds.) FORMATS 2008. LNCS, vol. 5215, pp. 233–249. Springer, Heidelberg (2008)
6. Bertrand, N., Legay, A., Pinchinat, S., Raclet, J.-B.: A compositional approach on modal specifications for timed systems. In: Breitman, K., Cavalcanti, A. (eds.) ICFEM 2009. LNCS, vol. 5885, Springer, Heidelberg (2009)
7. Bertrand, N., Pinchinat, S., Raclet, J.-B.: Refinement and consistency of timed modal specifications. In: Dediu, A.H., Ionescu, A.M., Martín-Vide, C. (eds.) LATA 2009. LNCS, vol. 5457, pp. 152–163. Springer, Heidelberg (2009)
8. Bulychev, P., Chatain, T., David, A., Larsen, K.G.: Efficient on-the-fly algorithm for checking alternating timed simulation. In: Ouaknine, J., Vaandrager, F.W. (eds.) FORMATS 2009. LNCS, vol. 5813, pp. 73–87. Springer, Heidelberg (2009)
9. Cassez, F., David, A., Fleury, E., Larsen, K.G., Lime, D.: Efficient on-the-fly algorithms for the analysis of timed games. In: Abadi, M., de Alfaro, L. (eds.) CONCUR 2005. LNCS, vol. 3653, pp. 66–80. Springer, Heidelberg (2005)
10. Čerāns, K., Godskesen, J.C., Larsen, K.G.: Timed modal specification - theory and tools. In: Courcoubetis, C. (ed.) CAV 1993. LNCS, vol. 697, pp. 253–267. Springer, Heidelberg (1993)
11. Chakabarti, A., de Alfaro, L., Henzinger, T.A., Stoelinga, M.I.A.: Resource interfaces. In: Alur, R., Lee, I. (eds.) EMSOFT 2003. LNCS, vol. 2855, pp. 117–133. Springer, Heidelberg (2003)
12. David, A., Larsen, K.G., Legay, A., Nyman, U., Wąsowski, A.: Timed I/O automata: a complete specification theory for real-time systems. In: HSCC (2010) (accepted)
13. de Alfaro, L., Faella, M.: An accelerated algorithm for 3-color parity games with an application to timed games. In: Damm, W., Hermanns, H. (eds.) CAV 2007. LNCS, vol. 4590, pp. 108–120. Springer, Heidelberg (2007)

14. de Alfaro, L., Henzinger, T.A.: Interface automata. In: FSE, Vienna, Austria, pp. 109–120. ACM Press, New York (2001)
15. de Alfaro, L., Henzinger, T.A.: Interface-based design. In: Marktoberdorf Summer School. Kluwer Academic Publishers, Dordrecht (2004)
16. de Alfaro, L., Henzinger, T.A., Stoelinga, M.I.A.: Timed interfaces. In: Sangiovanni-Vincentelli, A.L., Sifakis, J. (eds.) EMSOFT 2002. LNCS, vol. 2491, pp. 108–122. Springer, Heidelberg (2002)
17. Deng, Z., Liu, J.W.s.: Scheduling real-time applications in an open environment. In: Proceedings of the 18th IEEE Real-Time Systems Symposium, pp. 308–319. IEEE Computer Society Press, Los Alamitos (1997)
18. Garland, S.J., Lynch, N.A.: The IOA language and toolset: Support for designing, analyzing, and building distributed systems. Technical report, Massachusetts Institute of Technology, Cambridge, MA (1998)
19. Henzinger, T.A., Matic, S.: An interface algebra for real-time components. In: IEEE Real Time Technology and Applications Symposium, pp. 253–266. IEEE Computer Society, Los Alamitos (2006)
20. Henzinger, T.A., Sifakis, J.: The embedded systems design challenge. In: Misra, J., Nipkow, T., Sekerinski, E. (eds.) FM 2006. LNCS, vol. 4085, pp. 1–15. Springer, Heidelberg (2006)
21. Kaynar, D.K., Lynch, N.A., Segala, R., Vaandrager, F.W.: Timed i/o automata: A mathematical framework for modeling and analyzing real-time systems. In: RTSS, pp. 166–177. IEEE Computer Society, Los Alamitos (2003)
22. Kaynar, D.K., Lynch, N.A., Segala, R., Vaandrager, F.W.: The Theory of Timed I/O Automata. Synthesis Lectures on Computer Science. Morgan & Claypool Publishers, San Francisco (2009)
23. Larsen, K.G.: Modal specifications. In: Sifakis, J. (ed.) CAV 1989. LNCS, vol. 407, pp. 232–246. Springer, Heidelberg (1990)
24. Larsen, K.G., Nyman, U., Wasowski, A.: Modal I/O automata for interface and product line theories. In: De Nicola, R. (ed.) ESOP 2007. LNCS, vol. 4421, pp. 64–79. Springer, Heidelberg (2007)
25. Larsen, K.G., Nyman, U., Wasowski, A.: Modal i/o automata for interface and product line theories. In: De Nicola, R. (ed.) ESOP 2007. LNCS, vol. 4421, pp. 64–79. Springer, Heidelberg (2007)
26. Larsen, K.G., Steffen, B., Weise, C.: Continuous modeling of real-time and hybrid systems: From concepts to tools. STTT 1(1-2), 64–85 (1997)
27. Lee, I., Leung, J.Y.-T., Son, S.H.: Handbook of Real-Time and Embedded Systems. Chapman, Boca Raton (2007)
28. Lynch, N.: I/O automata: A model for discrete event systems. In: Annual Conference on Information Sciences and Systems, pp. 29–38. Princeton University, Princeton (1988)
29. Lynch, N.A., Tuttle, M.R.: An introduction to input/output automata. Technical Report MIT/LCS/TM-373. The MIT Press, Cambridge (November 1988)
30. Maler, O., Pnueli, A., Sifakis, J.: On the synthesis of discrete controllers for timed systems (an extended abstract). In: STACS, pp. 229–242 (1995)
31. Milner, R.: Communication and Concurrency. Prentice-Hall, Englewood Cliffs (1988)
32. Nicola, R.D., Segala, R.: A process algebraic view of input/output automata. Theoretical Computer Science 138 (1995)
33. Raclet, J.-B., Badouel, E., Benveniste, A., Caillaud, B., Legay, A., Passerone, R.: Modal interfaces: unifying interface automata and modal specifications. In: EMSOFT, pp. 87–96. ACM, New York (2009)

34. Stark, E.W., Cleavland, R., Smolka, S.A.: A process-algebraic language for probabilistic I/O automata. In: Amadio, R.M., Lugiez, D. (eds.) CONCUR 2003. LNCS, vol. 2761, pp. 193–207. Springer, Heidelberg (2003)
35. Thiele, L., Wandeler, E., Stoimenov, N.: Real-time interfaces for composing real-time systems. In: EMSOFT, pp. 34–43. ACM, New York (2006)
36. http://www.cs.aau.dk/~adavid/tiga/tio.html
37. Vaandrager, F.W.: On the relationship between process algebra and input/output automata. In: LICS, pp. 387–398 (1991)

The How and Why of Interactive Markov Chains*

Holger Hermanns[1,2] and Joost-Pieter Katoen[3,4]

[1] Dependable Systems and Software, Universität des Saarlandes, Germany
[2] VASY Team, INRIA Grenoble – Rhône-Alpes, France
[3] MOVES Group, RWTH Aachen University, Germany
[4] FMT Group, University of Twente, The Netherlands

Abstract. This paper reviews the model of interactive Markov chains (IMCs, for short), an extension of labelled transition systems with exponentially delayed transitions. We show that IMCs are closed under parallel composition and hiding, and show how IMCs can be compositionally aggregated prior to analysis by e.g., bisimulation minimisation or aggressive abstraction based on simulation pre-congruences. We survey some recent analysis techniques for IMCs, i.e., explaining how measures such as reachability probabilities can be obtained. Finally, we demonstrate that IMCs are a natural (and simple) semantic model for stochastic process algebras and generalised stochastic Petri nets and can be used for engineering formalisms such as AADL and dynamic fault trees.

1 Introduction

Designing correct and efficient distributed systems is a difficult task. As a challenging case take an offshore wireless sensor network that is designed to identify tsunami situations and relay tsunami warnings [61]. Once fully operational, will this network help to save human life? Can we guarantee its correct functioning, or is there a risk of failure at the very moment when it is seriously needed? To say it with Barendregt, correct systems for information processing are more valuable than gold [4]. In the tsunami context, a correct system is one that guarantees certain time bounds for the tasks it needs to perform, even in the presence of message losses or component failures. Correctness, performance and dependability are intertwined here, and so they are in many other contemporary IT applications. These applications ask for quantitative correctness properties such as: The frequency of system downtime is below one hour per year, and packets arrive timely in at least 99.96% of all cases.

* This research has been funded by NWO under grant 612.000.420 (QUPES) and DFG-NWO grant Dn 63-257 (ROCKS), by the EU under FP7-ICT-2007-1 grant 214755 (Quasimodo), and by the German Research Council (DFG) as part of the Transregional Collaborative Research Center "Automatic Verification and Analysis of Complex Systems" SFB/TR 14 AVACS.

F.S. de Boer et al. (Eds.): FMCO 2009, LNCS 6286, pp. 311–337, 2010.

Performance and dependability evaluation is a discipline that aims at analysing these quantitative system aspects. Major strands of performance evaluation approaches are measurement-based and model-based techniques. In *measurement-based evaluation*, experiments are performed on a concrete (often prototypical) realisation of the system, and timing information is gathered, which is then analysed to evaluate measure(s) of interest. These techniques are routinely practiced in the systems engineering world. They provide specific, precise and very concrete insights into the functioning of a real system. The drawback of these approaches is mainly the fact that they are not reproducible, are hard to scale, and difficult to generalise beyond the concrete setup experimented with. In order to increase reproducibility and reduce costs of larger experiments, distributed systems researchers often resort to *emulation* studies, where the real system code is executed on a virtualised hardware, instead of distributing it physically on the target systems. This especially allows for better concurrency control and thus improved reproducibility. However, it remains notoriously unclear to what extent the imposed control mechanisms tamper the validity of the obtained measures.

In *model-based performance evaluation*, a more general, and thus more abstract approach is taken. A model of the system is constructed that is deemed just detailed enough to evaluate the measure(s) of interest with the required accuracy. In this context the modelling process is an additional step that needs to be performed, and this is a non-trivial task. Process calculi [5] provide a formal basis for designing models of complex systems, especially those involving communicating and concurrently executing components. The underlying basis is the model of labelled transition systems, which represent system behaviour as transitions representing discrete system moves from state to state. The consideration of stochastic phenomena has led to a plethora of stochastic process calculi, cf. the survey in [36]. One of their semantical models is the topic of this paper: *interactive Markov chains* (IMCs, for short) [35]. It stands out in the sense that it extends classical labeled transition systems in a simple yet conservative fashion. IMCs arise from classical concurrency models by incorporating a second type of transitions, denoted $s \xrightarrow{\lambda} s'$, that embodies a random delay governed by a negative exponential distribution with parameter $\lambda \in \mathbb{R}_{>0}$. This twists the model to one that is running on a continuous timeline, and where the execution of actions is supposed to take no time —unless they can be blocked by the environment. (This is linked to the notion of maximal progress.) By dropping the new type of transitions, labeled transition systems are regained in their entirety. By instead dropping the old-fashioned action-labeled transitions, one arrives at one of the simplest but also most widespread class of performance and dependability models, *continuous-time Markov chains* (CTMCs). They can be considered as labeled transition systems, where the transition labels —rates of negative exponential distributions— indicate the speed of the system evolving from one state to another. Their benefits for stochastic process calculi is summarised in [16].

While this simple combination of LTS and CTMCs was at first viewed as a rather academic distinction, the last decade has shown and stressed its importance. First and foremost, IMCs have shown their practical relevance in applications of various domains, ranging from dynamic fault trees [11,10,12], architectural description languages such as AADL (Architectural Analysis and Design Language) [9,15,13,14], generalised stochastic Petri nets [40] and Statemate [8] to GALS (Globally Asynchronous Locally Synchronous) hardware design [22,19,23]. The availability of CTMC-based tool support [31] for IMCs has led to several of these applications. On the other hand, a rich set of algorithmic advances for the analysis and minimisation of IMCs have been recently developed that enable the analysis of large IMCs [49,66]. Whereas so far the analysis trajectory was restricted to CTMC models obtained from IMCs whose weak bisimulation quotient is free of nondeterminism, with the work of [66] this restriction has become obsolete. In addition, recent developments in compositional abstraction techniques for IMCs are promising means to analyse huge, and even infinite IMCs. This paper provides a survey of IMCs, some of their recent applications and algorithmic advancements.

Organization of this paper. Section 2 introduces IMCs, explains their semantics, defines some basic composition operators and considers (bi)simulation. Section 3 focuses on the analysis of measures-of-interest on IMCs, such as reduction to CTMCs and reachability probabilities of various kinds. Section 4 reports on compositional minimisation techniques for IMCs, including recent progress in aggressive abstraction. Section 5 describes the usage of IMCs as semantical backbone for industrially relevent formalisms such as fault trees and AADL, as well as of other modeling formalisms. Finally, section 6 concludes the paper and gives some propects for future research directions.

2 Interactive Markov Chains

What are IMCs? IMCs are basically labeled transition systems with a denumerable state space, action-labeled transitions, as well as Markovian transitions that are labeled with rates of exponential distributions. In the remainder of this paper, we assume the existence of a denumerable set of actions, ranged over by α and β, and which includes a distinguished action, denoted τ. Actions τ models internal, i.e., unobservable activity, whereas all other actions model observable activities.

Definition 1 (Interactive Markov chain). *An* interactive Markov chain *is a tuple* $\mathcal{I} = (S, Act, \longrightarrow, \Longrightarrow, s_0)$ *where*

- S *is a nonempty set of states with* initial state $s_0 \in S$.
- Act *is a set of actions,*
- $\longrightarrow \subseteq S \times Act \times S$ *is a set of* interactive *transitions, and*
- $\Longrightarrow \subseteq S \times \mathbb{R}_{>0} \times S$ *is a set of* Markovian *transitions.*

We abbreviate $(s, \alpha, s') \in \longrightarrow$ as $s \xrightarrow{\alpha} s'$ and similarly, $(s, \lambda, s') \in \Longrightarrow$ by $s \overset{\lambda}{\Longrightarrow} s'$. States are by the type of their outgoing transitions. Let:

- $IT(s) = \{s \xrightarrow{\alpha} s'\}$ be the set of interactive transitions that leave s, and
- $MT(s) = \{s \overset{\lambda}{\Longrightarrow} s'\}$ be the set of Markovian transitions that leave s.

A state s is *Markovian* iff $MT(s) \neq \emptyset$ and $IT(s) = \emptyset$; it is *interactive* iff $MT(s) = \emptyset$ and $IT(s) \neq \emptyset$. Further, s is a *hybrid state* iff $MT(s) \neq \emptyset$ and $IT(s) \neq \emptyset$; finally, s is a *deadlock state* iff $MT(s) = IT(s) = \emptyset$. Let $MS \subseteq S$ and $IS \subseteq S$ denote the sets of Markovian and interactive states in IMC $\mathcal{I}$.

A labeled transition system (LTS) is an IMC with $MT(s) = \emptyset$ for any state s. A continuous-time Markov chain (CTMC) is an IMC with $IT(s) = \emptyset$ for any state s. (The case in which $MT(s) = \emptyset = IT(s)$ for any s is both an LTS and a CTMC). IMCs are thus natural extensions of labeled transition systems, as well as of continuous-time Markov chains.

The semantics of an IMC. Roughly speaking, the interpretation of Markovian transition $s \overset{\lambda}{\Longrightarrow} s'$ is that the IMC can switch from state s to s' within d time units with probability $1-e^{-\lambda \cdot d}$. The positive real value λ thus uniquely identifies a negative exponential distribution. For a Markovian state $s \in MS$, let $\mathbf{R}(s, s') = \sum\{\lambda \mid s \overset{\lambda}{\Longrightarrow} s'\}$ be the *rate* to move from state s to state s'. If $\mathbf{R}(s, s') > 0$ for more than one state s', a competition between the transitions of s exists, known as the *race condition*. The probability to move from such state s to a particular state s' within d time units, i.e., the Markovian transition $s \to s'$ wins the race, is given by:

$$\frac{\mathbf{R}(s, s')}{E(s)} \cdot \left(1 - e^{-E(s) \cdot d}\right),$$

where $E(s) = \sum_{s' \in S} \mathbf{R}(s, s')$ denotes the *exit rate* of state s. Intuitively, it states that after a delay of at most d time units (second term), the IMC moves probabilistically to a direct successor state s' with discrete branching probability $\mathbf{P}(s, s') = \frac{\mathbf{R}(s,s')}{E(s)}$.

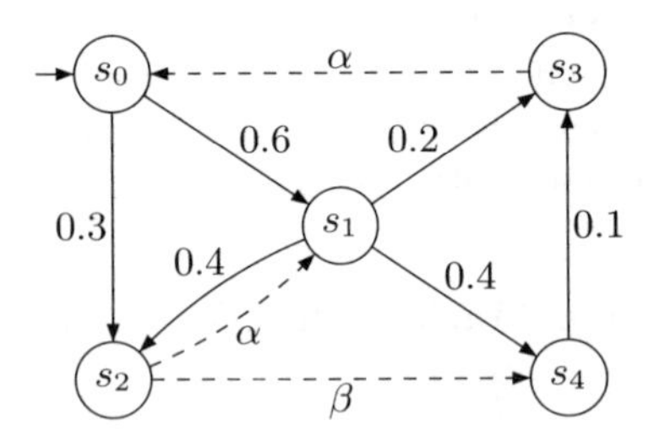

Fig. 1. Example of an IMC with Markovian and interactive states

Example 1. Consider the IMC $\mathcal{I}$ of Fig. 1 where dotted arrows denote interactive transitions and solid arrows Markovian transitions. We have $MS = \{s_0, s_1, s_4\}$ and $IS = \{s_2, s_3\}$. Markovian states behave like CTMC states, e.g., the transition $s_0 \overset{0.3}{\Longrightarrow} s_2$ expires within $z \in \mathbb{R}_{\geq 0}$ time units with probability $1 - e^{-0.3 \cdot z}$. The two Markovian transitions of s_0 compete for execution and the transition whose delay expires first is taken. In such a race the sojourn time in s_0 is determined by the first transition that executes. As the minimum of exponential distributions is exponentially distributed with the sum of their rates, the sojourn time of s is determined by its exit rate $E(s)$. In general, the probability to move from a state $s \in MS$ to a successor state $s' \in S$ equals the probability that (one of) the Markovian transitions that lead from s to s' wins the race. Accordingly, $\mathbf{R}(s_0, s_2) = 0.3$, $E(s_0) = 0.3 + 0.6 = 0.9$ and $\mathbf{P}(s_0, s_2) = \frac{1}{3}$. The probability to move from state s_0 to s_2 within 3 time units is $\frac{1}{3} \cdot \left(1 - e^{-2.7}\right)$.

Internal interactive transitions, i.e., τ-labeled interactive transitions, play a special role in IMCs. As they are not subject to any interaction, they cannot be delayed. Thus, internal interactive transitions can be assumed to take place immediately. Now consider a state with both a Markovian transition with rate λ, say, and a τ-transition. Which transition can now occur? As the τ-transition takes no time, it can be taken immediately. The probability that the Markovian transition executes immediately is, however, zero. This justifies that internal interactive transitions take precedence over Markovian transitions. This is called the *maximal progress assumption.*

Definition 2 (Maximal progress). *In any IMC, internal interactive transitions take precedence over Markovian transitions.*

Composition and hiding. The main strength of IMCs is that they are compositional.

Definition 3 (Parallel composition). *Let* $\mathcal{I}_1 = (S_1, Act_1, \longrightarrow_1, \Longrightarrow_1, s_{0,1})$ *and* $\mathcal{I}_2 = (S_2, Act_2, \longrightarrow_2, \Longrightarrow_2, s_{0,2})$ *be IMCs. The* parallel composition *of* $\mathcal{I}_1$ *and* $\mathcal{I}_2$ *wrt. set* A *of actions is defined by:*

$$\mathcal{I}_1 \,||_A\, \mathcal{I}_2 = (S_1 \times S_2, Act_1 \cup Act_2, \longrightarrow, \Longrightarrow, (s_{0,1}, s_{0,2}))$$

where $\longrightarrow$ *and* $\Longrightarrow$ *are defined as the smallest relations satisfying*

1. $s_1 \xrightarrow{\alpha}_1 s_1'$ *and* $s_2 \xrightarrow{\alpha}_2 s_2'$ *and* $\alpha \in A$, $\alpha \neq \tau$ *implies* $(s_1, s_2) \xrightarrow{\alpha} (s_1', s_2')$
2. $s_1 \xrightarrow{\alpha}_1 s_1'$ *and* $\alpha \notin A$ *implies* $(s_1, s_2) \xrightarrow{\alpha} (s_1', s_2)$ *for any* $s_2 \in S_2$
3. $s_2 \xrightarrow{\alpha}_2 s_2'$ *and* $\alpha \notin A$ *implies* $(s_1, s_2) \xrightarrow{\alpha} (s_1, s_2')$ *for any* $s_1 \in S_1$
4. $s_1 \stackrel{\lambda}{\Longrightarrow}_1 s_1'$ *implies* $(s_1, s_2) \stackrel{\lambda}{\Longrightarrow} (s_1', s_2)$ *for any* $s_2 \in S_2$
5. $s_2 \stackrel{\lambda}{\Longrightarrow}_2 s_2'$ *implies* $(s_1, s_2) \stackrel{\lambda}{\Longrightarrow} (s_1, s_2')$ *for any* $s_1 \in S_1$.

The first three constraints define a TCSP-like parallel composition [45]: actions in A need to be performed by both IMCs simultaneously, except for internal actions (first constraint), whereas actions not in A are performed autonomously (second and third constraint). According to the last two constraints, IMCs can delay independently. This differs from timed models such as timed automata, in which individual processes typically need to synchronise on the advance of time. The memoryless property of exponential distributions justifies independent delaying: if two Markovian transitions with rates λ and μ, say, are competing to be executed, then the remaining delay of the μ-transition after the λ-transition has been taken, is exponentially distributed with rate μ.

Definition 4 (Hiding). *The* hiding *of IMC $\mathcal{I} = (S, Act, \longrightarrow, \Longrightarrow, s_0)$ wrt. the set A of actions is the IMC $\mathcal{I} \setminus A = (S, Act \setminus A, \longrightarrow', \Longrightarrow, s_0)$ where $\longrightarrow'$ is the smallest relation defined by:*

1. *$s \xrightarrow{\alpha} s'$ and $\alpha \notin A$ implies $s \xrightarrow{\alpha}' s'$, and*
2. *$s \xrightarrow{\alpha} s'$ and $\alpha \in A$ implies $s \xrightarrow{\tau}' s'$.*

Hiding thus transforms α-transitions with $\alpha \in A$ into τ-transitions. All other transition labels remain unaffected. This operation is of importance for the maximal progress assumption of IMCs. Turning an α-transition emanating from state s, say, into a τ-transition may change the semantics of the IMC at hand, as after hiding no Markovian transition will be ever taken in s.

Bisimulation. To compare IMCs, we introduce the notions of strong and weak bisimulation. For set $C \subseteq S$ of states and state s, let $\mathbf{R}(s, C) = \sum_{s' \in C} \mathbf{R}(s, s')$. Intuitively, two states s and t are strongly bisimilar if any interactive transition $s \xrightarrow{\alpha} s'$ can be mimicked by t, i.e., $t \xrightarrow{\alpha} t'$ such that s' and t' are bisimilar. In addition, the cumulative rate of moving from s to some equivalence class C of states, i.e., $\mathbf{R}(s, C)$ equals $\mathbf{R}(t, C)$. Since the probability of a Markovian transition to be executed immediately is zero, whereas internal interactive transitions take always place immediately, there is no need to require equality of cumulative rates if states have outgoing internal transitions. Let $s \stackrel{\tau}{\not\longrightarrow}$ denote a predicate that is true if and only if s has no outgoing τ-transition. For state s, action α and $C \subseteq S$, let $\mathbf{T}(s, \alpha, C) = 1$ if and only if $\{s' \in C \mid s \xrightarrow{\alpha} s'\}$ is non-empty.

Definition 5 (Strong bisimulation). *Let $\mathcal{I} = (S, Act, \longrightarrow, \Longrightarrow, s_0)$ be an IMC. An equivalence relation $R \subseteq S \times S$ is a* strong bisimulation *on $\mathcal{I}$ if for any $(s, t) \in R$ and equivalence class $C \in S/R$ the following holds:*

1. *for any $\alpha \in Act$, $\mathbf{T}(s, \alpha, C) = \mathbf{T}(t, \alpha, C)$, and*
2. *$s \stackrel{\tau}{\not\longrightarrow}$ implies $\mathbf{R}(s, C) = \mathbf{R}(t, C)$.*

States s and s' are strongly bisimilar, denoted $s \sim s'$, if $(s, s') \in R$ for some strong bisimulation R.

The rate equality is adopted from the notion of lumping equivalence [18]. Two IMCs $\mathcal{I}_1$ and $\mathcal{I}_2$ on (disjoint) state spaces S_1 and S_2 respectively are bisimilar, denoted $\mathcal{I}_1 \sim \mathcal{I}_2$, if there exists a strong bisimulation R on $S_1 \cup S_2$ such that $(s_{0,1}, s_{0,2}) \in R$. The next property asserts that $\sim$ is substitutive with respect to parallel composition and hiding, so, e.g., $\mathcal{I} \sim \mathcal{I}'$ implies for any set A that $\mathcal{I} \setminus A \sim \mathcal{I}' \setminus A$.

Theorem 1. *[35] $\sim$ is a congruence wrt. parallel composition and hiding.*

As discussed before, τ-transitions play a special role in IMCs. Whereas strong bisimulation treats all interactive transitions in the same way, regardless whether they are internal (i.e., labelled by τ) or not, weak bisimulation takes an observer's point of view and cannot distinguish between executing several successive τ-transitions or a single one. This allows for collapsing sequences of internal interactive transitions by a single such transition. This acts exactly the same as for labeled transition systems. The treatment of Markovian transitions is a bit more involved, however. First, let us remark that the probability distribution of a sequence of exponential distributions is not an exponential distribution but constitutes a phase-type distribution. Therefore, it is not possible to define a weak version of the transition relation $\Longrightarrow$ as is done for weak bisimulation in labeled transition systems. The solution is to demand that Markovian transitions have to be mimicked in the strong sense, while they can be preceded and/or followed by arbitrary sequences of internal interactive transitions. The treatment of sequences of internal interactive transitions is similar to that of branching bisimulation [62]. As for strong bisimulation, rate equality is only required if a state has no outgoing internal transitions (maximal progress). Let $s \xrightarrow{\tau^*} s'$ denote that s' can be reached from s solely via zero or more τ-transitions; in particular $s \xrightarrow{\tau^*} s$ for any state s. For state s, action α and $C \subseteq S$, let $\mathbf{W}(s, \alpha, C) = 1$ if and only if $\{s' \in C \mid s \xrightarrow{\tau^*} \xrightarrow{\alpha} \xrightarrow{\tau^*} s'\}$ is non-empty.

Definition 6 (Weak bisimulation). *Let $\mathcal{I} = (S, Act, \longrightarrow, \Longrightarrow, s_0)$ be an IMC. An equivalence relation $R \subseteq S \times S$ is a* weak bisimulation *on $\mathcal{I}$ if for any $(s, t) \in R$ and equivalence class $C \in S/R$, the following holds:*

1. *for any $\alpha \in Act$, $\mathbf{W}(s, \alpha, C) = \mathbf{W}(t, \alpha, C)$, and*
2. *$s \xrightarrow{\tau^*} s'$ and $s' \overset{\tau}{\not\longrightarrow}$ implies $t \xrightarrow{\tau^*} t'$ and $t' \overset{\tau}{\not\longrightarrow}$ and $\mathbf{R}(s', C) = \mathbf{R}(t', C)$ for some $t' \in S$.*

States s and s' are weakly bisimilar, denoted $s \approx s'$, if $(s, s') \in R$ for some weak bisimulation R.

Theorem 2. *[35] $\approx$ is a congruence wrt. parallel composition and hiding.*

Bisimulation relations are equivalences requiring two bisimilar states to exhibit identical stepwise behaviour. On the contrary, simulation relations [46] are preorders on the state space requiring that whenever $s \preceq s'$ (s' simulates s) state s' can mimic all stepwise behaviour of s; the converse is not guaranteed, so state s' may perform steps that cannot be matched by s.

Definition 7 (Strong simulation). *For IMC $\mathcal{I} = (S, Act, \longrightarrow, \Longrightarrow, s_0)$, $R \subseteq S \times S$ is a* simulation relation, *iff for any $(s, t) \in R$ it holds:*

1. *for any $\alpha \in Act$ and $s' \in S$, $s \xrightarrow{\alpha} s'$ implies $t \xrightarrow{\alpha} t'$ and $(s', t') \in R$ for some $t' \in S$*
2. *$s \overset{\tau}{\not\longrightarrow}$ implies $E(s) \leq E(t)$*
3. *$s \overset{\tau}{\not\longrightarrow}$ implies for distributions $\mu = \mathbf{P}(s, \cdot)$ and $\mu' = \mathbf{P}(s', \cdot)$ there exists $\Delta : S \times S \to [0, 1]$ such that for all $u, u' \in S$:*

(a) $\Delta(u, u') > 0 \implies (u, u') \in R$ (b) $\Delta(u, S) = \mu(u)$ (c) $\Delta(S, u') = \mu'(u')$

We write $s \preceq s'$ if $(s, s') \in R$ for some simulation R and $\mathcal{I} \preceq \mathcal{I}'$ for IMCs $\mathcal{I}$ and $\mathcal{I}'$ with initial states s_0 and s_0', if $s_0 \preceq s_0'$ in the disjoint union of $\mathcal{I}$ and $\mathcal{I}'$. The last constraint requires the existence of a weight function Δ that basically distributes μ of s to μ' of s' such that only related states obtain a positive weight (3(a)), and the total probability mass of u that is assigned by Δ coincides with $\mu(u)$ and symmetrically for u' (cf. 3(b), 3(c)).

Theorem 3. *$\preceq$ is a precongruence wrt. parallel composition and hiding.*

Constraint-oriented specification of performance aspects. Let us conclude this section by describing how IMCs can be used to meet the challenges as put forward in the well-known paradigm of separation of concerns. We do so by showing that IMCs can be naturally used to specify performance aspects in the so-called constraint-oriented specification style [64]. This style is a format par excellence to support the separation of concerns principle when specifying the characteristics of complex distributed systems. It has been originally developed to support the early phases of the design trajectory. Put in a nutshell, constraints are viewed as separate processes. Parallel composition is used to combine these constraints much in the same vein as logical conjunction.

To illustrate how IMCs perfectly match the constraint-oriented specification style consider a given system model P that does not contain random timing constraints yet —i.e., P is a labeled transition system— and let α and β be two successive actions in P. To insert a random delay between these two actions, it now suffices to construct an IMC D_p with an initial state with outgoing transition α and a final state, i.e. a state without outgoing transitions, that can can only be reached by a β-transition. The state reached after performing α and the state from which the β-transition is emanating are connected by a CTMC, i.e., an IMC with only Markovian transitions. This CTMC models the random delay that we want to impose on the delay between α and β. The resulting system is now obtained as $P \,||_{\{\alpha,\beta\}}\, D_p$. The "delay" process D_p is thus imposed as additional constraint to process P. This procedure can now be repeated to impose delays between other actions in P. As CTMCs can approximate general probability distributions arbitarily closely, this is a powerful recipe. This is exemplified in [39] where a complex telephone system specification in LOTOS has been enriched with performance characteristics using a constraint-oriented specification style.

Now assume that we want to impose random delays on some of the observable actions from P and Q. Following the procedure just described, this yields

$$(P \,||_A\, Q) \,||_{A_p \cup A_q}\, (D_p \,||_\emptyset\, D_q)$$

where A_p are the synchronised actions with "delay" process D_p and A_q the ones with D_q. Note that the timing constraints are added "on top" of the entire specification. As it suffices to impose a single delay on each action, the processes D_p and D_q are independent, and thus need not to synchronise. In case D_p delays some local actions from P, and D_q delays local actions from Q, the above specification can be rewritten into the weak bisimilar specification:

$$\underbrace{(P \,||_{A_p}\, D_p)}_{\text{local constraints of } P} \quad ||_A \quad \underbrace{(Q \,||_{A_q}\, D_q)}_{\text{local constraints of } Q}$$

Note that in this system specification, the functional and performance aspects of each individual component are separated, as well as the specifications of the components themselves.

3 IMC Analysis

Assume that the IMC under consideration is complete, i.e., it is not subject any further to interaction with other components that are modeled as IMCs. This is important, as this means that actions cannot be further delayed due to a delay which is imposed by the environment. Formally, this means that we can safely hide all actions in the IMC at hand, i.e., we consider $\mathcal{I} \setminus A$ where A contains all actions occuring in $\mathcal{I}$. Accordingly, all actions are labeled by τ. The typical specification that is subject to analysis is thus of the form:

$$(\mathcal{I}_1 \,||_{A_1}\, \mathcal{I}_2 \,||_{A_2} \,\cdots\, ||_{A_N}\, \mathcal{I}_N) \setminus A$$

where A is the union of all actions in IMC $\mathcal{I}_i$, i.e., $A = \cup_{i=1}^{N} Act_i$. Due to the maximal progress assumption, the resulting IMC can be simplified: in any state that has a τ-transition, all Markovian transitions can be removed. Subsequently, sequences of τ-transitions can be collapsed by applying weak bisimulation. If nondeterminism is absent in the resulting IMC, in fact a CTMC remains, and all analysis techniques for CTMCs can be employed [34], such as transient or steady-state analysis or CSL model checking [2].

Time-bounded reachability. An alternative analysis technique is to compute time-bounded reachability probabilities. This does not require the IMC to be reducible to a CTMC, and can thus be applied to *any* IMC. Let us explain the kind of measure we are interested in. First, consider infinite paths in an IMC. An infinite path π in an IMC is an infinite sequence of the form

$$\pi \;=\; s_0 \xrightarrow{\sigma_0,t_0} s_1 \xrightarrow{\sigma_1,t_1} s_2 \xrightarrow{\sigma_2,t_2} \ldots$$

with $s_i \in S$, σ_i is either an action in Act or equals $\perp$, and $t_i \in \mathbb{R}_{\geq 0}$. The occurrence of action α after a delay of t time units in state s_i in π is denoted by $s_i \xrightarrow{\alpha,t} s_{i+1}$; in case of a Markovian transition after t time units delay, this is denoted by $s_i \xrightarrow{\perp,t} s_{i+1}$. As internal interactive transitions take place immediately, their occurrence is denoted $s_i \xrightarrow{\tau,0} s_{i+1}$. For time point $t \in \mathbb{R}_{\geq 0}$, let $\pi@t$ denote the sequence of states that π occupies at time t. Note that $\pi@t$ is in general not a single state, but rather a sequence of several states, as an IMC may exhibit immediate transitions and thus may occupy various states at the same time instant. An example path in the IMC of Fig. 1 is $s_0 \xrightarrow{\perp,3.0} s_1 \xrightarrow{\perp,2.0} s_2 \xrightarrow{\beta,0} s_4 \ldots$ which occupies the states s_2 and s_4 at time instant 5.0. Let $Paths^{\omega}(s)$ denote the set of infinite paths starting in state s. Using a standard cylinder construction, a sigma-algebra can be defined over the set of infinite paths of an IMC, and can be equipped with a probability measure [66], denoted Pr in the sequel.

Now, let $\mathcal{I}$ be an IMC with state space S, initial state s, and let $G \subseteq S$ be a set of goal states and $I \subseteq \mathbb{R}$ a time interval with rational bounds. The time-bounded reachability event $\Diamond^I G$ is defined as:

$$\Diamond^I G \;=\; \{\pi \in \mathit{Paths}^\omega(s) \mid \exists t \in I.\, \exists s' \in \pi@t.\, s' \in G\}$$

It thus contains all infinite paths starting in state s that hit a state in G at some time point that lies in the interval I. We are basically interested in the probability of the event $\Diamond^I G$. The problem, however, is that —due to the presence of non-determinism— this is not uniquely defined. To see this, consider the IMC of Fig. 1 with $G = \{s_4\}$. The probability of the event $\Diamond^{[0,2]} G$ for state s_2, for instance, now depends on how the non-deterministic choice between α and β has been resolved in state s_2. If β is chosen the probability equals one; otherwise it depends on the choice in state s_1. We therefore consider the probability of $\Diamond^I G$ relative to a specific resolution of the non-determinism in the IMC. Such resolution is defined by a total-time deterministic positional *policy* D, say. It goes beyond the scope of this paper to fully define this class of policies. For the sake of the remainder of this paper, it suffices to consider D as a function that takes as argument the current state s_i, say, and the total time that has elapsed along the path leading to s_i, including the time already spent in state s_i so far. Based on this information, D will select one of the actions of an outgoing transition of s_i.

Example 2. Consider again the IMC of Fig. 1. Assume the execution of the IMC so far is $s_0 \xrightarrow{\perp,3.0} s_1 \xrightarrow{\perp,2.0} s_2$. A choice between the actions α and β has to be made in s_2. An example policy D is $D(s_2, t) = \alpha$ if $t \leq 10$, and $D(s_2, t) = \beta$ otherwise. Thus, if the residence time in the current state s_2 is d time units, say, then α will be chosen if $d \leq 5$ (as 5 time units have passed until reaching s_2), whereas β will be chosen if $d > 5$.

We can now be more precise about the measure-of-interest: we are interested in maximizing the probability of $\Diamond^I G$ for all possible total-time dependent policies, i.e., we want to determine

$$p^{\max}(s, I) \;=\; \sup_D \Pr_{s,D}\left(\Diamond^I G\right) \qquad \text{for timed policy } D.$$

One may wonder whether we should not consider more powerful classes of policies, such as randomised ones, or policies that may base their decision on the entire computation so far, but this does not lead to a larger value for $p^{\max}(s, I)$:

Theorem 4. *[57] Total-time deterministic positional policies are optimal for maximising* $\Pr(\Diamond^I G)$.

Reachability probabilities. Before discussing how to compute $p^{\max}(s, I)$, let us first discuss a simpler variant of the event $\Diamond^I G$. This case occurs if $\sup I = \infty$ and $\inf I = 0$. As the time interval does not impose any timing constraint anymore, this amounts to a simple reachability event:

$$\Diamond G \;=\; \{\pi \in \mathit{Paths}^\omega(s) \mid \exists i \in \mathbb{N}.\, \pi[i] \in G\}$$

where $\pi[i]$ denotes the i-th state along π. Thus all paths are considered that hit G at some position, no matter how much time has elapsed upon hitting G. For such (unbounded) reachability events, positional policies suffice, i.e., there is no need anymore to "know" the total time that has elapsed along the computation so far. In fact, $p^{\max}(s,[0,\infty))$ can be determined by considering the discrete-probabilistic process that is embedded in the IMC at hand. The discretised counterpart of an IMC is an interactive probabilistic chain.

Definition 8 (Interactive probabilistic chain [23]). *An* interactive probabilistic chain *(IPC) is a tuple $\mathcal{P} = (S, Act, \longrightarrow, \mathbf{P}, s_0)$, where S, Act, IT and s_0 are as in Def. 1 and $\mathbf{P} : S \times S \to [0,1]$ is a transition probability function sastifying $\forall s \in S.\, \mathbf{P}(s, S) \in \{0,1\}$.*

A state s in an IPC $\mathcal{P}$ is *probabilistic* iff $\sum_{s' \in S} \mathbf{P}(s,s') = 1$ and $IT(s) = \emptyset$. As for IMCs, we adopt the *maximal progress assumption.* Hence, interactive internal transitions take precedence over probabilistic transitions and their execution takes zero discrete time steps. The embedded IPC of an IMC is obtained by considering the discrete-probabilistic interpretation of $\Longrightarrow$, i.e., $\mathbf{P}(s,s') = \frac{\mathbf{R}(s,s')}{E(s)}$ if $MT(s) \neq \emptyset$, and 0 otherwise. It then follows:

Theorem 5. *For any IMC $\mathcal{I}$ with embedded IPC $\mathcal{P}$: $p^{\mathcal{I}}(s,[0,\infty)) = p^{\mathcal{P}}(s,[0,\infty))$.*

The values $p^{\mathcal{P}}(s,[0,\infty))$ can be obtained by applying a slight variation of value iteration algorithms for MDPs [7].

Discretisation. The computation of $p^{\max}(s, I)$ with $\inf I \neq \emptyset$ can be done using discretisation, and as we will see, can also be reduced —though in a different way as explained above— to value iteration on MDPs.

Definition 9 (Discretisation [66]). *An IMC $\mathcal{I} = (S, Act, \longrightarrow, \Longrightarrow, s_0)$ and a step duration $\delta \in \mathbb{R}_{>0}$ induce the* discretised IPC *$\mathcal{P}_\delta = (S, Act, \longrightarrow, \mathbf{P}', s_0)$, where*

$$\mathbf{P}'(s,s') = \begin{cases} \left(1 - e^{-E(s)\cdot\delta}\right) \cdot \mathbf{P}(s,s') & \text{if } s \neq s' \\ \left(1 - e^{-E(s)\cdot\delta}\right) \cdot \mathbf{P}(s,s') + e^{-E(s)\cdot\delta} & \text{if } s = s'. \end{cases} \tag{1}$$

Let $p^{\mathcal{P}}_{max}(s,[k_a,k_b])$ for an IPC $\mathcal{P}$ with state s and step-interval $0 \leq k_a \leq k_b$ be the supremum of the probabilities to reach a set of goal states within step interval $[k_a,k_b]$, $k_a, k_b \in \mathbb{N}$. The following result allows to approximate this probability in the underlying IMC by a step-bounded reachability analysis in its discretised IPC. This discretisation is indeed *quantifiably correct*:

Theorem 6 (Approximation theorem [66]). *Let $\mathcal{I} = (S, Act, \longrightarrow, \Longrightarrow, s_0)$ be an IMC, $G \subseteq S$ a set of goal states and $\delta > 0$ a step duration. Further, let I be a time interval with $\inf I = a$ and $\sup I = b$ such that $a < b$ and $a = k_a\delta$ and $b = k_b\delta$ for some $k_a \in \mathbb{N}$ and $k_b \in \mathbb{N}_{>0}$. Then:*

$$p^{\mathcal{P}_\delta}_{max}(s,(k_a,k_b]) - k_a \cdot \frac{(\lambda\delta)^2}{2} \leq p^{\mathcal{I}}_{max}(s,I) \leq p^{\mathcal{P}_\delta}_{max}(s,(k_a,k_b]) + k_b \cdot \frac{(\lambda\delta)^2}{2} + \lambda\delta.$$

Given an error bound ε, we can choose a sufficiently small step duration $\delta > 0$ such that $\left|p^{\mathcal{P}_\delta}_{max}(s,(k_a,k_b]) - p^{\mathcal{I}}_{max}(s,I)\right| \leq k_b \cdot \frac{(\lambda\delta)^2}{2} + \lambda\delta < \varepsilon$ holds. Note that this can be done *a priori*. Hence, $p^{\mathcal{P}_\delta}_{max}(s,(k_a,k_b])$ approximates the probabilities $p^{\mathcal{I}}_{max}(s,I)$ up to ε. Further, $p^{\mathcal{P}_\delta}_{max}(s,(k_a,k_b])$ can easily be computed by slightly adapting the well-known value iteration algorithm for MDPs [7]. For an error-bound $\varepsilon > 0$ and a time-interval I with $\sup I = b$, this approach has a worst case time complexity in $\mathcal{O}\left(n^{2.376} + (m+n^2)\cdot(\lambda b)^2/\varepsilon\right)$ where λ is the maximal exit rate and m and n are the number of transitions and states of the IMC, respectively.

Example 3. (Adopted from [58].) Consider the IMC depicted in Fig. 2(a). Let $G = \{s_4\}$ as indicated by the double-circled state s_4. The only state which exhibits non-determinism is state s_1 where a choice between α and β has to be made. Selecting α rapidly leads to the goal state as with probability $\frac{1}{2}$, s_4 is reached with an exponential distribution of rate one. Selecting β almost surely leads to the goal state, but, however, is subject to a delay that is governed by an Erlang(30,10)-distribution, i.e., a sequence of 30 exponential distributions of each rate 10. Note that this approximates a deterministic delay of 3 time units. The time-bounded reachability probabilities are plotted in Fig 2(b). This plot clearly shows that it is optimal to select α upto about time 3, and β afterwards. The size of the IMC, its maximal exit rate (λ), accuracy (ϵ), time bound (b) and the computation time are indicated in Fig. 2(c).

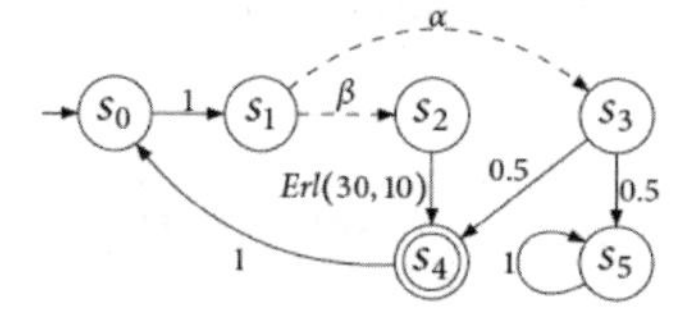

(a) The $Erl(30,10)$ model $\mathcal{M}$.

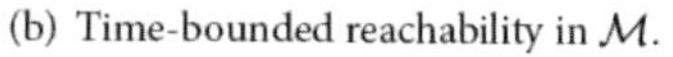

(b) Time-bounded reachability in $\mathcal{M}$.

problem	states	ε	λ	b	prob.	time
$Erl(30,10)$	35	10^{-3}	10	4	0.672	50s
$Erl(30,10)$	35	10^{-3}	10	7	0.983	70s
$Erl(30,10)$	35	10^{-4}	10	4	0.6718	268s

(c) Computation times for different parameters.

Fig. 2. Time-bounded reachability probabilities in an example IMC

Time-bounded reachability-avoid probabilities. To conclude this section, we will explain that determining $p^{\max}(s,I)$ can also be used for more advanced measures-of-interest, such as "reach-avoid" probabilities. Let, as before, s be a state in an

IMC, $I = [0, d]$ a time interval with rational d, G be a set of goal states, and A a set of states that need to be avoided before reaching G. The measure-of-interest now is to maximise the probability to reach G at some time point in the interval I while avoiding any state in A prior to reaching G. Formally, the event-of-interest is:

$$\overline{A}\,\mathsf{U}^{[0,d]}\,G \;=\; \{\pi \in \mathit{Paths}^{\omega}(s) \mid \exists t \leq d.\, \exists s' \in \pi@t.\, s' \in G \wedge \forall s'' \in \mathit{pref}(s').\, s'' \notin A\}$$

where $\mathit{pref}(s')$ is the set of states along π that are reached before reaching s' and $\overline{A}$ is the complement of A, i.e., $\overline{A} = S \setminus A$. The maximal probability of this event can be computed in the following way. The IMC is first transformed by making all states in G absorbing, i.e., for any state $s \in G$, the outgoing transitions are removed. This is justified by the fact that it is not of importance what happens once a state in G has been reached (via a $\overline{A}$-path); in addition, if a G-state is reached before the deadline d, this does not matter, as it will still be in G at time d since it is made absorbing. In addition, all states in $A \cap \overline{G}$ are made absorbing as the probability of a path that reaches an A-state which is also a $\overline{G}$-state to satisfy the event-of-interest is zero. The resulting structure is thus an IMC in which only the states in $\overline{A} \setminus G$ are unaffected; all other states are made absorbing. It now follows in a similar way as in [2]:

Theorem 7. $\underbrace{\sup_D \Pr_{s,D}\left(\overline{A}\,\mathsf{U}^{[0,d]}\,G\right)}_{\textit{in the IMC } \mathcal{I}} = \underbrace{\sup_D \Pr_{s,D}\left(\Diamond^{[0,d]}\,G\right)}_{\textit{in the IMC } \mathcal{I}'}.$

Here, IMC $\mathcal{I}'$ is obtained from $\mathcal{I}$ by making all states outside $\overline{A} \setminus G$ absorbing. As a result of the above theorem, computing time-bounded reach-avoid probabilities is reduced to determining time-bounded reachability probabilities, which can be determined in the way described earlier. It goes without saying that a similar strategy can be applied to (unbounded) reach-avoid probabilities.

4 Abstraction

As for any state-based technique, the curse of dimensionality is a major limitation for IMCs. Although its approximate analysis algorithms as described above are polynomial (with relatively low degree) in the state space size, state spaces of realistic systems easily consist of millions or even billions of states. In order to deal with such systems, aggressive abstraction techniques are required. In the following, we consider abstraction techniques that are based on partitioning the state space into groups of states. A possibility to achieve this, is to apply bisimulation minimisation.

Compositional bisimulation minimisation. An important property that provides the basis for such abstraction is the fact that for bisimilar states time-bounded (as well as unbounded) reachability probabilities are preserved:

Theorem 8. *[56] For any finitely-branching IMC with state space S, states $s, s' \in S$, $G \subseteq S$ and time interval I:*

$$s \sim s' \quad \textit{implies} \quad p^{\max}(s, I) \;=\; p^{\max}(s', I).$$

The above result opens the way to generate —prior to any (time-consuming) analysis— an IMC that is bisimilar to the IMC under consideration, but preferably much smaller. This is called the quotient IMC. For equivalence relation R on state space S and $s \in S$, let $[s]_R$ denote the equivalence class of s under R, and let $S/R = \{[s]_R \mid s \in S\}$ denote the quotient space of S under R.

Definition 10 (Quotient IMC). *Let $\mathcal{I} = (S, Act, \longrightarrow, \Longrightarrow, s_0)$ be an IMC and R a strong bisimulation on S. The* quotient IMC $\mathcal{I}/R = \big(S/R, Act, \longrightarrow',$ $\Longrightarrow', [s_0]_R\big)$ *where $\longrightarrow'$ and $\Longrightarrow'$ are the smallest relations satisfying:*

1. *$s \xrightarrow{\alpha} s'$ implies $[s]_R \xrightarrow{\alpha}' [s']_R$, and*
2. *$s \overset{\lambda}{\Longrightarrow} s'$ implies $[s]_R \overset{\mathbf{R}(s,[s']_R)}{\Longrightarrow}' [s']_R$.*

It now follows that for any IMC $\mathcal{I}$ and strong bisimulation, it holds $\mathcal{I} \sim \mathcal{I}/R$. (A similar result holds for weak bisimulation, replacing $\sim$ by $\approx$).

The next question is how to obtain the bisimulation quotient of a given IMC, and preferably even the quotient with respect to the coarsest bisimulation, as this yields an IMC of minimal size which is strong bisimilar to the original one. Using a variant of Paige-Tarjan's partition-refinement algorithm for computing strong bisimulation on labeled transition systems we obtain:

Theorem 9. *[35] For any IMC $\mathcal{I}$ with state space S and strong bisimulation R on S, the quotient IMC $\mathcal{I}/R$ can be computed in time complexity $\mathcal{O}(m \log n)$ where m and n are the number of transitions and states of the IMC $\mathcal{I}$.*

The results so far suggest to compute the quotient IMC prior to the analysis of, e.g., time-bounded reachability probabilities. This leads to significant state-space reductions and efficiency gains in computation times, as e.g., is shown in [47] for CTMCs. But, as the bisimulation minimisation is not an on-the-fly algorithm, it requires the entire state space of the original, i.e., non-minimised IMC up front. For realistic systems, this requirement is a significant burden. Fortunately, as IMCs are compositional —they can be put in parallel in a simple manner— and as bisimulation is a congruence wrt. parallel composition, bisimulation minimisation can be applied in a *component-wise manner*. This works as follows. Suppose the system-to-be-analysed is of the form:

$$\mathcal{I} \;=\; \mathcal{I}_1 \,||_{A_1}\, \mathcal{I}_2 \,||_{A_2}\, \cdots \,||_{A_N}\, \mathcal{I}_N,$$

i.e., a parallel composition of N IMCs. For the sake of our argument, let us assume that the size of $\mathcal{I}$ is too large to be handled, and therefore bisimulation minimisation cannot be applied. However, each component is of a moderate size that can be subject to minimisation. Let $\widehat{\mathcal{I}_i}$ be the quotient of IMC $\mathcal{I}_i$, for $0 < i \leq N$. Each such quotient can be obtained by the aforementioned partition-refinement algorithm. Thanks to the property that bisimulation is substitutive wrt. parallel composition, it follows from the fact that $\mathcal{I}_i \sim \widehat{\mathcal{I}_i}$, for $0 < i \leq N$, that:

$$\mathcal{I}_1 \,||_{A_1}\, \mathcal{I}_2 \,||_{A_2} \cdots ||_{A_N}\, \mathcal{I}_N \;\sim\; \widehat{\mathcal{I}_1} \,||_{A_1}\, \widehat{\mathcal{I}_2} \,||_{A_2} \cdots ||_{A_N}\, \widehat{\mathcal{I}_N}.$$

The worst case time complexity to obtain this reduced system is determined by the largest IMC $\mathcal{I}_i$ and equals $\mathcal{O}(\max_i(m_i \log n_i))$ where m_i and n_i are the number of transitions and states in IMC $\mathcal{I}_i$. Similar reasoning applies to weak bisimulation, with the exception that the time complexity for determining the quotient under weak bisimulation requires the computation of a transitive closure which is in $\mathcal{O}(n^{2.376})$. As weak bisimulation also preserves maximal time-bounded reachability probabilities, and is substitutive, an IMC can be minimised compositionally before any analysis:

Theorem 10. *For any finitely-branching IMC with state space S, states $s, s' \in S$, $G \subseteq S$ and time interval I:*

$$s \approx s' \quad \textit{implies} \quad p^{\max}(s, I) \;=\; p^{\max}(s', I).$$

Finally, for simulation preorders we obtain a slightly other preservation result. Intuitively speaking, whenever $\mathcal{I} \preceq \mathcal{I}'$, then $\mathcal{I}'$ can mimic all behaviours of $\mathcal{I}$, but perhaps can do more (and faster). This yields:

Theorem 11. *For any finitely-branching IMC with state space S, states $s, s' \in S$, $G \subseteq S$ and time interval I:*

$$s \preceq s' \quad \textit{implies} \quad p^{\max}(s, I) \;\leq\; p^{\max}(s', I).$$

One may now be tempted to first minimise an IMC wrt. simulation preorder or its corresponding equivalence $\preceq \cap \preceq^{-1}$, but it turns out that checking a simulation relation between probabilistic models such as IMCs is computationally involved [1,67]. In the sequel, we will see that simulation preorders are nonetheless crucial to obtain more aggressive abstraction techniques for IMCs.

Interval abstraction. Compositional bisimulation minimisation has been applied to several examples yielding substantial state-space reductions. It allowed the analysis of IMCs (in fact, CTMCs) that could not be analysed without compositional minimisation [39,30,32]. With the advent of increasingly complex systems, more radical reduction techniques are needed. In the sequel, we present a recent framework to perform aggressive abstraction of IMCs in a compositional manner [49]. The key idea is to (again) partition the state space, but rather requiring that each partition solely consists of equivalent (strong or weak bisimilar) states, we are more liberal, and in fact allow for any state space partitioning. As a result, a state s is not bisimilar to its partition (as for bisimulation), but instead its partition *simulates* s. Intuitively speaking, this means that all behaviour of s can be mimicked, but perhaps that the partition exhibits more behaviours than s. As the partition is aimed to be coarser than in the case of bisimulation, a central question is which measures are preserved, i.e., what does a maximal (time-bounded) reachability probability computed on the minimised IMC imply for the original IMC?

In the remainder of this section, we assume that IMCs are *uniform*.

Definition 11 (Uniform IMC). *An IMC is* uniform *if for any state s we have that $MT(s) \neq \emptyset$ implies $E(s) = \lambda$ for a given fixed $\lambda \in \mathbb{R}_{>0}$.*

The residence time in any state with at least one Markovian transition is thus governed by the same exponential distribution. Although this seems a rather severe restriction, there is an important class of systems for which this applies, viz. IMCs in which delays are imposed in a compositional manner using the constraint-oriented specification style. The point is that any CTMC can be transformed by a simple linear-time procedure into a weak bisimilar uniform CTMC [3]. Consider the specification $P \,||_A\, D_p$ where P is an IMC with only interactive transitions, i.e., P is an LTS, and D_p is a CTMC, probably enhanced with a start action α and end action β as explained before. The purpose of D_p is to impose a random delay between the occurrence of α and β in P. This is modeled as an arbitrary, finite-state CTMC. We can now transform D into its uniform counterpart $\widehat{D_p}$, say. As $D_p \approx \widehat{D_p}$ and $\approx$ is substitutive wrt. parallel composition, it follows that the non-uniform IMC $P \,||_A\, D_p$ is weak bisimilar to the uniform IMC $P \,||_A\, \widehat{D_p}$. (Several operators are preserving uniformity, see [38].)

Let IMC $\mathcal{I}$ be uniform. Our abstraction technique for $\mathcal{I}$ is a natural mixture of abstraction of labeled transition systems by *modal* transition systems [51,52] and abstraction of probabilities by *intervals* [27,48]. This combination yields *abstract* IMCs.

Definition 12 (Abstract IMC). *An* abstract *IMC is a tuple $\mathcal{I} = (S, Act, L, \mathbf{P}_l, \mathbf{P}_u, \lambda, s_0)$ with S, s_0 and Act as before, and*

- $L : S \times Act \times S \to \mathbb{B}_3$, *a* three-valued labeled *transition function*
- $\mathbf{P}_l, \mathbf{P}_u : S \times S \to [0, 1]$, *lower/upper transition* probability bounds *s.t.*

$$\mathbf{P}_l(s, S) \leq 1 \leq \mathbf{P}_u(s, S) \quad \textit{and}$$

- $\lambda \in \mathbb{R}_{>0}$, *an exit rate.*

Here $\mathbb{B}_3 = \{\bot, ?, \top\}$ is the complete lattice with the ordering $\bot < ? < \top$ and meet ($\sqcap$) and join ($\sqcup$) operations. The labeling $L(s, \alpha, s')$ identifies the transition "type": $\top$ indicates a must-transition, ? a may-transition, and $\bot$ the absence of a transition. $\mathbf{P}_l(s, s')$ is the minimal one-step probability to move from s to s', whereas $\mathbf{P}_u(s, s')$ is the maximal one-step probability between these states. Given these bounds, the IMC can move from s to s' with any probability in the interval $[\mathbf{P}_l(s, s'), \mathbf{P}_u(s, s')]$. Any uniform IMC is an AIMC without may-transitions and for which $\mathbf{P}_l(s, s') = \mathbf{P}_u(s, s')$. The requirement $\mathbf{P}_l(s, S) \leq 1 \leq \mathbf{P}_u(s, S)$ ensures that in any state s, a distribution μ over the direct successor states of s can be chosen such that for any s' we have: $\mathbf{P}_l(s, s') \leq \mu(s') \leq \mathbf{P}_u(s, s')$.

Let us now describe how to perform abstraction of an (A)IMC. As stated above, the principle is to partition the state space by grouping concrete states to abstract states. For concrete state space S and abstract state space S', let $\alpha : S \to S'$ map states to their corresponding abstract ones, i.e., $\alpha(s)$ denotes the abstract state of s and $\alpha^{-1}(s') = \gamma(s')$ is the set of concrete states that are mapped onto s'. α is called the abstraction function whereas $\gamma = \alpha^{-1}$ is known as the concretization function.

Definition 13 (Abstraction). *For an AIMC* $\mathcal{I} = (S, Act, L, \mathbf{P}_l, \mathbf{P}_u, \lambda, s_0)$*, the abstraction function* $\alpha : S \to S'$ *induces the AIMC* $\alpha(\mathcal{I}) = (S', Act, L', \mathbf{P}'_l, \mathbf{P}'_u, \lambda, \alpha(s_0))$*, where:*

- $L'(s', \beta, u') = \begin{cases} \top & \text{if } \bigsqcup_{u \in \gamma(u')} L(s, \beta, u) = \top \text{ for all } s \in \gamma(s') \\ \bot & \text{if } \bigsqcup_{u \in \gamma(u')} L(s, \beta, u) = \bot \text{ for all } s \in \gamma(s') \\ ? & \text{otherwise} \end{cases}$
- $\mathbf{P}'_l(s', u') = \min_{s \in \gamma(s')} \sum_{u \in \gamma(u')} \mathbf{P}_l(s, u)$
- $\mathbf{P}'_u(s', u') = \min(1, \max_{s \in \gamma(s')} \sum_{u \in \gamma(u')} \mathbf{P}_u(s, u))$

There is a must-transition $s' \xrightarrow{\alpha} u'$ if any concrete version $s \in \gamma(s')$ exhibits such transition to some state in $\gamma(u)$. There is no transition between s' and u' if there is no such transition from $s \in \gamma(s')$ to $\gamma(u)$. In all other cases, we obtain a may-transition $s' \xrightarrow{\alpha} u'$.

Example 4. Consider the uniform IMC depicted in the figure below on the left, and ket $S' = \{s, u\}$ be the abstract state space. Assume the abstraction is defined by $\alpha(u_0) = \alpha(u_1) = u$, and $\alpha(s_0) = \alpha(s_1) = s$. This yields the abstract IMC depicted on the right. As $s_0 \xrightarrow{\alpha} u_0$ and $s_1 \xrightarrow{\alpha} u_1$, there is a must-transition labeled by α from s to u. Although $s_0 \xrightarrow{\beta} u_0$, s_1 has no β-transition to u_0 or u_1. Accordingly, we obtain a may-transition labeled with β between s and u. As $\mathbf{P}(u_0, s_1) = \frac{1}{2}$ and $\mathbf{P}(u_1, s_1) = \frac{1}{3}$, we obtain that $\mathbf{P}_l(u, s) = \frac{1}{3}$ and $\mathbf{P}_u(u, s) = \frac{1}{2}$. The other probability intervals are justified in a similar way.

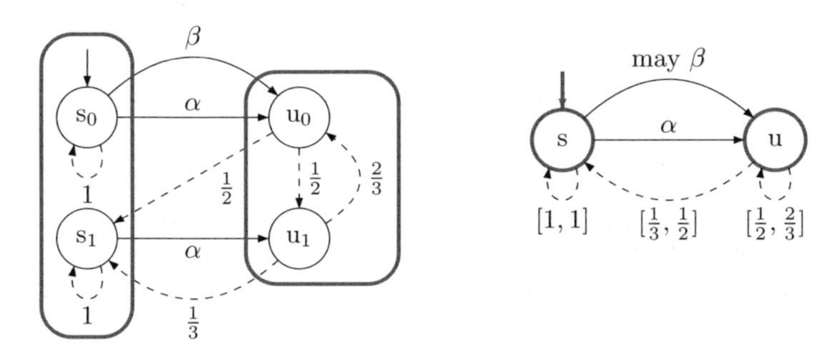

The formal relationship between an AIMC and its abstraction is given by a simulation relation which is in fact a combination of probabilistic simulation on IMCs as defined before (with a slight adaptation to deal with intervals) and the concept of refinement on modal transition systems [52]. Let $\mathbf{T}(s)$ denote the set of probability distributions that exist in state s and that satisfy all bounds of the probability intervals of the outgoing Markovian interval transitions of s.

Definition 14 (Strong simulation). *For AIMC* $\mathcal{I} = (S, Act, L, \mathbf{P}_l, \mathbf{P}_u, \lambda, s_0)$, $R \subseteq S \times S$ *is a* simulation relation, *iff for any* $(s, s') \in R$ *it holds:*

1a. for all $\alpha \in Act$ *and* $u \in S$ *with* $L(s, \alpha, u) \neq \bot$ *there exists* $u' \in S$ *with* $L(s', \alpha, u') \neq \bot$ *and* $(u, u') \in R$,
1b. for all $\alpha \in Act$ *and* $u' \in S$ *with* $L(s', \alpha, u') = \top$ *there exists* $u \in S$ *with* $L(s, \alpha, u) = \top$ *and* $(u, u') \in R$, *and*
2. $L(s, \tau, u) \neq \top$ *for all* $u \in S$, *implies for all* $\mu \in \mathbf{T}(s)$ *there exists* $\mu' \in \mathbf{T}(s')$ *and* $\Delta : S \times S \to [0, 1]$ *such that for all* $u, u' \in S$:

(a) $\Delta(u, u') > 0 \implies uRu'$ *(b)* $\Delta(u, S) = \mu(u)$ *(c)* $\Delta(S, u') = \mu'(u')$

We write $s \preceq s'$ if $(s, s') \in R$ for some simulation R and $\mathcal{I} \preceq \mathcal{I}'$ for AIMCs $\mathcal{I}$ and $\mathcal{I}'$ with initial states s_0 and s'_0, if $s_0 \preceq s'_0$ in the disjoint union of $\mathcal{I}$ and $\mathcal{I}'$.

Let us briefly explain this definition. Item 1a requires that any may- or must-transition of s must be reflected in s'. Item 1b requires that any must-transition of s' must match some must-transition of s, i.e., all required behavior of s' stems from s. Note that this allows a must-transition of s to be mimicked by a may-transition of s'. Condition (2) is the same as in the defininition of simulation for IMCs, except that the set of distributions in a state in an IMC is a singleton, whereas for AIMCs this set can be infinite.

Theorem 12. *[49] For any AIMC* $\mathcal{I}$ *and abstraction function* α, $\mathcal{I} \preceq \alpha(\mathcal{I})$.

As this abstraction is coarser than bisimulation, a significantly larger state-space reduction may be achieved and peak memory consumption is even further reduced. The notion of parallel composition and hiding, as defined for IMCs can now be lifted to AIMCs in a natural manner, and it can be shown that

Theorem 13. *[49]* $\preceq$ *is a pre-congruence wrt. parallel composition and hiding.*

This result provides us the means to carry out abstraction on (A)IMCs in a fully compositional manner. Suppose the system-to-be-analysed is of the form

$$\mathcal{I} \; = \; \mathcal{I}_1 \, ||_{A_1} \, \mathcal{I}_2 \, ||_{A_2} \, \cdots \, ||_{A_N} \, \mathcal{I}_N,$$

i.e., a parallel composition of N IMCs. Let $\alpha(\mathcal{I}_i)$ be the abstraction of IMC $\mathcal{I}_i$, for $0 < i \leq N$. Thanks to the property that strong simulation is substitutive wrt. parallel composition, it follows from the fact that $\mathcal{I}_i \preceq \alpha(\mathcal{I}_i)$, for $0 < i \leq N$, that:

$$\mathcal{I}_1 \, ||_{A_1} \, \mathcal{I}_2 \, ||_{A_2} \, \cdots \, ||_{A_N} \, \mathcal{I}_N \;\preceq\; \alpha(\mathcal{I}_1) \, ||_{A_1} \, \alpha(\mathcal{I}_2) \, ||_{A_2} \, \cdots \, ||_{A_N} \, \alpha(\mathcal{I}_N).$$

5 IMCs as Semantical Model

Much of computer science is about specification formalisms. Domain specific languages as well as universal notations are being promoted by various interest groups and taken up by standardization bodies. Some of them appeal due to their graphical notation convenience, such as the UML, others appeal because they clarify the aspects of a certain domain. One example of the latter is AADL, the Architectural Analysis and Design Language [28]. For many of these languages the work is considered done once the syntax is fixed, and an intuitive explanation of the semantics is provided. Formalizing these intuitions is sometimes a task for legions of scientists: The conception of Statecharts for instance has lead to several dozens of different semantics, and more are on the horizon. Still, one of the lessons generally learnt from these experiences is that a good semantics is compositional [29], a semantics that provides a meaning to an object based on a composition of the semantics of its parts. If the composition adheres to simple-to-grasp rules, this semantics can become consensus. Compositionality is a fundamental and highly desirable property of a semantics: it enables compositional reasoning, i.e. analyzing complex systems by breaking them down into their constituting parts. Examples *par excellence* of simple-to-grasp rules have been given before: parallel composition and hiding.

A clean and well-understood semantics is a necessity for model-based evaluation of such languages. It is as simple as that. Whenever performance figures or correctness claims are presented for UML fragments or the like, they are specific to the semantics chosen, and in case that semantics is neither commonly agreed nor easy-to-grasp, doubts remain concerning the general validity of such claims.

Dynamic fault trees. Let us consider a classical domain specific language, known as fault trees. Fault trees were first planted in the youth of civil nuclear energy, as means to systematically quantify the risk of a catastrophic hazard [63] in a plant. A fault tree is a diagrammatical variation of a boolean function, drawn in a tree-structured manner where the leaves correspond to boolean variables. These leaves represent basic operational units of the plant such as valves and pipes. The failure of an operational components flips the corresponding boolean value to true. If the entire function evaluates to true, a catastrophic event is supposed to be unavoidable. Fault trees have been standardised, and their use is prescribed in many engineering areas. A classical fault tree is static, the order of failure occurences is assumed not important, and components cannot be replaced dynamically by spare components. If considering such extensions, one arrives at the diagrammatical notation of dynamic fault trees (DFT) [25].

The semantics of a dynamic fault tree can no longer be mapped directly on a boolean function, but instead needs a state-transition graph representation to reflect the system dynamics. If one assumes that failure occurences follow exponential laws, which is a standard and sometimes justified assumption, it seems natural to expect that the resulting model is a CTMC. Actually, the first complete formalisation attempted [21] aimed at providing a CTMC semantics, but revealed a number of ambiguities in the DFT framework. Most notably, in some instances of DFTs non-determinism arises. This is where IMC and its compositionality property can play a pivotal role: The work of Crouzen *et al.* [12,11,10] provides a clean and elegant compositional semantics, a semantics that maps on IMC. More precisely, the semantics takes up ideas of I/O-automata [53], and uses *input/output* interactive Markov chains (I/O-IMC). I/O-IMC are restricted versions of IMC that allow for non-blocking communication. The semantics is fully compositional: The semantics of each DFT element is an I/O-IMC. The semantics of a DFT is then obtained by parallel composing the I/O-IMC semantics of all its elements.

Example 5. As an example, we demonstrate this approach for a SPARE gate, a functional unit that makes a redundant unit of functionality available (the spare), in case the original unit (the primary) fails [12]. Figure 3 shows the I/O-IMC semantics of a DFT consisting of a SPARE gate A having a primary B and a spare C.

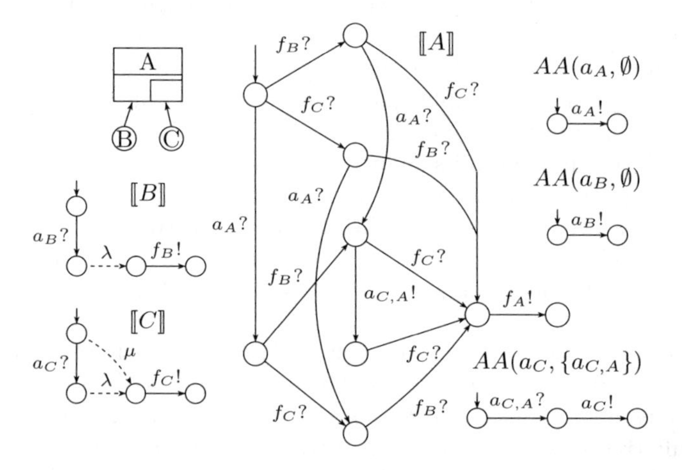

Fig. 3. A DFT example and six I/O-IMCs that model its behavior [12]

The I/O-IMC of the DFT is obtained by parallel composing the six IMCs, properly synchronised. The congruence property established before is inherited by I/O-IMCs and enables compositional aggregation to combat the state-space explosion problem existing in DFTs, see [10,12].

Archtectural Description Languages. Hardware/software (HW/SW) co-design of safety-critical embedded systems such as on-board systems that appear in the aerospace domain is a very complex and highly challenging task. Component-based design is an important paradigm here to master this design complexity while, in addition, allowing for reusability. As safety-critical systems are subject to hardware and software faults, the adequate modeling of faults, their likelihood of occurrence, and the way in which a system can recover from faults, are essential to a model-based approach for safety-critical systems. To overcome these shortcomings one needs an enriched practical component-based modeling approach with appropriate means for modeling probabilistic fault behavior.

To warrant acceptance by design engineers in, e.g., aerospace industry and the automotive engineers, efforts have been spent to based on the Architecture Analysis and Design Language (AADL) [28], a design formalism that is standardised by the Society of Automotive Engineers. Among these efforts, Arcade [9] has adopted the DFT work mentioned above to the recent AADL Error Model Annex, and provides a map of each of the components on an I/O-IMC, again in a fully compositional manner. This is in spirit similar to the work performed in the ESA project COMPASS [13,14,15], where IMC are targetted to model nominal and probabilistic fault behaviour, fault propagation and recovery, and degraded modes of operation. The integration of nominal behavior and error models basically boils down to a parallel composition of a variable-decorated transition system (which is a semantically an IMC) and an IMC.

Generalised stochastic Petri nets. Generalised Stochastic Petri Nets (GSPNs) are a well-established modelling formalism for performance and dependability evaluation, supporting stochastic timed behavior and weighted immediate choices [54,55]. To this end, timed transitions and immediate transitions are supported in a GSPN. Performance evaluation of a GSPN proceeds at the level of the reachability (or: marking) graph. That graph is transformed into a CTMC, for which efficient steady-state and transient solvers are at hand. This evaluation trajectory was pioneered by the tool GreatSPN [20], nowadays it is implemented in a plethora of tools.

However, it is notoriously overlooked that the above evaluation trajectory is incomplete. It is restricted to *confusion-free* GSPNs. Confusion arises if a firing sequence admits the simultaneous enabling of multiple non-conflicting immediate transitions. GSPNs equip immediate transitions with global priority levels and globally assigned weights to diminish the occurrence of such nondeterministic choices. But priorities and weights do not, and cannot, eliminate confusion in its full entirety. The presence of nondeterminism, however, makes it impossible to associate an unambiguous stochastic process to such nets.

Recently we managed to attack this principal problem [40]. We have taken up earlier thoughts on nondeterministic GSPN semantics [37] to come up with an IMC semantics for GSPNs. Actually, this semantics is not more than a reinterpretation of the marking graph as an IMC. With the analysis results reported in this paper, this means that also confused GSPNs can now be analysed. This was not possible before.

Example 6. Consider the GSPN depicted in the figure below on the left where solid bars depict immediate transitions and open bars represent delayed transitions. This GSPN is confused. In marking $(0,0,1,1)$, for instance, the set of reachable tangible markings is $\{(1,0,0,0),(0,0,0,1)\}$. If the enabled transition t_5 is chosen, the tangible marking $(0,0,0,1)$ is reached almost surely. However, if enabled transition t_6 is chosen, we enter the tangible marking $(1,0,0,0)$ almost surely. Hence, the next tangible markings depends on the way the nondeterminism in $(0,0,1,1)$ is resolved and cannot be quantified. The usual way to deal with this situation is to equip transitions t_5 and t_6 with weigths. The marking graph of the GSN is depicted in the figure on the right. Here, solid arrows depict Markovian transitions, and dashed arrows correspond to the firing of immediate transitions in the net, and are interpreted as τ-labeled IMC transitions.

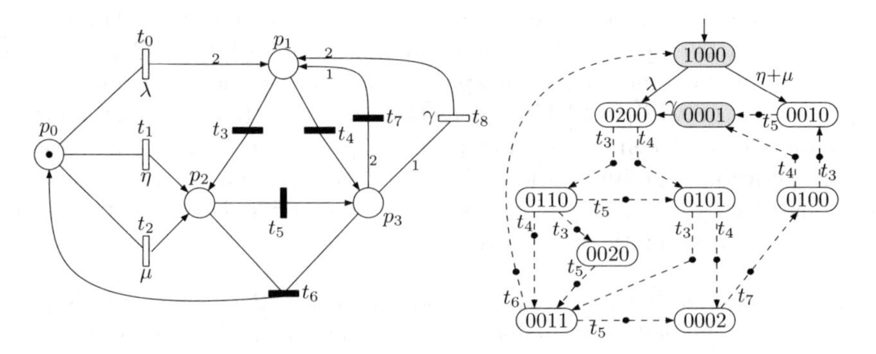

Statecharts. A modelling environment used by engineers in several avionic and automotive companies like AIRBUS or BMW is STATEMATE, a Statechart-based tool-set. To enable performance and dependability evaluation of Statemate designs, the German special research initiative AVACS has spent considerable energy to a connection between Statemate and IMC [8,38,65,42].

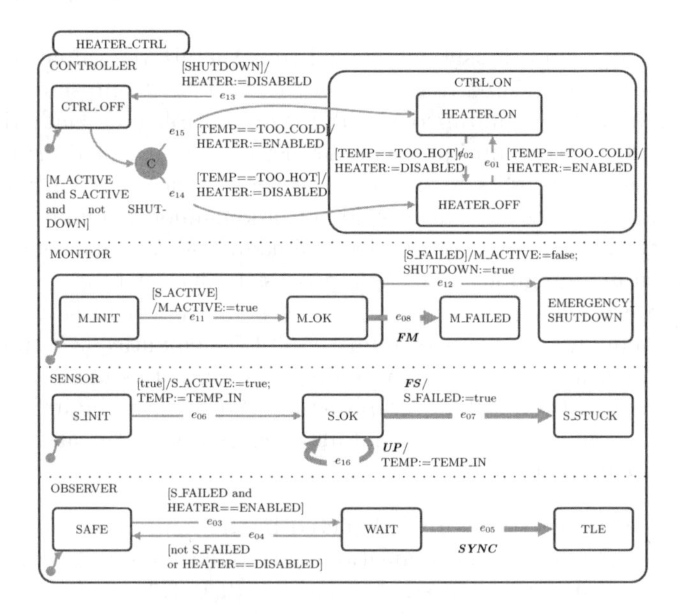

Fig. 4. A Statechart [8]

One key feature of this approach is that the model construction steps rely heavily on compositional properties of the IMC model, and employ precisely the constraint-oriented specification style advocated in Section 2. For this, the design comprises distinguished *delay transitions*. In the figure, these are FM, failure of monitor and FS, failure of sensor). These transitions have an effect or are affected by the advance of time. Mostly, delay transitions indicate component failures, but the concept is more flexible. *Delay distributions*, in the form of continuous probability distributions affecting the occurrence of the delay transitions are incorporated via the *elapse*-operator. Symbolic (i. e. BDD-based) representations and compositional methods are exploited to keep the model sizes manageable.

The complexity challenges posed by this problem domain could only be addressed by (1) performing a state space reduction on the non-deterministic part of the model by means of a *symbolic* minimisation capable of handling huge state spaces and (2) constraint-oriented specification of time-constraints *after* this reduction into the model. The developed technology was applied to a non-trivial case study from the train control domain with an explication of the improvements contributed by each of the relevant translation steps. In Figure 5 we quote a fraction of the relevant information from [8], illustrating the effects and costs of compositional minimisation.

Tracks –	Compositional Construction			Final Quotient IMC	
Choices	States	Transitions	Time (sec.)	States	Transitions
1 – 1	71	261	18.70	16	55
1 – 2	79	325	22.58	29	101
1 – 3	99	419	26.87	39	143
1 – 4	119	513	30.43	49	185
2 – 1	731	3888	31.72	187	1006
2 – 2	1755	11059	39.55	665	3442
2 – 3	3127	20737	47.71	1281	6991
2 – 4	4899	33495	57.83	2097	11780
3 – 1	10075	75377	50.01	2573	18260
3 – 2	53858	387501	293.53	16602	112011
3 – 3	134555	1061958	1114.82	44880	320504
4 – 1	143641	1343747	785.30	35637	313270
4 – 2	1350908	11619969	243687.33	416274	3452502

Fig. 5. Composition and minimisation statistics [8]

6 Concluding Remarks

This paper has presented an overview of foundational, algorithmic and pragmatic aspects of IMCs, a simple generalisation of both CTMCs and LTS with a fully compositional semantics. There are other approaches that give a compositional semantics in a continuous time Markov setting, among them popular formalisms such as PEPA [43], EMPA [6] or MTIPP [41], the latter being the semantic basis of the PRISM toolkit [44] in 'ctmc' mode. None of these formalisms has the properties that IMCs possess. In particular, they do not extend classical concurrency models in a conservative fashion. For each of these calculi the role of an atomic action is particular. This affects the synchronisation of actions, and thus the final performance results – in different ways for each of these calculi. It is not easy to explain what is happening precisely, and this is not the topic of this paper; the interested reader may consult [17]. In IMC, the separation of delays and actions allows to treat action synchronisation as in standard concurrency models. It is surprising that given the advantages of IMCs, recent approaches for CTMC-variants of process calculi for mobility and service-oriented computing [59] and interesting new developments in structured operational semantics for such calculi [50,24] do not adopt this approach.

An extension of IMC towards time-inhomogeneous continuous-time dynamics is provided in [33]. In the discrete time setting, a model class with similarly distinguishing properties is provided by probabilistic automata [60]. Probabilistic automata can be integrated into the IMC model, retaining full compositionality [26].

We have reviewed the theoretical basis of IMC, and have discussed two recent algorithmic achievements that foster the applicability of IMC: analysis techniques in the presence of nondeterminism, and compositional abstraction techniques. IMCs practical relevance has been highlighted by reviewing in applications of various domains, ranging from dynamic fault trees to generalized stochastic Petri nets. While the first generation of tool support, CADP, has found several academic and non academic uses, the recent algorithmic advances described in this paper are not yet fully integrated in a tool. This is a major topic of ongoing work.

References

1. Baier, C., Engelen, B., Majster-Cederbaum, M.E.: Deciding bisimilarity and similarity for probabilistic processes. Journal of Computer and System Sciences 60, 187–231 (2000)
2. Baier, C., Haverkort, B.R., Hermanns, H., Katoen, J.-P.: Model-checking algorithms for continuous-time Markov chains. IEEE TSE 29, 524–541 (2003)
3. Baier, C., Katoen, J.-P., Hermanns, H., Wolf, V.: Comparative branching-time semantics for Markov chains. Information and Computation 200, 149–214 (2005)
4. Barendregt, H.: The quest for correctness. In: Images of SMC Research 1996. Stichting Mathematisch Centrum, pp. 39–58 (1996)
5. Bergstra, J.A., Ponse, A. (eds.): Handbook of Process Algebra. Elsevier Publishers B.V, Amsterdam (2001)
6. Bernardo, M., Gorrieri, R.: Corrigendum to “A tutorial on EMPA: A theory of concurrent processes with nondeterminism, priorities, probabilities and time. TCS 202 254, 1–54 (1998); Theoretical Computer Science 254, 691–694 (2001)
7. Bertsekas, D.: Dynamic Programming and Optimal Control, vol. II. Athena Scientific, Belmont (1995)
8. Böde, E., Herbstritt, M., Hermanns, H., Johr, S., Peikenkamp, T., Pulungan, R., Rakow, J., Wimmer, R., Becker, B.: Compositional dependability evaluation for STATEMATE. IEEE TSE 35, 274–292 (2009)
9. Boudali, H., Crouzen, P., Haverkort, B.R., Kuntz, M., Stoelinga, M.I.A.: Architectural dependability evaluation with Arcade. In: Dependable Systems and Networks (DSN), pp. 512–521. IEEE, Los Alamitos (2008)
10. Boudali, H., Crouzen, P., Stoelinga, M.: A compositional semantics for dynamic fault trees in terms of interactive Markov chains. In: Namjoshi, K.S., Yoneda, T., Higashino, T., Okamura, Y. (eds.) ATVA 2007. LNCS, vol. 4762, pp. 441–456. Springer, Heidelberg (2007)
11. Boudali, H., Crouzen, P., Stoelinga, M.I.A.: Dynamic fault tree analysis using input/output interactive Markov chains. In: Dependable Systems and Networks (DSN). IEEE, Los Alamitos (2007)

12. Boudali, H., Crouzen, P., Stoelinga, M.I.A.: Rigorous, compositional, and extensible framework for dynamic fault tree analysis. IEEE Transactions on Secure and Dependable Computing 7, 128–143 (2009)
13. Bozzano, M., Cimatti, A., Katoen, J.-P., Nguyen, V., Noll, T., Roveri, M.: Codesign of dependable systems: A component-based modelling language. In: Proc. 7th Int. Conf. on Formal Methods and Models for Co-Design MEMOCODE, pp. 121–130. IEEE CS Press, Los Alamitos (2009)
14. Bozzano, M., Cimatti, A., Katoen, J.-P., Nguyen, V., Noll, T., Roveri, M.: The COMPASS approach: Correctness, modelling and performability of aerospace systems. In: Buth, B., Rabe, G., Seyfarth, T. (eds.) SAFECOMP 2009. LNCS, vol. 5775, pp. 173–186. Springer, Heidelberg (2009)
15. Bozzano, M., Cimatti, A., Katoen, J.-P., Nguyen, V., Noll, T., Roveri, M.: Safety, dependability and performance analysis of extended AADL models. The Computer Journal (2010)
16. Bravetti, M., Hermanns, H., Katoen, J.-P.: YMCA: Why Markov chain algebra? In: Proceedings of the Workshop Essays on Algebraic Process Calculi. Electronic Notes in Theoretical Computer Science, vol. 162, pp. 107–112. Elsevier, Amsterdam (2006)
17. Brinksma, E., Hermanns, H.: Process Algebra and Markov Chains. In: Brinksma, E., Hermanns, H., Katoen, J.-P. (eds.) EEF School 2000 and FMPA 2000. LNCS, vol. 2090, pp. 183–231. Springer, Heidelberg (2001)
18. Buchholz, P.: Exact and ordinary lumpability in finite markov chains. J. of Applied Probability 31, 59–75 (1994)
19. Chehaibar, G., Zidouni, M., Mateescu, R.: Modeling multiprocessor cache protocol impact on MPI performance. In: IEEE International Workshop on Quantitative Evaluation of Large-Scale Systems and Technologies. IEEE, Los Alamitos (2009)
20. Chiola, G., Franceschinis, G., Gaeta, R., Ribaudo, M.: GreatSPN 1.7: Graphical editor and analyzer for timed and stochastic Petri nets. Performance Evaluation 24, 47–68 (1995)
21. Coppit, D., Sullivan, K.J., Dugan, J.B.: Formal semantics for computational engineering: A case study on dynamic fault trees. In: ISSRE, pp. 270–282. IEEE Computer Society, Los Alamitos (2000)
22. Coste, N., Garavel, H., Hermanns, H., Hersemeule, R., Thonnart, Y., Zidouni, M.: Quantitative evaluation in embedded system design: Validation of multiprocessor multithreaded architectures. In: Design, Automation and Test in Europe (DATE), pp. 88–89. IEEE, Los Alamitos (2008)
23. Coste, N., Hermanns, H., Lantreibecq, E., Serwe, W.: Towards performance prediction of compositional models in industrial GALS designs. In: Bouajjani, A., Maler, O. (eds.) Computer Aided Verification. LNCS, vol. 5643, pp. 204–218. Springer, Heidelberg (2009)
24. De Nicola, R., Latella, D., Loreti, M., Massink, M.: Rate-based transition systems for stochastic process calculi. In: Albers, S., Marchetti-Spaccamela, A., Matias, Y., Nikoletseas, S., Thomas, W. (eds.) ICALP 2009. LNCS, vol. 5556, pp. 435–446. Springer, Heidelberg (2009)
25. Dugan, J., Bavuso, S., Boyd, M.: Dynamic fault-tree models for fault-tolerant computer systems. IEEE Transactions on Reliability 41, 363–377 (1992)
26. Eisentraut, C., Hermanns, H., Zhang, L.: On probabilistic automata in continuous time. In: IEEE Symposium on Logic in Computer Science (LICS). IEEE, Los Alamitos (2010)
27. Fecher, H., Leucker, M., Wolf, V.: Don't know in probabilistic systems. In: Valmari, A. (ed.) SPIN 2006. LNCS, vol. 3925, pp. 71–88. Springer, Heidelberg (2006)

28. Feiler, P.H., Rugina, A.: Dependability modeling with the Architecture Analysis & Design Language (AADL). Technical Note CMU/SEI-2007-TN-043, CMU Software Engineering Institute (2007)
29. Frenkel, K.A., Milner, R.: An interview with Robin Milner. CACM 36, 90–97 (1993)
30. Garavel, H., Hermanns, H.: On combining functional verification and performance evaluation using CADP. In: Eriksson, L.-H., Lindsay, P.A. (eds.) FME 2002. LNCS, vol. 2391, pp. 410–429. Springer, Heidelberg (2002)
31. Garavel, H., Mateescu, R., Lang, F., Serwe, W.: CADP 2006: A toolbox for the construction and analysis of distributed processes. In: Damm, W., Hermanns, H. (eds.) CAV 2007. LNCS, vol. 4590, pp. 158–163. Springer, Heidelberg (2007)
32. Gilmore, S., Hillston, J., Ribaudo, M.: An efficient algorithm for aggregating PEPA models. IEEE Trans. Software Eng. 27, 449–464 (2001)
33. Han, T., Katoen, J.-P., Mereacre, A.: Compositional modeling and minimization of time-inhomogeneous Markov chains. In: Egerstedt, M., Mishra, B. (eds.) HSCC 2008. LNCS, vol. 4981, pp. 244–258. Springer, Heidelberg (2008)
34. Haverkort, B.R.: Performance of Computer Communication Systems: A Model-Based Approach. John Wiley & Sons, Chichester (1998)
35. Hermanns, H. (ed.): Interactive Markov Chains. LNCS, vol. 2428. Springer, Heidelberg (2002)
36. Hermanns, H., Herzog, U., Katoen, J.-P.: Process algebra for performance evaluation. Theoretical Computer Science 274, 43–87 (2002)
37. Hermanns, H., Herzog, U., Mertsiotakis, V., Rettelbach, M.: Exploiting stochastic process algebra achievements for generalized stochastic Petri nets. In: Petri Nets and Performance Models (PNPM), pp. 183–192. IEEE, Los Alamitos (1997)
38. Hermanns, H., Johr, S.: Uniformity by construction in the analysis of nondeterministic stochastic systems. In: Dependable Systems and Networks (DSN), pp. 718–728. IEEE, Los Alamitos (2007)
39. Hermanns, H., Katoen, J.-P.: Automated compositional Markov chain generation for a plain-old telephone system. Science of Comp. Progr. 36, 97–127 (2000)
40. Hermanns, H., Katoen, J.-P., Neuhäußer, M.R., Zhang, L.: GSPN model checking despite confusion. Technical report, RWTH Aachen University (2010)
41. Hermanns, H., Rettelbach, M.: Syntax, Semantics, Equivalences, and Axioms for MTIPP. In: Herzog, U., Rettelbach, M. (eds.) Proc. of the 2nd Int. Workshop on Process Algebras and Performance Modelling. Arbeitsberichte des IMMD, vol. 27(4), Universität Erlangen (1994)
42. Hermanns, H., Johr, S.: we reach it? or must we? in what time? with what probability? In: Measurement, Modelling and Evaluation of Computer and Communication Systems (MMB), pp. 125–140. VDE Verlag (May 2008)
43. Hillston, J.: A Compositional Approach to Performance Modelling. Cambridge University Press, Cambridge (1996)
44. Hinton, A., Kwiatkowska, M.Z., Norman, G., Parker, D.: PRISM: A tool for automatic verification of probabilistic systems. In: Hermanns, H., Palsberg, J. (eds.) TACAS 2006. LNCS, vol. 3920, pp. 441–444. Springer, Heidelberg (2006)
45. Hoare, C., Brookes, S., Roscoe, A.: A theory of communicating sequential processes. J. ACM 31, 560–599 (1984)
46. Jonsson, B.: Simulations between specifications of distributed systems. In: Groote, J.F., Baeten, J.C.M. (eds.) CONCUR 1991. LNCS, vol. 527, pp. 346–360. Springer, Heidelberg (1991)
47. Katoen, J.-P., Kemna, T., Zapreev, I.S., Jansen, D.N.: Bisimulation minimisation mostly speeds up probabilistic model checking. In: Grumberg, O., Huth, M. (eds.) TACAS 2007. LNCS, vol. 4424, pp. 87–102. Springer, Heidelberg (2007)

48. Katoen, J.-P., Klink, D., Leucker, M., Wolf, V.: Three-valued abstraction for continuous-time Markov chains. In: Damm, W., Hermanns, H. (eds.) CAV 2007. LNCS, vol. 4590, pp. 311–324. Springer, Heidelberg (2007)
49. Katoen, J.-P., Klink, D., Neuhäußer, M.R.: Compositional abstraction for stochastic systems. In: Ouaknine, J., Vaandrager, F.W. (eds.) FORMATS 2009. LNCS, vol. 5813, pp. 195–211. Springer, Heidelberg (2009)
50. Klin, B., Sassone, V.: Structural operational semantics for stochastic process calculi. In: Amadio, R.M. (ed.) FOSSACS 2008. LNCS, vol. 4962, pp. 428–442. Springer, Heidelberg (2008)
51. Larsen, K.G.: Modal specifications. In: Sifakis, J. (ed.) CAV 1989. LNCS, vol. 407, pp. 232–246. Springer, Heidelberg (1990)
52. Larsen, K.G., Thomsen, B.: A modal process logic. In: IEEE Symposium on Logic in Computer Science (LICS), pp. 203–210. IEEE, Los Alamitos (1988)
53. Lynch, N.A., Tuttle, M.R.: An introduction to input/output automata. CWI Quarterly 2, 219–246 (1989)
54. Marsan, M.A., Balbo, G., Chiola, G., Conte, G., Donatelli, S., Franceschinis, G.: An introduction to generalized stochastic Petri nets. Microelectronics and Reliability 31, 699–725 (1991)
55. Marsan, M.A., Balbo, G., Conte, G., Donatelli, S., Franceschinis, G.: Modelling with Generalized Stochastic Petri Nets. John Wiley & Sons, Chichester (1995)
56. Neuhäußer, M.R., Katoen, J.-P.: Bisimulation and logical preservation for continuous-time Markov decision processes. In: Caires, L., Vasconcelos, V.T. (eds.) CONCUR 2007. LNCS, vol. 4703, pp. 412–427. Springer, Heidelberg (2007)
57. Neuhäußer, M.R., Stoelinga, M., Katoen, J.-P.: Delayed nondeterminism in continuous-time Markov decision processes. In: de Alfaro, L. (ed.) FOSSACS 2009. LNCS, vol. 5504, pp. 364–379. Springer, Heidelberg (2009)
58. Neuhäußer, M.R.: Model Checking Nondeterministic and Randomly Timed Systems. PhD thesis, RWTH Aachen University / University of Twente (2010)
59. Prandi, D., Quaglia, P.: Stochastic COWS. In: Krämer, B.J., Lin, K.-J., Narasimhan, P. (eds.) ICSOC 2007. LNCS, vol. 4749, pp. 245–256. Springer, Heidelberg (2007)
60. Segala, R.: Modeling and Verification of Randomized Distributed Real-Time Systems. PhD thesis, Laboratory for Computer Science, Massachusetts Institute of Technology (1995)
61. `http://portal.acm.org/citation.cfm?id=1451820`
62. van Glabbeek, R.J., Weijland, W.P.: Branching time and abstraction in bisimulation semantics. J. ACM 43, 555–600 (1996)
63. Veseley, W., Goldberg, F., Roberts, N., Haasl, D.: Fault Tree Handbook. US Nuclear Regulatory Commission, NUREG- 0492 (1981)
64. Vissers, C., Scollo, G., van Sinderen, M., Brinksma, E.: On the use of specification styles in the design of distributed systems. Theor. Comput. Sci. 89, 179–206 (1991)
65. Wimmer, R., Herbstritt, M., Hermanns, H., Strampp, K., Becker, B.: Sigref – a symbolic bisimulation tool box. In: Graf, S., Zhang, W. (eds.) ATVA 2006. LNCS, vol. 4218, pp. 477–492. Springer, Heidelberg (2006)
66. Zhang, L., Neuhäußer, M.R.: Model checking interactive Markov chains. In: Esparza, J., Majumdar, R. (eds.) Tools and Algorithms for the Construction and Analysis of Systems. LNCS, vol. 6015, pp. 53–68. Springer, Heidelberg (2010)
67. Zhang, L., Hermanns, H., Eisenbrand, F., Jansen, D.N.: Flow faster: Efficient decision algorithms for probabilistic simulations. Logical Methods in Computer Science 4 (2008)

Author Index

Printing: Mercedes-Druck, Berlin
Binding: Stein+Lehmann, Berlin